D0387027

LEWIS A. DRUMMOND

THE CANVAS CATHEDRAL

Publishers Since 1798

THOMAS NELSON PUBLISHERS®
a division of Thomas Nelson, Inc.

Nashville

This book is dedicated to my dear wife
and companion of more than fifty years,
Betty Drummond: faithful friend,
my strength, and one deeply loved.

THE CANVAS CATHEDRAL

Unless otherwise noted, Scripture quotations are from the New American Standard Bible ®. Copyright © The Lockman Foundation 1960, 1962, 1963, 1968, 1971, 1972, 1973, 1975, 1977. Used by permission.

Scripture quotations noted NKJV are from The New King James Version. Copyright © 1979, 1980, 1982, Thomas Nelson, Inc., Publishers.

Scripture quotations noted KJV are from the King James Version.

Scripture quotations noted NIV are from the Holy Bible: New International Version ®. Copyright © 1973, 1978, 1984 by International Bible Society. Used by permission of Zondervan Publishing House. All rights reserved.

Scripture quotations noted PHILLIPS are from J. B. Phillips: The New Testament in Modern English, Revised Edition, copyright © J. B. Phillips 1958, 1960, 1972. Used by permission of Macmillan Publishing Co., Inc.

Scripture quotations noted RSV are from The Revised Standard Version of the Bible, copyright © 1946, 1952, 1971, 1973 by the Division of Christian Education of the National Council of the Churches of Christ in the USA. Used by permission.

ISBN 0-8499-4310-8

Printed in the United States of America

03 04 05 06 07 — 5 4 3 2 1

CONTENTS

And He gave some as . . . evangelists.
—EPHESIANS 4:11

FOREWORD

OVER THE CENTURIES CHRISTIAN EVANGELISTS have sought to help people understand the Gospel message, and to call them to a personal commitment to Jesus Christ as Savior and Lord. This has been my own goal as an evangelist—but I know I am the only one of the latest in a long line of men and women who have gone before me.

In this book Professor Lewis Drummond outlines some of the most significant evangelistic movements since the first century, and I am humbled that he has chosen to examine our own ministry against this historical backdrop. As he clearly shows, throughout the history of the church the Gospel has been proclaimed in obedience to Christ's command to "Go into all the world and preach the good news to all creation" (Mark 18:15)—from ancient amphitheaters to modern television studios. Throughout his study Dr. Drummond highlights the crucial role of preaching in the work of evangelism, and the importance of declaring the Gospel message with clarity, integrity and urgency.

This is an essential book for students, pastors and others who want to understand how God has called and empowered His ambassadors in every generation to spread the good news of Jesus Christ. May it instruct and challenge Christians to a renewed commitment to the ministry of evangelism as we move forward in the 21st century.

BILLY GRAHAM

PREFACE

IT WAS, I BELIEVE, AN EPISCOPAL CLERGYMAN who lodged a complaint against Billy Graham during the 1949 "Christ for Greater Los Angeles" campaign. His criticism was that Billy Graham had set back the cause of religion one hundred years. Billy Graham's rejoinder was typical. "I did indeed *want* to set religion back," he said, "not just one hundred years but nineteen hundred years, to the Book of Acts, when first-century followers of Christ were accused of turning the Roman Empire upside down."[1]

This quip of Billy Graham's is a good example of his innocent humor in the face of opposition and of his ability to turn a critical comment to the advantage of the gospel. It is also an unselfconscious assessment of his ministry. He sees himself (and rightly so) as belonging to the mainstream of evangelical faith and witness as it has continued down the Christian centuries. So in his opening address at the Lausanne Congress in 1974, he was able to claim that "the Congress stands in the tradition of many movements of evangelism throughout the history of the church."[2]

Dr. Lewis Drummond's purpose in this book is to test this claim and to consider Billy Graham's place in history. His twelve characteristics of evangelism constitute a cluster of essentials that may also be found in the evangelistic message, methods, and motives of Billy Graham.

Readers will enjoy this opportunity to compare the contemporary with the historical and to evaluate the extraordinary ministry of Billy Graham by these twelve criteria. They form a substantial picture of evangelism. One might perhaps sum it up as follows:

Evangelism begins in the loving heart and sovereign will of Almighty God, as revealed in Scripture. It is essentially a bold proclamation by word and deed of Jesus Christ, incarnate, crucified, risen, reigning, and returning. It is undertaken in obedience to the Great Commission, whatever the cost and in dependence on the Holy Spirit. It summons all humankind to repent and believe and then to live a new life of godliness in God's new community, the church.

More simply still, evangelism is the proclamation of the revealed Word of God the Father, focusing on His Son, Jesus Christ, crucified and risen in the power of the Holy Spirit. Authentic evangelism is Trinitarian evangelism, and Billy Graham is essentially a Trinitarian Christian who stands in the central tradition of the church.

It is my conviction, however, that Billy Graham will go down in the history of the church as more than an evangelist. First and foremost, he is a *Christian*, determined by grace to follow in his Master's footsteps. In the increasingly permissive society of the last half of the twentieth century, Billy Graham has refused to bow before the winds of public opinion. He has maintained his personal integrity. He has walked humbly with his God. He has loved his enemies who have vilified him, bearing the pain and declining to retaliate. In sexual self-control and financial accountability (areas in which other evangelists have fallen), Billy Graham has been above reproach. In brief, he has embodied the gospel that he has proclaimed. The Manila Manifesto declares that "nothing commends the gospel more eloquently than a transformed life."[3] Billy Graham's testimony has been eloquent indeed.

Second, Billy Graham will be remembered as a *churchman*. He has never been a lone evangelist. He believes in the church. He has cooperated with the churches as much as possible. He has also called the church back to its mission. He has often said in my hearing that if the church were faithfully evangelizing, there would be no need for a person like him. He was exaggerating, of course, for there will always be some Christians whom God endows with the charisma of evangelists. Nevertheless, we take his point. If every individual Christian were a faithful witness, and if every local church were diligently reaching out into its own neighborhood, mass evangelism would not need to be so prominent as it has been in our generation.

Third, Billy Graham has been an *internationalist*. Although he is a patriotic American citizen, he has never been a nationalist or been infected by the spirit of nationalism that has been so pervasive in his day. In visiting 185 countries, he has always been respectful of other cultures. From the beginning of his ministry, he has opposed racism and refused to hold a racially segregated crusade. His internationalism has been acknowledged by world leaders, and he has been granted an audience by innumerable heads of state. Moreover, in these interviews he has always had the courage to go beyond protocol to testimony.

Fourth, Billy Graham has been a *statesman*. He has been wonderfully liberated from a preoccupation with his own ministry and has gladly recognized the importance of others' work. Consequently, he has brought training and encouragement to multitudes of fellow evangelists throughout the world. His concern for them culminated in Amsterdam 2000. There, in July and August, ten thousand evangelists assembled from 209 countries. It is said to have been the most representative gathering, secular or religious, in the history of the world. What a vision! Although Billy Graham was unable to attend owing to ill health, his influence brooded over the assembly, as evangelists the world over still look to him for inspiration. He was also the pioneer spirit behind the numerous congresses on evangelism (international, regional, and national), in particular Lausanne I (1974) and Lausanne II in Manila (1989). Nobody else could have created such a widespread and substantial evangelical unity.

I commend Lewis Drummond for undertaking the task that has resulted in this wide-ranging book. He has thoroughly researched the evangelistic ministry of Billy Graham in order to ascertain Graham's place in history. Although Drummond never descends to the level of hagiography, a careful reading of his book will convince us that, by God's providential grace, no single person in the twentieth century has been more influential for Christ than Billy Graham.

JOHN R. W. STOTT
December 2000

ACKNOWLEDGMENTS

MANY HAVE GIVEN INVALUABLE HELP in producing this work. Dr. and Mrs. Graham and their family members graciously shared of their time to help this author attain a grasp of many issues. Graham team members and others who gave interviews and presented their insights concerning Billy Graham's ministry proved most helpful. To all these I express my profound gratitude. A sincere word of appreciation goes to the Billy Graham offices in Minneapolis, Minnesota, and Montreat, North Carolina. Also, the Billy Graham Center in Wheaton, Illinois, provided significant resources. The personnel of all those institutions were most cooperative and helpful. And to Joseph Paul, executive vice president and editor-in-chief of Word Publishing, I express appreciation; his counsel likewise proved invaluable. Dr. David Bruce gave time and counsel that aided the work tremendously. I must also thank the secretaries who spent hours on the computer putting the manuscript in order: Michelle Joiner, Sherrill Hallquist, Tina Braswell, Mario Escobedo II, Lisa Tucker, Kathy Jauch, and Gail Gough. Gratitude must also be expressed to evangelist Frank Harber and his research students at Southwestern Baptist Theological Seminary and to Jason Motte for indexing the book. Several of my students at Samford University did excellent research as well, saving this author many hours of labor. Above all, full honor goes to God for His graciousness in allowing this author to undertake the work and to sense His help and leadership.

May He be glorified thereby and the Graham ministry find its proper place in posterity.

Lewis A. Drummond
Birmingham, Alabama

INTRODUCTION

WHILE IN MY THIRD YEAR OF COLLEGE, one of my friends and fellow ministerial classmates said to me, "Let's go down to the Tingley Tabernacle tonight. There is a young evangelist who is going to preach. I heard him a year or so ago at a Youth for Christ rally, and he can really preach." The Tingley Tabernacle was an independent church that met in the heart of the city. I asked, "What is the young preacher's name?" My friend replied, "His name is Billy Graham." I retorted, "I've never heard of him. I have too much studying to do; I can't go." BIG MISTAKE! Not many months later in a "canvas cathedral"—a large tent erected in Los Angeles, California—that relatively unknown young evangelist preached and was skyrocketed to world prominence. The Billy Graham epic began, and history was made.

It may seem redundant, if not presumptuous, to produce another volume on the ministry of Billy Graham and the evangelistic association he has led for more than half a century. Myriad accounts, biographies, and books of many varieties on the evangelist and his work have been written. Why, then, another?

As strange as it may appear, Billy Graham's legacy and his ministry's contributions to the church and the kingdom of God have never been evaluated in the context of evangelical church history. In my book *The Evangelist,* I detailed Billy Graham's legacy, but in this book I will consider in depth his method of evangelism in the broader context of biblical, evangelical church history. In this book, the questions will be raised: (1) Do Graham's evangelization efforts find a worthy place in that historical, evangelical, biblical context? and (2) Have Graham's life and ministry contributed to Christ's cause in the world? Many realities suggest Graham's ministry should be investigated from the historical perspective to answer these important issues. For example, no evangelist has preached the gospel to more people in the entire scope of the Christian movement, nor have more people responded positively to the gospel call from one man. Around the world Billy Graham is known and admired, and year after year polls recognize him as one of the ten most respected personalities in the world. He has preached the gospel to more people in live audiences than anyone else in history—more than 210 million people in more than 185 countries and territories—through various meetings, including the Mission World and Global Mission satellite projects. Hundreds of millions more have been reached through radio, television, video, and film. He has been honored by governments and myriad organizations, not to mention multiplied churches and countless people. An investigation and evaluation of his ministry as related to its historical, contributory perspective surely stands in order. That constitutes the purpose of this book.

The value of such an investigation is that it can hopefully answer the issue as to the integrity, historical authenticity, and genuine impact of the Billy Graham phenomenon. If he and his association fulfill the principles of biblical, historically authentic evangelical understanding of evangelism, then he not only has his place in the sweep of church history, but his ministry and contribution also stand vindicated and he deserves the respect of succeeding generations. That is important for the present hour and for years to come.

Therefore, with such a rationale for another volume on the Graham epic, this work undertakes a swift journey through two thousand years of church history to discover the essential principles of evangelism from an evangelical perspective along with an in-depth investigation of Graham's work and beliefs with the view to discover whether his ministry follows the basic principles of authentic evangelical evangelism and whether the final fallout is positive and contributory. If such be the case, Graham's contribution truly deserves an important place in history.

CHAPTER 1

THE EPIC BEGINS

Do the work of an evangelist.
—2 TIMOTHY 4:5

CAN THIS REALLY BE HAPPENING? We have never seen anything like this before! Do you think this is truly of God? I do not know! One can hardly tell at this stage! Such were the questions and exclamations that surrounded the phenomenon taking place in late September 1949 on the corner of Washington Boulevard and Hill Street on the edge of the skyscraper district of Los Angeles, California. A large tent affectionately called the Canvas Cathedral had been erected on the site, and people were flocking to it by the thousands. A casual observer might think because of its proximity to Hollywood that a magnificent entertainment program was in progress. Nothing was farther from the truth. Unbelievably the tent housed an evangelistic campaign conducted by a thirty-year-old North Carolina farm boy named Billy Graham. But what a "show" it was to behold.

THE BEGINNINGS AND BACKGROUND

It had all begun some months earlier through the means of a concerted prayer effort for California. A local Los Angeles Lutheran minister, Armin

Gesswein, had been challenging the evangelical believers in the Los Angeles area to give themselves to prayer. He had shared in the significant 1937 religious revival in Norway. He said, "Whenever God is going to do any kind of work, He always begins with prayer."[1] Another lesser-known personality who was significant in stimulating prayer concern in the Los Angeles area was a young Baptist minister named Joe Stevens. He had served as an officer in the United States Cavalry in World War II and was ministering with rich spiritual blessings attending his work. Others also had leadership roles in creating an atmosphere of prayer. They had discovered the secret that God moves in reviving power essentially in answer to fervent prevailing prayer. As the biblical commentator Matthew Henry said, "When God is about to pour out unusual blessings, He first sets His people a-praying." Los Angeles, in many respects, had fallen on its knees.

In the same general time frame, a group of Christian laymen felt a concern and burden that Los Angeles needed an evangelistic crusade, somewhat comparable to the former Billy Sunday meetings in the earlier decades of the twentieth century. They met and formed a committee to investigate such a possibility; some had actually played a similar role in one of the previous Billy Sunday crusades. The critics saw it all as a futile effort. The prevailing temperament of many Christians after the cessation of the hostilities of World War II centered in the conviction that the days of mass evangelism were over. Many argued that the world would be addressed with the gospel primarily through personal witness and by the ministry of local churches. The great days of significant American evangelists who preached to the multitudes, such as Jonathan Edwards in America's First Great Awakening, Charles Finney in the Second Revival, and well-known evangelists such as D. L. Moody and Billy Sunday, were now relics and icons of the past. The days of people meeting en masse to hear the gospel had ended.

Yet it can be correctly said that not all forms of mass evangelism had ceased. Youth for Christ rallies were being held across America during the war and in the immediate postwar period, and young people were responding well. There were also a number of evangelists who exercised some effect during those years, but certainly no significant personality had arisen to epitomize that method of evangelization as had been true of the past. But were the critics right? To say that God will discard any particular method of reaching people for salvation is a rather dubious pronouncement. At any rate, the Los Angeles committee invited Billy Graham to come and hold an evangelistic crusade. And now as we look back and reflect on that effort at mass evangelism in Los Angeles four years after the fall of Germany and Japan, we can see that God was about to do a marvelous work of grace once more. In His sovereignty, God can do as He wishes. A mighty move of God lurked in the wings, awaiting the crucial cue to enter center stage. Exciting days lay in store. But who was this evangelist named Billy Graham whom God was about to raise to world prominence?

THE EVANGELIST

Billy Graham had no unusual background to commend him to the task; at least so it would seem. Born into a typical Presbyterian farming family in 1918, Billy Frank, as his family and friends called him, grew up on the family dairy farm. He was reared in the typical Southern culture of Charlotte, North Carolina. He came to faith in Christ in an evangelistic crusade in September of 1934 under the preaching of evangelist Mordecai Fowler Ham. Being about sixteen years old at the time, Billy Frank experienced a true transforming conversion. In the same crusade in Charlotte, two friends, brothers Grady and T. W. Wilson, stepped out in a new commitment to Christ. God in sovereign grace began, even at that early stage, putting together a team that would ultimately impact the globe.

When Billy finished high school, he went for a short time to Bob Jones College in Cleveland, Tennessee. But he soon left Bob Jones and enrolled in Florida Bible Institute at Temple Terrace, a suburb of Tampa. Dr. Bob Jones, founder and president of the college, was disappointed and disturbed with Billy Graham's decision to leave his school. The president told the young man, "Billy, if you leave and throw your life away at a little Bible school, chances are you will never be heard of. At best all you could amount to would be a poor country preacher somewhere out in the sticks."[2] How wrong he was. One night, in the setting of his studies at the Bible institute, Billy wandered out on the golf course of Temple Terrace. On the eighteenth green he fell to his knees, giving himself in full surrender to do God's will, to preach His gospel, and to follow the Lord Jesus Christ wherever He may lead.

EARLY MINISTRY

Billy Frank finished his studies at Florida Bible Institute and moved to Wheaton College, west of Chicago. There he received his Bachelor of Arts degree in anthropology. At Wheaton he also met his future wife, Ruth, a medical missionary's daughter. After college days, Billy Graham became pastor of a small Baptist church in Western Springs, Illinois. His life seemed set. A definite call to preach had come, and now God had opened the door for him to become a pastor. There he started broadcasting *Songs in the Night,* a religious radio program featuring George Beverly Shea as vocalist. That too proved very providential, as shall be seen. The program met with good success. His friend Grady Wilson had also spent a year at Wheaton College, and the tie between Billy and the Wilson brothers deepened. After he left the Western Springs church, Billy threw himself into the evangelistic rally ministry of Youth for Christ International. He began to travel extensively in America. In the mid-'40s, Billy traveled to England and extended his ministry of itinerant evangelism overseas.

As Graham's involvement with Youth for Christ developed and demanded more of his time, he became convinced that he should devote himself entirely to itinerant evangelism. His wife, Ruth, longed to go back to the Far East and serve in Tibet. But Billy felt no such call and gave himself more and more to evangelism. At the same time, Dr. W. B. Riley, pastor of the First Baptist Church of Minneapolis, Minnesota, urged him to accept the presidency of Northwestern Schools, which Riley had founded. Somewhat reluctantly, Graham agreed and became an educational administrator along with his itinerant evangelistic ministry. At a spiritual life conference in North Carolina, Billy met Cliff Barrows. Cliff led the singing for the conference, and a new friend and fellow servant of Christ was bonded to Billy. The team was coming together. With Grady Wilson, George Beverly Shea, Cliff Barrows, and Billy all together, things were ready to erupt to the glory of God in Los Angeles. Yet, a most significant spiritual step in young Graham's ministry took place just before the Los Angeles crusade opened.

A NEW STEP

Billy had a very close friend and fellow Youth for Christ evangelist, Charles Templeton. He too was a young man with outstanding ability and a keen intellect. Although Billy had previously assumed he would go to seminary after graduation from Wheaton College, his ministry developed so rapidly that he never acquired further theological training. On the other hand, Templeton became convinced that the message they had been preaching was far too simple and that they had to sharpen their theological swords. Templeton enrolled in Princeton Theological Seminary and all but begged Billy to follow him. This threw Billy into a quandary of indecision. To compound the problem, in discussions with Templeton and others, Billy had begun to entertain some doubts about the total veracity and authority of the Scriptures. At the same time, however, he recognized that when he would quote the Bible in a sermon, convicting power gripped the people. This thrust him in the conflict between his conscience and his sharp, inquiring mind. A resolution had to be found.

As Billy struggled with his conscience and his intellect seemingly in conflict, the dilemma became threatening. Just before the Los Angeles meetings of 1949 were scheduled to begin, he served as a featured speaker in a student conference at Forest Home, a retreat center in the San Bernardino Mountains near Los Angeles, established by Henrietta Mears of the Hollywood Presbyterian Church. At Forest Home Billy faced again his friend Charles Templeton, who was also a speaker. The two debated the validity of the Bible, but it only deepened Billy's inner conflict.

In real turmoil, one night Billy went out for a walk in the pine forest surrounding Forest Home. He trudged about fifty yards off the main trail and sat down on a large rock. He spread his Bible out upon a tree stump in front of him. Struggling with his doubts, he had to face the question of the validity of the Scriptures and make a decision. And he did make a decision, one from which he has never veered or departed since. Actually, it has formed the foundation of his ministry. In a spirit of absolute surrender before God, in something of the same spirit he exemplified on the eighteenth green at Temple Terrace, he cried out, "Oh, God, I cannot prove certain things. I cannot answer some of the questions Chuck is raising and some of the other people are raising, but I accept this Book by faith as the word of God."[3] Billy made his choice. By faith he accepted the Bible as the fully truthful authoritative Word of God, and his ministry was transformed. A bronze tablet that identifies the actual "stone of witness" where Billy sat down and accepted once and for all the validity of the Bible stands there to this day. That deep and enriching experience and commitment to the absolute truthfulness and power of the Word of God not only relieved Billy of his conflicts and doubts, it set the stage for what took place in Los Angeles just a few days later on September 25, 1949—a date to remember.

After the enriching experience at Forest Home, Billy made his way to Los Angeles to start his campaign in the Canvas Cathedral. There the volcano of God's mercy erupted, and Los Angeles was shaken in a fashion that had not been seen in America since the dynamic days of America's First and Second Great Awakenings.

THE CRUSADE

The great Los Angeles crusade was scheduled to last for three weeks. The organizers wisely pitched the tent in a strategic location, a well-known intersection. The large tent could not but catch the eye and attention of the many passersby in that busy section of south Los Angeles. Still, few expected to see what actually transpired, least of all Billy and his team.

Although Armin Gesswein had challenged Los Angeles believers to fervent prayer, when Grady Wilson came on the scene he got the so-called prayer chains organized. Moreover, prayer groups were organized in churches and entire days for prayer were set aside. There were also all-night prayer meetings, as well as much fervent individual prayer. The Spirit of God was clearly setting the stage.

As the evangelistic services began to unfold, nothing of particular significance took place, except for the fact that just one conversion is important in the sight of God, and a few people came to Christ each night. But the crowds were hardly overwhelming; still the response seemed somewhat encouraging. As one week followed the other, things picked up considerably and it began to become clear that God was starting to move. Encouraged, Billy Graham wrote in a letter to a friend: "We are having by far the largest evangelistic campaign of our entire ministry. You would have been thrilled, if you could have seen the great tent packed yesterday afternoon with 6,100 people and several hundred turned away, and seen the scores of people walking down the aisle from every direction accepting Christ as personal Savior when the invitation was given. . . . There is some agitation that the campaign continue for several more weeks."[4]

The "Christ for Greater Los Angeles" campaign, as it was called, faced an important decision: Should the services end on a high note or should they carry on? As the committee addressed the issue, several felt the effort should stop. They had hit a significant stage and reasoned it would be best to end on that positive plain. Others, however, felt convinced that the work should be continued. People were still responding, and there seemed to be an ever-rising interest. The committee referred the question to a subcommittee of three. They in turn left it to Billy.

The evangelist found himself in a state of hesitation. He really did not quite know what God would have them do. He and Cliff prayed earnestly that the Holy Spirit would show them His will in an unmistakable way. They did as Gideon of the Old Testament ventured to do; they sought a sign. They put out the fleece, praying and watching for a sign. It came. Not with a wet fleece as in Gideon's case, but with a telephone call in the early hours of the morning.

THE "WET FLEECE"

Stuart Hamblen was a most unlikely candidate to become God's "fleece." Hamblen, a massive Texan in his late thirties, had become one of the most popular radio stars on the West Coast. This was before television emerged as the main media, and Hamblen's program was the most listened to radio broadcast in California, with tens of thousands tuning in to his program every day. He rose to become something of an icon to Westerners. He had also won the Pacific rodeo and was a successful racehorse owner, a big gambler, and a heavy drinker. His father had been a Methodist preacher in Texas, but when Stuart moved west, he said he left it all behind. His radio program was called the *Cowboy Church of the Air*. This made Hamblen a hypocrite, a fact he would gladly acknowledge later.

Hamblen's wife, Suzy, however, was a dedicated Christian woman with a vibrant faith. She had prayed for her husband for sixteen years. When Henrietta Mears started the Hollywood Christian Group for Bible study, Suzy enticed Stuart to attend the sessions from time to time. When Billy's crusade started in September 1949, Hamblen promised his wife he would go hear the young evangelist. Stuart, though, tried to back out, which led to a bitter argument with his wife. Biographer John Pollock tells the story:

Early that evening Hamblen shied, "Baby, you just drop me off at Brittingham's Bar and go on out to the meeting and pick me up on your way home."

Suzy flared, saying she had told everybody he was bringing her.

Stuart replied: "If that's the way you feel about it, let's get going! Get on your mule right now!"

They drove to Westwood. Unexpectedly Billy arrived an hour early too. [Billy said], "Stuart was rough, strong, loud and at times uncouth, but I was attracted to him. And because I was a Southerner he sort of took to me. And he said, 'Come and be on my radio show. I can fill your tent down there for you.'"

"That," Stuart comments, "was before I began hating the man."

Billy duly attended Warner Brothers studio for a live interview on KFWB. Hamblen then urged his audience to go to the tent, and to Billy's surprise blurted out, "I'll be there too."

The Hamblens sat in the front row, Stuart enjoying his patronage. "When the plate was passed I would put in three bucks—or maybe ten if I was sure someone of the Team was watching me." Ruth Graham had come West for the first days and Stuart took the Team out, to Chinatown to watch Ruth's skill at chopsticks, or elsewhere for Southern fried chicken.

In the second week at the big tent Hamblen grew angry. Billy's long finger seemed to be pointing right at him: "There is somebody in this tent who is leading a double life." Hamblen genuinely believed such remarks were deliberately aimed. After one more night he fled to the Sierras on a hunting trip, not returning until midnight on the supposed final Sunday, October 16.

With ill grace Hamblen was beside Suzy in the front row on Monday night. "When Billy Graham got up and preached a terrific sermon, I said, 'O that is a lot of malarkey, he is lying.' When they took up the collection, I said, 'That is a racket!' When they sang some wonderful hymns, I said, 'That singing is lousy.' The long finger pointed again. 'There is a person here tonight who is a phony.'" Stuart Hamblen rose from the seat in a fury, shook his fist at Billy and stormed out in the middle of the sermon.

"I went first to one bar and then to another, but I couldn't stand the taste of the drinks they poured me. Besides, their bands were hitting sour notes. At last I gave up and started home, and on the way Christ spoke to me." Hamblen fought back. "I was still fighting when I got home and woke my wife up, and I didn't wake her up gently. I stormed into the upper bedroom where she was asleep and I said, 'Woman, get out of that bed.' She jumped out of the bed with those brown eyes all wide and aflash and said, 'What is the matter with you?' I said, 'Let's pray.' We prayed, but I still couldn't make connections."

About 2 A.M. Stuart said that since Billy was the man who had upset him they would wake him up. Billy answered the telephone, could hear that Stuart had been both drinking and crying, and told him to "come right on down" to the apartment hotel where the Grahams and the Grady Wilsons shared an efficiency suite.

Stuart, with Suzy trailing behind, banged on the apartment door. It was opened by Billy in slacks and sweater. Stuart roared, "I want you to pray for me."

Billy replied, "No, I'm not going to do it." Stuart nearly knocked him down.

"Come in, Stuart," Billy said, "and I'll tell you why."

Billy knew that Stuart Hamblen was like the Rich Young Ruler and refused to help him to a selfish, easy faith. At one point in their talk Billy even said, "Go on back home. If you're not going to go all the way and let Jesus Christ be the actual Lord of every area of your life, don't ask me to pray with you, and don't waste anybody else's time."

At last, about 5 A.M., Stuart promised he would give up all that was mean and wicked in his heart. "We started praying and we weren't whispering. Billy prayed, Grady Wilson prayed, Suzy prayed, I prayed. And as I knelt by that chair I felt I was kneeling at the feet of my Jesus. 'Lord,' I prayed, 'you're hearing a new voice this morning.'"

When they got from their knees they all talked at once for joy. Stuart called his mother long-distance in Texas and heard her weep and shout at the news. Then they had breakfast, cooked by Grady, and therefore featured grits, a Southern dish that Stuart had always detested. But now he ate two helpings with relish, and when he asked for a third, Grady exclaimed, "Boy, you've been really converted!"

That very day Stuart Hamblen told his radio audience that he had given his life to Christ. "I've quit smoking and I've quit drinking." He would sell all his racehorses except one, which he would never race again. "Tonight at the end of Billy's invitation, I'm going to hit the sawdust trail."

The sensation was enormous. Hundreds of newcomers flocked to the big tent. On the next Sunday, and again the following week, Hamblen went on the platform to say, "I didn't know what it was like to be a real Christian. Do you know the thrill of it all? I like to talk about it. Boy, I talk about it everywhere"—including the bars he had most frequented. He learned that, quite seriously, the betting in "Gower Gulch" and along Hollywood Boulevard that Hamblen "wouldn't keep it up," dropped from 100-1 to 20-1; and after his second testimony, to 10-1.

Stuart Hamblen's conversion was Billy Graham's "fleece." The campaign was extended.

At the end of that week Billy, Cliff and Bev Shea put out another "Gideon's fleece," praying for a clear sign whether to extend once again.

The night on which they had to make up their minds to close or extend, Billy arrived at the tent to find the place swarming with reporters and photographers—a new, overwhelming and distracting experience. Flashbulbs exploded everywhere. Billy in the middle of the sermon had to ask a man to climb down from a stepladder he had placed right in front of the platform. All sorts of questions were flung at him afterward, and next day the Los Angeles *Examiner* and *Herald Express* carried banner headlines. Someone told Graham, "You've been kissed by William Randolph Hearst." The dispatch was featured in the other Hearst papers across the country, and was picked up by Associated Press.[5]

THE MEDIA

The story of William Randolph Hearst's committing his newspaper kingdom to publicizing the Graham crusade presents a fascinating tale in itself. The story goes that Hearst, at the urging of one of his house servants, became interested in Graham. As a result, he liked what he heard and penned a two-word note to his reporters: "Puff Graham." Some members of the family, however, later said that Hearst would not have expressed it that way. Regardless, the reporters were given some word from the newspaper tycoon and began to publicize the Graham ministry in an almost fantastic fashion. The die was cast.

ANOTHER CONVERT

At that stage another significant conversion took place. The West Coast "godfather" of syndicated crime at that time was Mickey Cohen. He became known as the Czar of the Los Angeles Underworld. Although many of his henchmen had been successfully prosecuted, authorities could not get enough evidence on Cohen to indict and convict him. One of his fellow crime masters was an electronic genius by the name of Jim Vaus. Vaus had been an officer in the U.S. Army during World War II and had developed incredible electronic skills. But even while in the army he had tampered with army equipment and was court-martialed. President Truman pardoned him, however, and thus he got off the hook.

Jim Vaus had a fascinating background. Being the son of a Baptist minister, to please his parents he attended a local Bible school for a period of time but did not enter into the spirit of the institution. He became editor of the yearbook his senior year but was expelled for embezzling the funds. From there he went into the military and carried on his escapades. Upon discharge, Mickey Cohen hired him to set up electronic surveillance and various electronic means of gathering information.

Vaus developed a wiretapping system whereby all he needed to know was the telephone number in a given area and he could tap into the conversation. He did not need to attach wires; he would just sit in his hotel room and listen to any conversation in the city if he knew the telephone number. As can be imagined, many Hollywood stars engaged him in that enterprise. Not only that, he developed an electronic mechanism that would interrupt the teletype messages transmitted from New York to Los Angeles, interpret them, and then feed the message back into the wire service without either party on the East or the West Coast knowing that their message had been intercepted and read. The purpose, quite obviously, was to find out what horses had won a race on the East Coast, place a bet on the winning horse, and then send the message back through the wire service. Using this system, large sums of money could be illegally won. Vaus truly was a genius. And being close to Mickey Cohen, he had a fantastic future in crime!

Like Suzy Hamblen, however, Jim Vaus's wife was a dedicated Christian. With all the notoriety Billy Graham received after Stuart Hamblen's conversion, she finally talked her husband into attending one of the crusade meetings with her.

Jim Vaus had come alive to Stuart Hamblen's commitment on Saturday, November 5, when he tuned his car radio to station KFWB in Los Angeles and heard Stuart give his Christian testimony. Vaus at first thought, *What that guy won't do for publicity!* However, when Stuart did his commercial for the sponsoring cigarette company and stated, "Folks! Smoking won't do you any good at all! In fact, you might as well quit! But if you have already got the habit, smoke "__s" (naming the sponsor), it struck Jim Vaus significantly.[6] He went to the service.

The night that Jim Vaus attended was just one day before Billy Graham's thirty-first birthday. Vaus had to admit that when "Billy stepped to the center of the platform I could not find anything wrong with him. . . . Something about the ease with which he moved, the flash in his eyes, the conviction in his voice, gripped me. His message was not new, I had heard it lots of times. What amazed me was there weren't any jokes. It was all Bible. And I knew he was telling the truth."[7]

When Graham gave the invitation, Vaus fell deeply under conviction. He clenched his fists as the Spirit of God moved powerfully in his heart. Then an old gentleman, a personal worker in the crusade, gripped his arm. The first thought that came to Jim Vaus's mind was to knock him down into the sawdust. But the old gentleman did not say a word; he just bowed his head and prayed. Uncle Billy Schofield, as all knew him, was holding Vaus's arm and praying earnestly for him, but Vaus wanted to run pell-mell out of the Canvas Cathedral. Right at that moment, Billy Graham said, "There is a man in this audience who has heard this story many times before, and who knows this is the decision he should make. Yet again he is saying no to God. He is hardening his heart, stiffening his neck, and he is going out of this place without Christ. And yet this may be the last opportunity God will give him to decide for Christ."[8] This thrust Jim into an even deeper conflict of heart and mind. Again Billy said, "This is your moment of decision." Finally, Jim Vaus muttered, "I'll go." The battle was over. Vaus headed for the front. He was taken to the small counseling tent, and soon his wife knelt by his side, making a deeper commitment to Christ. Jim prayed, "Lord, I believe this time from the bottom of my heart . . . it's going to be almost impossible to straighten out this bewildered, tangled life of mine. But if you will straighten it up, I will turn it over to you, all of it."[9]

The *Los Angeles Examiner* and *Herald Express* headlines the next morning read: "Wire Tapper Vaus Hits the Sawdust Trail." The news flashed across America. Armin Gesswein, on a train from Minneapolis to Chicago, heard the report on the train radio news bulletin. As soon as he reached Chicago he called Billy from the Youth for Christ office. Billy said, "Armin, you had better get out here fast. Something's happened and I don't know what it is. It is way beyond me."[10] Of course, the answer was that God had come in genuine reviving power.

MORE VICTORIES

There were other significant conversions too. Louis Zamperini, a track star who had won Olympic gold medals, came to Christ. This also made headlines. Los Angeles was stirred. Billy Graham's name was heralded across the country. This author was in his college dormitory room when the news came over the radio. What a startling revelation of God's marvelous doings! I ran to my next class, a course on preaching, and shared with the whole class that God had come in a powerful way to Los Angeles through a young evangelist by the name of Billy Graham. All rejoiced.

The "Christ for Greater Los Angeles" crusade turned out to be a startling event—an epic. How did it come about? In a very real sense of the word, it was the sovereignty of God, along with Billy's commitment to the Word of God and the faithful preaching of the gospel. As a result, the Holy Spirit fell. God's hour had arrived. And the rest is history.

THE HISTORICAL QUESTION

From Los Angeles, Billy Graham had gone from strength to strength. But the statement "the rest is history" raises the significant issue: Is the Billy Graham ministry genuinely a historical phenomenon that finds itself in the mainstream of evangelical thought and evangelistic credibility that has manifested itself throughout two thousand years of church history? Is the Graham phenomenon of the last half of the twentieth century something that will fade away and be forgotten, or will it find a legitimate place in the historical sweep of what God has done for two millennia in gospel proclamation and thus make its contribution to God's kingdom—and the world?

The purpose of this book is to attempt to discover the answers to these questions. It will mean trekking through these two thousand years, at least certain aspects of them, to discover what historical evangelism in practice and principle truly is; and then looking at the Graham ministry over the years, raising the question, Does the ministry of Billy Graham and the Billy Graham Evangelistic Association truly fit in the whole scheme of God's kingdom work in the declaration of the gospel? So the analysis of the Billy Graham epic will attempt a rather audacious thing: walking through those two millennia of church history to uncover the basic elements of authentic evangelism from an evangelical perspective. But it should prove to be a quite fascinating journey. Some incredible events have occurred in those two thousand years of God's great actions. Thus we will press on and divide the church's epochal movements into six basic periods:

> The Apostolic Age (1–100 C.E.)
> The Age of the Church Fathers (100–500 C.E.)
> The Middle Ages (500–1500 C.E.)
> The Reformation Age (1500–1650 C.E.)
> The Puritan/Pietistic-Revival Age (1650–1900 C.E.)
> The "Great" Age (1900–2000 C.E.)

Granted, these may seem to be arbitrary divisions, but they serve the purpose and hopefully do no violence to the unfolding of God's dealing in the evangelistic ministry of His church.

INTRIGUING PERSONALITIES

For each "age" listed above, this book will introduce two significant intriguing personalities with brief biographical sketches and then outline one historically authenticated principle of evangelism each personality epitomized. Space precludes any exhaustive, in-depth look at the theological truth these people symbolize. Still, the evangelical doctrinal outline presented would surely have their sanction and approval. In that fashion, twelve central principles will emerge that together culminate in an evangelism that can be recognized as a ministry of biblical, historical integrity.

The choosing of only one aspect of evangelism in these various historical personalities does not mean these giants of the church did not integrate other acceptable principles in their lives and ministries as well. They surely did; they were well-rounded servants of Christ. But the setting forth of one specific evangelistic precept in each personality is undertaken in light of the fact that each person investigated particularly contended for that specific principle as he carved out his evangelistic service. That approach hopefully justifies the endeavor and in the end will set forth the twelve essential, historical, authentic evangelistic principles by which to judge Billy Graham. Simply put, in each chapter, one salient personality and the principle of evangelism he personified will be set forth in his respective era of church history. Then the Billy Graham ministry will be thoroughly investigated to discover his approach to that respective truth. The work will thus unfold as follows:

The Apostolic Age
- The apostle Peter's evangelism, which was filled and directed and empowered by the Holy Spirit
- The apostle Paul's call to preach and herald the gospel in such a manner that communicated the entire message of Jesus Christ so that evangelism might be one of depth and biblical integrity

The Age of the Church Fathers
- Augustine's theology that God reveals Himself as sovereign in all of life and the experience of the church, the evangelistic ministry in particular
- Athanasius's contention that the Lord Jesus Christ stands at the center of all authentic evangelism; He must be fully understood for all the entire Bible declares Him to be

The Middle Ages
- St. Francis of Assisi's example of the fact that evangelism, to be truly biblical, must be expressed in a holistic manner
- Savonarola's contention for the gospel, which showed that often a severe price, even the price of suffering and death, must be paid

The Reformation Age
- Martin Luther's commitment to the reality that true evangelism emerges from the Scriptures, primarily and exclusively
- Ulrich Zwingli's argument that world evangelization and defense of the gospel demand boldness on the part of those who would declare Christ

The Puritan/Pietistic-Revival Age
- Richard Baxter's demonstration that the goal of evangelism is salvation that leads to a discipleship life of godliness and holiness
- John Wesley's demonstration that evangelism experiences its greatest reaping time during the periods of spiritual awakening

The "Great" Age
- William Carey's ministry that set forth the principle that the gospel is for all people and must be extended to the farthest reaches of the world
- Charles Haddon Spurgeon's demonstration that an evangelism of integrity that produces lasting results places the church at the emanating center of the endeavor

The result of this approach will hopefully be that these twelve principles will emerge in such interest and clarity that they can form the matrix of biblical, historical evangelism at its best so Billy Graham and his ministry can be grasped and evaluated in that light. The question will be continually raised: Do Billy Graham and the many ministries of the Billy Graham Evangelistic Association meet the standard of evangelistic church history, and have they truly contributed to God's kingdom and the world's good? It should be instructive and inspirational for the reader to see how and why God has used one man and his team to address more people with the gospel than any other evangelist in the history of the entire church.

As the various principles of historic evangelism and the Graham ministry are approached, it will become evident that to strictly "cubbyhole" each of the twelve criteria discussed in this work will be impossible. Many of the evangelistic principles merge and to some degree overlap. For example, the criticism and attacks on Billy Graham illustrate the principle of persecution and suffering for the gospel. At the same time, Graham's firm stand for his position is indicative of his boldness for the gospel.

Moreover, the Christian church generally recognizes that the Graham ministry must be seen and understood in the light of what has been termed the "New Evangelicalism." But when we say the "New Evangelicalism," we must recognize that evangelicalism dates back to the first century. As John Stott has said, "The evangelical faith is nothing other than the historic

Christian faith."[11] There have obviously been evangelicals since the birth of the church; yet, in the past century or two, there has been a quite radical resurgence of the evangelical approach to the Christian faith, hence the name "New Evangelicalism." In recent years, notables like John R. W. Stott, pastor; Carl Henry, theologian; Harold J. Ockenga, pastor and educator; and specifically Billy Graham, evangelist, have become household names. Graham has especially served as a symbol of the new thrust. Ockenga said that Billy Graham has become the spokesman of the convictions and ideals of the New Evangelicalism.

Space prohibits a detailed definition of the development of this "new" evangelical movement. However, D. A. Carson gives a succinct summary. Professor Carson presents a brief, but to the point, definition of evangelicalism with these words:

The term "evangelical" is colored with different shadings in various parts of the world. In North America until very recently, it was used to refer to Christians who are loyal to both a formal principle and a material principle. The formal principle is the truth, authority, and finality of the Bible. The material principle is the gospel as understood in historic evangelical Protestantism. While not wanting to minimize the theological and ecclesiastical differences in that heritage, we might summarize that heritage in terms such as these: We insist that salvation is gained exclusively through personal faith in the finished cross-work of Jesus Christ, who is both God and man. His atoning death planned and brought about by His heavenly Father, expiates our sin, vanquishes Satan, propitiates the Father, and inaugurates the promised kingdom. In the ministry, death, resurrection, and exaltation of Jesus, God himself is supremely revealed, such that rejection of Jesus, or denials of what the Scriptures tell us about Jesus, constitute nothing less than rejection of God himself. In consequence of his triumphant cross-work, Christ has bequeathed the Holy Spirit, himself God, as the down payment of the final inheritance that will come to Christ's people when he himself returns. The saving and transforming power of the Spirit displayed in the lives of Christ's people is the product of divine grace, grace alone—grace that is apprehended by faith alone. The knowledge of God that we enjoy becomes for us an impetus to missionary outreach characterized by urgency and compassion.

This summary, or something like it, most evangelicals would happily espouse. This sort of approach tightly ties "evangelical" to "evangel" . . . the gospel of Jesus Christ.[12]

A fuller summary description of the view can be found in the Lausanne Covenant, a document that came out of the 1974 Lausanne Conference in Switzerland sponsored by the Billy Graham Evangelistic Association. (See Appendix B.) Suffice it to say that evangelism, along with specific basic theological axioms, has become the key component in the context of contemporary evangelical Christianity.

It would seem appropriate at this juncture to present a definition of evangelism per se. This will give a working grasp of the term that will be used countless times as these pages unfold. Missiologist D. T. Niles defined the discipline as "one beggar telling another beggar where I found bread." That simple definition does get to the heart of the matter. A more developed definition that fills out Niles's basic statement is the following:

> Evangelism is a concerted, self-conscious effort to confront the unbeliever with the truth about and the claims of Christ with view to leading that unbeliever into repentance toward God and faith in the Lord Jesus Christ and thus into the fellowship of a local church where the spiritual maturation process can begin and be nurtured and provide an avenue for service in and through the body of Christ to establish God's kingdom in the lives of as many as the Lord God shall call.

And that is an important task, and a vital role for all the church to fill. As has been said, evangelism is not the *task* of the church; it is the church's very *nature*.

With these realities before us, we shall attempt to discover what the life, ministry, and impact of Billy Graham and his Evangelistic Association is all about and whether it truly measures up to authentic contributory evangelism. The church of Jesus Christ needs to know; future generations need to know. So to that intriguing task we now give ourselves, starting with the day the Spirit of God launched the Christian church on its kingdom enterprise, namely, the Day of Pentecost with the outpouring of the Holy Spirit. In that hour, the apostolic age was born and the gospel went forth with power.

INTRODUCTION TO THE
APOSTOLIC AGE

⁓

A RUSHING MIGHTY WIND, TONGUES OF FIRE, new languages, the power of God! Had we been visiting Jerusalem in the first century and witnessed that incredible event, we too would have cried out with the multitude, "What does this mean?" Yet the question should not have needed asking; Jesus the Christ told of it—even the Jewish Scriptures prophesied it. That great day testified to the fulfillment of our Lord's word that the Holy Spirit of God would come in power and establish the church through the apostles' witness. The new era of God's indwelling Holy Spirit had at last arrived. The Spirit was given and assumed control as the gospel of salvation spread over the land. The kingdom of God arrived in our very midst.

Those foundational days and succeeding events we call the apostolic age. And it all began by the outpouring of the Holy Spirit in that significant hour the church celebrates as the Day of Pentecost. Jesus had lived, died, and rose again; now, after His ascension, by the Spirit He had come to continue His ministry in and through His followers to establish His kingly reign on earth. The church was born, and the gospel raced forward on its worldwide mission.

The two outstanding personalities of that first century thrust were undoubtedly the apostles Peter and Paul. These men, their principles, and Billy Graham's understanding of their principles, deserve most careful attention. These aspects of evangelization are foundational to the evangelist's entire ministry. Thus, these issues shall be looked at in considerable depth relative to their basic contribution to the evangelistic thrust of the universal church. So we begin with Peter and the work of the Holy Spirit in evangelization. That is how it all got started, and in that way we can hopefully begin to grasp adequately the Billy Graham epic.

CHAPTER 2

THE HOLY SPIRIT IN EVANGELISM

~

PART I:
PETER AND THE HOLY SPIRIT

Peter, filled with the Holy Spirit, said . . .

—ACTS 4:8

INTRODUCTION

WHEN THE APOSTOLIC AGE DAWNED on the dramatic Day of Pentecost, one paramount principle projected itself in bold relief: Until Christ returns, this era is to be the "Age of the Spirit." As the Holy Spirit fell upon Peter and the 120 disciples in that monumental moment, a new dispensation of the kingdom of God had unquestionably broken in on the scene. Since that hour, *all* God's people have become recipients of the indwelling influence and impact of the Spirit of God. The creating God inaugurated an entirely new relationship between Himself and the believer. The promise of God's power and presence upon, in, and through His people had been foretold in the Jewish Scriptures and by Jesus Christ Himself; on that day it became a glowing reality. And the central figure in that dramatic scene was Simon Peter, the fisherman whom the Holy Spirit made a "fisher of men." The whole scene was just as Jesus said and the Old Testament Scriptures have prophesied.

THE OLD TESTAMENT PROMISE OF SPIRIT POWER

The outpouring of the Holy Spirit upon the Jewish believers in Jesus actually proved to be nothing new, at least in principle. The Spirit had manifested Himself countless times in Hebrew history. Many of the Jews had become quite knowledgeable regarding the fact that the Holy Spirit anoints God's people for ministry and service. The promises and the accounts of that heavenly work abound in the Old Testament Scriptures.

We are introduced to the doctrine of the Holy Spirit in the first verses of the Book of Genesis. After the foundational, creative statement that "in the beginning God created the heavens and the earth" (Gen. 1:1), the Spirit entered the scene: "And the earth was formless and void, and darkness was over the surface of the deep; and the Spirit of God was moving over the surface of the waters" (v. 2). The mighty hand of the Holy Spirit became powerfully manifest at the very outset of God's forming of the earth into a habitable planet for Adam, the crown of His creation. From that inception of the Spirit's work, the doctrine and activities of the Holy Spirit broaden and deepen through the pages of the Old Testament Scriptures like an ever-enlarging stream of truth and reality.

The promise of Joel, quoted by Simon Peter in his Pentecostal sermon (Acts 2), projects one of the most forthright Old Testament presentations of the promised bestowal of the Spirit of God. In that significant passage, Joel wrote:

It will come about after this that I will pour out My Spirit on all mankind; and your sons and daughters will prophesy, your old men will dream dreams, your young men will see visions. And even on the male and female servants I will pour out My Spirit in those days. And I will display wonders in the sky and on the earth, blood, fire, and columns of smoke. The sun will be turned into darkness, and the moon into blood, before the great and awesome day of the LORD comes. And it will come about that whoever calls on the name of the LORD will be delivered. (Joel 2:28–32)

Similar passages can be found throughout the Old Testament Scriptures:
Thou dost send forth Thy Spirit, they are created; and Thou dost renew the face of the ground. (Ps. 104:30)

This is the Word of the LORD. . . . "Not by might nor by power, but by My Spirit," says the LORD of hosts. (Zech. 4:6)

When they came to the hill there, behold, a group of prophets met him; and the Spirit of God came upon him mightily, so that he prophesied among them. (1 Sam. 10:10)

And Thou didst give Thy good Spirit to instruct them, Thy manna Thou didst not withhold from their mouth, and Thou didst give them water for their thirst. (Neh. 9:20)

The concept of the Holy Spirit moving mightily in and through God's people to accomplish His purpose became quite obvious to Israel's spiritual understanding. Surely Peter had some grasp of that wonderful reality. He had heard the Scriptures read in the synagogue; above all, he had sat at Jesus' feet. He surely knew that the Old Testament revelation of the Holy Spirit's work centered essentially in the anointing of the Spirit upon certain individuals at certain times for certain significant tasks. But now, since Pentecost, as Jesus promised, the Holy Spirit abides in *every* believer and animates *all* God's people in the service of Christ. Further, by His sanctifying power, the Holy Spirit forms Christ within redeemed believers, creating a life of godliness and holiness (Gal. 4:19). Peter and the early disciples had seen this exemplified perfectly in the Lord Jesus Christ. Every word, action, and miracle in His life was permeated with, motivated by, and empowered through the Spirit of God. Truly, the Spirit was given to Him "without measure" (John 3:34). The disciples had witnessed those wonderful realities. But Jesus said that by the Spirit they would do even "greater works" than He had done (John 14:12). Now the apostle and his fellow believers were set to experience something of it in their own lives. When the Day of Pentecost came, those promises found their overflowing fulfillment; and no one rose to the occasion more profoundly than Simon Peter.

PETER, THE HOLY SPIRIT, AND THE DAY OF PENTECOST

We know little of Simon Peter's life before he met the Lord Jesus. He was married, he had an impetuous personality, and he possessed a flare for leadership;

but he certainly had his foibles. Then came Pentecost and Peter stood as the personification of the Spirit-filled man. What a day Pentecost proved to be for Peter and his fellow believers. The Spirit was manifested in overwhelming majesty. Luke records the event in these words: "And suddenly there came from heaven a noise like a violent, rushing wind, and it filled the whole house where they were sitting. And there appeared to them tongues as of fire distributing themselves, and they rested on each one of them. And they were all filled with the Holy Spirit and began to speak with other tongues, as the Spirit was giving them utterance" (Acts 2:2–4). In that dramatic moment an event occurred that continues to this day. As commentator John Polhill has stated, "In a real sense, the church was born of the Spirit at Pentecost (chapter 2) just as the infancy narrative of Luke's gospel shows how Jesus was born of the Holy Spirit. . . . The presence of Jesus is experienced in the church through the Spirit. The Spirit is the abiding presence of Jesus; the Holy Spirit *is* the Spirit of Jesus."[1]

And the church expanded dramatically. The deduction from this primary truth centers in the fact that every significant breakthrough in the unfolding mission of Christ's church, as epitomized in Peter's early ministry, came about through the agency and auspices of the Holy Spirit. Frank Stagg, in his commentary on the Book of Acts, makes this principle paramount to understanding the Book of Acts. He points out that the initial breakthrough came on the Day of Pentecost through Peter's sermon. The next breakthrough occurred in the preaching of Philip to the Samaritans. That event constituted a major move for the church, for there were those in the Jerusalem congregation who thought the gospel was primarily, if not exclusively, for Jews and proselytes alone; all that despite the fact of what Jesus said in Acts 1:8 that the church was to make disciples of *all* nations. Another even more profound move forward came when Philip led the Ethiopian eunuch to faith in Christ (Acts 8:25–39). Not only Samaritans, but also now a Gentile heard the gospel, though the Ethiopian may well have been a convert to Judaism. Then a marvelous occurrence took place, again under the preaching of Peter (which we shall look at in more detail later), when he led a God-fearing Gentile and his entire household to faith in Christ (Acts 10). The conversion of Cornelius signaled a monumental breakthrough in the ongoing kingdom progress. Obviously, God has designed the gospel for everyone.

Stagg also points out a most interesting fact: The Book of Acts ends openendedly; the last word Luke wrote was the adverb "unhinderedly." This implies that the work of God continues to go on unhinderedly until the *parousia,* the return of Christ. The point is, these major breakthroughs were all effected and led by the powerful work of the Spirit of God. It took a while for Peter and the others to realize this revolutionary truth, but through this marvelous progression, the early Jewish Christians came to the understanding that the church must be an inclusive people, i.e., a people of God who break down all barriers of discrimination, prejudice, bigotry, and racism. As Stagg has shown, the church should always strive to present an "unhindered gospel."[2] Among the apostles, no one came to that realization any more significantly than Simon Peter.

PETER AND THE INCLUSIVE GOSPEL

The inclusive nature of the gospel gripped the apostle Peter; he was led to show the way of salvation to all (Acts 10), and that was revolutionary for a Jew—even a Christian Jew. But a new chapter in the life of the church opened. As William Barclay has said, "The tenth chapter of Acts tells a story that is one of the great turning points in the history of the Church. For the first time a Gentile is to be admitted into the fellowship of the Christian Church."[3] By the leadership and power of the Holy Spirit, the triumph of the gospel can impact the whole world.

The saga of how a small "Jewish sect" (as some saw the Christians) could so deeply influence the entire Mediterranean world in a matter of a few years staggered multitudes. So powerful did Peter and the early church's witness become that when the first missionaries came into a community, the antagonists threw up their hands and cried, "These that have turned the world upside down are come hither also" (Acts 17:6 KJV). As commentator Polhill said, "Only in being open to the Spirit of God were the witnesses of Acts able to fulfill the divine commission."[4]

PETER'S PREDOMINANCE AND THE SPIRIT

Peter clearly stands as the predominant figure among the twelve apostles, and as stressed, his witness is dramatically portrayed on the Day of Pentecost. That day must be viewed as a most insightful and instructive event on the working of the Holy Spirit in world evangelization, not only in Peter's life and ministry, but also for the entire community of believers for all time.

The message that Peter preached on the Day of Pentecost came to his hearers in an unbelievably convincing manner. Commentators and theologians have written volumes on the message of the gospel. This will be elucidated more clearly in the next chapter. Let it merely be said at this point that the message was straightforward, simple, and understandable, yet it was also most profound. As New Testament theologian Michael Green has pointed out, on the Day of Pentecost: (1) a person was preached, (2) a promise was presented, and (3) a response was expected. Green tells us Peter presented a three-point message concerning the *person* of Jesus Christ, i.e., the life, death, and resurrection of the Lord. In that context, Peter shared the *promise* of the forgiveness of sins, the gift of the Holy Spirit, and reconciliation to God. Finally, the apostle declared there must be a *response*. The response was threefold: repentance, faith, and baptism. This simple declaration struck deeply into the hearts of the hearers. Acts 2:37 states, "Now when they heard this, they were pierced to the heart, and said to Peter and the rest of the apostles, 'Brethren, what shall we do?'" The response was overwhelming. Three thousand were added to the church that single day (Acts 2:41). That type of response represents the ideal pattern for evangelism.

How does one explain the phenomenon of such reaction to the message? It certainly could not be found in the eloquence of Peter or even the fervency of his commitment to the gospel. It can only be attributed to the work of the Holy Spirit in and through the life of His servant. It was the direct fulfillment of the Word of the Lord in Acts 1:8, "You shall receive power when the Holy Spirit has come upon you; and you shall be My witnesses both in Jerusalem, and in all Judea and Samaria, and even to the remotest part of the earth." The power of God had fallen on Peter and the masses prostrated themselves before Christ's presence in repentance and faith.

When the Spirit of God fell on the disciples, as the Day of Pentecost makes clear, several primary evangelistic principles emerged that have guided the evangelical church ever since:

- The Spirit of God invades all believers (Acts 2:4).

- The Spirit of God uses believers in Christ to communicate the gospel (Acts 2:14).

- The Spirit of God empowers God's people to service (Acts 1:8).

- The Spirit of God bestows gifts of ministry on God's people to enable them to serve Christ with effect (Acts 2:4; 1 Cor. 12–14).

- The Spirit of God arouses deep and profound interest throughout the community (Acts 2:6, 7, 12).

- The Spirit of God reveals the full message of Jesus (Acts 2:14–36; John 14:26).

- The Spirit of God draws people to Christ (Acts 2:37).

- The Spirit of God regenerates repentant believers (Acts 2:41–42).

- The Spirit of God bears fruit in the believers to make them holy (Acts 2:42; Gal. 5:22–23).

On the basis of these spiritual dynamics, the mission of the church was launched.

In His commission, "You will receive power," our Lord spoke in the context of command. The future tense Jesus employed connotes an imperative sense: "you will [must] receive power," then "you will be My witnesses." The term Jesus used for "power" is the Greek word *dunamin*. The gospel writers employed the same word concerning the miracles of Jesus that gave such authenticity to His message. This implies, as pointed out by a New Testament scholar, "The Spirit of God was behind it all, and the gospel triumphed."[5] Power comes from the Holy Spirit, and He precipitates effective witness. God's people must be witnesses, and thus it becomes incumbent on the witnesses that they experience the power of the Spirit. That approach to evangelization epitomized Peter in his ministry.

Furthermore, the Holy Spirit not only empowers God's people for the task of evangelization, He also leads them in the grand enterprise. In the final analysis, the work is God's work, the *missio dei* as it has been called. The Spirit of God is the Leader and Director. Countless scriptural passages make this prime principle abundantly clear. The Book of Acts is replete with incidents of the principle, e.g., Acts 3:1–10, Peter and the healing of the cripple; Acts 8:4–25, Philip in Samaria; Acts 13:1–4, Paul on the first missionary journey; and Acts 16:9–10, the Macedonian vision. God does lead in evangelism by His Spirit.

As the gospel spread via the major breakthroughs mentioned earlier, all led by the Spirit, Peter preached and ministered with increasing power. In Acts 3:16, Luke recounts the Spirit-empowered healing of the cripple at the Beautiful Gate and the effective evangelism that ensued.

But persecution soon came on the witnesses, and the Jewish officials imprisoned Peter and John. The great word translated "witness" means "martyr." Persecution is inevitable. When the apostles were threatened and released, they returned to the gathered church and Peter shared the story of their encounter with the Jewish officials. Sensing the certainty of suffering for Christ, they lifted their voices in fervent prayer. Acts 4:29–30 records their plea before God: "And now, Lord, take note of their threats, and grant that Thy bond-servants may speak Thy word with all confidence, while Thou dost extend Thy hand to heal, and signs and wonders take place through the name of Thy holy servant Jesus."

Their prayer climaxed in the experience recorded in verse 31: "When they had prayed, the place where they had gathered together was shaken, and they were all filled with the Holy Spirit, and began to speak the word of God with boldness." Again the Spirit of God empowered them with boldness to declare the gospel of Christ as multitudes continued to press into the kingdom. New Testament scholar John Polhill describes the scenario as a unique period in which the people of God, filled with the Spirit, saw their church grow by leaps and bounds.

CHURCH GROWTH AND THE SPIRIT

After the conversion of Paul, persecution eased off for a period. Luke wrote, "The church throughout all Judea and Galilee and Samaria enjoyed peace, being built up; and, going on in the fear of the Lord and in the comfort of the Holy Spirit, it continued to increase" (Acts 9:31). When the Holy Spirit moves, the church expands and rejoices in the presence of God. We were previously introduced to the significant breakthrough for the church when Cornelius and his household came to faith in Christ. In the context of that major step forward, engineered by God, the Holy Spirit spoke very directly to Peter. Polhill points out, "Now it was the Holy Spirit . . . all was coordinated by the divine leading. The Spirit directed Peter to the three messengers standing at the gate and identified them as men He had sent."[6]

Recognizing the clear leadership of God's Spirit, Peter made his way with the messengers to the home of Cornelius. There he proclaimed Christ. Then Luke records these significant words: "While Peter was still speaking these words, the Holy Spirit fell upon all those who were listening to the message" (Acts 10:44). Peter raised the question: "Surely no one can refuse the water for these to be baptized who have received the Holy Spirit just as we did, can he?" (Acts 10:47). This fresh outpouring of the Spirit has been termed the Gentile Pentecost. The designation is quite appropriate. This event opened up the Gentile world to the gospel. Through the moving of the Holy Spirit in and through the life of Peter, similar breakthroughs in mission go on to this day. As one commentator has put it: "The pattern of a group demonstration of the Spirit invariably accompanies a new breakthrough in mission in Acts. We see it in the initial empowering of Pentecost, the establishment of the Samaritan mission, the reaching of former disciples of John the Baptist, and the foundation of the Gentile mission and its legitimization for the Jerusalem church."[7]

If this is the way God works, we must echo the words of Peter when he said, "Who was I that I could stand in God's way?" (Acts 11:17). The Spirit-filled ministry of Peter and the early church opened up the whole world for the message of Christ, and the church exploded with growth.

The only logical deduction to be drawn from this brief narrative of the early chapters of Acts as personified in the life of Peter can be set out in a threefold manner. First, all evangelists are to be Spirit-filled as they attempt to fulfill their gospel ministry. Second, all evangelism must be led and directed by the sovereign Spirit of God. Third, all evangelism is to be conducted in the power of the Holy Spirit and in submission to Christ's lordship. A brief comment concerning these significant concluding principles stands in order.

The fact that God intends all evangelists to be Spirit-filled is self-evident. It further implies that God intends *every* Christian to become an "evangelist," i.e., a *witness* in the purest sense of the word. This stands to reason because the Spirit was given to the whole church; therefore, the entire body of believers is equipped to witness and should do so.

Moreover, evangelism is to be directed and led by the Spirit of God. Those who would engage in the divine task of bringing Christ to the world, as Peter learned (Acts 10:15), must understand that the work is God's task. The Lord's people therefore are to cooperate intelligently with the Holy Spirit in the work of God.

The whole matter finds its roots in being submissive to the work of the Holy Spirit, seeking His power in all aspects of evangelization. These concepts and approaches were fully seen in Peter and in the history of the apostolic church. In the final analysis, God by the Spirit serves as the evangelist. That fact stands foundational to any effective ministry of evangelism. The Holy Spirit and true evangelism are one in the unity of the task.

A CONCLUSION

Therefore, it must be concluded that in all evangelistic efforts, whether they be mass evangelism or simple personal witness, the *power* and *leadership* of the Holy Spirit stands central. The evangelist who presumes to declare to people the eternal message of God's grace in Christ but is not filled with the Holy Spirit and empowered to speak with power is a travesty of biblical and historical evangelism. Much more will be said about the actual preaching of the gospel in subsequent pages, but let it be emphasized once more that all proclamation of the gospel of Jesus Christ must be Spirit-endued. Moreover, the world waits to see evangelism done on that foundation and evangelists like Peter who truly preach in the power of the Holy Spirit.

But what does all that mean theologically and pragmatically? What constitutes the biblical principles concerning the Holy Spirit that breathes authenticity into world evangelization? We begin with the life of Jesus.

THE DOCTRINE OF THE HOLY SPIRIT

We have seen something of the historical unfolding of the Spirit's work as epitomized in the apostle Peter; but to evaluate Billy Graham properly, the question must be raised as to what the Bible teaches concerning the Spirit's work as it relates to Christ and the church in world outreach. It should prove helpful first to look into the life of our Lord in respect to the Holy Spirit and His operation.

As summarily stated earlier, the Holy Spirit played a central role in Christ's earthly life and ministry. Starting with the incarnation, the entire Christ-event unfolded under the leadership, power, and unction of the Holy Spirit. Jesus Himself was conscious of this experiential reality. As James Dunn points out, "It is certain that Jesus believed himself to be empowered by the Spirit."[8] The principle of the Spirit's work in Jesus' life unfolds simply, yet most significantly:

- Jesus was born of a virgin, who conceived by the Spirit of God (Matt. 1:18).

- Jesus displayed unusual wisdom as a child under the touch of the Holy Spirit (Luke 2:41–51).

- At Jesus' baptism the Holy Spirit descended upon Him (Luke 3:21–22).

- Jesus was led by the Spirit into testing times (Matt. 4:1–11).

- Jesus' entire ministry of healing was empowered by God's Spirit (Luke 4:38–41).

- Jesus' teachings came in the wisdom of the Holy Spirit (Luke 4:14).

- Jesus delivered up His soul to the cross by the Holy Spirit (Heb 9:14).

- Jesus' resurrection was effected by the Spirit of God (Rom. 8:11).

- In summary, the Spirit was given unto Him "without measure" (John 3:34).

It becomes abundantly clear that the Holy Spirit served as the emanating source of all wisdom, power, and guidance in our Lord's ministry. As Leon Morris has pointed out, "The Spirit was on Jesus at all times, and his whole ministry sees the result of the presence of the Spirit."[9] Moreover, Jesus gave innumerable promises that the Spirit would come in like manner upon His disciples and minister through their lives as well. Some of the promises are:

I will ask the Father, and He will give you another Helper, that He may be with you forever; that is the Spirit of truth, whom the world cannot receive, because it does not behold Him or know Him, but you know Him because He abides with you, and will be in you. (John 14:16–18)

These things I have spoken to you, while abiding with you. But the Helper, the Holy Spirit, whom the Father will send in My name, He will teach you all things, and bring to your remembrance all that I said to you. (John 14:25–26)

Truly, truly, I say to you, he who believes in Me, the works that I do shall he do also; and greater works than these shall he do; because I go to the Father. (John 14:12)

As R. A. Torrey stressed, "The doctrine of the personality of the Holy Spirit is not only fundamental, but vital and immeasurably practical."[10] Suffice it to say, what occurred in the life of Jesus, the Holy Spirit effects in the life of the church. He teaches, leads, empowers, and uses God's people in kingdom advance. This leads us to what constitutes the biblical teaching concerning the person and work of the Holy Spirit that appears so essential to effective world evangelization for all God's people.

PNEUMATOLOGY: THE PERSON AND WORK OF THE HOLY SPIRIT IN EVANGELISM

The person of the Spirit raises the whole issue of the Trinity. The biblical concept of the *Triune* yet *One* God poses a true mystery. Perhaps all we can say with our limited ability to describe the infinite, Triune God is best expressed in the words of the Athanasian Creed:

There is one Person of the Father, another of the Son, and another of the Holy Spirit. But the Godhead of the Father, of the Son, and of the Holy Spirit, is all one, the glory equal, the majesty co-eternal. . . . And in this Trinity none is afore, or after other; none is greater, or less than another is. But the whole three persons are co-eternal together, and co-equal. So that in all things, as aforesaid, the Unity in Trinity, and the Trinity in Unity is to be worshipped.

Space forbids studying this central issue in any depth. We must content ourselves merely to say that the Spirit of God stands irrevocably as the Third Person of the divine Trinity with all the attributes and characteristics of God the Father and God the Son. He is omnipotent, omniscient, omnipresent, infinite, and ultimate; He is God. This is a mystery to be sure, but it is biblically true. Thus we accept that reality of the Spirit's divine personhood; but for our purposes here we restrict ourselves to His work in evangelization.

The Holy Spirit constantly operates in the world in manifold manners. However, one of the primary thrusts of the Holy Spirit in the human experience centers in His work toward evangelizing unbelievers. The key passage on this topic is found in John 16:7–11, in which Jesus said:

> Nevertheless I tell you the truth: it is to your advantage that I go away, for if I do not go away, the Counselor will not come to you; but if I go, I will send him to you. And when he comes, he will convince the world of sin and of righteousness and of judgment: of sin, because they do not believe in me; of righteousness, because I go to the Father, and you will see me no more; of judgment, because the ruler of this world is judged. (RSV)

The passage is rather difficult to interpret fully. As Raymond E. Brown has pointed out: "Several interpretations are possible. Augustine even avoided it because of its difficulties."[11] But surely the Spirit can lead one into the essential truth, because as Rudolf Schnackenburg points out, we can be "guided and enlightened by the Spirit, the Author of the Scriptures."[12] Another important word from Schnackenburg should be kept in mind in approaching this significant Johannine passage: "The Spirit, whose presence causes the Johannine community to rejoice is . . . inseparably bound to Jesus Christ. . . . He thus becomes Jesus' representative and in this way continues his revelation of salvation . . . and makes it effective and fruitful."[13] The Spirit of God is seen as the Presence of the resurrected Christ to lead and to enlighten people.

One thing is obvious in the rather complex passage under discussion: The words of Jesus reveal the threefold work of the Holy Spirit toward the unbelieving world. In fact, according to Leon Morris, it stands as "the one place in Scripture where the Spirit is spoken of as performing a work in 'the world.'"[14] The passage declares that the Spirit of God shows unbelievers their actual condition before God in a threefold manner.

THE HOLY SPIRIT CONVINCES OF SIN

C. H. Spurgeon correctly said, "The Spirit alone has power over man's heart."[15] Only the power of God can convince the human mind and heart of sin and thereby reveal to a person his true self. Melanchthon, theologian and companion of Martin Luther, once thought that by persuasion he could convince people of their sin. He learned differently when he entered the arena of the battle for souls.

He said, "Old Adam is too strong for young Melanchthon." The Holy Spirit, the *parakletos,* the "Advocate" who comes along by our side, He alone becomes the able "Convincer." C. H. Dodd put it this way; "The tables are turned. The Advocate becomes a prosecuting council and 'convicts' the world."[16]

The Holy Spirit creates conviction in the heart and urges people to face the reality of their true position before God and thus look to Him for mercy. In other words, to grasp fully the good news of the gospel, one must first come to understand the bad news of personal sin. Ethelbert Stauffer commented, "It was *necessary* that the Holy Spirit himself should open our eyes."[17] On our own, we human beings simply refuse to face the reality of personal sin. But the Holy Spirit steps in and convinces people of their sin of unbelief. Brown has told us: "The Paraclete will focus on the expression of disbelief that culminated in putting Jesus to death, but those who are guilty are a much wider group than the participants in the historical trial of Jesus. Those participants are only the forebears of men in every generation that will be hostile to Jesus."[18]

The scenario John's passage portrays is a world on trial before God. Through the Spirit-filled witness of the disciples to the Christ event, the world will have unveiled before its eyes the true nature of sin. Only the probing finger of God's Spirit can tap the deep recesses of the human heart and bring a person to that realization. And there is more.

THE HOLY SPIRIT CONVINCES OF RIGHTEOUSNESS

The Spirit of God not only convicts of sin; He convicts of righteousness. This term (Hebrew: *tsedeq*) to the Jews meant "straightness," action that conforms to a norm in Old Testament teaching. The New Testament uses *righteousness* (Greek: *dikaiosune*) in the sense of conforming to the righteous demands of God's will. What then constitutes the universal standard of God's righteousness? The answer: the Son's work on the cross, His resurrection, and His ascension. Morris has summarized it well: "The righteousness which is shown by Christ's going to the Father is surely that righteousness which is established by the cross."[19] Christ's life, death, resurrection, and ascension established and demonstrated the perfect righteousness of our God.

The point is that the Holy Spirit convinces the world that an acceptable standard of righteousness before the Lord does not depend on human efforts.

Even the Old Testament has told us "all our righteousnesses [deeds] are as filthy rags" (Isa. 64:6 KJV). Righteousness, or a "right standing" before God, a standing God demands, depends on the atoning work of Christ on Calvary. Jesus' words, "You no longer behold me" (John 16:10), "refer to the cross . . . or through the cross to the ascension."[20] Our righteousness is a result of God's reaching out through the life, death, resurrection, and ascension of Jesus Christ to atone for sins, thereby enabling God to establish people as righteous before His justice and holiness. The forensic idea becomes central: Believers are *declared righteous* because of Christ's atoning work. Paul expressed it this way: "He [God] made Him [Jesus] who knew no sin to be sin on our behalf, that we might become the righteousness of God in Him" (2 Cor. 5:21). Thus Christ's righteousness is set to the believer's account. This right standing with God is imputed through faith; blessed indeed is the person to whom the Lord imputes Christ's righteousness (Rom. 4:6). Such constitutes the dynamic, reaching-out righteousness of God in redeeming repentant, believing sinners (Rom. 4:1–8). Only the Holy Spirit can convince people of this essential truth. Virtually all humanity seeks to create their own righteousness, but that spells death. The Spirit *must* convict people of the truth concerning Christ and His righteousness freely given to us by grace.

Of course, in Christ believers are not only declared righteous, but in regeneration they are also *made* righteous. As Hoskyns emphasized, "The witness of the Spirit . . . is focused upon Jesus, and the nature of sin, of righteousness, and of judgment is exposed in relation to Him, and thereby shown to be present, concrete realities."[21] This does not imply sinless perfection in this life, but one does become different.

But how can this work of God be understood by the world? There is a problem, for as Paul wrote, the "natural man" (1 Cor. 2:14), i.e., the unbeliever, simply cannot grasp these things, for they are "spiritually discerned" (1 Cor. 2:14 KJV). Satan blinds and closes the eyes of unbelievers. But God has sent His Spirit to open the "natural" heart and mind, thus revealing the reality and need of God's righteousness. And unless the Holy Spirit does such a work, the unbeliever remains oblivious to the facts. Therefore, the Spirit's activities in revealing Christ assume a vital role for redemption. As Jesus said, "He shall glorify Me; for He shall take of Mine, and shall disclose it to you" (John 16:14).

THE HOLY SPIRIT CONVINCES OF JUDGMENT

The final work of the Holy Spirit, convincing the world of judgment, also has direct reference to the cross and resurrection. Jesus said, "The ruler of this world has been judged" (John 16:11). The "ruler," of course, is Satan, and the judgment is clearly the cross. Leon Morris stated, "The work of judgment is referred to the defeat of Satan on the cross."[22] As Beasley-Murray expressed it, "The ejection of the latter [Satan] from his vaunted place of rule took place as the Son of Man was installed by God as Lord of creation and Mediator of the saving sovereignty of God to the world."[23] And here is the sting for unbelieving people: This judgment on Satan "involves the judgment *of the world.*"[24] Because the world has subjected itself to its ruler and joined in the rejection of the Son of God, like the devil himself the world is fighting for a lost cause, that is, it has been judged. When the world condemned Jesus to death, it condemned itself. Brown summed it up well: "If the hour of passion and death represented the confrontation of Jesus and the Prince of this world, then in being victorious over death, Jesus was victorious over the Prince of the world. The very fact that Jesus stands justified before the Father means that Satan has been condemned and has lost his power over the world."[25]

Victory has now come by a cross and resurrection (they must be viewed as one). No one in himself will ever believe it, let alone accept the idea that in the cross human beings are judged with Satan (1 Cor. 18). However, the power of the mighty Holy Spirit can break through that fog of unbelief and reveal Christ as the only "hope" (1 Tim. 1:1). Our Lord not only defeated Satan at Calvary, He bore the punishment of sin in our place. Christ thus becomes our "Passover" (1 Cor. 5:7). He stands before God as the great and gracious "Substitute." Christ, the wisdom of God, has become our "life" (Col. 3:4). Christ is the gospel. And through it all, the "Spirit of truth" testifies of Jesus Christ to a world that desperately needs His grace (John 16:12–15).

Therefore, if no profound enlightening, convincing, convicting work of the Holy Spirit can be found, there will be no conversions at all. W. T. Conner had it right when he said, "Pentecost [the giving of the Holy Spirit] was just as essential for the realization in the lives of men of the values of gospel as was Calvary and the resurrection. Without the death and resurrection of Jesus there would be no gospel. Without Pentecost there would be no gospel so far as our apprehension and experience are concerned."[26]

The witness of the church has power only as it communicates the gospel in the strength and wisdom of the Holy Spirit. Jesus said, "No one can come to Me, unless the Father who sent Me draws him" (John 6:44). "Power belongs to God" (Ps. 62:11). Let it be said again, therefore, that those who would evangelize effectively must be "filled with the Holy Spirit," as exemplified so well in Peter and the first-century church (Acts 2:4). Only then can the people of God speak "the word of God with boldness" (Acts 4:31).

THE SPIRIT'S CONTROL

These truths imply that the Holy Spirit must have control and freedom to work in and through the life of the individual believer and the church collectively if the work of evangelization has any hope of accomplishment. He must lead. This immediately thrusts to the forefront the principle of all believers walking in the fellowship and fullness of the Spirit, bearing fruit and exercising their spiritual gifts with power. As Paul admonished the Ephesian believers, "Do not get drunk with wine, for that is dissipation, but be filled with the Spirit" (Eph. 5:18). The principle of a Spirit-filled life has been emphasized and written about endlessly. And correctly so, as repeatedly stressed, for without the fullness of the Holy Spirit there can be little fruitful evangelism and ministry of any kind. Remember, as Jesus said, "You shall receive power when the Holy Spirit has come upon you" (Acts 1:8). The church must seek that power. Our Lord commanded, "I send the promise of my Father upon you; but stay in the city, until you are clothed with power from on high" (Luke 24:49 RSV). Ten days later, Jesus kept His promise; Pentecost came. That event, as pointed out earlier, reveals several vital principles concerning effective evangelism. Some elaboration is called for here on the subject.

EVANGELISTIC PRINCIPLES ON THE HOLY SPIRIT

To begin, on the Day of Pentecost all believers in the Lord Jesus Christ received the Holy Spirit as God's gift (Acts 2:38). And since that day, whenever people put their faith in Jesus Christ as Lord and Savior, they immediately receive the gift of the Spirit. He takes up residency in every true believer. Second, these early Christians were not only invaded by the Holy Spirit for the first time, they also received an *infilling* of God's power. These first faithful followers received, from the Spirit of God, an endowment of extraordinary powers. Further, they received sanctifying grace. In a word, they received the Spirit and were filled with the Spirit simultaneously.

Pentecost was the Lord's day for the Holy Spirit to come and indwell and fill *all* believers for the first time. Thus it became a singular epic in the life of the church. In that sense Pentecost is no more repeatable than the cross of Christ or the glorious resurrection of our Lord. Yet at the same time, the passage surely implies that every Christian should have a deeper experience of the Holy Spirit than merely knowing that Christ lives in one's heart. The faithful are to be conscious of the Holy Spirit's *infilling* as well as realize He lives within.

THE FILLING OF THE SPIRIT

Paul's letter to the Ephesians presents a helpful insight into the concept of the Spirit-filled life. The apostle stressed the absolute necessity of the Spirit-filled life in the previously quoted verse: ". . . be filled with the Spirit" (Eph. 5:18). Paul saw no options. Walking with Christ, in all His fullness, was not to be approached casually or only if it aroused interest. The New Testament word *plerousthe* (translated "be filled") means "you *must* be *continually filled* with the Spirit." Paul's word is a positive command, just as the first section of the verse is a negative prohibition against drunkenness. Paul clearly saw the consistent Spirit-filled life as mandatory to the abundant life of holiness and effective service for every believer.

History also gives its testimony to the biblical mandate. For example, Dr. R. A. Torrey, Bible teacher and evangelist, gave his testimony in these words: "Take my own experience. I had been a minister for some years before I came to the place where I saw that I had no right to preach until I was definitely baptized [filled] with the Holy Ghost. I went to a business friend of mine and said to him in private, 'I am never going to enter my pulpit again until I have been baptized [filled] with the Holy Spirit and know it or until God tells me to go.'"[27]

Charles H. Spurgeon, the greatest of all Victorian preachers, on one occasion quoted in a sermon Luke 11:13: "If you then, being evil, know how to give good gifts to your children, how much more shall your heavenly Father give the Holy Spirit to those who ask Him?" Spurgeon then cried out to the eager congregation, "O, let us ask Him at once with all our hearts. Am I not so happy as to have in this audience some who will immediately ask? You that are the children of God—to you this promise is specially made. Ask God to make you all the Spirit of God can make you, not only a satisfied believer who has drunk for himself, but also a useful believer who overflows his neighborhood with blessing."[28]

THE CLEAR CONCLUSION

The fact of the Spirit-filled life and His complete dominance in evangelism is firmly established in Scripture and history. Most readily agree. But what will it mean to practical Christian living and evangelistic ministry?

First, the Holy Spirit is vital to a healthy, personal Christian experience. W. H. Griffith Thomas, a British scholar, states: "The only true immanence of God is the presence of Christ by the Holy Spirit in the heart and life of the believer. . . . It is in relation to the Holy Spirit that the Christian doctrine of God meets the deepest human need."[29] In a word, the Holy Spirit makes the divine immanence an experiential and dynamic reality wherein godly living follows. And that holds collectively for the church as the body of Christ as well as for the individual Christian. The church can then worship and minister in power and the believers discover the will of God as the Word of God comes alive. Actually, all spiritual life emanates from the Holy Spirit's work.

Second, as emphasized, the Holy Spirit enables Christians to live a holy life. He works as the "Sanctifier." Personal holiness is not an outmoded idea. He produces His fruit in the believer (Gal. 5:22). The Bible sets forth the concept repeatedly (e.g., 2 Cor. 7:1; 1 Thess. 4:7; Heb. 12:14). Living a holy life means developing a lifestyle pleasing to God and like God. "You shall be holy, for I am holy" (1 Pet. 1:16). For that, every believer needs God's fullness.

Further, the importance of the Spirit-filled life is directly related to growth toward Christian maturity and effective service on the basis of the spiritual gifts (1 Cor. 12:14). God's people grow as they "long for the pure milk of the Word" (1 Pet. 2:2), and the Holy Spirit serves as the "Instructor" in the Scriptures. Moreover, Spirit-filled, maturing Christians will result in a Spirit-filled, growing, ministering church. How desperately the world needs to see that kind of Christian congregation. And as stressed, the fullness of the Spirit makes for great evangelism—individually in the believer and collectively in the life of the church. Therefore, in the light of all that has been said, biblically, historically, and experientially, it can be concluded that God fully expects all believers, like Peter, to walk in submission to, under the leadership of, and in the fullness of the Holy Spirit. After all, it is His work that makes Christianity and world evangelization vital and alive.

A SUMMARY

The church's experience of the Holy Spirit, especially as it relates to evangelism, can be positively summarized as follows: As God's people "walk in the light as He Himself is in the light" (1 John 1:7), continually cleansed by His blood, they come to Him daily for the infilling of His wonderful Holy Spirit, thus finding life constantly overflowing with the divine presence and power and making their witness and service of true significance as the kingdom of God is advanced. This constitutes revived living, and it is God's way of being effective in evangelism to the glory of Jesus Christ. These principles are foundational to historic, evangelical Christianity.

We shall now attempt to see if the ministry of Billy Graham exemplifies these basic realities, thus giving him biblical, historical authenticity and effectiveness. Graham's understanding, experience, and practical ministry must reflect these essential realities concerning the Holy Spirit in evangelism and Christian service if he is to have biblical, historical credibility and thus make his contribution. Therefore, we will investigate his pneumatological convictions on:

- The power of the Holy Spirit

- The outworking of the Holy Spirit in the Old Testament and in Jesus' life

- The Holy Spirit on the Day of Pentecost

- The Holy Spirit and the Bible

- The Holy Spirit and the salvation experience

- The infilling of the Holy Spirit

- The Holy Spirit and Christian maturity

- The gifts of the Spirit and the fruit of the Spirit

- The leadership of the Holy Spirit in world evangelization

These many issues have been touched upon very briefly in the preceding Part I of this chapter. Now in Part II we turn to Billy Graham to investigate their presence, or lack thereof, in his life and ministry. This obviously constitutes a rather large order to fill. So we begin with a very personal story of Billy Graham himself and his early encounter with the Holy Spirit.

PART II:
BILLY GRAHAM AND THE WORK OF THE HOLY SPIRIT IN HIS EVANGELISTIC MINISTRY

And without that wooing of the Holy Spirit, you can't come to Christ . . .
—BILLY GRAHAM

INTRODUCTION: THE JOURNEY BEGINS

As the spring of 1946 dawned in London with its early wave of warm air and sunshine, Billy Graham made his first visit to Britain and Europe. Traveling with Torrey Johnson, they launched Youth for Christ in Europe. The movement took quick root in European soil, but Billy returned home with something of a saddened heart, burdened for the spiritual condition of the people. The great British revival of the eighteenth and nineteenth centuries had spent its force and secularism reigned. Back in the States, Billy spoke during a Bible conference at the Maranatha Bible Conference in Michigan. A man by the name of Clarence Benware heard Billy share something of Europe's desperate spiritual plight, especially in Great Britain. Benware came to Graham after the service and gave him one hundred dollars, saying, "You must go back." This struck a responsive chord in the evangelist's heart, and he determined to return to Britain as soon as possible. God opened doors and before long he again made his way to Europe, this time with singer Cliff

Barrows whom he had met at the Ben Lippen Bible Conference in North Carolina the previous year.

Billy had not been in England long when in October he and the team visited Tom Rees, a well-known English evangelist. They met at Hildenborough Hall, a few miles southeast of London. During the last night of a young people's conference being held there, Stephen Olford was the speaker. Olford had been brought up on the mission field in South Africa, and although he was only eight months older than Graham, it seemed to Billy he was a much older, mature Christian. Olford's message that night centered on Ephesians 5:18, "Do not get drunk with wine . . . but be filled with the Spirit." The message deeply touched Billy Graham, and he walked up to Olford after the message with, as Stephen described it, "that resolute look in his eyes, that determined thrust of his jaw and asked to know more,"[30] that is, about the Spirit-filled life. Billy wanted to converse with Stephen on the subject, but unfortunately, it was impossible for them to get together at that particular time as Billy and his companions had to leave for London.

After a short stint in the capital city, Billy Graham and Cliff Barrows began evangelistic rallies in the small Welsh town of Gorseinon. They also ministered in the Welsh city of Swansea, a mining center only eleven miles from Stephen Olford's home. God had been speaking to Billy's heart since the encounter in Hildenborough Hall. Billy later said that he was "seeking more of God with all my heart; and I felt that here was a man who could help me. I could sense that Stephen had something in his life I wanted to capture—he had a dynamic, a thrill, an exhilaration about him."[31] They met and what transpired proved to be in some sense dramatic for Billy. As biographer William Martin put it, the encounter was, "from the spiritual standpoint, the key development."[32]

Billy and Stephen closeted themselves in a little hotel at nearby Pontypridd with their Bibles open, seeking God's fullness for their lives. They turned pages together and shared the truths of God's Word. They labored over the Scriptures and gave themselves to much prayer. Stephen expounded, as biographer Pollock put it, "the fullness of the Holy Spirit in the life of a believer who was willing to bow daily and hourly to the sovereignty of Christ and to the authority of the Word."[33] Many of the things that the Spirit of God revealed to Billy and to Stephen in those hours were refreshing. They prayed, and as Stephen put it, "Like Jacob of old laying hold of God, crying, Lord I will not let Thee go except Thou bless me."[34] Billy and Stephen traveled spiritually step by step. As Olford said, "Billy just drank in everything I could give him."[35]

The first time Stephen Olford heard Billy Graham preach before Billy's spiritual experience, Olford evaluated Graham's preaching with these words: "Quite frankly, it was very ordinary. Neither his homiletics nor his theology nor his particular approach to Welsh people made much of an impact. The Welsh are masters of preaching, and the Welsh people expect hard, long sermons with a couple of hours of solid exposition. Billy was giving brief little messages. They listened, but it wasn't their kind of preaching."[36] The crowd reflected it; not many people attended, and the response to the strong invitation Billy gave produced little results. But in that little hotel, as Stephen and Billy shared together, Stephen related, "I gave him my testimony of how God completely turned my life inside out—and experienced the Holy Spirit in His fullness and anointing."[37] Billy responded, "Steve, I see it. That's what I want. That's what I need in my life." As they "prayed this through," Stephen said, "I can still hear Billy pouring out his heart in a prayer of total dedication to the Lord. Finally, he said, 'My heart is so flooded with the Holy Spirit,' and we went on praying to praising. We were laughing and praising God and he was walking back and forth across the room, crying out, 'I have it. I'm filled.' This is a turning point in my life.'"[38]

Would all this, however, make a significant difference in Graham's evangelistic ministry? At the very next service Billy seemed to be a transformed evangelist. Olford recalled, "For reasons known to God alone, the place which was only moderately filled the night before was packed to the doors. As Billy rose to speak, he was a man absolutely anointed."[39] As soon as he gave the invitation after preaching a sermon on the biblical story of the feast of Belshazzar, the Welsh people jammed the aisles making decisions for Christ. It seemed virtually everyone in the entire audience responded to Billy's appeal.

Olford went on to say, "My own heart was so moved by Billy's authority and strength that I could hardly drive home. My parents were still alive then, and when I came in the door, my father looked at my face and said, 'What on earth has happened?' I sat down at the kitchen table and said, 'Dad, something has happened to Billy Graham. The world is going to hear from this man. He is going to make his mark in history.' His response was absolutely wonderful, he said, 'It won't be the first time America has taken the lead in evangelism.'"[40]

And to repeat the cliché, *the rest is history*. Billy Graham's experience of being filled with the Spirit shaped the young evangelist into a man of God and the spiritual icon that he has become worldwide.

Billy Graham reflects back on that day as the definite turning point in his ministry of evangelism. He has said, concerning the experience, it was "a very significant moment."[41] His encounter with Olford has influenced to a large degree his whole understanding of the work of the Holy Spirit in evangelism. These foundational issues on the Holy Spirit in Graham's evangelism call for a full definition of the evangelist's position on the subject.

BILLY GRAHAM'S UNDERSTANDING OF THE PERSON AND WORK OF THE HOLY SPIRIT

It has been suggested that perhaps Billy Graham's most theological, yet very practical, book centers on the person and work of the Holy Spirit. His book *The Holy Spirit* (to which he later added a workbook) was written some thirty-two years after his meeting with Stephen Olford in Wales. It presents a clear insight to his general view of the work of the Holy Spirit as it relates to evangelistic ministry. He begins, as one would rightly expect, with the question "Who is the Holy Spirit?"

Raising this question and the practical issues that naturally follow is extremely timely, not only from the standpoint of church history as a whole, but particularly in the last half of the twentieth century. At one occasion in his earlier ministry, Billy spent a brief vacation time in Switzerland as the guest of Dr. Karl Barth, the noted theologian. In their conversation, Billy Graham asked Professor Barth what he thought would be the prime emphasis on theology in the ensuing years. Without hesitation, Barth replied, "The Holy Spirit." His prophecy proved true. Before his death, Pope John XXIII was asked what doctrine needed to be reemphasized today. He also quickly replied, "The doctrine of the Holy Spirit." He was on target as well. This can be seen in numerous movements such as the Keswick movement, the Pentecostal-Charismatic thrust, and the whole ethos that has been called "the Third Wave." The last half of the twentieth century, the main years of the Graham ministry, has seen a resurgence of pneumatology that has almost been unparalleled in the history of the church.

Billy Graham makes a valid and important point that the two great gifts God gives to His born-again children are (1) the gift of forgiveness that brings one into a proper relationship with God, and (2) the gift of the Holy Spirit. As Peter preached on the Day of Pentecost, "Repent, and let each of you be baptized in the name of Jesus Christ for the forgiveness of your sins; and you shall receive the gift of the Holy Spirit" (Acts 2:38). Graham has declared, "To the gift of forgiveness God also adds the great gift of the Holy Spirit."[42] As he expressed it, "The work of the Son of God *for* us, and second the work of the Spirit of God *in* us."[43] This constitutes the essence of the spiritual experience. Christian living depends on an understanding of the person and the work of the Holy Spirit. In that context Billy quotes a friend who said, "I need Jesus Christ for my eternal life and I need the Holy Spirit for my internal life."[44] In light of the fact that our Lord Jesus Christ laid strong emphasis on the promised coming of the Holy Spirit, when that climactic event took place on the Day of Pentecost, the church was readied to launch the evangelistic thrust that has been going on for two thousand years. But again, who is this Holy Spirit according to Graham's understanding?

THE SPIRIT'S PERSONHOOD

The first major point that Graham makes, as implied, is that the Holy Spirit must be understood as a *Person*. He must never be viewed as a mere force for good. He is a Person; thus He should not be addressed as an "it." This can be demonstrated, Graham contends, because of the various actions that are attributed to the Spirit in the Scriptures. The evangelist points out:

- He speaks (Acts 13:2).

- He intercedes (Rom. 8:26).

- He testifies (John 15:26).

- He leads (Acts 8:29; Rom. 8:14).

- He commands (Acts 16:6–7).

- He guides (John 16:13).

- He appoints (Acts 20:28).

- He can be lied to (Acts 5:3–4).

- He can be insulted (Heb. 10:29).

- He can even be blasphemed (Matt. 12:31–32).

Each of these activities obviously speaks of personhood. The Holy Spirit is not an impersonal influence, but a Person, as His actions and character make clear.

Moreover, the Bible emphasizes that the Holy Spirit possesses a divine nature. He stands as a member of the divine Trinity. This leads Graham to a second listing of scriptural verification of this most important claim:

- The Spirit is eternal (Heb. 9:14).

- The Spirit is all-powerful (Luke 1:35).

- The Spirit is everywhere present (Ps. 139:7).

- The Spirit is all-knowing (1 Cor. 2:10–11).

- The Spirit is called God (Acts 5:3–4; 2 Cor. 3:18).

- The Spirit is Creator (Col. 1:16–17).

Graham contends that it appears correct to deduce from these scriptural attributes that the Holy Spirit is God. Of course, this raises the aforementioned mystery of the Trinity. Billy Graham is at times somewhat confounded with the question of the Trinity. He confesses, "When I first began to study the Bible years ago, the doctrine of the Trinity was one of the most complex problems I had to encounter. I have never fully resolved it, for it contains an aspect of mystery. Though I do not totally understand it to this day, I accept it as a revelation of God."[45] What, then, does the evangelist conclude? He has written, "I can make in summary . . . there is nothing that God is that the Holy Spirit is not. He is very God of very God."[46] And, of course, Graham says the same for the Son, Jesus Christ. However, the doctrine of the Trinity still remains shrouded in mystery. We simply cannot fully grasp that Trinitarian concept with our finite, rational minds. But the Bible declares these Three are One; thus, we must "walk by faith, not by sight" (2 Cor. 5:7). Graham brings it together in these words: "All of the essential aspects of deity belong to the Holy Spirit. We can say of him exactly what was said of Jesus Christ. So we bow before Him, we worship; we accord Him every response Scripture requires to all-mighty God. Who is the Holy Spirit, He is God."[47]

But from the practical perspective, Graham sees several things relative to the divine Holy Spirit's work among people.

PRACTICAL OUTWORKING OF THE SPIRIT

Having come to realize something of the nature and personality of the Holy Spirit, it becomes obvious He does a very definite work in and among us. Graham contends there are three main expressions in the Old Testament that speak of the work of the Holy Spirit in and through human beings: (1) The Holy Spirit came upon people (2 Chron. 24:20); (2) He rested upon people (Num. 11:25); and (3) He filled people (Exod. 31:3). All of these works of the Spirit of God speak primarily of the impact of the Holy Spirit in forming godliness and holiness in believers and equipping them for service. More will be said on this concept later. But in summary, Graham's understanding of the Old Testament work of the Holy Spirit can be capsulated in these words: "The Holy Spirit was at work before the world began. Then He renewed and fed this creation. He was active throughout the Old Testament, both in the world of nature and among people, guiding and delivering them through the judges, prophets, kings, and others."[48]

NEW TESTAMENT REALITIES

Graham, moving to the New Testament revelation, points out that the Spirit's work in the four Gospels can be clearly seen as centering in the person and work of Jesus Christ. A further list surfaces from Graham's study of the four Gospels and related passages:

- Jesus was begotten of the Spirit (Luke 1:35).

- Jesus was baptized by the Spirit (John 1:32–33).

- Jesus was led by the Spirit (Luke 4:1).

- Jesus was anointed by the Spirit (Luke 4:18).

- Jesus was empowered by the Spirit (Matt. 12:27ff.).

- Jesus offered Himself as an atonement by the Holy Spirit (Heb. 9:14).

- Jesus was resurrected by the Spirit (Rom. 8:11).

- Jesus gave commandments by the Spirit (Acts 1:2).

Billy Graham insists that the Holy Spirit was fully operative in and through the entire life and work of Christ, beginning with His miraculous virgin birth. Although some dispute the doctrine of the virgin birth, Graham tenaciously holds, "Any suggestion that God the Holy Spirit was not capable of bringing the virgin birth to pass is nonsense. If we believe that God is God—and that He rules the universe—nothing is too great for his limitless power. At all times God does whatever he chooses."[49]

Graham's emphasis on the moving of the Holy Spirit in the birth, life, and ministry of Jesus is not to say that He was not at work among the disciples of Jesus before Pentecost. But the Day of Pentecost saw the outpouring of the Holy Spirit upon the church to equip God's people fully for ministry, godly living, and effective evangelistic kingdom progress.

PENTECOST

Graham is insistent that the coming of the Holy Spirit on the Day of Pentecost became the fulcrum for the movement of the kingdom of God and the history of the church. Pentecost, known as the Feast of Weeks, saw the great harvest, the first fruits of the Christ-event. Beginning with the birth of Jesus and culminating with the second coming of the Lord, this time has become, as Graham sees it, the age of the Spirit. And, of course, this falls in line with traditional evangelicalism.

Since the Holy Spirit's outpouring at Pentecost, Graham recognizes Him as performing a twofold work in the world. First, He reproves, or convinces, the world of "sin, and righteousness, and judgment" (John 16:8). We examined this passage earlier in this chapter. Graham fully believes the Holy Spirit reveals the good news of Jesus Christ to the convicted heart. Second, He draws them to the place of the decision, culminating in repentance and faith, which in turn precipitate spiritual birth.

Thus the work of the Holy Spirit in the preaching of the gospel is absolutely essential. Billy's strong emphasis on the necessity of the Spirit's touch in his preaching of the gospel is paramount in his understanding. This prime principle will be seen in more detail as this book develops. The Spirit's second work in the world, Graham contends, is to hinder the growth of lawlessness. That is to say, He has a "preserving" work. Paul states in 2 Thessalonians 2:7, "For the mystery of lawlessness is already at work; only he who now restrains will do so until he is taken out of the way." Moreover, in that "preserving" work, the Holy Spirit acts through the people of God. The Lord Jesus Christ termed His followers the "salt of the earth" and the "light of the world" (Matt. 5:13–14). The metaphors Jesus used are appropriate. Light enlightens and salt preserves. This places a tremendous responsibility on the part of the church to be "salt" and "light" in the hands of the Holy Spirit to do His convicting, preserving work. So as implied, the Holy Spirit not only works in the world, He also works in the church.

THE SPIRIT AND THE CHURCH

Graham lays down three prime principles on the point of the Spirit's work in the congregation of God. First, the church has its inception and lives a life of unity by the presence and power of the mighty Holy Spirit. Paul said, "For by one Spirit we were all baptized into one body, whether Jews or Greeks, whether slaves or free, and we were all made to drink of one Spirit" (1 Cor. 12:13). All believers constitute one body and are brought together to live in the oneness of the Spirit. Second, the Spirit of God lives in and animates the church. Ephesians 2:22 states, "in whom [Christ] you also are being built together into a dwelling of God in the Spirit." He indwells the individual members of the church, and He indwells the church as a unified body and imparts to it His life. The church is more than just the sum of its parts. The Holy Spirit works in and through every aspect of the church making it the living, unified body of Christ. Third, the Holy Spirit imparts gifts to the church: "And He gave some as apostles, and some as prophets, and some as evangelists, and some as pastors and teachers, for the equipping of the saints for the work of service, to the building up of the body of Christ" (Eph. 4:11–12). The final purpose of that significant work of the Holy Spirit is, as Paul expressed it, "until we all attain to the unity of the faith, and of the knowledge of the Son of God, to a mature man, to the measure of the stature which belongs to the fulness of Christ" (Eph. 4:13). These are obviously most important functions of the Spirit.

Graham points out that the Holy Spirit works not only in the church as a body, but as has been made amply clear, He works in the individual believer as well. First, He enlightens believers through the Word of God. One must be careful here, Graham points out. To be purely objective and intellectual with the Bible can lead to a legalism that stifles. One should also *experience* the Holy Spirit in the study of God's Word. The New Testament scholar George Beasley-Murray agrees, calling the Spirit of God "the Holy Spirit of revelation."[50] But at the same time, the Spirit works in a depth far more significant than a mere emotional experience. Christians must maintain a balance between biblical truth and a true spiritual existential experience to keep the Holy Spirit enlightenment on an even keel. Upon this principle Graham is most emphatic.

Moreover, the Holy Spirit actually indwells the believer's body (1 Cor. 6:19) to accomplish certain specific things. For example, Graham lists the following principles of the indwelling Spirit's actions:

- He comforts His people (Acts 9:31).

- He guides them into all truth and all of life (John 16:13).

- He sanctifies, that is, makes them holy (Rom. 15:16).

- He inspires his servants what to preach and to say concerning God's truth (1 Cor. 2:13).

- He directs in all of life, and aids us in all of our weaknesses (Acts 13:2; Rom. 8:26).

Therefore, it becomes vital, Graham contends, that one develop a proper understanding and experience of the Holy Spirit, as he did in England in 1946 under the inspired tutelage of Stephen Olford. One's spiritual life depends on the Spirit's working—and in that the Holy Spirit uses the Scriptures as His powerful "two-edged sword" (Heb. 4:12).

THE HOLY SPIRIT AND THE BIBLE IN GRAHAM'S UNDERSTANDING

Well known is the fact that Billy Graham stands absolutely committed to the concept of the Holy Spirit as the ultimate Author of the Bible. Hence, he argues, the Bible can be properly called the Word of God. More will be said about this position in a later chapter concerning Graham's view of the Scriptures and the role the Bible plays in the life of the church and evangelism. Yet, it will help to understand here how Graham views the Holy Spirit's hand in the formation and use of the Word of God.

Graham first points out that the Holy Spirit *totally* inspired the Scriptures. The Bible itself attests to this contention, as does the judgment of evangelical history along with the experience of multitudes of those who would walk with God. Peter wrote, "For no prophecy was ever made by an act of human will, but men moved by the Holy Spirit spoke from God" (2 Pet. 1:21). Graham also holds that the Holy Spirit not only inspired the Scriptures, but He also led in the selection of the sixty-six books that comprise the canon of Holy Writ. Simply put, in the entire process of forming Scripture, the Holy Spirit stands as the final Author. But He did not bypass human instrumentality. He inspired people to write and inspired the church in subsequent years to bring together the sixty-six books that comprise the Bible, putting a final period at the end of Revelation 22:21. The canon is closed; nothing more will be produced comparable to the Holy Bible in our earthly time frame. But what does inspiration by the Holy Spirit mean, as Billy Graham would understand it?

INSPIRATION

It must first be said that Graham does not hold to a dictation theory of inspiration, that is, that the inspired writers were merely passive "pens" in the hands of the Holy Spirit. Actually, the Bible itself does not state how the Spirit inspired the writers. But Graham does go on to say that the Holy Spirit moved in such a manner that the actual words as well as the ideas were inspired by the Spirit. He states, "I don't know how to get at the idea except through the words."[51] The words themselves did not escape the Spirit's guidance, although they were utilized in the writers' own stylistic, cultural, purposeful, historical, and theological fashion. Thus, Graham declares that the Bible can be relied upon as completely trustworthy and infallibly true even if it must be grasped by faith. His experience at Forest Home settled that issue once and for all time. He is quick to point out, however, that the inspiration by the Holy Spirit does not refer to any one translation or even to the ancient manuscripts now in hand. It refers basically to the original documents, or autographs, which we do not have. Still, the extant manuscripts are so close to the originals that one can rest upon the authoritative truthfulness of what we call the Holy Bible.

INSPIRATION IN READING

It must be said that the Holy Spirit not only inspired the Bible, but the Spirit also illuminates the heart and mind concerning what Graham calls "the unassailable truth."[52] Through faithful Bible study, the Holy Spirit has formed and shaped doctrinal and historical truth concerning God's dealings with the human race. The Scriptures serve as the source and vehicle for speaking to contemporary situations in regard to God and life. Therefore, as Graham quotes a Kenyan leader, "if the role of the Holy Spirit is to teach, ours is to be diligent students of the Word."[53] If the Spirit has inspired the Word, and serves as its interpreter of daily life; therefore, as Billy Graham has said, "I always come to the Scriptures with the Psalmist's prayer, 'Open my eyes that I may behold wonderful things from Thy Law'" (Ps. 119:18).[54]

All of this has a very definite application to evangelism, as Graham grasps it. He contends that all evangelistic preaching is to be rooted and grounded and emanating from the Word of God. He points out, "When we preach or teach the Scriptures, we open the door for the Holy Spirit to do his work. God has not promised to bless oratory or clever preaching, he has promised to bless his Word. He has said that it will not return to him 'empty' (Is. 55:11)."[55] Graham holds that the Word of God in the hands of the Spirit of God changes people's lives. On this point Graham quotes George Muller of Bristol, England: "The vigor of our spiritual life will be in exact proportion to the place held by the Bible in our life and thoughts."[56] Therefore, it can be correctly concluded that the Spirit transforms and inspires lives through that which He has originally inspired, the Holy Scriptures.

This inner evangelistic work of God's Spirit leads to Graham's views of the Holy Spirit and the salvation experience itself.

THE SPIRIT AND SALVATION

At the outset it should be said there is no question in the evangelist's mind about the absolute necessity of the Spirit's work in people coming to Christ. In an interview with talk-show host David Frost, Graham said, "I believe that the gospel is preached, however badly or with however many mistakes. . . . The Holy Spirit is the communicatory agent; that people are really not listening to me after about ten or fifteen minutes if I'm really preaching the gospel. I think they're listening to another voice inside, the voice of the Holy Spirit, and the Holy Spirit is applying and communicating."[57] Graham thus insists that the spiritual birth is essentially the Spirit's work using the truths of Scripture to convict and convert. Graham's book *How to Be Born Again* attests to this fact. In that work he wrote, "God Himself . . . He is the one who converts us. . . . He is preparing us for repentance by the conviction of the Holy Spirit."[58] He went on to conclude, "Salvation is of the Lord."[59] Billy points out that the Lord Jesus Himself saw spiritual regeneration as the accomplishment of the Holy Spirit when He said, "Unless one is born of water and the Spirit, he cannot enter into the kingdom of God" (John 3:5).

As might be suspected, Graham invariably turns to the third chapter of the Gospel of John, declaring that this passage constitutes one of the most clear, relevant passages in the Bible concerning the work of the Holy Spirit in the new-birth salvation experience. In a personal interview he said he fears people will tire of his constant preaching on John 3 and the new birth. But therein the gospel of salvation is forthrightly declared. Graham thus preaches it and constantly contends that this radical change Jesus spoke of, being "born again" (John 3:5), stands as the most vital need in the inner being of every person. If it were true for Nicodemus, a religious leader of the Jewish people (John 3:1), it certainly stands true for all. Moreover, this change cannot be earned or accomplished in one's own ability, nor can anyone else effect this dramatic experience in a person's life. Graham argues the new birth is solely the work of the Holy Spirit as He brings home to the human heart and mind the truth of the death and resurrection of Jesus Christ.

Graham sees the Holy Spirit playing a convicting, calling, and completing role in salvation. The Holy Spirit first convicts of sin (John 16:7–11). As Graham has said, "The Bible tells us . . . of the work of the Holy Spirit. What does He do? We are told that He convicts people of sin."[60] Therefore, Billy pleads, "you cannot come to Jesus Christ unless the Spirit of God brings you and unless you yield to the prompting and urging of the Holy Spirit. I beg of you to come to Christ while there is yet time."[61] Graham is much aware that Satan blinds people to their plights. As Paul stressed in 2 Corinthians 4:4, "In whose case the god of this world has blinded the minds of the unbelieving, that they might not see the light of the gospel of the glory of Christ, who is the image of God."

Graham insists that the Holy Spirit alone can remove the blinders and enable people to see their sin and need. Contemporary New Testament scholars agree. For instance, George Beasley-Murray has said the Gospel of John "underscores the necessity of the Spirit's illumination to grasp the revelation of God in and through His Son."[62] Thus the Holy Spirit is called "the Spirit of Truth" (John 14:17). It must therefore be concluded that apart from the convicting, convincing ministry of the Holy Spirit, no one would ever become conscious of his or her sin and lostness, let alone the truth of Jesus and His power to forgive sins and create new life. This is why Billy Graham feels he *must* give a solemn warning on the issue, and this is even more urgent because the Bible declares that a point can be reached in the hardening of one's heart against the Spirit's conviction where He will no longer strive to lead the unbeliever to Jesus Christ. Proverbs 29:1 states, "A man who hardens his neck after much reproof will suddenly be broken beyond remedy." That becomes an eternally tragic moment for any person.

But as the Holy Spirit enlightens concerning "sin, and righteousness, and judgment" (John 16:8), He also calls and draws the sinner to the Savior, revealing the risen Christ as one's only hope. He leads the open-hearted person into repentance and faith as he or she embraces the Lord Jesus Christ for all He is and all He has done. As Billy declared in his prophetic book *Approaching Hoofbeats*, "It would be completely futile for me to preach the gospel, as I have done to many people every year for the past generation, if the Holy Spirit were not convicting the hearers of their sin and prompting them to open their hearts to Christ."[63] As an evangelist, Billy Graham has stated, "The Holy Spirit is the great communicator. Without His supernatural work, there would be no such thing as conversion."[64] But when one does respond to the Spirit's call, in that moment of time, God effects the "washing of regeneration and renewing by the Holy Spirit" (Titus 3:5). There comes about a once-and-for-all radical change that has continuing impact on a person's life until the day one stands before God. The work is completed; that person is truly *born again*. Graham calls this the greatest of all miracles. The new birth spawns a whole new life. Time has been immersed into eternity, and guilt for sin has been eradicated as the very life of God itself is imparted to the new believer. That, the Spirit alone can do. Still, there is the human factor: A person must respond to the conviction and call before the act of salvation is completed.

THE RESPONSE TO THE SPIRIT

Evangelist Graham raises the question "How do you accept this gift?" He answers: by the simple act of faith in which you say yes to Christ. He urges the seeker to pray and "simply tell God you know you are a sinner, and you are sorry for your sins. Tell him you believe Jesus Christ died for you, and that you want to give your life to him right now, to follow him as Lord the rest of your life."[65] It becomes very evident that in every setting, Billy Graham has a heart that yearns to see people respond like that and come to Jesus. This burden in itself is born of the Spirit in the evangelist's life.

Billy Graham then addresses issues concerning the agency of the Holy Spirit in the life of the believer after he or she has been led to redemptive faith in Jesus Christ. He points out that we live in a time when contention concerning the inner work of the Spirit of God in the believer's life abounds. The advent of the Pentecostal-Charismatic movement has done much to precipitate the issues that have arisen. Though much good has come out of that and similar movements, considerable uneasiness and misunderstanding have also developed. Therefore, Graham feels that he must state his convictions concerning the work of the Holy Spirit in areas such as the baptism of the Holy Spirit, the infilling of the Holy Spirit, the Christian's warfare in the Spirit, and similar issues.

THE BAPTISM

Billy Graham first addresses what has basically arisen out of holiness and perfectionist movements known as "the baptism of the Holy Spirit." Graham has expressed his understanding of the baptism of the Holy Spirit by a personal illustration. While still a young student in Bible school in Florida, a preacher asked him, "Young man, have you been baptized with the Holy Spirit?" Billy replied, "Yes, sir." "When were you baptized with the Holy Spirit?" the preacher asked. Billy replied, "The moment I received Jesus Christ as my

Savior."[66] Although the preacher disagreed with him, that reply does reveal Billy Graham's basic conviction. He holds that the baptism of the Holy Spirit, initiated at Pentecost, becomes the experience of all who have received Jesus Christ as Lord and Savior. He contends all true believers are baptized in the Spirit at conversion, and he quotes as a scriptural reference 1 Corinthians 12:13: "For by one Spirit we are all baptized into one body." Is there more? Graham contends there is.

THE INFILLING

The principle of the Spirit-filled life and its importance for Billy Graham were approached in Part I of this chapter and in the story of Graham's own personal encounter with the Spirit under Stephen Olford. What does Graham actually say on this issue? Billy first points out there are definitely additional experiences of the Holy Spirit beyond the baptism, in particular being "filled with the Spirit" (Eph. 5:18). Graham expresses his basic position as, "one baptism but many fillings."[67] That is to say, when a person is saved he or she is baptized in the Holy Spirit, but the fact that the Ephesians 5:18 passage is a present imperative implies that God expects and commands people to experience the Spirit's continuing infilling. Graham grants there may be some differences in opinion that are merely semantic, but he contends that this particular approach is foundational to the inner work of the Holy Spirit in believers. He confesses, "During my ministry I have known many Christians who agonize, labor, struggle, and pray to 'get the Spirit.' I used to wonder if I had been wrong in thinking that having been baptized by the Spirit into the body of Christ on the day of my conversion I needed no other baptism. But the longer I have studied the Scriptures the more I have become convinced that I was right."[68]

Graham draws several conclusions from this position. First, he holds that when a person is "baptized in the Spirit" on conversion, he or she can also be simultaneously "filled with the Spirit." The gift of the Spirit can encompass both at the new birth. But the infilling must be continuous. His expression "*one* baptism but *many* fillings" comes into play here. Therefore, no Christian needs to strive or pray through *to get* the Spirit. He or she has already received the Holy Spirit when he or she invited Christ into their life through repentance and faith. This becomes obvious in the experience of Philip and the Ethiopian eunuch recorded in Acts 8. It certainly is true in the case of Paul's encounter with the Ephesians, who only had a partial understanding of the gospel (Acts 19). Thus Graham concludes that all true believers share in the Pentecostal event; as he states, "Since the baptism with the Spirit occurs at the time of regeneration, Christians are never told in the Scriptures to seek it."[69]

Using that as a starting point, Graham states that he has become convinced that many of the things some attach to the so-called *baptism* of the Holy Spirit actually belong to the experience of being *filled* with the Spirit. Graham lays much importance on the continuing infilling of the Spirit for believers. He goes so far as to declare, "I think it proper to say that anyone who is not Spirit-filled is a defective Christian. Paul's command to the Ephesian Christians, 'Be filled with the Spirit,' is binding on all of us Christians everywhere in every age."[70] Why should it not be seen as an option? Because, in the final analysis, being filled with the Spirit is no more or no less than complete surrender to Christ's lordship in daily living. As Graham has said, "*To be filled with the Spirit is to be controlled by the Spirit.* It is to be so yielded to Christ that our supreme desire is to do His will . . . as we grow in Christ, our goal is to be controlled by the Spirit."[71] And obedience to Christ's lordship matters most.

At the same time, Graham does not wish to be divisive. He strongly emphasizes that the Holy Spirit creates unity. The previously quoted Pauline passage, 1 Corinthians 12:13, speaks of the unity of the Spirit. In the end, the Holy Spirit's primary work in the believer centers in creating a life of holiness, purity, and Christian unity. And all Christians would certainly agree to that. But Graham does firmly hold that the life of holiness comes about by the infilling of the Holy Spirit. What does he mean by holiness?

HOLINESS

Billy Graham argues, as seen, that any believer who does not walk in the Spirit's fullness becomes a defective Christian. To fail on that point creates a pattern of carnality in the believer's experience. The devotional life tends to be erratic, the Word of God becomes neglected, prayer is a chore, and sensitivity to sin has been bludgeoned as with Lot in Sodom. He tells us, "We . . .

must understand that God commands us to be filled with the Spirit."[72] Only the Spirit creates a life of holiness. Paul calls it bearing the "fruit of the Spirit" (Gal. 5:22–23).

Not only is this truth evident in the writings of Paul, but the Lord Jesus Christ emphasized these principles as well. In our Lord's dialogue with the woman at the Samaritan well, He said He would impart to believers a well of water springing up to life (John 4:13–14). In John 7:38 Jesus said, "He who believes in Me, as the Scripture said, 'From his innermost being shall flow rivers of living water.'" That living water is life, the life of the Spirit, and it flows out in a life of godliness and holiness. As Graham put it, "This is not a pond of water, but an ever-flowing spring."[73] It certainly should be evident that God intends His people to be an ever-flowing source of this "living water."

These principles not only hold true for the individual Christian life, but they have also been the essence of great revivals when those dramatic events break on the scene. One of the prayers that came out of the Welsh revival of 1904–1906 reads:

> Fill me, Holy Spirit, fill me,
> More than fullness I would know:
> I am smallest of Thy vessels,
> Yet, I can much overflow.[74]

The purpose behind it all rests in the fact that when believers are filled with the Holy Spirit, they become vessels of holy blessing to the world. And whether that service is large or small in the eyes of the world, God smiles upon it.

Graham points out, however, that one must be careful in overstressing the sanctifying work of the Holy Spirit. Much unbiblical terminology and ideas are bandied about today, such as "the second blessing," or "the second work of grace." He points out that terms like these cannot be found in the Scriptures. He contends the Holy Spirit's work is not a "second" or a "third" or even a "thousandth." The Spirit operates on a *continual* basis in the Christian experience. Moreover, it can be spiritually perilous to seek constantly a new experience, because as Graham states, "filling does not necessarily imply 'feeling.'"[75] The issue in spirituality and holiness centers in *abiding in Christ* (John 15:4). Moreover, the central thrust of the idea revolves around not getting more of the Holy Spirit, but the Holy Spirit getting more of the believer. Thus one becomes an instrument in the hands of God for ministry and service to the glory of Christ.

MATURITY

Graham further sees the experience of the fullness of the Spirit as a vital necessity for spiritual growth and maturity. The Holy Spirit operates as the One who sanctifies, i.e., makes holy and matures, the yielded believer. When a person first comes to faith in Christ, his or her spiritual capacities and understanding are quite small. The Bible calls these new believers "newborn babes" (1 Pet. 2:2). But the Spirit-filled believer grows rapidly, and Christian maturity goes on a pace. Peter urged us to "grow in the grace and knowledge of our Lord and Savior Jesus Christ" (2 Pet. 3:18). That the Spirit effects.

Billy Graham injects another word of caution; as touched upon earlier, the experience of walking in the fullness of the Holy Spirit must not necessarily be equated with a deep emotional experience. Yet there are certainly times when God does give one a special touch. Billy Graham shares a striking illustration of this fact. In 1954 Billy and his wife, Ruth, set sail for London for his famous Harringay crusade. That crusade became one of those memorable moments in the history of British evangelism. It was the nearest thing to true revival that London had seen since the days of Wesley and Whitefield, although the Prayer Revival of 1860 impacted Great Britain a century before Billy's arrival. But on the way to Britain, sailing the Atlantic, Graham struggled in a deep spiritual battle. He confessed that he was all but overtaken with a sense of depression and a frightening feeling of inadequacy. He gave himself to prayer night and day. Later, Billy said he learned what the apostle Paul meant when he admonished God's people to "pray without ceasing" (1 Thess. 5:17). Then, he tells us, one day in a prayer meeting with his wife and colleagues, as he wept before the Lord, God granted him the deep assurance that He was faithful. Graham became convinced the Lord gave him a special anointing on that ship bound for England. And it proved true; the Holy Spirit took complete control for the work of the 1954 crusade. Billy prayed, and he prevailed. The Spirit of God always honors that. We shall be investigating later something of the power of the great Harringay crusade.

So we see, according to the evangelist, the Holy Spirit *baptizes, fills,* and at times for special needs *anoints* His people. What lies back of it all?

REASONS

Graham stresses that God fills His people with the Spirit for a very practical purpose. That purpose essentially expresses itself in enabling Christians to serve Jesus Christ with effect; in the case of Billy Graham, the Holy Spirit empowers the proclamation of the gospel for salvation. Billy has said, "If the power of the Spirit is not present, the work would be 'sounding brass or tinkling cymbal'"[76] (see 1 Cor. 13:1). Billy often quotes Paul's statement to the Corinthians: "And my message and my preaching were not in persuasive words of wisdom, but in demonstration of the Spirit and of power, that your faith should not rest on the wisdom of men, but on the power of God" (1 Cor. 2:4–5).

Graham grants the possibility of seeking the fullness of the Holy Spirit for wrong reasons, such as self-enjoyment or self-glorification. However, the ultimate purpose of the Spirit's infilling of any believer is that one's service might be effective and bring honor and glory to Jesus Christ and Him alone. The Westminster Confession has it correct: "The chief end of man is to glorify God and enjoy Him forever." The Lord Jesus Christ Himself said, "He [the Holy Spirit] shall glorify Me; for He shall take of Mine, and shall disclose it to you" (John 16:14). The Spirit does not even glorify Himself; He glorifies Jesus Christ. Thus Graham asks, "Why do we need the fullness of the Holy Spirit?" He answers, "Because only in the power of the Spirit can we live a life that glorifies God."[77] The Holy Spirit becomes the agent whereby a person can bring glory to God through a life of effective service and holiness.

These principles surely make it paramount that the Holy Spirit sustains, empowers, and strengthens—even physically—Spirit-filled preachers in gospel ministry. David Bruce, Billy Graham's executive assistant, tells of the many times he has witnessed in Billy's older years the evangelist's having to be assisted to the pulpit because of his age and illnesses. But suddenly, as Dr. Bruce put it, "the years seem to roll off him; and he preaches like a young man. It is the direct result of the empowerment of the Holy Spirit."[78] The Spirit-filled life is not optional for the effective proclaimer of Christ's good news. Little wonder Graham said, "I am convinced that to be filled with the Spirit is not an option, but a necessity. It is indispensable for the abundant life and for fruitful service. The Spirit-filled life is not abnormal; it is the normal Christian life. Anything less is sub-normal; it is less than what God wants and provides for his children."[79] The question now arises, How does Billy Graham understand it all comes about?

HOW?

What are the prerequisites for Spirit-filled Christian living in Graham's thinking? He brings it together with three key phrases: *understanding, submission,* and *walking by faith.* Understanding serves as the first step in being filled with the Spirit—understanding that God has given His Holy Spirit and deeply desires to fill His people with all His fullness. Furthermore, one must realize that such a blessing is not a mere option, but a command. Not only that, one must clearly grasp that unconfessed sin cannot be allowed. Graham says, "Before we can be filled with the Holy Spirit we must deal honestly and completely with every known sin in our lives."[80] He goes into considerable detail in that respect. This principle shall be approached in detail later in chapter 10. But it must be recognized that sin has to be dealt with in the area of the offense through confession, restitution, and a genuine broken spirit before God. The entire process of seeking the Spirit's fullness reduces itself to this: Who controls one's life, self or Christ? That leads to the second step, namely, submission.

Graham sees two steps in the concept of submission. The first centers in the area of confession and repentance as stated above. Anything in which the Holy Spirit has been grieved must be acknowledged and submitted to God so that the blood of Christ may cleanse that particular sin (1 John 1:9). Second, one must yield and submit oneself utterly and completely to the will of God. Paul pointed this out very forcefully in Romans 12:1–2: "I urge you therefore, brethren, by the mercies of God, to present your bodies a living and holy sacrifice, acceptable to God, which is your spiritual service of worship. And do not be conformed to this world, but be transformed by the renewing of your mind, that you may prove what the will of God is, that which is good and acceptable and perfect." Billy Graham believes that surrender is a definite and conscious act on the part of the believer to obey the precepts of the Word of

God. In a word, *obedience* assumes center stage in the Christian's life. Right there the third factor arises.

The Bible tells us that cleansed, obedient believers walk by faith. Billy Graham sees this as essential to the Spirit-filled life. Moving into the Spirit's fullness does not necessarily mean much agonizing and interceding and pleading with God; it rests upon reaching out in faith and bidding Him to fill us. Billy puts it this way:

> Now when we yield ourselves to Christ and follow Him as Lord of our lives, we know that something has happened. The Holy Spirit has taken over our lives, to guide and empower us. We are now to walk by faith, reckoning ourselves to be dead to sin and alive to God. We are filled with the Holy Spirit; now we are to live in light of this truth. This is not pretending; it is acting on God's promise.[81]

Graham points out that the experience of obedience comes about by faith in one's identification with Christ in death and resurrection. Quoting Paul, he states that we are to "consider [ourselves] to be dead to sin, but alive to God in Christ Jesus" (Rom. 6:11). The apostle brought it all together in Galatians 2:20, in which he said, "I have been crucified with Christ; and it is no longer I who live, but Christ lives in me; and the life which I now live in the flesh I live by faith in the Son of God, who loved me, and delivered Himself up for me." Graham's approach falls in line with the Keswick movement, where he has spoken. Stephen Olford and others of like persuasion have influenced him significantly regarding the doctrine of the Holy Spirit and the victorious Christian life.

Billy concludes his emphasis on the faith aspect of the Spirit's fullness by pointing out that if we are knowledgeable, understand our needs, have every known sin confessed, and are submitted to God, then we can reach out in faith and say, "I know I am filled with the Holy Spirit." And that is not presumption; it is simply taking God at His word (Luke 11:13).

SOME FURTHER CAUTIONS

At this juncture, Graham interjects words of warning that should be grasped. First, he tells us that we must remember that being filled with the Spirit does not depend on feelings or mere emotions; it centers on faith. That has already been stressed. Second, we must not delude ourselves into thinking that being filled with the Spirit means we live without sin (1 John 1:8). On the contrary, we must come before God regularly in confession, submission, and faith. Fullness, let it be stressed again, is not a once-and-for-all event, but a *continuing* experience. Yet in that abiding walk in the fullness of the Spirit, effective ministry and a godly life are generated wherein Christ is glorified. But another issue arises: the so-called "unpardonable sin" against the Holy Spirit.

THE UNPARDONABLE SIN

Billy Graham faces the issue of the unpardonable sin with sensitivity to the fact that one can sin against the Holy Spirit by blaspheming His work. This opens a controversial doctrine. Graham breaks down his views on the subject into two major categories. First, he states that the possibility of blaspheming the Holy Spirit does exist. He quickly points out that this particular sin, however, cannot be committed by Christians. The dangerous and serious sin of blasphemy against the Holy Spirit can only be experienced by those who have continually rejected Jesus Christ. But for those who would deny the possibility of such sin, Graham reminds us that Jesus said, "Therefore I say to you, any sin and blasphemy shall be forgiven men, but blasphemy against the Spirit shall not be forgiven. And whoever shall speak a word against the Son of Man, it shall be forgiven him; but whoever shall speak against the Holy Spirit, it shall not be forgiven him, either in this age, or in the age to come" (Matt. 12:31–32).

Billy interprets Jesus' words by pointing out that the essence of this most serious breach of God's will centers in the willful, persistent resisting of the Holy Spirit as He brings people to an awareness of their need for Jesus Christ. The Bible surely teaches that the Holy Spirit will not always strive with people; therefore, the possibility exists that the Holy Spirit may eventually stop striving with a person, and thus the individual stands in dire, mortal danger. Graham argues, "It is a sin that, when carried on long enough, leads to eternal doom. Only certain judgment remains for those who so resist the Spirit."[82] Therefore, true believers should lovingly and graciously urge people not to resist the Holy Spirit, but to surrender to Him and to receive Christ as Savior. To persist in a life of constant rebellion puts one in a very serious situation indeed. Then, second, can true believers offend the Holy Spirit?

WHAT ABOUT BELIEVERS?

A Christian can in some sense sin against the Holy Spirit, Graham tells us. Although Graham believes in the eternal security of the believer and thus that a Christian cannot commit the "unpardonable sin," he or she can *grieve* the Holy Spirit. To grieve the Holy Spirit means to offend His loving work in the heart. *Grieve* is a "love" word. The Holy Spirit loves, as do the Father and the Lord Jesus Christ. Thus Paul wrote, "And do not grieve the Holy Spirit of God, by whom you were sealed for the day of redemption" (Eph. 4:30). What grieves God's blessed Spirit centers in resisting His loving entreaties and acting in an un-Christlike, unloving manner in conduct, speech, or disposition. The Bible presents the Holy Spirit as the Spirit of truth (John 14:17) and grace (Heb. 10:29). He generates faith (2 Cor. 4:13) and holiness of life (Rom. 1:14). Therefore, anything false, doubting, bitter, ungracious, or unclean defiles the believer and grieves the Holy Spirit, curtailing His work in one's life. Nonetheless, the fact remains that the Holy Spirit will never leave the genuine believer. To resist His gracious inner work is deplorable in the light of His loving presence, but He will *never* forsake those who are truly born again.

Moreover, a Christian can *quench* the Spirit (1 Thess. 5:19). This too constitutes a sin against the Spirit, albeit not an eternal sin. The word *quench* means "to put out, to put a damper on." The New Testament metaphor presents the Holy Spirit as a fire. To quench Him simply means to resist Him in some area of one's life where He would lead into holiness and effective service. Therefore, the Christian must be sensitive and cautious in his or her personal relationship with the Holy Spirit and keep confessing his or her sins daily. But there are more positive realities regarding the inner work of the Spirit toward Christians.

THE SEALING OF THE SPIRIT

On a more positive note, Billy Graham points out that the Holy Spirit "seals" the believer. This implies security and ownership. Christians belong to God. Not only that, the Holy Spirit stands as God's pledge or earnest of one's relationship to Him. The Spirit, as it has been put in modern secular terms, serves as the down payment or pledge of God's purchase of believers through the blood of Jesus Christ. Paul uses this terminology in three different passages: "who also sealed us and gave us the Spirit in our hearts as a pledge" (2 Cor. 1:22); "Now He who prepared us for this very purpose is God, who gave to us the Spirit as a pledge" (2 Cor. 5:5); "who is given as a pledge of our inheritance, with a view to the redemption of God's own possession, to the praise of His glory" (Eph. 1:14). Little wonder, therefore, that the Spirit of God constantly bears witness to one's unbreakable relationship with God through His sealing and pledging work.

The wonderful, sealing, loving Holy Spirit also bestows gifts of ministry on His people. Graham places a strong emphasis on these "gifts of the Spirit," the *charismata*. The Spirit, baptizing all believers into the "body of Christ," bestows serviceable abilities upon every one, making the body a full functioning, ministering body to the praise of the Lord. This raises the issues as to the nature of these spiritual gifts. Graham points out several principles.

THE GIFTS

First of all, Billy makes it clear that the gifts of the Holy Spirit must be distinguished from natural talents. Natural talents are certainly blessed and used of God; however, not everyone abounds in talents, and as a consequence some may think they cannot serve Christ effectively. But Graham makes the point that every believer has at least one or more spiritual ministry gifts. First Corinthians 12–14 stresses that all Christians, because they are baptized into the body (1 Cor. 12:13), are placed in the body on the basis of their gift so that they may function in their Spirit-assigned role. Therefore, every Christian has an ability to serve the Lord Jesus Christ, and when they employ their gift, God honors it and uses it to His praise.

In the second place, Graham would have us to understand that these spiritual gifts are unquestionably supernatural. This stands true because they are endowments given by the supernatural Holy Spirit. They do not develop from the mere cultivating of one's native abilities. God bestows them upon believers so that they can take their proper place in the body of Christ and thus fulfill their responsibility as the body grows into the fullness of Christ (Eph. 4:16). In that manner a church becomes a ministering entity for the furtherance of the kingdom of God throughout the world.

Thus it becomes incumbent that all members of a local congregation discover and exercise their respective spiritual gifts. Moreover, the day will come when all believers will stand before the judgment seat of Christ *(bema)* to give an account of how faithfully they used the spiritual gifts imparted to them. Paul gave a solemn word of warning in 1 Corinthians 3:11–15 that if a member of the body does not build properly upon the foundation that Christ has laid through salvation and the giving of spiritual gifts, he or she will surely suffer loss. Serve Christ we must. How does Billy Graham understand the actual nature of these gifts?

THE NATURE OF THE GIFTS

Some nineteen gifts can be found in the Scriptures. The key passages are 1 Corinthians 12–14, Ephesians 4, and Romans 12. There are other references to spiritual gifts in the Old and New Testaments, but these constitute the major passages. Concerning the gifts listed, it should be recognized that these gifts are probably *categories* of gifts. As a case in point, the gift of teaching could vary quite significantly as the needs of the church arise. For example, some will be particularly gifted in teaching children the basic truths of the Scripture. On the other hand, the pastor of the church would certainly be expected to be a gifted teacher who can delve into the deeper things of the Word of God. This principle can be applied throughout the nineteen gifts listed in the Bible. But how can one discover one's gift? Billy Graham lays out several basic ideas.

DISCOVERING ONE'S GIFT

Billy Graham first urges believers to realize they do have at least one spiritual gift. Some may well have more, but all have at least one. Second, the discovery of one's spiritual gift comes primarily through thoughtful prayer. Third, one must be willing to use one's spiritual gift to bring honor to Christ and blessings of the Lord to the church. Fourth, seekers should delve into what the Bible says about the spiritual gifts, searching out examples of how they are employed. Last, one must acquire a knowledge of one's own self and abilities. Ask the question, How has God used me and what do I enjoy doing in the Lord's service? These steps may give insight into one's spiritual gift.

Graham grants that it may be a rather lengthy process to discover one's gifts, but we need to learn because it lays the foundation to effective ministry and service. Moreover, we should never think that one gift excels another. The hand is as vital to the body as the foot, the ear, or the eye. We bestow more honor upon the menial parts of the body, as Paul pointed out to the Corinthians (1 Cor. 12:22–24). And then there is the gift of the evangelist that the Holy Spirit gives to the church.

THE EVANGELISTIC GIFT

One of the gifts that Paul mentions is the gift of the *evangelist* (Eph. 4:11). Graham defines the term as "one who announces good news." As a case in point, Philip served as an evangelist (Acts 8). Moreover, the apostle Paul urged Timothy to "do the work of an evangelist" (2 Tim. 4:5). Graham sees this truth as the secret of his effective ministry of evangelism. He said to David Frost in an interview, "I think, David, that God gave me the gift of an evangelist. The Bible teaches that there's a gift of . . . an evangelist . . . that is a gift that God gives."[83]

Graham points out several things concerning this particular gift, especially in light of the fact that he acknowledges with gratitude to God that he has been given this ministering gift. He first states that the evangelist's message centers in the content of the gospel itself. If the evangelist has been given a special ability to communicate the gospel, his responsibility centers in presenting the full message, the good news of Jesus Christ, to those who need to hear. He does not necessarily do the work of a pastor; instead, the evangelist's message focuses on the life, death, burial, and resurrection of Jesus Christ and the call to repentance and faith in light of the fact that Jesus is coming again.

SOME CAUTIONS

Graham honestly acknowledges that some evangelists and their activities raise a question mark. The "Elmer Gantry" image of the errant evangelist has almost made the word *evangelist* a pejorative term, at least in the thinking of some. Evangelists can easily become the special targets of the devil; therefore, the evangelist must be a person of impeccable integrity, preaching the full gospel. God does not give the gift of evangelism to be abused.

It must also be realized that the exercise of the evangelistic gift speaks primarily to the intellect and will; it may or may not produce emotions. The evangelist calls people to decide *intelligently* for Jesus Christ. The evangelist challenges the unbeliever to exercise repentance toward God and faith in our Lord Jesus Christ (Acts 20:21). The Word of God thus becomes the basis of that which the evangelist communicates. These concepts Graham strongly stresses.

Graham also gives the caution that an evangelist can easily spend too much time planning how to achieve more visible results. He sees that as a trap for evangelists. He does not deny the desirability to see positive results, but the gift does not guarantee a large, immediate response. The Scriptures describe the evangelistic task as embracing a time for sowing, a time for cultivating, and a time for reaping. God stands as the One who gives the increase, and the evangelist must simply be faithful to the call and proclaim the entire message of Jesus Christ (1 Cor. 3:6–8), leaving the rest to God.

Furthermore, the gift of the evangelist does not imply ironclad methods or manifestations. Graham has said, "Evangelism is like an arrow. There's a sharp point, which is the gospel. But then the arrow broadens in many different styles. There are many different methods in evangelism but they all depend on the Holy Spirit."[84] The church stands in some danger today due to its emphasis and zealous efforts in programming evangelism. As Billy Graham has said, "Today in the face of vastly improved methods of communication, the power of the Holy Spirit is being neglected."[85] In the final analysis, as Graham states, "If the evangelist is to carry on a truly effective ministry to the glory of the Lord, the message must be backed by a Spirit-filled, fruit producing life. Jesus promised 'Follow me, and I will make you to become fishers of men'"[86] (see Mark 1:17).

Graham stresses one final word on the subject. All Christians are called by the Holy Spirit to witness and share their faith; all are expected to play their role in the fulfilling of the Great Commission (Matt. 28:18–20). One does not have to be a gifted evangelist to be a faithful witness for Christ and thus "do the work of an evangelist" (2 Tim. 4:5). With those principles in mind, Graham goes on to present his ideas on the more "spectacular" gifts of the Spirit and their importance in Christian ministry.

OTHER GIFTS

Graham spends some time discussing the gifts of tongues and healing in light of the fact that these gifts have attained such prominence in certain Christian evangelical circles in recent years. Billy takes a traditional evangelical stance on the gift of tongues. He tells us initially that the gift of tongues can certainly be genuine and of the Holy Spirit. Yet the possibility of creating a climate can arise wherein a person becomes merely psychologically worked up into a state of speaking in tongues. He also believes the possibility exists that tongues can be of satanic influence. With these ideas in the background, he discusses his views on the gift of tongues.

Billy makes a distinction between the gift of tongues manifested at Pentecost and the tongues Paul dealt with in 1 Corinthians 14. Some, of course, will disagree. But Graham holds to the position that at Pentecost the tongues were understood to be a definite foreign language. In the Corinthian Epistle, Paul is apparently dealing with ecstatic utterances. Now ecstatic utterances are not peculiar to Christianity. They can be found in various pagan religions as well, such as Hinduism.

Graham then places strong emphasis on the fact that the gift of tongues, like any of the gifts of the Spirit, should not be confused with the *fruit* of the Spirit. The gifts of the Spirit are for ministry and service; the fruit of the Spirit blossom out in holiness of life. Therefore, the gift of tongues does not necessarily elevate one Christian above another in spirituality. Graham further points out that Paul emphasizes the fact that the gift of tongues must be seen as one of the lesser gifts. Billy attempts to dispel the idea that the gift of tongues is equated with the baptism of the Holy Spirit. Again disagreement will arise, but he points out that the Bible and experience both wave a red flag concerning the gift. It has become clear that tongues can be abused, that they can even be dangerous as the gift can lead to spiritual pride and divisiveness. The gift of tongues is scriptural to be sure, but it must be guided by the Holy Scriptures.

Moreover, it must not be forgotten that the gifts of the Spirit are essentially for the building up of the body of Christ. Thus, tongues are not for personal satisfaction alone. Graham finds no problem in one exercising this gift of tongues. But if the gift is to be exercised publicly, it must always be accompanied by someone with the gift of interpretation so that the church may be profited. Paul stressed this (1 Cor. 14:1–19). And finally, surely not everyone has the gift of tongues. The body of Christ would not be a balanced body if everybody had the gift of tongues—it would be just one giant tongue, not a fully functioning body at all.

THE GIFT OF HEALING

Concerning healing, Graham gives an insightful word. In recounting the death of a faithful young Christian, he said, "This does not mean that God never heals in miraculous ways for I am certain that there are times when He does. But there are also many times when He does not. We cannot understand why. . . . But in the midst of the suffering, trials, and temptations, Jesus Christ provides His peace and joy."[87] Thus we must rest in faith that God is Love and does all things well. Our Lord does not heal everyone. Still, Graham grants that there is a gift of healing. He wrote, "I believe the gift of healing or miracles is one a believer has."[88]

But what about the *fruit* of the Spirit? How does Billy Graham see this important work of the Holy Spirit? A few words of the evangelist should be shared here, but the subject will be seen in more detail in chapter 10.

THE FRUIT OF THE SPIRIT

It has been pointed out that Billy Graham makes a sharp distinction between the *gifts* of the Spirit and the *fruit* of the Spirit. Paul enumerated this principle clearly in Galatians 5:22–23. Billy labors to expound the various aspects of the basic fruit of Christian love and to elucidate the absolute necessity of this grace in the believer's life. He has said, "We cannot love; we cannot have joy, peace, longsuffering, gentleness, goodness, faith, meekness, and temperance by ourselves. But the Holy Spirit who has lived in us since we received Christ as Savior is the one who gives us power to love. He gives us joy. He gives us peace. He gives up patience. He bears fruit in our lives."[89]

Such a life reflects holiness before the Lord and thus becomes a testimony to the world of the saving grace of Christ. And the Holy Spirit produces it all in the believer. In his *Christian Workers Handbook,* Graham brings it together by saying, "To be filled with the Spirit means that the believer will demonstrate the fruit of the Spirit in his or her life."[90] Let it simply suffice to say that Billy Graham places major emphasis on the godly life that comes about by the inner work of the Holy Spirit. Further, he stresses that evangelism must culminate in Christians becoming fruit-bearing believers; this constitutes the final mark in the goal of the purpose of God in all evangelization. This, in turn, impacts the world powerfully (Acts 2:42–47).

THE LEADING OF THE SPIRIT

Billy Graham sees the Holy Spirit playing a vital leadership role in every aspect of evangelism, and in the entire Christian experience for that matter. This means the Spirit not only controls and empowers, but He also *leads and directs* in all the affairs of ministry. If the question were ever asked: Does Billy Graham recognize that principle and has it been manifest in his evangelism? the answer to the question could be nothing but a most emphatic *yes*. The evangelist has said, "God has a specific will for the life of each Christian. It should be our highest purpose to determine just what His will is for us and then do it; whatever the cost."[91] Recognizing the Holy Spirit as the One who leads into God's purpose, Billy has given himself to follow that lead whatever the price.

This principle of the Spirit's leadership can be observed throughout Graham's entire ministry, not the least of which has been the bringing together of the team and the Billy Graham Evangelistic Association (BGEA) and the ministry that unfolded. We have seen how all that developed in the early days and has continued on. It would seem there is only one obvious answer: The Holy Spirit has directed it all. The camaraderie, mutual respect, and appreciation each team member and family expresses for one another is really quite remarkable. And the basic team has stayed together for more than fifty years. Only God by the Spirit could effect that. Yes, there has been a defector now and then. A few—very few—have been obliged to leave. But the way the organization has held together is really remarkable. At the time of this writing, Mr. Graham is in his eighties, Cliff Barrows in his late seventies, and Bev Shea in his nineties, and they still carry on. That is none other than Holy Spirit leadership, as He has always guided His servants throughout the history of evangelism. All evangelicals acknowledge that fact. And in Billy's personal life, God's bringing him his lovely helpmate, Ruth, and their five children was certainly led by the Holy Spirit. It would seem there is no question: The Holy Spirit has directed it all.

ANGELS

In the general context of the Holy Spirit's leading, Billy Graham introduces another dynamic: the work of holy angels. Billy confesses, "Angels belong to a uniquely different dimension of creation which we, limited to the natural order, can scarcely comprehend."[92] Yet, they are very real, and involved in human affairs. He elucidates this principle in his book *Angels: God's Secret Agents.* In that volume the evangelist develops a quite well-defined doctrine of angelology. He believes in angels and their activities on behalf of God's redeemed people. As always, he predicates his position on the Scriptures. Billy has said, "I believe in angels because the Bible says there are angels."[93] Theologians throughout history, such as Augustine, Thomas Aquinas, Karl Barth, C. S. Lewis, and others, agree. In his well-received book, Graham wrote, "Angels have a much more important place in the Bible than the devil and his demons."[94] Therefore, the church needs to be made aware of their existence and their position in ministry. That work centers essentially in "the affairs of the people," as the evangelist puts it. He agrees with Martin Luther in his definition as to the context of angelic ministry. Luther said, "An angel is a spiritual creature without a body created by God for the service of Christendom and the church."[95] Graham senses the importance of these biblical facts because an understanding in this area will be, in his words, "great comfort and inspiration to believers in God—and a challenge to unbelievers to believe."[96]

Graham tells us several things about angels. First, he agrees with Luther that they are created beings; yet, as Graham states, "they can change their appearance and shuttle in a flash from the capitol glory of heaven to earth and back again."[97] Second, as stated by Luther, angels serve God and regenerate believers. They are God's "messengers"; the word *angel* means "messenger." Often the Bible records angels coming from God to bring His message to His people. In that context, we can see angels in the Scriptures fighting the devil and his hosts. The classic case of this reality is when Daniel prayed and the devil tried to delay the answer. Michael the archangel came to defeat Satan's efforts and to win the victory (Dan. 10:10–21).

We see many incidents recorded in the Old Testament in which angels brought messages from God, fought for God's people, and gained victories for the Lord. Abraham entertained angels "unawares" (Gen. 13; Heb. 13:2). And the New Testament is no exception. Our Lord believed in angels. They aided Him, comforted Him, strengthened Him, and guarded Him. A classic case centers in the angels' ministering to Jesus in the agony of Gethsemane (Luke 22:43). The Lord said in the hour of His trial He could "appeal to [His] Father, and He will at once put at My disposal more than twelve legions of angels" (Matt. 26:53). And when Jesus returns, "He will send forth His angels with a great trumpet and they will gather together His elect from the four winds, from one end of the sky to the other" (Matt. 24:31).

The angels no doubt aid the Lord's elect people. This is true in the work of evangelism. Acts records the conversion of Cornelius, the Roman centurion (Acts 10). An angel appeared to him and beckoned him to send for Peter that the gospel might be communicated to him and his household. Then Peter was given a heavenly vision that made him open to going into a Gentile's house— forbidden by Jews—to share Christ. Angels do get involved in evangelism, even if they do not preach the gospel themselves.

The Bible abounds in many accounts of angels, archangels, and the heavenly hosts doing God's bidding to help the church establish the kingdom. It can all be summed up in the words of Hebrews 1:14, "Are they not all ministering spirits, sent out to render service for the sake of those who will inherit salvation?" That general statement covers the subject of angels quite well.

Space will not allow us to investigate all Billy Graham has said in the area of biblical studies and practical experience concerning angels and their activities. But his aforementioned book presents a full account of the beautiful doctrine and its relation to the Spirit's work.

All of this is to say that Billy Graham and his entire team are vividly conscious that the crusade and the entire work of the Billy Graham Evangelistic Association functions only because of the Holy Spirit's leading, power, and wisdom—and even angelic aid. Therefore, as Sterling Huston, crusade director, quotes Billy, "The secret of each crusade has been the power of God's Spirit moving in answer to the prayers of His people. I have often said that the three most important things we can do for a crusade are to pray, to pray, and to pray."[98] Prayer releases the Spirit. The incidents of God are leading and empowering, and using the team's ministry in answer to prayer could fill volumes. David Bruce has stated that Billy Graham's emphasis on the Holy Spirit and His work "runs throughout the entire Billy Graham Evangelistic Association, as they take their cue from the 'top,' Billy Graham."[99] But this reality will become self-evident as this book progresses. As Billy would say, in the words of an old hymn:

> In shady green pastures, so rich and so sweet,
> God leads His dear children along.
> There the water's cool flow bathes the weary one's feet.
> God leads His dear children along
> Some through the waters, some through the flood,
> Some through the fire
> But all through the Blood
> Some through great sorrow; but God gives a song
> In the night season and all the day long.

That is true, and the Graham ministry gives testimony to it. That is a contribution in itself.

A BRIEF SUMMARY

With all of these principles in mind, Billy Graham has constructed a thorough, if not elaborate doctrine of the Holy Spirit. To Graham, the work of the Holy Spirit stands foundational in his life and ministry of evangelism; it colors all aspects of his ministry as shall be continually seen in these pages.

The final issue to be faced concerning Graham's doctrine and emphasis on the Holy Spirit and His work centers in this: Does it basically conform to evangelical, historical understandings of the person and work of the Holy Spirit in evangelism, and has it made a lasting contribution to the cause of Christ in world evangelization? Clearly, this is the crux of the matter. To answer this query fully may take the rest of this book. Yet, it does seem quite correct to say, at least at this stage, that Billy Graham does definitely fall in line with traditional, historical evangelical thinking concerning the Holy Spirit and His role in the Christian experience. This leads to a final evaluation of the evangelist.

CONTRIBUTION OF BILLY GRAHAM
CONCERNING THE HOLY SPIRIT IN EVANGELISM

Few in the church today would deny that the body of Christ needs a "new Pentecost," that is, a true outpouring of the Holy Spirit to quicken and empower God's people for the task of extending the kingdom of God. It has happened many times in past history. Time and space fail to tell of the Spirit's work in great movements found in Old Testament accounts such as the Exodus under Moses, the returning of Israel to dedication to God under Elijah and Elisha, and many other spiritual epochs. In the New Testament and throughout subsequent history, the story is repeated. Men and women like William and Catherine Booth, who founded the Salvation Army; great missionaries such as William Carey and Amy Carmichael, who ultimately touched millions for Christ; along with a host of others were used by the Holy Spirit to revitalize God's people and propagate the gospel.

But notice these dynamics revolved around the mighty work of God's Spirit using a human instrument who understood biblically who the Spirit is, how He operates, and then placed his or her hand in the Spirit's grasp and permitted God to do His work. Those elements are *always* paramount when God moves mightily. All history attests to that fact. The issue thus becomes, does Billy Graham, as an evangelist, truly fall in that noble line?

The preceding investigation has hopefully provided an answer. It would seem that the only reasonable response could be affirmative. Graham does fill the role of the knowledgeable, committed, evangelical, Spirit-filled evangelist. Several things can be said in that regard. First, Billy Graham has a sound biblical theology of the Holy Spirit from the traditional evangelical perspective. There are, of course, those who disagree with some of his views. He does not please everyone. Yet he does basically adhere to what the church has held and taught for more than two millennia on the issues and doctrines of pneumatology. He has a basic historical, biblical, evangelical understanding of the teachings concerning the Holy Spirit.

Second, Graham has made a significant contribution in heralding the truths of the Holy Spirit, and many believers and churches have been richly blessed. Countless people have been challenged, deepened, and led into the fullness of the Spirit-filled, empowered life. This constitutes a most positive contribution in this vital aspect of spiritual Christianity. Surely, God has placed His anointing on Billy to be a prophet in this essential area of Christian doctrine and experience as well as his evangelization. Of course, it goes without saying that Billy's Spirit-filled evangelistic ministry has been the heart and core of his service to Christ, and has touched multiplied millions around the world. Many will be recorded in the Book of Life (Rev. 20:12) because of Billy Graham's Spirit-anointed ministry of evangelism.

Finally, as a consequence, many have been "saved" from futililty and mere ceremonial Christianity. A new freshness and spirituality has blossomed around Billy Graham's ministry. And this new spiritual vitality among God's people has significantly impacted many communities. Only God knows what the church, society, and the nations where he has ministered would be like today if he had not served them as God's Spirit-filled evangelist. He is owed a genuine debt of gratitude for his contribution to many different societies and cultures. And it all grows out of his understanding and personal experience of the Third Person of the divine Trinity: the blessed Spirit of God.

Thus it becomes quite appropriate to thank God for the life of devotion to the historical, biblical truth of the Holy Spirit that Billy Graham knows and practices so well. And that is not too effusive; it is reasonable and true.

CHAPTER 3

THE CALL AND THE GOSPEL IN EVANGELISM

～～

PART I:
PAUL: HIS CALL AND MESSAGE

. . . woe is me if I do not preach the gospel.
—1 CORINTHIANS 9:16

INTRODUCTION

All that has been said concerning the centrality of the Holy Spirit in evangelism as relating to Peter in his Jewish context certainly applies to the apostle Paul in his mission to the Gentile world. If ever there were a man who exemplified the Spirit-filled gospel ministry, Paul filled the role. And God profoundly honored his service in a most miraculous fashion.

Again, as in the case of Peter, we know little of the early life of Paul before his encounter with Christ on the Damascus Road. Still, from his own pen he tells us he was from Tarsus and a Roman citizen. He studied under the Jewish scholar Gamaliel and became a devoted Pharisee. Then, he met the Lord and was converted and called to the task of preaching the gospel. His life was never the same again.

Two powerful motivations compelled Paul to give himself without reservation to his task. Foundational was the deep conviction that God had called him to the work. Second, the apostle's grasp of the essence and nature of the gospel thrust him relentlessly into the world to share the saving message. The sincere evangelist of any age or culture must be captivated by those two vital convictions. We will look at the compelling call of God as Paul experienced it and the captivating gospel he preached. This chapter is quite extensive because it forms the very foundation of the evangelistic ministry in any age, Paul's or ours. We first examine Paul's call.

THE CALL

The apostle Paul rejoiced in his call. He said, "I magnify my ministry" (Rom. 11:13). The fact that the sovereign Lord God would place His hand upon a persecutor of the church and set him apart to minister Christ never failed to thrill him. It all began on the way to Damascus.

With hatred, vengeance, and murder in his heart, Saul wreaked havoc on the early church. Being a malignant menace to God's people, he later called himself the "chief of sinners" (see 1 Tim. 1:15). But in God's forbearance and mercy, He arrested the wild persecutor and not only brought him to faith in the Messiah he hated, but also called him to preach His message. What a radical transformation occurred in Saul when he heard, "I am Jesus whom you are persecuting, but rise, and enter the city, and it shall be told you what you must do" (Acts 9:5–6). The call had come, and Saul the persecutor became Paul the preacher.

Paul truly did rejoice in his call. He said to Timothy, "I thank Christ Jesus our Lord, who has strengthened me, because He considered me faithful, putting me into service" (1 Tim. 1:12). That commission elevated him to the rank of *apostle*, literally "one sent" from God. He knew the Lord had called and equipped him for the task by the indwelling Holy Spirit and the imparting of spiritual gifts (Eph. 4:12) for the ministry of evangelization. He exalted those facts. He began the introduction of the majority of his letters with the phrase "Paul, an apostle of Jesus Christ." To the Galatians, because of their question of his call, he stated very emphatically that his apostleship emanated "not of men, neither by man, but by Jesus Christ, and God the Father" (Gal. 1:1 KJV). Paul contended that God had "separated me from my mother's womb, and called me by his grace" (Gal. 1:15 KJV). In other words, Paul was predestined to preach Christ.

What constituted the essence of the apostle Paul's call? Simply put, the Holy

Spirit set him apart to preach the glorious gospel of Christ to the nations. Os Guinness expressed it in these words: ". . . my calling, as I have discovered it and tried to fulfill it, has been to make sense of the gospel to the world . . . and to make sense of the world to the church."[1] Paul would resonate with that. The world needs to understand the gospel, and the church needs the burden of the world on its heart. The apostle was so consumed with his call and its fathomless responsibility that it moved him to say, "For if I preach the gospel, I have nothing to boast of, for I am under compulsion" (1 Cor. 9:16). He felt his obligation so deeply that he endured stoning (Acts 14:19), imprisonment (Acts 22:23), rejection and ostracism (2 Tim. 1:15), and finally even martyrdom (2 Tim. 4:6). That is commitment, and it comes because of the *call of God.*

Furthermore, Christ's emphatic call cannot be confined to the first-century apostles. It has come to countless committed Christians through the centuries. It can be heard today. And the "Source" is the same—God; and the call is the same—declare the gospel. This stands true because God is the same "yesterday, today, and forever" (Heb. 13:8 NKJV), and the world struggles with the same profound need.

THE NATURE OF THE GOSPEL

Then, after the reception of the call, the nature of the gospel that God commissions His servants to proclaim must be clearly grasped, because that in itself thrusts one into the fields to reap the harvest. Paul certainly understood the good news and had absolute confidence in it. God had revealed the gospel to him (Gal. 1:11–12); thus, he could say, "I am not ashamed of the gospel, for it is the power of God for salvation to everyone who believes" (Rom. 1:16). Paul had such overwhelming assurance in the truth God had called him to share that he never altered his message throughout his life. This stands true for two vital reasons.

First, Paul saw the gospel as a divine revelation. It had been hidden for eons, but at last the Holy Spirit had made it known. As he said to the Colossians, "the mystery which has been hidden from the past ages and generations; but has now been manifested to His saints" (Col. 1:26).

Moreover, the message always strikes at the heart of the deepest human need. The gospel tells people how to be forgiven, how to enter into a dynamic fellowship with God, how to experience an abundant life, and how to be saved from wrath and live with God forever. It truly is a message of penetrating permanent power.

Little wonder Paul felt awestruck at the gospel. No other message compares to it. No philosophy, religion, or any human conception has approached the wonder and utter uniqueness of the gospel of Jesus Christ. It stands as God's ultimate truth—and He calls His people to declare it. As a result, Paul became a zealous proponent of the gospel and declared it to all people.

A true definition of the gospel immediately implies its universality. We shall look in depth at the global appeal of the good news in a later chapter; still, a short excursion on that central fact stands in order here.

THE SEGREGATION WALL FALLS DOWN

Perhaps the most significant verse concerning the universality of the gospel came from the pen of Paul and is found in the Book of Ephesians. The apostle wrote: "For He Himself [Jesus] is our peace, who made both groups into one, and broke down the barrier of the dividing wall" (Eph. 2:14). As implied above, when one arrives at a clear understanding of the essential message of Christ, its universal appeal is immediately evident. The gospel is applicable to every nation, regardless of ethnic, cultural, racial, or any other human barrier. This realization could hardly have been an easy thing for Paul to assimilate. Recall, he was "circumcised the eighth day, of the nation of Israel, of the tribe of Benjamin, a Hebrew of Hebrews; as to the Law, a Pharisee" (Phil. 3:5). The cultural and religious barriers that Paul had to overcome to arrive at the place at which he was able to say, "I have become all things to all men, that I may by all means save some" (1 Cor. 9:22), must have been monumental. Such a move no doubt constituted a revolutionary leap for a "Pharisee of the Pharisees." That revolution came on the Damascus Road. Paul's whole spirit and attitude, not only toward God but toward humanity as well, was transformed. The walls of segregation crumbled.

Through it all, Paul came to see that the gospel, by its very nature, is universal in its appeal. This principle of universality emerges out of the essence of the message. This can hardly be refuted because the good news of Christ reveals to the human heart:

- The path to forgiveness of sin (Acts 2:38)

- The route to peace with God (Rom. 5:1)

- The road to a full and meaningful life (John 10:10)

- The highway to heaven and eternal life (John 3:16)

All peoples need the assurance of such gifts of God's grace. Thus the gospel of Jesus Christ becomes the instrument of the Holy Spirit to break the human heart and to bring people to repentance and faith, thus to new life in Christ.

Paul fully recognized that he must defend, declare, and disseminate the message of Christ at all costs. In the light of this fact, his missionary journeys began. And in that ministry he had only one message to proclaim: "We preach Christ crucified" (1 Cor. 1:23). Paul and Barnabas, on their first missionary journey, created major events in the furtherance of the gospel. For example, in Pisidia, Paul preached Christ, saying:

> . . . To us the word of this salvation is sent out. For those who live in Jerusalem, and their rulers, recognizing neither Him [Christ] nor the utterances of the prophets which are read every Sabbath, fulfilled these by condemning Him. And though they found no ground for putting Him to death, they asked Pilate that He be executed. And when they had carried out all that was written concerning Him, they took Him down from the cross and laid Him in a tomb. But God raised Him from the dead. (Acts 13:26–30)

The incident culminates with this positive note: "When the Gentiles heard this, they began rejoicing and glorifying the word of the Lord; and as many as had been appointed to eternal life believed. And the word of the Lord was being spread through the whole region" (Acts 13:48–49).

A different incident occurred in Iconium. Paul proclaimed the gospel of Christ, but "the multitude of the city was divided; and some sided with the Jews, and some with the apostles" (Acts 14:4). Paul always seemed to be something of a divider of persons, at times even among some who called themselves believers. The primary reason centered in the fact that Paul was so convinced concerning the truth of the gospel of pure grace by faith that he would never allow it to have any sort of mixture. As a case in point, this "exclusivism" brought about serious conflict among the so-called Judaizers. These advocates argued that the Gentiles who would seek Christ must first adhere to the Jewish law, especially in circumcision and dietary restrictions. To oversimplify the issue, they contended a Gentile must become a Jew before becoming a Christian. Paul vehemently opposed this deviation from the essential gospel of grace. This situation precipitated the so-called Jerusalem Conference recorded in Acts 15.

THE JERUSALEM CONFERENCE

By the time of the Jerusalem Conference, the message of Christ had drawn many Gentiles to faith in Christ. In that context a dispute arose. The issue revolved around the question of how the Gentiles were to be accepted into the Christian community. The Judaizers were convinced that God had only one covenant and to be a member of that covenant, one must first submit oneself to Jewish initiation. Paul vehemently argued that God had inaugurated a new covenant, based on undiluted grace and faith in Jesus Christ alone. Thus a conference was called to settle once and for all the nature of the gospel.

At the forefront of the debate stood James, the leader of the Jerusalem church, along with Peter, the leading apostle. Into the fray Paul strode with his commitment to the exclusiveness of the message of grace. The decision would no doubt influence the future of Christianity with a profundity hard to imagine at the time.

Two central issues had to be faced and resolved. The first issue revolved around whether Gentile converts had to submit to the requirements of circumcision and keeping the Jewish traditions to be saved. As New Testament scholar John Polhill said, "A major barrier between Christians and Pharisees was the extensive use of oral tradition by the Pharisees, which Jesus and Paul both rejected as human tradition."[2] The second issue concerned how fellowship should be maintained between Jewish and Gentile Christians so as to celebrate together the Lord's Supper. So serious was the issue in the Galatian churches that Paul wrote the most stinging rebuke to be found in any of his Epistles:

> I am amazed that you are so quickly deserting Him who called you by the grace of Christ, for a different gospel; which is really not another; only there are some who are disturbing you, and want to distort the gospel of Christ. But even

though we, or an angel from heaven, should preach to you a gospel contrary to that which we have preached to you, let him be accursed. As we have said before, so I say again now, if any man is preaching to you a gospel contrary to that which you received, let him be accursed. (Gal. 1:6–9)

Obviously the issue had to be settled. What constitutes the pure gospel? How can one be saved? The conflict over who could eat the Lord's Supper together became especially volatile. For example, in Antioch, Peter refused to eat with his Gentile brothers and sisters in Christ. To this Paul reacted strongly. Paul shared with the Galatians the encounter:

When Cephas came to Antioch, I opposed him to his face, because he stood condemned. For prior to the coming of certain men from James, he used to eat with the Gentiles; but when they came, he began to withdraw and hold himself aloof, fearing the party of the circumcision. And the rest of the Jews joined him in hypocrisy, with the result that even Barnabas was carried away by their hypocrisy. (Gal. 2:11–13)

After the Antioch confrontation, Peter apparently saw the light and cleared himself on the issue. At the Jerusalem Conference, Peter argued along with Paul for the gospel of grace alone as the basis of fellowship with God and one another. One of the arguments made by Peter at the conference stressed the fact that keeping the Jewish law created a yoke no one could really bear. Although Jewish Christians were not asked to abandon the law, Peter and Paul both argued that faith in Christ alone constituted the only hope for salvation. James also rose to speak. He defended Peter's position that the Gentiles should not be required to embrace the Jewish law and submit themselves to circumcision. Paul declared that Jew and Gentile alike are brought together by faith into the single people of God "for His name's sake." It ended with the purity of the simple gospel of grace being set and sealed. The law does not save. The Gentile believers were asked out of graciousness and sensitivity to those of a Jewish background to do four things:

1. They should abstain from food offered to idols.

2. They should abstain from sexual immorality.

3. They should not eat meat of strangled animals.

4. They should not eat anything that contained the blood of animals.

These were mere courtesies that would keep the Gentiles from offending their Jewish brethren. They had nothing to do with the essence of the gospel itself, but rather living a life of Christian love and understanding. Thus the purity of the gospel was maintained. The contribution Paul made in his unswerving stance at the Jerusalem Conference became one of his most important contributions to the faith. And the gospel sped on.

Space forbids going into the multiplied instances of Paul's ministry of the gospel to the world. He stood before authorities, kings, even Caesar himself. During his imprisonments for the sake of the Christ, he communicated the message to everyone who would listen, whether centurion, fellow prisoner, Felix, or Agrippa. Paul recognized that the gospel is the power of God for salvation; therefore, it must be communicated to all people in all circumstances. Anything that falls short of that essential truth cannot be properly termed biblical evangelism.

CONCLUSION

The apostolic age, therefore, clearly communicates three essential truths in the unfolding saga of bringing Christ to the world. First, God calls His people to share in that ministry. Second, anyone who aspires to be faithful to that evangelistic call must minister under the leadership and unction of the Holy Spirit. Third, the simple but full gospel must be shared, and in the hands of the Holy Spirit it becomes the "power of God." And God desires that message of Christ to be communicated to all peoples.

This raises the fundamental issue: What actually constitutes the gospel? What makes up the biblical message that breaks down all barriers and addresses itself to all peoples? What is this message God calls His servants to declare? These questions must be answered to evaluate any evangelistic efforts, whether Billy Graham's or a simple layperson's witnessing to a lost friend. To these central issues we turn.

THE BIBLICAL NATURE OF THE GOSPEL

As we have seen, Paul placed a high premium on the fact that God had set him aside for the proclamation of the gospel. He cherished his call with its honor and high responsibility. When he instructed Timothy on the compelling nature of God's call, he urged—actually pleaded—with the young pastor of the Ephesian church: "O Timothy, guard what has been entrusted to you" (1 Tim. 6:20). As can be understood, Paul's admonition to Timothy to guard that which was committed to him can be nothing other than the full gospel of Jesus Christ. Paul felt such a commitment to the gospel that at times he called it "my gospel." What therefore constitutes the gospel for which Paul contended so fervently?

An illustrious history rests back of the gospel of Christ; the proclamation has been heralded around the world and must be seen as the Holy Spirit's key instrument in effecting salvation. As Paul said to the Corinthian believers, "For since in the wisdom of God the world through its wisdom did not come to know God, God was well-pleased through the foolishness of the message preached to save those who believe" (1 Cor. 1:21). In that verse we see in summary fashion the essence of the evangelistic dynamic of God.

THE ESSENCE OF THE MESSAGE OF JESUS CHRIST

Paul's word to the Corinthians bristles with stimulating ideas and principles. One of the most vital truths the apostle would have the entire church grasp is that, in all evangelistic endeavors, God uses as His primary instrument in redemption what Paul called "the message preached" (the Greek term *kerygma*). In other words, the *kerygma* serves as the "sword of the Spirit," which God wields to bring people to saving faith in Jesus Christ.

By the means of *kerygma*, people are brought to a saving knowledge of our Lord. This is what Paul meant when he wrote to the Romans: "I am not ashamed of the gospel *[euangelion]*: it is the power of God for salvation to every one who has faith" (Rom. 1:16 RSV). *Euangelion*—good news—and *kerygma*—the proclamation—are synonyms in the New Testament. And experience verifies the power of the message. The gospel was fully tested in the laboratory of life on the Day of Pentecost when "those who had received his word were baptized; and there were added that day about three thousand souls" (Acts 2:41). If the *kerygma*, in the hands of the Spirit through the agency of men and women, can accomplish those sorts of results, Christians should have it at their fingertips and be ready to share it gladly.

THE MEANING OF *KERYGMA*

The root of *kerygma* boasts various ideas. As Gerhard Friedrich stated, it signifies "both the result of proclamation (what is proclaimed) and the actual proclaiming."[3] Something quite profound emerges in the dual meaning of the term. It implies that the proclamation of the gospel is not a mere reciting of theological dogmas; it also speaks of a positive faith response with definite results. Such fruit is forthcoming because of the Spirit's activity in addressing real needs in the dynamic of proclamation. The ministry of Christ touches the total person. Therefore, when the *kerygma* was preached, miraculous results occurred: the conversion of lost sinners. Proclamation in the biblical sense does not attempt to persuade hearers by clever oration. As Paul said, the gospel comes in "demonstration of the Spirit and of power" (1 Cor. 2:4).[4] The reason for such a demonstration is clear; the apostle wanted to be certain that people's faith rested not on the wisdom of men, "but on the power of God" (1 Cor. 2:5).

This emphasis on the existential aspects of the gospel does not imply there is no definite theological, historical content in the message, however. Once more Friedrich is helpful: "The foolish message of Jesus crucified saves those who believe. . . . [It is a] message with a very definite content. The gospel of Paul is identical with that which Jesus Himself preached during His earthly life."[5] Paul's reminder in 1 Corinthians 15:1–4 makes it very plain that theology is important: "Now I would remind you, brethren, in what terms I preached to you the gospel. . . . For I delivered to you as of first importance what I also received, that Christ died for our sins in accordance with the scriptures, that he was buried, that he was raised on the third day in accordance with the scriptures" (RSV).

That word speaks of content. That is what the Jerusalem Conference was all about. The Holy Spirit takes the historical events of Jesus Christ and brings them home to the heart and thereby effects conversions. Paul knew the gospel contained both theological facts and Spirit-filled power. Therefore, when one sums up the gospel, several significant truths immediately surface:

- The gospel brings salvation (Eph. 1:3).
- The gospel brings the kingdom of God (Luke 4:21).
- The gospel brings immortality to light (2 Tim. 1:10).
- The gospel brings affliction (2 Tim. 1:8).
- The gospel brings truth (Col. 1:5).
- The gospel brings grace (Acts 20:24).
- The gospel brings peace (Eph. 6:15).
- The gospel brings labor (Col. 3:17).
- The gospel brings responsibility (1 Thess. 2:4).
- The gospel brings God (Rom. 15:16).

In a word, the gospel brings everything that pertains to life in the full God-given sense, because it brings men and women face to face with Jesus Christ. This is why it is called the "eternal gospel" (Rev. 14:6). All these truths should be proclaimed. *Kerygma* and *euangelion* are obviously most significant terms.

Now we need to answer the question raised at the outset: What constitutes the actual content of the proclamation, the good news?

THE CONTENT OF EVANGELISTIC PROCLAMATION

Although few appreciate the type of proclamation that grows out of a bigoted and narrow dogmatism, there must be no "uncertain sound" when the gospel is shared. As Douglas Webster reminded us:

A mood of uncertainty about the heart of the gospel, the Lord of the Church, and the Savior of the world, is unworthy of Christians and bodes ill for the future of missions if it is allowed or encouraged to persist. Describing the first mission to Thessalonica St. Paul wrote: "When we brought you the gospel, we brought it not in mere words but in the power of the Holy Spirit, *and with strong conviction,* as you know well" (I Thess. 1:5, NEB). Christian, even theological, humility is not synonymous with vagueness.[6]

What then is the message? What is this "foolishness of the message preached" (1 Cor. 1:21) that God uses to save the lost?

C. H. DODD'S APPROACH TO THE *KERYGMA*

Ever since New Testament scholar C. H. Dodd gave us his classic book *The Apostolic Preaching and its Development,*[7] much interest in New Testament studies has focused on the *kerygma.* Dodd approached this central concept by first making a definite distinction between *kerygma* and *didaskein. Didaskein* he defines as "teaching," i.e., ethical and moral instructions on the Christian life. *Didaskein* certainly contains theological doctrine, but *didaskein* is quite distinct from "proclamation." *Kerygma* is essentially the public declaration of Christianity to the non-Christian world with the view of converting that world. Dodd contended, "For the early church, then, to preach the gospel was by no means the same thing as to deliver moral instruction or exhortation. While the church was concerned to hand on the teaching of the Lord, it was not by this that it made converts. It was by *kerygma,* said Paul, not by *didache,* that it pleased God to save men."[8]

Dodd discerned six basic elements in the *kerygma* found in early Acts. First, the age of fulfillment has dawned and the Messianic age has arrived (Acts 2:16). Second, this new age has come through the ministry, death, and resurrection of Jesus Christ. Moreover, a brief account of these central acts of Christ's passion is always given. The concepts of the Davidic descent, the Lord's ministry of healing and helping, His vicarious death, and His glorious resurrection are presented without fail. Further, these truths are presented in the context of scriptural prophecy fulfilled as determined by the foreknowledge of God. Third, by virtue of the resurrection, Jesus has been elevated to the right hand of God as Messianic head of the new Israel (Acts 2:33–36). Fourth, God gives the Holy Spirit as the sign of Christ's present power and glory (Acts 2:33). Fifth, the Messianic age will reach its consummation in the return of Christ (Acts 3:21). Sixth, the *kerygma* in early Acts closes with an appeal for repentance, the offer of forgiveness, the gift of the Holy Spirit, and the assurance of salvation in the life of the age to come (Acts 2:38–39). Dodd then summarized, "We may take it that this is what the author of Acts meant by preaching the kingdom of God."[9]

Dodd saw some development upon this early Jerusalem *kerygma* in Paul's preaching. Paul's gospel, according to C. H. Dodd, can be summarized as follows:

- The prophecies are fulfilled, and the new age is inaugurated by the coming of Christ.

- Christ was born of the seed of David.

- Christ died according to the Scriptures to deliver us out of the present evil age.

- Christ was buried.

- Christ rose on the third day according to the Scriptures.

- Chrsit is exalted at the right hand of God, as Son of God and Lord of the living and the dead.

- Christ will come again as Judge and Savior.[10]

Dodd granted that the evangelistic message of Paul may have contained more than the above, but it normally had at least these seven points. That does not mean Paul preached all seven points every time he spoke, at least it is not so recorded in Acts. Yet they can all be found in Paul's writings. The reasons for the contrast—small as it is—between the Jerusalem and Pauline *kerygma* centers in the fact that Paul was preaching primarily to Gentiles. For example, presenting Jesus as Son of God rather than Messiah was far more relevant. Furthermore, Paul had time to work out a theory of the atonement relative to the cross. Consequently, he could say, "Christ died for us," that is, *for* our sins (see Rom. 5:6–11). In the days of the early Jerusalem proclamation, time simply did not allow for that sort of theological reflection. The practical implications for today are clear: Good evangelism is relevant, thoughtful, and culturalized.

Since the time Dodd wrote his classic, bookshelves have been filled with volumes that build upon his essential thesis. Wide and varied have been the approaches in these works. Criticism and development of Dodd's ideas have naturally arisen. Michael Green is a case in point.

MICHAEL GREEN AND THE *KERYGMA*

Chapter 1 presented a brief summary of Green's view of the biblical gospel in his book *Evangelism in the Early Church.* Now we look at his approach in a bit more depth. Green first contended that the background and understanding of the listeners significantly determined which aspect of the truth of Christ was to be shared. Green was not alone in this contention. Professor C. F. D. Moule, in his book *The Birth of the New Testament,* and Eduard Schweizer, in an essay found in *Current Issues in New Testament Interpretation,* take this line of argumentation.

The principle involved here should be stressed. Cultures, times, geographies, social mores, and philosophies differ—often quite dramatically. To communicate the gospel to a diverse world demands an acute sensitivity to that reality. The task of evangelism centers in sharing the unchanging gospel with a changing world. Let it be understood, the Word of God itself does *not* change, but it must be delivered in a relevant manner so that it communicates and makes sense within different scenarios. The wise and effective evangelist realizes this prime principle and adapts accordingly.

Still, Green argued, there remains a basic homogeneity in what the early church declared, and still should. What then makes up this basic homogeneity, as Green saw it? He suggested three basic points as essential to the gospel of salvation for all peoples of all times.

First, the early church preached a Person. Their message was frankly and unapologetically Christocentric. This gospel message was not so much on Jesus' life and public ministry; rather, it centered on His death and glorious resurrection.

Second, Green held that the infant church proclaimed the gift of forgiveness, the gift of the Holy Spirit, and the gracious gift of adoption and reconciliation. That kind of grace made "no people" the "people of God." Concerning the idea of gift in the gospel, the emphasis was placed upon the gift of forgiveness and the gift of the Holy Spirit.

Third, the first-century church looked for a positive response on the part of its hearers. The apostles were anything but shy in asking people to decide then and there, for or against Christ. These early preachers declared all people must do three things in the light of the gospel:

1. They must repent. This stands first and foremost.

2. They must exercise faith. A continuing life of faith is called for, but it must begin by a leap of faith. Moreover, true faith must be viewed as inseparable from repentance.

3. They must be baptized in the name of Jesus. This act of obedience serves as the seal on God's offer of forgiveness and the essence of one's overt response to that offer in repentance and faith.

Green thus presented his understanding of the *kerygma*. He also saw the essential proclamation as a definable, propositional body of theological truth.

JAMES STEWART AND THE *KERYGMA*

Another interesting approach to the theme of proclamation can be found in James Stewart's helpful book *A Faith to Proclaim*. Stewart declared the first axiom of evangelism is that the evangelist must be sure of his message. However, he did not, on his own admission, attempt to traverse again the ground that Dodd and others have covered in attempting to discover the primitive *kerygma*. His purpose was to find the bearing the *kerygma* has on present-day questions. From this pragmatic perspective, Stewart presented what he felt constitutes relevant gospel proclamation.

Stewart derived five principles that should be found in all evangelistic proclamation. It begins with the evangelist proclaiming the *incarnation*. The facts of the *kerygma* are historical facts; in other words, the doctrine of the incarnation means that "God has come right into the midst of the tumult and the shouting of this world."[11] Furthermore, the facts of the incarnation are not only historic, but they are unique. The kingdom of God, itself, has actually broken into the here and now. That is unique and unrepeatable.

The evangelist also proclaims *forgiveness*. This truth is always relevant to people's lives, for "wherever the Church truly proclaims the forgiveness of sins there the healing ministry is veritably at work."[12] The feeling of meaninglessness and loneliness so characteristic of an existentially oriented society must be recognized as essentially a problem of sin. Iniquity stands as the ultimate culprit in the loss of identity and feelings of futility, for sin separates one from

God, the source of all meaning. Therefore, as the church preaches forgiveness, it strikes at the heart of many problems. This brings the contemporary application of the gospel to the fore.

In the third place, Stewart stated that the proclaimer preaches the *cross*. The veil has been rent, the veil that kept people out of God's presence and shut God in. The darkness and mystery of God's "holy otherness" has now been dispelled. Reality can be touched. As Stewart expressed it: "The death of Christ gives me the very heart of the eternal, because it is not words at all, not even sublime prophetic utterance: it is an act, God's act, against which I can batter all my doubts to pieces. We preach Christ crucified, God's truth revealed."[13] Moreover, the cross speaks of atonement, guilt bearing, and expiation. Moreover, the demonic forces of the universe were defeated once and for all. Christ has overcome the world. "We preach Christ crucified" must always be the cry of the evangelist (1 Cor. 1:23).

Fourth, "the hour cometh, and now is" (John 4:23 KJV). The new age, the long-expected hope, has finally taken place: *Christ has been raised.* We declare a resurrected, living Lord. "This was indeed the very core of the apostolic *kerygma*," Stewart argued.[14] It was the theme of every early Christian sermon. The fact of the resurrection was no mere appendix tacked on the end of the apostles' proclamation. The resurrection is a cosmic event. It became far more than just a personal victory for our Lord; all history was shattered by this creative act of God Almighty. The resurrection means the whole world has died and a glorious rebirth has taken place. Nothing can ever be the same again. It must be clear, the apostolic message did not see Good Friday and Easter as two isolated events; they were always presented as one mighty stroke of God. As a result, things on this side of eternity have been immersed into things on the other side. God has effected His great act of justification. Stewart contended, "This is our gospel. For this is what Christianity essentially is—a religion of Resurrection."[15]

Finally, in summary, Stewart declared that the evangelist simply proclaims Christ. The message must never be seen as a cold, conceptualized theology or philosophy. A Person is preached, and He is the Helper, Shepherd, Companion, Friend, Light, and Bread of Life, our *Paraclete.* Christianity is an experience of a vital relationship to a living Christ. The world needs to make this discovery. How different contemporary society would become if it truly understood what the Christ-event means.

Stewart thus cast the *kerygma* in a pragmatic context. He applied all the essentials of the gospel to the living human situation. Surely this is what must be done in actual proclamation. Believers should thoroughly understand the message theologically, but it must be related in terms that address the *kerygma* to real life.

CONZELMANN AND THE *KERYGMA*

From a more critical perspective, Hans Conzelmann has told us: "No primitive Christian preaching has been transmitted to us. But the gist of the preaching is to be found in the epistles, from which types and patterns can still be reconstructed."[16] What, then, according to Conzelmann, are these "types and patterns" of the primitive *kerygma*? He lists the following:

- The promise of salvation, recognizable in Romans, Galatians, Colossians, and Ephesians, depicts the primacy of the saving event of the gospel; this is actualized in ethics.

- The connection with Scripture appears in surveys of the history of the people of God that end with a didactic conclusion: Acts 7:13ff.; Heb. 11; cf. 1 Clement.

- The newness of Christian existence in contrast to the past is depicted in the pattern "once . . . now"; once Gentiles in blasphemy and darkness, now enlightened (Rom. 7:5; Gal. 4:3ff.). Paganism is not described neutrally, but it is evaluated exclusively from the perspective of what is new.[17]

Many other writers have addressed the issue. Professor Harry Poe, in *The Gospel and Its Meaning*, points out that T. F. Glasson posed a *kerygma* containing five points: (1) the fulfillment of Scriptures, (2) the death of Christ, (3) the resurrection of Christ, (4) the forgiveness of sins, and (5) the apostolic witness.[18]

Professor Poe goes on to show that Bertil Gardner found seven elements in the *kerygma:* (1) the ministry of Jesus, (2) Jesus' suffering, death, and resurrection, (3) prophecies being fulfilled, (4) Jesus as the Lord and Messiah exalted to the right hand of God, (5) the bestowing of the advent and the judgment of the Lord, (6) the exaltation to conversion, and (7) the bearing of witness.[19]

This excursion through various thinkers' views of the *kergyma* definitely does not mean that there is no consensus as to the essence of the good news or that there cannot be found a simple biblical presentation of the message that we all can grasp. The heart and essence of the basic gospel that holds for all can be found in Peter's sermon on the Day of Pentecost:

- Old Testament prophecies fulfilled in Jesus (Acts 2:16–21)

- The incarnation of God's Son (Acts 2:22)

- The miraculous life of the Lord (Acts 2:22)

- The death of Christ as a substitute for our sins (Acts 2:23)

- The bodily resurrection of Christ (Acts 2:24)

- The call to repentance and faith (Acts 2:38)

- The promise of forgiveness of sins and new life in the Spirit (Acts 2:38)

It should be stressed that the New Testament church proclaimed the visible return of Jesus Christ (Acts 1:11; 3:20–21). Further, we will examine these salient points in some detail shortly relative to Graham's ministry of proclamation. We will then consider how Graham preaches the full gospel of Christ.

LESSONS FROM THE STUDY

Now what is to be learned from these several approaches to the *kerygma*? Two lessons seem vital. To begin with, whether we take a more rigid view of men like Dodd or a more flexible approach similar to Green, Webster, or Stewart, or even a more critical view like Conzelmann, the proclamation of Christ lies at the heart of the gospel. If evangelism aspires to be authenticated as biblical, then the redemptive realities of Christ must be fully declared in the message. The *kerygma* has a definite, definable biblical content. Although no one wishes to eliminate the demand for an existential response to the gospel, history and objective truth must be present in the proclamation.

Moreover, a balance must be maintained between content and personal appeal. The balance between the cognitive content of truth and the experiential element of coming to know God is beautifully displayed in Paul's prayer for the Ephesian church (Eph. 3:17–18). In his intercession Paul prayed that "being rooted and grounded in love" they might be able "to comprehend" (*katalabesthai*, that is, "with the mind") the breadth, length, height, and depth of God's love, and "to know" (*gnonai*, that is, "know by experience") His love, which "passes all knowledge." This is how one is "filled with all the fullness of God" and can thus serve and preach Christ in love. A balance between objective truth and subjective experience of God's love predicated on the truth must be kept at the heart of the *kerygma*, for that is what the term means. This sort of proclamation has impact and effect. People do respond to the truth spoken in love (Acts 2:41). Evangelists called by God need to know that.

The question can be raised, Why do people respond to the message of the gospel? The answer is simple but so very shattering: People are in sin estranged from God and face eternal judgment. The Bible makes much of this deeply disturbing reality. Paul elucidates the truth and seriousness of human sin in the Roman Epistle. Here are a few verses from that letter that drives the point home:

> For the wrath of God is revealed from heaven against all ungodliness and unrighteousness of men, who suppress the truth in unrighteousness. (Rom. 1:18)

> As it is written, "There is none righteous, not even one; there is none who understands, there is none who seeks for God." (Rom. 3:10–11)

> For all have sinned and fall short of the glory of God. (Rom. 3:23)

The consequence of our sin? Judgment. The writer of the Book of Hebrews declared, "It is appointed for men to die once and after this comes judgment" (9:27). Paul emphasized this eventuality also, saying, "The wages of sin is death" (Rom. 6:23). Sin is serious—eternally, deadly serious. And all stand guilty before a holy God. Is there any hope? Emphatically, yes; Jesus Christ came and now our sins can be forgiven. Restoration of fellowship with God can be effected. Eternal life can be had. That is the gospel, and that is why it is such good news. The *kerygma* is always presented in the context of need—the need of forgiveness of sins—and the promise of God's great love and grace in Christ.

CONCLUSION

Therefore, gospel proclamation, if true to the biblical idea, must be filled with dynamic *kerygmatic* content. That message alone moves people and meets their deepest need. That is the crux of the whole matter. Moreover, the call of God to declare the gospel of Christ and the nature of that good news immediately imply that it should be spoken with authority, in absolute confidence and in love. The message is God's message, and His messengers are to present it with the confident authority God conveys in the Word to His called servants. As Paul admonished Titus, "These things speak and exhort and reprove with all authority. Let no one disregard you" (Titus 2:15). The world always stands in need of such an authoritative declaration of God's love in Christ. We shall see if Billy Graham's preaching meets these tests.

PART II:
THE CALL AND THE GOSPEL IN THE LIFE AND MINISTRY OF BILLY GRAHAM

I'm going to preach His birth, death, and resurrection.
I'll preach it until Jesus comes.
—BILLY GRAHAM

INTRODUCTION

The New Testament, along with subsequent church history, attests to the fact that from the first century to the present hour, the call to share the gospel stands foundational to any successful endeavor in the ministry of evangelism. This is clearly evidenced in the life of the apostle Paul as outlined in the early pages of this historical work. Paul not only experienced a dramatic conversion in his Damascus Road encounter with Jesus Christ, but he also received a divine call to declare Christ to his contemporaries. Our Lord, instructing Ananias to seek out Paul, said, "Go, for he is a chosen instrument of Mine, to bear My name before the Gentiles and kings and the sons of Israel; for I will show him how much he must suffer for My name's sake" (Acts 9:15–16). Paul got the message and unreservedly committed himself to that divine call. On countless occasions he described his call using such words as "When He who had set me apart, even from my mother's womb, and called me through His grace, was pleased to reveal His Son in me, that I might preach Him among the Gentiles" (Gal. 1:15–16). Paul felt God's mandate so deeply that he exclaimed, "For if I preach the gospel, I have nothing to boast of, for I am under compulsion; for woe is me if I do not preach the gospel" (1 Cor. 9:16). The apostle was convinced of his call and convinced of the power of the gospel he was commissioned to declare.

Such constitutes the calling, conviction, and commitment of any true evangelist. Without those profound realities as a foundation, the evangelist normally accomplishes little in bringing people to faith in Jesus Christ. Therefore, the question arises, Has Billy Graham received such a call? Does he find himself in that noble train of God-called evangelists exemplified not only by Paul in the apostolic era, but also down through the two millennia of the Holy Spirit's work in setting certain persons aside for the task? Furthermore, does Graham have a firm grasp of the gospel message and preach it clearly with complete confidence? As implied earlier, this section of the chapter may well be the most extensive look at Billy Graham in this entire book. But that stands to reason due to the fact that the evangelist's understanding of the call and the nature of the gospel he preaches form the very core of his ministry. We must look at Graham in some detail to see if he actually does stand in the line of biblical, historical evangelism and thus does make his contribution. We begin with the call.

BILLY GRAHAM'S CALL

When evangelist Graham was converted in his teenage years, he immediately felt something of a burden to help others to faith in Jesus Christ. On completion of high school and one semester at Bob Jones College, he attended Florida Bible Institute in Temple Terrace, Florida. There he found spiritual nurture in the happy Christian environment of the institute. He faced many challenges in Florida, one of which grew deeper as the days went by. The question constantly confronted Billy, "Has God called me to preach His Word?" Many things fed into that spiritual query. The challenge of chapel services, classroom studies, and the counsel of spiritually minded leaders such as Professor John Minder seemed to force the confrontation with the call. Above all, the Holy Spirit's working in his life constantly raised the issue. Another factor, one that may seem somewhat irrelevant, was the breakup of his relationship with a young lady with whom he had fallen in love. Even this event aided in forcing the question as to whether God had His hand upon him for vocational ministry in preaching.

Graham soon rose above the heartache of his brief broken romance, and he resolved that Christ alone would come first in his life. He said, "The Lord Jesus shall have all of me, I am determined to follow him at any cost."[20] Young Graham began to realize that the deepening of his Christian experience was the most significant issue in his life and not his personal relationships, as meaningful as they can be. Christ must come first. Still, he did not have a convincing conviction that God's call to preach was upon him, even though he was already referred to by some as a "preacher boy."

Graham fully realized God's calling would cost him tremendously. He heeded well the Lord's admonition to "count the cost" (Luke 14:28 NKJV). He recognized that if God were setting him apart and he yielded to that call, he would have to forsake many other ambitions and goals. He had always wanted to be a professional baseball player, but becoming a preacher would be the end of that. He had to settle the issue. At the age of nineteen, the moving moment arrived. It is best recorded in his own words:

For some weeks, triggered by a profoundly searching sermon in chapel, I paced those deserted, echoing streets of Temple Terrace. In the moonlight, a soft southern breeze stirred the wispy Spanish moss that draped the trees on the golf course. I never felt so alone in my life—or so close to God. I walked through the late-night hours, struggling with the Holy Spirit over the call of God to be a minister. That was the last thing I wanted to be, and I had used all kinds of rationalizations to convince God to let me do something else.

I had the same sense of uncertainty in Charlotte nearly four years before, standing in the sawdust shavings of Mordecai Ham's tabernacle. There I did what I felt I should do: commit my eternal destiny to the saving grace of God in Jesus Christ. But was I now being asked to commit the rest of my life on earth to serving Him in a way that I did not particularly relish?

In the eighteen months since arriving at Florida Bible Institute, I exercised some gifts and began to develop some skills that I did not know I had. I knew that I loved to tell people the good news of God's salvation in Jesus Christ. On Sundays I often preached on the streets of Tampa, sometimes as many as five or six times a day. . . .

Many people responded to my preaching by confessing faith in Christ and being converted. My teachers and classmates seemed to affirm that this ministry was good and right for me. But did I want to preach for a lifetime? I asked myself that question for the umpteenth time on one of my nighttime walks around the golf course. The inner, irresistible urge would not subside. Finally, one night, I got down on my knees at the edge of one of the greens. Then I prostrated myself on the dewy turf. "O God," I sobbed, "if you want me to serve you, I will."

The moonlight, the moss, the breeze, the green, the golf course—all the surroundings stayed the same. No sign in the heavens. No voice from above. But in my spirit I knew I had been called to the ministry. And I knew my answer was yes.

From that night in 1938 on, my purpose and objectives in life were set. I knew that I would be a preacher of the gospel.[21]

God's call had come through a long struggle, and Billy Graham, future evangelist to the world, yielded to the will of God. The battle was over.

Graham did not feel a distinct call to be a full-time evangelist at this early stage of God's call to gospel ministry. All he felt convinced of was that God had called him to preach and that he must launch out in ministry. The "preacher boy" had become a Spirit-called preacher.

THE MOVE TO EVANGELISM

Graham's pilgrimage to full-time evangelism is a rather long story, one that his biographers have outlined in detail many times. It merely needs to be noted here that Graham's journey was launched as he began to receive invitations to preach in various churches and settings in Florida during his remaining days at the Bible Institute. One day, he was asked to preach a traditional "Bible-belt revival meeting" in a local Baptist church. As is common knowledge, Graham was reared in a Presbyterian home, but this evangelistic opportunity came from a Baptist congregation. In the context of that invitation, the pastor said that the congregation would not accept him if he were not a Baptist. In the 1940s, denominational lines were drawn quite strictly in the Deep South. So Graham submitted himself to baptism by immersion at the hands of a Southern Baptist pastor. By his own confession, Billy said it was a "glorious experience."[22] He has remained a Southern Baptist since, having for several decades held membership in the First Baptist Church of Dallas, Texas. It may appear that his Presbyterian convictions were not very strong, or perhaps even his Baptist understandings, but he was vitally concerned about God's call upon him as a preacher. And he gave himself to his calling so profoundly that he was willing to change denominations so that the doors of ministry might be opened. Regardless of whether his actions are commendable, they do show something of Billy Graham's absolute commitment to God's call upon his life.

MINISTRY GROWTH

Billy Graham's preaching ministry grew and developed during his remaining time in Temple Terrace. As one author put it, "The Billy Graham who graduated from the Florida Bible Institute in 1940 was quite different from the one who had entered Bob Jones College just a few years before. His commitment to Christ had not only been thought through but internalized."[23] Upon graduation, he enrolled for the Bachelor of Arts degree at Wheaton College in Wheaton, Illinois. On that Christian campus, his ministry was enhanced not only by study in the academic setting of Wheaton, but also through the dynamic Christian atmosphere that pervaded the college. Opportunities constantly came across his path for ministry. After graduation and marriage to Ruth Bell, daughter to missionaries in China, he became pastor of the Western Springs Baptist Church, a short distance from Wheaton.

In the setting as pastor, Billy carried an effective gospel ministry and saw a healthy number of people come to faith in Jesus Christ through his preaching. The Western Springs Church did much to enhance Billy Graham's preaching gifts and his call to share the gospel. At the same time he served as pastor, invitations kept coming for evangelistic rallies and to conduct Youth for Christ meetings in various parts of the country. The stage was being set for the sharpening of the call to the ministry of full-time evangelism.

CRYSTALLIZING THE CALL TO EVANGELISM

Ruth Bell Graham, as mentioned previously, had always intended to go to Tibet as a missionary, being especially burdened for that country. Yet she recognized that God's hand rested mightily upon her husband in evangelism and encouraged him in that work. Finally, Billy left the pastorate and went into full-time ministry with Youth for Christ under the direction of its founder, Torrey Johnson. While serving in Youth for Christ, Dr. W. B. Riley—pastor of the First Baptist Church of Minneapolis, Minnesota, and president of a Bible institute sponsored by the church—became quite ill. It was evident that his ministry was coming to a close. He insisted, virtually on his deathbed, that Billy become president of the Bible institute. For a short time, Graham took the job. But Ruth, absolutely convinced that God had called her husband to evangelism, constantly urged him to leave that post and devote himself to vocational evangelism. It was in those dynamic days that the great crusade in Los Angeles of October 1949 burst on the scene. That once and for all settled the fact that God had called Billy to the ministry of full-time evangelism.

Through these many avenues of experience, under the sovereignty of God and the leadership of the Holy Spirit, a new figure had arisen on the twentieth-century scene. It all came together to make an impact for Christ in the spreading of the gospel that has rarely been seen in the history of the church. Billy Graham, evangelist, received God's call; he responded and the world has had its eyes focused on him ever since. The foundation was laid: The call had come, and God's man had responded.

The question can be raised, Why did God call Billy Graham in particular for such a ministry? Billy Graham himself has often said that when he gets to heaven he is going to ask God, "Why me?" George Beasley-Murray, in his commentary on the Gospel of John, answered the question: "The privilege bestowed on the disciples was not on account of their worth but through saving electing grace."[24] Well said! This principle stands true for all believers; we are tokens of God's sheer grace, nothing else.

Few questions have ever been raised concerning Billy Graham's commitment to the work of the evangelist. Too many experiences, along with Graham's obvious gifts and usefulness in that spiritual arena, have convinced most people—even the critics—of the validity of God's call and the commitment that Billy made at the Temple Terrace golf course. The implication of this for Graham is very significant.

THE IMPLICATION OF THE CALL: COMMITMENT

Billy Graham is committed to this task, for he realizes that his commitment rests totally in the fact that God Himself has unquestionably called him. Therefore, there can be no swerving from that commission. One thing that all who know him affirm is his absolute commitment to God's call. And the implications thereof govern his entire life. He certainly has had opportunities to forsake that call, but his commitment has always remained true. As a case in point, T. W. Wilson, Billy's personal assistant for many years, who just recently passed away, tells the account of President Lyndon B. Johnson's asking Dr. Graham to become the head of a new social program for poverty-stricken Americans he was enacting during his administration in the White House. Billy responded that he would seriously consider it because he wanted people to know he felt a deep concern for the hungry, homeless, and needy. He pondered the offer for some time.

One day, in a hotel room with T. W., Billy told his assistant to get President Johnson on the telephone and tell him he would accept the position. As T. W. picked up the phone, Grady Wilson, associate evangelist with the BGEA, walked in. Billy said, "Grady, I have just told T. W. to phone the president. I am going to head the new poverty program. What do you think about that?" In his blunt but honest way, Grady replied, "Well this is the first time I have ever seen God call someone to the gospel ministry and then 'un-call' him." Then Grady walked out of the room.

Billy immediately told T. W., "Put down the phone, don't call President Johnson." He remained true to this call. That does not mean the evangelist lost his love and concern for needy people. By no means; we shall see in a subsequent chapter all the benevolent things he does for people in want. He has a great heart to meet all needs; but, above all, he knows God has called him to be an evangelist, and that ministry strikes at the heart of people's deepest need—salvation.

Even more dramatic was the fact that one day President Johnson said to Billy Graham, "Billy, I want you to run for president [of the United States]. I'll put my whole organization behind you." Billy replied, "I appreciate it, but

God has called me to preach, and I'll never do anything else as long as I live." Billy later recalled, "God kept me convinced that His calling was superior to any earthly appointment."[25]

Thus it virtually goes without saying that Graham realizes his call centers in being a preacher of the gospel. But this raises the fundamental issue, that which constitutes the heart of this specific chapter: Does Billy Graham truly preach the gospel? That is to say, does he understand and preach the full gospel as presented in the New Testament and proclaimed through the two thousand years of evangelical church history? We are prone to say he does. Yet, if we are to grant Billy Graham a proper place and role in biblical historical evangelism, that issue must be thoroughly analyzed. The question must be raised: Is Graham genuinely true to the apostolic, historical gospel, and has he been faithful to preach that good news through the many years of his ministry? If so, this will put the basic stamp of historical authenticity upon his work. Thus we must investigate the issue in some depth.

BILLY GRAHAM'S UNDERSTANDING OF THE GOSPEL

We have seen in Part I of this chapter on the work of the evangelist that the key word concerning the gospel is the Greek word *kerygma*. It therefore seems necessary to consider the salient points of Graham's preaching to discover whether they are in line with the essence of the *kerygma*, the proclamation. But before a detailed exegesis of these issues is undertaken, it will be wise to see upon what foundation Graham builds his understanding of the *kerygmatic* content of the gospel.

GRAHAM'S FOUNDATION OF THOUGHT

Graham establishes his grasp of the gospel on the basis of a biblically oriented theology. His oft-repeated phrase "the Bible says," which has almost become a trademark of his preaching, indicates his commitment to the Scriptures as the final authority of truth. In a subsequent chapter we shall see in detail his basic theology of the Bible. Suffice it to say here that Graham fully believes that what he preaches is rooted and grounded in the holy Bible, and he has a very foundational reason for so doing.

Graham has made statements on numerous occasions that confirm his view. He has written: "I . . . take my position on the basis of what the Bible teaches because the Bible is the revelation from God to man. The Bible tells us not only of God's love for us and how we can be saved, but also tells us how we should react to the problems and difficulties of life. . . . The Bible is the infallible rule of faith and practice."[26] Billy Graham clearly believes that God reveals Himself. He contends that in our finitude we can only come to know the infinite God by virtue of the fact that He breaks into one's human experience and reveals Himself. Graham asks, "Does He speak to us? Does He tell us where He is—how we can find Him—how we can be right with Him? . . . God has answered these questions in His Word."[27]

Billy Graham does grant that God reveals Himself in various ways. For example, He reveals Himself through nature. As the psalmist said, "The heavens are telling of the glory of God; and their expanse is declaring the work of His hands" (Ps. 19:1). God speaks in nature through His creative hand. Billy said, "In its own language, nature speaks of God's existence. . . . God speaks in the regularity of the seasons; in the movements of the sun, moon and stars."[28]

Not only does God speak through nature, He also speaks through conscience. Graham sees the moral principle deeply engrained in the very fabric of personhood. He would agree with philosopher Immanuel Kant's proposition of the "categorical imperative." This simply means that everyone has a conscience as to the nature of right and wrong because of the creating hand of God. God reveals Himself and speaks through one's conscience.

Supremely, however, God has revealed Himself in the person of His Son, the Lord Jesus Christ. As the writer of Hebrews has declared:

God, after He spoke long ago to the fathers in the prophets in many portions and in many ways, in these last days has spoken to us in His Son, whom He appointed heir of all things, through whom also He made the world. And He is the radiance of His glory and the exact representation of His nature, and upholds all things by the word of His power. When He had made purification of sins, He sat down at the right hand of the Majesty on high. (1:1–3)

Jesus Christ of Nazareth stands as God's final word concerning Himself. Therefore, the true Christian evangelist, beginning with the apostles and down through the centuries, is committed to the principle, as Paul expressed it, "We preach Christ crucified" (1 Cor. 1:23). Jesus is the supreme revelation of God. But this raises the question, How do we know anything of redemptive substance about Jesus of Nazareth? The answer, of course, is immediately forthcoming.

Graham stresses that we learn about the incarnation, life, death, resurrection, and saving grace of God in Jesus Christ through the propositional revelation of God in the Scriptures, the Old and New Testaments. He has stated, "The Scriptures say about Christ, 'In Him all fullness of Deity dwells in bodily form' (Cor. 2:9). This revelation is the most complete God ever gave to the world. Do you want to know what God is like? All you have to do is look at Jesus Christ."[29] Then very succinctly Graham brings it together, saying, "The Bible is the textbook of revelation,"[30] emphasizing the scriptural revelation of Jesus Christ. The Bible is the only basis for understanding the good news of God's Christ. Although God speaks through nature and conscience, He has fully revealed Himself in His incarnate Son and we learn of Him in the Scriptures. Consequently, we are bound to the Bible in the hands of the Holy Spirit to provide a full redemptive revelation of God. That is why the biblical story of Jesus, the gospel, "is the power of God for salvation" (Rom. 1:16). Therefore, any evangelist who aspires to be faithful to his calling to preach the gospel must see that his message is predicated on the Word of God. It is that simple, yet that significant and foundational. God has spoken in the pages of Holy Writ.

A FURTHER FACT

This does not mean that one should be abstract or intellectual alone in the pursuit of the revelation of God in the Scriptures. The Holy Spirit enlightens the mind and heart. Billy is very conscious of this fact. The previous chapter was devoted to the ministry of the Holy Spirit in the evangelistic enterprise. Hopefully it has become convincing that Graham fully believes that the Holy Spirit takes God's revelation in nature and conscience and supremely in the Spirit-inspired Bible and in that dynamic experience speaks to the human heart, pulls off the scales from the eyes, and reveals the truth of God as it centers in the good news of Jesus Christ. Billy knows this well; he has said,

"Whenever I preach the gospel anywhere in the world with authority, the Holy Spirit will drive it home to the human heart."[31] In other words, the objective propositional gospel of Christ, fused into the human experience by the Holy Spirit, moves people to true faith in Jesus Christ.

In light of this fact, Billy Graham is most sensitive to the content of the message as well as the moving of the Spirit in evangelization. He has said, "Evangelism is . . . 'spreading the gospel of Christ.' It is more than a method, however, it is also a message."[32] This again leads to the basic question already raised: Does Graham truly preach the saving gospel? Is he correct in his message as well as his method? He obviously predicates his gospel preaching on what he understands the Bible to say, but we must discover whether he is essentially true to the biblical revelation of God's redeeming message as attested by evangelical understandings for many centuries.

THE *KERYGMA* IN BILLY GRAHAM'S MINISTRY

We have seen that the apostle Paul was so committed in his call to preach the gospel that he said to the Galatians, "But even though we, or an angel from heaven, should preach to you a gospel contrary to that which we have preached to you, let him be accursed" (Gal. 1:8). The pure, unadulterated gospel must be tenaciously held at any cost. What, therefore, can we glean from a biblical perspective to test Graham's faithfulness to the Word of Life? We have examined several theologians' views in Part I of this chapter; perhaps a fuller digest of the significant previously outlined scriptural passage (Acts 1–3) will serve our purpose concerning the criteria by which we can judge Graham's proclamation.

THE PROCLAMATION

It would seem to this author that a proper view of the *kerygma* can be best summarized in the salient points of Peter's sermon preached on the Day of Pentecost along with the surrounding events as recorded in Acts 1–3. Ten basic principles emerge in that overall context. This becomes something of the litmus test for faithfulness on the part of any evangelist as he faithfully attempts to fulfill his calling in evangelism. The essential principles are as follows:

- Jesus Christ of Nazareth is the fulfillment of Old Testament prophecies concerning the coming of God's salvation through His Messiah (Acts 2:16–21).

- Jesus Christ was incarnated as the Son of God (Acts 2:22).

- Jesus lived a sinless, revealing, perfect life, doing many glorious miracles (Acts 2:22).

- Jesus Christ was crucified on the cross for the sake of the sin of the world (Acts 2:23).

- Jesus Christ was raised bodily from the dead, triumphing over sin, death, and hell (Acts 2:24).

- Jesus Christ is coming again to usher in the fullness of the kingdom (Acts 1:11; 3:20–21).

- People are called to repent and believe and to commit their lives to following Christ, as symbolized in baptism (Acts 2:38).

- Christians receive the promise of the forgiveness of sins (Acts 2:38).

- Christians receive the gift of the Holy Spirit (Acts 2:38).

- Christians experience a whole new life (Acts 2:42).

These essential points make up the essence of the gospel.

Theological nuances and many ramifications that space forbids presenting here emerge out of Peter's sermon. Volumes of theology have been written on each of these points. But it must be stressed here that these facts do constitute the heart of the gospel, and it therefore must be seen whether Billy Graham faithfully preaches these truths in his attempt to bring people into a right relationship to God through Jesus Christ. We shall look at them one by one.

First, it seems only fair to share a word from the evangelist. In a personal interview, Billy was asked about the Greek word *kerygma*. He replied, "I started using that term after I read the book by C. H. Dodd, *The Apostolic Preaching and Its Development*. I began to think of that in a depth I hadn't before. . . . It has been in recent years I feel the *whole* content (of the *kerygma*) must be in *every* sermon."[33] In an interview with David Frost, Graham said, "I have stuck to what is called the *kerygma*, which is the death, the burial, and resurrection of Jesus Christ and the fact that people need to repent and come to Christ by faith. And that has been the central core of my message everywhere. . . . I am determined that the cross is my message."[34] Graham's executive assistant, David Bruce, who knows the evangelist well, confirmed that statement when he said, "Incarnated in all his (Billy Graham's) preaching are the points of the *kerygma* that lead to salvation."[35] That does get to the core of the issue. We will now see how well Graham assimilates all the elements of the proclamation in his gospel preaching.

JESUS CHRIST: THE FULFILLMENT OF THE MESSIANIC PROMISE

C. H. Dodd makes the point that the Messianic reign was fully prophesied in Old Testament Scriptures and is a part of the apostolic gospel. There is a grand day coming. That constitutes an important element of the message. Graham agrees, saying, "His [Jesus'] death had been prophesied."[36] This particular aspect of the gospel especially appeals to Jewish culture or those with a biblical background. Yet there is even a utopian idea in Greek philosophy and written in the mind-sets of many cultures, especially in the West because of the influence of Greek thought. The idea of the "Golden Age" seems to be woven into the fabric of most people. Although Paul did not stress this when he spoke to the philosophers at Mars Hill in Athens, it still becomes a relevant point as the evangelist adapts it to the immediate culture in which he or she speaks.

As stated, Billy Graham fully accepts this prophetic element of the *kerygma*. He elaborates on the point, saying, "Fulfilled prophesies witness to the Bible's accuracy hundreds of years before Christ." It was predicted that He would:

- be born of a virgin (Isa. 7:14; cf. Luke 2:26–35)
- be born in Bethlehem (Mic. 5:2; cf. Luke 2:4–7)
- live a sinless life (Isa.53:9; cf. 2 Cor. 5:21)
- be put to death (Isa. 53:5, 7; cf. Matt. 27:35)
- cry from the cross, "My God, my God, why have you forsaken me?" (Ps. 22:1; cf. Matt. 27:46).[37]

In God's economy, this means the ushering in of the kingdom. It startled the Jewish people, because the Messianic kingdom came via the cross.

Graham clearly sees the coming of the Messiah, Jesus Christ, as the establishment of the kingdom of God on earth. He has made many pronouncements in this regard. Following are the more succinct and pointed statements of the evangelist: "The Messiah, God's anointed One, His only begotten Son . . . He would reign as Lord, the promised Messiah, the Lion of David in splendor and in power."[38] Expanding the theme, Graham went on to say, "The kingdom of God is not only a future hope, but a present reality. Wherever men and women turn to God in repentance and faith and then seek to do His will on earth as it is done in heaven, there the kingdom of God is seen . . . the kingdom of God 'already' present in the lives of the believers who glorify Him. . . . King Jesus has conquered Satan."[39] In a word, "The real kingdom is the kingdom of believers."[40] In the same spirit, George Beasley-Murray states in his commentary on John's Gospel that "the divine *basileia* [kingdom] is God sovereignly acting in judgment and salvation through the Son: accordingly the kingdom that comes through the Son is the kingdom of God in Christ."[41] All these utterances concerning the coming of the kingdom to establish God's reign lead to the gospel truth of the incarnation.

INCARNATION

As seen, the basic issue of the entire Christian faith points ultimately to this: Was Jesus truly God robed in human flesh? Is the incarnation a genuine historical reality? Or should Jesus be seen as no more than just a very gifted spiritual leader, as some would say? We shall devote an entire chapter later to Graham's understanding of Christology relative to our Lord's personhood and His centrality in all gospel presentation and ministry. Still, let it be stressed here that Graham has made himself clear on the subject of the incarnation in such statements as, "At the heart of that good news is Jesus Christ. He is God in human flesh."[42] As an evangelist he makes no equivocation on who Jesus is. Graham states, "Jesus Christ made the astonishing claim that He was God. Either Christ was God, or He was a blasphemous liar, or a maniac."[43]

As the question is raised about the reality of the incarnation, one of Billy Graham's fullest statements on the issue follows. He wrote as a true evangelist and follows it up with a personal appeal:

You cannot read the New Testament without realizing that Jesus claimed—frequently and clearly—that He was the divine Son of God, sent from Heaven to save us from our sins. It is also clear from the gospel accounts that His disciples did not believe His claims at first, but only gradually came to understand and accept them (particularly after the resurrection, which proved beyond doubt that He was who He claimed to be). . . .

Anyone could claim to be divine, of course, but did Jesus do anything to back up His claim? Yes! His miracles, which were witnessed by thousands, were an evidence of His unique nature. His resurrection verified His claim. But why is this important? It is important because only a divine Savior could truly save us from our sins. If Christ were just a great religious teacher, He would have no power to bring us forgiveness. But because He was God's only Son, He could die as a perfect and final sacrifice for our sins. Have you accepted the gift of forgiveness He offers you?[44]

From this statement, we see that Graham does accept the traditional, historical evangelical view on the incarnation. It can be concluded that Graham believes in, and preaches as part of his message, that Jesus, as Paul put it to the Philippians, "existed in the form of God, did not regard equality with God a thing to be grasped, but emptied Himself, taking the form of a bond-servant, and being made in the likeness of men" (Phil. 2:6–7).

CHRIST LIVED A REVEALING, VICTORIOUS, AND PERFECT LIFE

If we take seriously the fact that the incarnate Christ is the final revelation of God, then the life that He lived must be incredibly different. Three things need to be understood in this context. First, Jesus Christ lived a perfect life. He never sinned, "nor was any deceit found in His mouth" (1 Pet. 2:22). Second, Jesus Christ came and revealed God. In spirit, in attitude, and in word, Jesus Christ showed us what God is like. He was conscious of His role and said to Thomas, "He who has seen Me has seen the Father" (John 14:9). He became the revelation of God in our midst. Third, He lived victoriously. That is to say, He succeeded where Adam failed. Thus Paul calls Him "the last Adam." The apostle wrote, "So also it is written, 'The first man, Adam, became a living soul.' The last Adam became a life-giving spirit" (1 Cor. 15:45). Where the first Adam failed in the Garden of Eden, and since Adam was the federal head of the human race everyone fell with him; now Christ as the "last Adam" has succeeded victoriously, and since He is the federal head of the new Adamic race, all have life in Him. Paul labored this point, and it is tremendously significant to the life of the Lord Jesus Christ. What does Billy Graham say about the life of Jesus? He has said, "These essential truths concerning the humanity of Jesus I positively affirm."[45]

Next we come to Graham's central thrust in the *kerygma*: Calvary.

CHRIST DIED ON THE CROSS

Very few professing Christians would be unwilling to say with the apostle Paul, "May it never be that I should boast, except in the cross of our Lord Jesus Christ, through which the world has been crucified to me, and I to the world" (Gal. 6:14). Here we come to the crux of the matter: the cross of Jesus Christ.

One night, in an early crusade, Billy Graham gave his typical invitation, and few people responded. Riding back to his hotel with a layman, the evangelist asked, "What happened? Why did so few come forward?" The perceptive layman answered, "Billy, you did not preach the cross." These words struck Graham's heart deeply. Back in the hotel room he fell on his knees and prayed, "I'll never preach without stressing the cross."[46]

Since that moment the cross of Christ has remained central for Graham—and for his team. Associate T. W. Wilson stated, "He emphasizes this to all the Team."[47] Thus the question becomes, What does Billy Graham have to say concerning the crucifixion? Historic Christianity views Jesus and His cross as an atoning work, that is to say, Jesus died for the sins of the world. He became the great "Substitute," bearing human sin in Himself that forgiveness before a holy God may be possible. As Paul put it, "Christ died for us" (Rom. 5:8), and "Christ died for our sins according to the Scriptures" (1 Cor. 15:3). Peter said, ". . . obtaining salvation through our Lord Jesus Christ, who died for us" (1 Thess. 5:9–10). These and a multitude of other verses in the New Testament make unavoidable the insistence that Jesus suffered vicariously, in our place, and suffered the punishment of all our sins. Evangelicals have held this truth tenaciously for two thousand years.

Has Graham interpreted this doctrine properly in the light of evangelical thought? The evangelist has much to say in this area. Following are just a few of his many statements:

In the suffering of Jesus we have the participation of God in the act of atonement. Sin pierced God's heart. God felt every searing and spear. "He [God the Father] made Him who knew no sin [Jesus] to be sin on our behalf" (2 Cor. 5:21).[48]

The cross is the focal point in the life and ministry of Jesus Christ.[49]

The cross . . . has become the only remedy for the ills of each person, and of the world.[50]

Satan's power was broken at the cross.[51]

One of Graham's longest—and most eloquent—passages on the cross reads:

Man's only salvation from sin stands on a lonely, barren skull-shaped hill; a thief hangs on one cross, a murderer on another, and between them a man with a crown of thorns. . . . Who is this tortured figure, who is this man that other men seek to humiliate and kill? He is the Son of God. What brought Him to this place of horrors? You did and I did, for it was for your sin and my sin that Jesus was nailed to the cross. But sin overreached itself on the cross. The blow that crucified Christ became the blow that opened the gates for man to become free. Sin's masterpiece of shame and hate became God's masterpiece of mercy and forgiveness. Through the death of the Lamb of God upon the cross, sin itself was crucified for those who believe in Christ. His death is the foundation of our hope, the promise of our triumph! Christ bore in His own body on the tree the sins that shackle us. He died for us and rose again. He proved the truth of all God's promises to man; and if you will accept the Christ by faith today, you, too, can break the bonds of sin, and stand secure and free in the knowledge that through the love of Christ your soul is cleansed of sin and saved from damnation.[52]

To say the least, Graham does have a firm grasp of the atonement as understood by historic evangelicalism. He obviously adheres to the traditional substitutionary view of the atonement. It would be all but impossible to count the times he has quoted Paul's statement: "Christ died for our sins" (1 Cor. 15:3). But what about the resurrection of Jesus? Is He really alive, and does Graham preach the resurrection?

THE RESURRECTION

Considerable controversy surrounds the resurrection, particularly since the advent of the higher critical hermeneutic as personified in theologians like Rudolph Bultmann and others. Some of these thinkers have trouble with the concept of a bodily resurrection of Jesus, as traditional evangelicalism has held. This is a most important point, as we have tried to emphasize in the earlier sections of this work. What does Graham say about the resurrection of Jesus—its nature and its significance?

Billy Graham holds and preaches most emphatically the bodily resurrection of Jesus Christ. He calls the great Easter event the foundation of faith. In his popular work *How to Be Born Again*, he wrote, "The basis for our belief in Jesus Christ is in His resurrection."[53] Graham cites Karl Barth as saying that without the "physical resurrection of Jesus Christ there is no salvation." Graham goes on to declare, "If Christ were entombed someplace in a grave near Jerusalem where millions who visit Israel each year could walk by a grave and worship Him, then Christianity would be a fable. The apostle Paul said, 'If Christ has not been raised, then our preaching is in vain and your faith is in vain. . . . If Christ has not been raised, your faith is futile and you are still in your sins' (1 Cor. 15:14, 17). . . . Without the resurrection, the cross is meaningless."[54]

Graham contrasts the Christian faith in the resurrection with world religions—e.g., Judaism, Islam, etc.—and states, "Only Christianity claims resurrection for its founder."[55] He then goes on to show the evidence for the resurrection of Jesus, listing such realities as the empty tomb and the testimony of reliable witnesses. He quotes philosopher and theologian C. S. Lewis: "The first fact in the history of Christendom is a number of people who say they have seen the Resurrection. If they had died without making anyone else believe this 'gospel' no gospels would ever have been written."[56] Obviously, Billy Graham believes that without the resurrection of Jesus Christ, the Christian religion is a sham. He has said, "All of Christianity as a system of truth collapses if the resurrection is rejected. . . . Resurrection is central to the gospel. . . . A personal salvation experience is directly related to belief in the resurrection. . . . It couldn't be clearer in the Scriptures."[57]

Moreover, Graham is very emphatic about the bodily resurrection of Jesus. He argues for the bodily resurrection of our Lord. He affirms the tomb was empty. And it is important to understand that the cross and the resurrection must be seen as one divine event in the saving sovereignty of God. That is good news indeed. John Stott expressed in a personal interview that he would like to see Billy emphasize more the resurrection of Christ. Be that as it may, Graham does hold tenaciously, as he said, that "this event was unique in human history and is fundamental to Christianity."[58]

Billy Graham saw the importance of stressing the resurrection of Christ while in the Soviet Union. He asked Vladimir Sorokin, an Orthodox minister, if he had any advice concerning his preaching. The Orthodox preacher and professor insightfully urged Billy to emphasize more the resurrection of the Lord. Billy heeded the advice. Beyond any wisp of doubt, Billy Graham believes in and preaches the bodily resurrection of Jesus and understands it as an essential point in the *kerygma*. This leads to the next major aspect of the gospel.

JESUS IS COMING AGAIN: KINGDOM FULLNESS

"He is coming. One of these days the sky is going to break open and the Lord Jesus Christ will come back. He will set up His reign upon this planet, and we're going to have peace and social justice. What a wonderful time that's going to be."[59] With these words Billy Graham takes his stand on the biblical declaration that Christ will return to earth. He understands the promise of Christ's second coming very literally. He knows that on Ascension Day, the angels emphatically promised, "this Jesus, who has been taken up from you into heaven, will come in just the same way as you have watched Him go into heaven" (Acts 1:11). A new heaven and earth await the believer in Christ on the glorious day of Jesus' return (Rev. 21–22).

Graham presents five reasons that demand the return of Christ: (1) The prophecies of the Old Testament state it, (2) Jesus' own statements confirm it, (3) to deal with Satan, (4) to alleviate the present world crisis, and (5) to raise the dead. A brief excursion into the evangelist's actual views on the *parousia* (the return) of Jesus at the end of the age stands in order.

Billy Graham confesses that he believes in the so-called premillennial view of the Lord's return, as it offers the most comprehensive explanation of coming events. Yet in his preaching he does not stress in detail his eschatological convictions on premillennialism, although he is obviously of that persuasion. Graham's primary thrust in his evangelization concerning the end of the age revolves around the simple fact that Christ is coming. He believes all true Christians will be resurrected from the grave and that Jesus will usher in peace and social justice. Still, he does outline his basic views in *The Billy Graham Christian Workers Handbook*. In that volume he lays out the following sequence of events surrounding the return of Christ:

- Christ's coming is imminent: It could occur at any time (Matt. 24:42–44; 1 Cor. 15:52; Rev. 22:12).[60]

- The first stage of His coming is known as the Rapture: We believe that Jesus died and rose again and so we believe that God will bring Jesus those who have fallen asleep in him. . . . "For the Lord Himself will come down from heaven with a loud command, with the voice of the archangel and with the trumpet call of God, and the dead in Christ will rise first. After that, we who are still alive and are left will be caught up together with them in the clouds to meet the Lord in the air. And so we will be with the Lord forever" (1 Thess. 4:14, 16–17; see also Titus 2:13). This is the first resurrection (1 Cor. 15:52–57; 2 Cor. 5:4; 1 John 3:2).[61]

- Next comes the judgment seat of Christ for believers (2 Cor. 5:10). Believers will be judged for their faithfulness in life and service (1 Cor. 3:11–15; 4:1–5). However, Christians will not be judged for their sins. That was taken care of at Calvary (2 Cor. 5:21).[62]

- The Great Tribulation period comes next (Dan. 12:1; Matt. 24:21, 29; Rev. 7:14), and the man of sin (Antichrist) will be manifested (2 Thess. 2:3, 4, 8; Rev. 13:1–10).[63]

- Christ returns as King of kings and Lord of lords (Rev. 19:11–16). The decisive Battle of Armageddon takes place (Joel 3:12; Rev. 16:16; 19:17–21).[64]

- The Millennium (Christ's thousand-year reign) will follow (Rev. 20:4–6).[65]

- A second resurrection will bring together all who have rejected Christ throughout the ages. They will be judged "according to their works, by the things which [are] written in the books" (Rev. 20:13) at the Great White Throne Judgment: "And anyone not found written in the Book of Life [will be] cast into the lake of fire" (Rev. 20:15).[66]

- Finally, those who have been redeemed through faith in Christ will begin their everlasting life in the "new heaven and new earth" (Rev. 21–22). (All Scripture text from NIV.)[67]

Not all will agree with the evangelist on all these points; not even some evangelicals. But Graham does not insist that everyone must understand the details surrounding the Lord's return as he does to be a faithful evangelical. One must simply hold to the fact that He is coming again—hopefully soon. Rarely, if ever, does he go into any details of Christ's return in his preaching. He simply states that the Lord will return to establish fully the kingdom and all should be ready. After his proclamation of the incarnation, the life of Jesus, the cross, the resurrection, and the promise of the *parousia*, Graham gives the evangelistic appeal.

THE CALL TO REPENTANCE AND FAITH

Although *repentance* and *faith* must not be seen as synonyms, they are so united that they have been likened unto two sides of the same coin. This constitutes the expected human response to what Christ has done. Graham defines repentance and faith clearly as he issues his call to Christ and conversion. We begin with Graham's call to repentance and his understanding of what that means.

Repentance

Repentance holds a central role in conversion. Billy Graham labors to define repentance and make it clear and fully understood. He has written:

What did Jesus mean by the word *repent*? Why does it appear over and over throughout the Bible? If you look in a modern dictionary you will find that *repent* means "to feel sorry for, or to regret." But the original words that Jesus spoke meant a great deal more than that. They meant a great deal more than just regretting and feeling sorry about sin. The biblical word *repent* means, "to change, or to turn." It is a word of power and action. It is a word that signifies a complete turnabout in the individual. When the Bible calls upon us to repent of sin, it means that we should turn away from sin, that we should do an about-face and walk in the opposite direction from sin and all that it implies.

Too many modern Christians have lost sight of what the Bible means when it talks about repentance. They think that repentance is little more than shaking their heads over their sins and saying, "My, but I'm sorry I did that!" and then continuing to live just as they have lived before.

True repentance means "to change, to turn away from sin, to go in a new direction."[68]

Graham then points out that repentance is not *mere* emotions. There are three aspects of true turning from sin to God, according to Graham: "First, there is a knowledge of sin. . . . Second, emotions are involved . . . true emotions and depth of feeling. . . . Third, repentance involves the will . . . [and] only the Spirit of God can give you the determination necessary for true repentance."[69]

This is a large order to be sure, and Billy, in his own words, regretfully states: "There are thousands of people in America who have their names on church rolls . . . but they have never really expressed true repentance."[70] Graham must be seen as one who fully understands the biblical meaning and call to repentance. In his crusades, and on all occasions, he faithfully issues that call to turn from sin to God. It must be granted that Graham did not always emphasize the necessity of repentance in his earlier ministry as strongly as he does now. Having observed his evangelization for decades, his absolute insistence on repentance has grown through the years. Perhaps Billy Graham has become increasingly conscious of the problem of unconverted church members, especially in America. Be that as it may, he certainly gives proper place to repentance now and has for some time—and that is to his credit. This leads to the other side of the coin of the call: faith.

Faith

Coupled with repentance in genuine, biblical conversion is the presence of faith. The Bible stresses faith as a vital exercise in coming to know God. Scriptural passages that drive that reality home to the human heart appear on almost every page of the Bible. Following are a few that Billy Graham cites:

Believe Me that I am in the Father, and the Father in Me; otherwise believe on account of the works themselves. (John 14:11)

Believe in the Lord Jesus, and you shall be saved, you and your household. (Acts 16:31)

But as many as received Him, to them He gave the right to become children of God, even to those who believe in His name. (John 1:12)

Therefore having been justified by faith, we have peace with God through our Lord Jesus Christ. (Rom. 5:1)

For by grace you have been saved through faith; and that not of yourselves, it is the gift of God; not as a result of works, that no one should boast. (Eph. 2:8–9)

Graham always makes the point that a person is not saved by faith; rather, one is saved by *grace* through *faith*. Thus faith becomes the channel through which the saving grace of God flows. Obviously, that is important. So it must be asked, How does Billy Graham understand the faith principle and how is it practiced? He has said:

[Faith] is the hand that reaches out and receives the gift of His love. In Hebrews 11:1, we read, "Now faith is the substance of things hoped for, the evidence of things not seen." Weymouth has translated it this way, which makes it easier to understand, "Now faith is a confident assurance of that for which we hope, a conviction of the reality of things which we do not see." Faith literally means "to give up, surrender, or commit." Faith is complete confidence. . . . The Bible says, "Faith cometh by hearing, and hearing by the word of God" (Romans 10:17). We believe what God has to say about salvation. We accept it without question. . . . It is not some peculiar, mysterious quality for which we must strive. Jesus said we must become as little children, and just as little children trust their parents, so we must trust God . . . as in repentance, there are three things involved in faith. First, there must be a knowledge of what God has said. That's why it's so important for you to read the Bible. That's why it's so important for you to know something of the teaching of the Bible concerning the salvation of the soul. . . . [There] must be a knowledge that you are a sinner. You must have the knowledge that Christ died for your sins and that He rose again for your justification. The death, burial, and resurrection of Jesus Christ is the very heart of the gospel. That must be believed and accepted as a minimum for conversion. . . . Second, the emotions again are involved. The Bible says, "The fear of the Lord is the beginning of wisdom" (Proverbs 1:7). Paul said, "The love of Christ constraineth us" (2 Corinthians 5:14). Desire, love, fear—all are emotions. Emotions cannot be cut out of life. . . . There is going to be a tug at the heart. Emotion may vary in religious experience. Some people are stoical and others are demonstrative, but the feeling will be there. . . . The third is named "Will." Intellect says that the gospel is logical. Emotion puts pressure upon Will and says, "I feel love for Christ," or "I feel fear of judgment." And then the middle-man, called Will, is the referee. He sits there with his hand on his chin, in deep thought, trying to make up his mind. It is actually the *will* that makes the final and lasting decision. It is possible to have the intellectual conviction and the emotional feeling and still not be properly converted to Christ. Faith has legs. "Faith without works is dead" (James 2:20).[71]

Then after repentance and faith come wonderful promises.

THE PROMISES OF FORGIVENESS, SALVATION, AND ETERNAL LIFE

When a person hears and understands the essential *kerygmatic* content of the gracious work of Jesus Christ in life, death, resurrection, and return and then responds in genuine repentance and faith, many wonderful biblical promises burst upon the heart and mind.

Forgiveness

Billy Graham strongly stresses the fact that forgiveness and its attending peace of heart can be fully experienced. He has said, "You can lose your despised and sinful self and step forth a new person, a clean and peaceful being from whom sin has been washed away."[72] He put it this way in *How to Be Born Again:* "In place of a broken relationship between God and the sinner, 'atonement' results and 'he shall be forgiven' by God.'"[73] The evangelist brings it together in summary fashion with these words:

> "Your sins are forgiven you for His name's sake" (1 John 2:12). What a stupendous promise! Throughout the New Testament we learn that the one who receives Christ as Lord and Savior also receives, immediately, the gift of forgiveness. . . . God's forgiveness is not just a casual statement; it is the complete blotting out of all dirt and degradations of our past, present and future. . . . God's goodness in forgiving us goes even further when we realize that when we are converted we are also declared just which means, that in God's sight we are without guile, clothed forever with Christ's righteousness.[74]

Those key statements certainly cover the issue. In Christ we are forgiven, and we have peace at last; our guilt is genuinely gone. That too is part of the *kerygma* (Acts 2:38). But there is more in the full gospel than forgiveness of sins, as important as that obviously is.

The Gift of the Spirit

When a person comes to Christ in repentance and faith in Jesus Christ, he or she receives the gift of the Holy Spirit. The previous chapter has been devoted to this truth, but a remainder of what Graham says about the gift of the Holy Spirit is appropriate here. He has preached: "Each Christian has the Holy Spirit . . . [and] when we are yielded to God and His will, we are filled with the Holy Spirit." He emphasizes, "It is not how much of the Spirit we have, but how much the Spirit has of us."[75] This also is a wonderful truth that emerges in the gospel message (Acts 2:38).

A New Life

Furthermore, a whole new life becomes the consequence of God's salvation. Billy Graham has written an entire book on this theme, titled *The Secret of Happiness.* He sees the Christian life as one of victorious joy even in the midst of trials, tribulations, and sorrows. He declared:

Too many think of happiness as some sort of will-o'-the-wisp thing that is discovered by constant and relentless searching. Happiness is not found by seeking. It is not an end in itself. . . . Jesus once told His disciples: "Seek first the kingdom of God and His righteousness; and all these things shall be added unto you" (Matthew 6:33). . . . There, if we will take it, is the secret of happiness: "Seek ye first the kingdom of God . . . and all . . . shall be added unto you."[76]

Heaven

Finally, Jesus Christ ushers believers into His glorious presence forever. Billy Graham has written and preaches that there is an eternity to be faced that will be brought in all of its fullness at the second coming of Jesus Christ. Heaven is a beautiful place. As Graham put it, "Heaven is a place, designed by the greatest architect, and it is promised that there we will receive our glorious inheritance. I don't know exactly what kind of inheritance I will receive in heaven, but I know it will be magnificent."[77] Graham goes on to make several points about heaven that are found in the Bible. He tells us:

- Heaven is the city of our God.[78]

- In heaven there will be no fear.[79]

- In heaven there will be no night.[80]

- In heaven there will be no more suffering.[81]

- In heaven we will recognize and be recognized.[82]

- In heaven there will be no more sorrowful separations.[83]

- In heaven each of us will have a superhuman body.[84]

Then the evangelist hits the high mark when he tells us, "We will be like Jesus . . . in knowledge . . . [and] in love. . . . So the supreme benefit, the one which surpasses all others, is that we will be with Jesus Christ."[85] That is heaven, and Billy urges all to be ready for that grand day when we leave this temporal life and face eternity.

But will heaven be our home? That will not be true for some. That raises life's greatest question.

THE BAD NEWS

Billy Graham has said, "Now we know that God is a God of love. We know that God is a God of mercy, but the Bible also teaches that God is a God of wrath."[86] As there is a heaven to gain, an old preacher said, there is also a hell to shun. Graham definitely believes in a literal separation from God forever, which constitutes the essence of judgment and hell. As an evangelist has said, "Jesus specifically states that nonbelievers will not be able to escape the condemnation of hell (Matthew 23:33). . . . Probably one of the most graphic descriptions of hell in the Bible is given by Jesus in His parable of the rich man and Lazarus. . . . The rich man was sent to hell and was in torment. . . . It is a graphic description of the unbeliever's sufferings apart from God . . . and it was 'fixed' or permanent. There was no second chance."[87] But the doctrine has certainly raised questions. Graham goes on to point out some deviations from these truths that Jesus taught:

- Universalism—everybody will be eventually saved.
- Annihilation—nonbelievers will just cease to exist.
- Second Chance—there will be the opportunity to be saved after death.

All these errors Graham rejects; he believes hell is a real, eternal place of torment for the damned. And Billy states about the essence of the torment: "Hell, essentially is separation from God. Hell is the loneliest place in the universe."[88] The thought is horrifying. That is no doubt why, as Billy Graham points out, "Jesus Himself spoke frequently about hell. He warned of a hell to come. . . . There is no fellowship in hell except fellowship with darkness."[89] The judgment of God is a reality, a terrible reality; there can be no escaping God's arm of justice. As Scripture warns us, the "wages of sin is death" (Rom. 6:23)—eternal death. The writer of Hebrews tells us first comes *death*, and then the *judgment* (Heb. 9:27).

All of these principles and truths place in high profile the fact that people stand in desperate need of salvation. Of course, all of this has been implied in the *kerygma* itself. If Christ died and rose for the problem of human sin, evil, and corruption, then that problem must be of gigantic proportions. What does Graham have to say about this issue?

HUMAN SIN

First of all, the evangelist sees everyone as under sin. He declared, "The Bible says so. 'All have sinned and fall short of the glory of God' (Rom. 3:23). If there were no other reason, that in itself would be sufficient. But there is a second reason. . . . Any person who is not fully as good as Jesus Christ is a sinner. He alone is the world's only example of one who was without sin."[90]

Graham points out that the problem of sin all began in the Garden of Eden when Adam and Eve disobeyed God's specific command. He said, "This was the test . . . Adam made his choice . . . [and] the Bible states very clearly that the results of Adam's sin shall be visited upon every one of his descendants. [Thus] sin entered the human race through Adam."[91] This biblical concept finds it roots in the solidarity of the human race (Acts 17:26). Given the rugged individualism of Western thought, the idea is difficult to grasp. Still, it remains a biblical truth and must be accepted. In the final analysis, the human race is one.

Graham goes on to define the sins of which we are all guilty. He tells us these sins include: (1) "Lawlessness; the transgression of the law of God," (2) "iniquity, deviating from the right," (3) "missing the mark, falling short of the goal that has been set," (4) "the intrusion of self-will into the sphere of divine authority," and (5) "unbelief."[92] In one of his early books, *The Seven Deadly Sins,* Graham elucidates the pragmatic side of these root issues. In light of these truths and the fact that "all have sinned," there is little wonder that Billy Graham insists there is only one remedy. He states, "Man's only salvation from sin stands on a lonely, barren, skull-shaped hill."[93] It was there Jesus died; He "became sin for us that we might become the righteousness of God in Him" (2 Cor. 5:21). Jesus alone saves. And that, as Graham argues, explains the reason that the gospel message is so powerful and must be heralded worldwide. In a word, every living person needs to experience forgiveness and salvation. Thus it is understandable why Billy said, "The motto I have taken for my life is 'to evangelize the world in this generation, that every person might hear the gospel once before the others have heard it twice.'"[94]

CONVERSION: NEW LIFE IN CHRIST

This theme has been briefly touched upon earlier, but a closer look at Graham's understanding of conversion should prove helpful. The basic concept is clearly outlined in the ending paragraph of Acts 2. Luke describes the new church as a group of believers who had been radically and dramatically changed. The converts were benevolent, loving, sacrificial, and members of a vibrant community. Because of their conversion, Luke tells us, "they were continually devoting themselves to the apostles' teaching and to fellowship, to the breaking of bread and to prayer" (v. 42). The new believers became a highly respected people who precipitated great church growth throughout the conversion of a multitude of others: "The Lord was adding to their number day by day those who were being saved" (v. 47). That scenario pictures conversion in the fullest sense of the word. It can be expressed in this fashion: True repentance and faith initiate godliness of life, which in turn impacts the unbelieving community and enables evangelism to flourish. Billy Graham has several things to say about the meaning and the centrality of the experience. Here is a brief example:

> Conversion means "turning." The Bible is full of the concept and God pleads with man to turn to Him. . . . The new birth is not just being reformed. It's being transformed . . . through the new birth we can enter a new world. The contrast used in the Bible to express the change which comes over us when we are born again [converted] is very graphic; from lust to holiness; from darkness to light; from death to resurrection; from stranger to the kingdom of God to now being its citizen. . . . He [the converted one] receives a new nature and a new heart. He becomes a new creation.[95]

Graham correctly implies that the connection between repentance and conversion is close when he quotes Peter's admonitions on the Day of Pentecost: "Repent, therefore, and be *converted*"[96] (Acts 3:19). He then strives to make it very clear that "a person cannot turn to God to repent, or even believe, without God's help. God must do the turning. Many times the Bible tells how men and women did that very thing."[97] Billy brings it together when he states, "To be a Christian means to be 'Christ-like', and we cannot be like Him in any degree unless we are changed, *converted*."[98] So the evangelist sees our turning to God and God's turning to us; thus, we are converted, changed, and made daily more like Jesus. That is being a Christian by God's grace.

Surely these sobering truths motivate any Christian to present the gospel to people. It clearly motivated Billy. In light of this theological unfolding of the gospel in Billy Graham's ministry, it would be proper to see at this juncture how the Billy Graham Evangelistic Association has summarized the gospel in their Statement of Faith:

STATEMENT OF FAITH
THE BILLY GRAHAM EVANGELISTIC ASSOCIATION BELIEVES . . .

- The Bible to be the infallible Word of God, that it is His holy and inspired Word, and that it is of supreme and final authority.

- In one God, eternally existing in three persons—Father, Son, and Holy Spirit.

- Jesus Christ was conceived by the Holy Spirit, born of the Virgin Mary. He led a sinless life, took on Himself all of our sins, died and rose again, and is seated at the right hand of the Father as our mediator and advocate.

- That all men everywhere are lost and face the judgment of God, and need to come to a saving knowledge of Jesus Christ through His shed blood on the cross.

- That Christ rose from the dead and is coming soon.

- In holy Christian living, and that we must have concern for the hurts and social needs of our fellowmen.

- We must dedicate ourselves anew to the service of our Lord and to His authority over our lives.

- In using every modern means of communication available to us to spread the gospel of Jesus Christ throughout the world.

Most all would agree that Billy Graham has never swerved, wherever he may be, from the preaching of the full *kerygma* of Jesus Christ. Moreover, he has uncompromisingly and courageously contended for it. We shall see this clearly as this book progresses, especially in chapter 7. These salient *kerygmatic* truths have become the essence of his message. Graham has been faithful to his call. This fact is attested by his own statements. He tells the following story: "Mother always told me to preach the gospel, and keep it simple. Two weeks before she went to be with the Lord she admonished me with the same words. I said,

'Mother, I'm going to preach His birth, death and resurrection. I'll preach it until Jesus comes.' She squeezed my hand and said, 'I believe it.'"[99] Mother Graham was right and he has been true. His closest associate, the late T. W. Wilson, once said, "I have never heard him compromise. He is committed to the exclusiveness of the gospel."[100] Others give testimony to this reality. Franklin Graham, Billy's son, has stated in a personal corespondence, "One of the major things he [Billy Graham] has done . . . is to keep the gospel clear and at the forefront of his ministry. He has not deviated to the left or right in sixty years of preaching the gospel message." Surely the previously recorded scholars, Dodd, Green, Poe, and others would grant that Graham does declare the apostolic *kerygma*.

Carl F. H. Henry, theologian and first editor of *Christianity Today* magazine, said:

> Graham is not simply an evangelist, but is expressly an evangelical evangelist, and that implies at once an irreducible theological content and commitment to a complex of Bible doctrines. He has never vacillated on the fundamentals that evangelical orthodoxy championed against theological liberalism. When modernist and humanist critics accused him of turning back the clock of theological progress by a generation, he offered to escort them back 19 centuries to Jesus and the apostles.[101]

Therefore, it seems correct to conclude that Billy Graham is and always has been faithful to the gospel from a historical, biblical perspective. And that gives him credibility, not to mention his incredible contribution to so many lives.

Let it also be said that Billy Graham has been exceedingly zealous in his proclamation of the gospel. This can be seen in many avenues of his work—writings, media ministry, and other methodology—but especially in his crusades. Obviously, the primary work of Billy Graham has centered in crusade evangelism. This aspect of the Graham phenomenon deserves a brief look.

CRUSADE WORK

The crusades have consumed much of Graham's time and energies. Up to the present moment, since the Los Angeles crusade in 1949, he has conducted some 373 crusades and evangelistic rallies (see Appendix D). And this is not to ignore his earlier work prior to the Los Angeles crusade. While traveling with Youth for

Christ, in Europe, in England, and even as a young pastor, he has been faithful in proclaiming the cross in multiplied settings, often at serious sacrifice on his part.

As can be imagined, mass crusades have produced their critics. So the question arises, Do mass evangelism methods have biblical, historical roots; and if so, has Billy Graham employed that methodology in a manner befitting the gospel of Christ? This issue we must approach.

THE VALIDITY OF MASS EVANGELISM

Despite the fact that questions have been raised in various circles concerning the authenticity and effectiveness of mass evangelism, history is replete with positive examples of its use—we see it even in the Bible.

One need but look in the Old Testament to discover the principles of mass meetings to communicate God's message. The "solemn assemblies" proclaimed throughout the Old Testament present a classic case in point. Or see Moses addressing the masses of Israel as recorded in the Book of Deuteronomy. The New Testament is likewise no exception. There must have been several thousand assembled on the Day of Pentecost—three thousand were converted when for the first time they heard a full gospel presentation (Acts 2:41). And whether it was Philip in Samaria (Acts 8:4–24), Paul in Athens (Acts 17:16–32), or Peter and John at the temple (Acts 3), the masses gathered to hear God's Word.

When a serious investigation of the history of evangelistic methods is undertaken, the mass mode surfaces in every age. This can be seen clearly as a sweep through two thousand years of church history is undertaken.

HERITAGE OF PREACHING EVANGELISM

The Billy Graham Evangelistic Association produced a video presentation of such a historical sequence for the conference on evangelism called Amsterdam 2000. Following is a presentation of the script for the video. It makes it quite clear God has had His hand on the methodology of mass evangelism for two millennia:

Throughout history, God has called His people to the task of evangelism. And some He has called to the special ministry of preaching. Beginning with Peter,

Paul, Phillip, and others, Christian evangelists proclaimed the gospel in synagogues and market places throughout the Roman Empire.

In the second and third centuries, evangelists took advantage of the political unity of the Roman Empire to spread the gospel throughout the empire. Among these was Gregory Thaumaturgus, who began to preach in Pontus, where there were a handful of Christians in that city. At his death, thirty years later, there were only a few dozen who did not believe.

In the third century, Barbarian tribes from Mongolia invaded vast areas of the West, and Christian women were among the captives taken. Although forced into slavery, these women remained faithful and converted many of their captors to Christ. Ulfilas, a descendant of slaves, preached to the Goths and translated the Scriptures into their language. A native church arose and Gothic preachers took the gospel to other tribes in Europe.

The barbarian invasions continued, and by the sixth century the Roman Empire had lost much of its territory and power. To the East, however, the Nestorians became a force for the extension of the Christian faith. In addition, the eloquent and persuasive preaching of John Chrysostom and others in the eastern part of the empire won countless people to Christ.

Europe entered the so-called Dark Ages and Islam emerged as a powerful force, hindering the progress of Christian preaching in North Africa and slowing outreach in Asia. However, believers shared Christ across central Asia and Christianity began to grow in India.

In the West, the gospel continued to advance through evangelists like Columba, an Irishman who was the first to bring the gospel to the pagan tribes of Scotland. After establishing a Christian monastery on the small island of Iona, Columba converted many of the region's pagan cities to Christianity. Columba was just one example of how members of the monastic movement were a force for evangelism.

A century later, King Oswald of Northumbria, who was introduced to the gospel while living on Iona as a boy, invited several evangelists from the island to come and establish a monastery just a few miles from his castle in Northern England. On what is now Holy Island, devout men like Aidan and Cuthbert established a Christian learning center and would travel great distances throughout England and Scotland to deliver the gospel message.

Through the dedicated work of these men and other pioneering preachers, many northern Europeans abandoned their pagan gods and turned to Christ. In the Eastern Orthodox Church, the preaching and translation of the Scriptures by Cyril, Methodius, and others led to the conversion of vast numbers of people in Russia and elsewhere.

During the seventh century, many Christians traveled along China's "Silk Road," witnessing for Christ as they went. Their work resulted in several thousand Asian converts and left an impact for decades. But when a new dynasty arose in China, their work was hindered and Christianity was reversed.

By the eleventh century, Islam had spread from Spain to Indonesia. Between 1096 and 1272, the church in the West responded to Muslim expansion with eight military crusades intended to purge the world of Islam. In contrast to these crusades, Francis of Assisi preached the gospel of Christ's love and peace to the Muslims, attempting contact with them in North Africa and Spain.

Beginning in the fourteenth century, the Renaissance brought a renewed interest in art and learning, but the church failed to teach the Scriptures to the common people. God called John Wycliffe to preach to the English people and to translate the Scriptures into their language. The gospel spread to other parts of Europe. Jan Hus preached in Czechoslovakia, and in Italy God called Jerome Savonarola to proclaim a message of repentance and faith. In response to Savonarola's preaching, churches were crowded, but his message troubled the established order, and Savonarola was hanged and burned in the city square of Florence.

At the beginning of the sixteenth century, the Western church entered a time of unrest. A reformation movement challenged the growing corruption and abuse of authority in the church. Scholars like Erasmus, Martin Luther, John Calvin, and others sought the essence of the gospel message.

The dawn of the age of exploration provided new opportunities for the proclamation of the gospel. When French, Spanish, and Portuguese explorers set sail, they were often accompanied by clergy of the Christian church committed to evangelism. The much-feared pirates of the Caribbean produced some unlikely evangelists. After capture and imprisonment, some returned to their Christian roots and devoted their new lives to preaching the gospel to captors and to the people on the west coast of South America in Peru, Chile, and Ecuador. In Asia, Matteo Ricci, a scientist as well as a preacher, spent twenty years proclaiming Christ in China. Ricci took advantage of requests for scientific advice and preached as he worked. By 1650, his preaching had won a quarter million converts to Christ in China.

By the late seventeenth and eighteenth centuries, Europe had entered the age of reason. Great strides were made in science and medicine. Unfortunately for many, Christianity became a mere intellectual exercise and church attendance a formality. John Wesley, George Whitefield, and others felt the call of God and began to preach with new enthusiasm. Wesley preached an average of eight hundred sermons a year, to crowds as large as twenty thousand . . . and a great awakening of faith swept the English-speaking world.

By the late eighteenth century, the North American population was expanding westward. To reach these scattered people on the frontier, the Methodists developed a network of circuit preachers. These men covered areas of five hundred square miles or more on horseback. In 1800, camp meetings developed as another method of evangelizing the frontier. These events attracted people from miles around and sometimes lasted a week or more. The Spirit of God continued this renewal for evangelists like Charles Finney, Phoebe Palmer, and former slave Amanda Smith. Revival spread to other parts of the world as well. In Sierra Leone, hundreds of ex-slaves responded to Christian preaching. One of these, Samuel Crowther, preached Christ throughout Nigeria; and the evangelists he trained were the first to bring the gospel to many parts of West Africa. Revival also spread across Europe. In Germany, evangelists like Elia Shank, Samuel Keller, and Jacob Vetter joyfully proclaimed Christ in tent meetings and churches. Keller preached thousands of times during his twenty-five-year career and reached more than five million Germans with the gospel. In Latin America, Francisco Penzotti, an Italian immigrant, gave away Bibles and New Testaments all across the continent, which laid the foundation for thousands of converts.

In 1870, God called a shoe salesman named Dwight Moody to lead evangelistic meetings in America and England. Moody felt the urgency to reach large numbers and preached to nearly one hundred million people during his lifetime. His systematic approach introduced the world to the modern age of mass evangelism.

In 1891, God called Billy Sunday to leave a successful career in professional baseball to become an evangelist. The American public loved his unique, theatrical style of attacking sin and vice. Thousands were converted to Christ through Sunday's preaching.

Between 1914 and 1945, the world was ravaged by two major wars. But in

Africa, Asia, and Latin America, God spoke through His evangelists. In Japan, Paul Kanamori preached the message of salvation in mass rallies. Between 1916 and 1919, Kanamori recorded forty-three thousand decisions for Christ. In India, Sadhu Sundar Singh was converted following a vision of the Lord. Although ostracized by his family, he preached throughout India and Ceylon.

Following World War II, at the Christ for Greater Los Angeles Crusade in 1949, Billy Graham emerged as the leading figure of a new breed of evangelists. The use of radio, television, and film multiplied the impact of his crusades by reaching new and broader audiences. Mass evangelism now reached people who sat in the comfort of their own home no matter the technology; however, preaching remained paramount. Whether through electronic means or the public meeting, the preaching of the gospel has continued. Today, gifted evangelists around the world are proclaiming Christ.

Since the first preaching of the apostles, God has called men and women to proclaim the good news of salvation in Jesus Christ. There are many more wonderful stories of evangelists which could be told.[102]

Much of the work and methods of these leading biblical, historical evangelistic leaders centered in reaching mass audiences. Thus it would seem, at least in principle, that Graham's methods in crusades have the legitimate sanction of the Bible and evangelical history. As stated, this does not mean mass evangelism is without its critics. There are those quick to point out possible weaknesses. Some say such an evangelistic strategy can lead to a personality cult, or it can become too emotional, or people really do not know what they are deciding for. Of course, the largest criticism centers in the accusation that the "converts" do not last. And there are instances in the history of mass evangelism where all those pitfalls have to some degree been true.

William Thomas, in a Ph.D. thesis, makes a compelling point. He states that motivation, goals, and methods of crusade evangelism have arisen out of its spiritual origins, messages, and understanding of the socioreligious conditions of the times, as well as the spiritual experiences of the evangelists. When Christians today seek to apply this method of outreach (which is just one method of evangelism), they should take into consideration its historical development. Consideration should also be given to the process of communication.[103] In a word, mass evangelism—as shown—does have a legitimate history and in many contexts is sufficiently communicative. Furthermore, an atmosphere is created in a mass crusade that directs the minds of many to the things of Christ. That is important; it can be a seed sown that will bear fruit later. The final results are God's doings.

Moreover, as shall be seen in succeeding chapters, the work in the Billy Graham Evangelistic Association has been conducted on the highest level of ethical and moral standards. The Graham Association, and Billy Graham himself, strive for integrity in all the affairs of the work, crusades or otherwise. This shall become obvious as this book progresses. The actual workings of the crusades shall be presented in a succeeding chapter. But it does seem reasonable to say that Graham's crusade evangelism not only has the stamp of biblical, historical veracity, but it also serves as an effective method that God's Holy Spirit has honored and used for centuries. Thus it has validity and authenticity and has proved contributory to many lives.

Further, as stated, Billy Graham's impact goes beyond the crusades. A brief look into some of these areas of ministry is of interest.

WRITINGS

At present, Graham has written twenty-four books and dozens of tracts and booklets. Several of his books have been bestsellers. A number will go down as classic evangelistic writings. There is little question that a large number of people have been convicted and converted through reading Graham's books, especially his *Peace with God* and *How to Be Born Again.* Several of the evangelist's works also center on Christian discipleship. These too have been well received.

OTHER WIDESPREAD MINISTRY

Other aspects of Graham's faithfulness to the gospel are evident in the various ministries he has undertaken, most of which will be elucidated in more detail later. But as a case in point, the schools of evangelism that for years accompanied the major crusades and are now held in various parts of the world have proved most significant. The number of preachers, evangelists, and laypeople who have been inspired, challenged, and equipped to do evangelistic work around the globe is most encouraging. Along with these schools have been the world conferences such as the recent Amsterdam 2000. The impact of this ministry is most positive—as shall be seen.

Time fails to tell of the impact of the media ministry. Multiplied millions worldwide have heard the gospel through television, radio, and other media. One of the highlights of that particular aspect took place in March 1995 in the context of a crusade in San Juan, Puerto Rico. A worldwide network, made available by satellite, permitted the gospel to be heard worldwide. It was broadcast to three thousand mission points in 185 countries and territories, and heard by ten million people gathered at those mission outposts. It is estimated that one billion people heard the broadcast around the globe. Of course, no one knows the number of listeners who were moved Godward by this evangelistic outreach. Such is the impact of this faithful ministry. Other instances of this nature will be presented in the following pages.

PERSONAL WITNESSING

Billy Graham is not just an isolated, high-profile evangelist. He loves to tell people about Jesus Christ. This is evident in his interviews, his press conferences, and similar encounters. On a person-to-person basis, Graham serves as a most faithful and effective witness.

On one occasion, while speaking at a conference for some of North America's most talented and creative thinkers, Graham was approached by one of the leading Internet gurus. Following introductions, this young man invited Graham to join him for a return trip to the East Coast in his private jet—there was much he wanted to discuss. Though declining, Graham left open the door for future visits. Telephone calls and subsequent visits during the next several months led to a meeting in a hotel room in a crusade city where Graham was instrumental in leading this young man to the Lord. The man said in appreciation to Billy, "I have corporate jets in my company. Anytime you want to go any place in the world, just call me and a jet will be at your disposal."

Such incidents are indicative of the gratitude of just one man whom Billy Graham took time to lead to Christ. It also speaks of the spirit of Billy that such conversations occur on a regular basis, whether they be with a company CEO or just the average person. As a case in point of Graham's sensitivity to all sorts of people, during the Australian crusade in 1979, Billy and a coworker were taking an early morning walk through a park. A man quite intoxicated staggered by them. Billy walked a few more steps and then stopped and turned around. He walked back to the bedraggled street man, put his arm on his shoulder, and did his best to point him to Jesus. That is the heart of the evangelist. He truly does love people.

Billy Graham seizes every opportunity and every means, as led by the Holy Spirit, to communicate the glorious gospel of Jesus Christ, be it on a personal level or before thousands. He has remained faithful to the call that he received in Florida as a nineteen-year-old young man. He has been used significantly—in many respects unprecedented in evangelical history. The recently composed Amsterdam Declaration gives validity to these statements. It reflects what Billy Graham believes, preaches, and practices and serves as a guide for any sincere evangelist. (See Appendix C.)

All this does not mean that one cannot be faithful to the gospel and to the call to evangelism unless he or she becomes a world-renowned preacher and is involved in multiplied ministries. By no means. There are many God-called evangelists who are virtually unknown and in the eyes of the world seem rather insignificant. Faithfulness, not fame, stands as the ultimate criteria for greatness. Jesus was very emphatic about it when He said, "Be faithful until death, and I will give you the crown of life" (Rev. 2:10). Faithfulness creates validity and authenticity. In that regard, Billy Graham, regardless of all of the popularity and accolades that have come his way, has not deterred from his calling and his faithful commitment to share Christ regardless of circumstances. He has kept the promise he made to his mother just before her death to preach Christ. That grants him basic historical acceptance and presents the rationale for his worldwide contribution.

CONCLUSION AND CONTRIBUTION
OF BILLY GRAHAM AND THE GOSPEL CALL

The glorious gospel of Jesus Christ shines brightly around the world today. Sadly, not every single person has heard; there are still many people in tragic darkness. But more and more, the message is being heralded to the nations. It seems a new day for evangelism. But ever since the Garden of Eden, the message of Christ has gone forth from the heart and lips of those whom God has called and equipped with the message of salvation. Among the illustrious army stands Billy Graham. He has been in the trenches for more than half a century.

It has hopefully become undeniably evident that God has called Billy Graham to be an evangelist, a bringer of good news to the needy world. His experience at the eighteenth hole of the Temple Terrace Golf Course, and all that led up to it, can hardly be questioned. Surely that divine moment was engineered by God. The Bible says that God calls and enables His willing servants to evangelize and then gives them to the church as His gift. There is little doubt, at least in Billy's heart and mind, that such has been his experience. The manner in which our Lord has used Billy Graham to preach the gospel for more than sixty years attests to that reality. Few historians—or casual observers—would want to dispute that which has become so obvious: God has His hand on Billy.

Furthermore, Billy Graham does preach the full gospel. Again, it has hopefully become evident through this study that Graham grasps the nature of the gospel, and he preaches it in all its completeness. Rare is the evangelistic sermon from Graham in which every point of the whole *kerygma* is not set forth—and that in the power of the Holy Spirit. Surely that is what primarily precipitates the incredible response to his preaching. Evangelical history and contemporary evangelism sanction that approach.

Most would agree that the word *incredible* describes accurately the response of Graham's hearers to the gospel message. Granted, the praise directed to Billy Graham sometimes gets a bit out of hand. But Billy does not sanction that; he is a genuinely humble man. All who know him testify to that reality. He himself said, "I am not a great preacher, and I don't claim to be a great preacher. I've heard great preaching many times and wish I was one of those great preachers. I'm an ordinary preacher, just communicating the gospel in the best way I know how."[104]

Nonetheless, those who have heard and heeded his gospel message can be numbered in the millions. Around the world, among people of all cultures, countries, classes, and kinds, multitudes have responded to his call to "repentance toward God and faith in our Lord Jesus Christ" (Acts 20:21). That is what Paul told the Ephesian elders he preached, and so does Billy. But then, that constitutes the message that all faithful, biblically oriented evangelists have proclaimed throughout history. Further, as seen, Graham's crusade methodology has history's stamp of approval. In that historic line Billy Graham has found his place. He understands the gospel, he declares the gospel to the masses, and people are saved. These realities reveal the evangelist's great contribution. That is historical, biblical evangelism—no more, no less.

INTRODUCTION TO THE
AGE OF THE CHURCH
FATHERS

~~

TRAVELING THROUGH THE EARLY YEARS OF THE church of Jesus
Christ, one theological axiom becomes evident. This truth was declared decisively in the apostolic age and emphasized equally in the time of the church
fathers: *Evangelism is God's enterprise.* That is to say, the spread of the gospel,
as exemplified in faithful heralds like Billy Graham, finds its inspiration, direction, empowerment, and accomplishment through the dynamic work of God
Himself. The extension of God's kingdom is God's accomplishment. Yet, the
fact also remains equally true that God never works in a vacuum. In the *misseo dei* (mission of God), He uses human agency. There we have one of the
great paradoxes of the faith. In advancing His kingdom, the sovereign God
designs and fashions His people as His agents in His grand enterprise of world
evangelization. Still, it must be constantly emphasized, especially in our age of
pragmatic humanism, that God is sovereign in all things, thus exerting a pertinent and pointed impact on the evangelistic ministry of the church. Thus we
see the mystery of the interplay of divine sovereignty and human responsibility manifesting itself. Churches, as well as individual believers, cannot successfully engage in the evangelistic task until they visualize themselves in the light
of God's sovereign acts in the entirety of salvation history. But God always uses
His people in that history. The principle weaves that beautiful warp and woof
into a lovely tapestry of effective evangelism.

CHAPTER 4

THE SOVEREIGNTY OF GOD IN EVANGELISM

⁓

PART I:
AUGUSTINE AND DIVINE SOVEREIGNTY

To thee, the Creator and Governor of the
Universe . . . thanks were due to thee our God.
—AUGUSTINE

INTRODUCTION

Few in the history of the church have exemplified the truth of divine sovereignty and human responsibility more forthrightly than the notable church father Augustine. Therefore, it will be wise to attempt to follow his footsteps on the path of finding God's way of bringing the world to the foot of the cross.

For a man who knew no Hebrew and surprisingly little Greek, it is rather amazing that Augustine became "the finest theological mind of his age."[1] His two classics, *The City of God* and *The Confessions*, have become standard fare not only in theological circles, but they have also taken their place on the shelves of the great literature of history. But Augustine's beginnings were quite average for one destined to historical greatness.

Augustine was born on the thirteenth day of November 354, in Tagaste, Numidia, a part of the Roman Empire after the destruction of Carthage in 146 B.C. He was brought up in a normal middle-class family. His father, Patricius, and his mother, Monica, exerted strong parental influence over young Augustine, particularly his mother. Patricius served as a municipal official and did not become a Christian until the latter part of his life. But Monica was a lifelong Christian and served as a constant source of inspiration to her young son.

The future theologian had his early education in his hometown of Tagaste. He then attended a nearby university, about a dozen miles from his home, in the city of Madaura. From there he moved to Carthage in 371 to study law.

At the age of nineteen, while reading Cicero's *Hortensius*, Augustine faced the challenge of discovering the essence of religious realities. Throwing himself into the study of the various religious concepts of the day, he became captivated by Manicheism. This particular Greek philosophical approach had its roots in Platonic dualism, a system that undergirded most Greek philosophy. Manicheism spread its influence from Persia to the western edges of the Roman Empire. It virtually dominated philosophical thinking during the third and fourth centuries. Mani, the author of the system, was converted from the life of a magician to Christianity. Yet his views soon took a rather dubious turn. His approach centered in synthesizing Christian concepts with the dualism of Zoroastrianism. One of the basic tenets of Mani's thought structure declared that one could find salvation through ascetic living. Although Augustine was caught up in the system for a period of time, he later developed an interest in Neoplatonic thought. Both philosophical, religious systems were typical of Greek dualism. Yet through it all, Augustine began to realize that God stood as the source of all good. Finally, under the influence and inspiration of Bishop Ambrose, Augustine began to see the light of the gospel of Christ his mother had so ardently attempted to share with him.

AUGUSTINE'S CONVERSION

When Augustine was thirty-two years of age, living in Milan, where he had become a professor of rhetoric, he heard Bishop Ambrose preach for the first time. Deeply impressed by the godly man's message, Augustine began to question seriously Greek philosophical understandings, particularly his Manicheism. Ambrose's preaching of the pure gospel profoundly touched young Augustine and brought about a spiritual crisis that thrust him into the Scriptures. He fell under deep conviction of sin and began to pour out his heart with weeping for forgiveness. He met Christ—and was dramatically transformed. Augustine's conversion was sudden, but it proved deep and enduring. Although he completely and unequivocally dedicated his life to Jesus Christ, it proved a long pilgrimage to the cross for the astute young man. The dramatic story deserves a brief reading.

AUGUSTINE'S JOURNEY TO CHRIST

Augustine profoundly needed the moral and ethical reform that Christ could bring. Some years before his conversion, he had a relationship with a young woman he met while a student in Carthage. A son was born to them. He actually consorted with his mistress for more than a decade. After the breakup of the affair, their son, Adeodatus, lived with Augustine until the boy's premature death in late adolescence. Through all these years of immorality, Augustine's mother, Monica, fervently prayed for his conversion.

After four years of study in Carthage, Augustine moved back to his hometown to teach. Then in 383 he traveled to Rome, against the will of his mother. One year later he moved to Milan, where he received a professorship in rhetoric. There he heard the sermons of Ambrose. His mother at the time was living close-by with relatives. Shortly after Augustine's move to Milan, a good society marriage was arranged for him, which forced him to give up his mistress. Before his marriage, however, he had to wait two years before he could claim his bride, as his fiancée was underage. Being impatient and discontent, Augustine took yet another mistress. All the while his mother kept pressing the claims of Christ upon his life.

Augustine's conversion came about in a quite dramatic fashion. The climactic scene took place in a garden. Sitting with his friend Alypius in a private garden, suddenly, as he expressed it in his own words, "the deep consideration had from the secret bottom of my soul drawn together and heaped up all my misery into the side of my heart, there arose a mighty storm, bringing a mighty shower of tears."[2] Augustine got up and left Alypius. He then heard the voice of a child repeating the words "*Tello lege*" ("take and read"). With Bible in hand, he opened to the Epistle of Paul to the Romans and read from chapter 13, verses 13 and 14. Suddenly the darkness of doubt vanished, and peace and joy filled his heart—he had found Christ.

In 387, after forty days of preparation for baptism, in an Easter vigil night on Holy Saturday, Augustine and his son, Adeodatus, and friend Alypius were baptized into the Christian faith by Ambrose. The attractions of the great Roman Empire lost their charm and he began to see his own worldly ambitions of moneymaking as a teacher of rhetoric as hollow and sterile. Being a new man with a new vision, he returned to North Africa.

Quite sadly, while Augustine and a few Christian friends were delayed in the port city of Ostia near Rome, waiting for the ship to transport them back to Africa, Augustine's mother died. Monica's last word to her newly converted son was, "Son, for my own part I have no further delight in anything in this life." Her constant prayer for the conversion of Augustine had been fulfilled. She said, "My God hath done this for me more abundantly . . . what am I still doing here?" With those words she went to be with her Lord.

Two years later, in the coastal city of Hippo Regius, the church consecrated Augustine into the priesthood. During his ordination ceremony, when the laying on of hands was exercised, he literally burst into tears. Thereafter he devoted himself totally to understanding and sharing the truth of God's Word. His ardent study made him the formidable theologian that the world recognizes to this day.

AUGUSTINE'S MINISTRY

Augustine's ministry began by exposing the errors of the Manichean philosophy he knew so well. By 393, his talents were becoming recognized and appreciated. In that year he received the commission to preach a series of sermons in the place of his bishop. Two years later, the old bishop passed away, and Augustine assumed the responsibility of the church at Hippo. He remained in that pastorate until his death in 430. For thirty-five years, Augustine stood strong for the faith. He opposed the Donatists, an ultraconservative group embracing a philosophy decreeing that anyone who had apostatized from the faith under the persecution of Diocletian and then sought to return to the church in repentance was absolutely rejected. Against this hard stance Augustine rebelled, arguing ably from the Scriptures. He had become an astute biblical theologian. Despite his weakness in the original languages, he knew the Scriptures well and vigorously contended for the orthodox, evangelical faith.

Augustine, as implied, predicated his entire theological structure on the foundation of the revelation of God in Jesus Christ as recorded in Holy Scripture. To him, revelation constituted the essence of divine knowledge. For Augustine, revelation "functions in the order of knowledge as grace functions in the order of action, and right knowledge and right action are impossible without revelation and grace."[3] To learn of God, Augustine insisted on the power of grace and one's total commitment to God's revelation in Christ, as clearly presented in the Bible.

In light of this approach, it becomes evident why Augustine would insist on the sovereignty of God. The Scriptures declare this essential truth time and again. Of course, this raised for Augustine the issue of God's sovereignty and how human responsibility figures in the equation. Perhaps because of his philosophical background and a high view of the ultimacy of God's nature, he refused to attempt to resolve the issue. He understood that paradox is intrinsic to the revelation of God. So he simply accepted God's sovereignty and human responsibility and left it in the realm of the infinite mind of God.

This does not mean that Augustine had no firm theological convictions or avoided good scholarship. He held tenaciously to basic evangelical positions. He fully accepted the doctrine of the Trinity and the absolute deity of Jesus Christ. Augustine contended that the problem of evil could only be solved in the incarnation of the Son, the *logos* of God (John 1:1–12). This position was in direct conflict with his earlier Platonism, which held that all flesh was evil; therefore, God could never be robed in flesh. John's prologue to his Gospel (1:1–12) eventually undermined Augustine's confidence in Platonic thought. He sloughed off the Platonic-Greek dualism and developed a high Christology. Actually, this departure from Platonism led Augustine to a full commitment to the sovereignty of God and ultimately precipitated his conversion. He further articulated the essential work of the Third Person of the Trinity, the Holy Spirit, in bringing people to Christ. Central to Augustine's thought, as can be surmised, the sovereignty of God surfaced as one of the paramount theological truths he embraced. The Reformers of the sixteenth century, and the Puritans who followed, constantly referred to Augustine on this issue, quoting him with the ring of authority.

It goes without saying that Augustine was one of the most influential of the church fathers. Something of an "Augustinian Renaissance" arose just prior to the Reformation. Augustine's influence thus helped set the stage for the Reformation and its emphasis on God's sovereignty. This was particularly true for Martin Luther and John Calvin. Phillip Melanchthon, Luther's theologian, declared that the proclamation of the gospel through the ages had been most clearly set forth by five men: Isaiah, John the Baptist, Paul, Augustine, and Luther. This places Augustine on a high level, and to the present day many agree.

BATTLES

Numerous theological battles erupted around Augustine. He had a classic struggle with Pelagius, who held to a form of salvation by works. In response to the Pelagians, Augustine developed a full-blown doctrine of the sovereignty of God in election and predestination. For the Pelagians, salvation was essentially a reward for good works, i.e., salvation had to be earned. Against this unbiblical view Augustine strongly objected, arguing for the principle of the sovereignty of God in redemption and the absolute necessity of unmerited grace for salvation. Augustine saw redemption as a free, surprising gift of God. He said that in Christ his sins were "dissolved as if they were ice."[4] This position does not eradicate human freedom in the salvation experience. As Augustine stressed, he saw people as chosen and free. He said that God does not save us by ourselves; neither does He save us apart from ourselves. Augustine could live with the paradox and be appreciated for his stance. Thus for Augustine, the divine sovereignty of God reigned in all things for His ultimate glory.

It should be clearly understood that Augustine's high view of God's sovereignty should not be seen as relating to the idea of predestination and election alone. He also contended that the sovereignty of God is fully active and in complete control of the entire mission and ministry of evangelization. The mission is God's mission, and He works in every aspect of the enterprise as He pleases. God controls the task, and His people must intelligently cooperate with Him. That constitutes their responsibility in the light of God's sovereignty.

AUGUSTINE'S CONTRIBUTIONS

To evaluate the contributions of Augustine is impossible in this limited account. A few of his significant writings must be briefly mentioned, however. His book *The Confessions* will always stand as one of the great devotional classics of all time. His *City of God* outlines the entire kingdom enterprise of the sovereign God. In his treatise *Ad Simplicianum*, written about 396, he stressed the absolute omnipotence and sovereignty of God in divine grace. Still, as pointed out, Augustine took human responsibility seriously. As difficult as it may be to reconcile these seemingly contradictory statements, as D. A. Carson has said, "It is axiomatic that any truly monotheistic religion is going to experience the tension between divine sovereignty and human responsibility."[5] The tension must be kept, as Augustine attempted to do. On one occasion, someone came to Charles Spurgeon, who held strong views on the sovereignty of God and human freedom, and asked how these two ideas can be reconciled. Spurgeon replied, "I did not know you had to reconcile friends." Although Spurgeon put it simply, that gets to the heart of what the Bible says. As Augustine saw it, God is sovereign and will accomplish His task through His people. Wise evangelists gear their approach to winning unbelievers on that basis.

CONCLUSION

Thus, Augustine lived a life of exalting the gospel of Jesus Christ and the absolute sovereignty of God in all Christian endeavors to lead people to salvation. He learned, as perhaps his most quoted statement declares, "Thou madest us for thyself, and our heart is restless, until it reposes in Thee."[6] His ministry remains as a monument to his theological acumen and dedication. He died at Hippo on August 28, 430, while the city was being besieged by the Vandals. It was said of Augustine that he combined the creative powers of Tertullian and the intellectual breadth of Origen with the ecclesiastical sense of Cyprian. Augustine became a power for the whole life of the church, up until modern times. A notable life to be sure!

But the question arises, Does the Bible itself actually teach the unequivocal sovereignty of God in all things? To that doctrinal question we turn.

THE SOVEREIGNTY OF GOD IN EVANGELISM

History attests to the fact that many men of God like John Calvin, Martin Luther, William Perkins, and others relied heavily on the theology and thought of Augustine of Hippo. Having seen something of his spiritual journey, it becomes understandable why Augustine can be chosen as epitomizing the theology he so ably defended. The fact that God by His Spirit reached down in sovereignty and touched the life of a profligate young man and transformed him into a giant among the church fathers certainly presents an example and token of the centrality of God in the conversion experience. Thinkers of all persuasions, not just the Reformers, realize that there can be no true evangelism unless God puts His sovereign mark on the enterprise. Jesus said, "No one can come to Me, unless the Father who sent Me draws him" (John 6:44). The Lord went on further to point out that the Holy Spirit alone convicts of "sin, and righteousness, and judgment" (John 16:8). Clearly, the sovereign God becomes the Initiator, Convictor, Converter, and Sustainer of all evangelism. In a word, God is sovereign in evangelism. But what does the Bible mean by the sovereignty of God, especially as it relates to world evangelization?

GOD'S SOVEREIGN PERSONHOOD

In the first place, God is sovereign in His own personhood, as can be seen in His actions. A classic illustration of God's sovereignty manifested itself in the contest between Elijah and the four hundred prophets of Baal on Mount Carmel. In that well-known historical event, Elijah threw down the gauntlet to the prophets of Baal with the challenge: "'Call on the name of your god, and I will call on the name of the LORD, and the God who answers by fire, He is God.' And all the people answered and said, 'That is a good idea'" (1 Kings 18:24). At that moment on Mount Carmel a dramatic climax came on the wings of Elijah's prayer:

O LORD, the God of Abraham, Isaac and Israel, today let it be known that Thou art God in Israel, and that I am Thy servant, and that I have done all these things at Thy word. Answer me, O LORD, answer me, that this people may know that Thou, O LORD, art God, and that Thou hast turned their heart back again.

Then the fire of the LORD fell, and consumed the burnt offering and the wood and the stones and the dust, and licked up the water that was in the trench. And when all the people saw it, they fell on their faces; and they said, "The LORD, He is God; the LORD, He is God." (1 Kings 18:36–39)

The point had been made: The Lord God, *Yahweh*, manifested Himself as the sovereign God—the Creator, Sustainer, the Lord of all, who can and does act *as He wills*.

Many years before this climactic event, Moses learned the same essential truth. On Mount Sinai, another significant mountain peak in the revelation of God, Moses fell into an argument with the Lord (Exod. 3–4). Quite amazing is the fact that the sovereign God will permit us to argue with Him, but He is also a God of grace and mercy as well as the sovereign Lord. Finally, during his conflict with God, Moses asked, "Whom shall I say sent me to the Israelites? They will surely want to know." And God answered, revealing His personal name: "I am that I am." He is *Yahweh*—the God of all existence, the sovereign Lord, the Almighty, the Essence of Ultimate Reality. His name displays His sovereignty. That is who He is; and marvel of marvels, mere humans can come to know Him. Though He is the hidden One, He has also bared His arm in human experience, probably more than we will ever realize, and He declares His absolute sovereignty in grace and love. The very act of creation (Gen. 1–3) and all subsequent history attest to that wonderful reality.

It will prove helpful to see in more detail what we actually mean when we say God is *sovereign*.

GOD AND SOVEREIGNTY

Our quest to acquire more depth of understanding concerning God's sovereignty begins by pointing out a prevalent error. There are some today who project a very limited view of the sovereign Lord. They put a subtle question mark over His all-powerful, all-knowing, all-sufficient strength and wisdom.

This approach, perhaps for want of a better term, is called "process theology." In this theological matrix, a quite serious aberration of biblical truth concerning God's personhood has emerged. This particular theological deviation takes its lead from various considerations. The evolutionary hypothesis made its impact on the movement. Not the least of influences on process thinkers centers in God's seeming inability to cope fully with the perplexing problem of evil and suffering. Many years ago, this particular issue moved Edgar S. Brightman of Boston University to lay the early foundation stones in process theology structures. He projected the concept of a "limited God." But process theology takes its major current understanding from philosopher Alfred North Whitehead (see Whitehead's *Process and Reality*). To illustrate Whitehead's influence, leading process theologian John B. Cobb Jr. confessed, "I become more of a Whiteheadian than [ever] before."[7]

Whitehead projects the basic tenet that God exists in a process of becoming, as do human beings, even though He may be way ahead of us. In other words, God finds Himself not quite able to handle certain aspects of reality (like evil and suffering) at the present stage. Whitehead tells us God is "growing"; therefore, the day may come when He can cope. Simply stated, God is *not* at this time omnipotent, and His sovereignty is *not* ultimately all-pervasive. He certainly is *not* immutable. Consequently, absolutes virtually fall to the ground. If God is in process and not absolute, how could anything else be? In this context so-called postmodernism was born. Although these statements on process theology are something of an oversimplification of the concept, they do express the basic thrust of the view.

One of the key leaders of this movement has been Norman Pittenger of Cambridge University. Pittenger has said:

He [God] is always *related*, hence always *relational; he is eminently temporal,* sharing in the ongoing, which *is* time. His transcendence is in his sheer faithfulness to himself as love, in his inexhaustibility as lover, and in his capacity for endless adaptation to circumstances in which his love may be active. . . .

We live in a "becoming world," not in a static machine-like world. And God himself is "on the move." Although he is never surpassed by anything in the creation, he can increase in the richness of his own experience and in the relationships which he has with that creation. He is the *living* God; in that sense, we may say (as the title of a book of mine dared to do) that God is "in process."[8]

Although Pittenger's emphasis on the love of God and God's benevolent involvement in the affairs and struggles of His creation is most admirable,

Pittenger drains God of His sovereign immutability and shackles Him with a supposed failure to solve all questions. In his view, God is *not* sovereign.

Pittenger has rejected the theology built on the biblicism Augustine and all conservative evangelicals have contended for. He admits this, saying, "We cannot work with . . . sheer Biblicism in its fundamentalist dress."[9] In a similar spirit, Paul Tillich said, "The Protestant message cannot be a direct proclamation of religious truths as they are given in the Bible."[10]

However, process thought leaves one with disquieting theological and philosophical questions. Despite the relative popularity of the movement, these theologians project themselves into a precarious position. They place themselves on shaky ground, first of all, because most of them will grant that God is the Creator of all reality. But if their process presuppositions are true, then God has created an order of reality (space and time) that He is subject to and an order He cannot quite cope with, at least at this stage in time. They make God the Creator of space and time and yet subject to it. The question then immediately rears its stubborn head: How could God possibly create something, such as space-time,[11] greater or stronger than Himself? Anything God is subject to and cannot handle surely stands as stronger or greater than He. How then could God, who created space-time, be subject to it? That, of course, is nonsense. If God truly did create the entire space-time continuum, how could it ascend and hold sway over God? How could *any* creator create *any* order greater than himself? Actually, process thought makes space-time the ultimate principle, not God. The process thus becomes all but God itself. That projects a very questionable philosophy, not to mention an unbiblical one. The Scriptures state: "With the Lord a day is like a thousand years, and a thousand years are like a day" (2 Pet. 3:8 NIV). God certainly transcends time, not vice versa.

Therefore, process theology falls to the ground in a shambles of inner contradictions if not outright absurdities. God relates to people in their changing attitudes and actions, but God in His essence is true to Himself; He is a constant, sovereign Person who does not change. He is the transcendent "I am." The God of the Bible is ultimate, infinite, transcendent, sovereign, and immutable. He is infinitely beyond the bounds of creation and infinitely above the reasoning of all intelligent creatures. He is the transcendent Lord!

There are other views that cast question marks over the sovereignty of

God that are not quite as serious nor always pressed to the point as are the views of process theologians. So-called liberation theology arises as a case in point. The same could probably be said for some feminist theology as well. In the final analysis, we find ourselves forced back to the Holy Scriptures. They alone present an authoritative base upon which one can build a satisfying theology. And the Bible—along with experience—makes it abundantly clear that God is the sovereign Ruler of all, who wills and it is done. But now to a more positive presentation.

POSITIVE TRUTHS CONCERNING GOD'S SOVEREIGNTY

Jesus said, "With God all things are possible" (Matt. 19:26). The very words of our Lord make it clear that God is sovereign. We see this in the several concepts the Bible spells out as the *attributes* of God. These divine characteristics, though well known, bear repeating. Three specific ideas are central. First, the Scriptures declare God is *omnipotent*. The Bible states that "the Almighty reigns" (Rev. 19:6). The term "Almighty" means God is King, Lord, Ruler with limitless power and authority.

Several things can be said about this attribute of God. The almighty majesty of God is clearly implied in creation itself when God spoke *ex nihilo* this immense universe into being. He declared His sovereignty many times when He called Himself God Almighty (Gen. 17:1). The Hebrew term is *El-Shaddai*. This designation indicates that God must be recognized as all-powerful and impregnable. There is nothing He cannot do (Job 42:2). God has displayed His sovereignty in every aspect of life and has manifested that fact in the entire history of the church and all mankind. He stands as incomparable in quality. Thus the writer of the Revelation exalted with the words: "Worthy art Thou, our Lord and our God, to receive glory and honor and power; for Thou didst create all things, and because of Thy will they existed, and were created" (Rev. 4:11). God rules.

The Bible also testifies that God is *omniscient*. That is to say, everything in all time and space and eternity is visible and knowable to Him. Nothing exists that He does not perfectly contain within His personhood. He even knows the number of the hairs of our head (Matt. 10:30). He is aware of everything in the entire historical sweep of creation from the moment of the Big Bang until the appearance of "a new heaven and a new earth" (Rev. 21:1). God knows all, reads all our thoughts, realizes our every motive, sees our troubles, uncovers our sin, recognizes our faith, and determines our destiny. Transcending time and space, He holds the entire time sequence in His hand. Only sovereign knowledge could do that.

Finally, the Bible states that God is *omnipresent*. God is anything but a "localized" God. He is a far cry from the tribal deities of which the Old Testament speaks. We can never escape His presence. He always stands near, permeating all reality. The Bible says, "Where can I go from Thy Spirit? Or where can I flee from Thy presence? If I ascend to heaven, Thou art there; if I make my bed in Sheol, behold, Thou art there. If I take the wings of the dawn, if I dwell in the remotest part of the sea, even there Thy hand will lead me, and Thy right hand will lay hold of me" (Ps. 139:7–10).

God must not be seen as limited to our four-dimensional world of length, breadth, depth, and time. He stands above it by His infinite transcendent "Otherness." At the same time, He is in and through it all, but He exists beyond it as well. The Bible describes Him as "the High and Lofty One who inhabits eternity" (Isa. 57:15 NKJV). But there are other attributes of God the Bible discloses besides the three aforementioned characteristics; as a case in point, His holiness.

GOD IS HOLY

God must be recognized as absolutely, unequivocally *holy*. Theologians have called Him "the Holy Other." Were we to see God, the one overwhelming attribute that would strike us with awe would be His consuming holiness. Once again, look at Moses on the holy mount; he is distraught and at his wits' end. He cries out for a fresh vision of God. He pleaded, "I pray Thee, show me Thy glory" (Exod. 33:18). God answers graciously, saying that no one could see the Lord and live; yet He would cause all of His glory to pass before Moses. As He passed by, God promised Moses He would place him in the cleft of the rock, putting His hand over Moses' face lest he look upon the Lord and be consumed. Moses would just see the Lord with a backward glance as He was absorbed into the Shekhinah cloud of His glory. When Moses came down from that incredible encounter with Holy God, the Israelites shrank back in fear; Moses didn't realize that the very skin of his face glowed from just that fleeting backward glimpse of God who is "light, and in Him there is no darkness at all" (1 John 1:5). God is absolutely holy. That attribute speaks of His unequivocal sovereignty.

A QUESTION

All of this raises the question: If God is this kind of a sovereign God—omnipotent, omniscient, omnipresent, utter holiness—how can we mere humans ever encounter Him? He seems to be a God so utterly transcendent and so "Other" that in our sin and waywardness and inadequacies we could never come to know Him. But there the other wonderful attributes of God present an answer to the quandary. The Bible strongly emphasizes that God is Love (1 John 4:8). He is also gracious and merciful (Ps. 86:15). He is patient and long-suffering (2 Pet. 3:9). In a word, God in grace comes and relates to us. He is sovereign and a God of utter transcendence, but He also graciously enters into the very midst of our turbulent lives. How does He do it? God so loved us that He gave His only Son that we might have a relationship and meaningful fellowship with Him. The sovereign Lord becomes the loving, redeeming heavenly Father. Wonder of wonders, the sovereign, holy God is a God of grace and wonderful loving compassion who gives us His Son to die for us so as to conquer death. As Karl Barth said, "It is just His lordship over life and death that is the *omnipotence* of God the Father."[12] All these attributes and aspects of God's nature spell His sovereignty—and demand evangelization on our part. This now leads to the issue of how God acts in His sovereign grace in evangelization.

THE ACTIONS OF GOD

If God is all that the Bible and traditional Christianity have claimed Him to be, He acts sovereignly in evangelization. Human intellect, human striving, human sacrifice, religiosity, and anything generated on the human level will never attain the goal of salvation and an intimate relationship with God. Therefore, there is only one hope: God acting in sovereign *grace*. And that is exactly what He has done in the incarnation of Jesus Christ. Thus the message of the life, death, and resurrection of Jesus becomes the most vital, essential dynamic truth human ears can ever hear. That great message of salvation opens up the entire vista of God's redemption and brings His chosen ones into His holy presence. And God moves in sovereign grace and power through the gospel of Christ. What an act of grace and love in the fact that God has seen fit to reveal Himself redemptively in all of His glory to people like us. That is an act of sovereignty and love in its greatest expression.

As we consider the actions of God in His sovereign grace, we recognize that our Lord not only reveals Himself, but in the final analysis actually does the work Himself. It is "God who gives the increase" (1 Cor. 3:7 NKJV). This does not mean that God does not use His church and human agency to further the kingdom. This we have stressed. But we must fully recognize that the kingdom is God's, and He does the work in His sovereign power.

Still, it appears so often the church slips into what Stephen Olford calls "evangelical humanism," i.e., relying on human abilities, schemes, and plans to accomplish God's purpose. A serious word of caution stands in order, especially today it would seem; we must not forget, the sovereign God is the One who acts and accomplishes the task. All human efforts not motivated and led by the Spirit of God and empowered by His divine presence amount to nothing. Jesus said, "Apart from Me you can do nothing" (John 15:5). This demands a proper humble attitude of faith on the part of God's people and an utter reliance on His sovereign acts.

Therefore, it seems most wise to permit the sovereign God to become the focal point of life and gear all evangelistic activities in light of the truth that God reigns as sovereign in all.

CONCLUSION

Theologian Norman Geisler brought it together well when he wrote:

A God who is before all things, beyond all things, creates all things, upholds all things, knows all things, and can do all things is also in control of all things. This complete control of all things is called the sovereignty of God. As the *Westminster Confession of Faith* puts it, "God, from all eternity, did, by the most wise and holy counsel of His own will, freely, and unchangeably ordain whatever comes to pass" (chapter 3). Nothing catches God by surprise. All things come to pass as He ordained them from all eternity.[13]

If this is the nature and work of God, whom the church is attempting to proclaim in its evangelistic thrust, a proper attitude of humility and faith must grip the heart and mind of God's people. Only then can we be assured God will act in His sovereignty and reach out to those who would believe. These truths constitute a vital aspect of historical evangelistic understandings. God's usable evangelists have understood it and ministered on that basis. Does Billy Graham?

PART II:
BILLY GRAHAM AND THE SOVEREIGNTY OF GOD IN EVANGELISM

I believe in the sovereignty of God.

—BILLY GRAHAM

INTRODUCTION

The doctrine of the sovereignty of God in evangelism has at times created many theological and practical questions. Yet, the providence of God in sovereign action as it relates to the Billy Graham ministry stands out in bold relief. One can hardly deny that God has worked sovereignly in the life and ministry of the twentieth century's most renowned evangelist. The Scriptures declare unmistakably that God's sovereignty moves in the entire salvation phenomenon. This reality—and Graham's view of it—must be investigated.

GOD'S SOVEREIGNTY MANIFEST IN THE BILLY GRAHAM STORY

Billy Graham has come to understand that what has transpired in his own life personally, in the team collectively, and in the overall ministry of the

BGEA through the years has been a manifestation of the sovereign providence of God. As Graham states, "Christ comes . . . and says, 'I am Lord! There is no circumstance beyond my power, and you can trust Me.'"[14] Concerning his entire ministry, he has said, "I have no other answer . . . sheer sovereignty chose me to do this work and prepared me in His own way."[15] We have seen the drama of Billy Graham's call to the ministry on the golf course in Temple Terrace, Florida. Graham is convinced that the sovereignty of God moved in that gracious moment of calling him into the ministry. Moreover, he not only believes in God's sovereign call to ministry in a general sense, but he is convinced that God in sovereignty has called him to be a world evangelist. Recall he said, "I believe that God in His sovereignty . . . chose me to do *this work.*" Billy put his finger on it when he stated, "God is in control."[16]

Furthermore, nothing points to God's sovereign leading more than how the Graham team came together. That interesting phenomenon illustrates forcefully God's sovereignty in the forming of the Billy Graham Evangelistic Association (BGEA). Maurice Rowlandson, longtime associate of Billy and director for years of the BGEA London office, said, "If there is any one thing where God has given generously to Billy Graham, it is the gift of wisdom in the selection of colleagues. There can be very few organizations which can show the same loyalty and longevity of their staff and colleagues as is displayed by many of the Billy Graham Team members."[17] And the only answer to that fact rests in the sovereignty of God.

The director of Graham's Washington crusade, Elwyn Cutler, in like manner said that it is marvelous "just to stand back and see how the Lord worked, in ways beyond human understanding, to bring . . . the leadership he wanted."[18] The principle that Cutler expressed concerning the Washington crusade has permeated the entire organization and structure of the Graham ministry. But a human response is demanded. Torrey Johnson, the founder of Youth for Christ, with whom Billy worked for several years, expressed it this way: "God wants you to go."[19] God calls, sends, and works His work through His yielded servants who are willing to go to advance Christ's kingdom. Billy Graham's evangelistic ministry was launched under God's providence as the sovereign God brought the team together, and they responded. A quite fascinating story unfolds in that context.

THE TEAM IS BORN

We have seen in the chapter on the work of the Holy Spirit how God brought the original team together. A brief recap stands in order under the framework of God's sovereignty.

In one of Graham's early ventures in Youth for Christ, he spoke at a large rally in Minneapolis. That event forged a significant bond between Billy and George Wilson, who became Graham's business manager. The first foundation stone was laid in the Graham Association. Probably unknown to Billy Graham at the time, when he served as pastor of Western Springs Baptist Church, an important act of God transpired. Billy enlisted as his soloist on his radio program a man named "Bev" Shea. He has been with Billy Graham for more than half a century and still sings beautifully. Another act of God in sovereignty was set.

And we remember how Grady and T. W. Wilson, along with Billy, had an experience of Christ in the same Charlotte, North Carolina, revival meeting. All three went to Bob Jones College together. The foundations grew. Then in the summer of 1945, with his wife expecting their first child, Graham spoke at the Ben Lippen conference center in Asheville, North Carolina. Someone urged Billy Graham to enlist Cliff and Billie Barrows, two young musicians who were actually on their honeymoon. Cliff and Billie had attended Bob Jones College as had Graham, but they had never met. Cliff led the music and Billie played the piano at the conference. Billy was impressed; another bond was created under God's sovereign grace. Thus the central members of the team were bonded and have remained together in the ministry of evangelism to this day, fifty-plus years later. That is what the sovereignty of God can accomplish.

But God in sovereign grace was not through with bringing together just the basic team. While still working with Youth for Christ, Billy Graham often spoke to military servicemen. In that setting, he met Paul Maddox, chief of chaplains for the European command. Another relationship was forged, and Dr. Maddox spent many years after his retirement from the military with Graham as an assistant, researcher, and adviser. He made a significant contribution to the work. Not too long after the first Los Angeles meeting of 1949, Billy Graham held a three-week crusade in Columbia, South Carolina. The Laymen's Evangelistic Club was the sponsor of that particular effort. The organization hired Willis Haymaker to do the advance work for the Columbia crusade, since he had filled that role in the ministry of evangelists Bob Jones Sr. and Gypsy Smith. Haymaker proved so effective in that position that Graham invited him to join the team as his crusade organizer. It was also in the Columbia meeting that Graham met pianist Tedd Smith, and he too joined the team and has been with the BGEA since.

By 1951, the basic platform team of Graham, Barrows, Shea, Grady Wilson, and Tedd Smith were all serving together. Save the death of Grady Wilson in 1988, they have served since the early days. Little wonder Billy could write: "The Lord is sovereignly directing His own work of redemption."[20]

After the Columbia crusade, Graham traveled to New England for a brief mission at the Boston Gardens. He then launched a sixteen-city tour, followed by a press group led by Jerry Beavan. The journalist had taken leave from Northwestern Schools, where he was employed as the media and public relations director. He joined the Graham team and served as the executive secretary and public relations director. He worked with Graham for many years, ending his career with the Graham Association as director of the London office.

As the ministry expanded, the team obviously grew apace. In those early days, Billy Graham held a crusade in Portland, Oregon. There he was led into broadcasting. In a short time, he was speaking on the American Broadcasting Company's network on Sunday afternoon prime time. The president of the National Religious Broadcasters, Dr. Theodore Elsner, got Graham in touch with his son-in-law, Fred Dienert, an advertising and public relations man. Dienert and his partner, Walter Bennett, specialized in religious work and soon were employed by the Billy Graham Evangelistic Association. Another step forward had been taken.

The fact that Billy Graham broke into radio and television certainly demonstrates that the ministry was expanding under the sovereign purpose of God. The multiplied masses who have heard Graham through radio and television are virtually countless. And the number of converts likewise defies imagination. How God in His wisdom not only brought the team together, but also opened incredible doors of ministry is nothing short of miraculous. Sovereignty is the only answer.

Graham, always concerned that those who made decisions under his ministry had the opportunity for spiritual growth and maturity, sought ways to implement means to effect that vital work. Again, God was at work. The Holy Spirit brought together Graham and Dawson Trotman, the founder of the Navigators organization. In its early days, the Navigators was an evangelical work that ministered to military personnel. Bible memorization and Bible study helps were given to men and women in the military service. Trotman became a key man in the area of Christian growth and discipleship. Under God, Trotman became the leader in Graham's program of new believers' follow-up, later to be led by Charlie Riggs and Tom Phillips.

It has become obvious that through the years God has brought many different personalities into the Graham ministry. Most of them are not as well known as the high-profile personalities mentioned above; yet they have been most significant in the roles they have played. Fascinating is the story of men and women such as Robert and Lois Ferm, Sterling Huston, Walter Smyth, David Bruce, John Corts, John Akers, as well as the associate evangelists, a host of secretaries, and many others. And that is not to mention workers and local people who have volunteered to make the Billy Graham Evangelistic Association what it is. With offices in various parts of the world, the primary headquarters in Minneapolis, and Billy Graham's personal headquarters in Montreat, North Carolina, literally thousands have made their contribution and legacy. Therefore, as President Gerald Ford prayed with Billy Graham, "we acknowledge Thy sovereignty in the selection of our leaders."[21] That prayer was not offered in the sense of political leadership alone, but in all of God's doings. Graham fully acknowledges the sovereignty of God in bringing together his association for the spreading of the gospel to the glory of Jesus Christ.

Perhaps the clearest insight into the spirit of Billy Graham regarding God's hand in the work centers in the fact that he is not a man who seeks any acclaim for himself. He wants all the glory to go to God. He fully realizes the work was born in and continues under the sovereign lead of the Lord. Billy Kim, Graham's interpreter in the Korean crusade and now president of the Baptist World Alliance, relates that in the Korean meetings with multitudes coming to Christ, Billy Graham said, "We are just here watching what God in sovereignty will do."[22] This spirit of humility, no doubt, constitutes one of the reasons that God has so significantly magnified the Graham ministry. As the Reverend Maurice Wood, Bishop of Norwich and a member of the House of Lords in London, has said:

I believe that in each generation God raises up certain people he can trust with success. I would put Billy in line with the Wesleys and St. Augustine. Toss in (St.) Francis if you like. He's in that league, anyway. And what's extraordinary is that he (Graham) doesn't seem to know it. He doesn't want a Graham church. He is more interested in sharing the load than in grabbing the limelight. He wants to be a servant of the church, to challenge and spark the churches to be what they must be—the evangelizing agents of God and his word. But there's no doubt about it; he is the most spiritually productive servant of God in our time.[23]

This is a legitimate evaluation of a man well qualified to speak. So many of Graham's own team members testify to Graham's genuine humble spirit as well. The evangelist knows it is all God's work.

This leads to an evaluation of Graham's understanding of the sovereignty of God in his life and ministry.

GOD'S SOVEREIGNTY AND GRAHAM'S EVANGELISTIC MINISTRY

Beasley-Murray in his commentary on the Gospel of John uses the phrase "the saving sovereignty of God" countless times. Salvation operates under God's sovereignty. Billy Graham, well aware that God has been sovereignly at work in his ministry, essentially agrees with the New Testament scholar and thus related, "The longer I work in crusades the more convinced I am that salvation is of the Lord."[24] Billy went on to say, "I've learned my greatest lesson. It's not by power or might or any fancy sermon, it is wholly and completely the work of the Holy Spirit."[25] Graham acknowledges that in his earlier years he did not entertain strong convictions concerning the sovereignty of God and the work of the Holy Spirit. He confessed, "I used to think that in evangelism I had to do it all, [now] I don't believe any man can come to Christ unless God has drawn him."[26] Through the years, having witnessed the tremendous sovereign work of the Spirit of God, he fully realizes and acknowledges, "The Lord is sovereignly directing His own work of redemption."[27] Moreover, his basic conviction has deepened concerning the salvation experience itself. He said that in salvation, "the new birth is a divine work."[28] "Salvation is all of God."[29] And that is biblical. We must now attempt to get a grasp of what Graham means by these statements.

GOD'S SOVEREIGNTY IN THE PRAGMATICS OF EVANGELISM

Sovereignty is clearly portrayed in William Randolph Hearst's memo to his reporters to "puff Graham." Graham was virtually an unknown young evangelist when the Hearst empire got behind him. The result: Los Angeles, 1949. Then the sovereignty of God became most forcefully evident in the London Harringay crusade of 1954. In some respects that crusade remains the highlight of the Graham ministry. Concerning that mighty outpouring of the Holy Spirit and God's sovereign grace, Graham said, "I am sure that all of you that have been to Harringay have become aware that the atmosphere has been charged with the power of the Holy Spirit. . . . I felt like a spectator standing on the side watching God at work, and wanted to get out of it as much as I could and let Him take over."[30] Such experiences engrained in Graham an utter dependence on the saving sovereignty of God. And that principle is not only reflected in his theology, but in his whole approach to evangelism. He said on one occasion, "We dig our little trenches. 'God, You work right here; and if You don't work here then I won't work with You.' . . . We try to put God in a corner . . . but before you know it God comes out of the corner; . . . the mighty, sovereign God works in His own way."[31] He went on to say, "There's tremendous truth here. God, who is sovereign in bestowing His rewards, understands that some have little opportunity for their service and that their ability is limited, but He proves to them the liberality of His gracious heart."[32]

As stated earlier, understanding God's sovereignty in the work of evangelism has created a genuine spirit of humility in Billy Graham. During a London crusade, in a conversation between Graham and Sir Winston Churchill, the then British prime minister said, "I want to congratulate you for these huge crowds you've been drawing." Billy replied, "Oh well, it's God's doing, believe me." Churchill remonstrated, "That may be, but I dare say that if I brought Marilyn Monroe over here, and she and I went together to Wembley, we couldn't fill it."[33] He had a similar encounter with President Nixon. The president said to him, "It must be unimaginably gratifying to have accomplished such a host and such a reception." Almost instantly Graham replied, "I didn't fill the place; God did it. God has done this, and all honor, credit and glory must go to Him. You can destroy my ministry by praising me for this. The

Bible says that God will not share His glory with another."[34] An inspector in Australia, during a crusade there, said, "There is something here I don't understand. There is something here with depth that is beyond me—it can only be God at work."[35] It can be summed up best in Billy Graham's previously quoted words, "I have no other answer to this, sheer sovereignty chose me to do this work and prepared me in His own way."[36]

When it seems serious errors have at times intruded into Graham's work, God in sovereignty turns it to good. A story of the error in condemning socialism during the 1954 London Harringay crusade will be discussed in detail in a following chapter. Suffice it to say here the nation was upset over the issue. Yet God in His providential sovereignty turned it around for good. The incident gave Graham a high profile, and people came to see whether the "flap" was true. Graham, resting in the sovereignty of God's providence, was able to look back on the affair and say, "In the end, in God's providence, the entire flap . . . got us publicity far beyond anything we could have imagined."[37] But also in relatively minor matters, God's hand can be seen at work. Sterling Huston, North American crusade director, tells the story of the Washington, D.C., crusade in May 1986. The date was set and the Civic Center booked. One day Sterling received a telephone call from the director of the center saying that the Convention Bureau of Washington had double-booked an event at the same time Graham's crusade was to begin. Sterling, realizing the BGEA had more "clout" than the competing party for the venue, decided to lay it out in prayer before God and did not insist on his prerogative. So a new day was set for the Graham crusade. It resulted in getting the expenses for all the facilities at half price, and they were now able to engage the large outdoor stadium for a rally as well. The masses came, many of whom found Christ. God's sovereignty always works for the best. Alan Street was correct when he said, "Billy Graham believes that God has sovereignly called him and equipped him to evangelize the world. He feels he is on a divine mission, sent forth by the King of Heaven and Earth."[38] Such being the case, this leads to the consideration of Graham's own theological, doctrinal approach to God's sovereign work.

BILLY GRAHAM'S THEOLOGY OF SOVEREIGNTY

In his small but insightful book entitled *Evangelism and the Sovereignty of God*, theologian J. I. Packer has asked, "What, then, are we to say about . . . a hearty faith and the absolute sovereignty of God? It undergirds evangelism, and upholds the evangelist, by creating a hope of success that could not otherwise be entertained."[39] Packer, a committed, Reformed thinker, is also committed to evangelism in the context of affirming human freedom.

Here, of course, the problem of divine sovereignty and human responsibility once again rears its head. It would seem on the surface that the doctrine is an outright contradiction. Packer grants the issue is inexplicable, yet still true. Even though it appears to be an insolvable paradox to our finite minds, sovereignty and responsibility are both found in the Scriptures. Therefore, they must be faithfully held in dynamic balance, even if that balance precipitates tension. Through the years, discerning evangelists have seen this reality. To quote again C. H. Spurgeon: "They are two truths of Holy Scripture, and we leave them to reconcile themselves."[40] To this it seems Graham would basically agree. Graham himself has stated, "As human beings deprived of the unlimited vision that God originally intended His creatures to have, we cannot comprehend the glory and magnitude of the Spirit that lies so far outside ourselves."[41] Therefore, "our failure to comprehend God fully should not strike us as strange."[42] God alone can resolve the anomaly in His infinity, so again let it be said, we rest in faith. Thus one is forced to conclude that people are not only responsible to exercise their will in repentance and faith in the Lord Jesus Christ, but the sovereignty of God so operates in the salvation experience that apart from it there will never be any repentance or faith, and hence no salvation. The sovereignty of God constitutes a vital element in the entire program of the extension of the kingdom of God through the proclamation of the gospel and the conversion of the lost. Augustine, Calvin, Zwingli, Luther, the Puritans, and a host of others in the historic chain of examples in this book held such a position. How does Billy Graham think and gear his ministry in the light of this time-honored biblical truth? The answer has already been implied, but now it will be helpful to explore explicitly this particular issue regarding Graham.

BILLY GRAHAM'S APPROACH TO GOD'S SOVEREIGNTY

Billy Graham, in his approach to the problem of God's sovereignty in salvation, is quite conscious of the fact that when attempting to grasp the sovereignty issue one is left with many perplexing quandaries. He said, "Your finite mind is not capable of dealing with anything as great as the love of God. Your mind might have difficulty explaining how a black cow can eat green grass and give white milk—but you drink the milk and are nourished by it. God is utterly perfect and absolute in every detail. . . . He is the holy and perfect God."[43] As seen previously, Graham readily admits there are unresolvable anomalies. This is certainly true in the salvation experience if God is sovereign in His total personhood. Ultimately, sovereignty must impact human salvation. After all, that is life's most important issue. That is why Beasley-Murray, as mentioned earlier, calls it "saving sovereignty." Graham faces this issue and speaks to it.

A basic insight into Graham's view of the sovereignty of God in the salvation experience can be found in an interview with David Frost. Graham said concerning God's action in redemption, "He'll take over. And He won't make any mistakes. There is not going to be anybody in hell who was not supposed to be there, and there's not going to be anybody in heaven who wasn't supposed to be there. And I'll leave it at that."[44] But it must be said that the evangelist does not accept the concept of so-called double predestination, i.e., the view that God elects some to hell. He said, "This does not imply that if a person is lost, God ordained it so."[45] However, he does embrace the concept of eternal security, or better termed, the perseverance of the saints. He said, "Christian conversion is the transformation which we experience when we are born again. Since one is not born over and over again, we must think of Christian development in two phases: birth and growth."[46] Further, Graham states, when "the Holy Spirit seals us or puts His mark on us, we are secure in Christ."[47]

All that constitutes a quite forthright stance. As previously quoted, Graham declares, "Salvation is of God." He apparently means that in the most profound sense. At the same time, Billy Graham, as an evangelist, makes a strong appeal for a human response to the gospel. He calls for repentance and faith. He cannot be questioned about his commitment to full human responsibility. He seems quite content to rest in the paradox; and back of it all he believes in and rests in the sovereignty of God. He and Charles Spurgeon in some sense go hand in hand, although he might not have quite as strong a view on predestination and election as did Spurgeon.

THE BASIS

Graham predicates his view of God's sovereignty on the fact of His great creating hand. When one attempts to answer the question of why God acts as He does, Graham states, "The only possible answer is that all these things and many more are the work of a Supreme Creator. As a watch must have a designer, so must our precision-like universe have a great designer. We call him God. . . . The Bible declares that the God we talk about, the God we sing about, the God from whom all blessings flow is the God who created this world and placed us in it."[48] The creative hand of God must also be seen in bringing about the salvation of straying mankind, whom He has created. But this God remains inscrutable. Graham has said, "God is a spirit, infinite, eternal, the unchangeable. That definition of God has been with me all my life, and when a man knows in his heart that God is infinite, eternal, and unchanging spirit it helps to overcome the temptation to limit Him."[49] Although this great God transcends all, He is by our side to help us, guide us, strengthen us, and meet our needs. He is hidden, yet imminent. In the words of Francis Shaeffer, He is the "God who is there."

HISTORICAL TESTIMONY

Wayne Stanley Bonde, a biblical scholar, has contended that among the theological assumptions that constitute the basic tenets of Protestant evangelism is belief in "the sovereignty of God over human life."[50] Bonde states that the principle was held by many historical evangelistic luminaries, such as Roger Williams, Thomas Hooker, George Whitefield, Jonathan Edwards, and Billy Graham. Moreover, the position has a history of effective evangelism behind it. Bonde argues that in the doctrine of the sovereignty of God, classical Protestantism rests on the Bible; as found in Augustine, Aquinas, Luther, and more dramatically associated with John Calvin. He quotes from Calvin's *Instruction in Faith:* "We contemplate, therefore, in this universality of things, the immortality of our God, from which immortality have proceeded the beginning and origin of all things . . . for, the seed of the word of God takes root and brings forth fruit only in those whom the Lord, by his eternal election, has predestined to be children and heirs of the heavenly kingdom."[51]

Bonde, in his understanding of Billy Graham, sees the evangelist adhering to this basic reformed view. But again, at the same time, he is quick to point out that historic evangelism has also contended that "man has freedom of will to choose the grace of God."[52] Recognizing the enigma of divine sovereignty and human responsibility, he contends that Graham rests in that historic stream.

There is credence in Bonde's contention as Edward Vaughn, in an unpublished Ph.D. thesis, has quoted Graham as praying, "Our Father and our God, we pray in Christ's name, that all of those whom thou hast chosen in Christ will surrender their wills to the Savior tonight and we pray that the Holy Spirit will convict of sin and of righteousness and the judgment and point them to the Lamb of God that taketh away the sin of the world."[53] Graham further prayed on another occasion, "Our Father and our God, we pray that the Holy Spirit will draw those to thyself whom *thou hast chosen in Christ*" (emphasis added).

It does seem obvious that Graham's theology of divine sovereignty and human responsibility maintains the biblical balance that traditional evangelicalism has espoused through the centuries of church history. Graham feels quite comfortable to talk about "the Father's sovereign will"[54] and at the same time contend, "We must all enter the kingdom of heaven with the simple faith and trust as a child."[55] Again let it be made clear that Graham lives with the ultimate, suprarational truth that God is sovereign in salvation but that all mankind must respond in their free choice of faith and repentance.

As much difficulty as some people have over the issue, it can be summarized and to some degree resolved with what J. I. Packer states: "The root cause is the same as in most cases in error in the church—the intruding of rationalistic speculations, the passion for systematic consistency, a reluctance to recognize the existence of mystery and to let God be wiser than man, and consequence subjecting of Scripture to the supposed demands of human logic."[56] Thus accepting the revealed truth in God's Word, Packer has correctly said, "Faith and the sovereignty and governing grace of God is the only thing that can sustain [evangelism], for it is the only thing that can give us the resilience that we need if we are to evangelize boldly and persistently."[57] The whole Graham phenomenon stands, it would seem, as a token of that essential principle of the sovereignty of God in evangelistic ministry. Graham is very willing to let "God be God." In all the rational difficulties, one must remember that the infinite always will remain a mystery—a divine mystery. Philosopher John Newport speaks of the issue as "the silence of God's sovereignty."[58] Graham has correctly declared, "Christianity can never be reduced to reason alone."[59] In speaking of John's vision recorded in the Book of Revelation, Billy confesses, "God remained a mystery to John and to us—the mystery who was and is and will always be—[but] the mystery worthy of our glory and honor and power."[60] But at the same time, as stressed, the great infinite, mysterious God works very intimately with us for our salvation. Wonder of wonders!

Thus Billy Graham visualizes God working sovereignly in evangelism in a threefold sense: (1) Evangelism is *of* God, as stressed, (2) evangelism is *through* God, and (3) evangelism is to the *glory* of the sovereign Lord. A brief look at these major points and how they are illustrated in Graham's ministry seems apropos to close this particular aspect on God's sovereign work in world evangelization.

SALVATION IS OF THE LORD

The fact that evangelism emanates from the sovereign God, Billy Graham sees unfolding in a threefold fashion in the Scriptures. First, evangelism is God's plan for people's eternal redemption (John 3:16). "God's saving sovereignty is precisely life eternal," as Beasley-Murray points out in his commentary on John.[61] Second, evangelism, which centers in the *kerygma,* is God's command (Matt. 28:1–20; Acts 1:8). Third, obedience is the Christian response to God's sovereign command (John 14:21). To this threefold truth, Billy Graham resonates. As Paul wrote to the Romans, "For from Him and through Him and to Him are all things. To Him be the glory forever. Amen" (Rom. 11:36). In the final analysis, all ministry, and that means evangelism, rests finally in God. The mighty God is the Author, the Originator, and the Power and Presence in all effective service. Not only do the Scriptures make this truth obvious, but history also attests to its reality. Again, limitation of space forbids recounting the multiple incidents that illustrate the point. Perhaps one, from a personal perspective, is indicative of this concept in the life and understanding of Billy Graham.

In 1970, this author and his wife had the privilege of speaking and preaching in the Central Baptist Church of Moscow. These were difficult days for the church of the Lord Jesus Christ—Baptists, Methodists, Orthodox, and all religious groups. One of the seasoned leaders of the Moscow Baptist Church,

Reverend Mitzcovich, a dear brother who had suffered much for his faith, one day took us to a large sports stadium in the Moscow area. When we got to the stadium, he looked over the vast arena and said, "I am praying every day that the hour will come when Billy Graham will be able to preach here to the masses of Moscow." Quite naturally, we wondered if that prayer would ever be answered. The Cold War was at its height; the power of the Soviet Union with its nuclear arsenal was awesome. Atheism reigned. How could it ever come to pass? But God is sovereign in evangelism. Some years later, Gorbachev introduced the principles of glasnost and *perestroika.* The door for Billy Graham in Eastern Europe began to open. He preached in Hungary, and by God's sovereign hand, he was at last invited to Moscow. He conducted a traditional evangelistic crusade with all the preparation that he normally makes in any foreign country right in the heart of Moscow. God in sovereignty answered Brother Mitzcovich's prayer. Only God could accomplish such a feat of grace. As Dr. Tom Phillips, longtime associate in the BGEA, points out, in the context of difficult circumstances such as opposition, logistics, bad weather, or whatever, Billy is confident the gospel rests in the hands of the sovereign God and will call people to salvation. The evangelist has absolute confidence in that truth.

Moreover, through God's sovereign providence, virtually the entire world has opened to Billy Graham. And he has responded, as John Pollock, Graham's biographer, entitled his book: *To All the Nations: The Billy Graham Story.* Graham constantly lifts up the principle with the oft-quoted simple statement: "Salvation is of God."[62] Therefore, as one of Billy's team members said, "We must never presume upon the grace of God. Just because the Holy Spirit moves in amazing power once does not necessarily mean He is obligated to repeat revival in the same city."[63] Such sovereignty demands humility and submission.

Furthermore, not to sound repetitive, but it must be stressed, the principle of sovereignty that Graham espouses operates on a very personal individual level. The evangelist wrote, ". . . It is impossible for man to turn to God to repent, or even to believe without God's help! All you can do is call upon God to turn you. . . . When a man calls upon God, he is given true repentance and faith."[64] And all are certainly free and responsible to call upon God. That simple equation gets to the heart of Billy Graham's grasp of personal salvation. The evangelist is fully committed to the principle Paul elucidated in 1 Corinthians 1:26–29: "For consider your calling, brethren." God does call to salvation. The Scriptures forthrightly declare it. Graham believes that, saying, "In the Bible God has spoken verbally, and this spoken word has survived every scratch of human pen."[65] For the evangelist, the Bible says it, and that settles it. Salvation is of God.

SALVATION IS THROUGH GOD

The supreme power for evangelism rests in the moving of the Holy Spirit in the communication of the gospel. Two basic principles emerge from this truth. First, the Holy Spirit's work in the life of the unbeliever leads that person to salvation. As the author of the fourth Gospel put it, "When He comes, [He] will convict the world concerning sin, and righteousness, and judgment" (John 16:8). If anything can be said about Billy Graham, he is fully cognizant of the Holy Spirit's leading in salvation. He said in his autobiography concerning the London crusade, "I was almost filled with fear. In my entire life, I had never approached anything with such a feeling of inadequacy as I did in London. If God did not do it it could not be done."[66] He went on to say, "As the crusade gained momentum, I found myself becoming more and more dependent on God. I knew that all that we had seen happening in Britain was the work of God."[67] Graham fully acknowledges the work of the Holy Spirit in the context of God's sovereignty in addressing the gospel to people. As Graham has said, "God must prepare our hearts."[68] But all this has been made amply clear in the chapter on Billy Graham and the Holy Spirit.

Second, the Holy Spirit not only works in the life of unbelievers in convicting them of sin, righteousness, and judgment, but the Holy Spirit also moves in and through the life of the evangelist in the task of communicating the gospel effectively. John has said, "But the Helper, the Holy Spirit, whom the Father will send in My name, He will teach you all things" (John 14:26). Billy Graham testifies to this principle by saying, "I rarely leave without attempting to explain the meaning of the gospel."[69] He knows that the gospel becomes the instrument the Spirit of God uses in bringing the truth of Christ to the human heart in order to create conversions. Therefore, he must explain the "Good News" to people. At the same time, however, Billy confesses, "Now I know that I may preach it [the gospel] rather poorly and I know that maybe some evening I may not be feeling up to par physically and all the rest of it and I leave out many things that I wanted to say. But . . . God uses even that simple presentation that might have been poorly done and he applies it to the human heart because salvation, the Bible says, is of God."[70] Billy sees his proper role. The Holy Spirit uses the evangelist as the human agent, communicating the gospel, thus effecting redemption. Again from his autobiography, Graham said, "I was merely the preacher, the messenger. None of what was happening could have happened apart from God."[71]

Billy Graham realizes that not only he, but also the team members, must understand this principle and serve on that basis. And they do. The director of international crusades for many years, Walter Smyth, said on one occasion, "We can waste a lot of time and effort, we can promote, we can do all kinds of things; but if we don't have the blessing of almighty God, our work's going to be in vain . . . so it's not the work of a man—it's the work of the Spirit of God."[72] Smyth's reaction is typical of the Graham team. Billy has said, "With each passing year . . . [we feel] more dependence on the power of the Holy Spirit."[73] He is the supreme power for evangelism. Evangelism is *through* God.

EVANGELISM TO GOD

The culmination of biblical evangelism must rebound to the glory of the sovereign God. This presents the "why" of evangelism. Great glory accrues to God when His people, evangelists or laypeople, submit themselves to the sovereignty of God and share the gospel with unbelievers. This was true in the evangelistic ministry of our Lord. Paul stated, "For I say that Christ has become a servant to . . . the Gentiles to glorify God for His mercy; as it is written, 'Therefore I will give praise to Thee among the Gentiles, and I will sing to Thy name'" (Rom. 15:8–9). God is exalted when people in their need and in their sin come through the path of repentance and faith and experience the transforming power of Christ. Jesus said, "By this is My Father glorified, that you bear much fruit, and so prove to be My disciples" (John 15:8). The Bible even goes so far as to say that there is more joy in heaven over one sinner who repents than over ninety-nine righteous persons who need no repentance: "There is rejoicing in the presence of the angels of God over one sinner who repents" (Luke 15:10 NIV). When sinners repent, God's grace is magnified and He is thereby glorified; thus, the angels rejoice with exaltation and praise to the salvation that is of Him, through Him, and finally to Him. The motivation issue demands a few more words.

THE MOTIVATION

The natural outcome of these essential truths means that the task of evangelism must ultimately be motivated by seeking the praise and honor of God. That becomes the prime motivation. John Stott, in his work *Our Guilty Silence,* outlines three motives to evangelize: (1) God's command, (2) the unbeliever's need, and (3) the glory ascribed to God. God's glory is the supreme motivation. As the apostle Paul said to the Corinthians, "Whether, then, you eat or drink or whatever you do, do all to the glory of God" (1 Cor. 10:31). Can it be said of Graham that the glory of God is his basic motivation in evangelism?

It is no problem to hear Billy Graham expressing himself concerning his motivation in world evangelization. He is very conscious of the fact that God "is not going to divide His honor with anybody."[74] It would be easy for the evangelist to take credit for himself. With all the accolades Billy has received, the temptation for self-glorification must surely exist. But Graham always manifests the attitude, as he expressed it: "We could not help but be overwhelmed by the response we had seen almost everywhere. . . . But [it was] a response we could only attribute to God."[75] He told one writer, "There is something here with depth that is beyond me—it can only be God at work." Therefore, Graham always insists, as he said to President Nixon, "God has done this and all the honor, credit, and glory must go to Him."[76] That says it all.

Of course, there are those who criticize Graham for the extensive crusade publicity and what some would see as the exalting of his persona. He has said many times over he wishes he could dispense with all the advertisement using his name. As stressed so often in many interviews with team members and others, the testimony of his humility constantly surfaces. The reason for the publicity, however, rests in the fact that Graham recognizes that we live in a day, especially in the Western world, when people are drawn to personalities. Thus it seems wise to utilize that mentality for the good of the crusades. Moreover, we must remember that the sovereign God does use His people in evangelization and ministry. Therefore, with reluctance, he lets his name go forward. But his inner circle is very conscious of his genuine spirit of humility; he truly desires that the honor and glory for what is transpiring in his evangelistic ministry ultimately culminate in the praise of God. Salvation is of, through, and to the sovereign God. To this Graham has committed himself.

A BRIEF SUMMARY

Therefore, fully recognizing the sovereignty of God in the entire evangelistic enterprise of the universal church, Billy Graham strives to keeps a biblical, historical perspective. It seems fair to say, he attempts to keep the fact of God's sovereignty in his theology, in his work, and in his own life as well. For Graham, God is all in all in the winning of people to faith in Jesus Christ. The doxology of Jude thus befits the evangelist: "To God our Savior, who alone is wise, be glory and majesty, dominion and power, both now and forever, Amen" (Jude 25 NKJV).

CONCLUSION AND CONTRIBUTION OF BILLY GRAHAM CONCERNING GOD'S SOVEREIGNTY

The conclusion to this chapter can begin with the simple declaration: "God is sovereign." Yet such a declaration is profound indeed. It means there is nothing He does not know, no place He does not occupy, nothing He cannot do. God is in control. No event transpires that He does not sanction, no space-time principle He has not ordered, no human action He does not allow. This is His creation and He rules and runs it.

Granted, this truth possesses problems. How do evil and suffering figure in the issue? Where did evil arise and why does God permit it? What about human freedom of will and responsible choice? These and many more perplexities thrust themselves forward. And though there can be found no completely satisfactory answer on this side of eternity, it still remains true: God is sovereign. But it is also true that the day will come when all questions will be answered and God's sovereignty at last understood. Until that day, "we walk by faith, not by sight" (2 Cor. 5:7).

That is how Billy Graham grasps it all—as this chapter has endeavored to reveal. Moreover, he orders his life and evangelistic ministry on that basis. This can be seen in a multiplicity of ways. As has been pointed out in these pages, God has sovereignly bared His arm in calling the evangelist, putting together the team, preventing them from making tragic blunders that would undo the ministry, protecting them in the many onslaughts that have come their way, honoring the ministry with blessings and many won to Christ, keeping the team intact, and in a thousand other ways. And Billy knows it well.

But then, such divine action has been true through biblical times and in the entire course of evangelistic history. After all, the mission is God's and the kingdom is His. He will not ultimately let His work suffer defeat. The kingdom will one day extend to the far reaches of the entirety of creation. True evangelists of any age recognize this truth and operate on that basis, and that, it would seem, includes Billy Graham. In light of all that has been written in this chapter, the only logical conclusion is that Billy well recognizes and honors God's sovereignty. He knows that what has transpired in his own life and ministry can only be attributed to the sovereign Lord. His conversion, his call, the team, the open doors, the countless conversions, the entire work over the years attest to God's power. Billy gladly acknowledges that fact and lets it be known. One of his favorite statements, as we have seen, is, "When I get to heaven I am going to ask God 'Why me?'" Of course, he really knows the answer God will give: "Because I chose you; I am sovereign and I do as I wish." That will settle the question.

Is there a practical, legitimate contributory outcome because of the fact of God's sovereignty in the Graham ministry? The answer again is *yes*. Several things surface to verify that contention:

- It has given Graham a spirit of humility that is a challenge to others.
- It has inspired the faith of many to rest in God's sovereignty in the extreme circumstances of life.
- It has put God where He belongs in the thinking of many.
- It has guided the entire Graham team, and God has been pleased to bless the ministry to millions.
- It falls in line with the history of evangelism that gives it veracity.
- It has brought glory to God, which always blesses others.

That is a biblical, historical truth and a proper approach to evangelism. Graham has thus made his contribution and legacy and falls in the historic line of evangelical evangelism.

Still, there is more to Christian evangelism than just conducting giant crusades and holding to a strong view of God's sovereignty, as important as that is. Jesus Christ must be at the center and heart of it all. That is to say, a proper Christological foundation must be laid and permeate the entire enterprise. The next chapter will address that issue regarding the Graham ministry.

CHAPTER 5

CHRISTOLOGY IN EVANGELISM

∽

PART I:
ATHANASIUS AND THE CHRISTOLOGICAL
ISSUE IN EVANGELISM

For . . . His becoming Incarnate we were the object,
and for our salvation He dealt so lovingly.
—ATHANASIUS

INTRODUCTION

Athanasius was born in 296, some forty-two years after the death of the noted church leader Origen. At the departure of Origen in 254, considerable theological ferment began to infiltrate the Christian movement. Athanasius became the bishop of Alexandria, Egypt, the city of his birth, and in that context made his contribution. Historical evangelism owes Athanasius a deep debt, as we shall see.

By the third century, Egypt was fast becoming an important center in the

Christian movement. At the time, Alexandria boasted of being a leading intellectual center in the Roman Empire. Churches and educational institutions grew and multiplied. Athanasius himself received his education at the catechetical school in his native city. In his early ministerial years he became a deacon in the church and secretary to Alexander, then the bishop of Alexandria. Being active in theological issues from the inception of his ministry, he served as attendant to Alexander at the Council of Nicea in 325 and then succeeded him as bishop of Alexandria in 328.

THE COUNCIL OF NICEA

The Council of Nicea will always be recognized as a most important moment. A serious Christological controversy had permeated the church, and as a result that central issue dominated the proceedings. In the setting of the Council, Arius, a presenter and leader, entertained a very faulty view concerning the person of Christ. In essence, he denied the full deity of Jesus. Many had embraced his low Christology, however, and the controversy thus raged. But through the influence of Athanasius, and his skillful presentation of a sound Christology, the Arian heresy was defeated by the attenders at Nicea and a new creed was formulated. A biblical evangelical view of the person of Jesus Christ won the day. Of course, remnants of the battle carried on; error does not die simply because a council decrees it. But a severe blow was dealt to Arius and his followers. With the victory creed in hand, Athanasius continued his contention for a proper view of Jesus Christ. Gaining a firmer grasp of the issue will help to understand Arius and his views.

ARIUS THE THEOLOGIAN

Arius was no second-class scholar. However, as stated, he developed a quite faulty view of the person of Christ. Origen, who preceded both Arius and Athanasius, had written on the subject and written well, although some of his ideas were inconsistent and left a legacy of theological ambiguity. As might be expected, both Arius and Athanasius convinced themselves they were following Origen, at least as they understood him. Arius argued for the subordination of the Son to the Father. He saw that concept as an absolute, contending that Jesus lacked God the Father's full nature because the New Testament presents Him as the "first-born among many" (Rom. 8:29). Being begotten of the

Father, Arius argued, Christ could not be coequal with the Father in the full sense and thus not enjoy an equal status with the Father. Arius argued that the Father is "ruler of all," and therefore by logical deduction He would be something of a "ruler" over Christ, His Son. This would mean that in speaking of the attribute of omnipotence, for example, that designation must be restricted to God the Father. On the other hand, Athanasius contended for what he termed—leaning on Origen—the "eternal generation of the Son." That is to say, Christ was coequal and coeternal with the Father. It reduced itself to this: Arius embraced subordination of the Son, and Athanasius argued for the full deity of Jesus Christ. The problem of the Trinity had arisen again.

Interestingly, Arius served as a priest in Alexandria when in 318 he began his public campaign of negating the full deity of Jesus. No one questioned the intellectual acumen of Arius. He was trained at the theological school in Antioch, where he was no doubt deeply impressed by the Aristotelian philosophy that dominated the Antiochian school. Arius apparently imbibed the idea of the subordinate status of Jesus to the Father from an Aristotelian rationalistic epistemology, arguing that even the differences in the names of the Father and the Son implied a difference of substance. He would point out, for instance, that an apple was not a tree; that is why different names are given to them. The Father and the Son, therefore, must be different in substance as the divine Persons are named differently in the Scriptures. To Arius, this meant that if the Father was God, the Son could not also be God, at least not in the same full sense of the word. Arius granted that Christ could be divine, but His divinity would only be partial and derivative because of His sonship to the Father.

The two key verses from which Arius argued were Proverbs 8:22, "The LORD possessed me at the beginning of His way, before His works of old," and Colossians 1:15, "He [Jesus] is the image of the invisible God, the first-born of all creation." As Gerald Bray, theological historian, pointed out:

The result of all of this was Arianism, the belief that Jesus was a divine creature who had entered the human race. Its spiritual power lay in the attractiveness of having a savior who was like us (as a creature) yet more powerful (because he was a divine being). It avoided the crude adoptionism of Paul of Samosata, who had taught that Jesus was a mere man, without so far identifying Jesus with God as to make it impossible for him to experience human suffering and death. Arianism was a subtle heresy, which had an answer for everything, and it had a wide popular appeal. It was not stamped out in the Greek-speaking world until after the death of one of its champions, the emperor Valens, in 378.[1]

Of course, it goes without saying that many of the Arian arguments revolved around the struggle to find an answer to the doctrine of the Trinity. Many ideas arose in the attempt to unravel the mystery of the Trinity, often attacking the essential doctrine of Christ's deity. Some of these errors included Apollinarianism, Nestorianism, Adoptionism, etc. A serious battle raged, and it was fought out in various ways. Theological debate, writings, and conferences ensued. Arius himself even wrote hymns to convey his message. As one historian suggested, "This is a good example of heretical 'evangelism'!"[2] Taking the lead on the battlefield, Arius followed the approach of Aristotle and Plato, arguing vehemently that the Son and the Spirit were mere emanations from the ultimate Father God. Arius seemingly was too rationalistic in his epistemological approach to accept "mystery" in the Godhead. Against this, Athanasius stood strong for the total deity of Jesus Christ.

ATHANASIUS THE WARRIOR

Athanasius spoke out, argued, and wrote in his war against the Arian error. As a consequence, he incurred the enmity of the powerful Arianizing party, especially during the reigns of Constantine and Constantius. This conflict resulted in the deposing of Athanasius from his bishopric by these Roman emperors, sending him into exile. He was first banned to Trier in 336. Upon the death of Constantine in 337, Athanasius returned to Alexandria, but in 339 he was again forced to flee to Rome. There he established a close affiliation with the Western church. This move did not rupture his relationship with the Eastern church, however. Nonetheless, Athanasius continued in close contact with the West throughout the remainder of his life.

The emperor restored Athanasius to his position in Alexandria in 346. But in 356 he was again deposed from his leadership role in the church. Athanasius remained in hiding in Alexandria until the accession of Julian in 361, but one year later, Julian also exiled him. However, in just one year, in 363, Julian died and Athanasius once again resumed his position as bishop of Alexandria. He endured one more short exile in 365.

It was a turbulent time indeed for the contender of the faith. Of the forty-six years Athanasius served as bishop of Alexandria, seventeen were spent in exile. In his later years, Athanasius devoted the rest of his life to building up the Nicene party. And to the credit of his tenacity and willingness to suffer, his orthodox Christology finally triumphed victoriously over the Arian party in the decree of the Council of Constantinople in 381, some eight years after his death. Athanasius died in Alexandria the first week in May of 373, a victor in the battle for the heart and center of Christianity: the person of Jesus Christ.

After Athanasius's death, the creed for which he so strongly contended was included in the Church Council that met in 381. It reads as follows:

THE NICENE CREED

> We believe in one God, the Father, almighty,
> Maker of heaven and earth
> of all that is, seen and unseen.
> We believe in one Lord Jesus Christ, the only Son of God,
> eternally begotten of the Father,
> God from God, Light from Light,
> true God from true God,
> begotten, not made,
> of one Being with the Father.
> Through Him all things were made.
> For us and for our salvation
> He came down from heaven:
> by the power of the Holy Spirit
> he became incarnate from the Virgin Mary,
> and was made man.
> For our sake he was crucified under Pontius Pilate;
> he suffered death and was buried.
> On the third day he rose again
> in accordance with the Scriptures;
> he ascended into heaven

and is seated at the right hand of the Father.

He will come again in glory to judge the living and the dead,

and his kingdom will have no end.

We believe in the Holy Spirit, the Lord, the giver of life,

Who proceeds from the Father and the Son.

With the Father and Son he is worshipped and glorified.

He has spoken through the Prophets.

We believe in one holy Catholic and apostolic Church.

We acknowledge one baptism for the forgiveness of sins.

We look for the resurrection of the dead,

and the life of the world to come. Amen.

— BOOK OF COMMON PRAYER, 1990

Historians contend that some dispute arose as to whether it was actually the original creed. The issue was raised at the Council of Chalcedon in 451. However, as Gerald Bray points out, "this Creed is now included in the proceedings of the Council of 381 [Nicea], a place which is confirmed in the decrees of the fifth and sixth session of the Council of Chalcedon."[3] Regardless of the historical problem, it certainly expresses what Athanasius believed and taught and stood for. It remains as a tribute to his willingness to contend for full deity of Jesus Christ.

AN EVALUATION OF THE MAN, HIS BATTLES, AND THE IMPLICATIONS

It has been implied that Athanasius won his war completely. But he did not always emerge victorious, especially in some of the earlier skirmishes. One impediment to his early success rested in the fact that he had a faulty Greek translation of the New Testament Scriptures. Moreover, he did not know Hebrew. Thus he was inclined to accept a verse like Proverbs 8:22, cited above, as purely Christological. This weak hermeneutic did not help his argument in the beginning days of the battle. But he soon overcame these early handicaps and grew in scriptural knowledge and the wise use of the Bible. He became an able Bible scholar and exegete, employing the Scripture in a clear and forceful manner as he grew in his biblical grasp. For example, he departed from the questionable allegorizing tendency of the Alexandrian school; that constituted a major departure in that day. Athanasius sought to demonstrate the logic of Scripture as a whole, striving to demonstrate that the Bible made the incarnation of the Word of God inevitable. As one put it, "God did not become a man because some philosopher thought it would be a good idea, but because He has created man in His own image. It was because man was uniquely related to God—so uniquely that even angels did not share in their relationship—that only God could make good Adam's disobedience and restore the human race to fellowship with Himself."[4] Athanasius raised his banner high. He fought vigorously because he realized that attacking the person of Christ ultimately meant attacking the very foundation of the Christian faith.

The implications of Christology for salvation and redemption, not to mention the proclamation of a gospel of integrity, are clearly most profound. Thus Athanasius fought a crucial battle. As the war continued, Athanasius gained more and more strength. It can be said that Arius was essentially "dethroned" at the Council of Nicea, even though his ideas were far from being totally eradicated. In some respects the war still goes on today, especially whenever the divinity of Christ is impugned. Yet, one wonders where the church would be today had not Athanasius fought so valiantly. Athanasius made one of his most significant contributions on the Christological issue when he penned his renowned book, *De Incarnatione* (On the Incarnation). It remains in print to this day. The evangelistic context for the writing is patent; in essence, it was an evangelistic tract designed to win pagans to faith in Jesus Christ. In that work he did not attack Arius directly; he simply attempted to present an orthodox Christology that would defeat subtle heresies and win people to faith in Jesus Christ. If Jesus is not who the Bible claims He is, evangelism dies. Scriptural evangelism is first and foremost *Christ-centered*. To this truth, history puts its stamp of authenticity and approval.

Athanasius contended forcefully and convincingly that the whole of salvation history points up in bold relief the fact that the incarnation of Christ was the logical necessity in the redemptive plan of God. In his four *Discourses*, he attacked the Arians specifically and repudiated their interpretations of their favorite proof texts. His skillful use of the Scripture established him as the leading evangelical theologian of the time. As historian Gerald Bray put it, "His name became a hallmark of orthodoxy."[5]

ATHANASIUS'S ORTHODOX CHRISTOLOGY

Athanasius's argument in his famous *De Incarnatione*, which he penned while still in his twenties, contended that God the Son by His union with humanity had in His life, death, and resurrection become the restorer of fallen humanity back to the image of God. Christ overcame death and the consequences of sin. Further, Athanasius accepted the full humanity of Jesus; he was certainly not docetic (denying Jesus' humanity). He felt very comfortable holding the mystery of Jesus being fully man and fully God. Athanasius did not succumb to the rationalism of the Greeks. He could live with the tension of the God-man. The implications for evangelism are obvious.

The climax of the life and ministry and tenacious quest for Christological orthodoxy of Athanasius stands as a monument to the work of the Spirit of God in preserving the centrality of Jesus Christ. Although Athanasius himself had passed on, his work bore fruit and came to its culmination at the Council of Chalcedon in 451. That particular council, for all practical purposes, once and forever settled the issue of the nature of Jesus Christ for evangelicals. It came out of many years of controversy to be sure, but it stands as a monument to the dedication of this man of God. His name will always endure as one of the great contributors to orthodoxy and evangelistic zeal. True evangelism is Christ-centered in every aspect of the endeavor. It becomes the test of legitimacy and authenticity for the evangelist. But what does the Bible itself teach about the person of the Lord Jesus Christ? This must be seen in some detail.

BIBLICAL CHRISTOLOGY

The crucial question in Christological theology centers in what the Bible means by "the Word became flesh" (John 1:14), i.e., the meaning of the incarnation. Who was Jesus? New Testament scholar George Beasley-Murray contended, "In my judgment, the key Christological issue is the reality of the true manhood and real divinity of Christ (more exactly, his deity). The tendency of many is to insist that if Jesus is man, he cannot be God."[6] In this dynamic and controversial area of study, various concepts have emerged, expressed in three rather technical terms: *anhypostasia, kenosis,* and *lordship.* Of course, in the arena of Christological thought, theologians have set forth many positions.

This study must be restricted to the three ideas listed above that can produce problems; then we shall present a balanced, evangelical biblical view.

THE ANHYPOSTASIA CONCEPT OF THE INCARNATION

This view, quite current in some theological circles today, is anything but new. It centers on the idea that in the person of Jesus Christ there was no true full humanity, no distinct human *personality*. Adherents to this concept contend that Jesus of Nazareth was a divine personality merely assuming a human nature. That is to say, Christ was not really a *human* person, but a *divine* person who took upon Himself a human nature, but not a human personality. This ancient approach to Christology first found followers during the church's controversy with the Nestorians in the fifth century. Some say it had an even earlier expression, at least in incipient form, among the Apollinarians. At any rate, Cyril of Alexandria in his polemic against the Nestorians gave the concept its first full airing during the fifth-century theological controversies. The Nestorians argued that Mary gave birth to the human Jesus, but not to the eternal Son of God.

Emil Brunner, somewhat an exponent of the anhypostasia view, brought his unique interpretation to the issue. He declared a distinction is to be drawn between the "personality" of Jesus, which is a historical reality, and His "Person," which is the nonhistorical mystery of the Godhead. That is to say, the personality of Jesus is no more than human nature assumed by the Second Person of the Godhead, thus taking the place of a human "person" in Jesus.[7]

The weakness of Brunner's approach centers on the fact that any attempt to divide the ego is a sheer abstraction, for the ego is clearly a unity. As Donald Baillie expressed it, "It must be sheer nonsense to maintain that in the case of Jesus the one [nature] was divine while the other was human. For the transcendental and the empirical ego are not distinct entities at all, but the two sides of the same entity. . . . That is meaningless, for human nature thus separated is an abstraction."[8]

The problem with anhypostasia concepts centers on the apparent reluctance of its advocates to make Jesus genuinely and fully human while at the same time fully divine, which the Bible clearly teaches. And Donald Baillie's contention that one cannot destroy the unity of Christ's personhood certainly is correct. Chalcedon settled that issue. Anhypostasia can even degenerate into a docetism, which stresses the divinity of Jesus to the point that His humanity becomes drastically weakened.

THE KENOTIC THEORY OF THE INCARNATION

The kenotic concept is a relatively modern theory. It takes its primary lead from the Greek term *kenosis* ("emptied"). In Philippians 2, Paul wrote of Jesus, "Who, though he was in the form of God, did not count equality with God a thing to be grasped, but *emptied himself*, taking the form of a servant, being born in the likeness of men" (Phil. 2:6–7 RSV, emphasis added). The biblical origin of the *kenosis* idea is obvious. However, can the passage in Philippians, which is clearly poetic (or even a hymn), support all the theological weight it is called upon to bear in modern versions of the kenotic theory?

The basic thrust of this idea revolves around the contention that the Son of God, the divine Logos, laid aside His full divine attributes (omniscience, omnipresence, omnipotence, etc.), divested himself of His ultimacy for a period of time, and lived on earth with all the limitations of humanity. In other words, He "emptied" Himself *(ekenosen)* of His transcendence and became a man.

Will this approach, however, hold up to all that the word *incarnation* demands? Granted, Paul was certainly correct when he stated Christ "emptied" Himself. Moreover, Vincent Taylor argued convincingly that at least some form of kenotic Christology is essential to any "worthy doctrine of the incarnation."[9] But can the *whole* answer to the incarnation be found in *kenosis* alone? That is the problem we must answer.

First, as Donald Baillie asked, "What happened to the rest of the universe during our Lord's self-emptying period?"[10] The Bible tells us clearly the omnipotent Son of God continually sustains the universe (Col. 1:17).

Second, the kenotic theory in its extreme form sounds perilously close to an incarnation that is no more than some sort of theophany. That is, the Son of God, formerly the Transcendent One, changed Himself temporarily into a man. He laid aside His full divinity and took up humanity to reveal God. But as Donald Baillie properly contended, this idea is even akin to the pagan idea of metamorphosis. It hardly embodies the full Christian doctrine of the incarnation. Donald Baillie said, "The relation between the divine and the human in the incarnation is a deeper mystery than this."[11] The essential problem with the kenotic view of the incarnation is that it simply does not exhaust the truth of Jesus Christ.

All this does not deny the truth in the general kenotic idea. Jesus did lay aside a measure of His splendor, *but not His deity*. Perhaps the best approach to Philippians 2:6–7 is to see the core of the issue in the phrase "taking the form of a servant." The phrase presents an explanation of how the divine Son emptied Himself: He became a servant in the fashion of man.

LORDSHIP AND THE INCARNATION

Karl Heim of Tubingen formulated this Christological concept some years ago. In Heim's book *Jesus der Herr* (Jesus the Lord), an interesting existentially oriented theory is worked out. Heim argued that every person needs a leader and lord whom they can unquestionably and unreservedly follow. That Leader is the Lord Jesus Christ. Moreover, that leadership of the Lord must be personal, direct, and existential. The experience is an "I-Thou" relationship between the Lord and His followers. Furthermore, there must be absolute obedience on the part of His disciples. That raises a serious question: Is it possible to follow Christ in absolute obedience all the time? Yes, argued Karl Heim, for the Holy Spirit actualizes it. Consequently, one's relationship to God is forever changed, because Jesus came and by the Spirit has become our Contemporary, continually leading us to God. That constitutes the meaning of *leadership* and *lordship*.

The problem with Heim's quite radical approach rests in the fact that he has no Christology. His approach does not yield a true Christology because he fails to answer the question of how divinity and humanity combine in Jesus. Heim made Christ our existential Leader, but he went nowhere in solving the essential Christological issue.

Of course, many other approaches to incarnational theology exist today. Space limits their treatment here, but they have all been discussed in detail in myriad writings. The above concepts are mere samples of what some circles currently hold on this central Christian doctrine. Clearly, they fall short. But this acknowledged negative approach to Christology will hopefully point out positively the evangelical, biblical view. Therefore, we now turn to the scriptural teachings concerning God being in Christ, reconciling the world unto Himself (2 Cor. 5:19).

A BIBLICAL EVANGELICAL VIEW OF THE
INCARNATION AND CHRISTOLOGY

The incarnation delivers humanity its "supreme paradox."[12] The undeniable fact that the transcendent "Holy Other" became immanent in flesh and dwelt among us boggles the rational mind. Here we confront the ultimate "mystery."[13] Like the truth of the Trinity, in one's limited human power to comprehend, it remains beyond our ability. Therefore, in faith one must turn to the Scriptures as the only authoritative Word from God on the issue. But even after grasping all that the Bible declares, the mystery of the person of Christ still remains. So, relying on the Scriptures is all believers can do, for in the Bible alone do we have a propositional revelation of God's truth. This demands a launching out on faith, but to that venture we are compelled and rewarded. Faith pleases God (Heb. 11:6), and He speaks through the pages of our Bibles (Ps. 119:24). That is sufficient for our needs.

Concerning the concept of the incarnational God, it may prove helpful first to see some of the outstanding historical statements on the incarnation built upon the Word of God. The Scriptures form the foundation of these significant creedal statements. One of the most important declarations concerning the incarnation came from Athanasius. He wrote:

> For he [Jesus Christ] did not simply will to become embodied, or will merely to appear. For if he willed merely to appear, he was able to effect his divine appearance by some other and higher means. But he takes a body of our kind, and not merely so, but from a spotless and stainless Virgin, knowing not a man, a body clean and in very truth pure from intercourse of men. For being himself mighty, and Artificer of everything, he prepares the body in the Virgin as a temple unto himself, and makes it his very own as an instrument, in it manifested, and in it dwelling. And thus taking from our bodies one of like nature, because all were under penalty of the corruption of death he gave it over to death in the stead of all, and offered it to the Father—doing this, moreover, of his loving-kindness, to the end that, firstly, all being held to have died in him, the law involving the ruin of men might be undone inasmuch as its power was fully spent in the Lord's body, and had no longer holding-ground against men, his peers, and that, secondly, whereas men had turned toward corruption, he might turn them again toward

incorruption, and quicken them from death by the appropriation of his body and the grace of the Resurrection, banishing death from them like straw from the fire.[14]

The Westminster Confession reflects Athanasius's understanding. That document from Britain reads:

> The son of God, the second person in the Trinity, being very and eternal God, of one substance, and equal with the Father, did, when the fullness of time was come, take upon man's nature, with all the essential properties and common infirmities thereof, yet without sin; being conceived by the power of the Holy Ghost, in the womb of the Virgin Mary, of her substance. So that two whole, perfect, and distinct natures, the Godhead and the manhood, were inseparably joined together in one person, without conversion, composition, or confusion. Which person is very God and very man, yet one Christ, the only Mediator between God and man.[15]

Many such statements have been forthcoming for two thousand years. What are the writings attempting to say?

SOME POSITIVE POINTS

First, as theologian Millard Erickson pointed out, the incarnation is to be seen essentially as the eternal Son of God assuming or gaining human qualities rather than giving up divine attributes.[16] This is where an undue stress on *kenosis* (Phil. 2:6–7) can lead to error. Paul was not arguing that Jesus ceased to possess a divine nature during the days of His flesh. Colossians 2:9 makes this very clear: "For in him the whole fullness of deity dwells bodily" (RSV). The Son accepted some limitations while on earth because of His taking the form of a servant, but not at the loss of essential divine attributes. Incarnation was far more than some sort of Old Testament theophany. At the same time, in the incarnation the Second Person of the Trinity took on a genuine human nature and attributes. John tells us, "And the Word became flesh, and dwelt among us, and we beheld His glory, glory as of the only begotten from the Father, full of grace and truth. . . . No man has seen God at any time; the only begotten God, who is in the bosom of the Father, He has explained Him" (John 1:14, 18).

Second, the incarnation does not mean the two natures of Jesus, human and divine, functioned independently of each other. He was a unity: one Person. Remember Donald Baillie's argument: You cannot separate the ego. All the acts of our Lord were always divine and human, never human on one occasion and divine on the next. He was omniscient as God; but because He was incarnated, He limited Himself and was subjected to the human organism and process of acquiring knowledge through time (Luke 2:52). This is true of all the divine and human attributes in Jesus. Granted, the idea is very difficult to conceive because human rationality is limited. Nonetheless, full meaning must be given to the divine-human hypostatic union of Christ in the incarnation.

Third, preconceived ideas as to what constitutes true humanity must be laid aside. The Fall of our first parents has corrupted our humanity. None of us are truly human in the original, created sense. When Jesus came as a "servant, being born in the likeness of men" (Phil. 2:6–7 RSV), He did not take on a sinful nature. To the contrary, Jesus acquired the sort of humanity Adam and Eve enjoyed before they fell. Paul called Jesus the "last Adam" (1 Cor. 15:45). He was truly human, human as God originally intended. And it is not incidental that Jesus, as the "last Adam," succeeded where the first Adam failed.

Moreover, and of central importance, God is revealed, understood, and discovered in Jesus Christ. Human concepts of God are wrong if they conflict with what Jesus is like and what He said. Remember, in Him "the whole fullness of deity dwells bodily" (Col. 2:9 RSV). God became the Incarnate God. God has declared Himself in that manner. The incarnation is a *fact*—a redemptive fact—and believers accept it and cope with it as best they can, even if human cognition fails to explain it fully.

Fourth, the above argument assumes the principle that the incarnation originated and emanated from God, not from the earth. A human being did not become God; God became a human being. No human could ever become God (regardless of the claim of some religions), but it does not follow that the reverse is impossible. Remember, with God nothing is impossible (Luke 1:37), even the Son of God being born of a woman. Right here a word stands in order about the virgin birth of Jesus.

THE VIRGIN BIRTH OF JESUS

In relatively recent years, the doctrine of Jesus' virgin birth has become a sharply controversial issue. In what is known as the "fundamentalist-modernist" controversies, the acceptance or rejection of the concept of the virgin birth stood as the barometer of orthodoxy in the minds of many. It virtually became tantamount to the acceptance or rejection of Jesus' divinity. It may not be quite as hot an issue today; nonetheless, the issue deserves serious consideration because the Bible clearly teaches Mary was a virgin. Of course, the biblical emphasis rests more on the divine conception rather than on the fact that Mary was a virgin—although she was certainly that.

Because the Scriptures declare it, and evangelicals accept the authority of the Bible, we reject denial of the doctrine of the virgin birth. But this does not mean Christians must ascribe validity to any extrabiblical view or speculations, such as those held by some Roman Catholics. Thus, as pointed out, it may be best to call the doctrine the "virgin conception," not the virgin birth. This seems more in line with the biblical presentation. Perhaps Carl F. H. Henry has the best approach. Henry states:

> It may be admitted, of course, that the Virgin Birth is not flatly identical with the Incarnation, just as the empty tomb is not flatly identical with the Resurrection. The one might be affirmed without the other. Yet the connection is so close; and indeed indispensable, that were the Virgin Birth or the empty tomb denied, it is likely that either the Incarnation or the Resurrection would be called in question, or they would be affirmed in a form very different from that which they have in Scripture and historic teaching. The Virgin Birth might well be described as an essential, historical indication of the Incarnation, bearing not only an analogy to the divine and human natures of the Incarnate, but also bringing out the nature, purpose, and bearing of this work of God to salvation.[17]

Moreover, Erickson correctly argues that the virginal conception by the Holy Spirit demonstrates that salvation is all of God's grace and must be seen as a supernatural gift of His love and mercy. Moreover, it clearly points up the uniqueness of Jesus and becomes a token of God's absolute sovereignty over nature to salvific ends. The Bible states that Mary's virginal conception had a significant role to play in the incarnation of God's Son; therefore, we accept the truth and thank God for His sovereign grace and power.

Much more could and perhaps should be said concerning the incarnation of God in Christ. The entire doctrine of Christ fills volumes. But again, space forbids the exercise. Perhaps it is best simply to summarize by stating that one must realize that Jesus, a very complex personality, was and is humanity and divinity in one unified Person. Our task is to accept what the Holy Scriptures state and avoid the heresies. As Erickson expressed it:

> There are basically six [heresies], and all of them appeared within the first four Christian centuries. They either deny the genuineness [Ebionism] or the completeness [Arianism] of Jesus' deity, deny the genuineness [Pocetism] or the completeness [ApoHinarianism] of his humanity, divide his person [Nestorianism], or confuse his natures [Eutychianism]. All departures from the orthodox doctrine of the person of Christ are simply variations of one of these heresies. While we may have difficulty specifying exactly the content of this doctrine, full fidelity to the teaching of Scripture will carefully avoid each of these distortions.[18]

So we rest on the Word, thank God for the glorious reality of the incarnation that God became man, and realize some day believers will grasp it fully when we see Him face to face.

THE RATIONALE BEHIND THE INCARNATION

Why all this stress on Christology? Why is it so important? The answer is simple, yet most important to grasp: Redemption rests upon it. *Our salvation stems from who Jesus was and is and what He did.* Never, therefore, is He to be understood as anything but all God, all man, one hypostatic union. John made this very clear in his writings (1 John 2:22; 4:1–3; 2 John 7). One must not sever the eternal Lord and the historic Jesus: "Jesus is the Christ" (John 20:31). What the Gospels say of the incarnate, eternal, cosmic Christ is *historic* and *true.* If not so, our salvation evaporates.

The implications for evangelism of the above principles are obvious and exceedingly significant. For example, there are those who would tell us people can be saved and redeemed through the "cosmic Christ" apart from hearing the good news of the historical Jesus. This subtle syncretistic approach is rejected, and not because of a narrow conservatism. Syncretism fails because the New Testament reveals nothing of such an idea. The Bible declares the uniqueness of Jesus because of the meaning of the historical incarnation in Christ's redemptive activity. A weak Christology based on a weak view of Jesus will make for a weak evangelism and hence a shallow experience of God. Therefore, the world needs to know all it means to call the incarnate God by His incarnational, historical name: *the Lord Jesus Christ.* The whole *kerygma* (proclamation) of Christ must be shared and the Son of God given His rightful place in all evangelism. The Bible and history constantly attest to this reality.

CONCLUSION

Herein the one, essential truth surfaces: *Jesus is Lord.* In every aspect of the Christian experience, Christ reigns. And that surely encompasses the ministry of evangelism. Jesus Christ must inspire, initiate, lead, permeate, and bring to fruition all phases and attempts at evangelization. He is first and last in bringing His redemption to the human experience. Anyone who would attempt to evangelize must be vividly aware of this basic truth and place Jesus Christ in His proper place in the enterprise. That constitutes a biblical Christology for the evangelist.

When the truth of Jesus Christ is understood, believed, proclaimed, and assimilated in life, the church finds itself rooted and grounded on an unshakable foundation, and the work of evangelism goes forward as the kingdom of God permeates the whole world. Athanasius contended for this and fought the battle well in his day. Great warriors for Christ have done likewise down through the eras of church history. Does evangelist Billy Graham do the same in his day? That shall be examined in the next major part of this chapter.

PART II:
BILLY GRAHAM AND THE CENTRALITY
OF CHRIST IN HIS MINISTRY

It is simple: Jesus is God.
—BILLY GRAHAM

INTRODUCTION

Christianity is Christ! That statement has made up the core of the Christian understanding of the faith since the first century. Among the Christological controversies that have challenged the church for millennia, there have been those who have arisen and bravely stood strong for an orthodox, biblical Christology. This battle has been illustrated in Part I of this chapter when the Arian controversy arose and Athanasius courageously fought for a proper understanding of the person and work of Jesus Christ. As discovered, the results and lasting influence of Athanasius's work brought about in 381 the well-known Nicene Creed with its distinctly Christ-centered statements. In that creed the emphasis, as earlier seen, rests on the Christological statement: "We belive in one Lord Jesus Christ, the only Son of God, eternally begotten of the Father God from God, Light from Light, true God from true God."

To this statement, along with the Chalcedonian Formulation, Christ is presented as foundational to the entirety of the Christian faith. Thus the inevitable question must be asked: Does Billy Graham adhere to these essential, basic tenets of evangelical Christianity concerning the person, work, and position of Jesus Christ in the task of world evangelization? Does Graham march in that noble, historical train? No issue can be found of more importance than this.

BILLY GRAHAM'S CHRISTOLOGY

Graham has raised the issue, Why is Christianity so different from every other religion in the world? What makes the message of the evangelist unique? What is distinctive about Christian discipleship? The answer to all these questions focuses not on the practice of religion, nor primarily on a plan for living, but on the person of Jesus Christ. Jesus, Son of the Father and Second Person of the Trinity, is "the central figure in our evangelistic message."[19] As Graham evaluates his own personal ministry, he has said, "I have spent my lifetime proclaiming one central truth: there is good news for people of the world. At the heart of that good news is Jesus Christ."[20] Thus it seems correct to conclude at the very outset of this inquiry that Billy Graham's message in all his evangelistic endeavors is essentially Christocentric. Of course, something of this conclusion has already been seen in the earlier chapter on the *kerygma,* the gospel. Yet, such a vital truth needs a broader and more inclusive look at the evangelist.

Billy Graham is quite emphatic about his views on the person and work of Jesus Christ. In a personal interview, Graham was pointedly asked, "Who is Jesus?" He was quick to reply, "I believe in the 'virgin birth.' He was supernatural from the beginning. He was God." Billy went on, "Jesus, on the human side was so wonderful, the compassion He had. He was God in the flesh; all man and all God." Not only that, the evangelist declared, from a pragmatic perspective, "He is the centrality of evangelism and all else."[21]

An incident occurred that brings the evangelist's practical application of his Christological position to the forefront. When Graham was preaching the Harringay crusade in London in 1954, an Anglican minister came to him and said, "Mr. Graham, I attended every night for three months and you preached the same sermon every night." Billy Graham said later, "I thought I had preached a different sermon every night, but I knew what he meant. He meant that certain things have to be said in every gospel message, because it is the gospel. There has to be the love of God; there has to be the cross of Christ; there has to be the resurrection of Christ; there has to be the fact of sin and man's response by repentance and faith."[22] He does preach Christ. This principle is brought together in Graham's statement in his book *Storm Warning:* "I have spent my lifetime proclaiming one central truth: there is good news for the people of the world. At the heart of that good news is Jesus Christ."[23] As Lockard has pointed out, a "Christ-centered message presupposes a strong Christology."[24] Graham agrees; he has said, "At the heart of that good news is Jesus Christ."[25] But what does Graham actually mean by these sweeping statements concerning the person and centrality of Christ in all his endeavors? Simply put, how does his basic Christology unfold? We need to investigate his generalized claims. As implied, the following issues have been explored to some extent in the previous chapter on the gospel; however, they need to be seen in more detail as Graham relates them specifically to his understanding of Christology. The question for Graham is: *Who is Jesus?*

WHO IS JESUS? THE INCARNATION

It can be correctly said—and here is where it all begins—that Billy Graham holds a traditional, evangelical view concerning the incarnation of Jesus Christ. First of all, he is fully committed to the concept of the virgin birth of the Lord. He affirms, "The Bible claims he was born of a virgin. I believe that, and I believe it is important for our faith to believe it."[26] Graham not only strongly emphasizes the uniqueness of the birth of Jesus Christ, at the same time he is convinced many Protestants, evangelicals in particular, do not give due respect to Mary, who bore Jesus. Unquestionably, many in evangelical Protestant ranks have reacted against what they consider an unbiblical view of the person and position of Mary. Even if that were true, Graham contends it constitutes no reason for not giving Mary the proper place she should have. She was highly chosen of God; she became the one through whom the Son of God entered into the world. That is unique and unprecedented and always will be.

But the primary issue centers on the truth that the divine Son of God Himself actually did come into this world. Graham expressed it very forcefully when he wrote, "God walked upon the Earth in human flesh."[27] This may sound quite docetic, but the divine incarnation is an indisputable reality. And it must also be granted that the evangelist strikes a balance between the deity and the humanity of Jesus, as shall be seen. Graham takes most seriously Paul's description of Jesus in Philippians 2, in which the apostle said:

> Have this attitude in yourselves which was also in Christ Jesus, who, although He existed in the form of God, did not regard equality with God a thing to be grasped, but emptied Himself, taking the form of a bond-servant, and being made in the likeness of men. And being found in appearance as a man, He humbled Himself by becoming obedient to the point of death, even death on a cross. Therefore also God highly exalted Him, and bestowed on Him the name which is above every name, that at the name of Jesus every knee should bow, of

those who are in heaven, and on earth, and under the earth, and that every tongue should confess that Jesus Christ is Lord, to the glory of God the Father. (vv. 5–11)

Graham expressed Paul's principle quite succinctly when he stated:

You see, God has not left us wondering around guessing whether or not he exists or what he is like. Instead—and this is very important for you to understand— God has shown himself to us. How has he done this? He has done it in a way that staggers our minds. He did it by actually taking upon himself human flesh and becoming a human being. Do you want to know what God is like? Examine Jesus Christ, because Christ was God in human flesh. "He is the image of the invisible God . . . for God was pleased to have all fullness dwell in him" (Colossians 1:15, 19). Christ confirmed that he was the Son of God by rising from the dead after his death on the cross. I invite you to look with an open mind and heart at Christ as he is found in the New Testament.[28]

Graham reinforces this stance by stating, "Why is Christianity so different . . . ? The answer, folks, is not on a plan for living, but on the person of Jesus Christ: Jesus, the Son of God the Father and the Second Person of the Trinity."[29] Theologian Carl Henry applauds Billy Graham for his stand as he commends Graham for "his focus on the Christological center of the Bible."[30] This leads to a closer look at Graham's views on who Jesus is.

WHO IS JESUS? GOD

Billy Graham is obviously most careful that a full Christological incarnational message be declared and understood. This implies the evangelist's absolute commitment to the *full* deity of Jesus. Graham has written, "It is actually the deity of Christ that above anything else gives to Christianity its sanction, authority, power and its meaning."[31] This truth must be stressed, especially in settings where other world religions have exerted strong influence. For example, when Billy was preaching in Nagaland and many in the congregation had a Hindu, Muslim, or syncretistic orientation, he took great care to emphasize that the God in Christ he proclaimed was not "one of the gods," but "*the*

God."[32] This did not prove acceptable to everyone attending with their various religious backgrounds, but in the three days that Graham preached, more than four thousand people made a decision for Christ. Graham expresses the concept of the deity of Jesus quite forcefully in his well-known book *The Secret of Happiness*. In that early work he said, "Jesus was not only man, but he was God himself, come down from the glory of heaven to walk on earth and show us what God is like. Christ is 'the image of the invisible God' (Colossians 1:15)."[33] But what does Graham say about Jesus' humanity?

WHO IS JESUS? A MAN

It must be made clear once again that the statement of Billy Graham quoted above implies that Jesus Christ was also fully man as well as the infinite, incarnate God. One does not sense any extreme docetic perversions of the incarnation creeping into Graham's understanding of it. He insists Jesus was fully human as well as divine. This can be seen in his stress on the importance of Mary as outlined above. Graham contends that Jesus walked among us and experienced life in a fully human sense. He brings this out in his volume entitled *Facing Death and the Life After*. Speaking of the humanity of Christ, Billy wrote, "He loved life on this earth. He enjoyed the pleasures of walking with his disciples, holding children on his knees, attending a wedding, eating with friends, riding in a boat, or working in the temple at Passover time."[34] Graham further points out that our Lord was human enough that "Jesus did not take delight in his approaching crucifixion."[35] He even prayed, "Let this cup pass from Me." In a word, from the human vantage point, the Lord experienced the pleasures and the traumas of this life, as does everyone else. But Graham is certainly not Arian; he resonates with Athanasius completely. As pointed out, he strives to maintain a balanced view concerning the divinity and humanity of Christ.

At the same time, Graham is very careful to state that, though human, Jesus never sinned. Concerning the sinless perfection of Jesus, Graham declared, "All the days of his life on earth he never once committed a sin. He is the only man who ever lived that was sinless. He could stand in front of men and ask, 'Which of you convinceth me of sin?' He was hounded by the enemies day and night, but they never found any sin in him. He was without spot or blemish."[36] When

Jesus queried His critics, "Which one of you convicts me of sin?" (John 8:46), they had no reply. Yet, in his sinless humanity, as the evangelist says, "He humbled himself as no other man has ever humbled himself."[37] Not only did Jesus empty Himself (*kenosis*, Phil. 2:7), He died on the cross. In Graham's continual lifting up of the cross of Christ, he makes the point that it may seem difficult to understand that Jesus, "who knew no sin, would have to bear the sin and guilt of all men."[38] But that truth rests at the core of Christianity. He then quotes 2 Corinthians 5:21: "God made him who had no sin to be sin for us" (NIV). This fact Graham emphasizes time and again. Jesus did not sin Himself, but God in unfathomable grace and infinite holiness heaped human sin upon His Son when He died on the cross, thus paying the penalty for our transgressions. We shall see Graham's emphasis on this central issue in more detail shortly.

Graham puts it together by declaring the time-honored evangelical truth that the man Christ Jesus is coequal with God the Father, the eternal Son of God, the Second Person of the holy Trinity, manifested in the flesh as the living Savior. Evangelist Graham insists:

> He alone had the power and capacity to bring man back to God. But would he? If he did, he would have to come to earth. He would have to take the form of a servant. He would have to be made in the likeness of man. He would have to humble himself and become obedient unto death. He would have to grapple with sin. He would have to meet and overcome Satan, the enemy of man's soul; he would have to buy sinners out of the slave market of sin. He would have to loose the bonds and set the prisoner free by paying a price—that price would be his own blood.[39]

Billy Graham obviously holds a very high, yet balanced, Christology concerning the incarnation, deity and humanity combined in unity in Jesus Christ. True, He was a man, but He is also the immutable Lord God. Graham declared in a sermon, "We know that Jesus was a man. He was completely human."[40] Billy Graham also preached, "The Bible teaches that Jesus Christ was God." Then he resolves the paradox somewhat by lifting up the faith principle. He said, Jesus "was more than God, he was man. He was as much man as he was God. He was as much God as he was man. He was the God-Man." There we must rest in faith, for it is a biblical Christology.[41] As Graham has declared, "All other things may change, but Christ remains unchangeable. In the restless sea of human passions, Christ stands steadfast and calm, ready to welcome all who will turn to Him and accept the blessing of safety and peace."[42] Billy confesses, "This is a staggering, almost incomprehensible truth."[43] But it is a truth, grasped by faith.

A second aspect of the gospel of Christ, one that emerges out of Christ's incarnate humanity, revolves around the dynamic life the Lord lived. Graham has much to say in this area of Christology.

WHO IS JESUS? THE LIFE

No one disputes the biblical truth that Jesus lived a dramatically different quality of life. And His life was far more than one just free from sin, as marvelous and miraculous as that obviously is. Graham places a healthy stress on the fact that Jesus lived a life of sacrifice, love, and ministry profoundly touching the needs of others. "He went about doing good" (Acts 10:38). Graham contends that because of the exemplary life of Jesus Christ, "virtually every significant and social movement of western civilization—from the abolition of slavery to child labor laws—owes its origin and influence to Jesus Christ."[44] Jesus set the pace and gave the inspiration, because in His exemplary life there was no human need He did not meet. He spoke comfort to the sorrowing; He granted forgiveness to the erring; He gave food to the hungry; He imparted healing to the sick; He gave instruction to the seeker; He issued rebuke to the rebellious; He laid out the pathway of life and fullness to the seekers; He led people to their destiny with God. But such a listing scarcely tells of the incredible life of ministry and teaching of Jesus. As has been said, "Jesus was the 'ultimate man.'" To all of this Billy Graham gives strong affirmation. The incarnation and the matchless life of Jesus, the God-man, stands above any person who has ever lived before or after. However, it all led up to the cross. Here Graham takes an overt and unapologetic stance.

WHO IS JESUS? THE MAN ON THE CROSS

If Billy Graham had any one motto, it would be that of the apostle Paul when he said, "God forbid that I should glory, save in the cross of our Lord Jesus

Christ" (Gal. 6:14 KJV). The cross stands as the focal point of the Christian faith (coupled with the resurrection, which shall be discussed in a moment). The spotlight of God's revelation shines brightly upon Calvary. The Bible lifts up the cross as the junction of all history. There were those, of course, who saw it all as just another death of an "antagonist" against Rome. How wrong they were. But what does the cross actually mean? How does Billy Graham see the cross of Jesus Christ that he so glories in? What makes up his theology concerning the death of Jesus? As far as the Bible and historical evangelicalism are concerned, the *atonement* for human sin was effected on Calvary.

Many theories of Christ's atonement have been propounded through the years, concepts such as the moral influence theory, the dramatic view of the struggle between God and evil, the ransom theory, and several other approaches. The view emphasized by a large community of evangelicals, however, and that to which Billy Graham gives basic assent, centers in the so-called governmental or substitutionary view of the atonement. In simplest terms, the idea revolves around the fact of Jesus bearing the sins of the world in Himself, dying on the cross as a *substitute* for sinful humanity. When Jesus cried out, "My God, My God, why have You forsaken Me?" (Matt. 27:46 NKJV), in that moment of time, in the inscrutable wisdom of God, all the sin of the world fell on the Son and He bore the judgment and punishment for humanity's evil. As vast as the depth of that sacrifice, as all-encompassing as the love thereby expressed, and as difficult as it may be to grasp, the grace of God brought about in that act salvation for the world. Jesus died for us! The atonement has been made. God has been reconciled to sinners and sinners to God. Eden has been restored. Life with God in time and eternity now stands available to all. The cross strikes at the essence of all reality. As Stephen Neill has said, "In the Christian theology of history, the death of Christ is the central point of history; here, all the rules of the past converge; hence, all the roads of the future diverge."[45] To all this Graham gives his strong, unswerving allegiance. He expressed it quite eloquently in a sermon: "I want you to see as they [the heavenly hosts] gather in the great council hall of God, and the Lord Jesus Christ, the Second Person of the Trinity, says to God the Father and God the Spirit, 'I will go and save the world. I will go and become man's mediator. I will go and become man's substitute, I will go and suffer and die.'"[46]

Graham then presents some dynamic implications of the substitutionary atonement of Christ.

IMPLICATIONS

Graham resonates with John Stott's evaluation of the central meaning of the cross. Stott said, "Confronted by human evil, how could God be true to himself as holy love? In Isaiah's words, how could he be simultaneously a righteous God and a Savior?"[47] "At the cross in holy love God, through Christ, paid the full penalty of our disobedience Himself. He bore the judgment we deserve in order to bring us the forgiveness we do not deserve. On the cross, divine mercy and justice were equally expressed and eternally reconciled. God's holy love was 'satisfied.'"[48]

Billy Graham forcefully preaches this. In the first place, Graham is vividly aware of the agonizing suffering of the cross. On one occasion he said, "I want you to see what happens. When Christ went to the cross, they took off his clothes, and they took a long whip of thongs with steel pellets in the end and lashed him across his back until his back was in shreds. They put a crown of thorns on his brow, until his face was bleeding. They spat on his face. They mocked him. They laughed at him."[49] But Graham sees far more than Jesus' physical suffering. In the same crusade in which Graham stressed the physical agony of Jesus, he said, "You can't get to heaven with your sins, and the only way you can have your sins forgiven and be presented unblamable to God is through the death of Jesus Christ on the cross. That's what God did."[50] Graham got to the heart of the matter when he said, "I preach the blood of Christ because on that day Jesus Christ shed his blood for the sins of mankind. . . . No matter how moving and emotional it may become the real gospel is in the fact that Christ died for me as a substitute."[51] Therein is the deep "agony" of the cross discovered.

Carrying on with that central substitutionary theme Graham, in his well-known book *World Aflame*, wrote, "It is only because of the love and mercy of God in Christ on the cross that I have any claim in heaven at all. It was God who permitted Christ to die as my substitute. It was God who accepted his sacrifice when he died."[52] The heart of the cross of Christ, as Graham sees it, is epitomized in the pain of atoning for sin as God's great Substitute. Graham further said, "Jesus assumed the sin and guilt of man and God's condemnation of death as he died upon the cross. His death satisfied the demands of God's justice that his laws be obeyed. . . . By sending Jesus thus to die in man's place God also expressed his love for him."[53] Love is the motive for the great sacrifice. Billy stated, "Out of his love for men, God has provided in the crucifixion of Jesus that substitutionary atonement for sin. . . . If they repent of sin and submit to Christ, His atonement becomes effective in the forgiveness of their sins."[54]

It may appear redundant to quote Graham's views so often; yet the atonement of Jesus Christ rests at the very core of any evangelist's preaching and ministry. To misinterpret Graham on these issues would be serious indeed. Furthermore, several spiritual principles emerge out of these repeated statements.

THE SUMMARY PRINCIPLES OF THE ATONEMENT

These many quotes by Graham, and myriad others could be cited, make it explicitly clear that the cross for Billy Graham implies three essential principles. One, God's great, holy love for sinful humanity reached out in grace and sent His Son into the world to effect redemption. Two, when Christ died on the cross, it was preordained by God that His death would serve as a substitute for the full punishment of the righteous judgment of God against human sin, and thus pay the price for human rebellion and effect reconciliation. Three, the preaching of the cross in the power of the Holy Spirit draws people to the Lord in repentance and faith to receive that atonement, forgiveness, and the salvation effected on Golgotha's hill. Graham's emphasis in his preaching can be seen in a sermon preached to more than two hundred thousand people in Rio de Janeiro, Brazil. Overlooking the vast arena where the crusade was being held stands a huge statue of Jesus with outstretched arms. Dominating the city's whole landscape, it is known as the "Christ of the Andes." Pointing to the statue Billy cried, "Do not look here, at me—look up there." He certainly was not suggesting any form of idolatry; he simply wanted people to look in their heart to Christ, "who takes away the sin of the world" (John 1:29). Graham is Christ-centered in his preaching, as has been the case for historical evangelism for twenty centuries. And therein the evangelist makes his signal contribution.

But the cross cannot be divorced from the resurrection. Again we see the proverbial two sides of the coin. Christ not only died for sin, He was resurrected as the living Lord to bestow new life on all genuine believers.

WHO IS JESUS? THE RESURRECTED LORD

Billy Graham deeply senses the absolute necessity of Jesus' resurrection. As the substitutionary atonement stands vital for salvation, so does the resurrection. In a message by Graham produced in *Decision* magazine he writes, "Jesus Christ, who was crucified, has been raised from the dead. If Christ's bones lie decayed in a grave, then there is no GOOD NEWS, and life has no meaning. The headlines of the world would soon indicate that the world is coming to an end soon with no hope for the future and eternity if Jesus Christ had not been raised."[55] This statement by Graham clearly indicates that he believes in the literal, bodily resurrection of Jesus Christ, as stressed in an earlier chapter. In no sense of the word does he entertain a critical, rationalistic view that would explain away the *bodily* resurrection of Jesus as have some. In the Christology of Graham—and traditional evangelical orthodoxy—Jesus was historically, bodily resurrected. The tomb is empty. The bones of Jesus are not moldering away in some unmarked Palestinian grave.

A bodily resurrection is not only the high-profile declaration of Scripture, but philosophically it falls in line with first-century Jewish thought, except of course for that of the Sadducees. To conceive of a spiritual resurrection was quite foreign to the bulk of the earthy theologians of Judaism. In Jewish thought, Gnosticism was anathema. To speak of a resurrection as no more than the spiritual continuance of a person's memory is absolutely foreign to traditional Hebraic doctrine. When an orthodox Jew thought of resurrection, he or she just naturally thought of a bodily resurrection. Of course, this was in the mind of Paul when he preached on the resurrection of Jesus on Mars Hill (Acts 17:31–32). He obviously made it absolutely clear that he was speaking of a bodily resurrection. The Greek mind-set of his hearers, for the large part, rebelled at the thought of such a resurrection. But Paul stood his ground and refused to be forced into a Platonic, philosophical understanding of life after death. And surely this is what the apostle had in mind when he wrote to the Corinthian church:

> For I delivered to you as of first importance what I also received, that Christ died
> for our sins according to the Scriptures, and that He was buried, and that He
> was raised on the third day according to the Scriptures, and that He appeared to

Cephas, then to the twelve. After that He appeared to more than five hundred brethren at one time, most of whom remain until now, but some have fallen asleep; then He appeared to James, then to all the apostles; and last of all, as it were to one untimely born, He appeared to me also. . . .

But if there is no resurrection of the dead, not even Christ has been raised; and if Christ has not been raised, then our preaching is vain, your faith also is vain. Moreover we are even found to be false witnesses of God, because we witnessed against God that He raised Christ, whom He did not raise, if in fact the dead are not raised. For if the dead are not raised, not even Christ has been raised; and if Christ has not been raised, your faith is worthless; you are still in your sins. Then those also who have fallen asleep in Christ have perished. (1 Cor. 15:3–8, 13–18)

The New Testament elevates the resurrection of Jesus to the highest level. It stands to reason, therefore, that any true biblical evangelist must likewise do the same.

GRAHAM'S REASONINGS

Graham thus stands solidly on the truth of the resurrection of Jesus and gives reasons for that stand. He said, "Remember that after Jesus' resurrection, he came into all kinds of ordinary places to all kinds of ordinary people. He appeared to people near his tomb and to two men on the road to Emmaus: he came to others at the lakeside, he met with a group in a house. He shared their meals and their walks."[56] Continuing the emphasis and its significance in his sermon, Graham stated, "The New Testament teaches from one end to the other that Christ indeed is risen from the dead. The most thrilling fact of human history is the resurrection of Jesus Christ."[57] In a word, the evangelist basically reasons from the Scriptures and faith. In Graham's Christological emphasis, he preached, "He was the Son of God but he was also man. He was every inch a man and every inch the Son of God. None of us can understand the nature of Christ in that sense—how God could become man; how he was born as a man and how he suffered as a man. He became God's man. But he also became a man crucified on the cross . . . and the tomb was not emptied of Christ's body that first Easter because some faithful person believed it. The *fact* proceeded the faith."[58]

Again, it must be said that pages could be filled with statements that Graham has made concerning the bodily resurrection of Jesus. He holds tenaciously to this view; that is incontestable, as has been seen in Graham's stand on the *kerygma* presented earlier. This now leads to the final point of Graham's Christology, namely, the return of Jesus Christ.

WHO IS JESUS? THE ONE WHO IS TO RETURN

In the previous study, it should be amply clear that Billy Graham is essentially a premillennialist, and that in the sense of a pretribulation rapture and a literal reign of Christ on earth for a thousand years. Some claim that Graham's position on eschatology has grown out of the basic fundamentalism he received from his family and his conservative education. There may be an element of truth in this contention. Yet an extreme emphasis on premillennialism with charts and delineating dispensational views, etc., cannot be found in Graham's preaching and writing. He takes very literally the return of Christ and the setting up of the millennial reign, but he does it in the sense of motivating people to be ready for that day. Graham is first and foremost an evangelist, not a theologian, as he himself states. The motivation behind all his preaching centers in creating the sense of urgency to be prepared for that hour when Christ actually does come again.

Few evangelicals would contest the fact that the Bible teaches the visible return of Jesus. At His ascension, angels appeared to the disciples and gave the promise: "And as they were gazing intently into the sky while He was departing, behold, two men in white clothing stood beside them; and they also said, 'Men of Galilee, why do you stand looking into the sky? This Jesus, who has been taken up from you into heaven, will come in just the same way as you have watched Him go into heaven'" (Acts 1:10–11). Billy Graham obviously takes this word literally. On many occasions he has made his position clear. In a sermon Graham preached entitled "Three Keys to Youthfulness," he stressed evangelist D. L. Moody's pronouncement that the world was soon coming to an end; and then went on to say, "If the world seemed about to come to an end in Moody's time, how much closer must we be to the climax of history."[59] The climax of history for both Moody and Graham centers in the second coming of Jesus Christ. Billy contends that the imminent coming of Christ can find attestation more often than any other aspect of New Testament eschatology. He points out that the Bible alludes to the *parousia* (return of Jesus) more than three hundred times.

In Graham's early days he was somewhat prone to set dates on the Lord's return. He said on one occasion, for example, that Christ would probably come back within two years. Obviously, he was wrong. His strong premillennialism no doubt accounted for that. But through the years he has mellowed on dogmatic date setting and pronouncements. He now contends, "It is wrong and unscriptural to try and set a date for Christ's return. God alone knows when He will come."[60] He stated that even Jesus did not know the time, only God the Father knows (Matt. 24:36). He further argued that if one knew the date of Christ's return, it would destroy the air of expectancy. Still, Graham does declare the distinct possibility that Christ may come in the relatively immediate future. He preached, "I would like to say with emphasis, I do believe we are now living in the closing period of history as we know it."[61]

Graham sees the return of Christ as a glorious hope, a utopia for the earth when Jesus comes again. Billy believes that when the Lord returns all the world's problems will be forever solved. War, famine, racial discrimination, social injustice, and the like will perish as Christ establishes His reign on earth. He has not deviated from that basic premise. Whether one agrees with Billy Graham's premillennial view, it must be granted that the Scriptures give the truth of Christ's return a significant prominence, and Billy Graham's continued preaching on the subject is biblically legitimate.

History has also given its sanction to a balanced preaching on the return of Christ. Many faithful evangelists and preachers have proclaimed it through the years. The foundational principle of biblical eschatology revolves around Jesus' emphasis on the kingdom of God. How does Graham measure up on this point?

WHO IS JESUS? LORD OF THE KINGDOM OF GOD

Often overlooked by many evangelists is the fact that one of the essential messages of our Lord centers in the establishment of God's kingdom. Jesus taught His disciples to pray, "Thy kingdom come" (Matt. 6:10). He preached, as did His predecessor John the Baptist, "Repent, for the kingdom of heaven is at hand" (Matt. 4:17). One cannot hold to a well-rounded Christology unless due respect is given to Christ's emphasis on the arrival of the kingdom of God and His lordship in it. As George Beasley-Murray has said, the "waiting is over and the kingdom is to come . . . the time before the kingdom is finished, the time of the kingdom has begun."[62]

While this has been commonly acknowledged, its significance for interpreting Jesus has often not been emphasized. Therefore, in the light of this reality, the kingdom of God should be preached in evangelistic proclamation. The coming kingdom is true in the ultimate sense, but Jesus is also establishing the kingdom now as well as its futuristic aspects. The principle of "now and not yet" applies in kingdom issues. Graham has said, ". . . Men will never build the kingdom of God on earth, no matter how hard they might try. Only God can do that—and some day He will when Christ comes again."[63] It must be acknowledged that most evangelists have not given ample time to this theme, as has been stated. Perhaps even Billy Graham does not mention this as much as one would hope; yet, there is no question that Billy Graham entertains a biblical concept of the kingdom of God. He argues from the fact that when Jesus was crucified, "a superscription was written over Him . . . THIS IS KING OF THE JEWS. He was then, and still is, King, but we have failed to acknowledge Him."[64]

Moreover, Graham's implicit preaching on the kingdom of God can also be seen in his declarations relative to entering into fullness of life, coming into a right relationship with God, and having one's sins forgiven that one might spend eternity with God in heaven and share in Christ's rule of the universe. And, of course, the evangelist's stress on the return of Christ has definite kingdom implications. Graham also makes it clear that when one comes into Christ's salvation, one enters into the kingdom of God. Our citizenship in Christ is in heaven, i.e., in the kingdom. Yet it must be said again that perhaps more high-profile emphasis on the kingdom perspective would be helpful, as is true of most preachers today.

CONCLUSION TO BILLY GRAHAM'S PERSONAL VIEW OF CHRISTOLOGY

All that has been said concerning Billy Graham's doctrinal approach to the person and work of Christ is perhaps summed up in his book *The Secret of*

Happiness. He wrote, "Jesus was not only a man, but he was God himself, coming down from the glory of heaven to walk on this earth and to show us what God is like. Christ is the 'image of the invisible God' (Col. 1:15)."[65] Graham calls Jesus "the embodiment of all truth."[66] He then quotes the great physicist Blaise Pascal, who said, "Apart from Jesus Christ we know not what our life is, nor our death, nor God, nor ourselves."[67] Christ alone is the divinely appointed Savior who died for sinners, bearing their transgressions on the cross. And Jesus, as Billy states, demonstrated beyond all doubt that He was the divine Savior and Lord by being raised from the dead. The gospel is the good news of God "concerning his son, Jesus Christ our Lord, which was made of the seed of David according to the flesh; and declared to be the Son of God with power according to the spirit of holiness, by the resurrection of the dead" (Rom. 1:3–4).[68] In summary, Graham holds, "At the heart of understanding . . . God is Jesus, our Savior and Lord. . . . In Jesus, the Lord, we see all of God we need to see. From Jesus we learn all of God we need to know."[69] Therefore, Billy urges, "Ultimately, one way or another, or at one time or another, we shall be faced with the question: What think ye of Christ?"[70] That is life's final question.

Billy Graham has faced quite fully the issue of Christology and it seems incontestable that his pronouncements stress historical evangelical positions on this vital issue. Now the final question arises: What sort of practical effort does evangelist Graham make to put Christ in the very center of his entire evangelistic ministry?

BILLY GRAHAM'S EFFORT TO MINISTER IN THE CENTRALITY OF CHRIST

It may seem unnecessary to emphasize once again the fact that Billy Graham preaches Christ. It has been amply demonstrated that Graham understands that Christ is the essence of the gospel, and he has faithfully proclaimed that *kerygmatic* truth in all of his evangelistic work, be it preaching, writing, personal witnessing, or whatever medium employed. All that has been said up to this point and shall be seen in the enfolding pages of this book makes the issue obvious. Billy Graham puts Christ as Lord and Savior at the heart of all his communicative efforts. Typical is his statement "The Lordship of Christ means . . . He takes over control of your life."[71]

Graham, moreover, also exercises caution that nothing carried on in the name of the Billy Graham Evangelistic Association fails to put Christ at its head and heart. Everything undertaken, whether it be crusade preparation, social ministries, or the follow-up program to help new believers, *Christ is the center.* As a case in point, in the evangelistic association's follow-up literature entitled *Living in Christ,* sentences like this appear: "Salvation means deliverance from the penalty and consequence of sin. It means beginning a new life with the Lord Jesus Christ. . . . He gives to individuals a new life through faith in his Son Jesus Christ. Jesus did everything necessary for your salvation, you should acknowledge your need of the Savior, ask for mercy and fully trust him."[72] Further, "the Christian life is a personal relationship with God through Jesus Christ."[73] The promise of victory over temptation is stressed with these words: "The Apostle Paul has given us the secret of Christian living in Galatians 2:20, 'I have been crucified with Christ; and it is no longer I who live, but Christ lives in me; and the life which I now live in the flesh I live by faith in the Son of God, who loved me, and delivered Himself up for me' (NAS). Learn to take your eyes off your own weakness and put your trust in Jesus Christ."[74] Concerning Christian growth and maturity, the follow-up material presents Philippians 1:6: "He who began a good work in you will carry it on to completion until the day of Christ Jesus."[75] The material also includes a personal testimony by Robert Munger, who stated, "One evening I invited Jesus Christ into my heart. What an entrance he made! It was not a spectacular, emotional thing, but very real. Something happened at the very center of my life. He came into the darkness of my heart and turned on the light. . . . He filled the emptiness with his own loving, wonderful fellowship. I will never regret opening the door to Christ."[76] So the references go. Christ is presented as the essence of all that which Graham intends to instill in the life of those who make decisions.

Further, in the evangelist's understanding of Christian service and ethics, he once again places Christ at the center. This issue need not be approached in detail at this stage as the succeeding chapters on holistic evangelism and godliness will fully elucidate Graham's commitment to these Christ-centered principles. In every aspect of the work, Jesus is lifted up and one is thus compelled to grant that Billy rests and works on the principle of the previously quoted motto of Paul, "God forbid that I should glory, save in the cross of our Lord Jesus Christ" (Gal. 6:14 KJV). But is this understood by the watching world?

BILLY GRAHAM'S IMAGE

As far as members of the Billy Graham Evangelistic Association are concerned, relative to Graham's image in placing Christ first, there is no question. In interviews with several team members, verification of the principle was immediately forthcoming. For example, David Bruce, Graham's executive assistant—one very close to the entire BGEA—has said, "Billy Graham is Christ-centered in all he does. Moreover, his spirit and approach filters down throughout the BGEA. His example motivates and challenges us all."[77] And that testimony can be repeated by many in the Graham team.

One might expect members of the Billy Graham organization to make such statements, but their testimony has a genuine ring of reality—and they should know. Still, the question arises: Does the world as a whole see Graham in this light? There seems to be little doubt on this point as well. In the early days, criticisms abounded. He was known as a "hot gospeler." But all that has largely passed away. For the last twenty-five years he has been voted as among the ten most admired men in the world. And this poll is not conducted by a religious group; it comes from a purely secular polling organization. That is virtually unparalleled. He has been welcomed into the halls of the most prestigious courts and offices in the world. Presidents, monarchs, authorities, and personalities of all types deeply and profoundly admire him. This does not mean he has not been without his critics, even up to the present moment. But by and large, for a man in his eighties, Billy Graham's image in the world is virtually pristine pure. And why is this so? Because people sense his absolutely unapologetic commitment to the centrality of Christ in his life and ministry. The Modesto Manifesto, which shall be discussed in detail later, has held him in good stead through the years and has largely silenced the critics. He is a man of impeccable integrity. Whenever he is interviewed on television, or at news conferences, or thrust in the limelight where multitudes hear him, he obviously receives an incredibly positive reception. The only answer can be that he preaches Christ, lives Christ, and glorifies Christ.

But it is not only in the halls of the famous where Billy Graham is held in high regard. The average person who takes time to look into the life and ministry of the evangelist gives a similar testimony. Even in these last years, when his health has limited his public ministry, he still carries a dynamic impact for

Christ and the gospel. Billy Graham has become a household word in much of the world and is looked upon with high regard and respect in virtually all segments of society. And that is not just the evaluation of one person; to find a serious critic today concerning the Christ-centeredness and Christlikeness of Graham poses a difficult task. There are those who will disagree with him theologically, but few disagree with his efforts to exalt the Lord Jesus Christ as the core and center of his life and ministry.

CONCLUSION AND CONTRIBUTION OF BILLY GRAHAM AND THE CENTRALITY OF CHRIST

"Jesus is Lord!" (Rom. 10:9 KJV). That first-century public confession of faith typified the approach, the essence, and the evangelistic results of the apostle Paul. Three centuries later, Athanasius boldly stood for the same central truth of the person and work of Jesus Christ. The result: Christology was formulated and the church and gospel were saved. It is right to thank God for men like Paul, Athanasius, and a host of others. Christianity is Christ; take Him out or pervert who He is, and the curtain comes down on the faith.

Ever since the Jerusalem Conference recorded in Acts 15 and down through the annals of church history, the battle for a proper Christology and gospel has been waged. Even at the present moment, adherents to an extreme, purely rational hermeneutic contend for a Christ who stands a far distance from the biblical presentation of our Lord. The war is not over. Therefore, there must be champions for the faith in every generation. The church must not lose Jesus. The historical line that can be traced from the apostolic days to our own shines with valiant warriors—men like Athanasius, Luther, Baxter, Wesley, Spurgeon, and many in our own contemporary times.

In this chapter we have attempted to examine, at least in outline form, what doctrines these defenders of the truth held and practiced concerning the Son of God. What can we say about Billy Graham by way of evaluation in this regard? And what has been the contribution to the battle he has made? First of all, it has hopefully become evident that the evangelist does hold to a proper biblical, evangelical, historical theology concerning who Jesus is. As seen, he recognizes the paradoxical nature of such a theology. He knows that, according to Scripture, one must believe in the total manhood of Jesus and at the same time accept His total divinity. He was the God-man. This paradox can only be grasped and held by faith, but recognizing that fact, Billy Graham rests in faith and trusts the day will come when the shadows will disappear in the glorious light of the full revelation of the Lord Jesus Christ.

But what about the pragmatics and contribution such a stand assumes, and does Graham grasp them? Again, an affirmation must be given. Billy does preach and minister Christ for all He is. In his writings, service, and preaching, Graham exalts the principle uttered by Paul, "Jesus is Lord." For Graham, Christ is central; He is all in all. Billy employs every means at his disposal to spread that truth.

Moreover, the evangelist has made significant contributions in several aspects of the Christ-centered ministry: (1) He has encouraged others to embrace the same historic theology, (2) he has enthroned Christ as Lord in his own life and ministry, (3) Christ is central in all the work and ministry of the entire BGEA, and (4) all this in turn impacts and blesses all those to whom Graham personally and the BGEA collectively minister. Billy's message since his early years as an evangelist has always been the same to the needy, defeated, soul: "You can have complete and unqualified victory by surrendering completely to Christ."[78] And that too is historic, contributory evangelism.

INTRODUCTION TO THE
MIDDLE AGES

THE THOUSAND YEARS THAT FOLLOWED THE AGE of the church fathers has acquired a variety of nomenclatures: the Dark Ages, the Middle Ages, the Catholic Era, etc. Often, at least in some evangelical circles, it has been described as a very "dark age." Of course, some validity to that criticism can be demonstrated. At the same time, however, a number of sterling personalities arose on the scene. Men such as Bernard of Clairvaux stood out as spiritual giants and exercised a tremendously effective witness for Christ. Likewise, one should not fail to mention significant movements such as the Lollards, the Waldensians, and others. The general milieu may have been dark as far as evangelicalism generally was concerned, but several bright stars illuminated the rather dismal sky.

No two Christians shone more brightly during those years than St. Francis of Assisi and Savonarola of Florence. The legacy of godliness they left and the multitudes they won to redemptive faith in Jesus Christ have become legendary. They deserve a close look, for they exemplified principles of evangelism that must always be present in an evangelism of historical integrity.

CHAPTER 6

HOLISTIC MINISTRY IN EVANGELISM

~

PART I:

ST. FRANCIS AND HOLISTIC SERVICE

Lord, make me an instrument of Thy peace.
—ST. FRANCIS

INTRODUCTION

Little disagreement can be found in evangelical circles that the salvation of the individual soul assumes central importance for the church. The meeting of human need, manifest in the forgiveness of sins and restoration of relationship with the Creator, stands as the primary priority for compassionate believers. At the same time, however, the meeting of all human needs as much as possible emerges as incumbent upon evangelical Christianity. The apostle John went so far as to say, "If someone says, 'I love God,' and hates his brother, he is a liar; for the one who does not love his brother whom he has seen, cannot love God whom he has not seen. And this commandment we have from Him, that the one who loves God should love his brother also" (1 John 4:20–21).

In light of this truth, an evangelism that accepts the full revelation of God in Scripture must be holistic in nature. This means that human needs, whether they are spiritual, physical, cultural, or economic, must be addressed by God's people. Holistic evangelism assumes a vital place in the forward movement of the kingdom of God. Our Lord beautifully personified this principle in His own ministry. Moreover, no one saw this truth more clearly than the renowned medieval man of God, St. Francis of Assisi.

THE CULTURE OF ST. FRANCIS'S EARLY DAYS

St. Francis, born in 1182, entered the world at a time of serious political and social upheaval. As historian James Burns describes it, "On all sides there [were] unrest and insecurity, with war as the only serious occupation."[1] Russia struggled against the Mongols as the Roman Empire languished in turmoil and fear over the constant threat of invasion from the Turks and Arabs, along with the Bulgarians. In this same period, the Moors invaded Spain. England was torn by unrest and civil war as the Scots moved south to exert their claims.

Although Italy itself had been somewhat consolidated under Charlemagne, the empire felt the threat of a return to barbarism. Raids from the Normans, the Huns, the Wends, and the Czechs became the norm of the day. Fear, gloom, and apathy gripped the populace. As people sought political and physical safety, they developed the feudal system. But even this new social arrangement precipitated private wars. National patriotism virtually disappeared as the city-state social structure emerged. Little security was to be had, however, as city-states rose against each other in bitter rivalry. As Voltaire put it, "Each castle became the capital of a small number of brigands, in the midst of desolate towns, and depopulated fields."[2] By the close of the twelfth century, things had deteriorated badly. Did the church arise to the challenge of the hour and become the "salt of the earth" to save the situation?

THE CHURCH

The medieval church itself could hardly be commended as a model of stability and thereby make its contribution to in thise turbulent scene. Historians agree that as evil as were the political conditions throughout Europe, the spiritual condition of the church was even worse. The church suffered a division between the East and the West as papal power became virtually absolute. A prime example of this ecclesiastical authority can be seen when Henry IV of Germany defied Pope Gregory VII. The king was forced to stand as a penitent outside the pope's gate at Canossa, barefoot and almost naked in the dead of winter, humbly begging for forgiveness. The church held that priests could literally change the elements of the Eucharist into the actual body and blood of Christ; thus, they held the keys to the kingdom. As a result, the populace feared the clergy and followed them virtually without question.

In the midst of this incredible ferment, the people sank into poverty and wretchedness. More tragic than anything, few ever heard the simplicity and power of the gospel. Of course, some of the clergy and laity possessed a measure of genuine sincerity. Not only that—and of vital importance—a new spirit of awakening and hope began subtly to develop among the people. Small groups arose here and there, seeking spiritual realities. But a real leader had not been found. The time seemed ripe for the Holy Spirit to do an unusual work and raise up a true man of God. In the ferment, God brought Francis of Assisi on the scene.

YOUNG FRANCIS

The general situation led, as one historian put it, to "one of the most remarkable movements in history."[3] In 1181, Giovanni Bernadone—as Francis was called in his childhood—was born into the world. His father, Pietro, was a wealthy merchant who traveled most of the time and, consequently, never grew close to his son. Yet, Francis's mother felt convinced that God had destined her son for greatness.

In his early years, young Francis lived life to its worldly fullness. He moved in a circle of pleasure-loving friends and became a debonair young man. His father likened his son to "the son of a prince, not like our son."

Early spiritual stirrings, however, began to move Francis. On one occasion, for example, he met a beggar on the street. In something of a blasé manner, he thrust the beggar aside and went on his merry way. But his conscience smote him deeply over his selfish, arrogant act. He cried out, "I am no better than a clown." After that, he never refused to give alms to the needy. God's hand was molding young Francis's future.

At that stage, hostilities broke out between Assisi and Perugia. As a result, Francis went to war for Assisi in 1205 at the young age of twenty-two. He fully intended to make a name for himself on the battlefield, but the forces of Assisi suffered a humiliating defeat and Francis ended up in prison, humbled and disgraced. Upon his release, he returned to Assisi and took up his usual carnal lifestyle. At this juncture, Francis became very ill, and his life of pleasure and sensuality seemed arrested. He felt his life was empty and meaningless as he cried out for inner satisfaction. But when he recovered, he once more reverted to his old revelry.

Again, war broke out; and for a second time Francis mounted his steed, vowing he would return a prince. He came back the very next day, bereft of armor and sword. No one has yet discovered what exactly happened. Then once again, he fell seriously ill. However, when he recovered this time, he absolutely rejected his former lifestyle, even though his old friends tried to draw him back into the life of pleasure. The monumental turn of his conversion loomed on the horizon, as he seemed crushed by the convicting power of the Holy Spirit.

CONVICTION AND CONVERSION

Francis remained in the "dark night of the soul" for some time, praying earnestly. In that state of depression, he encountered a leper one day. He drew back from the leprous man, the normal thing to do in his time. But once again, his heart smote him and he literally went up and kissed him. Most significantly, these events—the beggar and the leper—framed Francis's future service for Christ.

Francis languished in his state of spiritual anxiety for some time. Then, in 1206, at the little nearby chapel of St. Damian, it all came to a climax. Able to bear the burden no longer, he cried out, "Great and glorious God, and Thou Lord Jesus, I pray Ye shed abroad Your light in the darkness of my mind." As he poured out his soul, he looked up on the chapel wall and saw a painting of Jesus. The Lord's eyes seemed fixed on him. Suddenly, the "enlightenment" burst upon his heart and life. Christ was the answer. And Francis became a new man. A genuine conversion experience transformed the young man as he realized that Jesus Christ stood as his hope and the only One who could meet all his needs. He had found God's forgiveness and new life through Jesus Christ.

The wayside chapel of St. Damian where Francis's conversion experience occurred stood in sad need of repair. He resolved to restore the little chapel. The concept of holistic ministry was beginning to form in the heart of Francis. When the Franciscan Order was finally instituted, the faithful monks traveled all over Italy and much of the Mediterranean region bringing the message of Christ. At the same time, they were deeply concerned about the poor, the sick, and the needy. Holistic evangelism emerged.

A NEW LIFE OF MINISTRY AHEAD

When Francis informed his parents of what had happened at St. Damian, the family thought he was mad. Francis took all the money he had, gave it to those in need, took an old gardener's brown cloak, and left home. His father threatened to bring in the authorities to punish him for "misappropriating his goods" by giving them to the poor, but Francis never wavered; he would meet human needs regardless of any obstacle.

The new convert returned to St. Damian Chapel to repair it. Penniless, he started begging, and thus another key aspect of the Franciscan Order emerged. Francis said that he had become wed to "my lady poverty." After completing the repairs at St. Damian, he went to work on the Church of St. Mary of the Angels. On February 24, 1209, while reading a passage from Matthew's Gospel, "As you go . . . do not acquire gold, or silver" (Matt. 10:7–8), he felt overwhelmed. He jumped up, leaping for joy; the apostolic call to preach Christ had come.

The next day after the call, Francis took to the streets of Assisi, preaching the gospel. More than one historian contends that this event ultimately gave conception to the Reformation that would be born some three centuries later. The message of the saving grace of Christ, along with the meeting of people's physical and emotional needs, swept over the young man, and the Franciscan Order was launched.

THE MESSAGE

Francis's message was simple and plain. He preached the need of repentance and the joy of obedience to the will of God. He stressed the shortness of life and the certainty of judgment. Above all, he proclaimed the love of God in Jesus Christ. He urged people to seek God's favor and forgiveness through the life, death, and glorious resurrection of the Lord Jesus. As one contemporary, Thomas of Celano, said, "His words were like fire, piercing the heart."

Though some thought Francis weird, his intense joy and sincerity fascinated the people. They stood in awe of the man. As can be imagined, disciples soon began to gather around him. Bernardo di Quintaballe, a wealthy nobleman, followed Francis's lead. He went into the streets of Assisi and distributed all his wealth to the poor. One can surmise the profound impression this made on the city.

When the faithful followers reached seven in number, Francis and the seven would go out two by two and preach in the streets, the marketplaces, wherever people would listen. The gospel of grace was being declared in a fashion not heard for many years. The message that had remained hidden for a long period was again being heralded, and it was coupled with concern to meet all human needs.

One of the important factors ingredient to the incredible ministry of Francis centered in the fact that he became a great man of prayer. And the Order grew apace. He named his group the Frate Minores, the "Minor Brothers." They all took the vow of poverty, chastity, and obedience; and the poverty vow was real, not merely symbolic. There would be no monasteries because they went afoot into the world to preach the gospel to all people and meet the needs as much as possible. They especially ministered to the poor, lepers, and other outcasts. Although they adhered to the Roman Church, canonical orders had no appeal for the brothers. The liturgy of Rome exercised no compulsion on Francis or his followers, although they did observe daily mass. In 1212, after the Order had been formally organized, a delegation of eleven or twelve traveled to Rome for papal sanction. Surprisingly, Pope Innocent III granted it. He said, "Go in the name of the Lord and in His strength preach repentance to all." From that time on, the Order expanded with explosive growth.

THE GROWTH OF THE ORDER

The movement soon spread throughout Italy. After only very few years of ministry, Francis became known over a wide area. At this time, Clara Safai visited St. Francis. A rare personality herself, she was so inspired that in 1212 she started the Order of the Poor Claras, a Franciscan order for women. The movement continues to this day.

The disciples carried on with the principle of sharing the gospel of Christ two by two. The numbers of "poor brothers" grew into the thousands. By 1219, there were five thousand members and five hundred who sought admission. Italy and many other areas were deeply stirred. They traveled as far west as Spain and as far east as Egypt. At times, the whole listening audience would stand up and dedicate themselves to a life of preaching Christ and ministering to human needs. However, Francis, in his wisdom, would not permit mass movements. He would speak to them individually and say, "I will find ways for you to serve God." The Lord would hardly call a whole city to be preachers, he reasoned.

After the Order was well launched, Francis's health began to deteriorate. It must be observed that Francis, while meeting others' physical needs, neglected to meet his own. He suffered many illnesses. But with his positive, joyous spirit he called his infirmities "his sisters." Even in times of severe pain, he would joke with his companions. In this setting, the so-called stigmata occurred around 1224. Francis had bleeding wounds in his hands and feet, as did the Lord at His crucifixion. No historical evidence can be found to refute the claim.

St. Francis's health continued to deteriorate until it became evident that his homegoing was imminent. Francis had been particularly harsh on his own body, apologizing to it before he died. As he lay on his deathbed and looked at his faithful companions, his last words were:

> Adieu. . . . My children, remain all of you in the fear of God, abide always united to Christ; great trials are in store for you, and tribulation draws nigh. Happy are they who persevere as they have begun: for there will be scandals and divisions among you. As for me, I am going to the Lord and my God. Yes, I have the assurance that I am going to Him whom I have served.[4]

On Saturday evening, October 3, 1226, St. Francis entered the gates of glory. At the very moment he passed on to be with Christ, a great flock of larks alighted on the thatched roof of his little room and sang. It seemed a fitting end to a life of holistic evangelism that he so beautifully exemplified and fostered in his life and ministry.

HOLISTIC EVANGELISM AND ITS IMPACT

St. Francis predicated his entire ministry on the great God who meets all human needs. In his "Canticle of the Sun," St. Francis prayed:

> O Most High, Almighty, good Lord God to Thee belong praise, honor, and all blessing! Praise be to my Lord God with all His creatures, and especially to our

brother the Sun, who brings us the day and who brings us the light; fair is he and shines with the very great splendor; O Lord, he signifies to us Thee.

Praise be my Lord for our sister the moon and for the stars which He has set clear and lovely in the heaven. Praise be to the Lord for our sister water, who is very serviceable to us and humble and precious and clean. Praise be to the Lord for our mother the earth, which doth sustain and keep us. Praise be to my Lord for all those who pardon one another for His love's sake and who endure weakness and tribulation. Praise be to the Lord for our sister the death of the body from which no man can escapeth. Woe to him that dieth in mortal sin! Blessed are they who are found walking by Thy most holy will, for the second death shall have no power over them.[5]

This prayer makes it evident that Francis was concerned about the totality of life: the material, the spiritual, the temporal, and the eternal. As a consequence of his holistic ministry, many people in the midst of their multiplied needs had their eyes lifted up from temporal needs to the Lord Jesus Christ, their deepest need.

The mistake can be easily made in world evangelization that only spiritual needs matter. Even though these spiritual needs are primary, as John Stott put it, "a hungry man has no ears." Often the gospel must be shared in the context of meeting temporal human needs before an openness to one's greatest need, forgiveness of sins in Jesus Christ, can be sensed. Moreover, the evangelist should attempt to touch needy lives regardless of whether a reception for the message of Christ emerges. The love of Christ demands such, as seen from the previously quoted passage in 1 John. But at the same time, those who practice evangelism in the holistic sense often become the ones who reap the greatest evangelistic harvest. This was true in the life and ministry of our Lord and the early church; it should be true for the evangelist of any generation. It is the biblical plan. But the principle has at times created conflict.

A BATTLE BEGINS

The early decades of the twentieth century saw a quite radical change in evangelistic understandings and methodologies, particularly in America. The dynamics that precipitated the "revolution" had actually begun in scholarly circles some years earlier in Western European church life. The situation gave birth to the battle now known as the "modernist-fundamentalist" controversy. The advent (many years earlier) of the so-called higher critical hermeneutic—a movement that essentially had its birth in German theological circles—made a profound impact on the evangelistic scene by the turn of the twentieth century. Those were turbulent times. A brief historical grasp of the conflict should prove helpful in understanding what so dramatically changed evangelistic ministry understandings.

A BRIEF HISTORY OF CONFLICT

Emanating out of a critical, rationalistic theological approach to Christian truth, serious questions arose concerning the doctrine of biblical inerrancy. For instance, it gave rise to the so-called quest for the historic Jesus of Strauss and others. These scholars contended that the historic Jesus could not be fully established by the New Testament. Also coming on the scene was the documentary hypothesis in the Old Testament studies of Wellhausen and others. As this particular approach to the Scriptures developed, it found something of its epitome in the existential theology of men like Rudolf Bultmann. Question marks were placed over many biblical statements. As could be imagined, it created considerable conflict and controversy in the life of the Western church.

From the European perspective, the battle can be epitomized in the ministry of Charles H. Spurgeon, the famous London pastor. Spurgeon took a bold, conservative stand and resisted the rationalistic movement quite vehemently. He strongly contended for scriptural infallibility. Around 1885, the conflict became known as the Downgrade Controversy. It came to its climax in 1887 when Spurgeon broke his relationship with the Baptist Union of Britain. Unfortunately, it proved to be a devastating blow to the great preacher.

The Spurgeon affair stands as something of a parable of what was going on all over Western Europe at that time. In the next two decades, the controversy grew to full bloom in North America and brought about the aforementioned modernist-fundamentalist controversy. The simple definition of the battle revolved around the fact that the "fundamentalists" accepted the inerrancy of the Scriptures and the "modernists" did not. It became a revisiting of age-old controversies that had raged through the early Christian church. It boils down to this: Is final authority found in the divine revelation of the Bible or in human rationalization?

THE POINT FOR HOLISTIC EVANGELISM

In the United States, the battle etched a particularly devastating mark on evangelism. One outcome of the controversy was that evangelism became equated with fundamentalism, and social action became synonymous with modernism. Prior to the controversy, these two aspects of ministry were well wed. This amalgamation of social actions and evangelism had held true through the history of the church, as portrayed in the life of men like St. Francis of Assisi. In more recent centuries, evangelists such as John Wesley fostered significant social movements. For example, Wesley became one of the first, at least in British history, to foster prison reform. At the same time, the ministries that emerged in the continental Pietistic movement were most profound. Hermann Franke at the University of Halle, as a case in point, created several social ministries in the city along with his fervent evangelization.

In America during the eighteenth and nineteenth centuries, this approach dominated the general motif of doing ministry. Evangelism and social action coalesced. When evangelist Charles Finney became professor of theology and president at Oberlin College in Ohio, he saw to it that Oberlin served as a major railhead in the North for the Underground Railroad, where runaway slaves could find freedom. Oberlin became the first coeducational college in America and would accept students of all races. Finney even had a health plan for the students at the college, called the Graham Plan. Spurgeon's church in London exercised more than twenty social and evangelistic ministries. Evangelist D. L. Moody founded an excellent Bible institute in Chicago. Further, no one involved himself more in the temperance movement in the early twentieth century than evangelist Billy Sunday. Then came the controversy.

The liberal strata in American Christianity lost much of its evangelistic fervor and devoted itself to social action. They apparently equated Pietistic evangelism with obscure fundamentalism. Those on the conservative side, as it appears, began to equate social action with liberal theology. In rejecting the new theology, they, to a degree, threw out the baby with the bathwater; they rejected social action and gave themselves to individualistic evangelism. Confusion resulted. For example,

Rauschenbusch's well-known volume, *A Theology for the Social Gospel,* was misunderstood by many people. Some conservative circles immediately banned it because they assumed that social action emanated from liberal theology. However, Rauschenbusch took care to strike a balance between social ministries and evangelism. Nevertheless, many rejected his work. The upshot of it all was that evangelism was divorced from social action in the minds of too many.

This cleavage between social ministries and evangelization did serious damage to the holistic approach of evangelism, and it persisted to a greater or lesser degree for decades. In recent years, however, a hopeful reassessment of the situation has begun to develop. A growing appreciation for holistic evangelism seems to be on the rise. More and more churches are seeking to meet human temporal needs along with eternal verities, recognizing that the two aspects of Christian ministry are not in opposition. Fortunately, the "divorced couple" is hopefully being rewed. Furthermore, overwhelming biblical evidence for holistic evangelism cannot be avoided for the honest student of Scripture.

THE BIBLICAL BASIS FOR HOLISTIC EVANGELISM

The Lord Jesus Christ, as stated, epitomized what the ideal ministry should be. In His service, He simply met needs as He encountered them. He straightened crooked limbs, opened blind eyes, unstopped deaf ears, gave comfort and peace, exorcized demons, fed the hungry, raised the dead; and most important, He forgave sins. Not only did He invade the human experience by forgiving sins and granting eternal life, but He fed the five thousand as well. Wherever a crisis existed, He acted. Our Lord realized, along with the proper prioritizing of human need, the prime importance and nature of the kingdom of God. Thus, He established in His holistic ministry the kingdom in human hearts and lives.

THE NEW TESTAMENT CHURCH

The New Testament church proved no exception to our Lord's example. The apostolic fathers ministered to the total person. The Book of Acts, for example, abounds in the expression "signs and wonders." Peter healed the lame man at the beautiful gate (Acts 3:1–11). He raised Dorcas from the dead (Acts 9:36–41). Paul exorcized demons (Acts 16:16–18). These "signs and wonders" were miraculous acts of the power of God that pointed to the truth of the gospel. As they ministered in that holistic sense, great results followed. Another instance of the principle occurs in Acts 6. The church faced a problem in the feeding of the poor widows with fairness and equity, and they met the need. The crisis also gave birth to a new office, the diaconate. This new office was predicated on the principle that the needs of God's people are to be met by God's people. Moreover, Paul gathered an offering for the poor saints in Jerusalem (Acts 24:17). He also outlined to Timothy the conditions for being a registered widow that the church might meet their physical needs (1 Tim. 5:1–16).

This principle of holistic ministry appears throughout the Old Testament as well. Space forbids elucidating the story of Israel's exodus from their Egyptian bondage. God not only sent salvation from heaven, but He also sent manna from above. The prophets and great figures of the Old Testament era reiterate the principle over and over again.

Perhaps it can be brought together in the realization that the entire universe is our Father's world. That world was perfect as God originally created it, but because of the Fall, the human race is now subject to numerous physical, emotional, psychological, and spiritual needs. It thus becomes incumbent upon God's people to be engaged in the task of seeing that those multiplied needs are met. Wise, indeed, is the church and the individual Christian who realizes that essential principle.

THE PRIMARY NEED

Notwithstanding the importance of holistic ministry, it must be emphasized once more that a person's greatest need rests in his or her spiritual experience. Better for people to languish away in poverty and know Jesus Christ than to live in the so-called lap of luxury and spend eternity separated from God. Evangelism does strike at humanity's most profound need. Little argument can be raised against that truth. But it does seem one can rather easily slip into the error of meeting only social and physical needs and fail to understand that all people need Jesus Christ above all, and vice versa. But once again, let it be understood that no antithesis exists between social action and individualistic evangelism. They do go hand in glove, and Christian love demands that the church minister in that fashion.

Moreover, with various governments being what they are today, the need arises for Christians to be involved in the actual structures of society itself. This involvement often means throwing oneself into the political arena to bring about the kind of change that will ultimately help and aid people in distress. This can be seen in such social issues as the drug problem, poverty, crime, and the like. God's people should give themselves to various aspects of the public arena to bring about the kind of political, social, and economic change that will help eliminate problems. God's people must do all they can to alleviate suffering.

CONCLUSION

The point has hopefully been made that the denial of holistic evangelism constitutes a gross error, an error that should be eradicated. To deny a holistic approach to ministry is not historically viable, pragmatically acceptable, or biblically justified. Holistic evangelism rests upon such a solid historical and scriptural foundation that failing to engage in the enterprise precipitates a restrictive evangelism as well as an inadequate social ministry. It is that simple. As one contemporary pastor put it, he built his church on the principle of "finding hearts and healing them." That has been the approach of great evangelism in the past, and it challenges our contemporary evangelization to regain that foundational principle of the church's ministry to society. That constitutes part of being a fully committed Christian evangelist. How does Billy Graham measure up?

PART II:
HOLISTIC EVANGELISM IN THE GRAHAM MINISTRY

I have preached on every conceivable social issue.
—BILLY GRAHAM

INTRODUCTION

Billy Graham deeply desires to see people come to Christ. And that commitment extends to all people in all their needs, social and spiritual. He has said:

I burned inwardly when once I stopped at a West Coast motel and saw them turning away a Mexican—just because he was a Mexican. I burned again, when on the East Coast, I saw a sign over a restaurant saying "Gentiles Only." Can a Christian stand aside and say, "Let those people suffer those indignities"? Did not Christ say, "And as you wish that man should do to you, do so to them"? Does the bible not teach, "You shall love your neighbor as yourself"? We must enter into their difficulties and burdens, and their burdens must be our burdens if we are to fulfill the law of Christ.[6]

What sparked this "burning"? What moved Graham to reach out to people in the multiplicity of their needs? Did he not see his ministry exclusively as "soul winning"? Apparently not! These basic issues must be addressed.

As we looked into the life and service of St. Francis of Assisi, we learned that the man of God was a fervent evangelist. Like Graham, he too longed to see people come to faith in Jesus Christ. But history also attests to the fact that Francis felt a deep burden for the physical and social needs of his fellowman. Hence he reached out, touched the leper, and fed the hungry, even taking the vow of poverty himself. Simply put, he had a profound social consciousness that not only ministered to people with their various problems, but also under-girded his evangelism in a most significant way as well. Could this be what Billy Graham is saying?

The answer to this fundamental inquiry seems to be self-evident. As one observer declared, "Graham has one of the most acute and social consciences of any man I ever met. All his sympathies, all his affections, all his personal passion is on the side of the dispossessed, the disinherited, the lost, the hungry, the lonely, the homeless, the downtrodden."[7] This constitutes a quite sweeping statement to make of a man whose image and persona essentially reflect an evangelic aura. But Billy himself said, "I firmly believe in the application of the gospel to the social order, for the gospel must relate to the social concerns of our day."[8] Still, few know of the care and concern of Billy Graham as he reaches out to those who need ministry in the temporal sense, as well as meeting their eternal needs. Graham truly does have such concern. One biographer has called him "The Unheard Billy Graham." That is to say, not many understand his deep commitment to a holistic approach to ministry. If such be the case, it certainly warrants an in-depth investigation of the Graham epic.

THE PRINCIPLE

It will be well to undertake this chapter on the social consciousness of Billy Graham by first laying down his basic philosophical principle concerning the meeting of people's needs. Little doubt can be raised against Graham's commitment and concern for solving social ills. But there are those, especially some sociologists, who disagree with Graham's basic approach. At the same time, others see his principle of social action as the ultimate logical course. What, then, is Billy Graham's philosophy?

In a word, Graham's major premise on social and ethical concerns has its roots in people coming to the new life Christ creates. Graham is convinced that social needs cannot be fully and totally met by governments, new laws, or even the benevolent ministry of the church. The individual must be changed. A whole new perspective on life must be generated in people. He sees the basic social problems of any culture as a manifestation of individual sinfulness, selfishness, and the lack of a relationship with God that a walk with Jesus Christ overcomes. Graham has said, "If we today could only realize that a nation can rise no higher, can be no stronger and no better than the individuals which compose that nation! There is nothing wrong with the world. The trouble lies with the world's people. If the world is bad, it is because people are bad."[9]

Graham's strong contention centers in the argument that "bad people" become "good people" only when they experience new life in Christ. But when that takes place and a Christian world-view is adopted, people are motivated to meet the needs of others in the love of Christ. This alone will ultimately and finally change the world and solve its perplexities. As Jesus said, His followers are the "salt of the earth" and the "light of the world" (Matt. 5:13–14). Only true "salt" and "light" can permeate the pollution and the darkness of the world's sin and social ills and thus give birth to a new society. Changed lives develop a changed society. This constitutes the essence of Graham's basic social outlook, approach, and strategy.

At the same time, however, Billy Graham is not so "individualistic" that he has refrained from decrying those things that erode society as a whole. During his British crusade, Aruth Smith, an editor of London's *Daily Sketch,* wrote, "Billy Graham is right in saying the things he does. The colossal and awful scale of drunkenness, gambling, divorce, banditry and immorality in this country does not evoke a word of protest from the Archbishops or the leaders of the free churches. Is it not time that someone like Billy Graham focus attention on them?"[10]

The editor was reflecting what Billy Graham said concerning his ministry to England. Graham openly confessed to the British, "I am going to insist that honesty and integrity . . . [play a vital role] in individual lives. I am calling for a revival that will cause men and women to return to their offices and shops to live out the teachings of Christ in their daily relationship."[11] As he emphasized, "It is the man inside the suit that really counts." Thus he reached out to people in the attempt not only to lead them to Christ, but also to lead them to a more fulfilling ethical life. The evangelist is convinced that Christ alone can create in the human heart that spirit which eventually transforms society. Thus it becomes self-evident that Graham does have an essential holistic approach to his evangelism. How did he arrive at these conclusions?

THE BIBLICAL FOUNDATION

This philosophy of social action, as Graham understands it, finds its roots in the Word of God. He has confidence that this is what the Bible says concerning social action and it must therefore be acted upon. Billy Graham's appeal to the Scriptures will be seen in more detail in a later chapter when his understanding of the Bible is investigated. Suffice it to share here just one of his quotes: "If ever I get to the place where the Bible becomes to me a book without meaning, without power, and without the ability to reprove and rebuke my own heart, then my ministry will be over, for the Bible has been far more than my necessary food."[12] Obviously, Graham holds a very high view of the Scriptures. As E. S. James pointed out:

America has seldom, if ever, heard a world-renowned evangelist put such emphasis on the authenticity, reliability, and effectiveness of the Bible in teaching and preaching. Without equivocation he urged that Baptists and others stop quibbling about problems encountered in their study of the Bible and give themselves rather to proclaiming it. He left no doubt that he believes it— all of it.[13]

Thus Graham's entire social action philosophy is predicated upon the Word of God and the scriptural insistence upon changing the individual human heart that in turn makes for a viable society. As Jesus said, "The thief comes only to steal, and kill, and destroy; I came that they might have life, and might have it abundantly" (John 10:10). Upon this philosophy Graham's social concern and ministry have emerged.

A QUESTION

An issue must be faced relative to this approach, however. The question arises, Does the Bible and the social philosophy that it espouses truly make a difference in society? One of the leading professors and scholars in the area of Christian social ethics contends that it does. Professor T. B. Maston has said:

> It also has been indicated that most world issues are basically moral and spiritual. This means that if Christianity does not have an answer for the major problems of the world, they will not be answered adequately. . . . The Christians who have turned the world upside down have been men and women with a vision in their souls, the resurrected Christ in their hearts, and the Bible in their hands.[14]

Graham strongly affirms this argument. He contends the new birth and the regenerating power of Jesus Christ not only transform a person spiritually, but socially as well. In that manner, and in that manner primarily, society can experience the radical change it needs. In Graham's book *World Aflame*, he has said:

> Thus the Bible teaches that man can undergo a radical spiritual and moral change that is brought about by God Himself. The word that Jesus used, and which is translated "gain," actually means "from above." The context of the third chapter of John teaches that the new birth is something that God does for man when man is willing to yield to God.—Man does not have within himself the seed of the new life, this must come from God himself.[15]

We have seen many times Graham's insistence that the new life in Christ can be brought into maturity only by the inner work of the Holy Spirit. In that context, the Spirit of God transforms the individual person, and through changed lives He changes the church and hence a force is developed that can transform society as well. It can be summed up quite well in a quote from Billy Graham:

> We have been trying to solve every ill of society as though society were made up of regenerate men to whom we had an obligation to speak with Christian advice. We are beginning to realize that, while the law must guarantee human rights and restrain those who violate those rights, whenever men lack sympathy for the law they will not long respect it even when they cannot repeal it. Thus the government may try to legislate Christian behavior, but it soon finds that man remains unchanged.[16]

This does not mean that laws and legislative measures should not be employed. Graham insists that governmental decrees play their role. But the key to a healthy society centers in the changed lives of the people. So back to the original question: Is this philosophy pragmatic, i.e., does it actually work? Do changed lives change society?

In answer to this basic query, it becomes important to understand Billy Graham's understanding of conversion itself. This was seen in detail in a previous chapter; but in the context of social action he defined his understanding of conversion with these words:

> My sin was committed against God. If God is content with what Christ has done on my behalf and is willing to pardon me, then I have nothing more to worry about. I am redeemed, I am reconciled, I am forgiven, I am assured of heaven—not because of any goodness or good works of my own. It is only because of the love and mercy of God in Christ on the cross that I have any claim on heaven at all. It was God who permitted Christ to die as my substitute. It was God who accepted His sacrifice when he died.[17]

Billy goes on to apply the conversion principle to social concern. Graham sees two types or aspects of conversion, the first being from the world to Christ, the second from Christ back to the world. As he put it, "'The fruit of a new life is love for one's neighbor which leads to social action."[18] Billy

Graham's approach has always been that which he verbalized in London in the 1954 Harringay crusade. He held up his Bible and said, "I am here to preach nothing but what is in this book and to apply to everyday lives."[19] In these few words, Billy Graham's philosophy of social action is expressed; his practical, workable approach is set forth. Moreover, he proclaims these concepts as he sees them in his evangelistic ministry.

ETHICS IN PREACHING

Clearly Graham has a highly ethical, social purpose in his preaching. Obviously concerned about the salvation of the individual, he also deeply desires to see the salvation of Christ exemplified in everyday life. He said on another occasion in that first London crusade that the preacher faces a twofold task: "One, to proclaim the gospel of Jesus Christ as the only answer to man's deepest needs. Two, to apply as best we can the principles of Christianity to the social conditions around."[20] Graham feels convinced that this sort of preaching makes a difference morally, socially, and spiritually. Perhaps some examples of the positive fallout of this kind of evangelistic preaching and understanding of conversion will help answer the basic question as to its practical relevance to life and social ills.

A classic example can be found in the life of Billy Graham's own son, Franklin. Through his teenage years Franklin was hardly a dedicated Christian. He had his problems, as do many young people struggling through early adolescent years. But Franklin came to a very definite experience of Jesus Christ. His testimony has a solid ring of reality to it. He now holds evangelistic crusades, as does his father. Moreover, most people know of Franklin's deep commitment to meeting social needs. He directs two worldwide organizations: Samaritan's Purse and World Medical Mission. Inspired by Billy Graham and Bob Pierce, Samaritan's Purse has no doubt relieved more hunger, pain, and privation than any comparable organization in today's needy world. Throughout the entire globe, when disaster strikes, Franklin and his ministry step in with multiple tons of food, clothing, and resources of every sort to relieve the hurt. Even in the evangelism conferences Billy Graham has held (Amsterdam '83, '86, and 2000), Franklin and his group have distributed clothing, books, and multiple supplies to needy evangelists all over the world.

One touching story stands in order: A poor preacher from Africa attended the conference in Amsterdam in 1986. He had a daughter back home who was to be married but had no suitable dress in which to get married. As the gracious providence of God would have it, Franklin had one, only one, lovely wedding dress in his supplies. The father got it and took it home to Africa, and the wedding was a most happy event.

Stories like that—and ones with much deeper need—can be multiplied over and over again. Franklin, like his father, has a benevolent heart to feed the hungry, clothe the naked, comfort the brokenhearted, and lead them all to Jesus.

And this is not to mention the work of Franklin Graham's World Medical Mission. Physicians and medical personnel volunteer their time to travel to remote and needy parts of the globe to minister to the sick and dying. The lives saved by this tremendous work, only heaven will reveal. It really is a marvelous work. Franklin stands as a classic case that the changed heart in Christ can mean a changed society. In his autobiography, Franklin Graham calls himself a "rebel with a cause." He was a rebel against spiritual things; now he is a rebel for Christ's cause against sin and need. He has made the Lord's cause his. He beautifully combines evangelism and social action. It would seem Billy's philosophy works; at least it did in this significant case. Franklin confesses his father has been an encouragement to him in the work as well as an influence for evangelism in his ministry.

Not only Billy Graham's son, but also many of Graham's converts have embraced a similar social commitment that grew out of their conversion experience. There is the story of Jim Vaus, the wiretapper converted in the 1949 Los Angeles crusade. Chapter 1 of this book recorded his conversion. Jim spent the bulk of his Christian life after being transformed by God's love in a storefront mission in a New York slum area ministering to rebellious young people. Christ does make a difference. And that type of account can be multiplied many times over. The influence of Graham in this regard is far more positive than many people realize. He said on one occasion, "Certainly we as Christians have no right to be content with our social order until the principles of Christ are applied to all men. As long as there is enslaved one man who should be free, as long as slums and ghettos exist, as long as any person goes to bed hungry at night, as long as the color of a man's skin is his prison, there must be a divine discontent."[21]

Therefore, it would appear safe to conclude that although Mr. Graham's approach is not the only approach to social concern and action, it certainly seems to be a solid one. Moreover, he himself is genuinely sensitive to the needs of people in the practical situations of life that he encounters.

BILLY GRAHAM'S ACTIONS

The needs of people truly touch the evangelist Billy Graham. In 1952, Graham traveled to Korea during the Korean conflict to minister to the troops. In December of that year he was in Pusan and there he saw the abject misery of the Korean people. Some eight hundred thousand refugees roamed the streets of Pusan. The weather was terrible, the streets were muddy, and the people were unbelievably dirty. What food that could be found was anything but appetizing. Beggars hung about on street corners. Lepers and those with other diseases crowded in on every side. Precious children searched through the garbage heaps for scraps of food. The city had become a city of decrepit shacks. This appalling scene did something to Billy Graham. The pathetic sight of orphan children and the desperate people made a deep and lasting impression. He left Korea a much more matured person with a new awareness of man's misery and determined to do something about human need. As he traveled throughout the world, he continually developed a deeper and more profound sensitivity to human need.

Dr. John Corts, president and COO of the BGEA, tells of Billy traveling to southern India after a terribly devastating monsoon season. The pitiful plight of the people deeply moved the evangelist. His ministry stepped in and shipped tons of food and clothing to the area. The people were so grateful they began to call their little village after Billy Graham. His own conversion certainly brought the peace of God to his life, but it also laid the foundation for an awareness of, and a deep commitment to, alleviate social ills. Further, he feels convinced that this must be true of any genuinely converted believer. God's love demands it. Christ leads into holistic evangelism and ministry. This principle manifests itself in a number of ways.

GRAHAM'S VIEWS ON RACIAL SEGREGATION

Billy Graham faced and settled the racial problem early in life. In 1940, when he left the Bible Institute in Florida and enrolled in Wheaton College west of

Chicago, it was the first time he ever shared classes with African-Americans. The love of Christ won the Southerner and the issue has never been a problem personally since.

One of the most significant stands that Billy Graham took, while still in his early years as a preacher, occurred in 1952. He felt terribly uneasy about segregated seating arrangements made by local committees in his early crusades. This drove him into a study of the Scriptures on the issues. He soon found the answer and determined he would set an example of what the Christian position should be. On March 15, 1953, more than a year before the Supreme Court made its monumental decision of May 17, 1954, Graham deliberately and unapologetically completely integrated all of his crusades. The first integrated crusade took place in the Deep South city of Chattanooga, Tennessee. In this particular crusade, the local committee actually constructed an auditorium for a nonsegregated meeting—much to the chagrin of many Southerners. Few had a biblical grasp of the evils of segregation, at least in that part of America. But Billy Graham told the crusade committee that African-Americans must be allowed to be seated anywhere. He overruled every protest, ignoring the "prophets of doom" who forecasted serious troubles. Graham has never been reticent to take a firm stand on what he considers to be a biblical mandate.

When the local committee in the Dallas, Texas, crusade attempted to modify Graham's policy, his strong personal convictions once again surfaced. As a single case in point, one day Billy got on an elevator in a Dallas hotel with an African-American friend. The bellman who was operating the elevator stopped them and told the African-American that he could not ride on that elevator. Billy Graham became quite indignant. He said, "Either he rides with me or I go to the back and walk up with him. You can take your choice!" That settled the issue, and Dallas capitulated.

A very serious racial crisis erupted in Little Rock, Arkansas, in September 1957. Governor Orval Faubus had called out the National Guard troops to bar black children from the public schools. Billy again took his strong stand. He was contacted by President Dwight Eisenhower for advice, and the president listened. Graham was asked to preach in Little Rock, but because of his strong stand on the racial issue, his speaking engagement had to be postponed for a period. Of course, the White Citizens Council criticized Billy quite vitriolically. But in 1959, he preached in Little Rock and was well received. When he held a crusade in Chattanooga in 1953 and sections were cordoned off for African-Americans, Billy personally tore down the barriers.

Some few years later, in volatile Birmingham, Alabama, Graham scheduled a large evangelistic rally at Legion Field, the football arena for the University of Alabama. This author's wife was working in the office preparing for the crusade. It proved to be a very volatile situation indeed. The FBI had to put guards on the office workers. Harsh words constantly came in. Just a short time prior to the rally, the notorious "Bessemer bombers" had bombed the African-American Sixteenth Street Baptist Church, killing four small girls in the blast. But regardless of threats or what many people would have considered an affront to the gospel itself, Graham took his stand. On the day of the rally, the stadium was packed to overflowing; some thirty thousand people attended, with about a 50/50 ratio of blacks and whites. At the invitation time, both races streamed to the altar. It was a beautiful picture. Both races went out of their way to be friendly to each other. John Pollock describes it as "the most completely integrated public meeting in Birmingham's history, and the beginning of a new day."[22] No incident occurred, and Birmingham took a major step forward because of the stance of Billy Graham. The evangelist well realizes the evils of racial segregation. As he said at the 1966 World Congress on Evangelism held in Berlin:

We recognize the failure of many of us in the recent past to speak with sufficient clarity and force upon the biblical unity of the human race. All men are one in the humanity created by God Himself. All men are one in their common need of divine redemption, and all are offered salvation in Jesus Christ. . . .

We reject the notion that men are unequal because of distinction of race or color. In the name of Scriptures and of Jesus Christ we condemn racialism wherever it appears. We seek by God's grace to eradicate from our lives and from our witness whatever is displeasing to Him in our relations one with another. We extend our hands to each other in love, and those same hands reach out to men everywhere with the prayer that the Prince of Peace may soon unite our sorely divided world.[23]

In all these racial upheavals, Graham kept to his basic philosophy, saying, "We are ultimately not going to solve the race problems in America until men truly love each other. And this love can only be brought about by God, as we yield to Him."[24]

John Corts relates a classic example of Billy Graham's principle of social action at one of his Deep South crusades, one completely integrated. A certain lady, a top socialite of the community, came forward at the invitation to make her commitment to Christ. A black counselor talked with her and led her to Christ. Afterward, her irate husband said, "Didn't you realize you were speaking with a Negro counselor?" She said, "You know, I didn't even notice the color of her skin." Billy himself remarked, "You see, in the spirit of that moment, in a moment of dedication, racial consciousness was in the background."[25] So the point is made: Changed lives mean changed attitudes.

Billy Graham is not only concerned about the stance he takes in his own crusades, but he also feels the burden of helping the entire world become aware of the evils of prejudice, racial segregation, and disharmony. Through it all, Graham adheres to what the Bible says concerning interpersonal relationships, be they racial, economic, educational, or social. He contends there is something of a brotherhood of all humanity because of God's creative hand. This does not mean everyone is a regenerate believer, but it does mean that God in creation has made the human race one. As the Bible says, God "hath made of one blood all nations of men for to dwell on all the face of the earth" (Acts 17:26 KJV). That principle must be exercised and propagated. It must especially be recognized and implemented in the lives of Christian converts. Then they in turn serve as the "salt of the earth" to lend their support and effort in helping others to a like stance.

It should be emphasized here again that Graham's individualistic approach to ethics and morals by no means implies that he believes there should be no laws to govern interpersonal relationships. When the United States Congress passed the significant Civil Rights Bill, Billy gave his fullest support. Yet, for full compliance, the heart must be changed. Senator Hubert Humphrey, along with Billy Graham, recognized that legislation alone cannot accomplish the ultimate solution. Only a new heart can do that. He expressed this to Billy Graham, and Graham later affirmed the principle of Humphrey's assessment, declaring it takes love, understanding, forbearance, and patience on the part of both races. And it only comes about by the new life in Christ. The final solution is the gospel, but laws have their place and play their role as well.

This position on racial issues has never been compromised by Graham or his association in their many years of ministry. They employ people regardless of racial background. Billy has enlisted associate evangelists who labor with him from the African-American community, India, South America, and other parts of the world. Since the launching of his early evangelistic crusade ministry, Graham has proved himself a sterling character and protagonist for racial harmony and mutual acceptance. He clearly sees and propagates the ethical dimensions of his holistic evangelistic approach.

GRAHAM'S VIEWS ON POVERTY

It has already been mentioned that Billy Graham is significantly touched by the economic plight of people as they struggle in poverty. He tells a touching hunger story during a preaching mission in India that speaks of his heart and illustrates his basic philosophy of holistic evangelism. It reads as follows:

> I saw a young girl in India with a five-gallon empty water drum on her head. She was walking from her home village to a dirty water hole several kilometers away. And I have watched older women return bent under the strain of that unbelievably heavy load. The water sources near their homes had dried up from a prolonged drought. As I stood watching, I knew that girl's spiritual thirst was more important than her physical thirst, but I couldn't force myself to separate the two. Like the woman at the well at Sychar in Samaria to whom Jesus ministered, there was a person who needed, physically and spiritually, the water of life. Our loving witness for a lost soul must go hand in hand with our loving concern for a dying body. We are called by God to bring the water of life for both soul and body. God created them both, and His purpose is to redeem them both.[26]

Billy was so moved by such scenes that in his crusade work in the early '80s he organized in the Boston meeting what became known as the Love in Action Committee to raise food and help for the needy. But even before that, in the Minneapolis crusade of July 13–22, 1973, he for the first time took up an offering of food for the hungry. At times Billy himself will take a basket of food to a hungry family. Rick Marshall, BGEA crusade director, states, "It now lies at the heart of the crusades."[27]

Of course, through the years, as shall be shown, this holistic spirit has developed into many areas of ministry. For example, the Graham organization has created the World Emergency Fund. This work has literally deployed millions of dollars' worth of relief to needy areas. Few recognize the tremendous contribution this aspect of holistic evangelism has made to many needy people. And in it all, Graham has kept a good balance between social action and evangelism. As John Stott has pointed out, "He has prioritized his ministry well."[28] Moreover, the evangelist has not been silent on social issues in many areas—including the political.

BROADER INVOLVEMENTS

In June of 1967, Graham went to Washington to make his influence felt and give his full support to the antipoverty program of the Lyndon B. Johnson administration. In that setting he spoke to some two hundred influential persons at a luncheon meeting and gave a strong affirmation for doing all that is humanly possible individually and collectively as a nation to alleviate the misery of poverty-stricken families in America. At that luncheon he made the following statement: "This is the first time in seventeen years that I have come to Washington to speak for or against a government program. But now I have come to speak to various Congressmen, in favor of the poverty program."[29] As is well known, Congress passed Johnson's poverty program, the president signed it into law, and it became a revolutionary new approach to meeting America's needs.

The story has been shared earlier that President Lyndon Johnson urged Graham to head his poverty program. This thrust Billy Graham into a quandary. He recognized that God had called him to preach the gospel, and to that he was absolutely committed. Still, he desired that people would know of his deep concern for the social needs of the many. But the fact that he seriously considered the president's invitation demonstrates his concern for all levels of human need.

Moreover, the many gestures that Graham himself makes and has encouraged others to make regarding reaching out to people in their need are really quite remarkable. This is true on a personal level as well as organizing for action. For example, there was a pastor who received an invitation to become a professor and teach a much-needed practical theological discipline in Europe. The new professor had no funds to move, nor did the institution. Billy

Graham heard of it and the BGEA funded the move: professor, family, and furniture. That sort of story can be repeated many times. Billy Graham has a heart much in tune with St. Francis himself. He and his wife, Ruth, do untold good on a simple personal level right in their own community in North Carolina. Billy regularly sends money, anonymously, to needy families, as does Ruth. And on a larger scale, he personally raised considerable funds to get oppressed Jewish people out of the Soviet Union in communist days.

In the context of the crusades, the Love in Action work goes on. An appeal is made for people to bring canned goods, nonperishable food, clothing, etc. to be distributed to the needy in the city of the crusade. And the response has been most encouraging. Many of God's people have brought an untold number of boxes of donations. Truckloads of food have been collected and distributed. Billy Graham has been an inspiration and catalyst to foster a Christian spirit of benevolence to meet many human needs. The generosity and gracious spirit of this man are most commendable.

Why does Graham see all this as so essential? In his own words he said, "Because we have the life of Jesus, the work of the saints, the apostles, and the church organizing itself to help the widows. . . . Jesus had compassion; He did not preach so much about it, He just did it. We must follow His footsteps in our personal lives. . . . I have felt this very strongly."[30] That, it would seem, constitutes motive enough.

POLITICS

But what about Billy Graham's political views? It has been intimated that he keeps himself open to influence right decisions by the government. In what ways does Graham involve himself in politics to alleviate human suffering?

Graham is clearly aware of the fact that the state cannot reform people and give them a new heart; only Christ can do that. One of the contemporary problems in a country like America (as well as some countries in Europe) is the popular view that the state can solve all problems, falsely assuming that people's hearts are always altruistic. As Graham has said:

> We have been trying to solve every ill of society as though society were made up
> of regenerate men to whom we had an obligation to speak with Christian advice.

. . . We are beginning to realize that, while the law must guarantee human rights and restrain those who violate those rights, whenever men lack sympathy for the law they will not long respect it even when they cannot repeal it. Thus the government may try to legislate Christian behavior, but it soon finds that man remains unchanged.[31]

This statement by Graham implies two principles. First, back to his initial philosophy, the human heart must be changed before any lasting cultural problems can be finally resolved. Second, the law still does have a role to play, and concerned Christians should involve themselves in the political arena to get the right kinds of laws passed. Graham is careful regarding his stand on this point. He feels that as a Christian leader he should not alienate people on political issues that do not have a moral or ethical element. When Christian principles are at stake, however, a stand must be taken; when they are not, neutrality seems the best stance. This has been his position through the years. Yet, being neutral on some political issues has not crowded him in a corner and made him a political, ethical nonentity. He takes a firm stand when moral and ethical Christian principles are afoot.

Graham has thus been supportive of many aspects of American foreign policy. For example, his concern for needy people, especially in emerging nations, has made him strongly supportive of certain forms of foreign aid. He feels that governmental policy should reflect Christian values, and he lets it be known. Recall again that he said on one occasion: "This is the first time in seventeen years that I have come to Washington to speak for or against a government program."[32]

As would be anticipated, there are those who feel Billy does not exercise his strong influence enough. A high-profile instance occurred in 1954 when Graham refused to become involved in Senator Joseph McCarthy's anticommunist crusade. Billy insightfully recognized that McCarthy was something of a political demagogue who was going much too far in his attempt to find communists lurking about everywhere. This by no means implies that Graham failed to speak out against atheistic communism. To the contrary; especially in his earlier ministry, he preached quite vociferously against what President Reagan later called the "Evil Empire."

What particularly moved Graham to speak out so strongly in the earlier days of his crusade work was the Soviet Union's invasion of Hungary.

Moreover, he voiced sharp criticism for the vacillating position, if not the outright impotence, of the United Nations concerning the aggression against Hungary. The free Hungarian radio had sent out its last message begging the free world to come to their aid. But the United Nations proved very ineffective. In that setting Graham posed the question: "Do we have the right to enjoy our privileges of peace while people are being trampled to death beneath the steel heel of godless communism? I feel it is my duty to warn the American people that a day of reckoning is coming. We cannot ignore the oppressed, suffering and helpless peoples behind the iron curtain without paying for it at the judgment of God."[33]

Although Graham did not identify himself with Joseph McCarthy in the witch hunt he conducted, he did at the same time give his affirmation to those who were reasonably and sensibly investigating the infiltration of communism in the American system. Graham was primarily concerned over the spiritual issues and the suppression of human rights problem that emanated out of the communist philosophy. He actually saw Marxism, at least as it was expressed in the Soviet Union, as a religion. He condemned it with these words: "The devil is their god; Marx, their prophet; Lenin, their Saint; and Malenkov, their high priest. Denying their faith in all ideologies except their religion of revolution, these diabolically inspired men seek in devious ways to convert a peaceful world to their doctrine of death and destruction."[34] He became absolutely convinced the only remedy for the situation was the gospel of Jesus Christ. Graham was a strong anticommunist because of the atheism of the system, the oppression of people, and the loss of freedom the communist countries espoused. That stance helped gain the attention of William Randolph Hearst and his newspaper syndicate, which was instrumental in elevating Graham into national prominence.

As the years passed, Graham mellowed on the communist issue. And now, since the fall of the Iron Curtain, he mentions it little. Still, however, he is outspoken on human rights issues. For instance, the introduction of his national best-selling book of 1991, *Hope for the Troubled Heart*, contains a note that all the royalties from the book will go to the East Gate Ministries, "a new organization helping to bring about understanding between [communist] China and the rest of the world through spiritual understanding."[35]

Still, criticism of Graham on political issues from various fronts constantly arises. In England during the 1954 Harringay crusade, the newspapers harshly criticized him for a number of reasons. Five years later the governmental press in Ghana severely criticized him, actually condemning Graham because he did not speak out concerning the impending French atomic tests in the Sahara Desert. But in it all, Billy Graham maintained his position that he must be neutral on that in which there are no moral issues involved; his primary task centers in the evangelization of the world. He refuses to get locked into unprofitable and unnecessary political entanglements. The principle that a Christian social order will only come about by personal individual conversions has guided all of his political decisions. He said on one occasion:

> We talk glibly about the establishment of a Christian order of society through legislation and social engineering, as though we could bring it down from the skies, if only we worked hard enough. The kingdom of God will never come that way. If the human race should suddenly turn to Christ, we would have immediately the possibility of a new Christian order. We could approach our problems in the framework of Christian understanding and brotherhood. To be sure, the problems would remain, but the atmosphere for their solution would be completely changed.[36]

God's rules can never be created by human politics or manipulation; His kingdom only comes about through personal conversions.

As pointed out, the evangelist has softened his rhetoric toward the communist regimes around the world, especially the Soviet Union. But another barrage of criticism came when Graham traveled to the Soviet Union to attend and speak at a peace conference. He wrestled with the issue of whether to accept the invitation. But he concluded it was God's will to go. As can be imagined, there was a vociferous outcry among many conservative evangelicals and fundamentalists. Some accused him of not only backtracking on his earlier stance, but even compromising with the "Evil Empire." But Graham, who has never been particularly deterred by criticism from what he considers God's will, traveled to Moscow. And his trip ultimately opened significant doors for the gospel. As John Corts pointed out in a personal interview, Billy realized the Soviets were using him, but he was using them to get the gospel behind the

Iron Curtain. And it worked. Billy was given permission to hold a crusade in Moscow, as mentioned earlier. It was a tremendous time, and many thousands came to faith in the Lord Jesus Christ. His political, holistic principles held.

It must be admitted that in the political arena, Billy has made mistakes on occasion. On July 14, 1950, he had an interview with President Harry S. Truman. After leaving the Oval Office, at reporters' requests, he demonstrated to them how he had prayed for the president. He got down on one knee on the White House lawn and simulated a prayer, at least that is how the press perceived and presented it. It raised a few eyebrows, but was soon forgotten— and the evangelist learned to be more discreet.

PATRIOTISM

At times, questions have been raised about Billy Graham's patriotism. But he obviously is an American who loves his country and wants the very best for it. Still, he believes that America will become what it should be only when it comes to faith in Jesus Christ. Thus he holds up that Christian ideal for the nation. He said:

> What would happen today if the Bible were the supreme authority in the United States? If every citizen loved, read, and obeyed the Scriptures? What would happen if every individual in America would accept Christ as Savior and begin to live up to the terms of the Sermon on the Mount? Jesus Christ could solve the problem which the nation faces. He could solve the race problem, the crime problem, the home problem, the international problems. He can also lift the burdens that we have as individuals; he can reach the problems down in the innermost recesses of our own souls.[37]

Moreover, as seen, Graham contends that people have the definite responsibility to be involved and aid the government in its quest for proper action, if by no more than casting their ballot. He pointed this out strongly in what he said about voting: "Nothing would please the racketeers, gangsters, and the underworld more than for all church people to stay away from the polls and to be uninformed about the goings on in Washington. I would urge every Christian to vote and to show a keen interest in the politics of his community."[38]

Further, he urges Christians to do more than vote if they have the opportunity. They should exercise themselves in campaigning for honest and ethical leadership. He commends Christians with high moral standards who will involve themselves in the political arena. In that regard he said, "I know men who are in government who have high principles, fine motives, and unquestioned integrity. They have dedicated themselves to a life of public service because they sincerely want to serve their fellow men."[39] He feels it is an obligation that people, for the welfare of their country, give themselves to such service. Graham holds one strong qualifier, however. He does not believe the church should speak on every social and political issue that comes along, unless it has moral or spiritual implications. The church as a body cannot speak for everyone, and hence Christians should be most careful in their statements and commitments.

Several times Billy Graham has been asked to run for political office, even challenged to run for the presidency of the United States. In the height of his popularity, he might well have seen himself elected. But each time he definitely declined, always arguing that it would be a tragedy if through the strategy of Satan he did anything that might be construed as purely political. In 1968 he was strongly urged to enter the presidential race. But he let it be known that he could not do so. Though he was concerned about good politics and good government, he refused to enter the arena because he had been called to preach the gospel. He has said, "I don't want to get into any kind of politics, left or right, Republican or Democrat, because I experienced that a few times in my years, and you can get into trouble real fast."[40] President Nixon said to the evangelist many times, "Billy, at all costs stay out of politics. . . . Your ministry is more important than my election."[41] Still, Graham said, "I will be a friend to men of both parties."[42] Consequently, he has been a positive influence to both.

PERSONAL MORALITY AND ETHICS

Much has already been said concerning Graham's holistic approach in ethical and moral issues on a broad scale, and in the forthcoming chapter on godliness we shall look at this area of Christian experience in some depth. Nonetheless, perhaps at this point something of a succinct presentation should be made concerning his views on personal morality, godliness, and ethical living. He is deeply concerned for true discipleship rather than just seeing decisions made at his crusades. He truly desires to see genuine change in the individual human heart, as has been stated so often.

Early in Billy Graham's life, two Christians whom he had profoundly admired were accused of serious moral problems. It shook Billy tremendously. He soon learned that a person may make a profession of Christianity and still become a "castaway" (1 Cor. 9:27 KJV). That particular experience caused Graham to determine that nothing would ever be allowed in his life or the association that would reflect upon his or their personal commitment and bring dishonor to the name of Christ.

One incident occurred that significantly affected the future organization of the Billy Graham Evangelistic Association. In one of his early crusades, a "love offering" was collected for expenses and an honorarium. The money was in a large paper bag, and a newspaper photographer took a picture of an usher holding the money. As can be surmised, the picture made the newspaper the next day with the strong implication that Billy Graham was making off with a lot of the local money. This deeply grieved him and led him to a conversation with Jesse Bader, Executive Secretary of the Federal Council of Churches. Dr. Bader suggested that Billy form an association and the incorporated association handle all the money, and he and the team be put on a straight salary. That is exactly what Graham did, as previously pointed out. This incident moved Graham to form the Billy Graham Evangelistic Association and to write what has become known as the Modesto Manifesto. That important document was drawn together by the early team members in Modesto, California. Cliff Barrows called it "historic."[43] This document will be examined in chapter 10.

Quite clearly, Billy Graham is vitally concerned that no reproach ever be leveled at him or his work for mistakes of judgment. This principle applies in what might seem insignificant details. He has experienced one or two possible situations that could have been tragic. As a case in point, Billy never enters a hotel room first; someone always precedes him lest a trap of some sort has been set. From time to time it has saved him from a bad situation. Moreover, he never allows himself to be alone with a woman regardless of the circumstance. He will not ride alone in a car with a woman. When the eyes of the world are fixed on a high-profile personality like Billy, these minor things can become most significant. The apostle Paul said, "Abstain from all appearance of evil"

(1 Thess. 5:22 KJV). Graham meticulously follows that principle. His moral standards are unequivocally above reproach. And he feels such must be true for all real believers. This basic spirit and approach has won respect for Graham throughout the world. He is seen as a man of uncompromised sincerity, humility, and integrity. As one professor has expressed it so well, "There is an authentic 'gospel reality' in Graham."

OTHER ISSUES

Many other social issues could be raised. Again, space forbids but their mention. AIDS is an issue. Graham suggests three things to do: (1) Educate yourself on the facts, (2) learn about organizations fighting the world epidemic, and (3) volunteer through your church or otherwise and join the battle. Good advice and strategy!

Abortion has been in the limelight and has become a divisive issue. Graham is a strong advocate of birth control. At the same time, he is not in favor of abortion, except in cases that involve rape or incest, or when the mother's life is in jeopardy. Graham was deeply disappointed in 1996 when President Clinton vetoed legislation banning partial birth abortion. Billy said, "I think the president was wrong in vetoing it. I had the opportunity of telling him that in person."[44] Still, he feels that extreme activism in the antiabortion camp, such as Operation Rescue, goes too far, and the cause has been hurt. The tactics ought to be "prayer and discussion,"[45] he declares.

Further, on the issue of war, the evangelist has said, "I am not a pacifist, nor am I for unilateral disarmament. Police and military forces are unfortunately necessary as long as man's nature remains the way it is. . . . From the Christian perspective, therefore, the possibility of a nuclear war originates in the greed and covetousness of the human heart. . . . There is a tragic and terrible flaw in human nature that must be recognized and dealt with."[46] Graham laments the trillions of dollars spent every year on armaments around the world while children are starving to death. Hunger moves him deeply. He declares most ardently, "War is not necessary."[47] Christians are to seek peace (Matt. 5:9).

Many more issues could be raised, such as the crime rate and juvenile delinquency, divorce, sex, etc. (some of which shall be discussed in chapter 10).

Tom Allan, a Scottish socialist, brought it together well when he said, "Graham has one of the most acute social consciences of any man I ever met. All his sympathies, all his affections, all his personal passion is on the side of the dispossessed, the disinherited, the lost, the hungry, the lonely, the homeless, the downtrodden."[48] That benevolent spirit has been used of God to impress many for Christ.

THE FOUNDATION PRINCIPLE

Billy Graham's moral and social principles are predicated on Romans 12:1–2: "I urge you therefore, brethren, by the mercies of God, to present your bodies a living and holy sacrifice, acceptable to God, which is your spiritual service of worship. And do not be conformed to this world, but be transformed by the renewing of your mind, that you may prove what the will of God is, that which is good and acceptable and perfect."

Not only does Graham take this stance himself, but he also lifts up the standard for his fellow evangelists. He said on one occasion, "It is my conviction that even though evangelism is necessarily confined with narrow limits, the evangelist must not hedge on social issues. The cost of discipleship must be made plain from the platform. I have made the strongest possible statements on every social issue of the day."[49] He grants that there have been times when perhaps he overstepped bounds and made socioeconomic statements that he wished he could retract; nonetheless, he holds his position and preaches on issues that matter to the man in the street.

Furthermore, his own actions, as has been seen, fulfill this basic quest for holistic evangelism, and he mobilizes others and challenges them to that end. In his many significant evangelism conferences, especially in Amsterdam '83, '86, and 2000, a strong emphasis was made on meeting the needs of the attendees. He helped raise funds and brought thousands of evangelists from all over the world to attend the congress. He paid their way and provided lodging and food for them. Some had walked many miles just to get to a railhead or airport to fly to Amsterdam where the conferences were held. And, as shown, literally tons of clothing and books and provisions for their physical, mental, and spiritual needs were distributed. These conferences presented a graphic picture of meeting the holistic needs of the attendees.

Reference has been made to the holistic ministry of Franklin Graham through Samaritan's Purse and through the medical mission program he conducts. Billy Graham gives his complete support to this work and throws his influence behind it. This is not true simply because he is Franklin Graham's father, but because these are his own deep convictions. Many feel it was Billy's holistic concern that challenged and so deeply ingrained the burden in Franklin to meet people's needs, regardless of the need or who the people were. When asked if he thought he influenced Franklin, Billy replied, "I hope so." Surely he did.

THE CRITICS

Of course, as in many areas of Graham's ministry, there have been critics. As mentioned, some think he does or says very little in the area of social action. As a case in point, a reader of Graham's daily newspaper column, "My Answer," asked why he did not take a firmer, more vocal stand on issues. His reply of August 1996 reads:

> I suspect if you examined my sermons in detail over the years, you would find that I have touched repeatedly on virtually every social problem imaginable— from alcohol and drugs, to racism and war. But the important question we can ask about this issue is this: why do we have these problems? Our deepest problem is a spiritual problem, and that is why our greatest need is to be reconciled to God and allow Him to change our hearts. And that is why Christ came—to reconcile us to God.[50]

At the same time, Graham is quick to point out to his critics, "Contrary to the opinion of some, the evangelist is not primarily a social reformer or lecturer or a moralizer. He is simply keryg, a proclaimer of the good news."[51] It seems fair, and according to Graham's philosophy of social action, it is an adequate view. Such criticisms are obviously incorrect. Billy Graham does far more than most people realize, but he does put it in a secondary role because of his deep conviction that God has called him primarily to be an evangelist. He does not trumpet his many benevolent activities. Yet the conclusion has surely been made amply clear that, in evangelism, it is biblical to be a holistic evangelist.

And Graham serves in the spirit of the historical precedent set by men of God like St. Francis of Assisi. Thus Billy Graham takes his stand unapologetically regarding those who criticize him. Therefore, as best he understands it, he is absolutely committed as an evangelist to his social obligations and at the same time preaches the gospel of Christ, seeing lives changed that ultimately change society.

RESULTS

Actually, excellent results have been forthcoming from Graham's position. Many people have been helped by the Graham ministry as it has deeply and profoundly touched difficult situations. Since 1973, the World Emergency Fund has helped to alleviate suffering and privation when war and natural disasters occur. And it makes a real difference. The BGEA officials make it clear that every dollar contributed to the World Emergency Fund goes to relief projects. Nothing is directed for administrative expenses.

Graham, as a consequence of his holistic evangelism, has become a world leader, a compassionate man, and a genuine Christian. Very little criticism has fallen his way that has not been silenced. It all stems from the fact that Graham possesses honesty, integrity, and godliness in his own life that manifests itself in a genuine love for people in meeting their deepest needs.

CONCLUSION AND CONTRIBUTION OF
BILLY GRAHAM IN HOLISTIC EVANGELISM

"I burned inwardly . . ." That is what Billy Graham said about his reaction to social injustice. But then, one would expect that from an evangelist. Billy's heart does burn inwardly to see unbelievers won. But in this case, it will be remembered he was deeply disturbed because of the plight of disenfranchised people. This evangelist is vitally concerned for human rights, feeding the hungry, and meeting the needs of the homeless and suffering; he has a heart for the needy as well as the lost. Thus Billy Graham reveals his commitment to step into hurting lives and in the name of Christ meet needs. Therein he reflects his Christian love and compassion. He keeps a beautiful balance between evangelism and social action. As he has said:

The gospel is both vertical and horizontal. The vertical signifies our relationship to God. The horizontal signifies the application of the principles of the teachings of Christ to our daily lives. At least a third of my preaching is spent encouraging and teaching people to apply the principles of Christianity in their personal and social lives. . . . I would like to say emphatically that any gospel that preaches only vertical relationships is only a half-gospel.[52]

It does not seem an exaggeration to say that Graham has probably shown more compassion for needy people than any evangelist in many years, and he has done something about it. This chapter has attempted to reveal the heart and hand of Billy Graham in that respect. He does follow the lead of his Lord in touching people where they hurt.

Yet in it all, Billy Graham has remained the evangelist. It has been emphasized many times in these pages that he well recognizes that the most profound human need lies in the spiritual. He has never compromised or cut short his evangelization to do other ministries. But the love of Christ does compel him to do all in his power to alleviate pain. Priorities have been kept in place. The demonstration of compassion by the BGEA in so many places has been inspirational. Not only that, Billy is always doing "little things" on a personal, one-on-one basis. Illustrations of that fact are endless. He reflects his Lord in that regard. Jesus was never too busy or in too big a rush to stop and minister to just one person; witness blind Bartemaeus and the woman with the issue of blood. Billy is like Jesus in such situations.

But the inevitable question exerts itself once more: What contribution has Graham made in this area of historical, holistic evangelism? Will he be remembered as an "instrument of Thy peace," as is the case with St. Francis of Assisi? He may not be as "famous" in those regards as was Francis, even though Graham's social consciousness is exemplary. On the other hand, Francis is not remembered so much for his evangelism even though he was a true evangelist. Billy will no doubt always be seen primarily as a proclaimer of the gospel, as Francis is remembered for his benevolence. But history will surely record that when needs have arisen, Billy has stepped in to feed, clothe, and give aid. When hurting preachers and pastors needed encouragement, Billy was there. And his stand on racial matters will never be forgotten. Moreover, Billy Graham has been an inspiration and challenge to countless Christian leaders, organizations, and laypeople alike. Much has been done to help people and Christ's cause, even if it is not recognized. David Lockard entitled his book on Graham's holistic approach *The Unheard Billy Graham;* that puts it all in proper perspective.

So we are back to the time-honored cliché: Only eternity will record the work done, the lives reached, the people rescued, the governmental officials influenced, and the multitudes of Christian believers who have thrown themselves into such a work because of Billy Graham's lead. It really is hard to fault the evangelist in this regard. And that is historical, biblical evangelism as it should be.

CHAPTER 7

SUFFERING IN EVANGELISM

꙳

PART I:
SAVONAROLA THE SUFFERER

My Lord has done so much for me.
—SAVONAROLA

INTRODUCTION

It often seems that people visualize evangelists as spiritual heroes. Many heap admiration and acclaim upon God's gospel messengers. At times this scenario can be not only disconcerting, but a temptation for evangelists to seek popularity and power. Yet, in the overall scope of church history, this phenomenon is relatively new. Stalwart people of God who faithfully proclaim Jesus Christ have historically been a suffering, persecuted people. In one of the classic books of church history, *Foxe's Book of Christian Martyrs,* the author shares story after story of those who have been persecuted for their faith, many unto death. The Book of Revelation paints the same picture:

And when He broke the fifth seal, I saw underneath the altar the souls of those who had been slain because of the word of God, and because of the testimony which they had maintained; and they cried out with a loud voice, saying, "How long, O Lord, holy and true, wilt Thou refrain from judging and avenging our blood on those who dwell on the earth?" And there was given to each of them a white robe; and they were told that they should rest for a little while longer, until the number of their fellow servants and their brethren who were to be killed even as they had been, should be completed also. (6:9–11)

Obviously, evangelism has historically entailed more persecution than praise. Such was certainly true in the life of our Lord. It also became a reality for a quiet, meditative monk of the Dominican order, Savonarola of Florence (1452–1498).

SAVONAROLA AND THE FLORENTINE MINISTRY

Many similarities surface between St. Francis of Assisi and Savonarola of Florence. Both carried out their spiritual ministry in Italy as Roman Catholics, serving in a monastic context. The tie that binds them together, more than all others, is their deep devotion to God and their consuming commitment to the gospel of Christ. As God honored the ministry of St. Francis, the Holy Spirit powerfully anointed the service of Savonarola.

The two monks did differ in temperament, however. Historians described Francis as a radiant day of spring while Savonarola seemed more like a turbulent autumn day. The Florentine monk nursed a deep hatred of iniquity and cultivated a fervent passion to bring people to repentance and faith in Jesus Christ. But then, so did St. Francis. Further, the circumstances of Savonarola's day were not dramatically different from those of St. Francis. Political turmoil and societal unrest characterized both their times. St. Francis predated Savonarola by two and one-half centuries, and many of the more stabilizing factors that had emerged in the thirteenth century began to decay. The feudal system itself was collapsing. A new move to centralization rose on the scene, and out of the chaos of the times, rampant materialism gained strength. Actually, modern Europe was dawning as the Renaissance had cast its first beams across the horizon.

THE RENAISSANCE

The Renaissance movement ultimately set Italy ablaze. The human mind had readied itself to throw off the gloom and depression of the Dark Ages, even if Savonarola saw it as an "autumn day." Scholars revived the philosophies of ancient Greece and Rome. In that setting, two tremendous events took place. First, Gutenberg produced the printing press. This invention would prove to be one of the most monumental events of the millennium. The common people could now have reading material in their own hands. What this boded for the gospel proved tremendous. Second, Constantinople fell to the Turks. The scholars of the Byzantine Empire scattered throughout Europe, and a profound intellectual movement spread across the continent. It became obvious that Italy would ascend as the early center of the new life and culture.

The Renaissance can actually be divided into three distinct periods. From the days of St. Francis to about 1400 the Gothic period dominated the day. Progress was rather slow and laborious, and cultural religion still determined the mind-set of most. The second period took place in the dynamic fifteenth century. Religion still dominated the arts, but a new liberty and freedom entered the stage. The beginning of the sixteenth century marked a period called the High Renaissance. Life became far more affluent as morality decayed. Perhaps even more seriously, skepticism gripped the minds of many, especially the poor, as cruelty grew to unbelievable proportions. Crime and civic terror infiltrated society. As one historian put it, "Italy was full of Bravoes and cutthroats, who, before they struck down their victims from behind in quiet streets, did not think it incongruous first to visit the cathedral, and kneeling down, ask for God's protection."[1]

The spiritual climate of the Roman Church had deteriorated drastically, much as it had in the days of St. Francis. The popes scandalized Europe. For example, Paul II was known for his cupidity, Sixtus IV for his cruelty, Alexander VI for his unnatural passion, and Julius II for his infidelities and continuous involvement in European warfare. As a classic example of this rampant deterioration, the Vatican planned the murder of Lorenzo de Medici, the leading citizen of beautiful Florence. The pope's nephew planned the murder, and the murderer was an archbishop of the church. They made a mistake and Lorenzo's brother was killed instead. Local police uncovered the plot and the culprits were executed for the crime. When this news arrived in Rome, the Vatican issued a bull of excommunication against the executioners. Such abuses characterize the corruption of the church in Savonarola's time. Even Machiavelli said in regard to the church and priests of Rome, "We Italians owe this obligation—that we have become void of religion and corrupt."[2] In such a wicked age, the country stood in desperate need of a revolutionary voice for righteousness. And God granted it. That voice was heard in the fiery, powerful preaching of Savonarola.

THE EARLY LIFE OF SAVONAROLA

On September 21, 1452, in Ferrara, Italy, a "new hope" came into the world; Savonarola was born. At the time, everyone saw Ferrara as a dazzling, luxurious city-state. But Savonarola did not engage in the frivolity that characterized the early life of St. Francis. As a boy, Savonarola walked the streets of his city lonely and dejected. The path of pleasure had no attraction to the young lad. He felt the call of God to righteousness early in life. Deeply saddened by the corrupt situation of his city, he would spend hours at the altar of his church in agonizing prayer. He seemed to have the crushing burden of the world on his shoulders. What so deeply concerned him revolved around the world's rejection of Jesus Christ and God's glorious salvation.

On April 24, 1475, after hearing a sermon from an Augustinian friar, he fled to Bologna and entered a Dominican monastery. After taking monastic orders, he served in the monastery for some seven years. His great intellectual ability and religious zeal became evident to all; it looked as though he would have a most significant role in the life of the order.

THE MONK

In the confines of his monastery life, Savonarola immersed himself in a serious study of the Scriptures. In those days, the Scriptures were seldom read, let alone studied in depth. Even when the Bible was approached, an excessive allegorizing hermeneutic encrusted the Scriptures with Greek philosophy. When Savonarola first began reading the Bible, he too interpreted the Word in this fashion. But the more he studied, the more he realized that allegorizing must give way to the concrete truth of what the Bible actually says. As a result, Savonarola came to the realization that the Scriptures stand as the final authority in matters of the Christian faith. That new light precipitated a major turning point for the monk. He began to see the serious errors of the Roman Catholic system. Even at this early stage, Reformation ideas became deeply ingrained in Savonarola's spiritual understanding.

After seven years at Bologna, at the age of twenty-nine, the englightened friar was sent back to Ferrara as a parish priest. There his first preaching ministry began. Unfortunately, at that time, his preaching seemed to have little effect. In 1481, the year that Savonarola began his preaching ministry, war broke out in Ferrara. Savonarola was sent to Florence to the monastery of San Marco (St. Mark's), which housed the first public library in Italy.

In Savonarola's early days in Florence, despite his keen mind, he displayed no unusual gifts as a prophet. Nonetheless, the monastery appointed him Lenten preacher at the Church of St. Lorenzo. The more he preached, the more the crowds dwindled. Then, in 1484, Pope Sixtus died. Hope for reform and a more spiritual and genuine Christian church arose. But Sixtus's successor, Innocent VIII, proved even worse than his predecessor. The deteriorating situation burned in the heart of the lonely monk. He set himself to fasting and praying night and day as he pored over the Scriptures.

Then something quite remarkable happened. The prophecies of Revelation came alive and gripped Savonarola's heart and mind. He became convinced in the last book of the Bible that the judgments of the apocalypse related dynamically to his own day. At last, he had found his prophetic message. At that exact time, the church authorities sent Savonarola to the city of Brescia to preach. He applied all the terrors of Revelation to current events. His sermons began to overwhelm his hearers. Almost immediately, his fame as a preacher began to spread throughout northern Italy. In Florence, Lorenzo de Medici heard of the monk, and because of Lorenzo's powerful political influence, he engineered Savonarola's summons back to Florence. Savonarola gladly obeyed, even though he saw the powerful de Medici family as the symbol of the evil of the day.

It is only fair to say that Lorenzo de Medici personified evil no more than the average person; nor did Florence appear more wicked than any other city. Nonetheless, Savonarola saw de Medici and Florence as the symbol of all that he detested. So preach against it he must. Lorenzo probably did not anticipate that.

THE PREACHER

Now in Florence, Savonarola received the commission to preach. On the first of August 1489, Savonarola preached his first sermon at San Marco Cathedral. He began preaching from the Book of Revelation and in a very short time, the cathedral overflowed with people. The entire city seemed to be cramming into the beautiful Gothic structure, which stands to this day. The monk lashed out at the vices of the city and dragged the scandalous sins of the people into the blinding light of God's Word. Moreover, he spoke out against the impurities of the church under the sway of secular Renaissance humanism. He was fearless and incorruptible. He held back nothing. He passionately cried for repentance. This became the primary theme of his message: People must repent or suffer judgment.

The following year Rome elected Savonarola as friar of San Marco. In light of the political and religious dynamics of Florence, this meant that he should have paid homage to the house of Medici; but he absolutely refused to do so. He said God gave him the position of friar, not Lorenzo de Medici. Lorenzo did not take offense at this, as one might expect. Actually, some time later when Lorenzo became very ill, he called for Savonarola to minister to him. Lorenzo said that even though Savonarola had been very critical of him, "I know no honest friar but this one."

The crowds dramatically increased and the power of Savonarola's preaching grew in like manner. One historian expressed it this way:

> So large was the concourse gathered to hear him that he had to transfer himself to the Cathedral. Here, day after day, the population of Florence thronged to see and hear him. Many were drawn by curiosity, but even the most superficial became awed as they listened to the burning words of the preacher. The crowds thronged and pressed each other so close that there was hardly room to breathe; they built seats against the walls in the form of an amphitheater, and still the space was insufficient. And how is it possible at this date to describe the preacher? The deep resonant voice, the flash of his deep-set, penetrating eyes, the impassioned gestures, the marvelous flow of his oratory as, swept along with the fiery vehemence of his great soul, he discoursed to men of the eternal verities, of the awful facts of death and judgment to come? First he would begin in measured

and tranquil tones, taking up the subject, turning it quietly round, suggesting some scholarly exposition, advancing some interpretation, dealing with it casually, critically, suggestively; then, suddenly, often without warning, he would change; the meditative style was flung aside as the mantle of the prophet fell upon him; fire flashed from his eyes, the thunder came into his voice; now in passionate entreaty, now in scorching indignation, the sentences rushed out, never halting, never losing intensity or volume, but growing and growing until his voice became as the voice of God Himself, and all the building rocked and swayed as if it moved to the mighty passion of his words. And what of the hearers? They were as clay in his hands. Tears gushed from their eyes, they beat their breasts, they cried unto God for mercy, the church echoed and re-echoed with their sobs.[3]

One can imagine something of the impression Savonarola made by the power of such preaching.

Savonarola's prophetic message can be summed up in three simple, yet most profound, principles: (1) The church must be renewed, (2) before renewal, God will surely strike Italy with fearful chastisement, and (3) these things would shortly come to pass. In that setting, he preached repentance toward God and faith in our Lord Jesus Christ.

SAVONAROLA AS A TRIBUNE

The unrest in Italy generally escalated, largely due to the excesses of the contemporary pope. Savonarola continued to preach judgment. Then Lorenzo de Medici died, and Piero, his son, came into the place of prominence and power. Unfortunately, Piero fell far short of his father Lorenzo's abilities. Then Charles VIII of France invaded Italy and struck Naples. No united front could be mustered to aid Naples, and the city bent the knee to Charles. It looked like Florence would be next on the French agenda. Lorenzo de Medici had been on good terms with France, but foolish Piero sent support to the king of Naples. This raised the anger of Charles and precipitated the real possibility that Florence would soon be under attack.

The citizens of Florence became so disturbed and anxious that they sent for Savonarola to help reduce the tension. Some sources indicate that he had begun preaching on the necessity of a political revolution in order to reform religion and morality. This dragged the friar into public affairs, although much against his will. Piero de Medici threw himself at Charles's feet, and France gave very humiliating terms to Florence. This so enraged the Florentines that Piero actually had to flee the city. Savonarola intervened and signed a treaty with Charles VIII and the French armies withdrew.

This general political situation, along with the tremendous influence of Savonarola's powerful preaching (he preached three hundred sermons on the Book of Revelation), put Florence into his hands. As he entered the political arena, he feared the possibility of eroding the spiritual revival that had its birth under his leadership. Still, he felt the move into the spiritual and political leadership of Florence came from God. Savonarola reasoned that the spiritual would reinforce the political and the political could be a means to purify the spiritual.

Now, with this newfound power and influence, Savonarola set out to make Florence a city of God. He took the same basic tack that some years later the great Reformer John Calvin initiated in the city of Geneva, Switzerland. A new city actually did arise with Savonarola as its head. He almost accomplished his goal. As historian James Burns wrote:

> On the days when the Prior of St. Mark preached, says Milman, the streets were almost a desert; houses, schools, and shops were closed. No obscene songs were heard in the streets, but low or loud chants of lauds, psalms, or spiritual songs. Vast sums were paid in restitution of old debts, or wrongful gains. The dress of men became more sober, that of women modest and quiet. . . . Nor were the converts only of the lowly and uneducated. Men of the highest fame, in erudition, in arts, in letters, became amongst the most devoted of his disciples; names which in their own day were glorious, and some of which have descended to our own.[4]

Florence so responded that, as someone said, the carnival seemed like Lent. But, as so often in such movements, the first wave of Savonarola's popularity began to subside.

A NEW WAVE

Savonarola continued, however, to lash out against the pope. A contemporary wrote that one of the pontiff's strongest passions was an insatiable greed for gold. He accordingly formed intimate relations with Moors, Turks, and Jews, regardless of all the customs of his age. The pope's life of sin and debauchery shocked many. "Licentious Rome" escalated the ire of Savonarola even more as he continued to denounce its evil. How could licentious Rome and regenerate Florence coexist?

The pope attempted to silence Savonarola by flattery and bribes; the monk was offered a red cardinal's hat and post. Savonarola replied, "I will have no hat but that of a martyr, red in my own blood." Little did he know at the time that such would be the case. At this juncture, the pope issued a commission to look into Savonarola's orthodoxy. The commissioners immediately condemned him as guilty of heresy, schism, and disobedience to the Holy See. In May 1498, the official bull of Rome arrived in Florence with three charges against Savonarola: (1) refusal to obey the summons to Rome to defend himself three years earlier, (2) teaching of heretical and perverse doctrines, and (3) refusal to unite St. Mark's with the Tuscana and Roman provinces. Savonarola took the papal bull quite undismayed. He did stop preaching for a short season but soon resumed, thundering out to the people, "I lay down this axiom, there is no man that may not deceive himself, the pope himself may err, you are mad if you say the pope cannot err!"[5] One can imagine the reaction in Rome.

Pope Alexander VI did offer absolution to Savonarola if he would recant. But would he respond? Savonarola cried out, "I should think myself guilty of mortal sin if I should seek absolution."[6] Why the stance? Savonarola said, "Our doctrine has enforced good living, much fervor, and perpetual prayer, yet are we the excommunicated, they the blessed. . . . The answer of Christ may be expected. . . . The Lord will be with the excommunicated, the devil with the blessed."[7]

As can be imagined, the pope flew into a rage. Serious consequences were inevitable for the friar. Savonarola boldly appealed to the entirety of Christendom. He wrote letters to all the sovereigns of Europe, asking them to form a council to depose the pope. This cut the cord and the final ax fell.

THE CLOSING DAYS

The net closed in on Savonarola. The man used by God to bring about a great religious revival to all of northern Italy stood in deadly jeopardy. The crowd, fickle as always—just as in the case of our Lord—grew negative. Not only that, a famine and a plague broke out. It too deepened the negativism growing around Savonarola. Then, the Dominican and Franciscan Orders fell into conflict. All of these factors conspired to crush the popularity and power of Savonarola. The Signory of Florence was commissioned to arrest Savonarola. Friends wanted to help him escape, but he refused, bade farewell to his disciples, and gave himself up.

The mob turned against their great preacher. They actually struck him from behind and shouted, "Prophesy who it was that smote thee." It was a repeat of our Lord's suffering. For ten long days, Savonarola endured examination and severe torture. He then lay in prison for a full month.

Rome gave the word that Savonarola must die, "even if he be another John the Baptist," said Pope Alexander. The pope wanted Savonarola sent to Rome, but the signory refused. He would die in Florence. Along with Savonarola, two close friends, Friar Domenico and Friar Silvester, were likewise condemned to death. On May 23, 1498, the authorities led Savonarola to the Piazza della Signora. He walked into the piazza in front of St. Mark's Cathedral, to see that the gibbet, to the awe of the huge crowd that had gathered, had been constructed in the form of a cross. When Savonarola saw where he would be hung, he said, "My Lord has done so much for me." The executioners put the noose around his neck, and the bishop cried, "I separate you from the church militant and from the church triumphant." Savonarola, in the bravery that only the Spirit of God can give, cried back, "Not from the church triumphant, that is beyond thy power."[8] The noose tightened, the trap door opened, and Savonarola was hanged. He died for Jesus and for the faithful preaching of the gospel. They took his body down from the cross and burned it. The ashes were then thrown into the beautiful Arno River, which courses through the center of Florence. The saga ended. Rome won. But did it?

As strange as it seems, the church that had taken Savonarola's life proposed now to canonize him. The blood of the martyrs truly does become the seedbed of evangelical Christianity.

The beautiful sequel to the story reveals that the new spiritual life that God used Savonarola to bring about, not only in Florence but in many parts of the Mediterranean world, actually grew and deepened after his death. As a case in point, Michelangelo pored over Savonarola's sermons.

THE CORE

What was the secret of Savonarola's tremendous evangelistic ministry? The answer is threefold: (1) He submerged himself in the Word of God and came to grips with the simple gospel of Jesus Christ, (2) he grew into a man of great prayer and devotion, and (3) he was willing to die for Jesus and the gospel. He counted no cost too high to pay for the evangelization of the world. And he did pay with his life. So often, suffering surfaces in the context of fervent evangelism. Has this *always* been true? Is this a biblical principle? The doctrine of suffering for Christ must be investigated.

GOD'S SERVANTS SUFFER

The history of the righteous suffering begins in early Genesis. Cain killed Abel because "Abel offered to God a more excellent sacrifice than Cain, through which he obtained witness that he was righteous" (Heb. 11:4 NKJV). This suffering will continue to the end of the age. Revelation tells us, "I will give power to my two witnesses, and they will prophesy one thousand two hundred and sixty days, clothed in sackcloth. . . . When they finish their testimony, the beast [will] overcome them and kill them" (Rev. 11:3, 7 NKJV). From Genesis to Revelation, the Scriptures are saturated with the blood of those who for their faithful witness became martyrs for the Lord Jesus Christ. What a noble train! As the writer of Hebrews said, "Others experienced mockings and scourgings, yes, also chains and imprisonment. They were stoned, . . . they were put to death with the sword; they went about in sheepskins, in goatskins, being destitute, afflicted, ill-treated (men of whom the world was not worthy), wandering in deserts and mountains and caves and holes in the ground" (11:36–38).

Well known is the fact that the words *witness* and *martyrdom* stem from the same Greek root. The implication is clear: Those who would be a consistent witness for Christ may well suffer persecution. Furthermore, it goes without saying that the suffering scenario of God's faithful was epitomized in our Lord Jesus Christ. No one suffered as He did. Not only did He endure the ridicule, rejection, and reviling of His contemporaries, but He permitted himself to be impaled on the cross and suffer the judgment of the sin of the entire world. That act of grace constituted the greatest of all suffering for the glory of God. Suffering does redound on the glory of God. But how can suffering magnify the Most High? That becomes a perplexing question for many faithful believers.

THE PROBLEM OF THEODICY

It may sound presumptuous to say that suffering brings glory to God. Yet the truth remains. In some inscrutable manner, which goes beyond our ability to comprehend, suffering magnifies our Lord. Yet at least something of a rationale for the sufferings of God's people can be found.

It should be said at the outset that the Scriptures do not approach the problem of suffering in a full systematic or philosophical manner. The Bible basically delineates the fact that believers suffer in various ways for their faith. Recall, Paul wrote, "For to you it has been granted for Christ's sake, not only to believe in Him, but also to suffer for His sake" (Phil. 1:29). At the same time, the Bible does present at least something of a rationale for persecution. The first clear scriptural answer revolves around the reality that a measure of suffering is the direct result of sin and evil in the world. It all began in the Garden of Eden with Adam and Eve being expelled because of their rebellion against God. Although this tragedy inaugurated the beginning of evil and suffering in the human family, the Scriptures do not explain the origin of evil other than the fact that in some way Lucifer, "the Son of the Morning," was full of pride and exalted himself against God, having been engaged in aggressive spiritual warfare against God and His creation ever since.

SIN SPELLS SUFFERING

In the Old Testament, the Semitic mind-set of the writers always dealt with evil and suffering in a very concrete matter. The prophets never approached the issue abstractly. The Hebrew ethos normally regarded suffering as a direct punishment for sin. The Bible abounds with the principle that the wicked will suffer for their rebellion against God. As the psalmist said, "Evildoers . . . will wither quickly like the grass, and fade like the green herb" (Ps. 37:1–2). Of course, many times God showed mercy and grace. Still, the wayward person or nation God will judge. The Jews projected the principle into their own personal experience; they normally saw their own suffering as a sign of God's displeasure. Because of their corporate understanding of life and society, the sins of the nation were their own.

As the revelation of God expanded in Israel's grasp of spiritual truth, the concept of suffering developed in like manner. For example, the prophet Isaiah came on the scene with an expanded understanding of the problem. He saw a larger purpose in suffering than the traditional view. He saw the possibility of the sufferer carrying the sins of others. Isaiah 53 sets forth the portrayal of the "suffering servant," sacrificed for others. The eschatological hope that developed in the thinking and theology of the Old Testament writers caused them to look forward to the day of the Lord, when all the righteous, regardless of the suffering they endured, would be vindicated.

THE NEW TESTAMENT PRINCIPLE

The New Testament clearly portrays this developmental understanding in the fullest sense: The Messiah suffered for humanity's sins. When Christ died on the cross, the whole concept of bearing the sins of erring men and women reached its epitome. The entire purpose of Christ's coming into the world and His passion centered in the truth that He might bear suffering for the sin of the whole human race. From today's perspective, this great act of grace put a sanction and benediction on suffering that the world often fails to recognize or appreciate.

In light of their Lord's suffering, the early Christians clearly understood the inevitability of their enduring persecution, ostracism, and even death as faithful witnesses to Jesus. The apostle Paul said, "All who desire to live godly in Christ Jesus will be persecuted" (2 Tim. 3:12). He even saw his own suffering as somehow helping to fill up the sufferings of Jesus (Col. 1:24). The Bible abounds with this principle. As the church carries out its mission of world evangelization, tribulation and opposition will inevitably come from numerous sources. Satan will see to that. Suffering must not necessarily be seen as the result of sin on the part of the sufferer; often the contrary is the case. The world, the flesh, and the devil stand in opposition to everything the Spirit of God would accomplish. Trials and suffering thus become the lot of those who would faithfully witness to the message of Christ, but in it all God is glorified.

Therefore, all suffering must not inevitably be understood as the result of personal evil, although a measure of suffering does emerge out of rebellion against the will of God. As Paul wrote to the Galatians, "God is not mocked; for whatever a man sows, this he will also reap" (Gal. 6:7). But for the Christian, suffering often rests on a much more positive level.

OTHER REASONS FOR SUFFERING

Further, suffering often possesses a corrective, remedial effect in the lives of those who endure it. The Bible states:

> My son, do not make light of the Lord's discipline . . . because the Lord disciplines those he loves, and he punishes everyone he accepts as a son. Endure hardship as discipline; God is treating you as sons. For what son is not disciplined by his father? If you are not disciplined (and everyone undergoes discipline), then you are illegitimate children and not true sons. Moreover, we have all had human fathers who disciplined us and we respected them for it. How much more should we submit to the Father of our spirits and live! . . . No discipline seems pleasant at the time, but painful. Later on, however, it produces a harvest of righteousness and peace for those who have been trained by it. Therefore, strengthen your feeble arms and weak knees. "Make level paths for your feet," so that the lame may not be disabled, but rather healed. (Heb. 12:5–13 NIV)

In this quite lengthy passage, the writer bestows a benediction on temporal suffering. It can produce godliness and holiness in those who are exercised thereby. This is a significant principle and a positive reason for the patient endurance of suffering. Our Lord's words to the church in Smyrna profile this point:

> I know your afflictions and your poverty—yet you are rich! I know the slander of those who say they are Jews and are not, but are a synagogue of Satan. Do not be afraid of what you are about to suffer. I tell you, the devil will put some of you in prison to test you, and you will suffer persecution for ten days. Be faithful, even to the point of death, and I will give you the crown of life. He who has an ear, let him hear what the Spirit says to the churches. He who overcomes will not be hurt at all by the second death. (Rev. 2:9–11 NIV)

Christ's admonition constitutes a wonderful promise, not only for the church of Smyrna in the first century, but for all of God's people of any age.

Actually, it can be a blessed experience when God's people patiently endure pressure, persecution, and peril for the Lord Jesus Christ. As Peter said, "In this you greatly rejoice, though now for a little while you may have had to suffer grief in all kinds of trials. These have come so that your faith—of greater worth than gold, which perishes even though refined by fire—may be proved genuine and may result in praise, glory and honor when Jesus Christ is revealed" (1 Pet. 1:6–7 NIV).

In the end, God Himself receives great glory. The paradox, rarely grasped by the world, centers on the fact that Christians under persecution and pressure can rejoice at the same time the burden bears heavily upon their shoulders. The reason for that fact rests in the beautiful truth that the Lord Himself steps in and gives His grace in the hour of trial. Thus again we see that suffering is not always the result of evil, but actually exercises a sanctifying role in the lives of believers that brings glory to God.

ANOTHER PARADOX

Again, in a paradoxical fashion, when persecution falls on God's people, the church always goes forward. Therefore, the oft-repeated but very true cliché has it right: "The blood of the martyrs becomes the seedbed of the church." Those forces that would oppose the kingdom of Christ, personified in Satan, the demonic hosts, and the world, often overplay their hand. Whenever the heavy hand of oppression falls on the church, be it governmental, cultural, or individual, the Christians who endure acquire such a ringing testimony to the praise of Christ that people are irresistibly drawn to the cross.

The classic example of this principle can be seen in the first century, when persecution first fell on the church and the believers were scattered. The persecution caused Philip to flee, enabling him to go to the Samaritans and declare Christ to them. This event precipitated a major breakthrough for the early church. It was quite inconceivable to the Jewish mind that the "Samaritan dogs," as they were commonly called, could actually come to know God. Yet, when Philip preached Christ, multitudes of Samaritans came to faith in the Lord Jesus. That principle is shown throughout the New Testament. The stoning of Stephen, recorded in

Acts 7, apparently made such an impact on Saul that it resulted in his conversion on the Damascus Road. Paul became the apostle to the Gentile world that resulted in innumerable people coming to faith in Jesus Christ.

Church history weaves the same story. Foxe, in his aforementioned classic *Foxe's Book of Martyrs*, reiterates this principle time and time again. For many years, no other book had more influence for the cause of Christ. When persecution falls, almost inevitably the kingdom of God goes forward. Hence, we discover another significant rationale for the suffering of God's people to His glory.

GRACE SUFFICES

Important also is the fact that in the midst of difficult times, the grace of God has always proved sufficient. It must be granted, there have been those who have fallen away in the midst of persecution. That seems inevitable. The visible church has those in its ranks who nurse a superficial faith. When extreme pressure comes, there will be those who succumb and repudiate their Christian profession. Yet, it must be understood that those who endure to the end become the ones who will be saved, and God's grace always proves sufficient for His chosen ones. They endure. As the apostle Paul said to the Romans:

> Who shall separate us from the love of Christ? Shall trouble or hardship or persecution or famine or nakedness or danger or sword? As it is written: "For your sake we face death all day long; we are considered as sheep to be slaughtered." No, in all these things we are more than conquerors through him who loved us. For I am convinced that neither death nor life, neither angels nor demons, neither the present nor the future, nor any powers, neither height nor depth, nor anything else in all creation, will be able to separate us from the love of God that is in Christ Jesus our Lord. (Rom. 8:35–39 NIV)

God does care for His people. God's grace always triumphs.

THE END: GOD IS GLORIFIED

In the end it can simply be reiterated that the suffering and persecution that fall upon the people of God rebound to our Lord's glory. It not only sanctifies the believer and furthers the cause of Christ, but it also creates a ringing testimony of the saving grace of Jesus Christ to God's honor. Moreover, it is far from incidental that the rewards of those who suffer faithfully for Jesus shall be great. In the Book of Revelation, we see this beautiful truth graphically portrayed:

> When he opened the fifth seal, I saw under the altar the souls of those who had been slain because of the word of God and the testimony they had maintained. They called out in a loud voice, "How long, Sovereign Lord, holy and true, until you judge the inhabitants of the earth and avenge our blood?" Then each of them was given a white robe, and they were told to wait a little longer, until the number of their fellow servants and brothers who were to be killed as they had been was completed. (Rev. 6:9–11 NIV)

However, we must be conscious that God never honors a superficial "martyr's complex." Yet He rewards the faithful. As one commentator put it, "We may be afflicted, persecuted, dispersed, but the ultimate blessing is assured."[9] For the chosen few whom God allows great suffering and persecution, their names will be inscribed in the annals of glory for eternity. As the old expression has it, "What a way to go." More profundity resides in that statement than one might realize.

THE EPITOME OF SUFFERING

As previously mentioned, the epitome of suffering was personified in the Lord Jesus Himself. Paul sets forth beautifully the incredible concept of the Lord's self-emptying His glory in his Philippian letter. It has been quoted earlier, but it bears repeating, "Your attitude should be the same as that of Christ Jesus: Who, being in very nature God, did not consider equality with God something to be grasped, but made himself nothing, taking the very nature of a servant, being made in human likeness. And being found in appearance as a man, he humbled himself and became obedient to death—even death on a cross!" (Phil. 2:5–8 NIV).

The church of Jesus Christ will never understand the profundity and depth of Paul's words until we see our Lord, become like Him, and can thus grasp what God did in sending His Son into the world. The fact that the infinite, transcendent, holy Son of God could lay aside His glory and celestial honor and robe Himself in human flesh is all but unbelievable. We have seen that in the chapter that stressed the incarnation. To have lived with the limitations of humanity—save a sinful nature—defies imagination. Yet He did become just that. The life He lived, sinless and perfect, revealed God personally. In conquering sin and evil as the last Adam, Jesus' life is beyond description. During His days on earth He suffered all the ignoble things that could be conjured up against Him. He endured ridicule, ostracism, hatred, spite, lies, betrayal, and every evil that the depraved mind of man could heap upon Him. Yet with a graciousness and beautiful forbearance, He endured it all with grace and love. Then they nailed Him on the cross. In that terrible hour, only He and God the Father fully understood it all. Although the physical suffering was excruciating, the spiritual suffering was infinitely unimaginable. That moment, in the inscrutable wisdom of God, He bore all the sin of the world as He cried out, "My God, My God, why hast Thou forsaken Me?" (Matt. 27:46). That was the agony of Calvary. But the story does not end there.

THE ULTIMATE VICTORY FROM SUFFERING

Jesus came forth from the grave, not resuscitated to earthly life, but *resurrected* to receive again the full glory that was His before His descent into our sinful scene. As the resurrected Lord, He burst out of the four-dimensional world in which we are encased and once again took up His full transcendence and glory. Ascending back to the Father, He entered the Holy of Holies, sprinkled the blood on the altar, sat down at the right hand of the Father as King of kings and Lord of lords, established the new covenant, sent His Holy Spirit to continue His work in and through His people, and remains at the Father's right hand to intercede for all the saints. What a picture of suffering and final triumph Jesus Christ exemplifies.

CONCLUSION

Therefore, God's people know that those who follow Jesus Christ and declare Him to the sinful world will endure suffering as He did. The Bible and history reveal this reality with a clarity no one can mistake. As Savonarola said when he faced the gibbet in the form of a cross, "My Lord has done so much for me," we too must arm ourselves for a like experience. Evangelism inevitably breeds suffering. But in that suffering, the triumph of God is made complete. Any Christian witness to the gospel who is not willing to take whatever Satan may throw across his or her path is not worthy of the name of Christ. Evangelism and suffering are twin sisters in the work of God's kingdom. But what about Billy Graham? Has he suffered and endured graciously? This we must attempt to discover.

PART II:
BILLY GRAHAM AND SUFFERING

We accept each hurt, each problem, each difficulty as from His hand.
—BILLY GRAHAM

INTRODUCTION

It has become clear as seen from the Scriptures and church history that all who "live godly in Christ Jesus shall suffer persecution" (2 Tim. 3:12 KJV). Classic histories have been written on the theme of Christian persecution. Incontestably, those who have born a fervent witness for the Lord Jesus Christ have often become Christian martyrs, but through their martyrdom they have inspired many to come to faith in Jesus. One cannot divorce evangelism from suffering. This has been true throughout the ages of God's dealings with a rebellious humanity and shall remain true until the final trumpet sounds. As the apostle Paul put it, "For to you it has been granted for Christ's sake, not only to believe in Him, but also to suffer for His sake" (Phil. 1:29).

But why should this be so? Why do Christians suffer? Billy Graham raises that question in his much-read volume *The Secret of Happiness*.

BILLY GRAHAM'S UNDERSTANDING
OF CHRISTIAN SUFFERING

Evangelist Billy Graham, who himself has been maligned and has endured much, as shall shortly be discussed, raises the issue of Christian suffering:

Who wants to be persecuted? We cannot see happiness in persecution. No one enjoys being maligned. Almost all of us want the good will of our neighbors, and it is difficult to see what blessedness there could be in the enmity of others. . . . We may have concluded as have others, that there is usually something wrong with those who are persecuted for righteousness sake, that there is some quirk in their disposition, some personality peculiarity or some religious fanaticism which causes others to mistreat them. No, that is not always, or let us say, that is not usually the case . . . nowhere does the Bible teach that Christians are to be exempt from tribulation.[10]

But again it is asked, why is this so? Graham attempts to answer this much-debated question, called the problem of *theodicy*.

Graham begins by making it clear that Jesus tells His disciples in unmistakable language that discipleship means a life of self-denial and the bearing of His cross. That is to say, His cross becomes their cross. As the evangelist has said in his book *Storm Warning*, "Jesus warned that the price of believing in him would be high. Mockery, laughter, persecution, even death would be common."[11] Thus the Lord urges those who would be His followers to count the costs carefully, lest they should turn back and apostasize when they encounter the inevitable suffering and onslaughts of this world.

Graham points out that some Christians think that because they are believers, they will have no problems or suffering. That is wrong. Jesus goes so far as to tell His followers that the world will actually hate them (John 15:18–19). He likens them to "sheep in the midst of wolves" (Matt. 10:16). Billy Graham reminds us of Christ's words: "They will put you out of the synagogues; indeed, the hour is coming when whoever kills you will think he is offering service to God" (John 16:2 RSV). Moreover, Graham points out that the apostle Paul makes this principle high-profile. The apostle told the early Christians at Lystra, Iconium, and Antioch that "through many tribulations we must enter the kingdom of God" (Acts 14:22). Statistics alone make it abundantly clear that God's people suffer. In the 1990s, some 290,000 Christian martyrs each year were recorded. Graham well understands that suffering is the believer's lot.

But still the question arises as to *why*. Before Graham attacks the perplexing problem of the inevitability of suffering for Christ's disciples, he contends that Christians should actually rejoice in the midst of their trials, tribulation, and suffering. After all, Christ says, "Blessed are you when men cast insults at you, and persecute you, and say all kinds of evil against you falsely, on account of Me. Rejoice, and be glad, for your reward in heaven is great, for so they persecuted the prophets who were before you" (Matt. 5:11–12). Not only do Christians inevitably suffer, Jesus says there is to be rejoicing in the midst of it all. Why? Because, as Jesus said, *great* is the reward in heaven. Paul said, "The sufferings of this present time are not worthy to be compared with the glory that is to be revealed to us" (Rom. 8:18). In this context Graham outlines his approach to the concept of Christian suffering, the "why" of the issue. The evangelist points out six principles of suffering:

1. Christians suffer because they are human. Christians are not exempt from human plight.

2. Christians are not excused from suffering when they sin and disobey God.

3. There is no Christian "fallout shelter."

4. God uses suffering and trials to discipline believers.

5. There is profit from discipline. Job came out of the testing fire "as gold."

6. God allows the fires of tribulation to come into our lives in order to make us, and keep us, human.[12]

Graham then elaborates by quoting an early Christian historian: "When the day of victory dawned, the Christians marched in procession from the prison to the arena as if they were marching to heaven with joyous countenance agitated by gladness rather than fear."[13] The evangelist gets to the heart of the thing as he points out, "We are not surprised that the early Christians rejoiced in suffering, since they looked at it in the light of eternity. The nearer death, the nearer a life of eternal fellowship with Christ." In A.D. 110, Ignatius, who was put to death for his faith, is said to have cried out, "Nearer the sword, then nearer to God. In company with wild beasts, in company with God." The apostle Paul reiterates this principle in Romans 8:17: "If indeed we suffer with Him in order that we may also be glorified with Him." Billy resonated with that when he said, "For Paul the Christian life was one of suffering."[14] Still, as Graham says, "In all ages, Christians have found it possible to maintain the spirit of joy in the hour of persecution."[15] Why is that so? Billy answers, "In the midst of the suffering, trials and temptations, He [God] will provide His peace, joy and fellowship."[16]

Graham is much aware of the fact that many kinds of persecutions arise. All Christian suffering does not necessarily entail death. Suffering and persecution can certainly come in the guise of discrimination, being scorned, maligned, laughed at, and rejected by friends and society. Mental and psychological suffering at times can be more painful than physical torture. A tragedy of this sort of persecution rests in the fact that it can arise even from the ranks of those professing the Christian faith. It seems some in the visible church will inevitably shoot their arrows of criticism and scorn upon those who take valiant stands for Christ. As Billy Graham has said, "There is no doubt that the Bible teaches that every believer who is faithful to Christ must be prepared to be persecuted at the hands of those who are enemies of the gospel."[17] And some of those enemies can be found in the professing church. The question persists: Where does it all come from? What lies back of such evil persecution?

THE SOURCE OF CHRISTIAN PERSECUTION

An insight as to the source of persecution and suffering God's faithful ones endure came several years ago from one of Billy Graham's sons. The evangelist had been under particularly heavy attack. He was in conversation about the situation with his son. The story unfolds:

"When some of those things came out this summer, which some of you have read, I talked to my son at the university," he reminisced. He said, "Dad, you shouldn't even think about it. You know where these lies are coming from, don't you?" I asked, "What do you mean?" He said, "Well, who's the father of lies?" "The devil," I said. "So that's where they're coming from," he told me. "You're in a spiritual battle." Jesus said, "Fear none of those things which thou shalt suffer." "I am a coward," Graham stated abruptly, wondering if he could stand up against modern torture. "Would I deny my Lord?" he questioned. "I've almost asked the Lord to preserve me from that trial. Yes, if that's God's will for me, that's what I want. Yet"—a thoughtful pause—"I don't want it." His puzzled eyes searched his Bible, seeking renewed strength: "Blessed are ye, when men shall revile you, and persecute you, and say all manner of evil against you falsely, for my sake." He read triumphantly. "Rejoice, and be exceeding glad; for great is your reward in heaven."[18]

That gets at the essence of the matter. Graham forcefully states that the ultimate source of all persecution and malignment that befall the people of God has its origins in the pits of evil and the devil. Demonology, like angelology, has become almost outdated in many circles. Yet it needs to be understood. But space again forbids venturing into a full presentation of Graham's theology on satanic and demonic activity. Let it be said, he takes a traditional, conservative, evangelical stance on these issues. On that basis, Billy outlines that stand. He said, "The world, the flesh, and the devil are enemies, with Satan the chief culprit."[19] Billy contends that Satan is "the son of the morning, . . . the anointed cherub" (Isa. 14:12; Ezek. 28:14 KJV), and he enjoyed a high standing in the hierarchy of God's created beings. But being lifted up with pride he cried out, "I am a god, I sit in the seat of gods" (Ezek. 28:2). In that moment Lucifer the anointed cherub became Satan the devil, the adversary. Graham believes from the Bible's teachings that in Satan's fall, a host of angels, possibly a third of the heavenly host, fell with him (Rev. 12:4). And now there exists a hierarchy of demonic evil spirits, superintended by Satan, with one goal: to thwart God's expansion of His kingdom.

Little wonder then that those who would evangelize become Satan's special targets. Since the kingdom advances by the winning of people to faith in Christ, it must be granted that this satanic host with unusual power and wisdom attacks the proponents of the cause of Christ. In the midst of a world that has essentially given itself to Satan and the demonic forces, believers valiantly attempt to bear a testimony for Christ and the gospel. John expresses the believers' battleground as, "all that is in the world, the lust of the flesh and the lust of the eyes and the pride of life, is not of the Father but is of the world" (1 John 2:16 RSV). Society truly is, as Billy Graham often calls it, "an upside-down world." It stands to reason, therefore, when God's people confront the world in the power of the Holy Spirit with the gospel of Christ, the people of the world cry out in consternation, "These that have turned the world upside down are come hither also" (Acts 17:6 KJV).

Because many in the world willingly, although perhaps unknowingly, give themselves to the satanic enterprise, they become pawns in the devil's hand to bring destruction upon those who would serve Christ. As Billy Graham points out, "Herein lies the fundamental reason for Christian persecution. Christ's righteousness is so revolutionary, so contradictory to man's manner of living, that it evokes the enmity of the world. . . . As long as Satan is loose in the world and our hearts are dominated by his evil passions, it will never be easy or popular to be a follower of Christ."[20]

Billy knows it personally all too well. Excerpts from his early diary confirm that fact: "Don't doubt for a moment the existence of the Devil! We see his power and influence everywhere. He is very personal and he is very real. And he is extremely clever." At the end of a long day of conferences preparatory to opening the All-Scotland crusade in Glasgow, he wrote in his diary, "Satan is very cunning. We recognize that on our way to Glasgow, as we are holding our meetings and planning our strategy and spending time in prayer that God will send revival, that Satan is also holding his councils, laying his plans to bring, if he can, God's work to naught." Prior to his mission in Cambridge University in the fall of 1955, he wrote: "During the past week I have felt the tremendous opposition of Satan. I seriously doubt if at any time in my ministry I have so felt the powers of darkness. It seems as though the demons of Hell had concentrated against this mission."[21] Were it not for the grace of God and the fact that Satan can do nothing apart from what God permits, the cause of Christ would soon fail.

WHY SATANIC POWER?

Much mystery surrounds the truth of Satan's hold on the world. The question constantly surfaces: Why does God permit such? How can God allow bad things to happen to good people? Why does the Lord give Satan leave to do his ravaging work in the world? It becomes very personal: *Why do I have to suffer?*

Graham faces these questions by granting that, in the inscrutable wisdom of God, when such problems arise, the final answer to the quandary must wait for eternity to reveal God's answer. In the meantime, God's people should arm themselves for the realities and gird themselves in the power of the Holy Spirit, even rejoicing in their suffering, knowing that it has an "eternal weight of glory" (2 Cor. 4:17). So the Christian refuses to "pay evil for evil" (Rom. 12:17), and heeds the admonition to "never take your own revenge" (Rom. 12:19). As Paul brought it together in Romans 12:21, "Do not be overcome by evil, but overcome evil with good."

Graham thus points out that believers are to "fight the good fight of faith" (1 Tim. 6:12). He tells us: "The world, the flesh, and the devil are our enemies. In times of war one hardly expects the good will of the enemy's forces. . . . A battle is also raging in the spiritual realm. The Bible says, 'We wrestle not against flesh and blood, but against principalities, against powers, against the rulers of the darkness of this world, against spiritual wickedness in high places' (Eph. 6:12)."[22] Graham takes this spiritual battle very seriously, as he states, "Jesus said that a cross is the Christian's lot" (Matt. 10:38).[23] Still, as the evangelist points out, "The very fact that they, the persecutors, are inclined to persecute us is proof that we are 'not of this world,' that we are in Christ."[24] Therefore, Graham sees all Christian suffering as "the privilege of persecution."[25] He gives Christians some cautions, however. First, as Christians we may suffer because of our own poor judgment, stupidity, and blundering. He contends, "There is no blessedness in this."[26] Furthermore, Graham insists, "we must be careful not to behave offensively, preach offensively, and dress offensively."[27] And one must never adopt or embrace a martyr attitude. Graham delineates the proper Christian attitude as found in the Sermon on the Mount (Matt. 5:12–44), saying as Christians we should:

- Rejoice and be exceedingly glad (Matt. 5:12)

- Love our enemies (Matt. 5:44)

- Bless them that curse us (Matt. 5:44)

- Do good to them that hate us (Matt. 5:44)

- Pray for them that despitefully use us and persecute us (Matt. 5:44)[28]

Graham also argues that persecution serves as tangible proof that we are on the right side and identified with the Lord Himself. Jesus tells us that when we suffer hatred, it is "for My name's sake," and His admonition comes: "It is the one who has endured to the end who will be saved" (Matt. 10:22).

Tragically, as pointed out earlier, persecution can come from the ranks of the organized church. Many times, because of carnality or unbelief, some members of the professing church who do not truly know Christ—or are carnal believers—have leveled their guns on those who would fervently serve Christ and evangelize the world. Graham knows this because the organized church has often attacked him and his work.

In the face of all these dynamics, Graham, true to the Scriptures, points out that we actually have need for sunshine and shadow. As Charles H. Spurgeon once put it, "Grace grows best in the winter." There is an eternity to be faced; moreover, God intends suffering to enhance His work of sanctification. In reality, easy times are not particularly conducive to Christian maturity and development. Graham further realizes, as emphasized, that the patient suffering of Christians often precipitates the conversion of people who would perhaps otherwise remain untouched. Finally, persecution and suffering identify one with Christ so that the martyr truly does become the witness. Sanders, a Christian martyr, once said, "Welcome the cross of Christ. . . . I feel no more pain in the fire than if I were on a bed of down."[29] That may seem unrealistic to many, but it makes perfect sense to those who have a true heart for Christ and the world's conversion. The ranks of the blessed willingly suffer and follow Christ's words, rejoicing in the midst of persecution. As W. C. Burns of India wrote, "Oh to have the martyr's heart if not the martyr's crown!"[30]

We may not all be called upon to suffer in a physical sense, but in some manner we shall suffer. And in it the work of Christ is perfected in and through us. The true martyr's heart rejoices with a true positive spirit constantly reminding one's self of all the promises of God. This has certainly been true of Billy Graham.

TIMES OF TRIAL AND TRIBULATION FOR THE EVANGELIST

Billy Graham has had his share of sufferings and persecutions, even though he has not suffered physically for his faith. A longtime friend and colleague, Grady Wilson, has pointed out, "People have tried to lump the BGEA with unsavory stereotypes of evangelism, especially in our early days. They accused us of being flamboyant and flashy, hypocritical Elmer-Gantry types."[31] As could be expected, persecution for Graham has come often in the form of severe criticism and ostracism. And as John Stott has said concerning Billy Graham's trials, "Slander is a vicious kind of torture."[32]

Some of the most severe and perhaps most far-reaching criticisms against Billy Graham have come from the extreme right and left wings within the church. This illustrates and verifies the fact that persecutions and pressures sometimes come from the professing church. What may seem strange, but perhaps not unusual, is that persecutions have come from both sides of the theological spectrum. That is to say, those on the far left have been quite critical of Billy Graham for his evangelical stance; at the same time, those on the extreme right, from their hyperfundamental perspective, continually attack Billy Graham. So the battle goes.

FUNDAMENTALIST CRITICISMS

One of the attacks that grieved Billy Graham, perhaps more than any other through the years, came from the president of his first college, Dr. Bob Jones Sr. When Billy decided to leave the college and attend a Bible institute in Temple Terrace, Florida, "Dr. Bob," as the students affectionately called him, requested that Graham come to his office. There, Jones admonished Billy not to leave, with the warning that if he were to leave Bob Jones College, he would never be heard of and would probably end up in an insignificant church having forfeited a much larger ministry. When Graham did come into prominence, Jones soon got Graham in the cross hairs of his critical guns and accused him of peddling a "discount type of religion" and "sacrificing the cause of evangelism at the altar of temporary convenience."[33] While Graham was still involved with Youth for Christ and serving as president of Northwestern Schools, the relationship between Bob Jones and Billy had been reasonably cordial. However, as Graham's fame increased, Jones's harsh criticisms grew apace.

At times, rather bizarre things took place in that context. For example, as preparations were being made for the New York Madison Square Garden crusade, a printing company in Greenville, South Carolina, the new location of Bob Jones College, received a contract to do the printing for the New York endeavor. Several Bob Jones students were working part-time at the printing firm. Bob Jones forced all of these students to leave their jobs or they would be "shipped" from Bob Jones University. It must be said that Billy did everything he could to heal the breach that was ever widening with Dr. Bob, but to no avail. Bob Jones went to his grave denouncing Billy Graham and accusing the evangelist of having "led thousands into compromise and alliance with infidelity and Romanism" and "doing more harm to the cause of Jesus Christ than any living man."[34] Jones finally went so far as to say that any student who would dare to attend one of Graham's services would be expelled. Concerning these things Billy Graham said, "Fundamentalist is a grand and wonderful word, but it has gotten off-track and into so many extreme positions. . . . I felt like my own brother had turned against me."[35] Billy lamented and he always points out that "one of the worst wounds we can receive or give is done with 'words.'"[36] But then Billy quotes evangelist D. L. Moody, who said, "If the world has nothing to say against you, beware lest Jesus Christ has nothing to say for you."[37]

A spin-off from this situation came about not too long after the great 1954 Harringay crusade in London. Billy invited John R. Rice, evangelist and editor of *The Sword of the Lord* periodical, to come and participate in the crusade. Rice gladly responded and came back, writing glowing reports. But Bob Jones, in his vitriolic attacks on Billy, soon influenced John R. Rice, and the editor-evangelist targeted the ministry of Billy Graham in his periodical. In an article entitled "Billy Graham's New York Crusade," Rice denounced the whole event as the breaking down of convictions. In the next months after the initial attack, virtually every issue of *The Sword of the Lord* had an article or editorial warning people of the danger of Graham and his "modernist New York Crusade." Rice criticized Graham's methodologies as well as his motives. He charged that Billy Graham wanted "the prestige, the financial backing and worldly influence of the so-called liberals."

Carl McIntire, as might be expected, also attacked Graham quite viciously. McIntire, always outspoken, said that Billy Graham's crusades could "very easily be the church of the anti-Christ, Babylon the great, the scarlet woman, the harlot church, described in Revelation 17–18."[38] Such attacks represent typical experiences of persecution and precipitated real suffering for the sensitive spirit of Billy Graham.

The vehement attacks of those who hold the same basic theology as Graham proved a very trying experience for the theologian. When Billy Graham traveled to Northern Ireland during a very volatile time, Ian Paisley, an ultraconservative Presbyterian, wrote, "Is he [Graham] not so gracious? Is he not so kind? Is he not a lovely man? *Satan can be transformed into an angel of light.* And no marvel, for Satan himself is transformed into an angel of light.

Therefore it is no great thing if his ministers also be transformed into ministers of righteousness, whose end shall be according to their works."[39] These sorts of situations constantly dogged Billy Graham's heels especially in his earlier years, and still the attacks go on.

The volleys from the right wing of the church zero in most vehemently against one of Billy Graham's methodologies, not his basic theology. They well know the evangelist believes in biblical infallibility, the virgin birth, the deity of Christ, the historicity of the miracles, the substitutionary atonement, the bodily resurrections, the premillennial return of Christ, and the absolute necessity of repentance and faith as the response to the gospel. And they are well aware Billy always preaches it. Then what is the complaint?

The problem for the fundamentalist camp, for which they have little patience, is that Graham invites churches of all persuasions to cooperate and participate in his crusades—even Roman Catholics. He permits them to work in the crusades as counselors, ushers, and choir members; he even has some of their leaders in the platform party. He has followed this procedure since the early days of the crusades. To some conservatives, this is viewed as compromising the gospel. As a result, they launch their attacks. Other minor matters arise to be sure, but this seems to be the crux of their complaint. Is there an answer to their charge of heresy?

THE ANSWER

In 1958, Dr. Robert Ferm, then dean of students at Houghton College in Houghton, New York, wrote a book entitled *Cooperative Evangelism: Is Billy Graham Right or Wrong?* In that work he set out to defend Graham's practice of what he termed "cooperative evangelism." He took a historical approach, beginning in the New Testament and then focusing on the relatively recent evangelists, starting with Jonathan Edwards and going through Billy Sunday.

Ferm starts off by raising the key issue, "With *whom* shall we evangelize?" This is the question! In fact, Ferm says, "in the minds of some, the question of association takes precedence over the fact that the gospel is preached."[40] Ferm thus begins his defense of Graham by outlining some of the startling results of the Graham crusades in the '50s. He declares, "The evangelism of Billy Graham and of the Billy Graham Team has restored mass evangelism to a place of dignity and effectiveness that commands the respect and consideration of men and women in all walks of life."[41] He then goes on to defend the work from a New Testament and historical perspective.

THE NEW TESTAMENT ARGUMENT

The conservative fundamentalists accuse the liberals of wrong motives and Graham for not heeding the scriptural mandate to "come out from among them and be separate" (2 Cor. 6:17 NKJV). But as Ferm points out, the Bible teaches both separation and *fellowship*. As shown, Graham believes in the inerrancy of the Scriptures like his conservative critics. The problem thus centers in just how far the principle of "separation" is to be carried. Ferm states it can certainly be carried too far. He then cites the approach of Jesus on the issue. He points out that Jesus had contact with the Temple and its authorities despite their corruption; case in point, Nicodemus. He taught in the Temple and worshiped in the synagogues. He sent His disciples out on missions and instructed them, "Into whatsoever city ye enter, and they receive you, eat such things as are set before you" (Luke 10:8 KJV). The Lord also reminded the disciples that "he that is not against us is on our part" (Mark 9:40 KJV). Thus, "cooperative evangelism" seemed to be the philosophy and method of the Lord, and it followed throughout the first century. Paul preached in the synagogues and on Mars Hill. Peter preached in the home of Cornelius, and Philip even preached to the Samaritans—and all these venues gladly "cooperated" with the evangelists. And it has been true through the history of evangelism.

THE HISTORY OF COOPERATIVE EVANGELISM

Ferm states that Graham's critics also try to make their case by referring to the methodologies of the great evangelists of history. They argue the notable evangelists of old certainly did not use the Graham methodology of cooperative evangelism. Can their case be made? Ferm says it cannot.

Dr. Ferm first cites Jonathan Edwards and his ministry during America's First Great Awakening. Edwards encountered much opposition in the context of the Awakening. Many critics arose, especially from the ranks of church leaders, but Edwards carried on, refusing to condemn their lack of understanding and love. He simply said, "We may represent it as exceedingly dangerous to oppose this work."[42] Regardless of the obstacles, the movement spread and engulfed all denominations.

In the same revival context, George Whitefield ministered powerfully in the American colonies and in England as well. Ferm points out, "Whitefield always preached wherever there was an open door; he took to the open fields because 'the Established Church gradually closed its doors.'"[43] Finally, he too faced the same things as Billy Graham. The churches split over him, becoming the so-called New Lights and the Old Lights. The Old Lights fought Whitefield; the New Lights accepted his methodologies and supported him.

The same can be said for Whitefield's close friend and fellow revivalist, John Wesley. Although Wesley came to America only once—and that before his dramatic Aldersgate experience—he too approached his ministry in the spirit of Whitefield. Ferm declares, "Like Whitefield, Wesley maintained a most inclusive attitude throughout his ministry."[44] Wesley himself argued that "all the children of God may unite, notwithstanding those smaller differences."[45]

Charles G. Finney of America's Second Great Awakening was no exception to the rule. No one, at least in America up to that time, received more criticism than Finney did for his so-called New Measures. The conflict grew to the proportions that the New Lebanon Conference was held by leading clerics of the day, basically to censure Finney. Finney would go into a city and enlist all he could to support the work. Actually, Finney gave birth to modern mass evangelism crusades. An ex-lawyer with a brilliant mind and skill in argumentation, Finney "won" at the Lebanon Conference; his work carried on and tens of thousands were converted under his cooperative evangelism motif.

When D. L. Moody arose on the scene, he simply took up where Finney left off. Moody is well known and is considered by some as—at least up to Graham—"perhaps *the* most outstanding evangelist" of history.[46] On one occasion he encountered a Roman Catholic bishop (and that was before Vatican II, which was quite revolutionary to the Roman Church). The conversations went as follows after the bishop asked Moody to join his church:

He [Moody] then asked the Bishop: "Do you mean to say that I could go to the Noon Prayer Meetings and pray with all kinds of Christian people—Baptists, Methodists, Presbyterians, all together—just as I do now?"

"Oh yes," replied the Bishop. "If it were necessary you might do that."

"So, then, Protestants and Catholics can pray together, can they?"

"Yes."

"Well, Bishop, this is a very important matter, and ought to be attended to at once."[47]

The bishop and Moody did pray together. The principle was set, and Moody went to Dublin, Ireland, to conduct a crusade. The place was inundated with Roman Catholics. Moody felt he was only doing what Jesus set a precedent for. It works! Professor Henry Drummond of Scotland said of Moody, "No other living man has done so much to unite man with man, to reach down personal grudges and ecclesiastical banners, bringing into united worship and harmonious cooperation men of diverse views and dispositions."[48]

And when the flamboyant Billy Sunday burst on the scene, he reached out to all. Ferm said, "It is quite evident that Billy Sunday accepted the cooperation of liberals as well as conservatives. . . . Sunday was inclusive, accepting support from and cooperation of those who disagreed with him."[49]

And so the historical trail leads to Billy Graham. What can be said to his critics of cooperative evangelism? Robert Ferm sums it up well: "Having examined the policy of Billy Graham from the perspective of history and the Scriptures, it has been shown that he is neither out of harmony with the major evangelists, nor is his policy contrary to the Scriptures."[50] Billy Graham's answer to that is: "We welcome all who wish to participate in presenting Jesus Christ to the community that people might be won. We welcome all who wish to support a clear presentation of the Bible as God's infallible Word to man."[51] That should essentially settle the problem.

At the same time, Graham is criticized for using mass media, careful planning, advertising, and many other methods he employs. To explore that issue and Graham's answer we must wait for a later chapter when the structure, methods, and work of the entire BGEA are digested. Let it merely be said here, Graham's critics in his evangelism have little firm basis for their criticism.

It is true to say, as William Martin in his excellent biography of Graham points out, "Not all of Graham's fundamentalist critics saw him as a willing tool of Satan, sent forth to do the work of the Anti-Christ."[52] But a true spiritual battle does rage on.

SPIRITUAL WARFARE

Graham is well prepared for such attacks; he knows suffering is inevitable for God's evangelists. The Bible says, "For our struggle is not against flesh and blood, but against the rulers, against the authorities, against the powers of this dark world and against the spiritual forces of evil in the heavenly realms" (Eph. 6:12 NIV). And that warfare deeply involves people: the people of God and the people of darkness. It has always been so since the Garden of Eden (Gen. 3). As Billy Graham says, "In his warfare against God, Satan uses the human race, which God created and loved. So God's forces of good and Satan's forces of evil have been engaged in a deadly conflict from the dawn of our history."[53]

Graham's commentary on his Dortmund, Germany, crusade states, "I felt in Germany that I was in hand to hand combat with the forces of evil, though I believe the victory was the greatest in the history of our work."[54] The evangelist stressed the reality of warfare, pointing out that a well-known highly visible pastor or evangelist is often a special target of Satan. This warfare has been very real for Graham. At times he really has been "tried with fire" (1 Pet. 1:7 KJV).

For example, during the Chicago crusade in the early '70s, a large number of Satan worshipers rushed into the auditorium and ran down the aisles chanting their satanic verses. A hymn was being sung at that moment, but Graham got up, went to the microphone, interrupted the hymn, and said, "There are three or four hundred Satan worshipers here tonight. They said that they're going to take over the platform. Now I am going to ask you Christian young people to do something; don't hurt them; just surround them and love them and sing to them. And if you can, just gradually move them toward the doors." That was the end of the demonstration.

CRITICISM FROM THE LIBERALS

Billy Graham, always sensitive to criticisms, stated in preparation for the New York crusade, "We face the city with fear and trembling. I am prepared to go to New York to be crucified by my critics, if necessary. When I leave New York, every engagement we have in the world might be canceled. It may mean I'll be crucified—but I'm going."[55] And he did receive severe criticism. The *Christian Century* derided the forthcoming crusade as a "trumped-up revival which would 'spin

along to its own kind of triumph.'" The writer went on to say, "The Graham procedure . . . does its mechanical best to 'succeed' whether or not the Holy Spirit is
in attendance."[56] But then Jesus said, if they persecuted Him, they will persecute
us, because "a disciple is not above his teacher" (Matt. 10:24). And as Billy
Graham said, "Jesus suffered. . . . [This] also points us to the suffering Savior as a
pattern of how we as His believing people, should endure our suffering."[57]

Thus, Graham has always been prepared for the inevitable attacks, especially
from the left. And they came—and he handled them in his typical Christ-
centered manner. For example, he confessed that many consider him a throw-
back to Puritan times; they saw his theology as hopelessly out of date. The
evangelist said, "Some extreme liberal and Unitarian clergies said I was setting
back the cause of religion a hundred years. I replied that I did indeed want to
set religion back—not just a hundred years but 1900 years, back to the book
of Acts where first century followers of Christ were accused of turning the
Roman empire upside-down."[58]

As a further case in point of liberal criticisms, the *Christian Century* published
an article that said, "[Some theologians] agreed that Graham is sincere, but
deplored his theological literalism and his personality, his sensationalism, his
publicity techniques and his burning conviction, that he is a latter day
prophet."[59] Graham was not only criticized for his conservative theology, but theologian Reinhold Niebuhr criticized him for his racial message. Niebuhr said:

> The question arises why an obviously honest man, such as Graham, cannot
> embody the disavowal of race prejudice into his call to repentance. Perhaps the
> answer to that question takes one into the very heart of the weakness of "evan-
> gelical" Christianity, particularly of evangelical Christianity in its pietistic ver-
> sions. This form of Christian faith relies on an oversimplification of the issues in
> order to create the "crisis" which prompts conversion and the acceptance of the
> Christian faith.[60]

Yet Billy Graham takes a very strong stand against racial prejudice; since his
early years he would not preach in any segregated setting, as we have labored
to make clear. He has always been a strong advocate of racial acceptance and
harmony. But Niebuhr continued his attack on what he viewed as Graham's
general lack of concern about social issues. He said:

The personal achievements of Graham as a Christian and as an evangelist should be fully appreciated; but they do not materially alter the fact that an individualistic approach to faith and commitment, inevitable as it may be, is in danger both of obscuring the highly complex tasks of justice in the community and of making too sharp a distinction between the "saved" and the "unsaved." The latter may not have signed a decision card but may have accepted racial equality with greater grace than the saved.[61]

The onslaught from the liberal perspective was not so much on Graham's theology per se, but upon Graham's supposed lack of social concern. Yet, as seen in the previous chapter on holistic evangelism, Graham's concern has continually increased through the years in the area of social responsibility. Graham himself has said, "My belief in the social implications of the gospel has deepened and broadened. . . . I am convinced that faith without works is dead."[62] Consequently, he has covered virtually every area of social concern.

But still the criticisms from the liberal camp continued. One British critic said of Graham, "His theology is fifty years behind contemporary scholarship. He gives no sign of having read any of it from the last three decades. He is completely out of step with the majority of ministers and pastors."[63] A London bishop once said, "He will go back to America with his tail between his legs." Of course, the bishop was quite wrong.

The liberal Christian press also attacked Graham for his methodologies. They accused him of being far more of a promoter than an evangelist. In the *Christian Century*, Eugene Todd wrote, "When we talk of Billy Graham's 'mass evangelism,' why not call it 'mass promotionalism' and be done with it? How long will America tolerate the false assumption that evangelism is piling up fantastic records of decision cards? . . . I do not accept the presupposition that 'mass promotionalism' is ideal evangelism, as the followers of Billy Graham proclaim."[64]

In an editorial during the New York crusade, a writer sarcastically predicted that Graham's success actually stems from his publicity barrage. He wrote, "By the time these words are read, the Billy Graham crusade will be generating its own kind of excitement and tabulating its own kind of success in New York City. . . . The Billy Graham campaign will spin along to its own kind of triumph because canny, experienced engineers of human experience have laid the tracks, contracted for the passengers and will now direct the traffic which arrives on schedule."[65]

Considerable criticism has also arisen against Billy Graham from religious circles outside of the Christian faith. On one occasion while Graham was preaching in Africa, a sizable group of native witch doctors gathered during the services and with their enchantments attempted to thwart the work. But that which personally grieves Graham more than all comes from professed fellow believers. Still, he takes a balanced approach to the situation. He has said, "The extreme 'liberal' feels that I am too conservative in my theology, and that I oversimplify the gospel; whereas the 'fundamentalist' feels that I am too wide in my sponsorship. He feels that I should limit my sponsorship only to themselves—only to the extreme 'fundamentalists within Protestantism.'"[66] So Graham attempts to track a middle road, hopefully staying true to the gospel and to the Spirit of Christ.

Of course, the suffering of Graham in these respects has been true throughout the course of the history of evangelism. A "middle road" always elicits criticism from the two factions within the scope of Christian profession. But even more merciless than the criticism from fellow Christians is the measure of suffering that comes against evangelists from the secular press.

BILLY GRAHAM AND THE SECULAR PRESS

Billy Graham has been perceived by many in the secular world, especially in his early years, as one who employs high-pressure American salesmanship in order to "get people down the aisle." At one time he was known as "God's machine gun" by the press. In a typical case of this line of criticism, the *London Evening News* castigated Billy Graham as an "American hot gospel specialist" during the Harringay crusade of 1954.[67] The article called him an "actor-manager of the show," saying that "like a Biblical Baedeker, he takes his listeners strolling down Pavements of Gold, introduces them to rippling-muscled Christ, who resembles Charles Atlas with a halo, then drops them abruptly into the Lake of Fire for a sample scalding."[68] The *Daily Worker*, a popular London newspaper, ran the headline "Atom Bomb Gospeler" just before Graham arrived for the Harringay crusade. The article went on to say, "We should be able to get some quiet fun out of Mr. Billy Graham when he gets here. . . . His mission is to cause a religious revival on the strength of scores of thousands of pounds provided by wealthy backers. . . . He will try to persuade us that the more atom bombs America piles up, the more certain is the victory of the Prince of Peace."[69] The press claimed, "Billy Graham not only had the gall to decide England's religious life needed reviving but had attacked a major aspect of its political life as well." That is a story in itself.

In advertising for the Harringay crusade, the Graham publicity office in America had prepared material to be distributed to the British people. The text of one of the pieces of literature contained an inadvertent mistake—a serious one. The text read, "When the war (World War II) ended, a sense of frustration and disillusionment gripped England, and what Hitler's bombs could not do, socialism with its accompanying evils shortly accomplished."[70] The intent was to state that *communism* was one of the factors that had put roadblocks in the advance of the evangelical church. Unfortunately, the word *communism* inadvertently came out *socialism*. The British Labor Party was socialistic in philosophy and political orientation. The brochure was never actually distributed, but in Minneapolis, George Wilson saw an uncorrected copy of the brochure and used the text in reference to socialism on a publicity calendar. Instead of the word *secularism*, which Wilson intended to be used, the version kept the word *socialism*. When the calendar was distributed, it hit Britain like a bombshell. The *London Daily Herald* columnist Hannen Swaffer, quoting the calendar, asked just which evils Graham was placing at the feet of socialism. He wanted to know whether it was the abolition of the poor law, the national health service, town planning, family allowances, or improved educational facilities. He demanded that Graham "apologize . . . or stay away." Labor MP Geoffrey de Freitas raised the same criticism and even challenged Graham's admission to England on the grounds that he was "interfering in British politics under the guise of religion."[71] The Central Council of the Socialist Christian League also went on the attack and saw Graham's words as a severe criticism on "the British labor government which was in power from 1945 to 1951."[72] Although an oversight on the part of the Graham association, the spiritual eruption that ensued reminded one of that which befell the early church.

Needless to say, when Graham stepped off the ship in Great Britain, a barrage of reporters stood ready to castigate him. The Graham association did all within its power to correct the misunderstanding, and to some extent, the criticism soon passed away. However, there were those who would never give in. One of the most critical and best-read British reporters wrote his articles under the name of Cassandra. Billy Graham offered to meet with him, and they did—in a pub. Cassandra had his beer and Billy Graham had a soft drink. After the meeting, which can only be described as a stroke of God's grace, Cassandra completely changed his mind and attitude toward Graham and wrote some quite favorable articles concerning the evangelist. But down through the years, the press has constantly criticized him.

It may seem rather ironic, but the calendar affair actually put Billy Graham and his crusade on the front page of the papers, which helped in the final analysis. Still, the critics carried on. One particular criticism came when Billy Graham stepped off the *Queen Mary* at Southampton Harbor and took the train to London's Waterloo station. Critics condemned him for coming to London on such a luxurious ship like the *Queen Mary* when Jesus Himself traveled every place on a donkey. Graham replied, "Well, Jesus traveled on a donkey; you find me a donkey that can swim the Atlantic, and I'll try to buy him." Later, an interviewer asked upon hearing that statement, "Has anyone come up with one yet?" Graham replied, "No, I haven't found a donkey that could swim the Atlantic. So I am afraid I'm going to have to continue to use the airlines and the ships."[73]

As might be anticipated, in Iron Curtain days, the Soviet Press castigated Graham with very cruel words. As one writer of the Red Army paper *Red Star* expressed himself on the Graham crusade in Washington, D.C., "Americans are in hysterics about Billy Graham—a charlatan and a quack. Meetings have been attended not only by simpletons inexperienced in politics, but also by correspondents, avid for sensations. . . . American Senators and members of the House come with humble looks and blissful smiles. They listen to the howlings of a preacher who goes into rantings."[74] Ironically, Billy Graham later preached in Moscow.

Perhaps the most serious media criticism, among the numerous little arrows that have constantly flown Graham's way, came in America in the 1980s. Billy Graham received a request for an interview from two reporters of Charlotte, North Carolina's daily paper, the *Charlotte Observer*. They had interviewed Graham before and had written positive articles about him. Graham had no misgivings, therefore, about giving a full interview to these two reporters.

In the setting of the interview, the reporters asked Billy several questions about his work and then raised the query as to what Graham had planned for the future. He replied that he hoped to build a large building on the campus of Wheaton College that might be both the repository for his archives and an academic center for research in evangelism. He went further to state that he hoped to build a conference center not far from his home in Montreat, North Carolina. The reporters asked how he intended to fund these two projects. Graham replied that he had set up a foundation to receive gifts and funds for the projects and that as soon as it was sufficiently large enough he would undertake the construction. No more was said.

In the next few days, the reporters investigated the foundation that Billy Graham had established for the projects. They discovered that it had risen to twenty-three million dollars, but that it was approved by the Internal Revenue Service and had been audited every year and given a complete approval by the government with everything in order. Nevertheless, they printed an article under the title "Billy Graham's Secret $23 Million Fund." That was the headline and the lead sentence of the article. It exploded across the nation. Television, radio, newspapers, and newsmagazines were blaring everywhere that Billy Graham had twenty-three million dollars secretly stashed away. It caused a real flap. In reading the first paragraph of the article, it did sound quite questionable; but continuing to read down the page, noting all the facts of the case, any thinking person came away with the thought, *Well, what is so bad about that?* It was no secret at all. As a matter of fact, Graham had sent out a press release more than once regarding his plans and the foundation. But at the time, it was so inconsequential in the thinking of the media that no one had even bothered to publish it. The general feeling was that the foundation was legitimate and these were two worthy projects that presented no personal gain to Graham. When it came out that he, as an evangelist, had a "secret" twenty-three-million-dollar fund, one can imagine how less-than-thoughtful people received it.

The battle raged on for some time. As a case in point, on the first page of a daily paper in Orlando, Florida, there was a picture of a dollar bill with Washington's face removed and Graham's superimposed under the heading "Billy Graham's Secret 23 Million Dollar Fund." This author was asked to appear on local television to answer some of the questions. Graham's board of directors soon settled the issue in their decree that nothing illegal or unethical had been done. Graham had deceived no one. Creating a foundation to hold the funds until the projects could be completed was the wise and ethical way to do it. Thus, the matter should be dropped and the work should continue on. Thankfully, the criticism faded away. In the next few years, the fund was sufficient to build the beautiful Wheaton Center for the study of evangelism and to house the archives. The building also serves the graduate school of Wheaton College. The Cove, one of America's most respected Christian conference centers, is now constructed in North Carolina and has been a source of spiritual encouragement to many thousands. At times, the press has been thoughtless and merciless in their pursuit of sensational headlines at Billy Graham's expense—and usually wrong. Though Graham has not been called upon to wear the martyr's crown, it has not been easy. As John Corts has said, "Mental suffering is greater than physical suffering."[75]

Of course, Graham has always been careful with statements that could easily become sensationalized, especially in press conferences. But he is capable of erring. As an illustration, T. W. Wilson tells the story of a news conference in South Africa, during which someone mentioned that a local twelve-year-old native girl had been raped by a gang of men. An African chief had commented that in his tribe they castrated rapists. One of the reporters asked Billy Graham what he thought about the tragedy of the rape and the African chief's solution. Graham said half-jokingly, "I think when a person is found guilty of rape he should be castrated. That would stop him pretty quick."[76] Wilson, recounting the story, tells of sitting behind a British reporter who had his head tucked down and his eyes closed as if he were asleep. When Graham made that statement, the reporter suddenly perked up and wrote on his pad, "castrated." Billy Graham thought to himself, *I must get back to that and clarify it because I put my foot in my mouth.* But the questions went on; he forgot it and never got back to rectify the statement. Needless to say, it made the newspapers all over the world. The *Rand Daily Mail,* one of South Africa's most prestigious papers, sneered at Graham for his view as well as his activities. It was also widely published in the United States. A *Chicago Tribune* columnist jumped to his own conclusions and published a bitter, sarcastic piece on Graham for his remarks. Strangely enough, sometime later, an eminent British psychiatrist wrote an article for the *London Times* stating that castration was probably the best therapy for compulsive rapists. But the criticism went on.

SEVERE PRESSURE

At times, however, there have been far more serious issues, even attempts on Graham's life, if not his reputation. Death threats are not unusual. Precautions have to be constantly made. On one occasion, this author visited Billy Graham in his hotel room during the Manila crusade in the Philippines. At the end of the hall there were army personnel with automatic weapons to ensure that no one entered the hall who was not officially invited. Moreover, there is tight security during the crusade services themselves. The area around the platform where Graham preaches is always surveyed for any unknown objects. Bombings are not unusual in this world. So the stories go on of persecution, criticism, malignments, and suffering. Though he is a man of worldwide fame, popularity, and respect, it has not been an easy path to tread. Although this is true of any high-profile personality, a man whose life centers in dedicated service to Jesus Christ is inevitably going to endure a double measure of difficulty and suffering. But what is Billy's approach to it all?

BILLY GRAHAM'S ATTITUDE TOWARD SUFFERING

Dr. Nelson Bell, Billy's father-in-law, had a motto concerning attacks, criticisms, and suffering. It read, "No attack, no defense, proclaim the truth." That has been Billy Graham's basic position, learned from Dr. Bell. Billy Graham wrote his book *Till Armageddon* to show another dimension of the Bible's teaching about suffering, "the dimension of hope."[77] Thus he has always taken two basic stands in the face of criticism. First, he refuses, except on rare occasions, to reply to his critics and detractors. Second, he seeks to love his detractors and desires reconciliation. As John Corts stated, Billy always says, "Pray for them." This approach has not only proved the best defense, it has been an inspiration to many. Dr. Frank Harbor, a young evangelist, has so admired Billy's approach that he has said, "When attacks come, I ask myself, what would Billy do? How would he react?"[78] Billy has learned through the years that to perpetuate the issue with some line of defense normally does nothing but deepen the problem. Those who want to believe the bad will do so, and those who wish to be fair will be knowledgeable of the true facts. There have been one or two occasions, however, when Graham has attempted to answer the attacks, as in the case of the calendars at London's Harringay crusade. But normally he refuses to raise any line of defense at all. On one occasion, Marshall Frady wrote a very scathing biography of Billy Graham under the title *Billy Graham: A Parable of American Righteousness*. There are so many slanderous accusations in that particular work that Graham was urged to consider taking the case to court for slander. But he did not, and the book soon died the death and was read by only a scant few. Through the years, Graham's strategy has proved effective. And through the years, probably as a result of this line of defense, the press has gradually turned quite positive. Of course, the *entire* media was never against Graham. There have always been positive articles written in newspapers during the crusades.

Further, one does not hear too much criticism anymore from the liberal or ultraconservative camps of the church. Billy Graham, as previously mentioned, has been voted one of the ten most admired men in the world for more than twenty-five years. That is unprecedented. The media, newspapers, television, radio, and newsmagazines, by and large, have come to highly regard Graham. A typical case is the very popular television interview show hosted by Larry King. One can see, though he is Jewish, that King has profound admiration for Billy Graham. He conducts interviews with Graham regularly, even at the contemporary moment with Billy Graham in his eighties and suffering from Parkinson's disease. Graham's strategy has certainly proved positive. God does see one through; there is hope. But there is a second vital aspect to Billy Graham's approach to the suffering that he has been called upon to endure for the cause of Christ.

CONFIDENCE IN THE PROVIDENCE
AND CARE OF GOD

Billy Graham is not a fatalist or a naive person who superficially takes everything that occurs as from the hand of God. Nor does he face suffering in a glib fashion. There have been times when he has been discouraged. He has said (perhaps half-jokingly), "In my own life, the pressures at times, mentally, physically, and spiritually, have become so great that I felt like going to the Cove and lying down in the cemetery to see how I fit."[79]

Such is the lot of many, Billy Graham being no exception. Yet in the face of it, he firmly believes, as does his Presbyterian wife, Ruth, that in the providence and care of God, nothing is going to happen to Billy Graham that escapes God's permission. This does not mean there will be no suffering or heartache or perhaps even death. But God cares. He shared in an interview, "I get [death threats] quite often [but] I'm clothed in the armor of God . . . and if He wants me killed, I'm happy to be killed."[80]

God's people who faithfully serve Christ must face these realities. But, as pointed out at the beginning of this chapter, there is biblical rationale for all that takes place in believers' lives: Nothing occurs among God's children that He does not, for some reason, permit. And even if severe suffering and even martyrdom do occur to believers, they will have "stars in their crowns" that will far supersede anything that this world could possibly imagine. Graham has been criticized for virtually everything imaginable. But to repeat what Paul said, "The sufferings of this present time are not worthy to be compared with the glory which shall be revealed in us" (Rom. 8:18 KJV). That is a glorious hope.

David Frost, the well-known British interviewer, once asked Billy Graham, "How do you suggest that Christians get ready for the hard times ahead?" Billy's answer was classic: "The most important thing we can do is to grow in our relationship to Christ. If we have not learned to pray in our everyday lives, we will find it difficult to know God's peace and strength through prayer when hard times come. If we have not learned to trust God's Word when times are easy, we will not trust His Word when we face difficulties. . . . The Scriptures speak to us in those moments when we look to the Lord for sustenance and strength."[81] Graham then gives a five-point outline to believers on how to endure the times of suffering. He urges fellow sufferers to:

1. Expect suffering. Don't feel surprised.

2. Don't look at anyone else and what he or she does or doesn't have to bear; comparisons are demoralizing either way.

3. Recognize that it doesn't take great wealth or social influence to be faithful . . . but it takes patience and endurance.

4. Remember that one day all earthly suffering will end, and will not touch us.

5. Keep in mind that, when one bears suffering faithfully, God is glorified and honored. The suffering servants of Christ will be honored in a special way.[82]

Good advice from one who knows. For example, on one occasion, President Harry Truman called him a "counterfeit."[83] But Billy carried on and learned from it.

When asked how he felt about his Parkinson's disease and if he thought that God was responsible for it, again in typical fashion Graham answered:

> I don't know. He allows it. And He allows it for a purpose that I may not know. I think that everything that comes to our lives, if we are true believers, God has a purpose and a plan. And many of these things are things that cause suffering or inconvenience or whatever. But it helps to mature me because God is molding and making me in the image of His Son Jesus Christ. Jesus Christ suffered more than any man that ever lived because when He was on the cross He was bearing the sins that you and I have committed.[84]

Perhaps Graham's basic attitude is summed up in his statement that Christians are not "exempt from the tribulations and natural disasters that come upon the world. Scripture does teach that the Christian can face tribulation, crisis, calamity, and personal suffering with a supernatural power that is not available to the person outside of Christ."[85] Simply put, Billy Graham has faced all of his difficulties, problems, criticisms, attacks, and the malignment that he has suffered for many decades with the Spirit of Christ that permeates his entire approach to life and reality. Therefore, he stands victorious as God's people have through the ages. True, he may never be hanged and burned, as was Savonarola, but with the spirit of Savonarola he would certainly be able to say with the great saint of old, "My Lord has done so much for me." And that really settles the issue historically and pragmatically for any day.

Therefore, Billy Graham contends that Christians, regardless of what may fall across their paths by way of affliction, are to be patient and rejoice and become exceedingly glad (Rom. 5:12). Billy repeated the previously quoted church father Ignatius when he cried out prior to his execution, "Nearer the sword, then nearer to God. In the company of wild beasts, in company with God that cannot be defeated."[86] Billy stresses, "Christians can rejoice in the midst of persecution because they have eternity's values in view."[87]

What will prepare us for the day of suffering? What is the secret of victory in it all? Billy says, "The most important thing we can do is grow—in our relationship to Christ."[88] After all, as Paul has promised, believers who live in Christ's intimate fellowship can be "more than conquerors" (Rom. 8:37 KJV). Paul himself had that confidence when he said to the Corinthian church, "With all our affliction, I am overjoyed" (2 Cor. 7:4 RSV). The apostle thus went on to say he was "content with weaknesses, insults, hardships, persecutions, and calamities" (2 Cor. 12:10 RSV).

In this "upside-down world," as the passage previously quoted declares, "all that will live godly in Christ Jesus shall suffer persecution" (2 Tim. 3:12 KJV). Graham has assimilated that basic principle and confesses, "I have found in my travels that those who keep heaven in view remain serene and cheerful in the darkest day. . . . Victory for such does not come easily or quickly. But eventually the peace of God does come and with it is joy."[89] This has been true of Christ-honoring evangelists throughout the history of the church. Graham qualifies. As Billy has said, "I don't want to get to heaven with out any scars."[90] He won't.

CONCLUSION AND CONTRIBUTION OF BILLY GRAHAM AND PERSECUTION FOR THE GOSPEL

The verse of Scripture that has meant much to Graham is the word of comfort Paul shared with the suffering church in Rome: "For I consider that the sufferings of this present time are not worthy to be compared with the glory that is to be revealed to us" (Rom. 8:18). In this beautiful truth, the Bible places a blessing and benediction on suffering. And as seen so often in the writing and preaching of Billy Graham, *all* committed Christians suffer and endure some form of persecution. Not all have had to endure physical pain, but there is a pain of ridicule and resistance to God's work. Billy understands that well from personal experience—as documented. What does all this mean and how has it become a contribution to Christ's kingdom?

First, the onslaught Billy Graham has received clearly identifies him in the long line of notable believers who have taken the fiery arrows of Satan. He stands in that noble historical train whose reward will be great (Rev. 2:9–10).

Second, Billy has endured criticism and attempts to label him as either a "liberal" or a "fundamentalist" or an "obscurantist" or a thousand other monikers, and he has done it with a marvelous display of Christian patience and love. In a personal interview he said, "I sort of glory in the fact I was counted worthy to suffer for the name of Christ. That's the position the apostles took."[91] And he has rarely remonstrated or fought back. About his many conflicts Graham has said, "I feel the Lord wanted me to be quiet and not say too much . . . [in] rebuttal."[92] He has borne his burdens well. Thus he has been an inspiration and instructor in this area of spiritual warfare to many. This author must acknowledge that in the spiritual battles he has had to face, the attitude and approach of Billy Graham have been not only an inspiration, but a pattern to follow; and victory has been forthcoming. There are many who can give like testimony.

Billy's commitment to Christ has always enabled him to seek reconciliation with his attackers. No case is more indicative of this spiritual principle than the evangelist's attempts to reconcile differences with Dr. Bob Jones. Although "Dr. Bob" refused to be reconciled, Billy never gave up on seeking harmony; Billy loved Dr. Jones. Again he set an admirable example of Christian charity that has inspired and guided many. He does feel, however, that perhaps he was too conciliatory at times; he said, "Maybe I have stayed out of controversy too much, but I have concentrated on one thing: preaching the gospel. I felt it was what the Lord wanted."[93]

Finally, Billy Graham has demonstrated that to follow the biblical pattern when facing persecution brings about inner peace and contentment. Often the opportunity arises to reconcile serious differences, and God is therein glorified. The Bible does say that patience and endurance will "heap burning coals upon his [the persecutor's] head" (Rom. 12:20). That fire can clear out the dross. Therefore, said the apostle, "do not be overcome by evil, but overcome evil with good" (Rom. 12:21). This gains the ultimate victory and also becomes a radiant testimony for Christ that encourages the suffering believers and finally produces an inspiring testimony to the world. It so often attracts people to Christ when they see what the Lord enables His people to face. That is a contribution; that is biblical; that is historical; that is Billy Graham. Heaven will surely verify it.

INTRODUCTION TO THE
REFORMATION AGE

⁓

LIKE THE ASCENDING SUN ON A DISMAL HORIZON, new hope began to rise for the dissemination of the truth of God. At the advent of the sixteenth century, a powerful movement dawned in Western Europe. It can actually be compared in some respects to the first century, which witnessed the early dramatic expansion of the Christian church. We call it the Protestant Reformation; and for the first time in a thousand years, the truth of the gospel in its purity and simplicity was heard far and wide. As a consequence, multitudes pressed into the kingdom. A recent evaluation scored it as the most significant event of the second millennium. Evangelism from an evangelical perspective once again gained the ascendancy in many places.

During those reforming years, the pure principle of evangelical evangelism surfaced after being submerged in sacramentalism and sacerdotalism that had all but drowned the gospel message in a bewildering sea of ecclesiastical confusion. The essential doctrines of the Reformation demand that we understand them in our quest for authentic evangelism. Two of those theological principles, and two Reformers who epitomized them, shall be investigated as we seek to uncover the truths of historical, biblical evangelism. The two men to be investigated are Martin Luther and Ulrich Zwingli. Of course, there were other giants of the Reformation such as Calvin, Knox,

Beza, and others; and many other vital aspects of the Reformation occurred. However, Luther and Zwingli personified two essential principles that need elucidating. We shall look at these two bright lights in some depth.

CHAPTER 8

THE BIBLE IN EVANGELISM

~⁓

PART I:
LUTHER AND THE BIBLE

Here I stand, I cannot do otherwise; God help me.
—MARTIN LUTHER

INTRODUCTION

At the Diet of Worms, as friar Martin Luther of the Augustinian Order stood before the august body of the Roman Catholic Church on April 17, 1521, he was ordered to recant his position. In the face of the threat of excommunication, Luther said, "Here I stand, I cannot do otherwise; God help me." Those courageous words have echoed around the world ever since. And the stand cost him. Two years later, his rupture with the Roman Church was effected and Luther, stellar star of the Protestant Reformation, was thrust on his own to carry out his revolutionary ministry.

Why the stance? Why defy one thousand years of church history and the incredible power of the established church? The answer is simple and of eternal significance: Luther discovered that the final truth of God rests in the Word of God, not in councils, dogmas, or church dignitaries. The Bible stands as the ultimate word of authority in the things of God. Luther defied councils, popes, and the entire Roman Church whenever they deviated from the authoritative teaching of the Holy Scriptures. Luther's view of the Bible, in his own words, declares, "God's Word . . . is a great and rich treasure and offers us most wonderful revelations about the invisible, supernatural things."[1] Little wonder, therefore, in his reply to the inquiry of Johann Eck, his prosecutor at Worms, as to why he took the stance he did, Luther replied, "Since then Your Majesty and your lordships desire a simple reply, I will answer without horns and without teeth. Unless I am convicted by Scripture and plain reason—I do not accept the authority of popes and councils, for they have contradicted each other—my conscience is captive to the Word of God."[2]

Luther contended that the Word of God and the Word of God alone forms the basis of all divine truth and subsequent authority. On one occasion, when asked how he was able to effect such a spiritual revolution in Europe, he replied, "I simply taught, preached, wrote God's Word; otherwise I did nothing . . . the Word did it all."[3] For Martin Luther, it was *sola scriptura:* the Scriptures only.

Moreover, Luther was far from being a mere passive, theoretical theologian concerning the Word of God. As historian Timothy George has said, "Defying the pope, subduing the peasants, intervening in political crises, teaching, preaching, marrying, and giving in marriage: Luther was certainly a *doer of the Word and not a hearer only.*"[4] Because of his study and lecturing on the Scriptures, particularly the Books of Psalms, Romans, Galatians, and Hebrews, he said, "In the course of this teaching, the papacy slipped away from me."[5] He came to experience God's grace in Christ personally and set out at all costs to share the truth of the gospel with the world. Thus the Reformation was launched, a thrust based on the deep conviction that the Bible stands alone as the final revelation of Christian truth and experience. Those who would win souls to Christ must come to like agreement.

It goes without saying, of course, that to reduce the Reformation period to just one or two men paints a grossly inadequate picture of those monumental days. Before that crucial launching moment on October 31, 1517, when Martin Luther nailed his 95 Theses on the Wittenberg church door, there had been a procession of insightful spiritual leaders who served as precursors of the Protestant Reformation. Men like Savonarola—presented in the previous era—and notables such as John Wycliffe of Britain, John Hus of old Moravia, and a host of others came to the essential truths that Luther so ably defended. And Luther's contemporaries were not a few. Many became historic notables, such as John Calvin and Phillip Melanchthon (Luther's theological mentor), not to mention reforming groups like the Anabaptists and the early British Puritans. All these well served the Reformation, as did Luther. An innumerable host was raised up by the Spirit of God to once again put the Word of God where it rightfully belongs. And the Reformation went forward at an incredible pace.

It was a long, difficult, treacherous journey Luther traveled to arrive at his destination. But as his great hymn declares, "A mighty fortress is our God . . . our Helper He amid the flood of mortal ills prevailing." Luther arrived at his goal because he rested in the power of God and the truth of Holy Scripture. What a fascinating journey it proved to be! It all began for Luther one stormy day.

LUTHER'S JOURNEY TO THE TRUTH

On a hot, sultry July day in 1505, Martin Luther, a twenty-one-year-old student at the University of Erfurt, was returning to school after a visit with his parents. Suddenly a thunderstorm blew in and lightning struck him to the ground. The thunderclap was deafening and the flash of light more than struck him to the ground; it seemed to thrust him into the very presence of God. There stood God, whom Luther visualized as the "all-terrible, Christ the inexorable, and all the leering fiends springing from their lurking places in pond and wood that with sardonic cachinnations that might seize his shock of curly hair and bolt him into hell."[6] Luther was so terrified that he cried out to his father's saint, the patroness of miners, "Saint Anne, help me! I will become a monk." And he did. Martin Luther immediately dedicated himself to a monastery of the Augustinian Order, one of the strictest monastic groups of the day. After a farewell party with a few friends, he walked to the monastery gate and presented himself for holy orders.

THE NEW MONK

Martin Luther became a novice. As the novice "mantle" was about to fall on him, the prior asked, "What seekest thou?" Luther, with his face on the floor, replied, "God's grace and thy mercy." The prior then raised up the prostrate novice and interrogated him concerning whether he was married or a bonds-man or had any secret diseases. If his answers were in the negative, the prior would describe monastic life with all its rigor and sacrifice. The novice would be required to renounce all self-will, live on a scant diet, wear rough clothing, and spend many nights in prayer and hard labor by the day—all for the mor-tification of the flesh. To break human pride, one had to beg and take the vow of poverty. When all of these were outlined before the young man, he was asked whether he would shoulder these burdens. Luther replied, "Yes, with God's help." That opened the door for a year of probation in the monastery.

Why would a person take such a vow and submit himself to such a life? For a new monk the meaning was simple: The salvation of one's soul rested in the hands of the Roman Church. Therefore, to become a monk constituted the surest way of being a recipient of God's grace and being assured of eternal life. Luther had set out upon that path, but he had no idea where the journey would finally lead him.

CLOISTER LIFE

Every day in the monastery was crammed with religious exercises and hard work. One rarely found a moment to rest. The monks in the Augustinian monastery in Erfurt where Luther served were required to pray seven times a day. They would be awakened between one and two in the morning as the cloister bell roused them from their sleep. At the very first clang of the bell, the monks would spring up, make the sign of the cross, and put on their white robes and scapulars. The rules prohibited any brother ever leaving his cell with anything on other than the traditional habit. A second bell then sounded, and the monks came to the church, sprinkled themselves with holy water, and knelt before the high altar in prayer. Then everyone took their place in the choir. These services, called Matins, lasted for three-quarters of an hour. This proce-dure of worship was enacted seven times every day.

Through it all, Brother Martin became convinced that he was walking the path of the saints and that eternal life would surely be his reward. After a year's probation, the enthusiasm and commitment of the young monk were excelled only by his thrill of being admitted to the order. He took his solemn vow with this prayer, "Lord Jesus Christ . . . May this Thy servant, Martin Luther, who takes the habit, be clothed also in Thine immortality, O Thou who livest and reignest with God the Father and the Holy Ghost, God from eternity to eternity. Amen." The vow had been taken; Martin Luther became a full-fledged monk of the austere Augustinian Order. Confident that he had found the sure way of salvation, he would spend his days in prayer, meditation, and the disciplined life.

THE FIRST MASS

As Luther went through all the religious rigors, the time came when he would say his first Mass. Another "thunderstorm" occurred at that very moment. The church saw the Mass as far more than a mere symbolic, spiritual experience. When the priest elevated the host and said the proper words, the elements of bread and wine were believed to become the literal body and blood of Christ. The church had committed itself to the doctrine of transubstantiation as originated in the ninth century from the writings of Paschasius Radbertus. These concepts were later proclaimed a church dogma in 1215 by the Fourth Lateran Council. This was what the church believed. Believing that the holy Son of God Himself would actually come down upon the altar to once again be crucified, the doctrine of transubstantiation was an awe-inspiring, terrifying thought for Luther. Moreover, the clergyman officiating at the Mass dare not make one mistake in the words of the liturgy. With all these thoughts swirling around in Luther's heart and mind, and for the first time taking his place before the altar to recite the beginning words of the Mass, he felt terrified. When he came to the expression "We offer unto Thee, the living, the true, the eternal God," he was absolutely awestruck. He afterward related:

At these words I was utterly stupefied and terror-stricken. I thought to myself, "With what tongue shall I address such Majesty, seeing that all men ought to tremble in the presence of even an earthly prince? Who am I, that I should lift up mine eyes or raise my hands to the divine Majesty? The angels surround him. At his nod the earth trembles. And shall I, a miserable little pygmy, say 'I want this, I ask for that'? For I am dust and ashes and full of sin and I am speaking to the living, eternal and the true God."[7]

The awe of Holy God became like the smiting of a new lightning bolt. Luther could scarcely hold himself at the altar to the end of the Mass, overwhelmed by the holiness and the infinite power of God Almighty. His heart filled with turmoil, pain, tremor, and panic. He felt as did John when meeting the Lord Jesus Christ as recorded in the last book of the New Testament: "And when I saw Him, I fell at His feet as a dead man" (Rev. 1:17).

Yet, through all the religious exercises of the monastery, Luther found no true peace of heart or consciousness of God's acceptance. As his turmoil continually deepened, he felt alienated from God and in sin. What was wrong? He had gone the limits of asceticism. Would he ever find peace? Could he ever satisfy God?

Luther attempted every way imaginable to find an answer to the pervasive, deepening uneasiness he felt. He determined that he would do everything he could do to save himself. Whatever the church prescribed, whatever came into his heart and mind as another sacrifice to God, whatever the price might be, he resolved to perform it. He fasted sometimes three days on end without a bite of bread. Actually, he found his times of fasting more restful than those of eating. Not only that, as historian and biographer Roland Bainton pointed out, to Luther, Lent was more comforting than Easter. Luther drove himself into vigils and prayers that far exceeded any of the others in the monastery. He would even go so far as to throw off the warm blankets at night in his little monkish cell and endure the hours half-frozen to death in the cold German winters.

PROUD YET MISERABLE

Luther became somewhat proud of his discipline and sanctity. He would actually say, "I have done nothing wrong today." But then that subtle lack of peace and conviction would grip his heart. He would ask himself whether he had fasted enough or whether he was poor enough, whether he had stripped himself of all that would be worldly. Luther spent hours confessing his sins. One day one of his confessors at the monastery cried out, "Martin, why don't you just go out and sin really well; then you would have something to bring before God."

Luther actually believed in later life that his asceticism had done permanent damage to his health. He said, "I was a good monk, and I kept the rule of my order so strictly that I may say that if ever a monk got to heaven by his monkery it was I. All my brothers in the monastery who knew me will bear me out. If I had kept on any longer, I should have killed myself with vigils, prayers, reading, and other work."[8] But strive as he would, Luther could find no inner peace. It seemed to him he could not satisfy God at any point in his life.

Martin Luther exhausted the Roman system. He attempted to rely on the merits of the saints. He hoped thereby that he could mitigate something of the pain of purgatory. Some years before, the presiding pope had declared that indulgences could be extended to purgatory, not only for the benefit of the living, but also for the dead. The church had created places where the merits of the saints were more accessible than others. As a case in point, Pope Leo X declared every relic of the saints in Halle would afford an indulgence for the reduction of purgatory by four thousand years. Of course, the greatest bank of relics, merits of the saints, and indulgences were to be found in Rome. For example, in the crypt of St. Callistus, forty popes had been buried, along with seventy-five thousand martyrs. Rome declared the crypt even possessed a piece of Moses' burning bush. The Vatican boasted they had the chains of Paul and the scissors by which Emperor Domitian had cut the hair of St. John. One of the churches in Rome claimed it had a coin paid to Judas for betraying Christ. Above all, Rome had the entire bodies of St. Peter and St. Paul. Spiritual indulgences could be had in incredible quantity. Luther decided he must make a pilgrimage to Rome. Perhaps he could find peace with God in the "holy city."

OFF TO ROME

When Luther walked atop the hill and for the first time saw the "eternal city," he cried out, "Hail, holy Rome!" Yet he had been there but a very short time when disillusionment gripped his heart. He first encountered an incompetent confessor. The seeking monk also found that many of the Italian priests were ignorant, frivolous, and almost slaves of levity. Luther stood amazed at their blatant stupidity. Some of the clergy in Rome were so irreverent and unbelieving that they would address the sacraments, saying, "Bread thou art and bread thou wilt remain, and wine thou art and wine thou wilt remain." This deeply shocked the devout monk from Erfurt.

Luther was all but totally disillusioned. However, there remained one hope. He felt that he could find some release by climbing the Scala Sancta. Tradition held that these were the steps of Pilate's palace, which the Lord Himself had been forced to ascend. The church had moved them to Rome and propounded the doctrine that if one would climb Pilate's stairs on hands and knees, repeating the Pater Noster on each step and kissing each one, it would deliver a soul from purgatory. Luther actually regretted that his mother and father were not dead and in purgatory that he might confer upon them their deliverance. So he resolved that he would release his grandfather, Heine. Tradition has it that Luther ascended halfway up, jumped to his feet, and cried out, "The just shall live by faith." No real historical evidence can be found for this claim. Luther did indeed climb the stairs to the very top and dutifully repeated the Pater Noster and kissed every step. When Luther reached the top, he exclaimed, "Who knows whether it is so?" Luther returned to Erfurt utterly depressed. As Bainton expressed it, "Luther commented that he had gone to Rome with onions and had returned with garlic."[9] The pilgrimage failed.

THE GOSPEL COMES ALIVE

When Martin Luther returned home, the order transferred him from Erfurt to Wittenberg. There he was destined to spend the rest of his life. Wittenberg was a small town with a population of only two thousand people. Johann von Staupitz served as vicar of the Augustinian Order in Wittenberg. Vicar von Staupitz had a sympathetic heart toward the distress of his fellow monks and became a great comfort to Luther. Martin actually said, "If it had not been for Dr. Staupitz, I should have sunk in hell." But he still found no real peace.

The church taught that if one's sins are to be forgiven, they must be confessed. Consequently, Luther spent hour after hour in the confessional. On this point Staupitz made a tremendous contribution to the distressed Luther. Being in the train of the mystics, Staupitz helped Luther realize that he could find help by giving his attention away from individual sins to the actual nature of his heart. Luther began to realize, "When Peter started to count the waves, he sank. The whole nature of man needs to be changed."[10]

Luther set out on the mystic route with his confessor. At times real joy and peace would seemingly touch his life, but then the dogged sense of alienation from God would return. The mystics call it the "dark night of the soul." Luther spent more times in the dark night than in the bright sunshine. His distress grew so deep that everything in his religious life seemed to fail him. Not even prayer afforded him any peace. Doubts began to swirl around in his mind about everything he believed. But the most devastating doubt that gripped his soul was the idea that perhaps not even God Himself was just. It drove him to the point that he said:

> Is it not against all natural reason that God out of his mere whim deserts men, hardens them, damns them, as if he delighted in sins and in such torments of the wretched for eternity, he who is said to be of such mercy and goodness? This appears iniquitous, cruel, and intolerable in God, by which very many have been offended in all ages. And who would not be? I was myself more than once driven to the very abyss of despair so that I wished I had never been created. Love God? I hated him![11]

Luther had blasphemed. Staupitz was concerned about his protégé. Hoping some diversion would help him, Staupitz suggested that Luther study for his doctor's degree and assume the chair of the Bible at the university. This became the monumental moment that changed the entire direction of Luther's life. He had exhausted the Roman system and found no peace. *At last Luther gave himself to the Scriptures.*

Luther set out to learn God's Word and expound it clearly. On August 1, 1513, he began a series of lectures on the Book of Psalms. Two years later, he lectured on Paul's Epistle to the Romans. Next came the Galatian letter, which he thoroughly digested throughout the academic year of 1516–17. As Bainton put it, "These studies proved to be for Luther the Damascus Road."[12] The third great thunderstorm occurred. How radically different it proved to be from the first two! The literal flash of lightning and clap of thunder at the age of twenty-one and the first Mass were nothing compared with what Luther now experienced. However, this thunderstorm broke not with thunder and lightning and great fear, but as a "still, small voice." As Bainton stated, "No *coup de foudre*, no heavenly apparition, no religious ceremony precipitated the third crisis. The place was no lonely road in a blinding storm, nor even the holy altar, but simply the study in the tower of the Augustinian monastery. The solution to Luther's problems came in the midst of the performance of the daily task."[13]

THE GOSPEL DAWNS

What particularly gripped Luther from the Book of Psalms was chapter 22. In the opening verse, the psalmist cries out, "My God, my God, why hast Thou forsaken me?" What could this mean? Luther came to the unmistakable conclusion that it must refer to what Jesus uttered on the cross. Luther knew that everyone, including the psalmist, sinned, but the Bible taught that Christ did not. The only answer must be that the Lord Jesus took our sins upon Himself and died in our place on Calvary. He began to realize that Christ had become the great Substitute for sinners. This realization so radically altered Luther's understanding of Jesus Christ that it became nothing short of revolutionary. A whole new view of God and His Son gripped Luther's mind. He came to understand, "The all-terrible is the all-merciful too, wrath and love fuse upon the cross."[14]

Of course, Luther wrestled with how all this could be rationalized. Finally, he came to face the fact that human learning cannot comprehend in full measure what took place at Calvary. Only faith can grasp a mystery of this magnitude. This is what the godless Corinthians called the "foolishness of the cross," but is actually "the wisdom of God" (1 Cor. 1:18–31). As Luther expressed it, "God hides his power in weakness, his wisdom in folly, his goodness in severity, his justice in sins, his mercy in anger."[15] But how was this to be appropriated? Finally, the light shone forth as he wrote:

> Night and day I pondered until I saw the connection between the justice of God and the statement that "the just shall live by his faith." Then I grasped that the justice of God is that righteousness by which through grace and sheer mercy God justifies us through faith. Thereupon I felt myself to be reborn and to have gone through open doors into paradise. The whole of Scripture took on a new

meaning, and whereas before the "justice of God" had filled me with hate, now it became to me inexpressibly sweet in greater love. This passage of Paul became to me a gate to heaven.[16]

Luther had his Damascus Road experience; he met Christ in a new, redemptive way.

Through the study of the Word of God, Luther had come to a glorious salvation experience. He had been "born again." Peace flooded his life. God's Word had done its work. Little wonder that Luther came to the vital realization that the Scriptures stand as the final authority in the entire Christian experience, the salvation experience in particular. This fact alone forms the foundation and presents the rationale for his famous statement, "Here I stand, I cannot do otherwise; God help me."

The rest of the unfolding life of Luther—and the entire Reformation movement—continued to revolve around the commitment to the truth and authority of the Bible in all matters of religious faith, which especially relates to evangelism and the gospel. But what constitutes Luther's doctrine of inspiration and biblical authority? And how does it relate to evangelism?

LUTHER'S DOCTRINE OF THE WORD OF GOD

Luther's debate with Johann Eck at the Diet of Worms centered on the relative merit of the Scripture versus church tradition. The Roman Church did not officially deny Scripture, but what happens if and when Scripture and tradition conflict? Eck held that one must yield to the church and its traditions as over against the Word of God. The Roman Church holds to that position due to the fact that the church is seen as the only true interpreter of the gospel. At one time, Eck held to the superiority of Scripture over the church. But as one put it, he ended at the opposite pole: superiority of the church over Scripture.[17] However, Luther insisted on *sola scriptura*. Of course, when Luther contended for "Scripture alone," this does not mean that other realities are not considered. For example, one's understanding of Scripture can be greatly aided by knowledge of the biblical languages, the history and the background of the writings, etc. Biblical criticism has a role to play, as well. Not only that, many inputs from church tradition have a proper place in the Christian experience.

But in the final analysis, The Bible stands as the arbiter and the *final word* of authority. That is the point of Luther's stress on *sola scriptura.*

Furthermore, Luther was always concerned about protecting both the divine and the human aspects of the Word of God. The Reformer was fully convinced that the Bible was totally inspired by the Holy Spirit. Some scholars say that Luther did not believe in the inerrancy of Scripture. But as Clark Pinnock points out, "In Luther's case, statements supporting complete inerrancy are so numerous and so uncompromising that the only conceivable way to make him teach anything else is to charge him with gross inconsistency."[18]

Luther constantly appealed to Christ as the essence of the gospel. With Jesus Christ Himself as the criteria, Luther went so far as to say that the Book of James, in which Christ is mentioned but very little, was a "strawy" epistle. Later, Luther changed his mind about James, but regardless of where Luther came down in certain areas of plenary inspiration, he declared, "No other doctrine should be proclaimed in the church than the pure Word of God, that is, the Holy Scriptures."[19]

It is also important to understand that Luther, like Calvin, rejected the concept of the dictation view of inspiration. They were concerned about protecting the human element; nonetheless, they saw the Bible as the pure Word of God. For the Reformers, the divine and the human aspects were just there, and they simply lived with it. This means Luther was a critical scholar, at least in a limited sense. For example, he was the first biblicist to question the Solomonic authorship of the Book of Ecclesiastes. As has been aforementioned, Luther questioned whether the Book of James and other portions of the canon should have been included as Scripture. This, as has been made clear, was because of Luther's insistence on the primacy of those books that preach Christ.

Moreover, Luther, at least to a large measure, rejected excessive allegorizing in the interpretation of the Scriptures, especially in using allegory to establish the authority of the church. Christ is the One who stands above mere human authority. Luther freely confessed that when he was a monk, he excelled in allegorizing. However, all that changed. He said, "Since that time when I began to embrace the historical meaning I have always abhorred allegories and have not used them unless either the text itself exhibited them or [allegorical] interpretations could be cited from the New Testament."[20] As Luther argued, "No believing Christian can be forced to recognize any authority beyond the sacred Scripture, which is exclusively invested with divine right, unless, indeed, there comes a new and attested revelation."[21] The break with Rome came, not only in the authority of tradition, but also in the use of allegorization. The Reformers insisted on the necessity of "one simple solid sense" for the meaning of the Scriptures.

Furthermore, Luther was convinced that the Word of God is clear and understandable as the Holy Spirit interprets it to the human heart. Luther, in his *Bondage of the Will,* wrote, "It is a pestilent dictum of the Sophists, that the Scriptures are obscure and equivocal."[22] Luther challenged the Sophists with the question: If such were the case, why did God give it in the first place? Moreover, Luther argued that an obscure book could not accomplish in the lives of people what the Scriptures do. A denial of the understandability of the Word of God is a denial of the *sola scriptura* principle in itself.

Luther also strongly stressed the role of the Holy Spirit, not only in the formation of the Scriptures, but also in the understanding thereof. He said, "Whoever does not understand the subject matter of Scripture, cannot elicit the meaning of the words."[23] The Holy Spirit stands as the final Interpreter, and He speaks to the heart of all true seekers of God's truth through the Word.

The conclusion of the whole matter can be quickly summarized by stating that, for Martin Luther, the Bible is the Word of God; and in the Word of God alone one finds the truth of Christ and hence salvation. That is so foundational in the whole Christian enterprise that to fail on this point is to fail in a most fundamental sense. As the apostle Paul put it, "For since in the wisdom of God the world through its wisdom did not come to know God, God was well-pleased through the foolishness of the message preached [*kerygma*] to save those who believe" (1 Cor. 1:21). The wise evangelists take their stand with Martin Luther on *sola scriptura* and say with Luther, "My conscience is captive to the Word of God,"[24] because thereby one can come to know God.

THE POINT FOR A THEOLOGY OF EVANGELISM

The whole issue of the necessity of the Bible in the total Christian experience revolves around the fact that God does not exist on a mere human, rational, empirical, limited plane. It has been previously stressed that God transcends our limited dimensions. He must be understood as One whom finitude cannot claw its way up to. As the psalmist expressed it, "Such knowledge is too wonderful for me; it is too high, I cannot attain to it" (Ps. 139:6). Therefore, it follows that an ultimate, infinite, personal God would in some sense be "forced" to reveal Himself to humanity in its finitude. Even if intuition or *a priori* knowledge gives people some sort of indication of His existence, *revelation is absolutely necessary* to know the ultimate Person personally and thus redemptively. God must come to mankind for people to acquire a true saving knowledge of Himself. What then is the answer?

CHRIST: THE ANSWER

A revelation of God is not only what humanity desperately needs, but that is exactly what has occurred. God has seen mankind's plight and has come to us in *revelation*. The Scriptures state: "'What no eye has seen, nor ear heard [empiricism], nor the heart of man conceived [rationalism], what God has prepared for those who love him,' God has *revealed* to us through the Spirit" (1 Cor. 2:9–10 RSV, emphasis added). Christians hold that God has graciously made Himself known in a number of ways and manners: "In many and various ways God spoke" (Heb. 1:1 RSV,). But there is one supreme way God has revealed Himself clearly and unmistakably. The Bible says, "There was the true light which, coming into the world, enlightens every man" (John 1:9). That "Light" comes in the incarnation of Jesus Christ. As Simeon in the Temple said when he saw the baby Jesus, this Child would be "a light of revelation" (Luke 2:32). The infinite God has finally and fully revealed Himself in Jesus of Nazareth. As pointed out previously, Athanasius saw this clearly, but it virtually boggles the mind. Remember, however, God had to do some revelational thing if human beings were to come into personal, knowledgeable, redemptive contact with His ultimacy.

It thus becomes logical that revelation is just what Jesus Christ came to perform. Christians firmly believe He did much more, but He did reveal God in a full and satisfying way. Jesus said, "He who has seen me has seen the Father" (John 14:9). He uniquely revealed God as fully as human limitations can intellectually and experientially grasp God. Jesus Christ as *Person* presented the very nature of ultimate reality, suprarational *Personhood,* on humanity's personal level. "The Word was God" (John 1:1).

One question still remains, however. If God has authoritatively and finally spoken in Christ, how do we know anything about Jesus Christ, God's supreme revelation of Himself?

LEARNING ABOUT THE REVEALED CHRIST

The answer to the above question is central to all thought about God and His salvation. The answer is simply this: God Himself has given us a Book that tells us about His redeeming Son. It dramatically and powerfully relates realities about Christ's life, His teachings, His ministry, His death, His victory over the grave, and the implications and meaning of the entire event. The Book? Let it be said again and again, that Book is the Bible! Actually, there is no other substantive source in which to discover the essential realities about Jesus and the meaning of His life, death, and resurrection. The Holy Scriptures alone tell us the full story. We are thus forced to the Word of God, the Holy Spirit–inspired Scriptures. There rests the primary source of authority in theology and evangelism. Luther learned that truth; so must any effective evangelist.

The church has historically held the view set out here. For example, the thirty-nine articles of the Church of England stated the Bible is "God's Word written" (Article XX). The Scots Confession of 1560 called the Bible the "written Word of God" (XVII). The famous Westminster Confession of 1647 declared the Scriptures are "to be received, because it is the Word of God" (I.i.iv). The "Short Confession of Faith" of 1610 by the early Baptists said, "In this only God in the Holy Scriptures is manifested and revealed." The Baptist London Confession of 1644 stated: "In this written Word . . . God hath plainly revealed whatsoever he hath thought needful for us to know." Go back as far as the church fathers and trace the issue through church history, and the evangelical church's position on the Bible is always virtually the same. For us revelation is both personal in Christ (subjective) and propositional (objective) in the Holy Scriptures.

Why have God's people for thousands of years held such a position? Because the Bible is inspired by the Spirit of God Himself. Yes, human hands penned it, but God's Spirit inspired it—all of it. Paul wrote, "All Scripture is inspired by God and profitable for teaching, for reproof, for correction, for training in righteousness" (2 Tim. 3:16). Peter said, "For no prophecy was ever made by an act of human will, but men moved by the Holy Spirit spoke from God" (2 Pet. 1:21). Those words settle the issue for God's people. That exactly describes what the Bible is all about: God personally speaking in objective, propositional form in the Scriptures. The Holy Spirit takes His inspired truth and then comes through the Word and communicates spiritual realities to the open heart. God speaks. Of course, it goes without saying, after one has discovered the fact that God's Word stands as the propositional revelation of Himself, another vital issue immediately surfaces. Adherence to the Scriptures demands that one properly interpret the Word. It does little good to hold a high view of the Bible and then fail to apply proper principles of interpretation, i.e., use good hermeneutics. But that opens up a field of inquiry far too exhaustive for these short pages. Let it merely be said that if a balanced grasp of God's truth is to be had, the Scriptures must be approached sensibly and carefully—and many excellent volumes have been written on that subject.[25]

CONCLUSION

So it stands. In the Holy Scriptures, God has given us a trustworthy, authoritative Word for Christian redemption, ministry, and understanding of God. It becomes obvious that any evangelism worthy of the stamp of historical credibility must emanate from the Scriptures. The Bible, God's authoritative truth, forms the basis and foundation for any meaningful evangelistic ministry. Moreover, this principle applies to methodologies and practice as well as the verbal proclamation of the gospel. The question for any evangelist or any evangelistic enterprise thus becomes: Is it rooted and grounded in the Scriptures in every aspect, all the way from the actual proclamation of the good news to methodologies and approaches? As J. I. Packer correctly put it: "The mental discipline of systematically submitting our thoughts, views, and purposes to the judgment of Scripture as it interprets itself to us in regard to our relationship with God, is more than one Christian tradition among many; it is a discipline intrinsic to Christianity itself."[26] The authentic evangelist must remember the words of the apostle Paul when he said, "Faith comes from hearing, and hearing by the word of Christ" (Rom. 10:17). Therefore, evangelism, to have the favor of God, be of any lasting effect, and make a positive contribution to the world, must be rooted in, grounded on, and emanate from the Holy Bible. When a high view of the Scriptures and faithful proclamation thereof have become the matrix of evangelistic endeavors, God's power attends the work and lives are changed. Luther was right; *sola scriptura* becomes the evangelist's only word of authority and power. And at the outset let it be said, most recognize that Billy Graham marches in that noble train—as shall hopefully be clearly demonstrated.

PART II:
BILLY GRAHAM AND THE BIBLE

The Bible says . . .
—BILLY GRAHAM

INTRODUCTION

"The Bible says!" Anyone who has heard Billy Graham has heard that phrase multiple times. His sermons are punctuated with that oft-repeated declaration. For Graham, the Bible and the Holy Scriptures serve as the essential foundational core in the preaching of the evangelist. Actually, no instrument in the ministry of the entire Graham association has played a more central role than the Word of God. Even though the Bible has been maligned by critics, ignored, and gathered much dust, no book has resided more at the heart of Billy Graham in his evangelization than the Scriptures. Here is a Book to be dealt with, and Billy Graham has dealt with it extensively and significantly in his grasp of the Christian faith and the ministry of preaching Christ. As John Stott has said, "He's a man of the Bible."[27]

THE ISSUE

We have already discovered the Reformation principle of *sola scriptura:* the Scriptures only. Although church tradition, theology, hermeneutics, and a host of other disciplines play an important part in discovering the truth of God, the supreme and final authority for the Reformation giants always rested in the Scriptures. When a final verdict on truth is demanded, the Bible alone stands supreme. That epistemological principle not only pervaded the Reformation period, but it has been the mainstay of evangelicalism generally through the millennia of church history. Now we must look into Graham's biblical understandings concerning the validity and place of the Scriptures in the Christian experience, and especially in evangelization.

BILLY GRAHAM'S VIEWS OF THE BIBLE

Billy Graham once raised the issue as to whether the Bible has anything to say to us today. He answers the query very positively. For the evangelist, the Scriptures are as alive and relevant to every human need today as they were on the day they were written. Graham's basic views of the Holy Scriptures and their perpetual relevance can be seen in his convictions concerning the actual nature of God's Word. He takes his positive stance on the Bible as authoritative truth to meet life's issues for several reasons.

INSPIRATION

In the first place, Billy Graham holds a high view of the Bible because of his commitment to the proposition that the Scriptures are divinely inspired. When Graham speaks of inspiration, he speaks of *plenary* inspiration, i.e., each *word* counts, not just the idea behind the words employed. When the question is raised, "Do you believe in the plenary, verbal inspiration?" Graham answers, "I do, for the mere, simple reason that the words are mere signs of ideas, I do not know how to get at the idea except through the words."[28]

Graham believes that God has spoken in a unique sense in the Scriptures; therefore, the Bible stands as the revealed truth of God. Totally inspired by the Holy Spirit, it has the stamp of infallibility upon it, and thus the ring of authenticity. Graham said, "I came to believe with all of my heart in the full inspiration of the Bible."[29] Billy, of course, is conscious of the fact that the human pen played its part, as were Luther and the Reformers. But back of it all, God the Spirit moved the writers in such a manner that they wrote under His divine sovereignty. The end product is an inerrant transcript of the thoughts and truth of the triune God. Graham would agree with Martin Luther when he declared that we must read and wrestle with Scripture in such a way that we understand it as God Himself speaking the words. The Bible is replete with the statement, "Thus saith the Lord." Graham sees such a statement as a vindication of the inspiration and absolute truthfulness of the Scriptures. The Bible stands as the very Word of God; it is "God-breathed." Graham's approach can best be grasped when he declared, "God breathed life into man and made him a living soul, so also He also breathed life and wisdom into the Word of God."[30] He went on to elaborate, "I believe the Bible is the Word of God. By that I mean the full verbal inspiration of the Scriptures. I can accept no compromise with the teaching of the Scripture."[31]

Billy Graham also holds to the view that the Holy Spirit has led and preserved the Bible in such a way that today we have in the canon of the Scriptures an authentic version of God's revelation. Even though the original autographs are missing, we have in hand a fully reliable body of God's truth. Graham said, "God has spoken verbally, and His spoken Word has survived every scratch of human pen."[32] His approach can be summarized in the statement he made while penning an article under the title "Ambassadors." He wrote, "Our generation, especially in the West, has occupied itself with criticism of the Scriptures and all too often questioning divine revelation. Don't make that mistake. Take the Bible as God's Holy Word."[33]

In a word, Graham adheres to the total verbal inspiration and infallibility of the Bible, hence to the inerrancy of the Word. He does prefer to use the word *infallibility* rather than *inerrancy* due to the baggage the latter term has acquired. He said in light of this, "I decided to use the word *infallibility* . . . [still] they mean the same."[34] This also implies another principle: authority.

THE AUTHORITY OF THE BIBLE

Graham not only believes in the total inspiration of Scripture, he further believes in its absolute authority. The authority of the Bible grows out of its God-breathed nature. He wrote, "There is a second word that we would discuss when we talk about the Bible. Not only is the Bible inspired, but it is 'authoritative.' When we say that the Bible is 'authoritative,' we mean it is God's binding revelation to us. We submit to it because it has come from God."[35]

Graham holds that the Bible's authority is expressed in a unique way. He not only believes that the original texts were inspired of the Holy Spirit, but he is confident that the Spirit of God inspired the selection of the sixty-six books that comprise the canon itself. He grants that the choice of the books that make up the canon came through human hands; yet it was certainly not a mere human choice. God worked in and through the scholars who fashioned and compiled the canon. What we have, therefore, is again an absolute authoritative Word. Of course, all this implies a multiplicity of things, but it certainly means that the Bible is the final authoritative word in all matters of ethics, doctrine, theology, and in understanding life as a whole. It surely forms the core of the preaching of the gospel. Graham sums it up by saying, "God 'designed' the Bible to meet the needs of all people and all ages."[36] But how did the evangelist arrive at this position?

GRAHAM'S JOURNEY

Billy Graham's particular approach to understanding the nature and authority of the Bible did not come easily. Although he had been reared in a Christian home where the Bible was regularly read, he encountered several struggles over the Scriptures in his life. His aforementioned encounter with Charles Templeton concerning the highly critical method of interpretation proved a very difficult time for young Graham. Well known is the story, outlined earlier, of his endeavor to come to grips with the nature of the Bible at the California Forest Home retreat just prior to the Los Angeles crusade of 1949. At that juncture he made his faith commitment to the absolute validity of the Bible. Billy confesses that it was "a crucial moment" in his ministry.[37] Stephen Olford states it was in that experience that his most famous phrase, "the Bible says . . . ," was born.[38] But several steps led to that critical moment.

Graham's first major step came when he realized that aspects of the Scriptures would never be reconciled on a purely rational level. Billy said, "As a Christian, I am under no obligation to attempt to reconcile the Bible teachings with modern philosophy. Biblical truth does not parallel human opinion of any generation; it usually opposes it."[39] Those who declare the Bible is riddled with contradictions and myths project the implication that the gospel of Jesus Christ is somewhat anti-intellectual. Graham refutes that position. He has said, "It's a strange thing about this book [the Bible]. There are many things in it I don't understand and can't explain. Some of the questions I have asked about it I am sure will never be answered this side of Heaven."[40]

Billy is not saying the Bible is self-contradictory or nonsensible. His arguments set forth the principle that the Scriptures transcend mere human intellectualism. Therefore, the evangelist knows well that one must rest in faith in a God that exists above finite human reason. At the same time, however, Graham points out, "Skeptics have attacked the Bible and retreated in confusion. Agnostics have scoffed at its teachings but are unable to produce an intellectually honest refutation. Atheists have denied its validity, but must surrender to its historical accuracy and archeological information."[41] There are reasons to believe. Principles and precepts of apologetics can be employed to convince the open-minded.

In the case of science versus religion, Billy declares, "There is never any conflict between true science and Christian faith."[42] He sees the Bible as essentially "a book of faith, not necessarily science."[43] He stresses, "The Bible is a book of redemption."[44] And science, as all acknowledge, is not a "book" of religion. Actually, Graham contends, "the fact of the matter is: science and faith complement each other."[45] Many thinkers contend the Bible actually opens the door to scientific investigation and is something of the source of the modern quest for truth concerning the universe. The Bible believer cannot be charged with naive anti-intellectualism, although faith plays its vital role in the acceptance of biblical claims.

Graham's views can be summarized as follows: The Bible is totally inspired by the Spirit of God. Yet, one should not attempt to define the methodology by which God inspired the human writers. God brought the Bible together so that, in the form in which we have it today, it can be properly called the composition of God. Divine inspiration serves as the foundation for the validity and the authority of the Bible. It has the ring of authority because it wears the ring of God's inspiring hand. Therefore, being God's Word, the Bible is always relevant to the human situation. The Scriptures not only spoke to the Jews of old and the first-century church, they remain alive and relevant to every succeeding generation. This stands true because the Bible points the way to the answer of humanity's deepest needs and presents the solution in Jesus Christ. Thus the evangelist not only builds his own ministry on the Scriptures; he has contributed in helping many gain a new confidence in the Bible—and that is no mean contribution.

A CONFIDENT CONCLUSION

One can confidently conclude that Graham must be seen as a "revelationist" far more than as a pure rationalist. For Graham, if God's revelation as we have it in the pages of the Bible conflicts with rational reason, he opts for revelation. As Luther said, "We must consider the Word alone and judge according to it."[46] Still, though he rests on that epistemological base, he maintains an appreciation for research. He has said, "Every scientific fact that man has so far discovered adds luster and testimony to the value and integrity of the Bible."[47]

Graham would agree completely not only with Luther, but also with John Calvin, who said, "Those who penned the Bible 'were sure and genuine scribes of the Holy Spirit,' and their writings are considered to be oracles of God. . . . We therefore teach that faithful ministers are now not permitted to coin any new doctrine, but they are simply to cleave to the doctrine to which God has subjected all men without exception."[48] Graham is thus very emphatic that the Bible must be understood, assimilated, and lived out. As seen from the experience prior to the Los Angeles crusade at Forest Home, he came to that position after agonizing over the problem for several months. So Billy takes the Bible by simple faith and argues that faith alone can grasp God's truth. All these dynamics of inspiration, authority, and faith lay the foundation to understand the Scriptures as the very Word of God. But how does one interpret such a unique Book?

GRAHAM'S HERMENEUTICS

Hermeneutics—principles of interpretation—are vitally important in understanding the Scriptures. Some church fathers, leaders like Origen and Jerome, often used an allegorical method of interpretation. There has been for years a generally negative reaction to this approach, especially since Reformation days. Of course, some allegories are used in the Bible itself; for example, Paul's use of the Abraham-Hagar-Ishmael incident (Gal. 4:22–31). But excessive use of this hermeneutical method has been condemned because it can lead to quite faulty interpretation. The church has often suffered as a result.

When the Reformation burst on the scene of church history, Martin Luther, as briefly mentioned, revolted against the method, or at least the excessive use of the hermeneutical principle. He said, "I do not care much for allegories. . . . I became an enemy of allegorizing . . . the very [Scripture] narrative in itself [is] far more meaningful than is the allegory. . . . All who invent allegories . . . will not only be deceived but also greatly harmed. . . . Therefore, we should either avoid allegories altogether or undertake them with the greatest care and thought."[49]

This approach of Luther's strikes a resonating chord in most contemporary evangelical Bible students, Billy Graham being no exception. One finds little if any allegorizing in Graham's sermons. He stands in basic alignment with Luther and the history of good interpretation principles. Moreover, adhering to the infallibility of the Scriptures, one is not surprised to see that Billy Graham's basic hermeneutical approach is centered in a literal interpretation of the Bible. This can be encountered repeatedly in his preaching and writing. Yet he is not an extreme literalist by any means. He realizes that the Word of God contains many literary genres. Thus when he approaches a poetic passage, he recognizes it as such and interprets it as such—historical as historical, parabolic as parabolic, and so on. That lines up with sound traditional, historical evangelicalism.

These biblical presuppositions dictate several things for Graham's understanding of the pragmatic experiences of the Christian life and ministry.

THE PRACTICAL ASPECTS OF GRAHAM'S VIEWS ON THE BIBLE

To stress this point once more, Graham holds tenaciously to the principle of the Bible as authoritative in the totality of the spiritual experience, particularly as it relates to ethics and morals in Christian spirituality. Graham has said, "Every area of our lives is to be under the Lordship of Jesus Christ. And that means the searchlight of God's Word must penetrate every corner of our lives."[50] He quotes John R. W. Stott's statement that "we submit to the authority of the Scripture . . . submission to Scripture is fundamental to everyday Christian living, for without it Christian discipleship, Christian integrity, Christian freedom, and Christian witness are all seriously damaged, if not actually destroyed."[51] Turning to passages of Scripture such as John 15:3, "You are already clean because of the word which I have spoken to you," Graham states that we "should be obedient to all of it—that is, the Word of God."[52]

Concerning the Bible's role in developing Christlikeness in one's spiritual life, Graham quotes George Mueller, the founder of the great orphanage in Bristol, England, in the nineteenth century: "The figure of spiritual life will be in exact proportion to the place held by the Bible in our life and thoughts."[53] It is the Bible that instructs one in making correct moral and ethical decisions. Graham said, "I believe that God never leads anyone contrary to the Bible. So if you have a feeling that is contrary, it isn't God, but it might be the devil."[54]

In summary, for Graham, the development of one's spiritual experience as it relates to moral and ethical living is based on the lordship of Christ, with the Bible serving as one's strength and guidance. As Peter put it, "Long for the pure milk of the word, that by it you may grow" (1 Pet. 2:2). This emphasis is seen in Billy Graham's stress on Bible study for those who make decisions for Christ in his crusades. His program of new believers' orientation, which has made such a contribution to those receiving Christ, will be discussed in a subsequent chapter.

Billy Graham is quite specific on morality and the place God's Word holds on such issues. As a case in point, he takes up the evil of drunkenness. He wrote:

> The Bible is not silent about any force which threatens the souls of men. It lashes out at any and all of Satan's tricks and devices, and it is very clear on this denunciation of drunkenness. The Bible said, "Woe to the crown of pride, to the drunkards of Ephraim . . ." The Bible again says, "Woe unto him that giveth his neighbour drink, that puttest thy bottle to him and makest him drunken also." "And take heed to yourselves lest at any time your hearts be overcharged with surfeiting and drunkenness." Again the Bible says, "Let us walk honestly, as in the day; not in rioting and drunkenness." "Woe unto them that rise up early in the morning, that may follow strong drink; that continue until night." Again the Bible says, "Do not be drunk on wine, wherein is excess."[55]

And what Graham has said about the morality of abusing alcohol and the use of Scriptures, he applies to other specific ethical issues. Although so-called postmodernists would disagree, Billy Graham fully believes that God's decrees in the Scriptures are *absolutes*—moral absolutes. Billy Graham has said,

"According to the Bible, morals are not relative—they are absolute and unchangeable. There is nothing in the Bible that would lead us to believe that God has ever lowered His standards."[56] And in all Christian experience, the Holy Spirit through the Scriptures becomes the believer's guide and strength.

THE SPIRIT INSTRUCTS

Billy Graham fully recognizes the importance of the Holy Spirit creating understanding in the reading of the Scriptures. For Graham, the Holy Spirit not only stands as the One who inspired the Word of God, He also instructs believers in its truth, its ethical principles, all aspects of theology, and living the Christian life. The evangelist has said, "The moment we receive Christ, God gives us a key for understanding the Bible so that we can unlock and understand the message of God to us. The Holy Spirit becomes our teacher. The Holy Spirit helps us to interpret the message. He applies it to our hearts. The Bible is an infallible guide for life."[57] In that way the Bible comes alive to the open reader. The Spirit of God instructs the seeking believer in morals and doctrine. Thus the truth of God can be grasped. Again to quote Luther, the Reformer wrote on this point, "The ear hears and the heart understands through the illumination of the Holy Ghost."[58]

BILLY GRAHAM AND DOCTRINE

What does all this mean in establishing Graham's theological stance? Throughout the course of this book we have seen various doctrinal positions Billy Graham holds; therefore, it seems best here merely to outline his essential views as developed from years of personal Bible study:

- God Almighty is fully omnipotent, omniscient, and transcendent as the Creator and Sustainer of the entire universe.

- God is a God of compassion and love and created humanity to express that love and bring glory to Himself.

- Jesus Christ came into the world for the redemption of all peoples.

- Jesus Christ was fully God and fully Man in one hypostatic union.

- Jesus Christ lived a perfect life, revealing God and accomplishing what Adam failed to do in the Garden of Eden.

- Jesus Christ died a substitutionary death bearing the sins of the world upon Himself when He was crucified at Mount Calvary.

- Christ was bodily resurrected from the grave as the resurrected, living, and eternal Lord.

- Jesus ascended into heaven, entering the Holy of Holies, and was seated at the right hand of God the Father, as King of kings and Lord of lords, establishing the covenant. He with the Father sent the Holy Spirit to continue His work in and through believers and now intercedes for them before the throne of grace.

- Jesus Christ is coming again to judge the world in truth and righteousness.

- Believers will spend eternity in the heavenly Jerusalem. Unbelievers will be cast into the eternal lake of fire. Thus, history will come to its consummation with a new heaven and a new earth.

Concerning these essential evangelical doctrines Billy Graham has said, "God caused the Bible to be written for the express purpose of revealing to man God's plan for his redemption. God caused this book to be written that He might make His everlasting laws clear to His children, and they might have His great wisdom to guide them and His great love to comfort them as they make their way through life."[59] For a fuller view into Billy Graham's doctrine, see Appendix C, where the 2000 Amsterdam Declaration is presented. It represents the basic theological positions of the BGEA, based on the Bible and instructed by the Holy Spirit.

THE PLACE OF THE BIBLE IN BELIEVERS' LIVES

All these things being true, Graham obviously appeals to people to see the necessity of reading the Bible and to be instructed by God's Spirit into the truth. It must do more than collect dust on the shelf. Studying the Word of God is vital to one's entire spiritual experience. Billy said on one occasion:

The message of Jesus Christ, our Savior, is the story of the Bible—it is the story of salvation; it is the story of the gospel; it is the story of life, peace, eternity in heaven. The whole world ought to know the story of the Bible. But if this gospel is hidden today from any American reading these words, it is hidden because you have never opened your Bible, or you have opened it with a closed mind. The Apostle Peter summed it up when he wrote, "The longsuffering of our Lord is salvation; even as our beloved brother, Paul, who also according to the wisdom given unto him, has written unto you; as also in all of his epistles, speaking in them of these things; in which are some things hard to understand, which they that are unlearned, unstable, wrest, as they do also other Scriptures, to their own destruction."[60]

In a work produced by the BGEA under the title *Our Bible*, the evangelist went on to say, "The story of the Scriptures is the story of your redemption and mine through Jesus Christ. The Scriptures teach the death, burial and resurrection of Christ. Jesus Christ is the gospel. His death, burial and resurrection is the gospel story, without him you are lost and doomed."[61]

Believers are to understand these truths and share them with unbelievers. The Bible reveals the reality of God's plan for world redemption through Jesus Christ; therefore, the biblical gospel is to be fully proclaimed and declared. People desperately need to hear that message. Every Christian shares in the responsibility of communicating it. For the evangelist, the Scriptures stand as the final word concerning eternal truth.

Moreover, it is not incidental that the Bible speaks about the future all must face. Graham's eschatology is completely predicated on the Scriptures and what it teaches concerning "things to come." He once said on a lighter note, "I am an optimist, because I believe the Bible. I know the end."[62] And it is true. Graham certainly takes a historical, evangelical position—one that needs heeding today.

At the same time, although high praise of the Bible stands in order, one must be careful not to fall into bibliolatry, i.e., worshiping the Bible rather than the One who gave it. Billy Graham sounds this warning: "The mistake many make is that they worship the Bible. The Bible becomes sort of a fetish and we have it in our homes."[63] Good advice—and a balanced approach! This opens the door to investigate how Graham employs the Bible in his ministry as an evangelist.

BILLY GRAHAM'S USE OF SCRIPTURE IN EVANGELISM

In the evangelistic preaching and ministry of Billy Graham, the first point to be addressed centers in the fact of the evangelist's confidence in the *power* of biblical truth. Graham has said, "It [the Bible] has power like a sharp, two-edged sword."[64] He continually stresses that the Bible speaks to the lost world, and that in the unction of the Holy Spirit, "it is the textbook of revelation."[65] The Bible is the essential source of the good news of God unto salvation. Billy well understands that.

Furthermore, Graham and the team strive to use the Bible in a proper ethical manner in their evangelization. Rick Marshall, crusade leader and director of follow-up, says, "We never use the Scriptures as a hammer. We use it authoritatively, but not to 'fight' people."[66] In a spirit of humility, Graham gladly acknowledges that God's Spirit has used him significantly because of his proper use of the Bible and the high priority he gives it. He said, "I have found that when I present the simple message of the gospel of Jesus Christ with authority and simplicity, quoting the word of God, He takes that message and drives it supernaturally into the human heart. It is a supernatural message, a supernatural authority, a supernatural power by the Holy Spirit."[67]

Graham has preached the gospel message on every continent and in multiplied nations. Through it all he has become fully convinced that the gospel of Christ as found in the Holy Scriptures is a message of power and relevance for any generation or culture—wherever people may be found. In the hands of the Holy Spirit, it has the power to change and transform lives. He has said, "I know one thing [about the Bible]: It contains a mysterious power to direct all kinds and conditions of people into changed lives, and helps to keep them changed."[68] He gives personal testimony to that fact, saying, "I have found that the Scriptures have become a flame that has melted away unbelief in the hearts of people and moved them to decide for Christ. The Word has become a hammer breaking up stony hearts and shaping them into the likeness of God."[69]

Graham is quick to state that if the church ever turns from the simple proclamation of the gospel of Jesus Christ as found in the pages of Holy Writ, it stands in actual opposition to the Holy Spirit. The Bible must have primacy in the preaching Christ. He said:

I believe effective preaching must be biblical preaching whether it is the exposition of a single word in the Bible, text, or chapter. The Word is what the Spirit uses. So the important element is, the Word of God proclaimed . . . when we preach or teach the Scriptures we open the door for the Holy Spirit to do his work. God has not promised to bless oratory or clever preaching. He has promised to bless his word. He has said that it will not return unto him "empty."[70]

It is important to recognize Graham's use of the Scriptures, stated in his own words: "[In] my use of the Bible, I do not quote [verses] . . . to uphold my views. I try to take my position on the basis of what the Bible teaches."[71] That constitutes a wise use of Holy Scriptures and a good lesson for any that would share Christ. Graham has not moved from that stance in any significant way throughout his many years in his ministry of evangelism. For Billy Graham, the Bible always speaks to all peoples; therefore, he uses it to the fullest. It has been estimated by a team member that Billy quotes up to forty or fifty Bible verses in each sermon.[72] It may well be that in his adherence to and proclamation of God's Word, Graham has made one of his greatest contributions; he has turned many to a new confidence in the Holy Scriptures.

THE DEVOTIONAL LIFE

Graham also sees the Scriptures as a vital element in his personal devotional life. Scripture provides "food for the soul." He told an interviewer, "Every morning I read five Psalms and I read one chapter of Proverbs. That's been a longtime policy and practice of mine. . . . I have my devotions. And then after breakfast when I'm home . . . [and] I don't have any appointments in the morning, I spend another half hour just reading the Bible without studying, just reading, just feeding my soul."[73] John Corts gives testimony to Billy Graham's commitment to devotional reading of the Scriptures. He states, "Billy is constantly with the Bible; not just to find verses to quote, but to find strength, vitality and reality from the Bible."[74] Further, Billy believes in Bible memorization. He asks, "What has happened to Bible memorization? . . . What verses have you stored up for the future?" He admonishes all believers, "Get the Scriptures and its principles ingrained into [your] souls—precept upon precept, line upon line."[75] Good advice!

We will look more closely at Billy Graham and his devotional life in the chapter on godliness, but quite obviously, the Bible plays a major role in the disciplines of discipleship. And when life's problems pile up and one desperately needs solutions to difficulties, he says, "Outside the Bible, I cannot offer true, unfailing solutions."[76] The Scriptures meet the need in difficult times. After all, Jesus Himself faced the onslaught of Satan armed with the Word of God—and won (Matt. 4:1–11). In taking up the "whole armor of God" in spiritual battles, one must be able to wield the "sword of the Spirit, which is the word of God" (Eph. 6:17). The evangelist declares that Jesus Christ is the central story of the Scriptures and therefore, "the whole world ought to know the story of the Bible."[77]

THE RELEVANCY OF SCRIPTURE TO ALL CULTURES

Graham is not locked into a use of the Scriptures in evangelism that would make it irrelevant to modern culture and its problems. He has been described as preaching with the Bible in one hand and a newspaper in the other. Figuratively speaking, that is true. He has stated many times that the Bible is more up to date than the morning newspaper.[78] At the same time, Billy stresses the fact concerning the gospel itself, "I do not have to make the gospel relevant; it is always relevant in any part of the world . . . [and] I must get the whole gospel in [every] sermon."[79]

How he strives to make the Bible relevant to the culture where he preaches rests primarily in his introduction and illustrations. But the gospel is always the same. He holds to the truth tenaciously; as he said, "the Bible shows the timelessness of God's eternal truths."[80] Graham also said, "I don't think there is a single problem man faces that cannot be solved by Scripture."[81] Baptist evangelist Larry Walker has said of Billy Graham, "He has an amazing 'cross-over' ability with different societies. He becomes 'all things to all men' to win them."[82] Perhaps this is one of the reasons for his popularity. He strives to be aware and relevant to people where they are in life and share the message of Christ.

In his crusades even the music has changed as different modes of music appeal to changing societies and generations. For example, "youth nights" have been conducted for years on Saturday night in each crusade. Since the 1994 Cleveland crusade, the music has changed quite dramatically on the youth nights. The coliseum resounds with gospel rock music and special lighting as young people by the tens of thousands attend, many of whom make decisions for Christ. True, the older generation does not always like these dramatic changes, but remember, as Mrs. Graham has said, "you don't have to like worms to go fishing." To see the excitement of the teenagers jumping and waving their hands to the gospel in music is a phenomenon; but when Billy enters the pulpit, a hush falls over the entire mass of young people. The success of his ministry to teenagers, even though he is now in his eighties and suffering with Parkinson's disease, is nothing short of phenomenal. The response of that age group is due to the simple gospel message made alive and relevant to their contemporary culture. Actually, Graham sees a higher percentage of decisions today than at any given period in his entire ministry. As he said, "I have found that the Scriptures have become a flame that has melted away unbelief in the hearts of people and moved them to decide for Christ. The Word has become a hammer breaking up stony hearts and shaping them into the likeness of God. Does not the Scripture say, 'I will make my words in thy mouth fire.' And, 'is not my word like a fire . . . and like a hammer that breaketh the rock in pieces.'"[83]

As touched upon briefly, the power of the Word applies to spiritual maturity and growth in grace as well as for salvation. Another brief look at this principle, although from a different perspective, is in order here.

THE BIBLE AND GROWTH IN GRACE

Graham also believes that the Word of God has power to accomplish God's purpose in deepening and broadening the spiritual lives of believers. It becomes a primary resource for spiritual maturity and strength, especially in difficult times. In a sermon Billy lists involvement in God's Word as a major element in what he calls "Your Spiritual Survival Kit." He stated, "We need to read and memorize Scripture."[84] Graham has a program for the survival and development of the new convert in the Christian life. In it he stresses Bible reading, prayer, and fellowship. A full presentation of that program will be included in the chapter on godliness. As seen, Billy is personally convinced that the Bible has the answer to every problem, for the new believer and those more mature in the faith as well. Because it is God's Word, it appeals to *all* believers of all levels of spiritual maturity.

Thus Graham makes sure his preaching and instructing is Bible-based and practical. He stresses, in the words of the pslamist: "Wherewithal shall a young man cleanse his way? by taking heed thereto according to thy word . . . Thy word have I hid in mine heart, that I might not sin against thee" (Ps. 119:9, 11 KJV). But not all agree with the evangelist.

THE CRITICS

It goes without saying that Billy Graham has his critics concerning his use of the Bible. A former chaplain of St. Andrews College once said, "Graham encourages biblical ignorance by believing in a docetic Christ, clay-made man, a floating zoo, an amphibious-footed Jesus, a son of God who demonstrated his divinity as a homebrew artist . . . and topped it off with an ascension that looks like a Cape Kennedy blastoff."[85] This sharp criticism obviously comes from old-school liberalism, which along with Strauss many years earlier went on a search for the "historic Jesus," thus deviating from the evangelical view of the Scriptures. One would think that such an approach of old-line liberalism had been laid to rest, but it still lurks about to some extent.

Others think Billy Graham's faith is too naive and thus is not relevant to modern needs. There are those who would like to label his message as obscure and out of touch with the times. Nonetheless, multitudes still hang on his words on a worldwide basis. As one has said, "In a way never witnessed before, the world continues to be the parish of this evangelist."[86] Why does Graham take the position he does relative to his use of the Bible in his evangelism? Much has already been said in this regard, but a few final words should help in understanding his use of the Scriptures and why he has made such a contribution to biblical Christianity.

BILLY GRAHAM'S ASSUMPTIONS: A SUMMARY

By way of summing up this point concerning Billy Graham and the Bible, it must never be forgotten that Graham is first and foremost an evangelist; moreover, he is a conservative evangelical evangelist. Therefore, there are certain presuppositions that he brings to his understanding, interpretation, and use of the Bible. First, he recognizes that the final authority concerning the truth of God does not rest in him, but in the Holy Scriptures. He believes in the moving of the Holy Spirit to bring that truth home to the human heart and mind in the dynamics of people's daily lives. Thus he sees his use of the Scriptures as the core of his message as vital and absolutely essential to effective evangelism. Graham agrees completely with the principle Martin Luther expressed when the reformer wrote, "He who undertakes anything without the divine Word will labor in vain."[87] These assumptions definitely shape the evangelist's interpretation and preaching of the Bible.

As Billy Graham travels the world, he brings these basic convictions to bear on his hearers wherever he might be. He preaches Christ, the Christ found in the Bible, in "high" places and in the "lowly." The effect has been monumental. But such has always been the case through the course of the history of Bible-centered evangelism.

CONCLUSION AND HISTORICAL CONTRIBUTION OF BILLY GRAHAM AND THE BIBLE

It certainly appears that we can confidently conclude that Billy Graham is a biblicist in the historical, evangelical sense of the word. His entire world-view is Bible-based. In his book *World Aflame*, he states, "In this book, my thesis is based on the biblical philosophy of man and of history."[88] He also states, "We are called to live under the authority of Jesus Christ and the authority of the Scriptures."[89] Not only that, as stressed, he has been faithful to his convictions through the many decades of his evangelistic ministry. He has grown and matured in his approach, realizing ever more the importance of being faithful to the Word of God in all of life and ministry. Thus he essentially falls in line with biblical, historical evangelicalism. Professor Robert Ferm contends that Graham's approach to Bible-centered evangelism is historical evangelism. He said, "This is the first-century gospel as preached by the apostles."[90] And, it might be added, preached by faithful evangelicals for two thousand years.

Thus we conclude that the *written* Word of God, the Bible, and the *living* Word of God, Jesus Christ, together effect conversions. This reality Graham has grasped and implanted at the very heart of his ministry. That stands true of the entire BGEA. Henry Holley, overseas crusade director, declares, "It is our anchor."[91] And that is important because in the great moments of history, when the church has gone forward with lightning speed, the Word of God, with its truth and its power to move men and women to Jesus Christ, has assumed a paramount place. Effective evangelism that contributes to the conversion of the masses has always been a Bible-based evangelism. This we know quite well, and it has been stressed almost to the point of tedium. But a cursory study of church history makes that fact indisputable.

God reveals and declares Himself in His Word. In that way people learn who God truly is. As Luther held, "We must think of God as He has revealed Himself to us in His Word . . ."[92] As the Word is communicated, God shows Himself; and when people grasp Him in all His love, grace, compassion, holiness, and judgment, they are drawn by the Holy Spirit to embrace Christ and His salvation. And that, in the final analysis, stands as the only hope for the world and a viable society.

In a word, the evangelist who faithfully declares the gospel, may it be said again, becomes the "light of the world" and the "salt of the earth." In the Bible and throughout history these biblical facts cannot be gainsaid, and it is on this subject that Billy Graham has made one of his greatest contributions to his day. He has faithfully proclaimed God's Word, as well as inspired and trained many others so to do. That is no little feat. Evangelical history will no doubt put its stamp of approval on him, and contemporaries ought to be grateful to God that we have witnessed such a moving of the Spirit through a man in our time. In light of these realities, we can only say *soli deo gloria.*

CHAPTER 9

BOLDNESS IN EVANGELISM

～

PART I:
ZWINGLI, THE BOLD REFORMER OF SWITZERLAND

Do not be afraid . . . God is on our side.
—ULRICH ZWINGLI

INTRODUCTION

"Do something bold for God's sake!" cried Martin Luther. Ulrich Zwingli took that word as his guiding motto, and he lived up to his commitment. Zwingli, the Swiss Reformer, became a man bold for God in the proclamation of the gospel. As historian Timothy George has said, "From his first sermon in Zurich to his last stand at Kappel, Zwingli's career was characterized by steadfastness and courage in the face of considerable opposition. . . . He knew that his life belonged not to himself but to his Lord."[1]

Zwingli paid dearly for his boldness and courageous convictions. On October 11, 1531, he strapped on military armor, picked up a sharp two-edged sword, and went to battle against the enemies of the gospel in the countryside surrounding the monastery at Kappel. He was struck and killed. The

Catholic armies, after discovering that he whom they considered a heretic had died by the edge of the sword, burned his body and mixed his ashes with dung. An ignoble end? Not really!

Boldness often brings tragedy in the earthly realm but great victories in God's kingdom. Boldness has its price, but it also has its eternal reward. The noble train of the bold for Christ creates a glorious entourage. The Book of Revelation tells us, "They overcame him because of the blood of the Lamb and because of the word of their testimony, and they did not love their life even to death. For this reason, rejoice" (Rev. 12:11–12). Ulrich Zwingli, the bold Reformer of Zurich, filled the role and rejoiced.

THE EARLY LIFE OF ZWINGLI

In the little village of Wildhaus, high in the Swiss Alps in the canton of Toggenburg, on January 1, 1484, little Ulrich was born. That was just fifteen years before the martyrdom of Savonarola. Boldness for the truth had enlisted Savonarola in the army of the martyrs; it would be the same for Zwingli, but not before an illustrious ministry of the gospel.

Young Zwingli loved the mountains. His writings often speak of the joy of his early years in the Alps. However, more than just the beautiful countryside shaped Zwingli's early days. He saw himself as a Swiss patriot through and through. He loved his country and would willingly go to any length to see it prosper and remain secure. The second strong influence in the young man's life centered in the Renaissance philosophy of Erasmus. Although the philosopher held certain views that evangelicalism would reject, Erasmus did possess a foundational commitment to Christ. This basic approach gripped Zwingli. He described himself as "a Swiss professing Christ among the Swiss."[2] He worked out that profession by serving as a chaplain in the Swiss army, often accompanying the troops on their campaigns. However, in one particular battle, ten thousand Swiss soldiers were killed. It instilled a deep horror of war into the very fabric of Zwingli's soul. He cried out, "Oh, Lord, grant us peace." Yet, in battling for the gospel he willing gave his life. That is boldness.

Although Zwingli was an ardent advocate of peace and recognized war as a despicable thing, he never became a pacifist in the purest sense of the word. He believed a faithful citizen should undergo military training in order to protect his country. Armed neutrality formed his basic commitment. And amazingly, the Swiss have been able to keep that stance through many centuries of European upheaval. Zwingli's dream for the twelve cantons (counties or states) of Switzerland visualized them as corresponding to the twelve tribes of Israel. Simply put, Zwingli was a patriot with a deep concern for the social and political implications of the Christian faith.

ZWINGLI AND THE RENAISSANCE

Zwingli's basic philosophy may well account for something of his warm attitude toward the Renaissance humanism that enjoyed considerable popularity during his day. The movement, at least from a scholarly perspective, had as its goal a reformed society. The *modus operandi* revolved around applying classical philosophy to practical, contemporary life. In the Reformation period, no one individual was more influential in this particular approach to one's entire lifestyle than Erasmus. His philosophy nursed a definite humanistic strain, but the thinker also had a true commitment to the Christian faith. Philosophy and theology had not been divorced in his time as is so often the case today.

Zwingli's background made him receptive to the thought of Erasmus and others of like persuasion. At the universities of Vienna and Basel, Zwingli had become well versed in the humanities. In that context, Erasmus made his significant impact in the earlier years of Zwingli's education. This spawned in the philosophy of his life an amalgamation of scholarly achievement and Christian piety and ultimately led him to Christian ministry.

ZWINGLI'S MINISTRY

Zwingli served not only as a patriot and politician, he became a pastor of great influence and a very able theologian. He combined politics and faith remarkably well. He contended that the kingdom of Christ is not only spiritual, but also social. For Zwingli, spiritual Christianity implied social reform and a stable government for the well-being of people. He said, "God's word will make you pious, God-fearing folks. Thus you will preserve your fatherland."[3] Many contemporary believers hold strong views on the separation of church and state, but it proves helpful to recall Zwingli lived in sixteenth-century Europe.

The entire sociological-religious ethos was radically different from today, at least in most Western nations. But he had the kernel of the gospel.

THE GOSPEL

Zwingli came to the position that salvation rests solely in the grace of God through faith in the Lord Jesus Christ. He fully grasped the essential gospel of Christ. Although he had gone through all the necessary prerequisites to become a Roman Catholic priest and parish pastor, this new reformed concept of the Christian faith moved Zwingli to abandon his traditional Catholic belief system and embrace basic Reformation theology.

In 1516, Erasmus published his version of the Greek New Testament. As a pastor deeply concerned about the essential verities of the Christian faith, Zwingli gave himself to an ardent study of Erasmus's Greek New Testament. Between 1516 and 1518 he held a preaching post at Glarus and Einsiedeln, the same period in which Luther took his bold stand with the posting of the 95 Theses in Wittenberg. Zwingli committed himself so thoroughly to the study of the Greek text that his successor at Zurich, Heinrich Bullinger, stated that Zwingli had memorized in Greek all the Pauline Epistles. He obviously possessed a very fertile mind and became a very able scholar. His firsthand knowledge of the Greek New Testament laid the foundation for his powerful, expository preaching and biblical teaching. It made him an evangelist in the full biblical sense.

Later in life, as Zwingli's theology and ministry matured, he broke ranks with Erasmus in many respects. Yet at the same time, this exposure to the humanistic approach of Erasmus significantly influenced his understanding of the Christian faith as it related to social issues. Perhaps above all, the influence of Erasmus manifested itself in Zwingli's grasp of the spirituality of God and his openness to reason. He grew into a true Reformer.

ZWINGLI, THE BOLD REFORMER

Zwingli's repudiation of many of the trappings of the Roman Church and his embracing of a solid Protestant position came about in 1516 when, as he said, "led by the Word and Spirit of God I saw the need to set aside all these [human teachings] and to learn the doctrine of God direct from his own Word."⁴ In 1519, he became priest of the Great Minster Church in Zurich. As he began his ministry on January 1 of that significant year, he announced to the congregation that he would no longer follow the traditional lectern of published sermons. He declared he would preach from the Gospel of Matthew, beginning in chapter 1, and preach the entire book straight through. He then moved into the Acts of the Apostles and then to the Epistles of Timothy and on to Galatians. By 1525 he had preached through the entire New Testament and then turned to the Old Testament. Zwingli's dynamic and dramatic exposition of the Scriptures laid the foundation in Zurich for the Reformation, which soon infiltrated the entire country.

Zwingli did not actually sever himself from the Church of Rome until some years after his ministry began in Zurich. As could be expected, he was very aware of Luther and the events taking place in Germany. He profoundly appreciated Luther's courageous stand at the Diet of Worms and saw the German Reformer as another Elijah. As much as he admired Luther, however, he refused to be labeled as a full follower of the German movement. He said, "I did not learn my doctrine from Luther, but from God's word itself."⁵ His boldness also precipitated a fierce independence.

In the year that Zwingli began his ministry in Zurich (1519), a serious plague swept through the countryside. Two thousand people died in Zurich alone, and Zwingli himself almost succumbed to the plague. It became a profound spiritual experience for the Reformer. When he recovered from his illness, he resolved he would give himself in total dependence upon God and the furtherance of His kingdom.

This spirit of submission to God played a vital role in bringing him to an understanding of the Protestant doctrine of justification by faith. He did not exactly experience a Damascus Road revelation as was true of some of the other early Reformers; his experience was more of a developing realization of the all-sufficiency of Christ in salvation. His study of Erasmus set him on the path; then through diligent searching of the Scriptures, by the early 1520s Zwingli understood the doctrines of grace well and had experienced redemption through Jesus Christ alone. This set him in basic opposition to Roman doctrine. The crisis had come that he must separate from Rome. It became an hour for true boldness.

THE BOLD BREAK

It may be somewhat difficult to realize today what a wrench it was to leave the Roman Church in the sixteenth century. Life revolved around Rome. But Zwingli took the plunge, and two major steps emerged in his break with the Roman Church. In 1520 he gave up his papal pension. Then, two years later, on October 10, 1522, he resigned his office as priest of Zurich. That was bold; it meant expulsion from the church. But the city council immediately hired him as "preacher" to the entire city. God provides for His bold ones. Zwingli, now in a position to preach courageously with official sanction, effected the reformation of Zurich. As a result, many came to saving faith in Jesus Christ.

Although the Protestant movement marched forward through much of central and northern Europe, the Roman Catholic Church still exerted strong influence. Against the inevitable onslaught, Zwingli courageously took his stand. The Roman bishop of Constance, where Zwingli lived, was deeply alarmed at Zwingli's unashamed preaching of the simple gospel of Christ and feared people would conclude that the Roman system brought no redemption. The bishop thus set out on the propaganda path to denigrate Zwingli so as to maintain the unity and authority of the church. But the mass of the common people adhered tenaciously to the reformed doctrines of Zwingli. The bishop argued that Christ is one and so the church. But Zwingli boldly stood against that view; not that Christ Himself could be divided, but that the true church does not necessarily need to be one in organizational structures. In almost humorous fashion, when accused of not listening to the bishops, Zwingli replied, "Nothing is easier, since they say nothing." He began to admonish parishioners to leave "Holy Mother Church" and to follow the truth of the Scriptures. Erasmus, who was still totally committed to the Roman Church, severely criticized Zwingli for his stand. But the die was cast, and Zwingli stood unswervingly for the full doctrine of evangelical salvation and Protestant understandings of the organized church.

THE DEBATE

On Thursday morning, January 29, 1523, six hundred people at Zwingli's invitation gathered for a debate on the issue, two hundred of whom were members of the town council along with all the clergy of the canton. It became known as the First Zurich Disputation. The issue on the table? Protestant theology. The Reformer saw the assembly not as a mere local town council meeting, but a general council of the church universal. No one brought an accusation of heresy against Zwingli, although some subtle action was attempted by the Catholic bishops.

Zwingli stood strong and insisted that the sixty-seven articles he had formulated be addressed. A lively debate ensued. And to God's glory, the councilmen gave the verdict that Zwingli could "continue and keep on as before to proclaim the Holy gospel and the correct divine Scriptures with the Sprit of God in accordance with his capabilities."[6] The upshot of it all was—and a most significant conclusion it proved to be—the city of Zurich became the first official Protestant city by decree of the city council. Zwingli had boldly taken his stand for the truth of the Scriptures and prevailed. The Reformation had won a decisive victory among the Swiss people. Zwingli rejoiced as he exclaimed, "God be praised and thanked whose divine word will reign in heaven and upon earth."[7] His courage projected Zwingli in the minds of the people as a significant model of the Reformation.

ZWINGLI'S REFORMATION THOUGHT

The Swiss Reformation marched forward and its influence spread broader and deeper. As the work progressed, Zwingli expressed it well when he said, "Fearless is your armor! You must watch and be ready for battle; for God sends His prophets everywhere to warn the sinful world."[8] A proper theology and commitment to the gospel makes for boldness. In turn, this makes its impact for Christ. In his excellent book *The Theology of the Reformers,* historian Timothy George, upon whom much of this biographical material is dependent, points out several aspects of Zwingli's theology. George shows that the Reformer was committed to:

- Creator rather than creatures—God is supreme.

- Providence rather than chance—God is in control of all; it is not a capricious world.

- Holy Scripture rather than human traditions—the only authority for the Christian faith is the Word of God.

- True religion rather than ceremonial piety—true religion centers in the heart.

- Eternal kingdom rather than privatized morality—the social, political, and cultural aspects of society must be radically changed as well as the individual.

THE SPLIT

On this basis, the work flourished, but it precipitated problems. Well known is the fact that Zwingli and Luther came to odds over several issues, especially the doctrine of the Lord's Supper. Although Luther had rejected the Roman doctrine of transubstantiation, Luther had taken what historian Bainton calls the "middle road." Luther adhered to the doctrine of consubstantiation, that is, although the elements of the Eucharist are not transformed into the actual body and blood of Christ as Rome teaches, the body and blood of Christ are "comingled" with the elements. Luther saw the Eucharist as a "testament"; Zwingli preferred the word *memorial*. Where Luther saw the Lord's Supper as Christ's gift to the church, Zwingli saw it as a service of commemoration wherein the church proclaims the Lord's death until He comes. This variance over the meaning of the cup and the bread brought a serious split between Luther and Zwingli.

The split spelled something of a tragedy. To divide the Reformation over the issue raises serious questions. Luther and Zwingli both adhered to the essential gospel, and that matters most. Moreover, they both strongly and boldly affirmed the doctrine of the person of Christ that came out of the Council of Chalcedon, which stated that Christ was "one person in two natures"—as we have seen in the chapter on Athanasius. Zwingli ultimately prevailed in the Eucharist debate as the Reformation developed through the centuries. His position has become the position of most Protestant bodies today.

It has hopefully become obvious that Ulrich Zwingli stood as a man bold for God as he confronted the ecclesiastical evils and devious doctrines of his day. He stated, "If the shepherd would read the prophets then he would find nothing other than an eternal battle with the powerful and vices of this world."[9] Resting wholeheartedly on the realities of the absolute authority of

Scripture, salvation by grace through faith alone, the centrality of the eternal kingdom of God, and true religion rather than ceremonial piety, he fought on. Zwingli came on the scene as a Reformer in the fullest sense of the word, a Reformer with the boldness of his convictions that enabled him to confront authority and courageously proclaim the gospel of Jesus Christ. And he ministered in the midst of a milieu that was anything but conducive to the evangelization of the world's masses. Nonetheless, he stood tall as a man of strength, dauntless resolve, and courageous action.

The life of this bold man of God can be simply summarized with the statement that he was a strong heart for Jesus Christ even unto death—he did die for his faith. He went out on the battlefield to save his country for freedom and the gospel, and he was killed for his actions. That utter commitment to the Lord Jesus and the truth of the gospel gave him a boldness that etched his name in Christian history that will never be erased. True evangelists are bold people. They stand for the truth at all costs.

Boldness always plays a vital role on the stage of biblical, historical evangelism. This truth leads to an investigation of the biblical meaning of Christlike boldness.

THE SCRIPTURAL MEANING AND MANDATE FOR BOLDNESS IN EVANGELISM

The dictionary defines *boldness* as "possessing, showing, or requiring courage; audacious; fearless, spirited."[10] Thayer, in his Greek lexicon, defines the word as "freedom in speaking, unreservedness in speech, openly, frankly without concealment." Thayer goes on to give nuances to the word such as "free and fearless confidence, cheerful courage, . . . assurance." He tells us boldness means "the confidence in telling one to do something of the thing to be done."[11] In light of the meaning of the term, Paul wrote, "According to my earnest expectation and hope that in nothing I shall be ashamed, but with all boldness, as always, so now also Christ will be magnified in my body, whether by life or by death. For to me, to live is Christ, and to die is gain" (Phil. 1:20–21 NKJV). Quite clearly, boldness must be understood as a Christian grace, exemplified in Jesus Christ. The implications of such a strong word are obviously multifaceted.

In the evangelistic context, boldness in the effort to win people to faith in Christ stands as absolutely essential. The Scriptures are replete with illustrations of this essential principle. Witness Noah on the dry plains constructing an ark of mammoth size. For 120 years, he boldly preached to the mocking crowd, declaring the imminent judgment of God. The fact that he endured slander and ridicule demanded a boldness hard to imagine. For Moses to confront and demand of Pharaoh, "Let my people go," took great courage. True, he had met God in a most incredible fashion and had received a direct call; still, to appear before Pharaoh and his magicians and make such an appeal called for a boldness that far superseded the normal encounters of everyday life. This principle of boldness surfaces again in the commission of God to Joshua to cross the river Jordan and possess the Promised Land. An implication of the passage in Joshua 1 implies that Joshua apparently lacked the qualities of bold forthrightness that had characterized Moses. Three times in that pivotal passage, God's commission came to him with the word of admonition, "Be strong and courageous" (vv. 6, 7, 9). Joshua, being a man of God, heeded that word of encouragement for boldness, courageously led the people over the Jordan, and witnessed the walls of Jericho tumbling down.

Witness also the bold preaching of the prophets. One can picture Amos, the "farmer-prophet," as he confronted the erring Israelites and cried, "Prepare to meet your God." That took courage. Or see Jeremiah thrust down into a well because of his bold proclamation of the Word of God. Though he languished away under persecution and pressure, he uncompromisingly took his stand.

Perhaps the picture of the bold prophet is epitomized in Isaiah. In his vision of God the Holy One, the call came: "Whom shall I send, and who will go for Us?" In boldness of spirit Isaiah responded, "Here am I. Send me!" (Isa. 6:8). God made it clear that the people's reaction would be anything but receptive: "And He said, 'Go, and tell this people: "Keep on hearing, but do not understand; keep on seeing, but do not perceive."' Make the heart of this people dull, and their ears heavy, and shut their eyes; lest they see with their eyes, and hear with their ears, and understand with their heart, and return and be healed" (vv. 9–10 NKJV). Upon hearing that, Isaiah cried out, "Lord, how long?" (v. 11 NKJV). God answered:

> Until the cities are laid waste and without inhabitant, the houses are without a
> man, the land is utterly desolate, the LORD has removed men far away, and the for-

saken places are many in the midst of the land. But yet a tenth will be in it, and will return and be for consuming, as a terebinth tree or as an oak, whose stump remains when it is cut down. So the holy seed shall be its stump. (vv. 11–13 NKJV)

A divine commission is a high honor, but the content of the commission can be extremely difficult to fulfill. For Isaiah it meant preaching to people who would not listen; yet, he was compelled to go on until there was no one left to hear. That demands a boldness and a commitment that only God by His Spirit can engender in the human experience.

NEW TESTAMENT BOLDNESS

In the New Testament, this spirit of boldness reaches the heights. When Peter and John stood before the Sanhedrin and made their defense before the ruling body of the land, they courageously proclaimed Christ. Luke tells us that "when they [the Sanhedrin] saw the boldness of Peter and John, and perceived that they were uneducated and untrained men, they marveled. And they realized that they had been with Jesus" (Acts 4:13 NKJV). That experience typifies the apostles in all they did. They endured ridicule, imprisonment, persecution, even death. But they were bold for God and ultimately won multitudes to Jesus Christ. And the same spirit can be seen in many others in those early years of the church.

When one speaks of boldness in the New Testament era, the apostle Paul immediately comes to the fore. No matter where he found himself, Paul fearlessly and courageously shared Jesus Christ. After his conversion in Damascus he boldly preached Christ until a citywide rebellion rose up against him. Or see him before kings and authorities. Whether it was Caesar or the Sanhedrin, he took his stand. Perhaps the classic case occurred when Paul defended his faith before King Agrippa and Bernice. Standing before the pompous Agrippa, bound in chains, he made his case. Paul seized all occasions as an opportunity to preach Christ. Bold people do. In some exasperation, Agrippa broke in and exclaimed, "You almost persuade me to become a Christian" (Acts 26:28 NKJV). Paul boldly replied, "I would to God that not only you, but also all who hear me today, might become both almost and altogether such as I am, except for these chains" (Acts 28:29 NKJV).

But boldness is not exclusively exercised in the context of opposition and persecution alone. At times, situations demanded boldness in the circle of the church itself. In the Jerusalem Conference (Acts 15), Paul stood against a number of fellow believers as he forthrightly contended for the purity of the gospel of grace. As previously emphasized, the outcome of that event was monumental. Once and for all, it settled the fact that salvation comes by grace through faith alone, not by works of the Law. How grateful the entire church should be that Paul boldly took his stand.

THE RECORD OF HISTORY

Church history, along with the Scriptures, attests to these realities. Picture again Savonarola as he gives himself to the hangman's noose rather than recant his faith. Multitudes of martyrs have likewise given their lives through the years. To the current day boldness for Christ can at times mean death. In 1935, some thirty Korean believers assembled in their church. The foundation of the building can still be seen; that is all that remains. An invading army surrounded the building and demanded that the Korean believers deny their faith or face death. The believers boldly held their ground as the flames of fire consumed their lives. And at the very hour these pages are being penned, multitudes of Christians are choosing death because of their faith in Christ. That is boldness. All of this leads to the issue of how, especially in evangelism, Christian boldness can be attained.

ATTAINING BOLDNESS IN CHRIST

Several principles undergird the motivation and ability to be bold in evangelism. Initially, the courage to evangelize in all circumstances emerges out of God's Word. Believers are instructed in the Bible to be bold to believe, defend, and proclaim God's gospel. It may seem paradoxical to say that one has to be bold to defend what God has clearly revealed, but the truth of God is not always well received. For this reason Peter said, "Always [be] ready to make a defense to everyone who asks you to give an account for the hope that is in you" (1 Pet. 3:15). In some settings resistance to such a proclamation flares up to the point of persecution. Thus a bold stand for truth becomes necessary.

Why do such situations arise? Paul answered that query in his letter to the

Corinthians: "A natural man does not accept the things of the Spirit of God" (1 Cor. 2:14). Human pride often rejects God's truth. And at times it goes beyond a mere rejection of what God attempts to reveal. Because of rebellion in the human heart—which constitutes the essence of sin—the Word is resisted to the point of attempting to stamp out God's message, and that may well mean the stamping out of God's messenger.

As a result of such resistance, persecution can easily fall upon those who would share the gospel. This can be seen clearly in the stoning of Stephen recorded in Acts 6–7. When that man of God delineated the history of God's revelation and then applied the truth to the immediate situation, an outrage erupted and Stephen was dragged out and stoned to death. This somewhat typical incident points up the depravity of the human heart and the resistance that often comes from the proclamation of Jesus Christ. Moreover, Satan and his hosts incite such reactions. The church must never forget that spiritual warfare is inevitable for God's people. But the truth of God is at stake, and the vindication of God's grace hangs in the balance. Believers must boldly stand and battle on. True, the proclaimer often pays a heavy price, but the Scriptures admonish believers to be courageous regardless of circumstances. That forms a motivation. But there is more.

GOD'S CALL

Boldness also becomes vital in the context of the call of God. God sets His people apart to witness faithfully to His grace. The call of Isaiah, delineated earlier, stands as a clear example of the principle. In a very real sense, God's call— "Whom shall I send, and who will go for Us?"—comes to *all.* And the answer of *all* God's people ought always to be that of Isaiah, "Here am I. Send me." When one accepts the fact that the omnipotent God actually employs His people in the task, it becomes a thrilling call. It constitutes a high motivation to respond, but to heed the call requires profound courage; suffering is sure.

WORLD NEEDS

Moreover, the needs of the world demand courage. All that has been said up to this point makes it evident that the pressing problem of an alienated world is a central element in the call for evangelism and a bold response. The entire theology of the evangelistic enterprise can be summarized in three simple yet profound statements. These three declarations explain the evangelistic motive. First, the world and its people are lost, alienated from the "commonwealth of Israel" (Eph. 2:12), and abide under the judgment of God. Some criticize evangelists for majoring on what they consider the negative side of human experience. But the lost condition of multitudes is disturbingly true. Ever since the expulsion of Adam and Eve from Eden, humankind cannot crash through the gates of God and regain paradise by their own efforts. This world is lost and stands in dire need of hearing the gospel.

Second, there is only one answer to the human dilemma. People may travel many avenues seeking restoration to the beautiful original state of creation, but all to no avail. The Bible says, "There is a way which seems right to a man, but its end is the way of death" (Prov. 14:12). Although it may sound too exclusivistic, perhaps even arrogant to some, the Scriptures are clear: Jesus Christ is God's *only way* to restoration of fellowship with Himself. Jesus decisively declared, "I am the way, and the truth, and the life; no one comes to the Father, but through Me" (John 14:6). Very few Bible scholars fail to emphasize that Jesus used the definite article three times in His significant statement. The implication is clear: Christ is the *only way* to God. This truth the people of the world desperately need to know and assimilate in their lives.

Third, in the setting of the world's need and the solution of the dilemma through Jesus, God uses His people. The gospel has been committed to the church. The extension of God's kingdom depends on God's people and their response to His call. This truth was seen earlier in the significant calling of Peter to the home of Cornelius. That important principle cannot be avoided. These three truths demand great boldness. One never finds it easy to tell the world of its need and the impending judgment of God. Tragically, some will ridicule and reject those who attempt to help them face these realities. But evangelism must be done. So once again, let it be said, courage is in order.

THE SOURCE OF BOLDNESS

But can God's call to evangelize be heeded? The Scriptures answer with a resounding yes. Believers have access to the power of God. Therein lies the ability to be bold. The writer of Hebrews admonishes us, "Let us then approach the throne of grace with confidence, so that we may receive mercy and find grace to help us in our time of need" (4:16 NIV). The call of God to evangelize can be positively accepted because believers can boldly claim grace through Jesus Christ. That is the quality and basis of boldness that great evangelism has always exercised.

Reducing the task to its basic terms, the world's needs and the evangelist's call to meet those needs, demands a boldness of heart. Moreover, the Spirit of God will empower believers as He thrusts His people into the languishing world to share Jesus Christ. Simple faithfulness to God and a reliance on Him permeate the entire task of evangelism. That fact has a most important implication. The faithless church soon becomes the extinct church. The bold church, launching out on the commission with a consciousness of the need and calling on God for strength, wins victories for Jesus Christ. As our Lord said, "Be faithful unto death, and I will give you the crown of life" (Rev. 2:10 RSV). Nothing substitutes for faithfulness and obedience to Jesus Christ. As often stated, it may well mean making many sacrifices. There will be those who will not understand. Others will think it foolish. Those who would evangelize are often called fanatics and fools. Some rebel so strongly they persecute the witness.

But it should not be forgotten that few people remember the detractors of the bold evangelists. The names of those who opposed Luther, Zwingli, and in recent years Charles Finney, D. L. Moody, Billy Graham, and others, have long been forgotten. Who remembers the persons who threw the rotten eggs at John Wesley and George Whitefield as they preached? Who can name those who criticized Billy Graham for preaching behind the Iron Curtain? The names of those who withstood the giants of the faith have long been forgotten. And who knows the name of the person who slung the last stone that blotted out the life of noble Stephen? But we remember Savonarola and Finney and Graham and all the other bold stalwarts of the faith. God honors the faithful witness, the bold person.

And not only is that true for those who have been remembered by history, but many believers whom the world never acclaimed, but were faithful to Jesus Christ, share in the reward. They all shall be eternally remembered. "Those . . . will shine brightly . . . who lead the many to righteousness, like the stars forever and ever" (Dan. 12:3). That reward is well worth the sacrifice. As Zwingli discovered during Reformation days, bold faithfulness finally conquers. The weak, halting, compromising person never makes a lasting impact for God or contribution to the needy world. The bold alone make a mark for God and the well-being of humanity. It is the bold who contribute—and receive. Faithfulness to God will carry one through.

CONCLUSION

Therefore, we can confidently conclude that courage has great benefit and is experienced through the presence and power of God in the proclamation of the gospel. Human strength will fail, but the Holy Spirit creates boldness in the yielded, obedient believer. God gives the call to declare His truth. The Holy Spirit presses the human need on the heart of devoted believers and generates a boldness that brings honor to Jesus Christ. Those principles create the rationale to be "strong in the Lord, and in the strength of His might" (Eph. 6:10). That reveals the secret of successful service for Jesus Christ and the winning of the world to faith in Him. Boldness is vital to effective evanglism. Has Billy Graham been such? It has been implied he is bold; we shall see.

PART II:
BILLY GRAHAM AND BOLDNESS

We have and now declare war on spiritual apathy . . . and moral evil.
—BILLY GRAHAM

INTRODUCTION

Boldness: "showing a readiness to take risks or face danger." That definition has strong implications for those who would preach Christ. In light of the fact that the world stands in "enmity" (James 4:4 RSV) in relation to God and His truth, those who would declare kingdom realities must be very courageous and be constantly ready to take risks and face danger for Christ's cause. Heroes of the faith are a people bold for Christ. This principle is particularly applicable to Billy Graham. Through many experiences, Graham has come to realize this reality.

BILLY GRAHAM'S UNDERSTANDING
OF BOLDNESS FOR THE GOSPEL

Billy Graham's understanding of boldness can be found in an incident that occurred in the setting of the 1949 Los Angeles crusade. One of the notable converts, as has been seen, was Jim Vaus. He worked for the California godfather Mickey Cohen. When Vaus came to faith in Christ, he immediately arranged a meeting with Billy Graham and Cohen. Graham agreed to meet with the notable criminal and saw it as an opportunity to share Christ. However, Graham recalled, "I remember having a little feeling of uncertainty and hesitation, and yet inside me there was a boldness and courage, because I knew that I was going to witness to a famous man in the name of Jesus Christ."[12] Mickey Cohen later confessed that he felt uncomfortable too. But Billy boldly shared Christ, regardless of how Cohen would react. In his own words, the evangelist said, "I explained the gospel to Mickey, from A to Z, as simply, as forthrightly, and as best I could, praying subconsciously all the time that God would help me to find the right words." Although Mickey Cohen did not surrender his life to Jesus Christ, before they left Billy Graham had the boldness to ask if he could lead in prayer—and he did. Graham said, "From that day on, I began to pray seriously and hard for Cohen's conversion."[13] Billy Graham has always been bold and courageous to share the gospel in any setting with anyone. That is evident to all who have observed him. But there are other contexts where courage is called for in the life and ministry of the evangelist.

CONCILIATORY BOLDNESS IN MANY CIRCUMSTANCES

Another aspect of Graham's boldness along with his forthright sharing of the gospel can be seen in his reaction to the controversies his critics have attempted to force him into. It has been mentioned earlier that whenever Graham has been attacked, he has refused to engage in dialogue with his detractors, except on rare occasions. Some have called this reaction spineless. Billy calls it Christian, citing as his authority the Sermon on the Mount, where our Lord clearly stated, "Love your enemies, and pray for those who persecute you" (Matt. 5:44). The apostle Paul also took this basic approach when he wrote to the Roman church, "Bless those who persecute you; bless and do not curse them" (Rom. 12:14 RSV).

Billy has learned, "When reviled, we bless; when persecuted, we endure; when slandered, we try to conciliate" (1 Cor. 4:12–13 RSV).

Graham cites the prophet Nehemiah as his model for a conciliatory spirit. God lifted up the Old Testament prophet as the restorer of the ruined city of Jerusalem. When his enemies attempted to thwart his work by ridicule and criticism, he said, "I am doing a great work, so that I cannot come down. Why should the work cease?" (Neh. 6:3 NKJV). In a word, Nehemiah had a vision for God's kingdom and refused to engage in battle, verbal or otherwise. In that spirit, Billy Graham has said, "I have learned through the years not to reply to critics. Many of them want to fight and are hoping I will answer. If I'd replied, I would have bogged down in controversy years ago. In evangelism, we are simply too busy, this is God's work, and He will answer in His own time."[14]

This stand of Graham is not spinelessness, as some of his critics would have the world believe. It often takes far greater boldness—not to mention love—to refuse to engage in a controversy than to join in battle. The flesh wants to fight; the Spirit encourages conciliation and love. One of Billy Graham's longtime friends saw this and said of the evangelist, "I don't know how good a scrapper he would be in a fight, but I know he can out love any man I ever saw."[15]

Billy Graham's response to the firestorms of criticism that often rage about him is to display courtesy and love, simply refusing to fight back. That is boldness in the highest sense of the word, and it strikes at the heart of Billy Graham's basic approach to the issue of standing firm for the gospel. Many examples of such boldness can be found throughout the life and ministry of the man of God.

BILLY GRAHAM AND EXAMPLES OF BOLDNESS

Living in the American culture with the liberty, freedom, and civil rights that the American Constitution guarantees, Billy Graham has not too often had to face the perplexities, problems, and perils that many of God's people have endured through the ages. Yet he has not been widely free from facing situations where the call for boldness has been sounded. For example, Billy has often appeared on the Larry King TV interview program. A young evangelist and professor at Southeastern Baptist Theological Seminary, Frank Harbor, much admires Graham in this sort of setting. Dr. Harbor has said, "When Larry King asks, as he always does, is Jesus the *only* way? Billy always boldly says yes, never compromises, although that is far from being 'politically correct' today."[16]

At other times, entirely different situations call for boldness on Billy's part. On one occasion, in the early days, Graham was holding a citywide campaign in Augusta, Georgia, along with Grady Wilson. He had already assumed the presidency of Northwestern Schools and was engaged with Youth for Christ as well. At the hotel where he and Grady were staying, a wild party erupted one night in the room next door. The revelry woke Grady up from a deep sleep; he came to Billy's room and complained that he could not sleep because of the noise. Billy replied, "I can't sleep either, and tomorrow is a big day."

So Billy decided to put a stop to it. He put on his bathrobe, went out, and pounded on the door. A drunken man responded to the knock and wanted to know what he wanted. "I want to speak to this crowd," said Billy. He had fully intended just to tell them to please be quiet so they could get some sleep. But then, as he expressed it, the preacher in him came out. "I'm a minister of the gospel," he said. The moment those words fell from his lips a dead silence fell over the rowdy crowd. They knew what a Southern Bible Belt evangelist was. Billy went on, "I'm holding a revival campaign in this town. Some of you may have read about it in the paper." Suddenly a spirit of conviction fell on the group. Billy said, "I know God is ashamed of you." One man confessed that he was a deacon, another a Sunday school teacher. Billy did not know exactly what to do, but then and there he preached an evangelistic sermon. That is not the usual way to get a hearing for the gospel, yet it shows something of the genuine courage of the young evangelist and his willingness to endure ridicule, which he fully expected. Boldness wins.

COURAGEOUS PERSONAL SHARING

Billy has always been eager to share the gospel. John Stott deeply admires Billy's bold witness, especially to world leaders and personalities. Graham is willing to go against convention and do whatever seems necessary to get a hearing for the truth, regardless of possible attacks and rejection. Whether with world leaders at the Massachusetts Institute of Technology, on radio or television, or with just a man on the street, Billy shares Christ. Some of these incidents have been alluded to in previous chapters, but they illustrate boldness well.

For instance, when Billy led Stuart Hamblen, the West Coast cowboy radio personality, to Christ during the 1949 Los Angeles crusade, Hamblen invited him to be a guest on his radio show. Billy confessed that he hesitated at first to respond, concerned what some church people might think of him being on that sort of a program (a tobacco company sponsored the show). But as he considered the matter, the boldness of Christ welled up and he realized the opportunity he would have to share the gospel with millions. So he gave himself to the task. He reasoned, "Hadn't Christ himself spent time with sinners? Hadn't he then been criticized by the religious leaders of his day for that very thing? Why should I not take the risk? I said yes!"[17] After Billy Graham had been on the show for a short time, Stuart Hamblen, in his rather rough-and-ready cowboy manner, said, "Go down to Billy Graham's tent and hear the preaching. I'll be there too."[18] Many responded. This event may seem somewhat trivial, but in that sort of situation satanic opposition to the sharing of the gospel always arises. It takes the courage of Christ to stand strong and help others to the Savior, even in seemingly small matters.

One of the boldest things that Billy Graham ever did centered in his response to the aforementioned invitation to speak in the Soviet Union. While the Iron Curtain was still intact, he was invited to Moscow to speak at a peace conference. He realized if he accepted the opportunity, many people would severely criticize him. Even Senator Mark Hatfield said, "You will get the strongest criticism from the Christian right, because they will feel somehow that you're compromising with the devil." Criticism from the fundamentalist camp was hardly anything new to Graham; still it always grieved him.

So Graham prayed and prayed and finally became convinced that God would honor his trip to that communist country. Since 1959 he had asked that God would one day open the door for him to go to the Soviet Union and share the gospel. It seemed a dream, but God does all things in His own way and time. Perhaps, Billy Graham reasoned, this would open the door for a later crusade. Still, controversy seemed inevitable; and controversy did erupt. Nevertheless, Graham said:

> I knew it was going to be highly controversial so on the Sunday before I went, Vice President George Bush invited me to lunch at his home, because we had been friends for many years. And before the lunch, he said, "You know, I don't

think the Reagans have anybody here. . . . I think I'm going to call them and see if they'll come over." He called, and President and Mrs. Reagan came. I said, "Mr. President, I'm going, as you know, to Moscow to speak at a Peace Conference," and, I said, "I know your stand on this and you probably know mine." "Oh," he said, "don't worry about it." He said, "It will come out all right." He said, "I'm going to be praying for you." Neither one of them said don't go. Neither of them even hinted that I shouldn't go.[19]

Graham went, and God worked marvelously. Billy did get to share the gospel, in a limited sense to be sure, but it opened a door later for him to have the Moscow crusade that he had so longed for. In the center of the communist bloc, Billy Graham was finally able to preach the gospel of Jesus Christ fully and freely. That story has been related, and it was wonderful to see the prayers of many Russian believers answered. That called for real courage in the face of opposition from the religious world. God honored it greatly.

THEOLOGICAL BOLDNESS

Much has already been said concerning the opposition Billy Graham receives from the two extremes of the Christian spectrum, the extreme right and the extreme left. But regardless of where Graham finds himself, he holds his ground and fully declares the truth of Christ as he understands it. As shown, the most severe criticism he receives from the religious right centers in his openness to invite cooperation in his citywide crusade from all Christian groups, even Roman Catholics and so-called liberals. Some see this as a compromise of the gospel, as pointed out in a previous chapter. Yet, Graham holds a deep conviction that if anyone is willing to cooperate, realizing that he is going to preach an uncompromising, evangelical gospel, they are welcome to participate. In the early days, many in the Roman Catholic Church would not come near the crusades.

While this author was a seminary student in Fort Worth, Texas, Billy held a citywide crusade in that city. My wife was in a Catholic hospital for surgery, and one of the nurses, a nun, kept asking, "What is the crusade like?" Roman Catholics were forbidden by their priests to attend. My wife would explain to the nun all she knew about Billy Graham and the crusade to win people to

Christ. That scenario has now radically changed, and Catholic involvement is extraordinary. But the far right is convinced this action is heretical and a denial of evangelical Christian faith. Still, Billy holds his ground and boldly preaches the full gospel, making no compromise concerning the message. As a result, multitudes have come to faith in Jesus Christ. Boldness makes its contribution in the lives of others.

Billy did not have to die at the stake as did some, but many situations in which he finds himself certainly call for a genuine spirit of boldness for the Lord. It can be correctly said, whether Billy is interviewed on television, at a press conference, or simply sitting beside a person on an airplane, he always courageously grasps those opportunities to share Christ. This author can honestly say he has never heard Graham on an interview show be it television, radio, press conference, or whatever the situation may be, when he has not seized the situation to declare the gospel; and this has been true of the evangelist for more than fifty years. Graham displays a boldness that few have acquired.

BOLDNESS AND RACE RELATIONS

Perhaps in the area of race relations Billy Graham has shown the greatest boldness and made his most significant social contribution. In the beginning of his world ministry, he laid down the principle that his meetings would be fully integrated. We have already seen some of the dynamics of that situation in an earlier chapter. But one or two incidents should be recorded here.

As the 1958 New York crusade was drawing to a close, a series of Federal Court orders were established to end school segregation. In Charlotte, North Carolina, Billy Graham's hometown, a fifteen-year-old African-American girl by the name of Dorothy Conts, whose father was a pastor, was driven away from school by a pelting of rocks and sticks as she tried to enter the previously all-white Harding High School. The crisis so moved Billy that he wrote her a strong letter of encouragement. It read:

> Dear Miss Conts,
> Democracy demands that you hold fast and carry on. The world of tomorrow is looking for leaders and you have been chosen. Those cowardly whites against

you will never prosper because they are un-American and unfit to lead. Be of good faith. God is not dead. He will see you through. This is your one great chance to prove to Russia that democracy still prevails.[20]

That letter, in itself, took boldness, and it truly helped the desegregation effort.

The big crunch, briefly mentioned, came at the Central High School in Little Rock, Arkansas. Governor Orval Faubus precipitated a showdown as African-American students attempted to integrate the high school. Obviously, Graham would be asked for a comment. Billy wholeheartedly urged the white citizens of Little Rock to submit to the court order that the school be fully desegregated. He said, "It is the duty of every Christian, when it does not violate his relationship to God, to obey the law. I would urge them to do so in this case." Billy was conscious of the fact that the image being created around the world was detrimental to the democratic principles of America. He said it was "giving the communists one of their greatest [propaganda] weapons in years."[21] So again, Graham took his stand, unpopular as it was in many circles.

Of course, on the other side of the ledger, there were some who said that Graham did not go far enough. For example, he was criticized because he did not actually travel to Little Rock on the particular occasion when Governor Faubus issued his decree. He chose to stay away because he did not feel he should go without an invitation. His choice drew criticism from some:

> This response may have been a model of thoughtful courtesy, and it surely reflected Graham's distaste for conflict, but it hardly exemplified the stance of the biblical prophets, whose passion for justice sometimes took them into settings where their presence was not entirely welcome. Graham's quite genuine but restrained support of the movement inevitably left many dissatisfied. They saw him as the critic and opponent that he was, that indeed he was. Those pushing hardest against the barriers to equality labeled him an equivocator and compromiser, always ready to step back from risking the popularity on a bold and courageous stand.[22]

Some feel that such a criticism is valid; others feel that Graham did the wise thing. Whatever the case may be, he did what he felt the Spirit of God was leading him to do, and he did make his contribution.

Billy Graham's reputation as a committed integrationist did create real conflict, but at the same time it also set a positive example. He looked at each situation cautiously and acted in a "measured fashion that irritated his critics but kept him out of trouble."[23] He did his work as a bold Christian contending for the truth of Christ and the welfare of all peoples.

In September of 1959, Graham was invited back to preach in Little Rock for two large rallies. The Ku Klux Klan and the White Citizens Council distributed thousands of leaflets attacking him for his integration views and for inviting Martin Luther King to take part in the New York crusade. But the pastor of one of the large Baptist churches in Little Rock, Dr. W. O. Vaught, who had done much to still the troubled waters in the school integration crisis, told the evangelist, "There has been universal agreement in all the churches and out across the city that your visit here was one of the finest things that ever happened in the history of Little Rock. So very many people have changed their attitude, so many people have washed their hearts of hatred and bitterness, and many made decisions who had never expected to make such decisions."[24] That's a contribution. Even many years later, Vaught remembered the day well and wrote, "The influence of this good man was a real factor in the solution of our racial problems here in Little Rock."[25]

During those turbulent times, Billy Graham planned a South Carolina one-day revival. Sixty thousand people attended the event. It was heralded as "the first non-segregated mass meeting in South Carolina's history" and "the largest religious gathering ever held in the Southeast."[26] John Sutherland Bonnell of New York wrote to Billy Graham, commending him with these words: "The stand you took was very courageous and I believe truly Christian. Even the *Christian Century* had to take off its hat to you! I know that such a stand costs you a great deal in the matter of relations with some of the brethren in the South, but God will be able to use you even more effectively as the result."[27] Graham's position in the matter of integration is now legendary, and in the final analysis the results have been most positive.

CRUSADE BOLDNESS

Many of the crusade dynamics have called for braveness on Graham's part. After the great Harringay crusade in London of 1954, Billy was invited back on several occasions to conduct similar crusades. Some thought, however, that the evangelist had done all he could do and the crusade days were over for Britain. But in 1966, Graham carried on, despite considerable opposition, and plans went forward for a crusade in London's Earls Court Arena. The *Daily Mail*, one of London's more popular daily papers, took a rather blasé attitude when they wrote, "We've grown accustomed to his faith." But this did not deter Graham. Robert Ferm noted, "Billy was brave even to have it." And the crusade did well. These and similar situations have been the lot in virtually every crusade. From one perspective or another, opposition arises against Graham coming to town. The gospel always creates critics, but as Henry Holley, overseas director for the BGEA, stated, "Boldness comes by confidence in the truth."[28] And Billy always stands on the truth of Scripture. God honors that. So he carries on with a gracious spirit, and the Word goes forward.

POLITICS AND BOLDNESS

Billy Graham has also been very sensitive to situations that have a political ring along with a basic religious connotation. He visited Ireland in May of 1972. It was his hope that by engaging both Protestants and Catholics, along with the political leaders in Northern Ireland and the Republic of Ireland, he might be helpful in laying some groundwork for an eventual crusade that would not only bring many people to Christ, but would release some of the tensions between the warring factions. He had certainly been instrumental in America in bettering relationships between blacks and whites during his crusades. It was symbolic in that his visit to Northern Ireland came just a few days after he completed the successfully integrated crusade in Birmingham, Alabama. But could it happen in Northern Ireland? Graham's dialogue with the leaders of both groups made a positive impression. Graham not only dealt with the leadership of the opposing sides, he spent time on one occasion standing in a bombed-out dwelling, speaking words of comfort to a bus conductor whose wife had been killed by a terrorist bomb.

While in Belfast, Graham preached at the Raven Hill Presbyterian Church on Sunday evening. He had preached in that church in 1946 during his Youth for Christ tour. At that time, the most prominent Protestant preacher in Northern Ireland, Ian Paisley, preached a "counter sermon" in his own church and condemned Graham severely because of his "compromising" attitude toward Roman Catholics. He said, "The church which has Billy Graham in its pulpit will have the curse of the Almighty upon it."[29] Two years before Graham's visit, Paisley had written a book entitled *Billy Graham and the Church of Rome: The Startling Exposure.* Paisley was very negative toward the evangelist, but Billy stood his ground.

Graham met with hundreds of Northern Ireland's political, religious, and popular leaders. He spoke at Queens University in Belfast. That invitation came from both the Roman Catholic and the Protestant chaplains. He appeared on Ulster television several times as well as on the BBC. Of course, there were those who maligned him as not really understanding the depth of the situation. They particularly attacked him for saying that a genuine spiritual awakening could sweep the problems into the sea. Perhaps that was a bit of a generalization, but if the critics understood what really happens in a genuine spiritual awakening, they might not have been quite so vociferous in their comments. As one biographer said concerning the situation, "Ultimately, example proved more important than utterance. In every meeting Graham insisted that both Catholics and Protestants be present in proportion as equal as feasible. A requirement that brought together people who had never met or, if they knew each other at all, had certainly never sat down to eat or talk or pray with one another."[30] It was not an easy time, but the bravery and the courageous spirit that Graham manifested made its impact. And even though the problem still persists, at least at the moment of this writing, the evangelist did his best. Hopefully the situation will one day be resolved and the two parties can come closer together.

COURAGE IN CONFLICTS

It has been briefly stated above that at times it has taken considerable courage even to launch an evangelistic crusade. Such was the case when Graham was invited to Nagaland, a state in northeastern India. The region was in turmoil; yet, paradoxically, Nagaland is recognized as one of the most Christian spots on earth. Early in November of 1972, the Baptists of Nagaland celebrated one hundred years of ministry. They invited Graham to come for an evangelistic endeavor and to preach during the celebration ceremonies. He accepted. But the civil strife in Nagaland had grown to such proportions that a number of people were killed in various conflicts raging through the countryside.

The situation became so tense that several of Graham's advisers, even his Indian associate evangelist Akbar Abdul-Haqq, advised Billy to cancel the crusade. They feared that the guerrillas might stage an uprising and kill many innocent people. Billy Graham was in Bangkok at the time and decided to cancel the meeting, although he did it very reluctantly. He had never before canceled a crusade except for illness.

Meanwhile, back in Calcutta, Robert Cunville, an Indian and fellow evangelist, was deeply disappointed at Graham's cancellation. "God can still do a miracle," Cunville argued. He put in a call urging the many people who were gathered at Kohima in Nagaland to pray that God would change Billy's mind and bring him to their land. The very next morning, someone was knocking quite violently on Billy Graham's door. It was a young American missionary to Nagaland. He looked at Graham and said, "I have come here as the servant of the Lord. You've got to go to Nagaland."[31] He then explained the whole situation and how the people were fervently praying for Billy. He challenged Graham's faith as he reminded Billy that God has promised to protect His servants from danger. Graham saw this as a sign from God. He himself had a sleepless night and was praying earnestly that God would have His way in the situation. The answer had come; Graham immediately gathered his team, and off to Nagaland they went.

He wrote later in his diary, "Tears came to my eyes. I felt rebuked that I had even doubted about coming to these mountain people to minister the gospel. I felt terribly unworthy." He stayed in Kohima, Nagaland, for four days, speaking in morning Bible sessions and conducting typical evangelistic crusade services in the late afternoon. Twenty different interpreters translated his messages into the regional dialects. Not everything was peaceful, however. During the Wednesday morning Bible class, where tens of thousands had gathered, gunfire was heard on the edge of the crowd close to the jungle. No panic ensued as Graham urged the people to be calm. One man had been shot to death by a guerilla. But the outcome of it all was a great encouragement to the Nagas and it resulted in the salvation of many. Graham's boldness had once again seen him through to victory.

As could be expected, Billy has often been asked to give opinions about various problems erupting around the world, and that from the highest circles.

Graham has had the ear of presidents from Eisenhower on down. He has spent time in the White House with every president since Eisenhower, actually having led President Eisenhower into a full assurance of his salvation in Jesus Christ. Graham expressed his stance on the Vietnam situation in this way: "In regard to the conflict in Southeast Asia, I have avoided expressions as to who was right and who was wrong. Naturally, I have come under criticism from both hawks and doves for my position. During all this time, though, I had repeatedly indicated my hope for a rapid and a just peace in Southeast Asia. I have regretted that this war has gone on so long and has been such a divisive force in America. I hope and pray that there will be an early armistice."[32]

He went on to say, "I have never advocated war, I deplore it! I also deplore the violence everywhere throughout the world that evidences man's inhumanity to man. I am therefore praying for every responsible effort which seeks true peace in our time."[33] Both the hawks and the doves leveled criticisms against him, but he bravely took that middle-of-the-road stance. But the essential reason the evangelist refrained from "taking sides" in the Vietnam conflict was, in his own words, "I just decided that there was such a divisive and emotional issue in America that my job was to preach the gospel to the people on both sides. If I took a stand on one of these sides or the other, half the people would not hear what I was saying about Christ."[34] And this is something of the Lord's approach. Jesus' strongest word of judgment against a Roman leader was to call him a "fox" (Luke 13:32). And He said, "Render to Caesar the things that are Caesar's; and to God the things that are God's" (Matt. 22:21).

THE WATERGATE CRISIS

Billy Graham found the Watergate affair exceedingly difficult. He had been as close to President Nixon as to any of the presidents. And when he read the transcript of the Watergate tapes he was reduced to tears. But he did not compromise his moral convictions, though he did not directly attack Nixon. Again, criticism came his way, but he felt that silence was the stance he should take. Whenever Graham became convinced of the avenue that the Spirit of God would have him to travel, he boldly took his stand regardless of the onslaughts.

It must be borne in mind that Billy Graham sees himself essentially as an evangelist. He is reluctant to give advice or to make pronouncements on controversial matters that do not have definite Christian connotation. Of course, some feel that Watergate did have a definite moral connotation. Graham's philosophy does bring about misunderstanding and criticism; but as repeatedly stressed, he stands by his convictions of his role and his place in society's structures. That is a manifestation of boldness in itself whether one agrees with his stance in every situation.

CONCLUSION AND HISTORICAL CONTRIBUTION ON BILLY GRAHAM AND BOLDNESS

It appears somewhat judgmental to credit too much boldness, or not enough, upon any one Christian's life and service to Christ. We will all stand before the judgment seat of the Lord. Yet it does seem fair to say, despite what some have understood as vacillating or retreating from an uncomfortable situation, Graham has stood strong in his convictions. Many times the stance he has taken on controversial issues has been misunderstood by both ends of the spectrum. Nonetheless, he contends he does only that which he feels is the purpose and will of God for him as an evangelist.

It may well be true that his generous conciliatory spirit sometimes makes him appear to be vacillating and weak, and perhaps at times he should have defended his position more vigorously. Nonetheless, he attempts to maintain a Christian spirit in all matters. Thus it seems fair to say that by and large Billy Graham has been genuinely bold, especially when it mattered most. Even taking the middle ground in a matter often calls for real courage. Therefore, the evangelist can be found in the line of those who have suffered criticism, ostracism, and misunderstanding and, in the face of it all, continued to stand.

Moreover, Graham has never compromised his forthright declaration of the gospel of Jesus Christ in every given situation in which God has seen fit to place him. He has said, "To stand for the gospel has *never* been difficult."[35] He went on to say, "I feel if I don't [share Christ], the Lord will never give me another chance. It is God that has allowed me to have this opportunity."[36] And that is boldness in the biblical sense that can be seen as most productive in the history of kingdom progress.

Graham's attitude and commensurate action have truly been contributory to the kingdom of God and in many instances to society in general. One wonders where the civil rights and racial situation would be today had Graham not taken the position he has. Or what if he had vacillated in going to various "hot spots" to minister the gospel? Or how often has he inspired presidents and world leaders to make moral, ethical decisions? Above all, what if he had taken the easy road in the battles over his crusades and just opted out or given in to either the far right or the far left in theological and methodological conflicts?

But Billy has stood bold. He has not been martyred like Stephen or Savonarola, or lost his life in battle as did Zwingli, but he has paid a price. As a result, untold numbers have been encouraged, many errors avoided, and supremely, multitudes have been won to Christ. Boldness does make its contribution, as two thousand years of Christianity have amply demonstrated. Few would deny that evangelist Billy Graham marches in that noble army of the faithful bold ones.

INTRODUCTION
TO THE PURITAN/
PIETISTIC-REVIVAL AGE

~~⌐~~

ONE OF THE GREATEST ERAS OF CHURCH HISTORY saw its inception in what can be described as the Puritan/Pietistic-Revival years. As the Reformation waned and the curtain began to fall on the sixteenth century, God did a marvelous reviving work that transformed Britain and Central Europe; even the early American colonies received blessings. Secular historians, however, have not always been kind to the movement spearheaded by the Puritans and Pietists. Perhaps the problem rests in a lack of knowledge about the true nature of the movement, but the terms have taken on a negative connotation in the thinking of many people. To put the record straight, it should be pointed out that the Puritans for the better part were not legalistic bigots, nor the Pietist otherworldly dreamers. In its purist form, the movement can best be described as a genuine God-inspired revival. They proved to be great days for the church—and the land.

The movement can properly be expressed in the singular because the spiritual essence of the Puritans in Britain and the Pietists on the Continent was really one and the same. Historian Ernest Stoeffler, in his work *The Rise of Evangelical Pietism*, has pointed out, "The fact is that the essential differences between Pietism and what we have called Pietistic Puritanism cannot be established because they are non-existent. The pressure toward a certain pattern of piety within the Calvinistic tradition . . . whether in England, the Low Countries, the Rhineland, or elsewhere was basically the same."[1] Moreover, a historical chain reaction between the two can be demonstrated (see Appendix B). It all revolved around the Holy Spirit breathing new life into the lives of leaders like Richard Baxter, the epitome of Puritanism, and John Wesley, whose work culminated in a great revival movement. Not that other spiritual giants did not arise, nor was the thrust confined to Europe and America alone, but these two men stand as symbols for an evangelism that leads to godliness as best expressed in biblical revival. With these concepts in mind, we enter into one of the most exciting times in the history of the church.

CHAPTER 10

GODLINESS IN EVANGELISM

~⌒~

PART I:
RICHARD BAXTER: GODLINESS TO THE FOREFRONT

I found that the transcript of the heart hath the
greatest power in the hearts of others.
—RICHARD BAXTER

INTRODUCTION

As the drama of the Puritan/Pietistic awakening unfolds, one cannot but be immediately struck with the awesomeness of the movement. Few times in the history of the church has there been a more profound thrust of the Spirit of God among His people. The impact of the gospel in Britain, Europe, and America in the dynamic seventeenth and eighteenth centuries can rightly be compared to the first century. The evangelistic ministry of the church, coupled with the quest for godliness, reflected the apostolic age in a marvelous fashion.

In a very real sense, fervent evangelism merged into a quest for holiness in a manner that the two disciplines were beautifully wed.

During this significant period, names surfaced that made a mark on their era and have persisted to this day. In the Puritan wing of the movement, men like William Perkins, Thomas Goodwin, John Owen, Richard Sibbs, Arthur Hildersham, and countless others exercised a great ministry for Christ. On the Continent, notables like Johann Arndt, Philipp Spener, Hermann Francke, Count Nikolaus von Zinzendorf, and the Dutch Pietist Lodenstein are long to be remembered. To single out only one person and permit that individual to personify the Puritan/Pietistic spirit may seem rather historically dubious. At that same time, however, no single person exemplified the spirit of the hour in a more mature and effective fashion than Richard Baxter of Kidderminster, England. His life deserves exploration.

THE EARLY LIFE AND MINISTRY OF RICHARD BAXTER

Richard Baxter, born in 1615, was the son of Richard Baxter Sr. of Eaton-Constantine, near Shrewsbury. Being born into a Presbyterian family, the parish register records his baptism as the sixth of November. A key founder of the Puritan thrust, William Perkins, died in 1602. As one great Puritan passed off the scene, God prepared Britain for blessings with another.

Baxter's ancestry can be traced back to Henry VI. Even though his father became known as Baxter of Eaton-Constantine, he was actually born in Rowton. Richard's father left a bit to be desired. He lived a rather loose life and in his youth gambled away his freehold property. As a result, he left himself in debt and financial difficulties. Baxter described his father as "called a gentle-man for his ancestor's sake."[1] The story of Richard Baxter's father does not end in a cloud, however. He began a thorough searching of the Scriptures and fell under conviction because of his sin. About the time that his son, Richard, was born, he underwent a profound Christian conversion experience. It affected his life deeply and changed his entire character.

The local congregation where the Baxters worshiped had its problems. During a six-year period, for example, "readers," i.e., those who conducted worship services and led the church, were all ignorant men, two of them grossly immoral. Yet that pattern epitomized more than one such congregation in Baxter's day. Later, in his *Third Defense of the Cause of Peace*, Richard Baxter spoke out boldly enough to expose the names of erring clergy and readers. The tragedy of the situation centered in the fact that these illiterate and discredited clergymen were the only teachers that young Richard had. During the first four years of his elementary education he studied under four successive curates of the parish High Ercall; two of them drank themselves into poverty. When Richard was ten, his family sent him to Eaton-Constantine to live with his grandfather. One of the curates there officiated under forged documents, and he became Richard's schoolmaster. During the days of Baxter's study under the questionable curate, the curate only preached once, and even then he was drunk.

NEW HOPE

Fortunately, a man of moral character and some ability became Baxter's next tutor. Historian Marcus L. Loane said Baxter "was grateful to the master from whom he acquired his knowledge of Latin."[2] Later, his parents sent him to the free school in Wroxeter. By the gracious providence of God, he studied under a dedicated Puritan leader. Things improved quite dramatically for Richard. He spent the remaining years of his primary education under good guidance. At the age of nineteen he finished his formal schooling, never to attend the university. Throughout his life, Richard Baxter regretted his lack of higher academic training. In his work *Religuise Baxterianae*, he made "humble and passionate lamentation, over his early schooling." He wrote on one occasion, "As to myself, my faults are no disgrace to any university; for I was of none. I have little but what I had out of books, and considerable helps of country helpers. Weakness and pain help me to study how to live; and that set me studying on how to live; and I'm studying the doctrine from which I must fetch my motives and comforts."[3]

Richard could have been admitted to Oxford University, but his mentor, John Owen, recommended he place himself under the tutelage of Mr. Richard Wickstad, chaplain to the council at Ludlow. Baxter thought he would receive the kind of education that he had long sought, but Wickstad gave him very little help. Nonetheless, Baxter gave himself to serious research on his own and became a self-taught man.

BAXTER'S CONVERSION

At the age of fourteen, Bishop Morton confirmed Baxter into the life of the church. However, it did not prove to be a conversion experience. Yet at the same time, the conviction of the Holy Spirit deepened in his life and he began to be troubled about his soul's salvation. Richard Baxter's father had become a dedicated believer and served as a challenge to his son. In his fifteenth year, he got a hold of an old, torn book that had been given to his father. The book was entitled *Bunny's Resolution*. This work led him to Richard Sibb's *Bruised Reed* and later to William Perkins's book *On Repentance*. God used these Puritan writers to influence Baxter profoundly. He soon found Christ and experienced a sound conversion. A deep desire to become a minister settled on his heart and mind.

On leaving Ludlow in 1633, Richard Wickstad, Baxter's negligent tutor, persuaded him to give up any idea of entering the ministry. Wickstad painted a delightful picture of a courtier's life. He convinced Baxter that he could find fulfillment in that lifestyle. Baxter responded to Wickstad's words and went to court to serve Henry Herbert. However, a month at Whitehall in London proved to be enough—the life of the court disgusted him.

When Richard returned home to Eaton-Constantine, he found his mother in extreme pain and suffering. She lingered on until her death on the tenth of May in 1634. After his arrival home, he also learned that John Owen, who had been so significant in his life, had died of consumption.

COMMITMENT TO MINISTRY

The death of his mother, along with his leaving the court, once again rekindled in Richard's heart the desire to become a minister of the gospel. As a result, Baxter put himself under the tutelage of Reverend Francis Garbet, the parish clergyman of Wrexeter. There he studied theology despite a continual battle with poor health. Regardless of his health problems, he gave himself earnestly to theological reading and sharpening his intellectual acuteness. He studied men like Thomas Aquinas, Duns Scotus, Ockham, and others.

Up to this point, Richard had been a conformist and reasonably satisfied to live his life in the established Church of England. He did have some encounters with nonconformity, particularly with Darnell of Uppington, but the man did not impress Baxter. When Richard turned twenty, however, he encountered two very able nonconformists: Joseph Synonds and the well-known Walter Cradock. Their fervent piety and faithful preaching influenced him and warmly attracted him. For their faithfulness, they had suffered persecution at the hands of bishops who were anything but equals in piety and effective ministry. In Britain at that time, considerable persecution had fallen on the nonconforming Puritans. Parliament passed several bills making it most difficult for the nonconformists.

FIRST SERMON AND NONCONFORMITY

In 1638, while serving as a headmaster of a new school at Dudley, Richard Baxter preached his first sermon in the Upper Church of Dudley. From there he began to preach in the surrounding villages. He then became the established minister in Dudley. Baxter at that stage had entertained no idea of leaving the established church. While serving in Dudley, however, several evangelical nonconformists became close friends. They shared with Richard the reasons for their nonconforming stances. Along with his study of nonconformist literature, Baxter made the momentous decision to become a nonconformist minister himself. One thing that turned him away from the Church of England centered in the church's lack of discipline and the thoughtless presenting of the Lord's Supper to drunkards and swearers and immoral people. A further most decisive factor was the "Et Cetera Oath," required of established clergymen. That moved Baxter to his nonconformative commitment.

In 1640, additional anti-Puritan legislation by Parliament was passed. In that setting, the people of Kidderminster in Worcestershire drew up a petition against their conforming minister. The townfolk accused him of being a "vicar who used to haunt the taverns and was content to preach only once a quarter."⁴ However, the petition resulted not in the immediate discharge of the minister, but in the seeking of a new curate who would come and preach and share the work of the church. As a consequence, Baxter became their new lecturer and preacher of the church on the fifth of April, 1641. The old vicar soon passed off the scene as the Spirit of God set the stage for the great ministry of Baxter of Kidderminster; he became vicar of Kidderminster.

When Richard came to Kidderminster, he met lovely Margaret Charlton.

She had moved to the town with her devoted mother. She seemed at first a frivolous young lady, but Baxter's sermons soon led her to Christ. They married later in London in 1662. She proved to be a godly preacher's wife and a tremendous help and encouragement to Richard. He greatly appreciated her, saying he "believed that he had never deserved God's gift of Margaret."

NEW SERVICE

The incredibly effective ministry of Baxter at Kidderminster has become a high mark in history. As one historian put it:

> Before his coming thither, the place was overrun with ignorance and profaneness, but, by the Divine blessing on his wise and faithful cultivation, the fruits of righteousness sprung up in rich abundance. He at first found but a single instance or two of daily family prayer in a whole street; and on his going away but one family or two could be found in some streets that continued to neglect it. And on Lord's days, instead of the open profanation to which they had been so long accustomed, a person in passing through the town in the intervals of public worship, might overhear hundreds of families engaged in singing psalms, reading the Scriptures and other good books, or such sermons as they had taken down while they heard them from the pulpit. His care of the souls committed to his charge, and the success of his labors among them, were truly remarkable; for the number of his stated communicants rose to six hundred, of whom he himself declared there were not twelve concerning whose sincere piety he had not reason to entertain a good hope.[5]

God blessed the ministry of Richard Baxter so profoundly that the entire town experienced a glorious revival.

Baxter had been at Kidderminster only two years when the Cromwellian Civil War broke out that resulted in the execution of Charles I. Under Cromwell, the British Parliament switched religious and political sympathies. Although Baxter stood with Cromwell and Parliament against the monarchy, the two men held several differences of opinions. Cromwell saw Baxter as harboring too much "narrow dogmatism." Nonetheless, Baxter left Kidderminster and became a chaplain to Colonel Whalley's regiment, making his contribution to the spiritual life of the men engaged in the civil war. History records that Cromwell's forces won the day and the monarchy fell.

During those days Baxter's health had deteriorated quite seriously. He lived in virtual semiretirement. He battled ill health for several years and coined the well-known phrase: "I preach as a dying man to dying men." Baxter meant it in a physical sense rather than with a spiritual connotation. After some rest, he began to recover somewhat and finally returned to Kidderminster. In 1650, back in Kidderminster, he finished his classic, *The Saints' Everlasting Rest*, written largely during his recuperation period. It stands today as one of the greatest works on godliness of all time. Baxter began to realize that God had endowed him with a writing gift, and he gave himself to the pen. Baxter's most enduring book is *The Reformed Pastor* (1656). The book is not a contention for reformed theology, but for the reformed life of holiness and godliness that the Lord requires of those who would lead Christ's church.

Although he still remained quite physically weak, he continued with his writing ministry. His best-known works on evangelism include *Call to the Unconverted* (1657) and *Methodus Theologiae Christiane* (1681). He served well as an evangelistic pastor and writer.

THE KIDDERMINSTER MINISTRY

While Baxter labored as minister of the church in Kidderminster, he also became quite prominent as a political leader. He involved himself in many critical affairs of the day, one of which revolved around his opposition to re-establishing the monarchy under Charles II. Baxter's stand on the issue did not sit well with many Englishmen; they wanted a restoration of the monarchy. But as history said of him, "he feared no man's displeasure nor hoped for any man's preferment."[6] He was first and foremost God's servant and sought God's pleasure in furthering Christ's kingdom.

The work went forward under God's blessings, and Baxter's impact on Kidderminster is legendary. As pointed out, he became such an influence that the town formerly known for its rogues and drunkards became renowned for its godliness and piety. Baxter would visit every home and take time with every member of the family, guiding them in the things of Christ. The town became virtually a completely converted community.

In 1660 Baxter left Kidderminster for a short period to live in London. There he made a deep impression for the gospel of Christ and godly living. He preached before the House of Commons on the third of April of 1660. He also preached before the Lord Mayor and many Londoners in St. Paul's Cathedral. His notoriety spread, but he was a nonconformist.

PERSECUTION

The restoration of the monarchy witnessed new pressure against the nonconformists. On one occasion, Baxter was imprisoned for six months because of his nonconformity. After his release, further charges were leveled against him by irate Loyalists. He stood before the court and received a stiff fine and imprisonment until the fine was paid. For a year and a half he languished away in prison under deplorable conditions. Finally, a resolution was found and Baxter received a full pardon. He was released on the twenty-fourth of November 1686 with the fine remitted.

Baxter suffered many cruel wrongs, but he bore them in meekness and patience. In the pressure of those days, he served as a great reconciler of people and church denominations. Baxter was committed to the biblical principle of God's people living in harmony and accepting one another regardless of denominational difference. After all, they were all bound together by the gospel and Christian love.

LAST DAYS

Baxter was now an old man. Five years earlier his wife, Margaret, had passed away. She had been a strong and helpful companion, sharing in his quest for bringing people to Christ and the life of holiness. During his last lonely years, Baxter continued to write and influence many by the challenge of his pen. One day someone said to him that he had done incredibly well by his books. He answered, "I was but a pen in God's hands, and what praise is due to a pen?"[7] Richard Baxter, man of God, slipped away to be with his Lord at four o'clock in the morning on Tuesday, the eighth of December, 1691. He was interred beside his beloved wife in Christ Church, London. William Bates preached the funeral sermon with great power and pathos. An excerpt from his eulogy reads beautifully:

In his [Baxter's] sermons there was a rare union of arguments and motives to convince the mind and gain the heart. All the fountains of reason and persuasion were open to his discerning eye. There was no resisting the force of his discourses, without denying reason and divine revelation. He had a marvelous facility and copiousness in speaking. There was a noble negligence in his style, for his great mind could not stoop to the affected eloquence of words; he despised flashy oratory, but his expressions were clear and powerful; so convincing the understanding, so entering into the soul, so engaging the affections, that those were as deaf as adders who were not charmed by so wise a charmer. He was animated with the Holy Spirit, and breathed celestial fire, to inspire heat and life into dead sinners, and to melt the obdurate in the frozen tomb. His books, for their number (which it seems were more than one hundred and twenty) and variety of matter in them, make a library. They contain a treasure of controversial, casuistic, and practical divinity. His books of practical divinity have been effectual for more numerous conversions of sinners to God, than any printed in our time; and while the church remains on earth, will be of continual efficacy to recover lost souls. There is a vigorous pulse in them that keeps the reader awake and attentive.[8]

God's great man had gone, but the challenge for godliness in evangelism he left can never be erased. He epitomized all the Puritan/Pietists who stood in their zeal for the furtherance of the kingdom of God through the salvation of needy souls leading the redeemed into the godly life. Real evangelism culminates in godliness—always and forever. Baxter has shown us that. So the issue arises: What constitutes genuine, biblical holiness?

EVANGELISM AND GODLINESS

Evangelism in contemporary culture has been criticized for often precipitating "decisions" for Christ with no follow-up in developing godliness and holiness in the lives of new converts. The results: a carnal church. Perhaps a measure of justification can be found in this negative evaluation of some evangelists and their work. The quest for "success," understood in terms of the number of decisions recorded, has been a millstone about the neck of more than one proclaimer of the gospel.

It must be confessed that merely seeking decisions misses the biblical mandate for evangelism. Any evangelization that does not culminate in the quest for spirituality and a disciplined lifestyle is unworthy of the name "evangelism." But why do we see the problem constantly rearing its head? One would think the situation would be resolved. There has probably been more emphasis placed on and more books written on Christian discipleship than on any other aspect of Christian experience. Strong emphasis on holiness arises from many quarters. And rightly so, for our Lord said, "If anyone wishes to come after Me, let him deny himself, and take up his cross, and follow Me" (Mark 8:34). The evangelistic call to Christ entails a call to discipleship. The Bible, and evangelism at its best, always holds up Christ's demands as the ultimate standard for any evangelistic endeavor. The principle of evangelism for discipleship dominated the quest in the Puritan-Pietistic era. Godliness, as the Puritans realized, always shines forth as the ultimate mark to which evangelism must strive. We have seen this epitomized in the life of Richard Baxter. That spirit and approach to evangelization must be recaptured. The problem of a shallow evangelism must be solved. In the words of Dietrich Bonhoeffer in his classic work *The Cost of Discipleship*, "cheap grace" has no place in biblical evangelism.

That raises the question: How does the Bible present the principle of godliness? The core principle can be found in Paul's appeal to the Romans. He wrote:

> Therefore, I urge you, brothers, in view of God's mercy, to offer your bodies as living sacrifices, holy and pleasing to God—this is your spiritual act of worship. Do not conform any longer to the pattern of this world, but be transformed by the renewing of your mind. Then you will be able to test and approve what God's will is—his good, pleasing and perfect will. (Rom. 12:1–2 NIV)

The life of godliness has its roots in a Christ-centered, yielded, obedient life. Godliness and holiness spring from abandonment of the will to Christ's lordship.

FELLOWSHIP WITH CHRIST

The key phrase in living the Christ-honoring life of submission is found in 1 John 1:7: "If we walk in the light as He Himself is in the light, we have fellowship with one another." *Fellowship with God* is John's way of describing the fullness of the Christian experience and the goal of biblical evangelism. It means walking with God in the light of His holy presence.

A DISTURBING DILEMMA

At this point, a serious dilemma develops. God is holy light. No darkness can abide in His presence. "Light" and "darkness" are totally incompatible. Simply put, no one can walk with the God of light and still abide in darkness, the darkness of unresolved sin. Herein is the sting of the dilemma. John reminds us, "If we say we have no sin, we deceive ourselves, and the truth is not in us" (1 John 1:8 RSV). Human sin is the culprit, and we all stand guilty. How does one, therefore, deal with the problem? A solution is demanded. Dynamic Christian experience and godliness are predicated upon the solution to the sin situation.

THE ANSWER TO THE DILEMMA

The fundamental truth that John projects as the answer to the dilemma is found in his words: "If we walk in the light as He Himself is in the light, we have fellowship with one another, and the blood of Jesus His Son cleanses us from all sin" (1 John 1:7). The key phrase in John's statement is: "The blood of Jesus . . . cleanses us from all sin." This simply means that if one aspires to walk in the light of God's presence, he or she must be constantly cleansed by the power of Christ's forgiveness. The force of the verbal tense John uses implies a continual, daily cleansing of sins by the efficacy of Christ's blood. It needs to be pointed out here that the issue is *fellowship* with God, not *relationship*. The relationship with God is confirmed at conversion; fellowship is one's walk with God in developing holiness. What, therefore, constitutes the pragmatics of the principle of Christ's continual cleansing to maintain that fellowship?

CONFESSION OF SINS

In a word, the Bible tells us we are to confess our sins. John forthrightly states, "If we confess our sins, he is faithful and just, and will forgive our sins and cleanse us from all unrighteousness" (1 John 1:9 RSV). What does John mean when he urges us to bring our sins to God in confession?

It is quite fascinating to see the intriguing implications of the word *confess.* In the language of the New Testament, it is a compound word. John wedded two different words, and the union gave birth to a rich truth. The term is composed of the verb *to say* and the prefix *the same.* Thus the word translated "confess" in our English Bibles literally means "to say the same thing as, to assent to, or to agree with." Confession means we "agree with" concerning our sin.

With whom, however, do we agree? This precipitates a further question: Who convicts us of sins? The biblical answer is obvious: the Holy Spirit (John 16:7–11). The Spirit of God puts His convicting finger on specific and individual sins that have intruded into one's walk with Jesus Christ. Therefore, for Christians to confess sins scripturally is "to concede to" or "to agree with" the convicting Spirit of God that some *particular* act of rebellion *truly is a sin.* It means to get out of one's own self and stand by the Holy Spirit, be objective about the issue, and "agree" with Him. Simply put, it demands coming face to face with one's individual sins. In a walk with Christ, a general, nonspecific confession of sins does not reach the goal. True confession necessitates lingering before God long enough to permit the Holy Spirit to search one out, convict of specific sins, and place His finger on those particular deeds that constitute evil and then agree with Him. Of course, one must forsake those sins in the context of confession.

OTHER IMPLICATIONS

A secondary problem emerges, however. What if some sins rupture fellowship with others as well as one's fellowship with God? In such an instance, merely to confess them to God alone proves insufficient to experience the full liberty of Christ's forgiveness. They are to be confessed to God; this is obvious. But in His Sermon on the Mount, Jesus said, "So if you are offering your gift at the altar, and there remember that your brother has something against you, leave your gift there before the altar and go; first be reconciled to your brother, and then come and offer your gift" (Matt. 5:23–24 RSV). One cannot avoid the simple truth outlined by our Lord Jesus Christ: If one sins against another person and fellowship is thereby marred, restitution must be made to the offended person as well as to God. If one fails to acknowledge one's sin and seek forgiveness from those individuals sinned against (as much as is possible in the present circumstances and as God leads), then one cannot really expect deep fellowship with God or with one another. The godly learn that.

God places a high moral, ethical standard before His people. The essence of holiness centers in growing in Christlikeness to meet that goal. The biblical term for this process of maturing in consecration and purity is "sanctification." And that means dealing with the sin issue. That places before all believers step number one in seeking godliness. Of course, this principle is predicated on the foundational commitment to Christ's absolute lordship in one's life. But it is an essential discipline for those who would walk with God "in the light." But now we turn to the more positive side of the issue.

THE POSITIVE SIDE AND HEART OF THE MATTER

The essence of the sanctification process is found in Galatians 4:19: "Oh, my dear children, I feel the pangs of childbirth all over again till Christ be formed within you" (PHILLIPS). In this passage, the pathos of Paul surges to the surface as he yearns over these early Christians, pleading that "Christ be formed within." And this yearning is but a pale reflection of how God the Father yearns over all His children. His whole work in our lives is to form Christ within. This is what sanctification is all about. It culminates in bearing the "fruit of the Spirit."

The fruit of the Spirit—that quality of "fruit" that Christ epitomized in His character—constitutes the essence of *holy living*. This principle of Christian fruit-bearing is fully outlined in Galatians 5:22–23 where Paul wrote: "The fruit of the Spirit is love, joy, peace, patience, kindness, goodness, faithfulness, gentleness, self-control; against such things there is no law." Paul pleads with God's people to permit the Holy Spirit to develop a quality of Christlike holiness in their lives through His indwelling fruit-bearing work. The Christian, as a branch grafted into the Vine, Jesus Christ, is to abide and draw life-giving sustenance from the Vine. When this abiding state is maintained, marvelous fruit is produced on these "grafted branches." And Christ is thus formed within. The godly life is actually an embodiment of Jesus Christ Himself. This level of spirituality makes God's people, as Paul described the Philippians, "shine like stars in the universe" (Phil. 2:15 NIV); and "you hold out [fast] the word of life" (v. 16 NIV). This is godliness as the Bible defines it.

A BIG ORDER

God desires "fruit-bearing branches." But is it really attainable? Yes, for when God's people as branches abide in the Vine, Jesus Christ, His own life-giving power in the person of the Holy Spirit flows into life and fruit-bearing becomes natural. In the entire fruit-bearing process, it is vital to realize that Christ *Himself* is formed in the personhood of the believer by the power of the Holy Spirit (Gal. 4:19). Let it be stressed, Christian consecration is not mimicking Jesus. Christ's own life is actually infused within and expressed through the surrendered, abiding child of God.

Strictly speaking, Christians are not an *imitation* of Christ. Attempting to imitate Jesus in one's own strength can soon degenerate into legalism. Rather, let it be stressed, Christians are to be an *embodiment* of the Lord, yielded to Him (Rom. 12:1–2), keeping sins under the blood and simply abiding in Christ. In that way alone God can glorify Himself, because only in that manner does the Christian reflect His Son and hence bear His fruit. As one author expressed it, Christian living is not our living with Christ's help; it is Christ living His life in us. Therefore, that portion of our lives that is not His living is not Christian living. Paul said, "For to me, to live is Christ" (Phil. 1:21).

The Christian life is "rest," a rest of faith. Martin Luther said, "Therefore, we must nestle under the wings of this mother hen, and not rashly fly away trusting in the powers of our own faith, lest the hawk speedily tear us in pieces and devour us."[9] Staying on the ground of surrender to God's will, continually walking in faith with Christ and cleansed, and letting His life of beauty and power and fruit-bearing be lived through us—that is God's way to holiness. Thus one grows into a beautiful manifestation of Christ that brings honor and glory to God. In basic terms, the self-life is exchanged for the Christ-life.

ABIDING IS THE KEY

Abiding in Christ's fellowship thus becomes the key to biblical godliness. And that means diligently keeping the daily disciplines of full surrender, confession of all known sins, faithful Bible study and prayer, being filled with the Spirit, serving Christ joyously, and witnessing to His love and grace. Exercising these disciplines is absolutely essential. That is godliness, and that is life. When the church, the people of God, reach that level of holiness, multitudes will see, be challenged, and come to Christ. And that is evangelism God's way.

CONCLUSION

Thus we see in the dramatic late sixteenth century, when the Puritan-Pietistic movement was birthed through men like William Perkins and epitomized in others like Richard Baxter, not only did godly living flow, but effective evangelism swept the scene. Godly believers *always* seek the lost for Christ—just as Jesus Himself did. Thus, the church reached one of its finest hours. Any true evangelism that is worthy of the name must fulfill its role in the quest for godliness among the converts. So, again we raise the inevitable question, Has Billy Graham clearly seen this and thus fallen in step with that historical understanding of kingdom progress? What contribution has he made in this area of spiritual experience?

PART II:
GRAHAM AND GODLINESS

Godlikeness of character is the Christian's proper heritage in this earthly walk.
—BILLY GRAHAM

INTRODUCTION

Pentecost was the Day! The Book of Acts, chapters 1 and 2, describes the dramatic events surrounding the Day of Pentecost. These chapters, most New Testament scholars agree, present the pattern for New Testament and historical evangelism. After Peter declared the gospel of Christ, Luke records, "Now when they heard this, they were pierced to the heart, and said to Peter and the rest of the apostles, 'Brethren, what shall we do?'" (Acts 2:37). Peter immediately replied, "Repent, and let each of you be baptized in the name of Jesus Christ for the forgiveness of your sins; and you shall receive the gift of the Holy Spirit" (Acts 2:38).

The gospel was presented, and the Holy Spirit, who was given on that day, convicted those who heard. The apostles made a direct appeal for people to repent and believe in Christ, and the response was all but overwhelming. Luke tells us, "So then, those who had received his word were baptized; and there were added that day about three thousand souls" (Acts 2:41). That day became one of the early church's greatest evangelistic ingatherings.

But it did not end there. Immediately following the climactic account of those who were converted during that significant event, the Scriptures state, "They were continually devoting themselves to the apostles' teaching and to fellowship, to the breaking of bread and to prayer" (Acts 2:42). This description of the church's disciplined lifestyle, including the many new converts, stands as a classic example of the godliness of the Lord's people and the goal for all authentic evangelism, including Billy Graham's ministry. Does he measure up?

THE QUEST FOR GODLINESS IN BILLY GRAHAM: THE BASIC PRINCIPLE

In this quest for godliness, Billy Graham has struck a favorable stance in his evangelism. That fact and principle will become obvious as we delve into Graham's ministry. Billy Graham clearly understands, as the writer of the Book of Hebrews declared, "without holiness no one will see the Lord" (12:14 NIV). The fact that Graham has taken this principle very seriously is acknowledged by even his severest critics. But upon what basis does Graham see the holy life emanating from the Christian's experience? The principle is basic: Graham believes that true believers will seek a life of holiness when they understand the true nature of their conversion to Christ. An unbeliever might embrace a reasonably moral, ethical life, but godliness and holiness of life in the full biblical sense come about only by and through the Spirit of God. The activity and sanctifying power of the Holy Spirit in one's life serve as the source of a genuine conversion experience and the subsequent quest for a life that reflects Jesus Christ. As defined earlier, the Bible calls it "sanctification," i.e., being "set apart" from sin and "set apart" to God. And that lifelong process is God's purpose for every Christian. Paul said, "For this is the will of God, your sanctification " (1 Thess. 4:3). Graham's own life certainly stands as an example of that basic truth.

It may appear that an inordinate amount of space is being given to investigating Billy Graham's personal quest for godliness. But in light of the failures of some evangelists on this issue, it seems important. Still more vital does this in-depth look at Graham and personal godliness become because of the fact that his quest has shaped and colored the entire landscape of his evangelistic ministry. Therefore, it must be understood quite thoroughly. So the question arises, Does the evangelist measure up to biblical, evangelical principles of godliness and holiness of life?

GRAHAM'S PERSONAL QUEST

As has been briefly seen in previous chapters, Billy Graham was converted as a teenager under the preaching of Mordecai Ham, a Baptist evangelist from Kentucky. In that salvation moment, God in His grace granted Graham the "gift of the Holy Spirit" (Acts 2:38), and his life was transformed. Billy called it "the 180-degree turn." He gives testimony to this radical change of life in his autobiography:

> Before my conversion, I tended to be touchy, oversensitive, envious of others, and irritable. Now I deliberately tried to be courteous and kind to everybody around me. I was experiencing what the apostle Paul had described: the old has gone, the new has come! (2 Cor. 5:17). Mother especially, but other family members too, thought there was a difference. Most remarkable of all—to me at least—was the uncharacteristic enthusiasm I had for my studies![10]

The life of godliness—even in details such as teenage study habits—had begun. And it has carried on unceasingly since that divine moment when he was granted salvation. The foundation for all godliness is laid in Christ, and His salvation. When a person is truly saved, godliness follows. Salvation and sanctification are united. That principle expresses Graham's theology of holiness in simple form.

Billy Graham's early tutoring in godly Christian living came from his parents. Every Sunday the family got in an old automobile and drove five miles to the small Associate Reformed Presbyterian Church. In 1933, Billy's mother came into a new experience of Christ. She joined a Bible class at the urging of her sister, Lil Barker. She said about the experience, "The Lord has come in and lives in our hearts. I had never known that truth before."[11] Billy's father, Frank, was injured about that time, and after he recovered, the Lord spoke profoundly to both parents. They dedicated themselves to finding more time for Bible study and prayer. They started reading devotional writings to the children and had prayer regularly in a family worship time. The pattern of godliness had been set before Billy, but at that early stage he had no experience of it in his own life. He had the form, but not the substance. Then came conversion.

After Graham's salvation experience, he understood the importance of his parents' commitment to a holy lifestyle. He began to see the significance of prayer and Bible study. Furthermore, the desire to see others brought to faith in Christ began to grow in his heart and life. The foundation had been laid, and he now set out on the road to personal godliness. After Graham's call to the ministry, that spiritual quest for himself and for his converts deepened significantly. He had grasped what Luke was saying in the events that surrounded the Day of Pentecost. He learned that godliness and evangelism are traveling companions on the road to spirituality. That principle and its pragmatic implications for the evangelist need to be explored.

BILLY GRAHAM'S "PROGRAM" FOR GODLINESS

Billy holds that "God wants us to long for Him,"[12] and such a longing lays the spiritual groundwork for godliness. After the foundation is put in place through conversion, Graham recognizes that the cornerstone of all spiritual growth and maturity centers in continued absolute commitment to Jesus Christ as Lord. Spiritually mature Christians develop a lifestyle of seeking God's kingdom first (Matt. 6:33). Billy Graham expressed the principle this way: "In reality, Jesus Christ is the perfect fulfillment, example and demonstration of (godliness)."[13] The Lord Jesus becomes the challenge and example to all believers.

JESUS THE PATTERN

The Lord set the pattern for the principle of holy living when He cried out in the Garden of Gethsemane, "Not as I will, but as thou wilt" (Matt. 26:39 KJV). Graham has said, "If we would find genuine happiness, we must begin where Jesus began."[14] In that absolute commitment of Jesus Christ to His heavenly

Father, the challenge to holiness comes to all the people of God. As Graham has pointed out, "One must come to the end of 'self' before one can really begin to live."[15] Paul got to the heart of the issue in his Roman letter: "I urge you therefore, brethren, by the mercies of God, to present your bodies a living and holy sacrifice" (Rom. 12:1). Obedience and righteous living constitute the crux of the matter. Graham makes it clear that God "puts reins upon our wayward souls that they may be directed into 'paths of righteousness.'"[16] That means a life of practicing the discipline of God on the basis of obedience to the Lord. These are certain things that must be done to experience the disciplined life that leads to personal godliness.

THE DISCIPLINES OF GOD

The first discipline that God lifts up before His people centers in a life of Christlike purity. The evangelist works this out in a very down-to-earth fashion. He begins on a negative note, saying in a sermon, "You can't cover up sin; we only think we are getting away with it."[17] In the same sermon, Billy points out that as Solomon said, "he that covereth his sins that shall not prosper" (Prov. 28:13 KJV). Graham illustrates that truth by referring to Moses and the experience of *hitting* the rock that it might bring forth water instead of *speaking* to the rock, as God commanded (Num. 20:8–13). Graham preached, "In the wilderness Moses disobeyed God by striking the rock to obtain water rather than speaking to the rock. And God said that Moses could not go into the Promised Land because he had disobeyed Him."[18] He brought the application home with these words, "God says to us, 'I will not bless you, I will not give you victory. I will judge you unless you put away the sin that you are trying to cover up.'"[19] Sin and holiness are totally incompatible. In his excellent book on godliness, *The Secret of Happiness*, Billy simply points out, ". . . It is not God's will for us to continue in sin."[20] Purity is predicated on that principle.

Graham is quite forthright in laying down the principle that before purity of life and "the secret of happiness" can be experienced, all sin must be confessed and forsaken. Graham makes it a priority that we must be "sensitive to the presence of hidden sins . . . wrong motives, wrong attitudes, wrong habits, wrong relationships, wrong priorities. It may even be that . . . [you] will have to make restitution if you have stolen anything, or you may have to seek out someone and ask forgiveness for a wrong that you have committed . . . hold nothing back, as the songwriter says, 'give them all to Jesus.'"[21] Thus he says, "Happy are those who 'let go and let God.'"[22] Billy urges, "Christ is calling Christians today to cleansing, to dedication, to consecration and the full surrender."[23]

At this point, Graham gives a word of encouragement: "You can confess your sins right now, bring them to God and say, 'Lord here they are.' The Bible says, 'If we confess our sins he is faithful and just to forgive us our sins and to cleanse us from all unrighteousness' (1 John 1:9). God says, 'who so confesses and forsaketh [his sin] shall have mercy' (Prov. 28:13). . . . It doesn't matter how ugly or dirty the sin is, you can bring it to God and call it by name and ask for forgiveness. God loves you and He will forgive you, He will cleanse you, He will wash away your sins. You can shout from the mountaintops what God has done for you!"[24] That opens the gate to the road of godliness.

THE POSITIVE SIDE

Billy learned the "secret" of Christian victory in another meaningful encounter with Stephen Olford. It was reminiscent of the time in Wales in 1946. While in Montego Bay, Jamaica, Stephen was speaking at a Keswick convention. Billy and Stephen spent several days together in a hotel where Stephen laid out the principle of the victorious Christian life as espoused by the Keswick message. That teaching stresses the believer's identification with Christ in death and resurrection (Gal. 2:20), and that it is by faith—not works. God's power within overcomes the world, the flesh, and the devil. That principle is most important in living the godly life. As previously quoted, "One must come to the end of self before one can really begin to live."[25] The spiritual believer stops striving and begins trusting in God's power for victory because of his or her relationship with Christ in death and resurrection (Rom. 6:1–12). Billy got the message, thanks again to Stephen Olford. But how does it come about in the believer's actual experience?

Graham strongly stresses that the Holy Spirit, in His sanctifying work, will create purity and victorious fruit-bearing by faith. We have explored earlier Graham's doctrine on the work of the Holy Spirit, but another word of admonition of the evangelist needs recording. Graham states:

We are told that He [the Holy Spirit] sheds the love of God abroad in our hearts. He produces the fruit of the Spirit: "love, joy, peace, longsuffering, gentleness, goodness, faith, meekness, temperance" (Gal. 5:22–23). We cannot possibly manufacture this fruit in our own energy. It is supernaturally manufactured by the Holy Spirit that lives in our hearts! I must yield to Him . . . surrender to Him . . . give Him control of my life.[26]

Graham gives a word of caution here, however. We must remember, he points out, "the pure heart does not mean that I must live in a 'straitjacket.' There is liberty in Christ and that liberty is to do his will."[27] When a person lives the Spirit-filled life, he or she lives a life of godliness in the freedom and liberty of the Spirit through faith. Again, let it be emphasized, godliness is a walk of faith, not living under the law. The former approach to Christianity creates a life of purity and joy, predicated on daily commitment to the absolute lordship of Christ in life.[28] Of course, there are basic exercises that are necessary to maintain a walk in fellowship with Jesus Christ. As Billy said, "The inward journey is that lifelong pilgrimage of spiritual growth and maturity."[29]

Three personal disciplines—Bible study, prayer, and witnessing—cultivate the life of godliness and keep it alive and growing. Billy Graham has said, "Nothing can take the place of a daily devotional life with Christ. . . . Our quiet time, our prayer time, the time we spend in the Word is absolutely essential for a happy Christian life. It is impossible to be a happy, dynamic and powerful Christian apart from a daily walk with Christ."[30] Graham holds that each one of these disciplines is indispensable to godliness. As a preacher of the Word of God, he has always stressed the importance of the disciplines. This shall be seen as his ministry continues to unfold.

BIBLE STUDY

The study of the Bible has always been a vital part of the life of Billy Graham and his team. We have seen in a previous chapter that he has the highest regard for the Scriptures. To reiterate his position on the Bible, in an interview with David Frost, the evangelist said, "I believe that the Bible was inspired by God. . . . [It tells us] how to live and how to be saved."[31] But he would have us understand, as he once said, "I am going to heaven, not on my good works . . . or reading the Bible. I am going to heaven because of what Christ did on the cross."[32] As important as the Bible is to Billy Graham, Jesus Christ and His cross stand supreme.

Nevertheless, Graham is absolutely committed to faithful devotional reading of the Scriptures and memorizing verses of the Bible. Remember, he said, "Every morning I read . . . the Bible without studying, just reading, just filling my soul." Being in the Word of God regularly enables the Holy Spirit to develop in one the "mind of Christ." As Billy pointed out, "Our mental powers are to be brought under the control of Christ. 'Let this mind be in you which was also in Christ Jesus,' says Paul in Philippians 2:5."[33] With the mind of Christ we can discern the "good, and acceptable, and perfect, will of God" (Rom. 12:2 KJV). In an interview, David Frost asked Graham, "With . . . much reading of it [the Bible], I know you feel it's the Word of God and so on, but do you, in simple human terms, ever get bored with the Bible?"[34] Graham answered, "Never."[35] The Bible is central. Years ago, he penned a small book, *The Bible Says*. The book contains only Scripture. That speaks of his regard for the Word of God.

PRAYER AND GODLINESS

Along with enthusiasm for the Scriptures, Billy Graham is likewise committed to the absolute necessity of prayer for Christian godliness and maturity. When asked what he would do if he had to live his life over again, he invariably says he would "spend more time in study and more time in prayer."[36] He tells us, "Prayer is for every moment of our lives, not just for times of suffering."[37]

Graham knows that success in God's work revolves around prayer. He has said, "If Christianity is to survive in a godless and materialistic world, we must repent of our prayerlessness. We must make prayer our priority."[38] He fully understands that his work in evangelism is essentially the work of the Holy Spirit in and through his life and ministry. He constantly states that if he were to take any credit for himself, his lips would turn to clay. The Holy Spirit does the work; and persistent, prevailing prayer "releases" the Spirit to accomplish the task.

Not only does Graham see this as true for his own ministry, but it stands true for the entire kingdom of God. In a message on the power of prayer, he said, "Today the world is being carried on a rushing torrent that is sweeping out of control. Only one power is available to redeem the course of events, and that is the power of prayer. . . . How can we go on unless there is a renewed emphasis on prayer?"[39] Billy contends we must again look to Jesus, for He set the example of a life of prevailing prayer. Graham always exalts Jesus Christ as the pattern and source of meaningful prayer. In the Garden of Gethsemane, Christ prayed to the point of "great drops of blood" bursting out on His forehead (Luke 22:44 KJV). Further, as Graham said, "So fervent and so direct were the prayers of Jesus that once when he had finished praying, his followers turned to him and said, 'Lord teach us to pray' (Luke 11:1). They knew that Jesus had been in touch with God, they wanted to have such an experience."[40] Prayer is always to God and brings one into fellowship with Him. Jesus set the pattern, and those who have developed a life of godliness have grasped and implemented the principle of prayer.

BACKGROUNDS OF MEANINGFUL PRAYER

Graham points out that those who have turned the tide of history have turned it by prayer. It all begins in many great Old Testament accounts. In a message on prayer, Billy relates how King Hezekiah prayed, and as a result the entire army of the Assyrians was destroyed and the nation spared. He further points out that Elijah, a great man of prayer, lifted up his voice to God and fire from heaven fell and consumed the offering.

In the New Testament, the evangelist cites the apostle Paul's dynamic prayer life. As a result of the apostle's fervent intercession, churches were born throughout Asia Minor and Europe. And down through the pages of history, Graham contends it was men of fervent prayer such as John Wesley, Jonathan Edwards, and others who accomplished great feats for Christ. "Time after time," Graham declares, "events have been changed because of prayer. If millions of us would avail ourselves of the privilege of prayer, we could go to our knees in believing prayer and change the course of events."[41]

PRACTICAL PRINCIPLES OF PRAYER

Graham thus urges all believers to "pray without ceasing" (1 Thess 5:17). He declares, "This should be the motto of every follower of Jesus Christ. Never stop praying no matter how dark and hopeless it may seem."[42] Graham gives some helpful advice: "I would urge you to select a place where you can meet alone with God . . . that can be one of your greatest blessings."[43]

Again, in a practical manner, Graham urges the church to pray for those who do not know Jesus Christ. He stated that on one occasion, "I listened to a discussion of religious leaders on how to communicate the gospel. Not once did I hear them mention prayer. And yet I know of scores of churches that win many converts each year by prayer alone. If there is a person in our acquaintance that needs Christ in his life, then we need to start praying for him."[44] Graham is convinced that with God nothing is impossible.

Graham fully realizes the centrality of prayer in his crusades. Prayer preparation and prayer ministries permeate his every evangelistic effort. Prayer has been an essential part of the crusades, beginning in Los Angeles in 1949. Recall Armin Gesswein and the prayer ministry he inaugurated. The more formal prayer preparation in the crusades started worldwide with Billy Graham asking Mrs. Millie Dienert to travel to England to prepare for an upcoming crusade with prayer. Through the years, prayer preparation programs have grown tremendously. Now in the crusades a chairman and chairwoman are selected to lead out in prayer ministries for God's power to fall on the crusade. It blossoms out in ministers praying with ministers, women praying in small groups in homes, and churches using many avenues to intercede. Out of it have come what are termed "Prayer Triplets," three people joining together in concerted prayer for God's power to fall. Millie Deinert tells of women remarking, "We have learned to pray like never before."

God's people get excited about prayer. Billy's goal is to see revival take place because of faithful prayer in the home and in the church. Prayer does change things. As the Bible states, there is no task or problem too difficult for the power and love of God to intervene and meet the need (Gen. 18:14). Thus Graham programs for prayer, earnest prayer, in all his crusades. For the evangelist, "prayer is natural. We were fashioned in the beginning to live a life of prayer."[45] In a word, prayer is absolutely vital in one's own personal life and service. Billy emphasizes that a person is simply not godly if he or she does not pray. But there is a third discipline in a growing godliness: sharing one's faith with lost people.

WITNESSING

It may seem needless to express the fact that Billy Graham views witnessing as constituting the third major personal discipline in godly living. As Cliff Barrows has said, "We were committed to witness from the beginning."[46] Graham and the team personally witness to people constantly. Billy has said, "One faithful witness is worth a thousand mute professors of religion."[47] And Billy practices it himself. He tells the following story:

Some years ago I was in Washington, D.C., in the office of a very powerful and well-known politician. I suddenly looked in his eyes and said, "Sir, have you ever received Christ as your Savior?" He hung his head and didn't say anything. After at least a full minute, he said, "You know, no one has ever asked me that question before." I asked him if he wouldn't like to receive Christ right now and have confidence of eternal security.

As I held out my hand, I said, "It means repentance." I explained that it means faith in Christ and Christ alone. He was silent for two or three minutes, and I didn't say any more. Then he held out his hand and said, "I'll receive Him now," and we prayed. He was a church member. He had been around Christianity all his life, but he had never made that personal commitment. Nothing on earth is more important. Nothing.[48]

Daughter Anne Graham Lotz tells the story of one instance when Billy and Ruth were on a short vacation, staying in the beach home of some friends. Suddenly, Billy disappeared. After an hour, Ruth got concerned and went to look for him. She finally found him out in the backyard with the gardener. Billy had won him to Christ. As Anne pointed out, it is great to see the thousands coming to Christ in a crusade, but Billy is thrilled over leading just one person to Jesus Christ. He sees this discipline as vital and essential to a happy and prosperous life of godliness. He remembers very well the words of the Lord Jesus when He said, "You shall be My witnesses" (Acts 1:8).

Billy is vitally concerned that *all* believers engage in personal evangelism. Therefore, he has devised a program called Operation Andrew, which encourages witnessing for Christ. This program is implemented primarily in the context of his crusades. He enlists all who will make an effort to witness and help get people to the crusades. The basic program reads as follows:

> Operation Andrew is a simple plan. It helps us pray for, befriend, invite and bring to the special evangelistic event people we know who need Jesus Christ. Join with other Christians in your community who are trusting God to work through them to reach their neighbors, friends and family with the Good News of new life in Christ.

MY OPERATION ANDREW LIST

1._____

2._____

3._____

Use this card as a daily prayer reminder.[49]

Graham urges everyone in every way possible to share their faith. And in a very real sense he stands as a true example of the discipline. As biographer William Martin has said, "Without doubt, it is Graham's prowess as a soul winner that commends him most powerfully to Evangelical Christians, since no activity has a higher standing in their minds than bringing the lost to Christ."[50]

OTHER FACTORS IN GODLINESS

It is axiomatic that *fellowship* assumes an essential place in the development of godliness (1 John 1:3). That key word implies a twofold application as John's first Epistle makes clear. First and foundational, it applies to the individual believer and his or her relationship to God. That connotes the concept of, as our Lord put it, "abide in Me" (John 15:4). There will be little growth in godliness unless one abides in the dynamic fellowship of Jesus Christ. Our Lord's discourse on the theme recorded in John 15:1–11 makes that abundantly clear.

The second implication expands the term to the wider fellowship of the church. All who would walk with Christ must also learn to walk in harmony and fellowship with other believers. Thus, the church plays a significant role in

aiding growth and maturity in the Lord. These God-appointed spiritual principles must be held tenaciously, and, as shall be made obvious in chapter 13,
Billy Graham holds to these principles unswervingly.

Graham is also sensitive to the fact that godliness must express itself in relationship to all people. Interpersonal relationships stand at the core of a meaningful society. This is why the evangelist states, "Anger is one of man's most
devastating sins."[51] Moreover, a life of holiness is directly applicable in one's
moral life. Graham has "a passion for sexual fidelity."[52] Billy has said, "Impurity
is one of the most revolting of sins because it twists and distorts one of God's
most precious gifts to humans, human love, and drags it down to the level of
the beast."[53] Graham has kept himself absolutely pure. He sees it as a gross sin
to be unfaithful in sexual matters. His commitment to his lovely wife, Ruth, is
exemplary. As one biographer has said, "Billy Graham's spotless record as a
faithful husband is an accomplishment his followers regard with due appreciation."[54] Even Marshall Frady, who was quite critical of Graham in his biography, granted that the evangelist is a man with "exactly that quality of raw
childlike unblinking goodness" possessing "a staggering passion for the pure,
the sanitary, the wholesome, and the upright."[55] T. W. Wilson, Graham's personal associate for many years, commented there would have been no Billy
Graham as we know him today had it not been for Ruth and his faithfulness
to her. God has made them a great team, "a model couple."[56] Their commitment to one another is kept on the highest level.

THE FAMILY

Early in Billy Graham's ministry, he was in conversation with the widow of former evangelist Billy Sunday. Ma Sunday, as all affectionately knew her, said,
"Boys, whatever you do, don't neglect your family. I did. I traveled with Pa all
over the country and I sacrificed my children. I saw all four of them go straight
to hell."[57]

Billy Graham has been exemplary as a father as well as a husband. He confesses nonetheless, "I have felt I was a failure as a father due to my extensive
absences from home."[58] Billy has said of his wife, "Ruth was strong enough
and spirited enough to be both father and mother at the times the children
needed it."[59] But when Billy was home, they always had family devotions.

Although he has traveled much, the children and grandchildren have the highest regard for "Daddy."

At the time of this writing, Franklin Graham is engaged in a worldwide ministry, in many senses of the word succeeding his father. The three daughters, Gigi, Ruth, and Anne, are all living dedicated Christian lives serving the Lord Jesus Christ. Daughter Anne is a marvelous speaker and teacher herself. Youngest son Ned is engaged in a ministry in the Far East. It is not that the children did not have their times of difficulty in the spiritual realm, but through it all God has used the testimony of Billy and Ruth and the godliness of their lives to inspire and lead the family. Billy Graham has created what he calls the "Ten Commandments for the Home." They read:

1. Establish God's chain of command. The Bible teaches that for the Christian, Jesus Christ is to head the home, with the wife under the authority of a Christlike husband and the children responsible to their parents.

2. Obey the commandment that you love one another.

3. Show acceptance and appreciation for each family member.

4. Family members should respect God's authority over them and the authority God has delegated down the chain of command.

5. It is important to have training and discipline in the home and not just for the family dog!

6. Enjoy one another and take the time to enjoy family life *together*. Quality time is no substitute for quantity time. Quantity time *is* quality time.

7. Do not commit adultery. Adultery destroys a marriage and is a sin against God and against your mate.

8. Everyone in a family should work for the mutual benefit of the family. No child should be without chores or without the knowledge that work brings fulfillment.

9. Pray together and read the Bible together. Nothing strengthens a marriage and family more. Nothing is a better defense against Satan.

10. Every family member should be concerned about whether every other member of the family is truly saved. This extends after the immediate family to grandparents, uncles and aunts, cousins, and in-laws.

He then points out, "No one is truly a success in God's eyes if his family is a mess."[60]

Billy's middle daughter, Anne, tells the story of how her father exemplified the spirit of Jesus in family matters. The year she graduated from high school, Billy was to bring the baccalaureate address to Anne's class. On that Sunday, Anne received permission to use her mother's car to pick up some friends and drive to the service. On the way she had an accident and badly damaged the car, though none of the riders were hurt. She drove on to the baccalaureate service and parked the car with the damaged side near some bushes where no one would see it. When Billy got up to speak, Anne sank down in her chair, very nervous, although she felt sure her father knew nothing of the event. Father Graham gave his address, telling how proud he was of his graduating daughter and what a wonderful Christian she was and had never caused the family any problems. With that the service concluded.

Anne drove ever so slowly back to her home. As she was about to enter the house she hoped against hope that her father would be in his study and she would not have to face him right then. She just couldn't face up to confessing the accident at that moment after all the sweet things he had said about her. She was scared to death.

As Anne walked in the house, there stood her father, right in front of the door. He just looked at her. Anne burst into tears and threw her arms around him, sobbing, and confessed it all. Billy said, "Anne, I knew all along you had wrecked the car. A lady came up to me before the baccalaureate address and told me all about it. I've been waiting for you to come. I want you to know I love you. I'm glad you were not hurt. We can fix the car, and you will be a better driver now."

Reflecting on that event, Anne said:

In that one day I learned more about God than ever before. You know, we all get involved in "wrecks" and God knows all about it. He is just waiting for us to come and tell Him about it. We should not hide from God or run away. He will forgive us, He will tell us He loves us and make us a better person for it. That's how our heavenly Father is. Daddy has made it easier for me to know God and love Him. I've seen Godliness lived out in my parents. Mother said, you cannot make your children like spinach if every time they see mother or dad eat it they gag.[61]

Billy does exemplify a gracious, understanding, Christlike character in the family. All the children give a like testimony to Billy Graham as a father. Gigi said, "I saw Daddy live what he preached." Anne stated, "They set the tone for our lives by the way they lived theirs." Bunny said, "As busy as Daddy was, he spent time with me, he loved me, he prayed with me, he cried with me, [and] that will always be a special memory." Franklin stated, "I think back on those lonely times and say it was worth it all to sacrifice that time with Daddy so they [unbelievers] could come to faith in Christ." Ned said, "Their love and prayers have guided me all my life, including my own commitment to Christ."[62] Ruth, Billy's wife, summarized it well when she said, "Your attitude to God, your husband and your family must create an atmosphere of love, appreciation, and encouragement which every family needs."[63] And that too is very much Christian godliness.

HUMILITY

One of the reasons that Billy Graham relates so well, not only to the family, but to all people, is his incredible humility. He has said, "Spiritual pride, because it trusts in one's own virtue rather than the grace of God, is earmarked for God's judgment."[64] As pointed out so often, Billy Graham's humility is evident to all. When he first went to Hungary to preach, the only thing the Methodist superintendent knew of Billy was his reputation as "God's Machine Gun." After he met and got to know the evangelist, he said, "I know now the strength and power of Billy Graham—his humility."[65] Billy truly does want all glory to go to God. He always says, "Anybody can preach better than I can." He means it. Anne Graham Lotz says her father is actually rather timid. He has no unwarranted pleasure in all the accolades he receives, but he thanks God for the marvelous ministry our Lord has granted him. As Martin's biography pointed out, "Graham's humility stands in paradoxical tension with his understandable delight, also real, in his fame and accomplishments."[66]

In Billy Graham's quest for godliness he also strives for Christ-honoring relations with his team. In many interviews of team members by this author, they without exception hold Billy in highest regard for his humble godliness; and that is not simply because he is their "boss." Their admiration is real.

Furthermore, Graham's godliness manifests itself in the context of his holistic approach to the ministry. When Billy's children were young, he had a concern to help them learn to share in the needs of others. So when the children received a gift of money, which they often did, the parents created a "Help Fund." All the gifts the Graham children received were put in the fund. When a needy person came to their attention, the fund would be opened and that need met. The lesson was learned. Anne said, "My father's entire ministry came from his own person; he genuinely loves people." And perhaps that genuineness was displayed most clearly when Billy Graham was confined at the Mayo Clinic in Rochester, Minnesota, in the summer of 2000. He was very ill and felt perhaps that God's time to call him home had come. He had wonderful peace and anticipation of meeting Christ. He was in the same frame of heart as John Wesley in his last days when the founder of Methodism said, "The best of all, God is with us."

Despite all the pain Billy experienced in those difficult days, he showed genuine concern and affection for the nurses and medical staff. He always displayed sincere interest in them and attempted to minister to them. His focus, as daughter Anne said, "was on Jesus; he had such a sweetness and gentleness while under great pressure and discomfort." On one occasion earlier when Billy was confined in North Carolina, the nurse, not a committed Christian, said of the evangelist, "I have seen Christ in him." That personifies godliness.

THE SOURCE

The essence of Billy Graham's personal quest for godliness emanates from his understanding of the work of the Holy Spirit as so often seen. He has said, "In the struggle for righteousness, there is nothing more helpful than being passionately related to Christ through His Spirit."[67] The essence of it all is, as Paul expressed it to the Galatians, the Spirit "forms Christ within" (Gal. 4:19).

In this "forming" process Graham sees several definite steps. These moral principles are *absolutes*. Billy has said, as seen, "According to the Bible, morals are not relative—they are absolute and unchangeable."[68] The postmodern world-view, which denies moral absolutes, would do well to hear and heed Billy's word. Moreover, these discipleship precepts are not a burden. As Graham has said, "This invitation to discipleship is the most thrilling ever to come to humankind."[69] But Billy does not cut corners on the cost of discipleship. He states, "To take up the cross means that you take your stand for the Lord Jesus no matter what it costs. It means crucifixion of self."[70] He outlines these costly absolutes as follows:

- We must recognize our spiritual poverty.
- We must make sure we have received Christ as our personal Savior.
- We must maintain a contrite spirit.
- We must be sensitive to the needs of others.
- We must not be a half-Christian.
- We should be filled with the Spirit.
- We must be grounded in the Bible.
- We must witness for Christ.
- We must practice the presence of God.
- We must develop a taste for spiritual things.
- We must not be critical of others.
- We must not be envious of others.
- We should love everybody.
- We should stand courageously for the right.
- We should learn to relax in Christ.
- We must not be victims of paranoia.
- We must remember that we are immortal and live forever.

In this prescribed manner, Graham sees godliness achieved.[71] It is a tall order to be sure; but as Billy has said, "Christ gives you supernatural power to live the Christian life."[72] In a word, "The Christian life is not a way 'out' but a way 'through' life."[73]

SUMMARY

What can now be said by way of summary of Graham's grasp of personal godliness? It can all be brought together quite succinctly in Billy's own words: "We need to keep close to our Shepherd."[74] One observer has pointed out that Graham is a man with a passion to stay close to Jesus and do God's will. Melvin Graham, Billy's younger brother, said, "I have never met a person so concerned to do the will of God. He is steeped in prayer, shedding tears to find God's will."[75]

John Stott has said, "What is most captivating about Billy is his sincerity. There isn't an iota of hypocrisy in the man. He is real."[76] T. W. Wilson called him "the most completely disciplined person I have ever known."[77] Perhaps it can be reduced to this: Graham exemplifies pure integrity. He himself has said, "Integrity! That is what I have worked for all of my life: integrity."[78] Graham thus presses on as he sets before himself the quest for godliness and deeply desires to see it in his own life and ministry and that of his entire team and converts. It should be clear that his personal passion for godliness has colored his entire ministry. That leads to this next major point.

GODLINESS FOR THE TEAM

One of the first moves that Graham and the team made in their early ministry was the framing of the aforementioned Modesto Manifesto. They were sensitive to the image that mass evangelists had acquired through the years. The well-known novel by Sinclair Lewis, *Elmer Gantry*, had focused on scraps and pieces from the lives and ministries of various evangelists. Lewis put it all together, personalizing it in the life of his character Elmer Gantry. Gantry was a stereotype of insincerity, exploitation, and fleecing of followers. Later a Hollywood movie was made based on the book.

When Graham and the early team were conducting a crusade in Modesto, California, he and his associates became exceedingly sensitive to how some people felt about evangelists. They determined something must be done that would dispel possible accusations that he and his team were not operating on the basis of purity, integrity, and honesty. In a word, Graham wanted godliness to permeate not only his own personal life, but also that of the entire team, creating a positive image for his work. Billy well understood. As he himself said, "It seems to me that an evangelist, and the clergy for that matter, especially faces temptations in three areas: pride, money, and morals."[79]

In that context, in November 1948, before the great 1949 Los Angeles crusade burst on the scene, Graham called Bev Shea, Grady Wilson, and Cliff Barrows to his hotel room and said, "God has brought us to this point, maybe he is preparing us for something that we don't know. Let's try to recall all the things that have been a stumbling block to evangelists in years past, and let's come back together in an hour and talk about it and pray about it and ask God to guard us from them."[80] The group left, then they reassembled and began to look at the various pitfalls and possible problems that could lie in the future.

The first issue to be addressed, quite obviously, would be money. Evangelists have often been accused of fleecing the people. That had to be dealt with. The second problem was personal purity. There has always been the innuendo that some in the Lord's workers were guilty of sexual sins. Two other problems surfaced as well: inflated publicity—making statements that were not true about the success of a campaign—and criticism from local pastors. They determined they would be ethical and act with integrity on all of these issues.

Billy and his companions formulated an outline for themselves of simple, effective rules that would keep them from "all appearance of evil" (1 Thess 5:22 KJV). They drew up a document that—with later modifications following the formal organization of the Billy Graham Evangelistic Association—included the following:

THE MODESTO MANIFESTO

Honesty: It was resolved that all communications to media and to the church would NOT be inflated or exaggerated. The size of crowds and number of inquirers would not be embellished for the sake of making the B.G.E.A. look better. . . .

Integrity: It was resolved that financial matters would be submitted to a board of directors for review and facilitation of expenditures. Every local crusade would maintain a policy of "open books" and publish a record of where and how monies were spent. . . .

Purity: It was resolved that members of the team would pay close attention to *avoiding* temptation—never being alone with another woman, remaining accountable to one another, etc. A practice of keeping wives informed of their activities on the road and helping them feel a part of any and all crusades they undertook would be encouraged. . . .

Humility: (Encouragement and edification of ALL believers) It was resolved that members of the team were never to speak badly of another Christian minister, regardless of his denominational affiliation or differing theological views and practices. The mission of evangelism included strengthening the body of Christ as well as building it![81]

This summary of the Manifesto, supplied by Cliff Barrows, is developed in Billy Graham's autobiography *Just As I Am.* Billy Graham has taken all these commitments so seriously that, as Sterling Huston quotes him, the evangelist has said, "If ever I were to do anything dishonoring to Christ, I would rather He take me home to heaven before I did it."[82] That sums it up quite well.

As the ministry grew, the Manifesto grew in like manner. The basic foundations had been laid, but the principle had to be applied in many new areas of service (see Appendix E).

A recent development of the principle of godliness contained in the Modesto Manifesto came out of the great Amsterdam 2000 Conference for itinerate evangelists. It reads:

A COVENANT FOR EVANGELISTS
AMSTERDAM 2000

As a company of evangelists called and gifted by God to share the good news of Jesus Christ throughout the world, we earnestly pledge ourselves to:

1. **Worship** the one true and living God. Father, Son and Holy Spirit (Deut 6:4);

2. **Submit** to the Holy Scriptures, the infallible Word of God, as the basis for our life and message (II Tim 3:16–17);

3. **Proclaim** the gospel of Jesus Christ, God's Son and our Redeemer, the one and only Savior of the world (Acts 4:12);

4. **Seek** always to preach and minister in the power of the Holy Spirit (Acts 4:29–31);

5. **Live** a life of constant personal prayer, Bible study and devotion to God, and also be a part of a local fellowship of believers (James 4:10; Heb 10:25);

6. **Pray** that all persons of all languages and cultures may have access to the gospel and the Bible (Acts 1:8);

7. **Practice** purity in both singleness and marriage, caring for our family and bringing up our children in the nurture of the Lord (Eph 5:25; 6:1–4);

8. **Walk** humbly before God and our fellow human beings, renouncing arrogance, pride and boastful self–promotion (Micah 6:8; Eph 4:1–2);

9. **Maintain** financial integrity and accountability in all of our activities, so that the cause of Christ may not be discredited (I Tim 6:10–11);

10. **Serve** the needy and oppressed, remembering the mercy and compassion of Jesus (James 2:14–17);

11. **Encourage** the discipling and nurturing ministry of local churches (Matt 28:19–20);

12. **Work** together in unity with our brothers and sisters in Christ (John 17:23);

13. **Equip** others for the practice of evangelism, giving special care to involve new believers in the sharing of their faith (Eph 4:11–13);

14. **Stand** in solidarity with our brothers and sisters in Christ who suffer persecution and even martyrdom for their faithful gospel witness (II Cor 1:8–11).

Knowing that apart from Jesus Christ we can do nothing, we make these pledges with prayerful reliance on His help. As we do so, we ask for the prayer and support of Christ's followers so that world evangelization may be advanced, the church built up and God glorified in ever-increasing measure.

There is little doubt that in the final analysis, the effect of such efforts at godliness for the BGEA and all evangelists has been most positive despite criticisms that are bound to arise, such as the false round of criticism concerning the so-called twenty-three-million-dollar "secret fund." As mentioned previously, that negative media blitz and its quick demise stands as a token of the moral integrity of the Graham team and the realization that the innuendos of the *Charlotte Observer* were unfounded. No evangelist has enjoyed a greater reputation of integrity than Billy Graham or an organization like the BGEA. All criticisms have virtually fallen to the ground. The principles of the Modesto Manifesto worked. They guided Graham and the team and have projected an image of positive acceptance among the general populace. Rare anymore is the accusation of any impropriety on the part of Graham or his team. And the challenge he has given to others has no doubt saved many an evangelist from pitfalls.

Significant is the fact, as stressed, that Billy Graham wanted godliness not only in his own life, but obviously for the entire team. He realizes, as he has said, "Those entrusted with leadership bear a special responsibility to uphold the highest standards of moral and ethical conduct, both publicly and privately."[83] Of course, there have been problems on rare occasions when a member of the BGEA has fallen into error, serious error. But with the hope of redemption that person is counseled, prayed for, and helped in every way possible in hope that the error might be rectified and the person, whoever he or she may be, would come back into fellowship with Christ. However, if all efforts failed, the person was quietly dismissed and rarely were accusations made public. In this way the BGEA has kept intact its image of a genuinely godly Christian organization.

It is needless to say that team members are encouraged to engage in the Christian disciplines. Not only that, Graham does all he can to instill the principle of godliness in those who make decisions for Christ.

GODLINESS FOR THE CONVERTS

Graham deeply desires to see those who come to Christ during the crusades and the various BGEA ministries grow into godly Christian maturity. He has said, "Converts (or 'inquirers' as we call them) need encouragement and instruction. Evangelism is more than simply encouraging decisions for Christ. It is urging people to become disciples, followers of Jesus Christ."[84] Billy points out, "Parents do not abandon a baby at birth, but nourish and protect the life of that child. So evangelists are to assume responsibility for those born into the family of God under their ministry."[85] Billy Graham is most sensitive to the fact that when the Word goes forth, as Jesus taught in the parable of the sower, not everyone who hears the gospel will be moved to the extent that they will end up as a fruit-bearing Christian. In an interview Graham was asked, "As you see people coming forward in your campaigns . . . to make their decision, what do you think when you see hundreds of people coming forward? What thoughts are going through your mind?" Graham answered:

> The "Parable of the Sower" in which Jesus indicated there were four types of soil that the Word of God lands upon. A fourth of those will go on to grow in the grace and knowledge of Christ and become true disciples, but three fourths of those will not. For various reasons they will drop out. Maybe the pressure and allurements of the world, or maybe the materialism, or whatever it may be will wipe it all out. And Jesus spelled it out very carefully in the gospels and I don't know that one could say that a fourth—he didn't say a fourth—but he had four different categories and I have always thought in any group that comes forward to make a commitment, if I preached the gospel faithfully, a fourth of them will be there five years from now or ten years from now.[86]

So Billy is quite conscious of the reality that there will be those who will "fall away." Nevertheless, he does not take this casually. He is most concerned about seeing holiness developed in the lives of those who do respond to his invitation to receive Christ. This endeavor takes various forms. In that aspect of ministry, much is owed to Dawson Trotman of the Navigators organization and Charlie Riggs, who for years developed the entire program of follow-up for the inquirers at the crusades.

COUNSELING

The Billy Graham Evangelistic Association trains the counselors who deal personally with each individual who makes a decision during the crusades. Below is an outline of the steps they are taken through and the principles in which they are instructed to help responders make genuine commitments to Christ. A general introduction is presented and then four basic subjects are addressed in four sessions as follows:

General Introduction

Welcome to the Christian Life and Witness Course. You are joining thousands of others who through the years have attended a similar course in preparation for Christian service. Before the course begins it will be helpful to answer a few basic questions.

Who is the Christian Life and Witness Course for?

It is for every Christian who wants to know Jesus Christ better and wants to share Him with others. When you became a Christian, He gave you new life by the power of His Spirit in you. It is the knowing and sharing of this new life that this course is designed to strengthen. All followers of Jesus Christ can benefit from sharing together in this way.

Why is this course necessary?

It is always a good thing for Christians to have this type of course for preparation and training. In the Christian life there are always new lessons to learn. For those who are participating in the upcoming evangelistic event it is of special importance. This course will equip each of us to effectively share our faith. In addition, anyone who desires to be used as a counselor must attend the course.

Lesson One

   The Effective Christian Life

Lesson Two

   The Victorious Christian Life

Lesson Three

   The Christian's Witness

Lesson Four

   Follow-up and the Care of New Christians[87]

When a person makes a decision, that very night his or her name immediately goes to a central place in the city where the crusade is held. After every card is processed, the type of decision, along with the name and address of the person, is sent to a local pastor and church that same evening. The purpose, of course, is that the church will follow up on those who do make commitments. On a night when many decisions are recorded, it is not unusual for the workers to be up until one o'clock in the morning processing the decision cards so that a local church will have the information as soon as possible. Moreover, the counselors are required to make a personal contact with each inquirer within forty-eight hours of their decision at the crusade.

Furthermore, each person who makes a decision is not only personally counseled when he or she comes forward and then contacted within two days, he or she receives a packet on helpful materials on how to begin his or her walk with Christ.

One set of materials is entitled *Living in Christ*. It contains a copy of the Gospel of John, a section on "Words of Encouragement from Billy Graham," and instructions on how to use the booklet along with many promises that the Bible gives to believers. There are also a number of Bible lessons that the new convert can study. Scripture memorization cards are included as well. Four aspects or disciplines of living for Christ are presented under the following headings:

1. The Bible is food for the spiritual life.

2. Prayer is your lifeline to God.

3. A Christian is to be Christ's witness. You are an ambassador for Him wherever you go.

4. You can't be an effective Christian on your own . . . get involved in a church.[88]

These are sound words of advice and encouragement for the new believer.

Moreover, there are special guides and helps for children who make decisions for Christ. One booklet is entitled *Thank You Jesus; Discovery Book* and another *Jesus Loves Me*. Following the general line of the adult programs and helps, these booklets are designed to help children begin their walk with Christ. Actually, the program is quite thorough. It significantly helps the young convert to acquire a beginning understanding of living the Christian life.

Another book given to inquirers is entitled *30 Discipleship Exercises: The Pathway to Christian Maturity*. This is a Bible study book for small groups. It deals with subjects concerning the Lordship of Christ, the Assurance of One's

Salvation, Obedience to the Lord in the Christian Experience, How to Pray, How to Walk in Victory, the Place of the Church in the Believer's Life, Understanding the Fruits of the Spirit, Love, God's Providential Care, etc. It quite thoroughly covers the gamut of Christian experience. Not only does this help new converts, but it also aids those who make recommitments to Christ. And, of course, *Decision* magazine is given to help in the spiritual maturity process.

A booklet entitled *Friendship Evangelism* outlines a five-step program on sharing one's faith. It reads:

1. Look AROUND—Your missions field is right where you live, work or go to school. List names of individuals you know who need Jesus Christ. Pray for them regularly.

2. Look UP—God changes people through prayer. Pray each day for the people on your list, asking God to give you opportunities to talk about His love with them.

3. Look OUT—Find ways to cultivate friendships with the people on your list. Earn their confidence; spend time with them . . . Friendships open the way to talk about Christ.

4. Look FORWARD—Talk with each person on your list about attending a special evangelistic event with you. Choose a specific date and invite them.

5. Look AFTER—Those who respond to Christ or show interest in the gospel need your encouragement. Continue to pray for those who respond to the gospel and those who do not.[89]

This too helps develop believers in their quest for spirituality.

CONTINUED CONTACT

The BGEA keeps in touch with those who make decisions for at least one year after the decision is recorded. Bible study groups are often organized in cities where a crusade has been held. The pastors are contacted to see if they have followed up on the contacts. Then the pastors are contacted again. The BGEA does all it can to see that those making decisions are cared for and nurtured.

Churches that rise to the opportunity and attempt to assimilate inquirers into the life of the church have usually seen quite remarkable growth.

DO THE CONVERTS LAST?

Through the years, as pointed out, a major criticism of mass evangelism has been that converts don't "stick." Graham is most sensitive to this accusation. Of course, he realizes from the parable of the sower that some will fall away; it was true even in Jesus' ministry. But it surely has become evident that Graham does all within his power as a mass evangelist to mitigate the problem. The BGEA spends large sums of money to give help and guidance to the inquirers. Billy wants to see discipleship and godliness emerging out of the crusades. The churches that involve themselves in the crusades and follow the BGEA's guidelines in most instances receive a positive response in numbers and in their own spiritual maturity. As a case in point, when this author taught in Spurgeon's Theological College in London, he found many in the ministry today are there because of the British Graham crusades. And like testimonies are forthcoming from many parts of the world, America being no exception. To amass these sorts of statistics is most difficult if not impossible. But it does seem fair to say the lasting results of the crusades are quite good, as good at least as most churches experience in their own evangelistic ministries. And it cannot be refuted that Billy Graham is most sensitive to developing lives of godliness and Christian maturity in those who make decisions in his meetings and doing all he can as an itinerant evangelist to see it come about.

A FINAL ISSUE

Finally, it seems quite correct to state that the spirit that surrounds the Graham ministry profoundly touches many. The impact on the converts is obvious in multitudes of lives. The effects of the crusades among the ministers are also quite phenomenal. Those who volunteer for the work are likewise often deepened in their spiritual life, especially the counselors. An interesting statistic emerges in that setting. Ten percent of those who take the counselor training program come to personal faith in Jesus Christ themselves; that is, they experience for the first time Christ's salvation. Others, uncertain concerning their spiritual experience, often find the assurance of salvation in their training to help others.

It seems indisputable that the spiritual impact of the ministry in an area where Graham holds a crusade is most positive. It may well be true that the very fabric of society, if not transformed, is surely influenced positively for Christ and civic righteousness.

CONCLUSION AND HISTORICAL CONTRIBUTION OF BILLY GRAHAM TO GODLINESS IN EVANGELISM

Billy Graham is a man of God, and he genuinely wants that for every phase of his personal life and work. Once in an interview he was asked what he would like the first line of his obituary to read. Billy answered, "He was faithful and . . . he had integrity. I would like to be considered a person who loved God with all my heart, mind and soul."[90]

This explains why there is such a positive spin-off from the life and ministry of Billy Graham. Society can be glad for a godly man with that emphasis. The Bible says, "Righteousness exalts a nation, but sin is a disgrace to any people" (Prov. 14:34). This being true, it may be right there that Graham has made one of his greatest contributions. When just one sinner repents, there is not only rejoicing in heaven, many on earth do the same. The godly are the "light of the world" and the "salt of the earth." The more "light" and "salt," the better the world. The influence of Graham on society and culture because of the millions who have been converted and now live changed lives is really significant for the conservation of a viable social structure. True, the crime rate and immorality still climb, but one wonders what it would be like if Graham had not led many to Christ and into a life of godliness.

Not only that, Billy Graham has become a role model for many. This can be seen from three perspectives. First, Billy has set a high standard for other evangelists, pastors, and preachers. Church leaders, with few exceptions, hold him in high regard and emulate his life and commitment to the cause of Christ. Second, Graham has been a challenge to the spirituality of a multitude of true believers. The church of Jesus Christ looks to him as an example of godly living and faithful service to his Lord. Finally, Graham, because of his godliness, has been something of a challenge to the many who have not yet come to faith in Jesus Christ. It is difficult to ignore such a man of God. When he speaks, many listen, even if they may disagree. And he leads those who do listen with an open mind out of the "world" into the kingdom. Most societies are groping for role models and heroes. Graham has made his contribution filling that need. Truly, "a little leaven leavens the whole lump" (1 Cor. 5:6). And what is that "leaven"? It is love. The basis, root, and fruit of all godliness is love, God's quality of love. This is the "fruit of the Spirit" Billy Graham exemplifies.

Many years ago, in a city about to be destroyed, Abraham prayed that the destruction be diverted. God said, "I will not destroy it on account of the ten [godly men]" (Gen. 18:32). Think, if only ten godly people were in the city, God would have preserved the whole city. Society is far more dependent on godly believers than it ever realizes. Therein, evangelist Billy Graham, a man utterly committed to leading everyone he touches to Christ and godliness, makes his mark. Biblical evangelism emanates in godliness and holiness. That is historically and contemporarily a rich blessing indeed.

CHAPTER 11

REVIVAL IN EVANGELISM

~~∽~~

PART I:
JOHN WESLEY AND THE
EIGHTEENTH-CENTURY AWAKENING

About three in the morning, as we were continuing instant in prayer,
the power of God came mightily upon us.
—JOHN WESLEY

INTRODUCTION

The Puritan-Pietistic era reached something of its climax in the dramatic spiritual awakening that epitomized Western Christianity in the eighteenth century. Britain, Europe, and America experienced true revival. As Britain moved into the new century, the dawn of the Great Awakening sent its first ripples of the tide to come. Giants of the revival arose, men such as George Whitefield in England, Howell Harris in Wales, William McCulloch in Scotland, Jonathan Edwards in New England, and Theodore Frelinghuysen in New Jersey. Perhaps above all, John Wesley of Oxford personified the spiritual movement. At the time, revolutionary change dominated Western culture. The ferment of those days needs to be understood. The sociological upheaval in one sense created the hunger for God to do something unusual and great.

AN ERA OF UPHEAVAL

Strong elements in the general British political religious establishment lashed out against the Puritans. For example, the "Expulsion of the Non-Jurors" was directed to undermine Puritan influence and power. "The Suppression of Convocation" that culminated in the Conformity Act of 1711 brought extreme difficulties to dissenters. Not only that, the established clergy had seriously degenerated. Many clergymen never saw their own parish but still received a handsome stipend. They lived lives of revelry in London, never opening their Bibles.

The political scene was even worse. In Green's short history of the English people, he said:

> Of the prominent statesmen of the time the greater part were unbelievers in any form of Christianity, and were distinguished for the grossness and immorality of their lives. Drunkenness and foul talk were thought no discredit to Walpole. A later Prime Minister, the Duke of Grafton, was in the habit of appearing with his mistress at the play. Purity and fidelity to the marriage vow were sneered out of fashion, and the Lord Chesterfield in his letters to his son, instructs him in the art of seduction as part of a polite education.[1]

Samuel Johnson observed, "The apostles were tried regularly once a week on the charge of committing forgery."[2] Such indictments depicted the decline in theological and moral standards. Deism was on the ascendancy and had been enthroned by many.

Morally and ethically, the situation among the general populace of Britain appeared every bit as degenerate. A slogan bandied about declared, "Get drunk for a penny or dead drunk for two pence." The pubs and brothels enjoyed a roaring business. The crime rate rose at an alarming pace with little effective police action. Renaissance rationalism from Europe had invaded British society, and with it came the collapse of the basic values that the Puritan era had ingrained into the British populace. But right in the midst of it all, God powerfully intervened and sent a great revival.

A NEW CLIMATE DAWNS

The new awakening witnessed its early beginnings in Wales. In the seventeenth century, a significant work of grace had manifested itself in the ministry of Walter Cradock. Then, Griffith Jones began his preaching ministry in Wales as the eighteenth century dawned. It became something of a precursor of the Wesley-Whitefield revival.

In 1716, Jones took up his service as rector of Landdowror. He also served as a traveling evangelist. Although many of the established clergy refused their pulpits to him, the common people heard him gladly and he made a significant impact on the masses with many coming to faith in Jesus Christ. He actually became the founder of Welsh Methodism. The notable Daniel Rowland was converted under his ministry. As previously mentioned, Howell Harris, known as the most successful preacher who ever ascended a pulpit or platform in Wales, made his ministry felt. He significantly impacted the Welsh-Calvinistic Methodist movement. Even though Harris began in an obscure fashion, conducting worship services in his mother's home, his ministry exploded over the land. He was warmly supported by the Countess of Huntingdon, as God did a great work through him.

ACROSS THE ATLANTIC

Under the preaching of Increase and Cotton Mather, an awakening was born in the American colonies. The well-known Gilbert and William Tennent also made their contribution to the American version of this awakening. They had been influenced by Theodore Frelinghuysen, a leading Pietist. Of course, the life and ministry of Jonathan Edwards in early America constitutes an epic in itself. Space precludes going into further detail, so suffice it to say, Edwards's service to Christ in Northhampton, Massachusetts, spawned the revival that became known as America's First Great Awakening. His famous sermon, *Sinners in the Hands of an Angry God,* stands as a literary classic and is read and studied even in secular universities to this day. Again, evangelism flourished. They were wonderful days.

THE MAN OF REVIVAL

Now we must look at one particular figure who so beautifully embodied the movement: John Wesley. It may seem almost a crime not to give equal space to George Whitefield. Some historians contend that Whitefield was actually more influential in the British Awakening than John Wesley, at least in the early years of the movement. Few would disagree that in pulpit eloquence and persuasive power Whitefield was perhaps equaled only later by Charles H. Spurgeon.

But the reason Wesley is better known than Whitefield centers in the fact that Whitefield died young and did not possess the organizational skills of Wesley. Moreover, his writings were rather meager. On the opposite end of the pole stood John Wesley. He lived well into his eighties and ministered and published prolifically right up to the end. Furthermore, he excelled as an organizer and administrator. He synthesized and structured the movement in a lasting fashion. Virtually every Methodist church in the world—for it ultimately became a worldwide movement—acknowledges Wesley's contribution. Thus we look to the life of John Wesley as the champion of revival for evangelism.

WESLEY'S LIFE AND EARLY MINISTRY

Historian James Burns calls the Wesleyan movement "one of the most important events in modern religious history."[3] Most agree. John, along with his brother Charles, ultimately made an incredible contribution to the evangelistic scene of the entire world.

The Wesley brothers grew up in the town of Epworth in Lincolnshire. Their father served as vicar of the local Anglican church. Their mother, Susanna, will always be remembered as a spiritual giant. She gave birth to nineteen children and would take time each day to tutor each child in the things of Christ. John's great-grandfather, an Anglican priest, was turned out of his parish by the Act of Uniformity in 1662. Their grandfather suffered imprisonment due to the Five Mile Act. John inherited a diverse but wonderful heritage.

John Wesley was born in 1703, four years before the birth of his younger brother, Charles, the great hymnologist of the eighteenth century. Congregations around the world still sing Charles Wesley's hymns every Sunday. While the children were yet quite young, their home became engulfed in flames. The family fled, but when Susanna counted the children she realized one was missing. Suddenly in the window of the second story of the home stood little John. A local citizen rushed to his rescue and dragged him out to safety. John always considered himself "a brand plucked out of the fire" (Zech. 3:2 KJV).

The Wesley home constantly struggled for the necessities of life. Father Wesley could hardly be called an astute man with his resources. He saw himself as a writer and spent a good deal of time in London attempting to get his works published. Nevertheless, the family fared reasonably well, and John and Charles gained admission to Oxford University to prepare for the Anglican ministry.

While at Oxford, John and Charles (although some years separated their venture in Oxford) formed the Holy Club. Charles started the club, and John joined later when he came on staff. In the Oxford Holy Club setting, George Whitefield became a close friend of the Wesleys. The term "Holy Club" did not have a derogatory connotation in those days. The negative nickname they received was the "Methodists." They got that moniker because of their methodical way of attempting to achieve holiness. They were up at four o'clock each morning for the study of the Word of God and prayer; their religious enthusiasm and zeal knew no bounds.

John had studied at the Charter House School in London before settling in Christ's Church College in Oxford where he took his Master of Arts degree in Latin, Greek, Hebrew, French, and logic. In that setting he read Jeremy Taylor's *Holy Living and Holy Dying*. This classic Puritan work impressed him tremendously. After a period of time, John Wesley traveled to America. He went as a missionary ready to win the Native Americans to Christ and establish an orphanage work.

THE TRIP TO AMERICA

On Wesley's voyage to America, his small ship ran into a terrible storm. He was beside himself, simply terrified. On the same vessel, a group of Moravian missionaries were on their way to minister in America as well. The contrast between the peace and assurance that the Moravians seemed to have and the turmoil in John's mind struck him significantly. He wondered how anyone could have such peace in the midst of such a situation. When he landed in

America, he became acquainted with a Moravian missionary by the name of Spangenberg.

During one conversation with John, Spangenberg asked him, "Do you know Jesus Christ?"

"I know he is the Savior of the World," John replied.

"True," Spangenberg affirmed. "But do you know that he has saved you?"

Wesley replied, "I hope he died to save me."

Later Spangenberg said, "I fear they were vain words."[4] John had no assurance of his salvation, even though he had given himself to the Anglican priesthood, graduated from Oxford University, and even served as a missionary to primitive America. He spent eighteen months in North America and boarded a ship back to England with this testimony: "I went to America to convert the Indians, but, oh, who will convert me?"

CONVERSION

Back in Britain, John and Charles met another Moravian minister by the name of Peter Boehler. He deeply influenced the seeking brothers; they had to find peace in their hearts. Then on May 21, 1738, Charles came to a dynamic conversion experience. But John still languished in spiritual turmoil. Then three days later came the famous citation in his journal on May 24, 1738. John penned these words:

> In the evening, I went very unwillingly to the Society in Aldersgate Street, where one was reading Luther's preface to the Epistle to the Romans. About a quarter before nine, while he was describing the change wrought by God in the heart through faith in Christ, I felt my heart strangely warmed. I felt I did trust Christ, Christ alone, for salvation; and an assurance was given me that He had taken away my sins, even mine, and saved me from the law of sin and death. I began to pray with all my might for those who had in a more especial manner despitefully used me and persecuted me. I then testified openly to all there what I now first felt in my heart.[5]

At last, after a tremendously difficult struggle, salvation had come to John Wesley. Even after this dramatic experience, Wesley had his times of doubt. He said, "It was not long before the enemy suggested this cannot be faith . . . for where is thy joy?" He finally learned that the transports of joy that attend the beginning of saving faith sometimes fade. He was beginning to learn to walk by faith. But God had more to give the Wesleys and Whitefield. It became known as a little Pentecost, but more of that in a moment.

Later John married Mary Vaseille. It proved to be a very unfortunate marriage. Many of his friends had urged him not to marry Mary, but he insisted. Home life degenerated into a most disruptive relationship, so bad that at times she would literally grab John by the hair and pommel him. He said, "My wife is the secret of the success of my ministry—she kept me on my knees." He did not mean that as facetiously as it may sound. One day Mary left. To this day, no one has discovered what took place that precipitated the separation and her virtual vanishing off the pages of history.

After his conversion, John Wesley traveled to Herrnhut and to the estate of Nikolaus von Zinzendorf, where he again came under the influence of the Moravian movement. But now we must come back to the important event that took place a few months after John's saving experience of Christ.

THE FETTER LANE LITTLE PENTECOST

On January 1, 1739, just a few months after John's Aldersgate experience, he met with a group of Moravians welcoming in the New Year with Bible study and prayer. Early on the New Year's morning in a little building on Fetter Lane in central London, God's power fell on the group. The quotation from John's journal is so significant that it must be quoted just as he wrote it:

January 1, 1739
Mr. Hall, Kinchim Ingham, Whitefield, Hutchins, and my brother Charles, were present at our love-feast in Fetter Lane, with about sixty of our brethren. About three in the morning, as we were continuing instant in prayer, the power of God came mightily upon us, insomuch that many cried out for exceeding joy, and many fell to the ground. As soon as we were recovered a little from that awe and amazement at the presence of His Majesty, we broke out with one voice, "We praise Thee, O God; we acknowledge Thee to be our Lord."[6]

The Fetter Lane dramatic outpouring of the Spirit actually launched the great revival.

THE WESLEYAN REVIVAL

Several significant things immediately began to take place in the context of the awakening that began to break over Britain. First of all, the common people heard the gospel, regardless of the fact that many pulpits were closed to the Wesleys. George Whitefield rose to the challenge, breaking new ground by preaching in the open air, though at first Wesley thought it strange. In his early reluctance to preach in the fields, John did not believe anyone could be saved outside a church building. He learned differently, though he found it difficult in those first days of the awakening. He said on one occasion, "I submitted to be more vile 'standing on a little grassy mound,' preached . . . to a great crowd from the words 'the Spirit of the Lord is upon me because he hath anointed me to preach the gospel to the poor.'"[7] But God used the new method powerfully. Wesley yielded to God's leading and people responded by the tens of thousands.

Taking to the fields, this approach actually became something in the inauguration of the modern mass evangelism. That boded to be most significant for future evangelism. At times, especially in the larger metropolitan areas like London, people would gather in numbers of twenty to thirty thousand. The effectiveness of John's preaching in this setting is well known. As an example, one observer wrote:

> What was the secret of Wesley's power as a preacher? asks Fitchett. In many respects it might be imagined that he was the last man to sway an eighteenth-century crowd. He was a gentleman by birth and habit, a scholar by training, a man of fine and almost fastidious taste, with an Englishman's uneasy dislike of emotion, and a High Churchman's hatred of irregularity. He had little imagination, and no descriptive power. He told no anecdotes, as a rule, and certainly fired off no jests. What fitness had he to talk to peasants, to miners, to the rabble of the city, to the slow-thinking farmer drawn from the plough-tail? Yet he stood up, a little, trim, symmetrical figure; his smooth black hair exactly parted; his complexion clear and pure as that of a girl; his hazel eyes flashing like points

of steel. And beneath his words the crowd was melted and subdued until it resembled a routed army shaken with fear and broken with emotion; men and women not seldom falling to the ground in a passion of distress. . . . There was something in his discourse—a note in his voice, a flash in his eye—that thrilled the crowd with awe, awe that not seldom deepened into dread. The mood of the speaker was one of perfect calmness. But it was the calm of power, of certainty, of an authority which ran back into the spiritual world.[8]

Wesley's preaching took on a style that appealed to the average, working person, leaving the strictures of the sophisticated sermons to the established clergy. John's method was quite simple. First, he would preach God's law, and when conviction of sin ran deep, he would preach grace. As a preacher, John, along with George Whitefield, became the epitome of what constitutes great evangelistic preaching. Moreover, evangelism through music made its impact in those days. Charles Wesley, of course, excelled here.

WESLEY'S LABORS

Wesley labored tirelessly, preaching for more than fifty years. In true revival spirit, he was virtually obsessed with reaching people for Christ. As one historian put it:

In those fifty-one years he was said to have traveled 250,000 miles, in days when there were no railroads, and when the roads themselves were dangerous; and to have preached 42,400 sermons, or an average of more than two per day for every day in these fifty-one years. Nor were the sermons themselves of ordinary length, sometimes lasting for two hours, and addressed to crowds reaching even to 30,000 people. As a mere feat of physical endurance this is perhaps without a record. He relates, for instance, that in one day he rode a distance of more than ninety miles, and at the end was little more tired than when he rose in the morning. No hardship of storm or weather deterred him. His engagements were made in advance, and on he went through snow or sleet or rain, encountering a thousand obstacles, yet scarcely ever acknowledging defeat. Often when he had entered some quiet spot, after some exhausting journey, the temptation to rest presented itself to him in alluring forms. Here are some characteristic entries:

March 17, 1752: At the Foundry. How pleasing it would be to flesh and blood to remain at this little quiet place, where at length to weather the storm! Nay, I am not to consult my own ease but the advancing of the kingdom of God. Ten thousand cares are no more weight to my mind, . . . than ten thousand hairs on my head.[9]

This is certainly not to say John was a mere activist. On the contrary! In his home, which still stands on the site once called the Foundry, one can enter a small room and see a little kneeling bench. Every day for two hours John Wesley fell on his knees on that bench. He prayed and sought the salvation of all he could reach. His well-known motto read: "The world is my parish."

THE LAST LABORS

The time would come, however, when John would be called to be home with the Lord. He had reached eighty-six years of age, and now his tireless work began to show signs of weakness. In 1789, for the first time, this admission appears in his journal: "I now find I am growing old."[10] The following year, he also penned in his journal, "I am now an old man, decayed from head to foot. My eyes are dim, my right hand shakes much."[11] Yet, the evangelistic fire still burned in his soul and he added to this last citation, "I can preach and write still."[12] He did continue to write and to preach, and that very effectively. But the end drew near.

Wesley preached his last sermon in the magistrates' room at Leatherhead on Wednesday, February 23, 1791. He chose as his text, "Seek the LORD while He may be found" (Isa. 55:6). His evangelistic fervor still burned. The last letter he penned was a protest against the slave trade. Holistic evangelism, like St. Francis, gripped his heart. In his London home, he met death with the same magnificent fortitude that had characterized his long life. Actually, he greeted it with a cheer. His last words as he lay on his deathbed: "The best of all, God is with us." He went to be with his Lord on the second of March, 1791, worn out by incessant labors, but undefeated in faith and with great peace in his heart. John Wesley will always be known as a revivalist. And out of the revival evangelism with power ensued, as it always does. It will now be helpful to attain a grasp of the nature of real revival and how it directly spawns evangelism.

EVANGELISM PREDICATED ON
SPIRITUAL AWAKENINGS

It has been stated that when a true spiritual awakening settles on a people, evangelism explodes in unprecedented power and effect. History is replete with this principle, and the Bible itself undergirds that reality. In the days of the Old Testament, in times of awakening such as the Hezekiah revival, tremendous influxes of people joined the ranks of dedicated believers. The New Testament, as would be expected, epitomizes the principle of evangelism growing out of spiritual awakening. The Day of Pentecost stands as the classic example of the principle of spiritual awakening and the subsequent ingathering of thousands of new converts to the church of Christ.

THE PRINCIPLES OF SPIRITUAL AWAKENING

In his historic work *Revival, Their Laws and Leaders,* James Burns proposes several "laws," or biblical principles, of great awakenings or revivals. Some writers make a distinction between the terms "revival" and "spiritual awakening." But the majority of historians use the words interchangeably, which shall be done here.

Burns tells us that the essence of real revival can be seen in the fact that it always generates new spiritual life in and through the church. This in turn culminates in great evangelistic results. In that dynamic process several scriptural realities, or "laws," come to the fore.

THE LAW OF PROGRESS

Burns's first point is that God always progressively works in the world. This progressive work of the Holy Spirit is not a steady move upward, however. It ebbs and flows. There seems to be a protracted period with little movement, then suddenly a fresh surge of the Spirit lifts the church to the heights. Although the general trend of God's work is always upward, the progress is characterized by "ups and downs." The "ups" are the revival times. How vital these revival seasons are! Burns states:

Revivals are necessary for the spurring of man to high endeavor, and for the vitalizing of life. Were progress to be uniform—no part of man's nature moves until the other parts move also—advance would be so slow that life would stagnate. There could then be no high hopes, no springtide of exulting life, no eager and impetuous rush forward. Progress would be so slow as to be imperceptible, and man, robbed of high inspiration, would cease to hope, and cease to struggle. By the breath of revival life, however, God keeps the world in eager activity, and keeps the human heart ever fresh with hope. The consequence: progress and growth. Something like this kind of progress always typifies true awakenings.[13]

THE LAW OF SPIRITUAL GROWTH

Revivals serve as God's instrument for revitalizing spiritual life. When an awakening occurs, Christians are never quite the same again. Lives are radically changed. As seen earlier, the fifteenth-century Florentine revival under Savonarola reshaped Florence, Italy, into a veritable city of God on earth. The Welsh Revival of 1904 radically altered the entire Rhondda Valley of Wales, and the church of Wales came alive as never before. For months many churches stayed open twenty-four hours a day. Tens of thousands were converted. Civic righteousness became so pervasive that crime virtually ceased. It seemed incredible!

Revival results are always the same: profound spiritual growth. This proves true whether limited or extensive in geographical impact, for "the law which moves the mighty tides of the ocean is the same which ruffles the surface of the little pool made by the rain of a summer afternoon."[14]

THE LAW OF PERIODICITY

Law implies an orderly sequence of movements. Do awakenings occur at definite intervals? If so, can these sequences be discerned? If that were possible, we could forecast their appearance with some precision. But this obviously is not the case—history abounds with instances when churches have felt a desperate need for revival only to experience little blessing. Then when least expected, the heavens open. Clearly, the term "law" in this context must not be interpreted legalistically. The Spirit moves as He wills. Yet we may believe that these periodic movements operate on what may be called "divine law," on the basis of the sovereign purpose of God.

This law of periodicity reveals several important facts. First, God is in control of His church and will give His people what they need when they need it. Second, God's wisdom far supersedes ours, and we must always place the timing of these awakenings in the divine economy of things. Third, revivals do not come by caprice because the church does certain things in a formal, structured fashion. Although the people of God have their part, the sovereignty of God stands central in real revival. The law is not mechanical. Perhaps it can be best summarized by saying the needs and activity of the church and the sovereignty of God form the warp and woof of genuine awakening. A general defection from "the faith once delivered to the saints" usually infects the church before revival comes. Dullness and lethargy pervade God's people. Then comes the *fullness of time*. The ebbing spiritual tide has its limits as surely as the ebb tide of great oceans. Apathy and coldness has its end. Actually, the further the tide ebbs, the greater power and force it often gains to return and overflow the arid land.

This ebb tide seems to create among God's true people a deep sense of dissatisfaction. A period of gloom settles in—even to the point of weariness and exhaustion. Sick in soul and heart, men and women turn to God with a deep sigh. Longing for better things, they pray with Jacob of old, "I will not let you go unless you bless me" (Gen. 32:26). And though God may well touch their thigh and they limp through the rest of their days, they prevail. *Revival is always born in prevailing prayer.* This is an unalterable, central principle of awakenings. Prayer opens the door to the fullness of time.

Then comes what Burns calls the *emergence of the prophet*. Revivals have leaders—sometimes one, sometimes many. These leaders tend to be the incarnation of the movement; they personify the awakening in its most intense form. The leader is critically important. He or she gathers up all those intangible longings and ideas dimly felt and then personifies them, epitomizes them, sharpens them, expresses them, and gives them startling visibility.

The prophets effect the movement and vice versa. What kind of people are they? Burns puts his finger on this issue when he says, "Each of these great leaders has in common with all the others an unshakable faith in God, an overwhelming sense of a call to great service, a mysterious equipment of spiritual power which moves mountains, and a determination to do the work he is called of God to do even at the expense of life itself. In the Picture Gallery of the good and great, such men occupy the noblest place."[15]

THE LAW OF VARIETY

Each revival has a uniqueness of its own. No awakening is exactly identical to any other. Society changes from one generation to the next. People differ in temperament and culture. Therefore, the revival must vary to be relevant to its time and place. There seemingly cannot be a single movement that reaches all peoples and all cultures at one and the same time.

Another striking feature centers in the vast variety of appeals in awakenings. At times, the emotional impact predominates, as in the frontier revival of nineteenth-century America. At other times, theological aspects dominate, as was true in the Reformation. Then again volitional decision becomes paramount. The Wesleyan movement pictures that approach. But each movement wins its way because of the particular needs of particular people at particular times. Yet in it all, God works and thus effects a biblical balance. And through the law of variety, the Spirit of God builds up the church. The next consideration Burns calls the law of recoil.

THE LAW OF RECOIL

Every revival ends. Luther said that thirty years was the outer limit of an awakening. Though Luther is probably correct concerning most cases, some revivals have lasted considerably longer—others shorter. The first check of an awakening often comes when the initial emotional tidal wave has run its course. The many who were swept along on the merely emotional level soon fall away. Of course, the more stable effects endure long after the first emotional excitement dies. The church and society are always left on a higher plane.

But even when an awakening is long-lasting, the long-term effects eventually evaporate and decay once again sets in. The Fransiscan revival is an example. In the midst of a corrupt religious scene, Francis of Assisi burst on the scene and God used him to precipitate, as one historian put it, "one of the most remarkable movements in history."[16] Yet within a hundred years the vow of poverty had turned to riches, humility to tyranny, monasteries to palaces, and confession to manipulation. The deterioration so eroded the positive influence of the revival that it finally turned it sour. Therefore, when the awakening comes, this law of recoil must be recognized and prayerfully anticipated. This can help minimize the impact of the reality and save many a tragedy.

THE LAW OF THEOLOGY

Theology changes during revival times. There always seems to be a return to conservative evangelical thought. It takes this course:

1. *A return to simplicity.* Believers break through complex, abstract, obscure theology and get to the basic practical truth of the Scriptures.

2. *A return to New Testament spirit and methods.* There is a quest for the apostolic faith and way of doing things.

3. *The message of the cross.* The gospel, which centers in the cross of Christ and His resurrection, becomes the focal point of preaching.

4. *Liberal, rationalistic, speculative theology fades.* That kind of thought system never brings about awakenings. This does not mean revivals spawn anti-intellectualism. That too is a perversion of the Spirit's work. And at the opposite end of the spectrum, extreme fundamentalism mellows.

5. *Cold orthodoxy is reawakened.* Conservative theological systems can cool and stagnate. Nothing is much "deader" than a dead, cold, rationalistic conservatism. But when revival comes, although the actual theological position of conservatives may not substantially change, it suddenly comes alive and glows.

6. *The salvation of Christ as humanity's greatest need becomes paramount.* In awakenings, evangelism thrusts itself to the fore. Secondary ministries—as important as they are and must be done—are put in their proper secondary place and winning people to personal faith in Christ becomes primary. This is most vital to grasp.

Revivals spawn fervent evangelism, but more of that in a moment.

THE LAW OF CONSISTENCY

Revivals differ, as stressed. Yet there are certain consistent elements that always seem to appear. First, when the awakening breaks, a deep sense of sin will be awakened. For example, Jim Vaus, a man whom we met earlier, was involved in syndicated crime before his conversion in Billy Graham's 1949 crusade in Los Angeles. After his conversion he made restitution for all he had stolen. It wiped him out financially. Vaus even changed his testimony in a court case in which his perjury had sent an innocent man to jail. It was as Paul said, "I exercise myself, to have always a conscience void of offense toward God, and toward men" (Acts 24:16 KJV).

Second, the *fullness of the Spirit* is sought. Another facet in our revival jewel that always glistens brightly centers in the fullness of the Holy Spirit. After cleansing comes fullness. The Bible abounds with this idea. On the Day of Pentecost, "they were all filled with the Holy Spirit and began to speak in other tongues, as the Spirit gave them utterance" (Acts 2:4 RSV).

Then comes *fullness of joy*. After cleansing and fullness, God pours out His Spirit of love, joy, and peace (Gal. 5:22). The happiest people who have ever lived are the revived. Burns states, "There is a joyousness and elasticity of spirit, and a hopefulness. . . . This is the effect of a revival wherever it appears. It irradiates the atmosphere; it leaves in its track numberless happy men and women whose faces are aglow with a new light, and whose hearts throb with an intense and pure joy."[17]

Finally, *effective evangelism* follows the effulgence of joy. Joy must be shared. The church burns to bring others to Christ, and the unbelieving community is so attracted by what is going on in the church that they come by the multitudes to discover what is happening (Acts 2). When the reviving Holy Spirit falls on the church, the multitudes come and are "bewildered" (v. 6), "amazed and marveled" (v. 7), and finally throw up their hands in intellectual despair and cry out, "What does this mean?" (v. 12). This becomes the context of great outreach. When unbelievers begin to ask questions instead of criticizing, then the gospel can be effectively communicated.

In a word, when God breaks in on the church and truly revives His people, then the Spirit reaches the lost in unprecedented numbers. It all comes about because God's people are at last purified and geared for ministry and witness. All the people of God engage in the warfare. When an awakening arrives, the whole company of Christians are so revived that service for Christ abounds. Acts 2 climaxes with the words, "The Lord was adding to their number day by day those who were being saved" (v. 47). Every awakening gives testimony to this principle.

CONCLUSION

In light of all that has been said, surely hearts well up with the cry of the psalmist as he prayed:

> When the LORD turned again the captivity of Zion, we were like them that dream. Then was our mouth filled with laughter, and our tongue with singing: Then said they among the heathen, The LORD hath done great things for them. The LORD hath done great things for us; whereof we are glad. Turn again our captivity, O LORD, as the streams in the south. They that sow in tears shall reap in joy. He that goeth forth and weepeth, bearing precious seed, shall doubtless come again with rejoicing, bringing his sheaves with him. (Ps. 126:1–6 KJV)

That is when the church will evangelize as God intends it to do.

In such a setting, John Wesley did his monumental work. Great spiritual awakenings have always unfolded on the basis of these principles set forth. Again let it be said, the pouring out of the Holy Spirit and the infusion of new spiritual life into the church of Jesus Christ always lays the foundation for great evangelism. To the degree that the Holy Spirit is operative in and through the life of the church, to that degree evangelism becomes effective.

A simple poem puts it rather succinctly. It may not be in the best of English styles or theological acumen, yet it makes the point. The poet wrote:

> A city full of churches
> Great preachers, lettered men
> Grand choirs, organs' music
> If these all fail, what then?
> Good workers, eager, earnest
> Who labor hour by hour?
> But where, oh where, we ask

> Is God's almighty power?
> Refinement, education
> They have the very best
> Their plans and schemes are perfect
> They give themselves not rest.
> They give the best of talents
> They try their uttermost
> But what they need so clearly
> Is God the Holy Ghost.

The great need of the hour always is, in the words of Habakkuk the prophet, "LORD, I have heard the report about Thee and I fear. O LORD, revive Thy work in the midst of the years, in the midst of the years make it known; in wrath remember mercy" (3:2).

May God move the contemporary church in awakening power. So we must ask, Has Billy Graham seen this biblical and historical perspective of evangelism and made a contribution to that end?

PART II:
BILLY GRAHAM AND REVIVAL

Revival is essential.
—BILLY GRAHAM

INTRODUCTION

"Western culture had its fruits and its foundations in the Bible, the Word of God, and in the revivals of the seventeenth and eighteenth centuries."[18] With these words Billy Graham has struck the note that Western civilization owes much of its spiritual richness to great revival periods. He appears quite sensitive to spiritual awakening and its centrality in the shaping of church and culture. Right at the start of this look at Billy Graham and revival, it will be well to hear more of the evangelist's own words on this issue.

BILLY GRAHAM SPEAKS ON REVIVAL

In his book *Storm Warning*, Billy Graham sends out the alarm, "Without a sudden and massive world-wide revival of God's people and a return to the morality and the values set down in the Word of God, the earth is already under the condemnation of God, and its judgment will be swift, unavoidable, and total."[19] This theme has been sounded through the history of evangelism, and Graham has taken up the chorus with the multitudes that have gone before.

Graham is quick to recognize that if evangelism is to be effective in reaching the multitudes for Christ, it rests solely in the hands of the Holy Spirit using God's people as His agents. This has been reiterated often. When the church fails in its task or becomes spiritually "unhealthy," it stands to reason that Graham makes an appeal for a true reviving move of God upon Christian believers. Thus, in the setting and in the context of his crusades, Graham appeals for revival and awakening among the people of God. Effective evangelism depends on it. In a sermon entitled "America's Lost Frontier," published in 1962, he laid down this dictum: "What do we need? I say tonight at the outset of this crusade, we need a great national spiritual awakening. We need a revival from God. We need to hear from the heavens. We need to come apart and listen to God. Or, I tell you here tonight, we're in for judgment."

One writer has raised some pertinent questions in the light of such declarations from the evangelist. He asked, "What is the phenomenon called a 'Great Spiritual Awakening'? What, precisely, does 'to hear from heaven' mean? How, exactly, can individuals fulfill the need for such an awakening?"[20] Pertinent questions, to be sure! But it must be granted that Billy Graham is alive to what occurs during a great spiritual awakening and its importance. He knows, for example, what revival has meant to Western culture. He states, as already quoted, "Western culture and its fruits had its foundations in the Bible, the Word of God, and in the revivals of the seventeenth and eighteenth centuries."[21]

Moreover, it is noteworthy that something of at least a national spiritual stirring occurred in the early years of Graham's ministry. William McLoughlin, a writer in this area, contends that from 1945 to 1970, America's "Fourth Great Awakening" coursed through the American culture. There are those who will take issue with McLoughlin's thesis, however. For example, Wayne S. Bonde, in a Ph.D. thesis submitted at Southern Illinois University in 1973, said, "From all indications, America has been experiencing, from 1945 to the present, not a 'Great Awakening' but rather a religious awareness."[22] Christianity was riding the crest of the wave of popularity. Church attendance soared, contributions mounted, and unprecedented sums were spent on new church buildings. Perhaps something of the climax of the spiritual stirring of these years can be seen in the "Jesus movement" of the 1970s. That phenomenon touched multiplied numbers of that segment of the American population known as the "hippies." Many young people, caught up in the movement, were profoundly touched with the gospel of Jesus Christ. Further, there has been a significant continuation of those refreshing days in the founding of the so-called megachurches. Thus there is a positive lingering effect to the movement. But was it a true spiritual awakening, or is Wayne Bonde correct in stating that the movement was very positive but did not attain the profundity of a great awakening?

It does seem correct to say that though America was perhaps not experiencing a spiritual awakening of the magnitude of the First Awakening under Whitefield, Edwards, and others, it was an important time during which the church did grow and attained a new level of spiritual health. Many of the American people became alive to the importance of religious faith to a far greater degree than before. Churches grew as evangelism flourished.

Billy Graham is sensitive to the phenomenon because it was in this context that he launched his crusade ministry. Thus it becomes understandable why Graham would be sensitive to the reality of spiritual stirrings and plead for a deeper, more profound experience of God's reviving Spirit. As the religious spirit of the 1950s and 1960s declined, his appeal for revival became increasingly relevant.

Graham, conscious of the growing secularization and materialism of American culture, continually calls the nation to spiritual awakening. As a case in point, while speaking on one occasion from the podium of Caesar's Palace, in Las Vegas, Nevada, while coins were cascading into nearby slot machines, he said, "A spiritual awakening in this state could do more to touch America than any other state." Graham makes continual pronouncements to that end for the nation. As late as 1997, in the San Francisco crusade in October of that year, he said to the thousands gathered, "I hope when this crusade is over, we won't let the spirit that has developed die. And that we will see a great spiritual awakening."

As American society continues to deteriorate with the escalation of crime, corruption, violence, secularism, and immorality, more and more the need of revival asserts itself. In the face of these facts, Billy Graham cried out that only a great revival "would purge America of the rats and termites that are subversively endeavoring to weaken the defense of this nation from within."[23] Setting forth the need of revival, Graham wrote a small work entitled *Revival in Our Time*. In that volume he said, "We need a Holy Ghost, heaven-sent revival!"[24] Then he quoted 2 Chronicles 7:14: "If my people, which are called by my name, shall humble themselves, and pray, and seek my face, and turn from their wicked ways; then will I hear from heaven, and will forgive their sin, and will heal their land" (KJV). He summarized it by saying, "I believe that God is true to His Word, and that He must rain righteousness upon us if we meet His conditions."[25] Graham does appear to understand well the nature and need of true revival for a degenerate society.

THE WORLD'S NEED

Graham feels the concern and need for revival far beyond the confines of American society, however. He clearly longs for revival wherever he goes in the world. In the Japanese crusade in 1994, he said, "We revel in the joy and renewal He is bringing to this land. Yet we know this is only the beginning: the church in Japan is now being awakened—the full harvest is yet to be gathered." One of the most thrilling experiences for the evangelist, as he acknowledges, was to see the revival spirit throughout South Korea. Mention has already been made of the tremendous gathering in Seoul when more than one million came together to hear him preach the Word of God. It would seem the Pacific Rim is on the verge of revival, and in some places the movement has already broken out. Billy Graham, conscious of the need worldwide, lifts up that standard.

In Berlin, Graham recounted before a crowded church how Martin Luther and other spiritual giants had ministered in that country in Christ's name. He said to the German people, "I believe that a strong revival can spring from Germany, if Germany does not miss the chance."[26] He then asked each person to make a new commitment to Jesus Christ that night to seek revival, and hundreds of hands went up. Billy said, "There was, indeed, a sense of renewal and revival in that church."[27] Such has been the evangelist's approach around the world. When Graham was preparing for his Toronto crusade of 1955 he listed five purposes: "(1) To stir the city out of religious indifference; (2) To arouse hundreds to commit their lives to Christ as Lord and Master; (3) *To bring a spiritual revival to the churches and church members;* (4) To see a definite moral and spiritual as well as a social impact left in the community; and (5) To exalt not Billy Graham, but the 'Lord and Savior, Jesus Christ who died on the cross for our sins.'"[28]

Perhaps Graham's awareness of the need for worldwide revival is best expressed in a London sermon, in which he said:

> I would call you back to the God of Wesley and Whitefield. I would call you back to the God that your fathers and mothers worshipped. And I would call you back to the God that made Britain the greatest nation that the world has ever known. I would call you back to the principles that govern British life, spiritually and morally. I would call you back to home life that once we knew on these islands, and once we knew in the United States and Canada.

Quite obviously, Graham is calling the nations to return to God. And simply put, that constitutes the essence of revival. Hopefully, it has become clear that Graham visualizes a great awakening as the greatest need of the hour. This now leads to Billy Graham's basic views and more detailed understanding of a true spiritual awakening.

BILLY GRAHAM'S CONVICTIONS

In an insightful volume entitled *Revival and Revivalism*, Ian Murray has said:

> What happens in revivals is not being seen as something miraculously different from the regular experience of the church. The difference lies in degree, not in kind. In an "outpouring of the Spirit" spiritual influence is more widespread, convictions are deeper, and feelings more intense, but all this is only a heightening of normal Christianity. True revivals are "extraordinary," yet what is experienced at such times is not different in essence from the spiritual experience that belongs to Christians at other times. It is the larger "earnest" of the same Spirit who abides with all those who believe.[29]

James A. Stewart has likewise observed, "A church that needs to be revived is a church that is living below the norm of the New Testament pattern. . . . It is a tragic fact that the vast majority of Christians today are living a sub-normal Christian life. . . . The Church will never become normal until she sees revival."[30] It would seem that Billy Graham essentially agrees with Murray and Stewart. Revival is a return to "normal" New Testament experience. And the church and individual believers certainly need that reviving touch.

In this light, Graham confesses that his crusades are not revival in the historic, "overwhelming" sense of the word such as the Great Awakenings of the eighteenth century. As Lockard in *The Unheard Billy Graham* points out, "He [Billy Graham] is careful to clarify the distinction between evangelism and revival. He is an evangelist, but God alone brings the revival."[31] As has been made clear, Graham sees his role as essentially that of an evangelist, declaring the gospel to the unconverted. At the same time, however, he most sincerely and ardently prays that his work would help to spark real revival, or at least make some contribution to a genuine spiritual awakening. That is to say, that biblical, "normal" Christianity will be practiced. And that for a very good reason, as Billy explains:

> Revival and evangelism are not the same. Revival is concerned with the renewal of God's people; evangelism is concerned with those who have never known Christ. But the two are ultimately connected. When God's people are truly revived and renewed spiritually, it results in a new vision for a lost world and a new commitment to reach out to those who do not belong to Christ. Evangelism is the fruit of revival.[32]

Billy is aware of the difference between—yet interdependence of—revival and evangelism. He summarizes it by saying, "In preparation of evangelism, *revival is essential*."[33] And when the two unite to impact the world for Christ, that gets at the heart of what Ian Murray calls "normal" Christian experience.

Others share that same view and anticipation of revival. As a case in point, in the Rio de Janeiro, Brazil, crusade in 1974, one of the leading pastors in the city, Dr. Nilson Fanini, was reported as saying, "Dr. Graham's coming could have a catalytic effect in initiating the revival he longs to see."[34] Concerning the crusade in Boston in the early days of Billy Graham's ministry, one has evaluated

Graham's influence and contribution with these words: "If what followed fell short of the great awakening, short of Jonathan Edwards and George Whitefield, it did cause dry bones to rattle in normally sedate New England. To the degree revival came, it sparked a commensurate measure of evangelism."[35] But the question is, What does Graham see as the conditions of true revival?

GOD'S SOVEREIGNTY IN REVIVAL

Graham understands, as of first importance, that revival emerges from the sovereign grace of God. God sends revival, and He does it as He pleases in His own way and timing. Billy would agree completely with Jonathan Edwards, God's spokesman in America's First Great Awakening. Concerning revival, Edwards said, "Its beginnings have not been of man's power or device and its being carried on depends not on our strength or wisdom."[36] It comes, Edwards contends, as God wishes. Yet our Lord uses human instrumentality. And what constitutes that human element in a spiritual awakening? God moves in answer to the prayers of His people.

PRAYER BRINGS REVIVAL

Graham fully recognizes that revival, in the purest sense, comes through persistent prayer along with the faithful declaration of the Word of God. As Billy Graham tells us, "John Wesley prayed, and revival came to England, sparing that nation the horrors of the French Revolution. Jonathan Edwards prayed, the revival spread throughout the colonies. History has been changed time after time because of prayer. I tell you, history could be altered and changed again if people went to their knees in believing prayer."[37] This appeal goes out to the entire church; but pastors, preachers, evangelists, and leaders should especially give heed. Billy, in his *Biblical Standard for Evangelists,* appeals for revival prayer, and he also gives a succinct definition of what happens in a real revival. He said, "The . . . appeal in this final affirmation is for 'the Body of Christ' to join us in prayer and work . . . for revival. The greatest need for God's people today is a true spiritual revival—a fresh outpouring of the Holy Spirit on the Church, a profound experience and turning from sin, and a deepening commitment to God's will in every aspect of life."[38]

Prayer, the Word, and the sovereignty of God always weave the pattern of genuine revival. As the church begins to sense the need of an awakening and engages in fervent prayer, the sovereign God is at work. Thus Graham makes much of the necessity of prayer and prays for a real revival himself. Melvin Graham, Billy's brother, has said, "Billy prays for revival more than anything else."[39]

One of the evangelist's early prayer experiences for revival praying occurred some six months before the Spirit's outpouring in Los Angeles in 1949. During a Youth for Christ all-night prayer meeting at Winona Lake Conference Center, Indiana, Billy Graham stood up at three o'clock in the morning and read Joel 3:14: "Multitudes, multitudes in the valley of decision: for the day of the LORD is near in the valley of decision" (KJV). In that meeting God fell mightily upon them and they experienced a true touch of personal revival. Six months later came the Los Angeles crusade. From such encounters with the Holy Spirit Billy declares, "Understanding the consequence of sin and arrogance, I believe it should be the duty of every Christian to pray for repentance and revival in the land. We must do the work of believers, as Paul instructed, we must also seek the face of God as never before. I believe it is time we led the world to pray."[40]

Graham applauds prayer movements such as the National Day of Prayer, calling it "a remarkable event." Communities across America engage in prayer vigils on the steps of their city and town hall buildings and various venues— Washington, D.C., being no exception. Tens of thousands meet to pray for a revival of the Christian faith in the land. Graham said, "I believe this is the kind of commitment we must make in order to turn things around."[41] One year in Spokane, Washington, more than 180 teenagers gathered to pray for solutions to the problems of drugs, violence, and promiscuity in their schools. In Atlanta, Georgia, church members met on the steps of the state capitol to pray. Texas witnessed twenty-five hundred teenagers meeting for a concert of prayer in their city's coliseum.

In his administration, President George Bush Sr. decreed a National Day of Prayer, and as Graham described it, the day was "a wonderful outpouring of God's Spirit." He went on to say, "This is precisely the kind of fervor and dedication it will take on a nationwide scale to bring about the change and revival in our land." Graham clearly recognizes prayer as essential. It is all quite encouraging, for as Sterling Huston has recently said, "Prayer in the last ten years is unprecedented."[42] God sovereignly moves in response to prevailing intercession. But what about human instrumentality; does God need a man or woman if He chooses in His sovereignty to revive the work?

HUMAN INSTRUMENTALITY

It will be well remembered that James Burns in *Revivals: Their Laws and Leaders* states that one aspect of a genuine awakening is normally what he calls "the emergence of the prophet." There may be an occasional exception to the rule such as the Prayer Revival of 1858, during which no one leader arose. Still, normally, in most revival movements a great man or woman usually arises on the scene, lifted up by God's sovereignty. The Bible is witness to this principle. For example, Deborah led a significant revival whereby God brought victory to Israel. In church history the same pattern has constantly emerged. Time fails to tell of men and women like Jonathan Edwards in early America and Madame Guyon of France. Even in the contemporary moment revivals are flaming around the world and great prophets are on the scene.

Now if it is true that human instrumentality does not conflict with the sovereignty of God in such movements, then does Billy Graham see himself in the role of a revival prophet? He certainly longs to see revival and stresses the need constantly, but he is the first to admit he is not a revivalist in the strict sense of the word. Yet it must also be said that he does from time to time see a touch of real revival, and such moments always thrill him tremendously.

Perhaps the closest to an awakening came in Graham's early ministry. The Los Angeles crusade of 1949 surely saw something of a true revival spirit in that Southern California setting. Then almost immediately after the close of the Los Angeles meeting, Billy and his team traveled to the Boston area. Allen Emery, who served for many years as chairman of the board for the BGEA, relates the incredible sequence of events that took place in New England. The high points unfold as follows:

- Saturday night a rally was held in a large hall with much criticism from certain church circles. Nonetheless, the hall was filled to overflowing.

- A Sunday afternoon rally was planned for 3:00 P.M. By 1:30 P.M. the hall was jammed and the fire marshal closed the doors. Many inquirers came forward at the invitation.

- Then the Symphony Hall was acquired. It was filled to capacity.

- Next the Opera House was acquired and it overflowed.

- Finally, Boston Garden opened its doors and the largest crowd ever assembled in that venue gathered to hear the evangelist.

And through it all, multitudes were converted from every walk of life: newspaper reporters, people in bars, and many more. It was a true touch of God's reviving hand in that part of America that gave birth to the First Great Awakening. Then there were London and Harringay. This story has been related earlier, but it will help to see it from a revival perspective.

THE HARRINGAY CRUSADE

As a pattern in all revivals, initially a sense of need arises. In 1954, Britain had come through the Second World War battered and bruised. There was a feeling of futility in the minds of many. Rather strangely, in a nation that in the Victorian era had been known for its church attendance and Christian approach to life, the British people had all but vacated the churches. Most churches were more than half empty on the Lord's Day. A pervasive secularism reigned.

In that setting, hundreds of churches in London invited Billy Graham to conduct a crusade. Would he be the emerging prophet whom God could use to rectify the dismal spiritual scene? Graham began preparation by bringing as many people as possible together for prayer. Billy well knew that prayer stands as the key instrument of assault on the spiritual vacuum of any country. Many believers sensed the need and gave themselves to fervent intercession. An air of expectancy began to grow as Billy boarded the ship and sailed to England. Again, as is often the case when revival seems near, Graham met much opposition and resistance. The liberal theologians were hard on the attack. One such critic wrote, "His theology is fifty years behind contemporary scholarship."[43]

At the other end of the religious spectrum, the strict Calvinists objected to his use of the invitation. And it cannot be forgotten, there was still a lingering streak of anti-Americanism in the British people at that time. Then there was the aforementioned problem that developed over the calendar and the mistaken attack on socialism. That caused no small stir. The press claimed, as seen, "Billy Graham not only had the gall to decide that England's religious life needed reviving but attacked a major aspect of its political life as well."[44]

Graham perceived all these dynamics as the harbingers of revival: the desperate need, fervent prayer, opposition to a movement of God, recognition that this was entirely God's work, and the Word being preached. As the "emerging prophet," fully recognizing the work of God's Spirit in revival, Billy Graham preached the gospel with incredible power. Soon the signs of true awakening began to manifest themselves. Converts began to multiply in incredible numbers. Harringay Arena was packed, and people found new life and salvation in Christ through the simple declaration of the Word of God. That is always one of the clear marks of revival. It did seem that revival was on its way to old London.

As already stated, revival begins with its impact on the church. And such was the case in 1954 in London. John Yarbrough, Baptist evangelism leader, believes the Graham ministry has revived many churches in many cities around the world.[45] In the very traditional London scene in 1954, Christians would leave the arena and board buses, the underground, and trains going back to their homes and literally burst out singing. To go down into one of London's underground stations and hear a hymn being raised by a multitude of people, or to ride a London transport bus on which passengers were singing a hymn of praise, was unprecedented in the British scene. The church itself was mightily moved.

Finally, the whole London area came alive to what God was doing. Newspaper, radio, and television commentaries on the movement became daily fare. These unusual things happened in that touch of revival. As one writer put it:

No crusade looms larger in the collective memory and ethos of the Graham organization than the twelve-week effort at London's Harringay arena in 1954. This campaign so defied expectations, so triumphed over skepticism and opposition, and so captured the attention and imagination of the English-speaking world, particularly the British empire, that participants found it easy to believe that they were living in the days foreseen in the rousing revival standard: "From victory unto victory/His army shall he lead/Till every foe is vanquished/And Christ is Lord indeed."[46]

If only in a limited sense, London saw a measure of real revival.

This brings us to the final evaluation concerning Billy Graham and his contribution to historical spiritual awakening.

THE GRAHAM CRUSADES AND THEIR GENERAL IMPACT FOR REVIVAL

All that has been presented above can be summarized in two or three basic concepts. It must be said initially that at times a touch of real revival does break in on the Graham crusade scene. As seen, what occurred in London at Harringay Arena, in Rio de Janeiro, and in Nagaland did precipitate a sense of revival. In the early years in Boston, Billy Graham himself said that he wished he had not been so obligated to other places and could have stayed in the New England area. Graham stated that had he been able to stay longer, perhaps a deep revival would have broken out in that part of the country. He is probably quite correct in that evaluation, because revival seemed right on the horizon and about to dawn in the Boston area.

Second, Graham sees a measure of revival when people become stirred and begin discussing religion. In an interview with David Frost, Graham said that it was his hope that wherever he goes he could "get millions talking and discussing—even arguing—religion. In other words, cause a religious stir. In the book of Acts, wherever the apostles went, there was a 'stirring.' It is better than apathy."[47] This phenomenon often occurs in the Graham meetings and in that sense contributes toward revival. Of course, it is only correct to say that Graham does not always cause a stir in a city. For example, as reported concerning the San Francisco crusade, "The great metropolitan area was barely touched. There was no lifting of the crime rate. The upper stratus of San Francisco and peninsula society, with few exceptions, remained supremely uninterested. There was no outbreak of revival in the traditional sense in the churches."[48] It cannot be said that the crusades have always precipitated a spirit of revival; nevertheless, great steps for the kingdom of God have often been taken in many crusades.

The main point is, however, Billy Graham has a grasp of what constitutes revival and its importance, particularly in a spiritually deteriorating culture. And he longs to see revival in the profound historical, biblical sense; he attempts to impact that need to the churches and calls them to prayer.

Furthermore, it would seem correct to say that the crusades (some more than others) have seen a true touch of revival and have certainly "revived" many an apathetic believer. In Billy's early days, as daughter Anne has said, her father felt he could ignite the whole world to see a great awakening. Now in his older years, he is content to let God be God, knowing he did what he could to spark and foster spiritual awakening. He has always carried a burden of the sense of failing, but as he himself said, "I have done what I could."[49]

Graham has no doubt done far more than he realizes, but still the longing is there. And he well realizes, great evangelism grows out of great awakenings. If asked what would be his greatest desire concerning the outcome of his work, it would be that revival might take place. As previously quoted, he has said, "Without a sudden and massive worldwide revival of God's people and a return to the morality and values set down in the Word of God, earth is already under the condemnation of God, and His judgment will be swift, unavoidable, and total."[50] Graham longs for revival.

CONCLUSION AND HISTORICAL CONTRIBUTION OF BILLY GRAHAM AND REVIVAL

Therefore, it must be granted that as revival plays a vital role in biblical evangelism, Graham deeply desires to see God's actions in such movements through his ministry. Clearly he longs to be used by the Holy Spirit to spawn another Great Awakening to the honor of God and the Lord Jesus Christ and the salvation of souls. Furthermore, as seen, Graham has attempted to light the fire of revival and has in a limited sense been used by the sovereign God to experience at least a measure of revival in his crusades. That is historically valid and it makes a significant contribution to a viable society. Billy Graham the evangelist cries out as a prophet, "Yes we need to be saved—saved from ourselves. . . . Hosea the prophet urged the people of his day, 'Sow to yourselves in righteousness, reap in mercy, break up your fallow ground; for it is time to seek the Lord till He come and rain righteousness upon you' (Hosea 10:12)."[51] And all that speaks well for Billy Graham's decades of ministry—and for the world also. Every generation needs a prophet who will cry out for revival. That is indeed historical evangelicalism and evangelism in its best expression.

INTRODUCTION TO THE
"GREAT" AGE

~

AS SIGNIFICANT AND SWEEPING AS THE eighteenth-century revival proved to be, the movement saw something of its final, full reaping in the nineteenth and twentieth centuries. Historian Kenneth Scott Lataurette called the nineteenth century "the Great Century." It was; and likewise the twentieth century. The firm foundation established by the Puritans and Pietests, coupled with the Great Awakenings that followed, witnessed a rich harvest of converts for two hundred years. The movement gave the gospel such impetus that the church of Jesus Christ at last grasped the whole world in its vision. Two personalities of the two great centuries, symbolic of many others, epitomized the new spirit of the age. William Carey became a missionary to India, and Charles Haddon Spurgeon of London saw kingdom progress rooted in and emanating essentially from the local church. The principles personified by these men and their grasp of kingdom understandings bring to a climax what the Bible and history mean by an evangelism of integrity and authenticity that contributes to the well-being of many people.

We begin our final trek through two thousand years of God's work with the life, labor, and thought of William Carey, an extraordinary missionary.

CHAPTER 12

WORLDWIDE MINISTRY IN EVANGELISM

~⌐

PART I:
WILLIAM CAREY AND THE BIRTH OF THE WORLDWIDE MISSIONS

*[People] cry loudly for every possible exertion to
introduce the gospel amongst them.*
—WILLIAM CAREY

INTRODUCTION

"Through him Christ's great command was born anew." So said T. H.
Holyoak in his sonnet on William Carey. Northamptonshire, England,
boasts of the man known and eulogized as "the father of modern missions."
Although many missionary movements have arisen since the inception of the
gospel ministry through the early apostles, the commitment to bring Christ
to the whole world saw a new birth under the leadership of a simple cobbler
from central England. It must be granted that far more was afoot in those

significant years than the ministry of just one man; actually, the entire modern era of world evangelization had its inception in those days. And Carey served as a key.

CAREY'S PHILOSOPHY

All who knew William Carey recognized him as a keen student, even though he lacked formal university training. He became a master of languages and gave himself to the disciplined study of the Christian faith, particularly Christian history. As he delved into the past concerning the worldwide thrust of the gospel, he came to the conviction that the missionary mandate of Jesus Christ was integral to the very essence of Christianity. He took with deep seriousness the call of our Lord in the Great Commission (Matt. 28:19–20). He knew the message of salvation must be proclaimed to all people.

Through his study, Carey became well acquainted with the successes and failures of the Christian movement through the preceding near two millennia. As a case in point, it disturbed him deeply that a "flood of corruption" had engulfed the church in the wake of the Constantinian revolution. He realized that the quality of professing believers created a situation wherein, as he expressed it, "the professors of Christianity needed conversion as much as the heathen world."[1] Carey recognized the church had had its down times. However, on the heels of a spiritual "slough of despond," to use John Bunyan's words, great awakenings came. That is exactly where Carey found himself. The church needed to rise out of the valley and once again climb to the missionary mountaintop.

As depicted in the previous historical era, the Puritans and Pietists had acquired something of a grasp of the world mission cause. For example, a group of Pietistic students from the Universities of Halle in Germany and Utrecht in the Netherlands banded together some ninety years before Carey embarked to India and sailed to that nation, bringing the gospel to the people. Moreover, the Moravians, who had been significant in the conversion of Wesley, exemplified a fervent missionary zeal. These forerunners Carey saw as most significant to the cause of world evangelization. When the great eighteenth-century revival broke on the scene, the hope for a new worldwide thrust of the gospel began to be realized.

A NEW SPIRIT

That new spirit had its birth in prayer. In 1784, at the Northamptonshire Baptist Association meeting, a leading pastor, John Sutcliff, preached to the assembled ministers and messengers. He called upon his fellow Baptists to inaugurate a "concert of prayer" in their churches. He challenged them to meet on the first Monday of every month and seek God for revival and the spread of the gospel. The churches responded. Andrew Fuller, a very significant personality in the missionary movement, recorded in his diary: "December 6, an affecting meeting of prayer of this evening for the revival of real religion." Carey himself participated in the prayer meetings as revival began to touch their lives significantly. A new day was dawning.

But what kind of a man was this simple cobbler from Northamptonshire? That query yields a fascinating story.

THE EARLY LIFE OF WILLIAM CAREY

William Carey came into the world on August 17, 1761. The Wesley-Whitefield revival had been in full force for more than two decades. A marvelous harvest was being reaped as a significant new spiritual atmosphere swept across Britain. The revival impacted not only the church, but much of society as well. As often pointed out, historians—even those of the secular world—contend that the awakening saved Britain from the bloody fate that wreaked havoc across the English Channel during the French Revolution.

The obscure village of Paulerspury, in the county of Northamptonshire, was the site of Carey's birth. As is so often the case, as one giant passes off the scene, another is born. In the year that William Carey came into the world, William Law, a giant of evangelical spirituality, went to be with the Lord. Could Carey take his place?

William Carey was the firstborn of five children who came into the home of Edmund and Elizabeth Carey. Edmund worked as a weaver until William was six years old. Everyone recognized little William as a precocious child. He could read the Scriptures while still a small boy. His father said, "He was always attentive when a boy."[2] Although he read in many areas of science and history, his favorite book—like that of Charles Haddon Spurgeon, whom we shall meet in the next chapter—was John Bunyan's *Pilgrim's Progress*. He devoured every page of Bunyan's classic.

As a child, William loved his land. He would walk through the English countryside, admiring God's wonderful creation. This fascination with nature seemed to destine him for life as an agriculturalist. However, by the age of seven, he had developed several severe allergies. So his parents apprenticed him to a shoemaker. Working indoors he could avoid the pollens and irritants of the verdant countryside. At the early age of fourteen, William moved to the nearby town of Piddington, where he practiced his trade. Cobblers in those days made shoes as well as repaired footwear. This profession provided him his livelihood until he reached the age of twenty-eight. Yet his heart was not in it.

CONVERSION

William had been brought up, as had virtually every English lad, in the established Church of England. The local vicar baptized him in that communion, but Carey said that it had left him "wholly unacquainted with the scheme of salvation by Christ . . . real experiential religion, I scarcely heard anything till I was fourteen years of age."[3]

During that general period, he met John Warr, a fellow worker in the cobbler shop with William, who was a very effective witness for Christ. John had led many to the Lord. Through Warr's witness, God began speaking to William's heart. Slowly, Carey came to the realization of the seriousness of his sin and his total lack of ability to do anything to save himself. As a young man, he had lived an unholy life. As God's Spirit continued to speak to his heart, his conviction of sin deepened.

Carey did try to change his lifestyle. He resolved he would not live and speak and act as he did. But as the Holy Spirit continued to convict him on a Christmas trip to the city of Northampton, he came to the realization of how shameful he really was. He knew he must experience an entire change of heart if he would ever find peace with God. At long last, he was brought, as he said in his own words, "to depend upon a crucified Savior for pardon and salvation; and to seek a system of doctrines in the Word of God."[4] He found Christ.

Immediately upon his dramatic conversion, Carey began to share his faith with others, as his friend John Warr had shared with him. When he would travel back home to Paulerspury, he always witnessed to his relatives and friends. For William Carey, winning people to Christ became so central to his faith that he simply had to see others experience the wonderful salvation of Jesus Christ. A burden for the extension of the kingdom of God was deepening in young William's life.

CAREY AND THE DISSENTERS

On Sunday, February 10, 1779, King George III proclaimed a national day of fasting and prayer. The prayers centered in seeking God's grace in their recent defeat by the American colonies. Again, William's friend John Warr rose to the occasion and urged Carey to go with him to a worship service in a dissenting, nonconforming congregation. It seemed strange for a zealous Anglican to go a dissenters' meeting. The service was held in Carey's village of Piddington. There were an ample number of dissenters in England at the time. For example, in 1662, more than two thousand Anglican clergymen left the Church of England when Parliament passed the Act of Uniformity.

It must be granted that Carey held some prejudice toward the dissenters. But at the meeting in Piddington, Thomas Charter, a guest preacher from Olney, brought a stirring message on the cost of discipleship. In his sermon, Reverend Charter quoted Hebrews 13:13: "Let us go out to Him outside the camp, bearing His reproach." Those words so struck the heart of William that he realized God's purpose for his life meant he must go "outside the camp," bearing the reproach of Christ, and attach himself to the dissenters, also known as nonconformists.

Not long afterward, in the summer of 1782, Carey attended a Baptist dissenters' meeting at Olney. Early giants of the Baptist faith attended this meeting, men such as John Ryland, John Sutcliff, and Andrew Fuller. Fuller preached and deeply moved William. By this time Carey had become a full-fledged dissenter, but he was not quite sure about the particular Baptist distinctives Fuller espoused. Carey continued to give himself to the study of the Scriptures and soon arrived at the conviction that believer's baptism should be by immersion *after* one had come to faith in Jesus Christ. As this conviction gripped his heart, he applied for baptism at the hands of John Ryland. William Carey gathered with John Ryland and three deacons from the College Lane Church on the banks of the river Neane on a Sunday morning in October 1783. Willliam was baptized "in the name of the Father, the Son, and the Holy Spirit," and the die was cast.

THE NEXT TEN YEARS

Ten years after William Carey's baptism, in 1783, he boarded a ship headed for India as a Baptist missionary. It cannot be emphasized too strongly what a significant moment it proved to be when Carey set his face to the East. The ten years prior to his sailing had not proved easy for Carey, however. He always struggled with a very limited income. He also suffered with sickness and many hardships that fell across his path. In 1781, Carey married Dorothy Plackett at the church in Piddington. He was not quite twenty years old and she twenty-five. Dorothy was illiterate and even had to mark her own marriage license with an "X." Everyone knew her as "Dolly." The hope for a happy home followed.

Sadness soon struck the family, however. Their firstborn daughter, Ann, died at only two years of age. Carey himself contracted the same fever that took his lovely little daughter, and he came close to death. During William's illness, his mother came to care for her son. One day she asked a friend whether he felt William would ever become a preacher. The friend replied, yes, "and a great one, I think, if spared."[5]

God did spare William, and he became a very effective preacher. William continued to work at the cobbler's profession as his commitment to evangelism kept growing in his life. More and more he realized the entire world needed Christ, not just his English friends and acquaintances. The call to preach had come, and a new vision was born.

THE PREACHER AND PASTOR

Carey's formal preaching ministry began when the dissenters at Earl's Barton called him to preach every other Sunday. Then John Sutcliff felt that Carey should be set aside for the ministry in a regular ordination service. Carey united with Sutcliff's church in Olney. The Olney church had been touched by the evangelical awakening. John Newton, who penned the words to

"Amazing Grace," had been rector in Olney at one time. Pastor Sutcliff arranged a trial sermon for William in the summer of 1785. The record of the church relative to the event reads, "W. Carey, in consequence of a request from the Church, preached this evening. After which it was resolved that he should engage again on suitable occasion for sometime before us, in order that further trial may be made of his ministerial gifts."[6] The church duly set him aside for the ministry, after which he received a call to become pastor of the Baptist Church in Moulton.

God blessed the ministry at Moulton. Many new converts came into the fellowship of the church. The first time Andrew Fuller heard Carey preach, he was gripped by the young man's message. On that occasion he walked up to William, seized his hand, and exclaimed, "We must know more of each other."[7] Thus another gigantic step was taken, probably unrealized to either William or Andrew at the time.

Carey's life was hard at Moulton. But as difficult as things seemed, Dorothy and William were very happy in their married life and in the service of Christ. Dorothy submitted herself to believer's baptism in 1787. William rejoiced when he immersed his wife in the waters of baptism.

A NEW CHALLENGE

At that juncture, a much-publicized book came off the press: *The Journal of Captain Cook's Last Voyage.* Cook had been killed by natives in Hawaii in 1779. As Carey read the adventure of Cook's world travels, he became increasingly conscious of the need of bringing the gospel to all nations. The expansion of British influence around the world had centered on financial gain; why could England not bring the gospel of Christ to that world? Carey began to study everything he could lay his hands on concerning the distant lands and the people of the world. He put a large map on the wall of his cobbler's shop (he still made shoes as well as serving the church as pastor) and would work on shoes and pray for the world at the same time. That story is legendary.

The conviction of the need of world missions grew until Carey could no longer contain the burden he felt in his heart. He began to plead with the people to be gripped with a consciousness of Christ's call to the whole world. Through his preaching, his church members began to assimilate the message, as did fellow ministers. Carey pressed his case on Baptist leaders such as Andrew Fuller, John Sutcliff, and John Ryland. Finally, they too were caught up in a fervor to bring Christ to the world.

As William's burden grew deeper, he acquired Greek grammar and soon mastered the Greek New Testament. Before long he had quite well assimilated the Hebrew language as well. His gift for languages held him in good stead for the future. God was preparing him for his great translation work.

A NEW VENTURE

In April of 1789, Carey received an invitation to become pastor of a church in Leicester. Carey felt a wrench to leave the Moulton church, but became convinced that God had called him to his new post. In May of that year he moved his family to Leicester and became pastor of the Harvey Lane Baptist Church. The pastorate in Leicester did not prove an easy one. The membership declined to some extent, as did the people's giving. Discipline problems arose and Carey went through a difficult time. As the problems grew, the church set aside days of fasting and prayer.

Then suddenly a fresh renewal swept the congregation. By the spring of 1791, the situation at Harvey Lane had been reasonably resolved as the challenge of missions continued to deepen in William's life. At this stage, he published a book under the title *Inquiry*. In his work he made a plea for world evangelization. It received a wide circulation and soon Carey's appeal to the churches was heard over an extended area. George Smith has called Carey's book "the first and still greatest missionary treatise in the English language."[8]

Approximately one year later, in May 1792, at the annual Spring Baptist Associational Meeting, a number of ministers and messengers assembled at the Baptist chapel in Friar Lane from twenty-four associated churches. On Wednesday, after an extended time of prayer, William Carey stood up to preach. Carey laid the burden of worldwide evangelization on all those assembled. In his sermon he made the statement for which he is best known, "Expect great things. Attempt great things." Subsequent redactors have changed it somewhat to "Expect great things *from* God. Attempt great things *for* God." But the six words were the original words in Carey's sermon. The sermon became known as the "Deathless Sermon." The world must hear of Christ. It electrified not only the Baptists, but evangelicals of various sorts. Out of that climactic event came the proposal by Andrew Fuller that a Baptist society for propagating the gospel among the "heathen" be instituted. The delegates agreed, and the rest of that story is history.

Carey sailed to India in 1793. After many logistical problems, he boarded the *Princess Maria*. As they sailed past the white cliffs of Dover, Carey visualized the world hearing the gospel—and the Christian world caught the challenge with him.

THE RESULTS

Carey was only one missionary; the Baptists were a relatively small group. Yet this event became such a monumental moment in the ongoing life of worldwide evangelism that it stands as an epic in the furtherance of the kingdom of God. The whole world had at last been recognized as the field for evangelization. The high moment of modern missions had arrived.

After many arduous years of labor in India with its great disappointments and challenges—yet glorious victories—in 1834, William Carey died. As previously pointed out, at the death of one giant of the faith, a new giant often arrives on the scene. That same year, Charles Haddon Spurgeon was born in Kelvedon, England. The torch was passed, as our final chapter in this volume will make amply clear. As Cowper of Olney said, "God moves in mysterious ways, His wonders to perform."

But before we turn to Spurgeon and the principle of church-centered evangelism, we must look at the biblical teaching on the concept of worldwide evangelism and how Billy Graham fits in.

THE SCRIPTURAL BASIS OF WORLD MISSIONS

Missiologist Bill O'Brien has insightfully said, "One of the mysterious paradoxes . . . is the gap between the great love of our Lord held by those in our churches, in missions agencies, missionaries on the field, and their inability or unwillingness to close the gap between the Good News Haves and Good News Have-nots. Have we missed something of the heartbeat and purpose of God?"[9]

One cannot but answer O'Brien's probing question in the affirmative. It does seem the church has so often missed something in our Lord's command for world evangelization. And if so, the church has misunderstood, or perhaps even ignored, the scriptural principle inherent in its responsibility to bring Christ to all the nations.

WHAT THE BIBLE SAYS

As the disciples gathered prior to the Lord's ascension, Jesus delivered what the church calls the Great Commission. He said, "Go therefore and make disciples of all the nations, baptizing them in the name of the Father and the Son and the Holy Spirit, teaching them to observe all that I commanded you; and lo, I am with you always, even to the end of the age" (Matt. 28:19–20). That word should settle the issue once and for all. Worldwide evangelization is God's agenda. But much more can be found in the Holy Scriptures concerning world mission than merely proof-texting the principle with a few isolated passages. A sweep through the entire Bible highlights what constitutes God's mission in the world, the *missio dei*.

THE OLD TESTAMENT MESSAGE

It all began in the Garden of Eden. After the ignoble Fall of Adam and Eve, the Bible tells us that God gave the fallen couple a verbal promise along with a dramatic picture of the restoration of their status before God. The Scriptures declare that the Lord slew animals and clothed them in skins. The Lord God not only covered their nakedness, but by innuendo, some Old Testament scholars believe, God's sacrifice of the animals pictured the great sacrifice that would one day effect complete reconciliation with God. From that moment, God by His Holy Spirit set out on a mission to restore alienated sinful mankind to Himself. Space fails to present a detailed account of the multiplicity of Old Testament accounts that demonstrate God's mission of world redemption. But the overall principle can be seen, for example, in the saving of Noah and his family from the deluge. Then, when Abraham came on the scene and God's commission came to the patriarch, the very essence of the *missio dei* was explicitly declared:

> Now the LORD said to Abram, "Go forth from your country, and from your rel-
> atives and from your father's house, to the land which I will show you; and I
> will make you a great nation, and I will bless you, and make your name great:
> and so you shall be a blessing; and I will bless those who bless you, and the one
> who curses you I will curse. And in you all the families of the earth shall be
> blessed." (Gen. 12:1–3)

God's plan of world redemption moved forward dramatically in the monumental moment of Abraham's call.

Nothing in the Old Testament epitomized God's reconciling redemption
more dramatically than the exodus from Egypt. Although slavery and privation for some four hundred long years plagued the Israelites in the latter part
of their Egyptian sojourn, God graciously stepped in. Crying out to God in
their misery, and God hearing in His mercy, He sent the mighty deliverer,
Moses. The exodus from Egypt stands as a high point of God fulfilling His
saving mission. Through the Red Sea, through forty years of wilderness wandering, then through the river Jordan, Israel entered the Promised Land as
the walls of Jericho fell. God's deliverance of His children from their
bondage is used in the New Testament as a dramatic picture of the ultimate
redemption that would finally come to the whole world in the person of
Jesus Christ.

For centuries, Israel traveled an erratic spiritual journey, climbing spiritual
heights only to be dashed down into the spiritual "slough of despond." In and
through it all, God worked by sending deliverer after deliverer until finally we
enter the four hundred silent years. Then, suddenly, bursting on the scene
came John the Baptist, announcing the revelation of God's own Son. The "new
exodus" from spiritual Egypt was as hand.

CHRIST COMES

The message and mission of Jesus, as He Himself declared, was "to seek and to
save that which was lost" (Luke 19:10). Redemption for all people at last
became a reality. The omnipotent One who sat on the throne with His Father,
out of love and compassion, came to fulfill all the promises of God. As Paul
expressed it in these oft-quoted verses:

Christ Jesus, who, although He existed in the form of God, did not regard equality with God a thing to be grasped, but emptied Himself, taking the form of a bond-servant, and being made in the likeness of men. And being found in appearance as a man, He humbled Himself by becoming obedient to the point of death, even death on a cross. Therefore also God highly exalted Him, and bestowed on Him the name which is above every name, that at the name of Jesus every knee should bow . . . and that every tongue should confess that Jesus Christ is Lord, to the glory of God the Father. (Phil. 2:5–11)

In that poetic passage Paul presented the incarnation as the miracle of miracles. It became the climax of God's redemptive mission. History was split in two. Through Jesus Christ, the "last Adam," God worked world redemption (1 Cor. 15:45). By Christ's death on the cross, along with His glorious resurrection, He purchased victory over sin, death, hell, and the grave. This message the world desperately needs to hear. Redeeming love has thus become the theme of the church. Little wonder that Charles H. Spurgeon had these words engraved on his tombstone in the Norwood Cemetery of London, England: "E'er since by faith I saw the streams thy flowing wounds supply, redeeming love has been my theme and shall be till I die."

The entire New Testament gives testimony to the reality of God's love and grace in worldwide redemption. Professor of evangelism Michael Green states that the bulk of the New Testament is essentially "the incidental literature of evangelism and world missions." As barriers were beginning to be broken and the church burst out of its Jerusalem cocoon, a fascinating scenario unfolds. The Book of Acts records the progress.

THE ACTS

New Testament scholar Frank Stagg outlines the Book of Acts in a fascinating fashion, as outlined in chapter 2. It will be recalled that he contends that Luke wrote to Theophilus to answer the question as to how a small, insignificant "Jewish sect," emanating from an obscure part of the Roman Empire, could in a matter of a few decades impact significantly the entire Mediterranean world. Stagg argues it came about because of major breakthroughs the church experienced as they cooperated with God's mission in the world.

The first major move occurred in the city of Jerusalem on the Day of Pentecost. The disciples had gathered, and after ten days of prayer, Luke records, as seen in an earlier chapter:

> And when the day of Pentecost had come, they were all together in one place. And suddenly there came from heaven a noise like a violent, rushing wind, and it filled the whole house where they were sitting. And there appeared to them tongues as of fire distributing themselves, and they rested on each one of them. And they were all filled with the Holy Spirit and began to speak with other tongues, as the Spirit was giving them utterance. (Acts 2:1–4)

This event created the glorious beginning of God's world mission. On that day, many nations had gathered in the city of Jerusalem; in a limited sense, the world had assembled. The gospel was preached, three thousand came to faith in Christ, and the Christian church was born.

As the Book of Acts unfolds, breakthrough after breakthrough comes until the Book of Acts ends in its fascinating fashion. As previously pointed out, the last word in the narrative is the adverb *unhinderedly*, the principle being that the work of God is designed to go on "unhinderedly" around the world. William Carey came to realize that God's mission must be understood as a *worldwide mission*. The message of Jesus Christ must be shared with all people of all times in all places. Several reasons for this fact immediately surface.

A THEOLOGICAL RATIONALE FOR THE MISSION OF GOD INTO ALL THE WORLD

The theological foundation for the advance of the church into all the world finds its source in the essential nature of God and His creative hand. Genesis 1:1 tells us, "In the beginning God created the heavens and the earth." Whatever the *modus operandi* of God in creation happened to be, God stands behind it as the sole Author. He created our vast universe *ex nihilo* (out of nothing), but not without purpose, goal, and meaning, and He did so as an expression of His creative power and love. God had a purposeful motive in creation and that purpose permeates every vestige of His universe. And although we cannot plumb the depths of God's rationale for it all, we do know that He formed mankind in His image from the dust of the ground and made us for the purpose of bringing glory to Himself through a life of intimate fellowship. All this not only points out the purpose of God, it brings out in bold relief that *God is love*.

A salient truth concerning the nature of God rests in the reality of His infinite love (1 John 4:8). The Greek word that the biblical writers overwhelmingly used in reference to God's great love, whether in the Septuagint of the Old Testament or the New Testament Greek, is *agape*. It is an utterly self-giving, unquestioning, reconciling, self-abandoning love. That quality of love characterizes the very nature of our gracious God. And He loves *all* of His creation, no exceptions. No race, color, cultural barrier, economic classification, geographical limitation, or any other humanly devised category removes people from the fathomless love of God. And how is that love perfectly expressed? Paul told us when he wrote, "God demonstrates His own love toward us, in that while we were yet sinners, Christ died for us" (Rom. 5:8). This does not mean that God excuses sin, evil, and the corruption of the human family. Still, God's love transcends any barrier that would cause His love to cease. As the apostle Peter recognized, "The Lord is not slow about His promises, as some count slowness, but is patient toward you, not wishing for any to perish but for all to come to repentance" (2 Pet. 3:9). The essential nature of God's love permeates His creative hand, and that truth creates the universal appeal of the evangelistic message.

THE NEED OF SALVATION

Another salient feature of the centrality and necessity of transcending all barriers to bring Christ to the world can be seen in the world's deep need of redemption. This has been amply stressed earlier in this work, but the Scriptures emphasize the truth time and again: "There is none righteous, not even one; there is none who understands, there is none who seeks for God; all have turned aside, together they have become useless; there is none who does good, there is not even one . . . for all have sinned and fall short of the glory of God" (Rom. 3:10–12, 23).

The conclusion is clear: Every human being stands under the condemnation of the Law. The root of the issue rests in the fact that God is not only love, He is also holy. The holiness of God should be seen on equal par with His all-embracing love. When Isaiah caught his vision of God in the Temple, his eyes were opened to the fact that hovering over the throne the Seraphim continually cry, "Holy, Holy, Holy is the LORD of hosts" (Isa. 6:3). The holiness of God, in the light of human sinfulness, demands divine judgment. Paul made it clear in his Epistle to the Romans that "the wages of sin is death" (6:23). Judgment awaits all. The Book of Hebrews states, "Inasmuch as it is appointed for men to die once and after this comes judgment" (9:27). Judgment stands as a universal certain fact for the entire human family. Therefore, the human need is universal and profound beyond understanding.

But Christ's universal salvation becomes available to all who will repent and believe (Acts 2:38). In the life, death, and resurrection of Jesus Christ, God in love has redeemed and has established the mission of world redemption. Lost people need Christ's salvation. Moreover, John tells us: "My little children, I am writing these things to you that you may not sin. And if anyone sins, we have an Advocate with the Father, Jesus Christ the righteous; and He Himself is the propitiation for our sins; and not for ours only, but also for those of the whole world" (1 John 2:1–2). No one lies outside the efficacious work of Jesus Christ if he or she will turn to Him in repentance and faith (Acts 20:21). His shed blood forever stands sufficient for the entire human race from Adam until the final trumpet sounds. That demands worldwide evangelization.

THE CALL OF THE SPIRIT

The all-inclusive gospel of Jesus Christ and the infinite love of God immediately implies a universal call to salvation. The Holy Spirit with His searching hand reaches out to every man, woman, boy, and girl on the planet to convince them of their sin, their need of righteousness, and the certainty of judgment if they reject God's call of grace (John 16:7–8).

Moreover, in that setting and context, the Holy Spirit reveals the Savior. Jesus said prior to His crucifixion:

These things I have spoken to you, while abiding with you. But the Helper, the Holy Spirit, whom the Father will send in My name, He will teach you all things, and bring to your remembrance all that I said to you. . . . But when He, the Spirit of truth, comes, He will guide you into all the truth; for He will not speak on His own initiative, but whatever He hears, He will speak; and He will disclose to you what is to come. He shall glorify Me; for He shall take of Mine, and shall disclose it to you. (John 14:25–26; 16:13–14)

The Holy Spirit in His convincing, convicting, converting work uses the church to convey His message. That constitutes a serious situation, because if God's people fail to take the gospel to the world, the message will not be heard. And today multiplied millions, if not billions, know little or nothing about the glorious good news of Christ. As Paul said:

There is no distinction between Jew and Greek; for the same Lord is Lord of all, abounding in riches for all who call upon Him; for "Whoever will call upon the name of the LORD will be saved." How then shall they call upon Him in whom they have not believed? And how shall they believe in Him whom they have not heard? And how shall they hear without a preacher? And how shall they preach unless they are sent? Just as it is written, "How beautiful are the feet of those who bring glad tidings of good things!" (Rom. 10:12–15)

In the final analysis, the church finds its rationale for existence in *worldwide mission*. Yet, as has been stated throughout this chapter, God is actually the One on mission. He stands as the ultimate Author of the challenging task. As David Bosch has said, "Missions is what God is doing to and through the servant, not what the servant does."[10] God works powerfully in and through the life of the church to accomplish His mission, and therein the church finds its challenge and strength for the task, namely, the establishment of the kingdom of God. We must evangelize. But that has surely been made crystal-clear in the preceding pages.

THE PRAGMATICS

It has become obvious that from all that has been revealed to the church through Scripture, theology, history, and logical deduction, God intends His people to cross every barrier and bring the good news to the very last person on earth. This being God's mission, and hence the church's mission, no reason can be raised for the church not throwing itself totally into the task. William Carey was absolutely right: A genuine burden for the entire world must settle down on the hearts of God's people. Regardless of the problems that the exclusiveness of the gospel precipitates, expressed in the age-old question, "What about the heathen who have never heard?" the task still remains to bring Christ to those "heathen." The Bible does not give an exhaustive philosophical answer to the question; it simply declares that people without Jesus Christ die in their sins and are morally responsible for that fact. Therefore, the church's responsibility is to get the message of salvation to them. Simply put, the Scriptures answer the query on a pragmatic basis. And if the church fails to assume its role seriously, it fails its Lord, thwarts the *missio dei*, and spells its own demise. God uses those who make themselves available.

CONCLUSION

What, therefore, does God expect of the church? It can be summarized simply by saying: God's people should be much in prayer, laying aside all prejudices and restrictions, permitting the Holy Spirit to burden every professing Christian with the worldwide task, and making the sacrifice necessary to see Christ brought to the whole world. As we previously learned, the word *witness* can be translated "martyr." Sacrifice rests at the heart of the mission. There is a price to pay, mountains to surmount. But our God is able, for "nothing will be impossible with God" (Luke 1:37). God will fulfill His mission, and happy is the church and every believer who joins in the endeavor. What a glorious task! It is life for death. Did Billy Graham make his contribution to that task? This we must look into.

PART II:
BILLY GRAHAM AND HIS WORLDWIDE MINISTRY

Let's put our arms around the world and love them.
—BILLY GRAHAM

INTRODUCTION

When the Lord Jesus Christ was born, the angels announced that His birth and its significance was for all people (Luke 2:10). Right at the outset, let it be said that this principle has undergirded the life and ministry of Billy Graham since the early years of his kingdom service. As one enters his small Montreat, North Carolina, office, on a wall beside the reception desk hangs a relief map of the world with the challenge of our Lord printed prominently: "And this gospel of the kingdom shall be preached in the whole world for a witness to all the nations, and then the end shall come" (Matt. 24:14). It speaks volumes of the evangelist's spirit and worldwide vision. Billy Graham, sensitive to the far-reaching implications of this biblical truth, in his own words laments, "The sad thing is that now, almost two thousand years after his [Christ's] birth, many of the earth's people have not heard the Good News and, consequently, do not know the joy of his salvation."[11]

NEW VENTURES

Determined to do something unusual and significant, Billy Graham broke new ground in bringing the gospel to the whole world. As touched upon earlier, nothing captivated the world nor expressed the heart of Graham more dramatically than did the Billy Graham Global Mission in San Juan, Puerto Rico, the week of March 16 through 18, 1995. The late Bob Williams, who served as director of International Ministries for the Billy Graham Evangelistic Association, set a lofty mission goal. The ministry was to be far more than a typical crusade in San Juan. Through satellite technology Billy Graham would broadcast his series of crusade messages to the entire world. Graham had attempted similar projects on a much more limited scale in past years. Satellite crusades had been conducted in the Far East, Africa, and Germany, for example. But this was something new: broadcasting the gospel to the whole world during one crusade. It involved incredible technology and unprecedented cooperation from numerous sources around the globe, but the results proved to be unprecedented. Uplinks went to 185 countries, and it is estimated that ten million people a night heard Graham's message with more than two million registered decisions.

The next year, in 1996, Billy telecast a single program entitled "Starting Over." It was transmitted to two hundred countries, translated into forty-eight languages, and reached a potential two and one-half billion people. Cliff Barrows said, Billy Graham was "preaching to more people than any other person in the history of the world."[12]

Such efforts demanded extensive preparation. First, the broadcasts had to be targeted to specific strategic areas. Crusade services would be recorded, then edited and translated into various languages and fed by satellite to the nations of the world. Second, because Graham felt it vital that people who responded be integrated into the Christian community, Christian workers had to be trained in all of the downlink sites throughout the world. Moreover, there would need to be workers enlisted for advertising, visiting, and staging the event in each country. But most important of all, spiritual training, counseling, and maintaining a follow-up program for those who would commit themselves to Christ had to be instituted. Bob Williams, now with the Lord, did a wonderful thing—it all "worked."

BILLY GRAHAM AND KINGDOM WORK

The project proved a vast undertaking. But it must be seen in the context of that which expresses the heart of Billy Graham. He understands that his ministry is a kingdom ministry. And the kingdom of God extends itself far beyond the confines of North America, where he has given the bulk of his time in evangelization. Graham's grasp of kingdom business gives him the worldwide vision that he has, not only to undertake a project like the San Juan, Puerto Rico, telecast, but to seize every opportunity to share the gospel worldwide. As Cliff Barrows pointed out, "Ever since their trip to England in 1946, Billy has had a worldwide vision."[13] He has even named two of his ministry agencies World Wide Pictures and World Wide Publications. This speaks volumes of his attitude to kingdom involvement.

In 1990, after Billy Graham had completed a mission in Hong Kong, he was in conversation with Henry Holley, a team member assigned to international work. Billy asked him, "Where can we go next?" Holley replied, "You have been practically everywhere in the world, except one place. This place I have prayed for because of my love for the region." When Billy Graham asked him where it was, Henry immediately replied, "North Korea." The conversation sparked a concern and created a challenge for Billy to visit that communist-held part of the Far East. Through various Korean contacts like Steven Linton, a scholar at Columbia University Center for Korean Research, Billy was put in touch with Ho Jong, the North Korean ambassador to the United

Nations. Negotiation went on for a period of a year. Finally, from the Korean Protestant Federation, representing the nation's several thousand Protestants, an official invitation arrived for Billy to go to Pyongyang.

Although the Koreans were somewhat suspicious of Graham, he brushed that aside and immediately made his way to the East. He spent a few days in Tokyo recovering from jet lag and then flew on to Pyongyang with members of his team. They arrived in the North Korean capital on March 31, 1992. Immediately upon their arrival they were escorted into a reception room at the airport for a formal greeting. The welcoming committee was composed of a delegation of Christians representing the Protestant and Catholic churches, along with the chairman of the Korean Protestant Federation, Kang Yong Sop. Billy addressed the group with these words: "I do not come as an emissary of my government or my nation, but as a citizen of the kingdom of God. As Christ's ambassador, I have come first of all to visit the Christian community—to have fellowship with my brothers and sisters in Christ, to pray and to worship with them, and to preach the gospel of Jesus Christ in your churches."[14] Clearly, Graham sees himself as an ambassador of the kingdom of God, and because the kingdom is universal, it is for all people at all times. This principle lays the basic foundation stones of his entire approach to his worldwide grasp of the ministry of evangelism.

One of the salient features of Billy Graham's kingdom approach rests in his understanding of the ecumenical motif of the kingdom of God. Billy Graham is an unapologetic Baptist, having held membership in the First Baptist Church of Dallas for decades. Nevertheless, he has certainly not restricted his ministry to Baptists. God's kingdom extends far beyond any particular denominational group, not to mention its universality in cultures, geography, or any man-made restrictions. Graham thus insists that any cooperating Christian group can play its role in his evangelistic crusades and endeavors wherever they may be. As seen, he welcomes all who will attend and take part in the evangelization of their constituency. Consequently, his crusades have a very broad base of involvement. Pentecostals, evangelicals, mainline churches, Roman Catholics, even many of the more liberal persuasion throw their time and influence and resources into the crusades. This spirit highlights Graham's worldwide consciousness; he will go and welcome cooperation wherever he feels God is leading regardless of the criticism and ostracism he has received. The contribution often made in such an approach, Billy Graham feels is well worth the criticism he endures. As a case in point, his trip to Russia yielded marvelous results. Concerning the 1984 trip, Billy said:

> In all, I gave over fifty sermons, lectures and speeches—the most intensive schedule in my entire forty years of ministry. . . . A high point was my sermon at the Church of the Epiphany in Moscow, the most important Orthodox church in the country. It was packed with people, and I preached on how to be born again—the same message I give everywhere I go. . . . I took advantage of that one moment when they invited me to come back. . . . I thought it was worth [the risk] . . . for the sake of preaching the gospel, and, secondly for the cause of world peace.[15]

The details of the Russian ministry need not be rehearsed again; simply suffice it to say that God honored the move, and this world-conscious posture was certainly true of other great evangelists such as Billy Sunday, D. L. Moody, Charles Finney, in the eighteenth century men like Wesley and Whitefield, and a host of others through the course of church history. It can all be capsulated in Billy's statement: "I felt God had called me to love all people."[16]

WORLD PEACE

At the same time, Graham shares a deep concern for world peace as well as preaching the gospel to all people. He feels it constitutes part of the church's responsibility as well as evangelism. This is God's world, and effort must be made to meet *all* needs of *all* people. Graham sees that. And his influence with world leaders has made a contribution to peace, perhaps more than most realize. Still, world evangelization holds top priority. At a conference for evangelists in Louisville, Kentucky, Billy read to the many evangelists there the following affirmation: "We affirm our commitment to the Great Commission of our Lord, and declare our willingness to go *anywhere*, do *anything* and sacrifice *anything* God requires of us in the fulfilling of that Commission."[17] And he himself has obviously lived it out.

It has been stated that Graham's view of the kingdom of God and the significant role of the church in the kingdom provides another vital aspect of his understanding of the entire scenario. This theme will be approached in more detail in the final chapter of this work on Billy Graham and his "church-centered" approach. It needs only to be said at this point that Billy Graham recognizes the church as a vital part of the kingdom of God and therefore his work must be centered in the church. But what actually constitutes Graham's theology of the kingdom of God?

THE NATURE OF THE KINGDOM

It appears quite correct to say that Billy Graham does not visualize the church as the sum and substance of the kingdom of God. The kingdom certainly goes beyond that point, as important as the church may be. There is an eternity past and future, and the kingdom extends infinitely beyond our space-time universe. The kingdom of God far exceeds human comprehension. The eternal kingdom is God's nonrestricted rule and reign over all, as seen in the chapter on God's sovereignty. There are angels (remember Billy wrote a best-selling book on the subject), cherubim and seraphim, Satan and demons, and realms we know not of. And God rules in it all. This is Billy Graham's basic premise. And that glorious kingdom has broken in upon us. Professor George Beasley-Murray states, "The faith of the Old Testament rests on two certainties, equally profound and indesolveably bound together. The first is that God has come in the past, and that he has intervened in favor of his people. The other . . . is the hope that God will come anew in the future."[18]

That hope of Israel came to a glowing reality in the advent of Jesus. As He entered the human scene, He cried out, "Repent, for the kingdom of heaven is at hand" (Matt. 4:17). The kingdom has come to us in the life, death, resurrection, and ascension of the Lord Jesus Christ, and it will be seen in fullness at the *parousia*, when Jesus returns. In the great anticipated second advent, Handel in his magnificent oratorio *Messiah,* has expressed it well from the Scriptures: "The kingdoms of this world have become the kingdoms of our Lord and of His Christ, and He shall reign forever and ever!" (Rev. 11:15 NKJV). And the fact that the gospel is heralded to the whole world as never in the history of the church, Billy feels, is "one of the signs that we are to look for as we approach the end of history."[19] In Billy's thinking the full kingdom may soon come.

Therefore, he says, "there is hope for the future."[20] For that hour, the evangelist warns, we must "be ready" (Matt. 24:44).

Such being the nature of the kingdom in the thought of Billy Graham, again may it be emphasized, this basic theology compels commitment to the entire world. The Lord made that fact very clear in the Great Commission (Matt. 28:18–20). Thus Graham has given himself to a worldwide ministry. This leads to a reflection of Billy Graham's concern for the world and his efforts at world evangelization. We have touched upon some highlights to set the scene; now a more systematic study is called for.

BILLY GRAHAM'S CONCERN AND WORK
FOR THE WHOLE WORLD

One biographer has said, "By 1956 Billy Graham no longer was merely an American preacher. What he said, or did, or was could make for good or ill across the world."[21] Billy Graham's world consciousness and influence began early in his ministry. We have already touched on this fact in the introduction of this chapter. But it helps to see how it all got started. Billy Graham's studies at Wheaton College no doubt planted some early seeds of world concern. Graham had majored in anthropology. This gave him insight of the true nature of humanity. He recognized that by the creative hand of God we are all of one family; the gospel, therefore, must be proclaimed to all in that bond of oneness. He could not divorce himself from any people group because we are all one in Adam, and all desperately need to be brought by redemption into the "last Adam," the Lord Jesus Christ (1 Cor. 15:45).

Graham's growing global awareness had its inception in the spring of 1946 when Youth for Christ became an international organization. As seen, Charles Templeton, Torrey Johnson, singer Stratton Shufelt, and Billy undertook a forty-six-day tour of Britain and the European continent. Wesley Hartzell, a reporter for William Randolph Hearst's Chicago *Herald-American,* accompanied the team. Graham returned to Britain later that year, in the fall of 1946, for a six-month tour. On this trip he invited Cliff Barrows and his wife, Billie, to serve as his musical entourage. In that international context, Cliff said of Billy and himself, "God really knit our hearts together in a special way."[22] During the six-month tour of Great Britain, Graham spoke at 360 meetings and had extended campaigns in Manchester, Birmingham, Belfast, and London. A world consciousness and concern became deeply implanted in his heart.

Graham's world concern grew through the following years. Then the great London Harringay crusade, delineated earlier, took place. In the triumph of that crusade Graham determined to do his best to fulfill the words of the Lord Jesus Christ when He said, "Preach the gospel to the whole creation" (Mark 16:15 RSV). He received the vision of becoming a world evangelist.

Immediately after the Harringay crusade, Billy and his small group engaged in a whirlwind tour of European cities. Bob Evans, an old Wheaton College friend who served in Paris for years, planned a series of rallies for the team. Because of the tremendous impact of the gospel that London experienced in the Harringay crusade, every city hired the largest stadium for Graham; and the response was all but overwhelming. Crowds overflowed every venue to hear the good news preached. In Stockholm, for example, sixty-five thousand people crammed into the Skansen Arena for the largest evangelistic meeting ever held in Sweden. In Copenhagen, fifteen thousand people gathered in pouring rain in the city square as Billy stood up to declare Christ. The attendance in Amsterdam reached forty thousand. Billy held a four-day short crusade in Paris. This was the first time in the history of modern France that all the Protestant churches rallied behind a major evangelistic effort. It proved to be a monumental moment. The very next year Graham picked up the challenge of the Far East. It did seem that the world was at his feet. And his concern escalated through the many years of worldwide ministry.

Thus Graham's early international trips, Cliff Barrows says, crystallized the worldwide vision of Bill Graham.[23] As a result of his early experience, Billy committed himself "unto the uttermost parts of the earth."[24] And the burden deepened. On the night before the team left for another English crusade in 1964, Billy, along with Lane Adams and Bob Ferm, knelt in prayer, dedicating themselves to serve the British people in the gospel. Bob Ferm said, "We all three knelt down, and I have often thought that if I could have had a copy or recording of that *ad lib* prayer, it would have broken the heart of Great Britain to realize that an American citizen [Billy Graham] had Britain so much in his heart, cared so much, longed so much for the best of God to come to those people."[25] Such was the depth of Graham's worldwide concern and commitment. That spirit moves people.

BILLY GRAHAM'S IMPACT ON WORLD
EVANGELIZATION

An account of Graham's crusade work around the globe would fill many volumes. He has virtually spoken to the entire world. And it is not just the crusades in themselves. As a former associate of Billy Graham put it:

> A five-day crusade with Billy Graham in the pulpit is just the tip of the BGEA iceberg. From its Minnesota incorporation in 1950 the association has grown into a multi-faceted ministry that could easily compete for a distinction once bestowed on the British Empire: the sun never sets on BGEA, either. People on every continent of the planet are touched by Billy Graham's ministry around the clock:
>
> - a listener to the "Hour of Decision" in China;
> - a reader of a Graham book in Brazil;
> - a viewer of a Graham movie in South Africa;
> - a subscriber to DECISION magazine in Australia;
> - a recipient of a Billy Graham tract in Russia;
> - a writer to the "My Answer" column in California;
> - a child watching a Graham home video in London;
> - an inquirer at an associate's crusade in India;
> - a seminar participant at The Cove in North Carolina;
> - a visitor to the Billy Graham Center in Illinois;
> - a victim receiving humanitarian aid in Rwanda.
>
> Even the imaginary snapshots above cannot completely capture the worldwide vision of the pulpiteer Billy.[26]

Graham's ministry to the military has proved powerful around the globe. His visits to Vietnam and other crucial areas through the years have been well received and most effective. In these settings, as always, he presents the gospel, conscious that some of those young men and women may soon meet God. Multitudes in the military have been impacted with the gospel, if not by Billy

Graham in person, at least through his writings, the media, and the ministry of his associate evangelists. And that is not an exaggeration. Statistics prove it.

This now leads to another important ministry of the Graham worldwide thrust: the great evangelistic conferences that have been sponsored by the Billy Graham Evangelistic Association.

BERLIN

In 1966, the Berlin conference on evangelization was convened. People gathered from many parts of the world and from various Christian groups to hammer out a viable evangelical theology. The theme of the conference read: "One Race, One Gospel, One Task." The conference was well received. It did have one weakness, however; it was predominantly Western in its makeup. But then came Lausanne.

THE LAUSANNE CONFERENCE

In August 1974, *Time* magazine wrote:

> Millions of Christians still take the Commission of Christ literally, still believe that one of their foremost tasks is to preach the gospel to the unbaptized. . . . Last week, in the lakeshore resort of Lausanne, Switzerland, that belief found a formidable form, possibly the widest-ranging meeting of Christians ever held. Brought together largely through the efforts of Reverend Billy Graham, some twenty-four hundred Protestant evangelical leaders from 150 countries ended a ten day international Congress on World Evangelization that served notice of the vigor of conservative, resolutely biblical, fervently mission minded Christianity.[27]

The Lausanne Congress for World Evangelization had come to pass. The large evangelism conference called by Graham in Berlin, 1966, proved a rich time, but the Lausanne Congress hit a spiritual high point.

The Lausanne Congress was actually reminiscent of the great Edinburgh Conference of 1910. In that mission milestone, John Mott challenged the evangelical world with the well-known phrase "the evangelization of the world in this generation." The Edinburgh conference eventually led to the founding of the World Council of Churches (WCC) some years later. Though it had a noble beginning from the evangelical, missionary perspective, the WCC slipped into something of the liberal persuasion and lost a large measure of its evangelistic fervency. As something of a counteraction to that loss, Graham organized the Lausanne Congress in 1974. As Billy Kim of Korea has said of Billy Graham, "He sees the world in focus."[28]

Twenty-four hundred representatives from evangelical circles around the globe gathered for one of the most significant meetings of the twentieth century. It certainly stands on par with the Edinburgh Conference of 1910. This author, having had the privilege of being in that gathering in Switzerland, can testify to the fact that there was a marvelous spirit of fellowship and camaraderie. The inspiration and challenge of those days highly motivated the attendees to fulfill the Great Commission in our generation. Furthermore, strong emphasis was laid upon the pragmatic aspects of the task. Seminars on virtually every aspect of world evangelization were provided. Everyone could honestly say they were helped to engage wisely in Christ's Great Commission. A new milestone had been laid. It constituted a most significant contribution to world evangelization. As Maurice Rowlandson said, "Looking back [on Lausanne] almost twenty years later, it is clear that Lausanne became a watershed for evangelicals . . . the growth of the influence of the evangelical wing [of the church] can be largely traced back to that congress."[29] And there was a BGEA follow-up to Lausanne a few years later in Manila called Lausanne II, sponsored by the Lausanne Continuation Committee.

AMSTERDAM '83 AND '86

The success of the Lausanne Conference spurred Graham to sponsor two significant conferences in the 1980s. In Amsterdam, the Netherlands, two conferences specifically geared to itinerant evangelists were convened. The first took place in 1983, the second in 1986. Graham had subsidized the Berlin and Lausanne conferences; now he raised a very large sum to bring evangelists from all over the world to Amsterdam. The conferences were a rewarding experience. The stories of the sacrifice and what it meant to participate in a world meeting of that magnitude transformed many delegates.

A large number of the attendees were from very remote parts of the earth. It was not unusual for some of the evangelists to travel long distances before they could even reach an airport to fly to the Netherlands. Traveling from remote areas of Africa, India, and other parts of the globe was a great physical hardship in itself. But they were well taken care of in the conference and the benefits proved most positive.

A theological note was sounded in the Amsterdam conferences, but the emphasis rested primarily on the inspirational and practical. The delegates met by geographical areas as they heard instruction and challenges concerning new and relevant ways to reach their nations for Jesus Christ. Many returned home with a fresh vision and new "equipment" to make an impact with the gospel.

Many stories emerged out of these conferences that are quite fascinating— even touching. Franklin Graham, president of Samaritan's Purse, assembled a large store of clothing, books, and other amenities for the many less-privileged delegates. They went away not only better equipped to fulfill their ministry, but also decently dressed and with helpful material for evangelization. It truly was an enriching moment for all the delegates, whether from an affluent society or from poverty-stricken nations. Needs were met, physical and spiritual, and a great impetus to world evangelization permeated the entire atmosphere. Graham's holistic approach to evangelization was now full grown and the conferences reflected it. The largest conference for itinerant evangelists was yet to come; however, that high hour needs a fuller presentation.

AMSTERDAM 2000

Again, Billy Graham called together evangelists from around the world. They were monumental days. As reported, they assembled

for one simple purpose . . . they came from the great cities of the world: Buenos Aires, London, Los Angeles, Moscow, Nairobi, Nanjing, and Sydney. They came from villages so small that the names don't appear on most maps. They came— 10,732 of them from 209 countries and territories around the world. They came together to focus on one simple purpose: to find new and more effective ways to proclaim the gospel throughout the world.[30]

In capsule form, that was Amsterdam 2000, a nine-day conference for evangelists and evangelism leaders held in the Netherlands from July 24 through August 6 at the turn of the millennium. The rationale for such a venture centered in strengthening evangelists and providing challenges and practical helps to strengthen the local church and to further the kingdom of God, bringing glory to Jesus Christ.

The theme of Amsterdam 2000 was: "Proclaiming Peace and Hope for the New Millennium." It struck a responsive chord in the more than ten thousand attendees from 209 countries. With outstanding speakers such as John Stott, Ravi Zacharias, Stephen Olford, the Archbishop of Canterbury, Anne Graham Lotz, Franklin Graham, Charles Colson, and others, along with two hundred workshop leaders, three major task force groups, and other programs, the conference provided a plethora of resources from which to choose. Moreover, the unity and fellowship experience across the church spectrum and from around the world was really quite overwhelming. In Billy Graham's words of welcome he stated, "This conference could be the catalyst for the most productive advance of the gospel ever. . . . You and I are poised to see from Amsterdam 2000 an enormous increase in the harvest." And it could well be true. Several most positive steps were taken.

Important documents surfaced in the effort. The early Statement of Faith of the BGEA was presented. It reads as follows:

THE STATEMENT OF FAITH FOR THE BILLY GRAHAM EVANGELISTIC ASSOCIATION
Serves as the basic theological framework for the Amsterdam 2000 Conference of Preaching Evangelists

The Billy Graham Evangelistic Association believes . . .

- The Bible to be the infallible Word of God, that it is His holy and inspired Word, and that it is of supreme and final authority.

- In one God, eternally existing in three persons—Father, Son and Holy Spirit.

- Jesus Christ was conceived by the Holy Spirit, born of the Virgin Mary. He led a sinless life, took on Himself all our sins, died and rose again, and is seated at the right hand of the Father as our mediator and advocate.

- That all men everywhere are lost and face the judgment of God, and need to come to a saving knowledge of Jesus Christ through His shed blood on the cross.

- That Christ rose from the dead and is coming soon.

- In holy Christian living, and that we must have concern for the hurts and social needs of our fellowmen.

- We must dedicate ourselves anew to the service of our Lord and to His authority over our lives.

- In using every modern means of communication available to us to spread the gospel of Jesus Christ throughout the world.

The Covenant for Evangelists (presented in chapter 10) was followed by the adoption of the Amsterdam Declaration. This larger work will guide many evangelists for years to come. As previously pointed out, the complete text is seen in Appendix C.

Strategic planning in evangelism was undertaken much to the profit of many. Franklin Graham was there again with food, clothing, books, and other supplies from Samaritan's Purse. A major part of the travel, lodging, and food (except for evangelists from America and Western Europe) was provided by the Graham organization. The comments of attendees from around the world were quite wonderful. From the Philippines one evangelist said, "Witnessing the fusion of the past and the present to teach the next generation has really moved me." A lady from Fiji stated, "For the first time I have realized that God has so many people—they are different colors, different languages, different hair styles, but in Him we are all one." From England a pastor related, "It reinforced the urgency of the gospel." A delegate from Sri Lanka said, "It was an encouragement to see how Billy Graham has evangelized." A South African declared, "It is a lonely road for evangelists—here I have found others—a real blessing." And on go the positive reactions. Rarely was a negative note sounded.

Most unfortunately, Billy Graham himself could not attend due to his illness. But the delegates saw and heard him as he spoke to them via satellite; his presence was sensed and the thousands of fellow evangelists expressed gratitude to the evangelist for such an event.

Amsterdam 2000 reached its climax when ten thousand–plus people gathered and observed the Lord's Supper. Richard Bewes of London officiated at the Eucharist. To gather around the Lord's Table with those from more than two hundred countries proved a rich experience indeed. The entire conference will long be remembered; and as said so often, only eternity will tell the ultimate outcome and the tremendous contribution of those days.

In 1812 William Carey had what he called a "pleasing dream." It was to gather together believers from around the world in a great conference in Cape Town, South Africa, for the furtherance of the gospel worldwide. That dream was not realized until the 1910 conference in Edinburgh, Scotland. Now, almost a century later, Billy Graham picked up the dream again in Amsterdam 2000 along with Lausanne, Berlin, and other events, and that flaming torch of the gospel is being passed on. Willem Visser 't Hooft, first general secretary of the World Council of Churches, said these conferences are a "reincarnation of John Mott."[31] As one evaluator put it, specifically citing the Lausanne conference, "The Lausanne covenant furnished evangelical Christianity with a rationale for social action that it had lacked since the days of Charles Finney."[32] Concerning the several conferences through the years, Billy himself has said that they are "the major part of our history."[33]

Amsterdam 2000 carried on the tradition and will probably be the last such one that Billy Graham himself will inspire and implement. But the legacy will carry on worldwide.

WORLDWIDE COVENANTS—A SUMMARY

Statements of faith and covenants were produced at each of the Graham conferences, much through the efforts of John Akers. They all more or less grew out of the original BGEA Statement of Purpose drawn up by George Wilson in the early years. That simple statement reads: "to spread and propagate the gospel of our Lord Jesus Christ by any and all . . . means."[34] The Lausanne Covenant is seen as a significant statement of evangelical thought (see Appendix B). It evolved from several months of study directed by John Stott. At the time, Stott was serving as president of the British Evangelical Alliance, along with his pastorate of All Souls Church in the heart of London. An outstanding preacher and writer, Stott, along with his committee, produced a significant statement concerning world evangelization and ministry. Not only were the tenets of evangelism laid down, but the necessity and importance of meeting people's full needs also found a place in the document. Billy Graham has said that that is about the only statement he has actually signed. As seen, a "Declaration" came out of Amsterdam 2000 (see Appendix C). These documents contribute tremendously to the evangelistic understanding and commitment of evangelical churches. It should be made clear that Graham in no sense intended the Lausanne conference or any of the others to be construed as a reaction to the more liberal World Council of Churches.

A continuation committee of the Lausanne conference was organized and has continued to work for many years. The committee is designed essentially to foster world evangelization. The Lausanne Continuation Committee holds meetings in local areas around the world. For example, a series of meetings in Singapore in 1977 and 1978, supported by Billy Graham, gave rise to a new awareness for evangelism in that part of the world. Strategic issues and strategies and theological papers were produced that brought the evangelical world together in a unique way. As one expressed it:

In these myriad extensions of what has come to be called the Spirit of Lausanne, the Lausanne covenant has played a major unifying role—again, particularly in the third world, where it provided a formal basis on which Baptists, Mennonites, Methodists, Pentecostals, and others, including evangelical members of the WCC-affiliated denominations, could agree to work together. It's a coalescence of the spirit of evangelism as exemplified by Billy Graham. . . . The international bulletin of mission research has asserted that the covenant may now be the broadest umbrella in the world under which professing Christians can be gathered to pray and strategize for the salvation of their cities.[35]

Furthermore, regional conferences for itinerant evangelists have emerged out of the various meetings. For example, in 1994, Billy Graham sponsored a large gathering of evangelists from North America in Louisville, Kentucky, entitled the North American Conference of Itinerant Evangelists (NACIE). At the time of this writing, Amsterdam 2000 has just ended, and already one hundred follow-up regional and national conferences are being planned. Not only that, excellent literature has been forthcoming out of these conferences, e.g., *A*

Biblical Standard for Evangelists (1983) and *Biblical Affirmations for Evangelists* (NACIE '94). And that is not to mention the large volume of addresses and workshop materials that have been produced from the conference by the BGEA. They all make a positive contribution in themselves. The world has been touched through the Graham-sponsored conference—indicative of the evangelist's worldwide concern.

WORLD CRUSADES

As far as Graham's personal world-crusade ministry is concerned, a most significant work centers in his penetration of Eastern Europe during communist days. He began to feel a burden for Eastern Europe as a tourist in 1959. He prayed with Grady Wilson and a few others in the vast Moscow stadium that he might one day preach the gospel in Moscow. We've seen the fulfillment of that prayer along with the prayer of Reverend Mitscovich. Dr. Alexander Haraszti played a vital role in all of Graham's endeavors in Eastern Europe. Haraszti, a medical doctor, was Hungarian by birth. Being a committed Christian, he learned of Billy Graham in the mid-1950s while still living in Hungary. He had received some typewritten pages in Hungarian concerning Graham's ministry. In 1955 he acquired a copy of Billy Graham's *Peace with God,* which he translated into Hungarian. That opened the door for a close relationship between Graham and Haraszti, who then began to orient Billy Graham concerning the communist bloc of Eastern Europe and its desperate spiritual need.

Billy's first venture in Eastern Europe was in Yugoslavia under the leadership of Joseph Horak, pastor of the Baptist church in Zagreb. As doors began to open, Graham extended his ministry into Poland, Hungary, and other Eastern European bloc countries. We have related the incident when Billy Graham first went to the Soviet Union to the Peace Conference—and the furor it precipitated. But doors opened more and more as he invaded the Iron Curtain.

A NOTE OF DEFINITION

This book is not intended to be a biography of Billy Graham. The actual stories of Graham and his overseas crusades have been fully outlined in the numerous biographical works on the evangelist. What is important to see here centers in the fact that few barriers have kept Billy Graham from his worldwide efforts at global evangelization. When one realizes the obstacles that have been overcome and the resistance that has been quelled for the furtherance of the kingdom of God, all honor must go to the Lord. Graham's commitment to kingdom extension has been played out in his life and ministry in a most positive fashion. And that is, in principle, historical evangelism and most contributory to world evangelization and kingdom progress.

This implies that Graham has been very successful in the endeavor. Is this true or has there simply been much publicity about his worldwide travel? This final issue must be addressed.

BILLY GRAHAM'S "SUCCESS" IN
WORLD EVANGELIZATION

Graham's "success" has come in many guises. As pointed out, he has been on the world's most-admired list for many years, presidents have called him in for prayer and counsel, newspapers have given him and his crusades front-page coverage, and he has been constantly in demand for television talk shows. But that in itself does not spell success in the final analysis, not in kingdom endeavors.

What then constitutes success in God's kingdom? It is certainly not mere numbers of attendees at the crusade or even necessarily the number of "decisions" recorded; certainly not how the media may evaluate the work. The best definition of success no doubt is found in the Scriptures when Jesus said that when one lost sheep is brought into the fold, there is more rejoicing over it "than over the ninety-nine which have not gone astray" (Matt. 18:13). Seeing people truly saved from eternal damnation matters most.

If genuine conversions serve as the final criteria for success in the task, it does seem fair to say that Billy Graham has been most successful. Testimonies of transformed lives abound. As stated, statistics do not tell us everything. But even there, Graham's insistence on integrity of reporting crusade results lends credence to the statistics of the Graham ministry (see Appendix D). It does seem correct to say that the multitudes who have made decisions for Christ are generally genuine. Moreover, on a percentage basis, it is interesting to note that the largest number of results has not been in America or the Western world where the gospel is reasonably well known; the greatest responses have been from some of the more remote parts of the globe. Again, not that numbers alone spell success, but these sorts of statistics can be something of an indicator of the fact that many responders to Graham's invitation have truly come to repentance and faith in the Lord Jesus Christ. Billy Graham strives with all his energy to effect just that. And that spells success on a worldwide scale in biblical evangelism. God honors that sort of effort and grants blessings and positive results.

Another of the reasons for Graham's "success" in world evangelization centers in the fact of his adaptation to the culture wherever he preaches. In the setting of all his international ministries, Graham is surprisingly relevant in his message. He does his homework. This author has heard him in many venues around the world. Graham is consistently well informed on the culture, history, and social dynamics of the country where he is ministering. He is quite comfortable in many different cultural settings. Of course, the gospel does not change, Billy always preaches the essential *kerygma,* but he informs himself on how to communicate it in a fashion that "makes sense" wherever he is. He knows how to culturalize the good news. In an interview on one occasion, he outlined how many international newspapers and newsmagazines he reads each day.[36] And he has good advisers as well. That is wise evangelism. The world will listen to a man like that.

Graham is an evangelist who truly does impact the world. That is no exaggeration; it is simply the facts of the case. As might be expected, some have thought that Billy has spent too much time overseas. Graham disagrees, however. Concerning his decisions as to where to hold crusades, in America or out of the country, he has said, "the Lord gave a right balance."[37] Such does seem true; at least most agree with his statement.

CONCLUSION AND HISTORICAL CONTRIBUTION OF BILLY GRAHAM TO WORLDWIDE EVANGELISM

In one of Graham's later works, *Storm Warning,* the evangelist brings the worldwide thrust of his ministry together with the words of Jesus: "This gospel of the kingdom will be preached in the whole world as a testimony to all nations, and then the end will come" (Matt. 24:14 NIV). Graham goes on to say, "Today, for the first time in history, we are witnessing the preaching of the gospel on a global scale such as the world has never known, using radio, the printed page, and television. It is one of the signs that we are to look for as we approach the end of history."[38] And that constitutes a significant contribution to many societies.

So what can be said? First, it must be granted that the evangelist has a sincere and magnanimous heart to reach the whole world for Christ. Very few would doubt his sincerity and integrity on that score. His ministry gives testimony to that fact time and again.

Second, the list of endeavors in world evangelization is truly impressive. Here are a few:

- world conferences such as Lausanne and Amsterdam

- actual crusades in many nations of the world

- literature, media, outreach, and various helps being constantly distributed to foster and aid evangelism in many countries

- offices that promote evangelism in leading world cities

- his attempt to be well informed on world events

- evangelistic missions he has sponsored and encouraged around the world, such as Mission to England '84 and Euro '70

- sending relief to stricken areas

- making at times real sacrifices to minister in needy areas

- employing associate evangelists from other countries and nationalities

And these are just a few, but important, ministries Billy Graham and the BGEA make to world evangelization. Of course, the final tally of positive results and the contribution to kingdom progress will have to wait for the verdict of heaven. But it does appear the Graham ministry falls well in line with historical, evangelical evangelism and has made its positive contribution, thus constituting his legacy. It can perhaps all be capsulated in these words from the evangelist himself: "Every Christian must grasp the vision and begin to see the world the way God sees it."[39] It would seem Billy does.

CHAPTER 13

THE CHURCH IN EVANGELISM

~⌒

PART I:
CHARLES HADDON SPURGEON AND THE CHURCH

It is wise to go there to worship God.
—C. H. SPURGEON

INTRODUCTION

Charles Haddon Spurgeon will always be known as "the Prince of Preachers." The designation is deserved; no one in the English-speaking world, save perhaps George Whitefield, displayed such pulpit acumen as Spurgeon. The masses flocked to hear him. For thirty-seven years, wherever he preached, he filled every venue, be it church building, auditorium, or music hall. During almost four decades of London ministry, his Metropolitan Tabernacle Church grew into the largest evangelical church in the world.

Further, Spurgeon not only excelled as an outstanding pastoral preacher, but he was a very gifted evangelist as well. An itinerant evangelistic ministry took him all over Britain and parts of Europe. Historians agree that Spurgeon was a pastor/evangelist par excellence. However, it must be recognized that whether he was on the road preaching evangelistic rallies or swaying the thousands who gathered every Sunday to hear him at the Metropolitan Tabernacle, Spurgeon was above all a churchman. His evangelism thrived and produced a lasting effect because of his commitment to exercise his evangelistic ministry basically in the context of the local church. Commitment to the church stands as vital for a dynamic, biblical evangelism of integrity. It all began for Spurgeon some years earlier, when he was just a teenage lad.

SPURGEON'S DAYS IN STAMBOURNE

Charles came into the world on June 19, 1834, in the Essex village of Kelvedon. When Charles was a ten-month-old baby, his father, John, moved the family to nearby Colchester. For reasons that have never been quite verified, Charles was sent off to live with his grandparents in the town of Stambourne. Grandfather James served as the minister of the nonconformist, reformed church in the community. Charles spent the next six years of his life with his grandparents. James Spurgeon had pastored the Stambourne Congregational Church for several years. He fulfilled the archetype of a typical Puritan divine. He wore knee britches and buckled shoes just like his spiritual ancestors. The grandparents' home became a wonderful training ground for Charles. The grandfather and grandmother were a godly couple, and their spinster daughter, Anne, became very close to Charles. The boy loved his aunt Anne deeply.

One day Charles wandered into one of the old upstairs rooms of the parsonage. It exuded the dusty odor of ancient volumes, old Puritan works. Charles, a very precocious little fellow, could already read well. He felt he had discovered a treasure. He said, "In my time it was a dark den; but it contained books, and this made it a gold mine to me. Therein was fulfilled the promise 'I will give thee the treasures of darkness.' . . . Out of that darkened room I fetched those old authors when I was yet a youth, and never was I happier than when in their company."[1]

In that room, Spurgeon found John Bunyan's classic, *Pilgrim's Progress*. The captivated little fellow devoured every page. In fact, Spurgeon read Bunyan's work more than one hundred times in the fifty-seven years of his life. Allusions to Bunyan's beautiful allegory abound in Spurgeon's sermons.

BACK TO COLCHESTER

At the age of six, Spurgeon's family brought their firstborn to Colchester, where he lived into his midteens. The parents were also godly people and influenced Charles tremendously, especially his mother. Charles's father said of his wife, "She was the starting point of all the greatness and goodness that any of us by the grace of God have enjoyed."[2]

Charles and his parents would often spend their summer holiday time in Stambourne with James and his family. On one occasion when Charles was ten years of age, Richard Knill, a well-known preacher, came to spend some time with them in Stambourne. The preacher made a most unusual prophecy. Charles's brilliance and his unusual perception of spiritual things—though he had not yet come to personal faith in Christ—deeply impressed Knill. He took the boy out in the back garden and prophesied that he would become a great preacher, preaching to thousands. Not only that, Knill prophesied that Charles would one day preach in the chapel of the famous British Baptist minister Rowland Hill. Richard Knill felt so convinced of the certainty of his prophecy that he made young Charles promise that when he did preach in Mr. Hill's chapel, he would sing the hymn "God Moves in a Mysterious Way, His Wonders to Perform." As the ministry of Spurgeon unfolded in later years, the prophecy did see fulfillment—and they did sing that very hymn.

Spurgeon spent his maturing years in various schools. At the age of fifteen, while home during the Christmas holidays from the school in Newmarket that he was attending at the time, he became deeply concerned about his personal relationship with Jesus Christ. He felt much like Pilgrim in Bunyan's allegory, trudging about with a great burden on his shoulders. He had hoped that he could find someone who would point him to "yonder wicket gate" where the burden might fall off and give him some relief and peace. He determined that he would go to every church in Colchester during the holiday season, hoping that some preacher would unveil to him the secret of salvation.

CONVERSION

One Sunday morning early in January 1850, a terrible snowstorm blew in. Charles, on his way to church, trudged down the street. He passed a little dead-end lane known as Artillery Street. There he recalled his mother had told him about a primitive Methodist chapel on the short lane. The weather being so miserable, he laid aside his first plan and decided to enter the little Methodist church. Perhaps there he could hear the message of salvation and redemption.

When the fifteen-year-old lad entered the church building, he made the fifteenth worshiper. He sat about two-thirds of the way back from the front of the church on the preacher's right hand. The pastor himself did not arrive, and a simple, nearly illiterate preacher from the congregation stood up to preach. Spurgeon shared and wrote about the event many times in the succeeding years. Let him tell us of that wonderful day in his own words:

A very thin-looking man, a shoemaker, or tailor, or something of that sort, went up into the pulpit to preach. Now, it is well that preachers should be instructed; but this man was really stupid. He was obliged to stick to his text, for the simple reason that he had little else to say. The text was, "LOOK UNTO ME, AND BE YE SAVED, ALL THE ENDS OF THE EARTH."

He did not even pronounce the word rightly, but that did not matter. There was, I thought, a glimpse of hope for me in the text. The preacher began thus: "My dear friends, this is a very simple text indeed. It says, 'Look.' Now lookin' don't take a deal of pains. It ain't liftin' your foot or your finger; it's just, 'Look.' Well, a man needn't go to college to learn to look. You may be the biggest fool, and yet you can look. A man needn't be worth a thousand a year to be able to look. Anyone can look; even a child can look. But then the text says, 'Look unto Me.' Ay!" said he, in broad Essex, "many of ye are lookin' to yourselves, but it's no use lookin' there. You'll never find any comfort in yourselves. Some look to God the Father. No, look to Him by-and-by. Jesus Christ says, 'Look unto Me.' Some of ye say, 'We must wait for the Spirit's workin'.' You have no business with that just now. Look to Christ. The text says, 'Look unto Me.'" Then the good man followed up his text in this way: "Look unto Me, I am sweatin' great drops of blood. Look unto Me; I am hangin' on the cross. Look unto Me; I am dead and buried. Look unto Me; I rise again. Look unto Me; I ascent to Heaven. Look unto Me; I am sittin' at the Father's right hand. O poor sinner, look unto Me! Look unto Me!" When he had gone to about that length, and managed to spin out ten minutes or so, he was at the end of his tether. Then he looked at me under the gallery, and I daresay, with so few present, he knew me to be a stranger. Just fixing his eyes on me, as if he knew all my heart, he said, "Young man, you look very miserable." Well, I did; but I had not been accustomed to have remarks made from the pulpit on my personal appearance before. However, it was a good blow, struck right home. He continued, "and you always will be miserable—miserable in life, and miserable in death—if you don't obey my text; but if you obey now, this moment, you will be saved." Then, lifting up his hands, he shouted, as only a Primitive Methodist could. "O young man, look to Jesus Christ. Look! Look! Look! You have nothin' to do but to look and live." I saw at once the way of salvation. I know not what else he said—I did not take much notice of it—I was so possessed with that one thought. Like as when the brazen serpent was lifted up, the people only looked and were healed, so it was with me. I had been waiting to do fifty things. But when I heard that word, "Look!" what a charming word it seemed to me! Oh! I looked until I could almost have looked my eyes away. There and then the cloud was gone, the darkness had rolled away, and that moment I saw the sun; and I could have risen that instant, and sung with the most enthusiastic of them, of the precious blood of Christ, and the simple faith which looks alone to Him. Oh, that somebody had told me this before, "Trust Christ, and you shall be saved." Yet it was, no doubt, all wisely ordered, and now I can say,

> E'er since by faith I saw the stream
> Thy flowing wounds supply,
> Redeeming love has been my theme,
> And shall be till I die.[3]

Charles had found the answer; Christ had come into his life. He truly did experience the burden "loosed off his shoulders."

After his conversion, Reverend Catlow baptized Charles in the Lark River. A short time later he finished his work at Newmarket School and transferred to Cambridge, where he attended school and also served as a tutor. He joined the St. Andrew's Street Baptist Church and the future was set for him, denominationally. Although he had been reared in the Puritan context of the Congregational church, he became convinced that a person should be baptized by immersion after their conversion experience as a testimony to the grace of Christ. At the St. Andrew's Church another significant event occurred.

THE PREACHING MINISTRY

Many small Baptist congregations in Britain could not acquire ordained ministers to fill their pulpits. As a result, a lay-preacher movement was instituted to fill the vacuum. The director of the lay preachers' organization, a member of the St. Andrew's Street Church, invited Charles to preach in a little cottage congregation in Teversham. It went well and a new ministry was born. Then, on October 12, 1851, at the age of seventeen, Charles received the assignment to supply the pulpit for a small Baptist church in Waterbeach, some six miles north of Cambridge. Rowland Hill, the famed Baptist minister, preached his first sermon in that church. Spurgeon was very well received and became pastor of the Waterbeach church in January 1852. As biographer Pike said, "He was a marvelous example of a preacher leaping at a bound full-grown into the pulpit."[4]

After two dynamic, growing years at Waterbeach, Spurgeon received the call to New Park Street Baptist Church of London, England. The church has an illustrious history. The great theologian John Gill, the superb preacher Benjamin Keach, the famous pastor John Rippon, and others had filled the same pulpit. But by the middle of the nineteenth century, the church struggled with hard times. The first Sunday morning that Spurgeon preached to the congregation, only eighty people arrived, even though the building held fifteen hundred. Yet, within the year, two thousand people crammed themselves into the fifteen-hundred-seat auditorium. On many Sundays, up to one thousand people were unable to gain entrance. People sat, almost spellbound, listening to the nineteen-year-old lad declare the Word of God in a fashion they had rarely heard.

For the next thirty-seven years, Spurgeon was the talk of London. His ministry unfolded in an unbelievable fashion. His popularity scarcely has a parallel in British preaching history. The newspapers wrote editorials; artists penned cartoons for publications; all London and England seemed astir. It was all but a revolution in nineteenth-century British church life.

THE MINISTRIES

Spurgeon created manifold ministries. More than twenty different organizations were carried on in the Metropolitan Tabernacle, as his church came to be known. These ministries included the Stockwell Orphanage, the Loan-Rock

Tract Society, the Ordinance Poor Fund, the Lady's Benevolence Society, the Lady's Maternal Society, the Metropolitan Tabernacle Poor Ministers Clothing Society, and many other works. Spurgeon and his church had a great heart. He believed in church-centered, holistic evangelism.

Spurgeon had, at one time, considered resigning his pastorate and becoming an itinerant evangelist. However, his heart always basically revolved around the church. When the growth of the New Park Street Church exceeded its capacity, the great Metropolitan Tabernacle was built. Spurgeon felt perfectly satisfied and stayed there the rest of his life. He realized that God had ordained the church to meet the needs of people, and that was his heartbeat.

THE COLLEGE

One particular work to which Spurgeon gave his deepest devotion, which he called his "first-born and best beloved," was the Pastor's College, now known as Spurgeon's Theological College. He founded the institution to train pastors and proclaimers of the gospel. It serves to this day and ministers as the largest Baptist theological school in Britain. Many notables have come through that institution and taken their ranks as missionaries, evangelists, professors, and pastors around the world.

THE CONTROVERSIES

It must be granted that Spurgeon became something of a controversial figure. He found himself embroiled in several spiritual battles. The most serious of all came in the last five years of his life, called the Downgrade Controversy. The rationalistic, critical theology of the Continent had invaded his beloved denomination, and he took his stand against it. Spurgeon strongly contended for the "faith which was once for all delivered to the saints" (Jude 3). Much to the deep sorrow and surprise of many, the Baptist Union did not rally behind him. As a result, he and his church separated themselves from the Union. He did not leave the Baptist denomination, however. He and his church united with the Surrey and Middlesex Baptist Association. Spurgeon spent his last years in that fellowship. The church and its fellowship with like-minded congregations always assumed a central place in his entire ministry.

The great preacher had battled illness for many years, being a victim of rheumatic gout. Compounding the issue, his wife, Susannah, was a semi-invalid in her later years. But the two struggled on, ministering in an incredible fashion despite their physical infirmities.

As Spurgeon suffered from his maladies, especially in the cold, damp London winters, he would often travel to the south of France to the beautiful coastal town of Mentone for recuperation. In the late fall of 1891, he and his wife journeyed to the Mediterranean for that purpose. Settling down in the Beau Rivage Hotel in Mentone, he hoped to recuperate and gain his strength. People would gather at the little hotel and he would minister to them in Bible study and preaching. But unfortunately, his physical condition seriously deteriorated.

THE END

It became clear that the end was approaching. Charles had been a faithful pilgrim and had traveled the road of Bunyan's character on his own spiritual journey. In the latter part of January, Spurgeon slipped into a coma. On January 31, 1892, at five minutes past eleven on the Sabbath night, in the words of Bunyan's *Pilgrim's Progress:*

> After this it was noised abroad that Mr. Valiant-for-Truth was taken with a summons by the same post as the other, and had this for a token that the summons was true, that his pitcher was broken at the fountain. When he understood it, he called for his friends, and told them of it. Then said he—I am going to my Father's; and though with great difficulty I have got hither, yet now I do not repent me of all the trouble I have been at to arrive where I am. My sword I give to him that shall succeed me in my pilgrimage, and my courage and skill to him that can get it. My marks and scars I carry with me, to be a witness for me that I have fought His battles, who now will be my rewarder. When the day that he must go hence was come, many accompanied him to the river-side; into which as he went, he said—"Death where is thy sting?" and he said—"Grave where is thy victory?" So he passed over, and all the trumpets sounded for him on the other side.[5]

The pilgrim had arrived home.

SPURGEON'S INFLUENCE

There may not have been a preacher in the last two centuries who had quite the influence of Spurgeon. To the present day, there remain more books in print written by Spurgeon than by any other English author of any literary genre. Yet that which distinguished the great preacher was his love for the church and his commitment to ministering in and through the life of the local congregation. His building of the extensive ministry in the Metropolitan Tabernacle of London, his planting of more than two hundred new congregations in Great Britain, the channeling of all his ministry in and through local congregations, and his faithfulness to his Baptist commitments despite the controversies all stand as a token of that which the New Testament declares: "Christ loved the church and gave Himself for it" (Eph. 5:25). Charles Spurgeon likewise loved the church. He realized that, as Professor Charles Erdman has pointed out, "the Christian church . . . [is] the appointed guardian of the sacred deposit of revealed truth."[6]

Thus Spurgeon realized that for evangelism to be lasting and of true significance it must be channeled in and through the local church as much as possible. This principle also stands true for mass evangelism. In a very real sense of the word, Spurgeon served as a mass evangelist in the context of his itinerant ministry. But he always saw to it that the local church received the benefit and played a vital role. Again, let it be said, he was a churchman. That is biblical, historical, and sensible; it makes for an evangelism of integrity and leaves a legacy. Spurgeon personified this legacy, as have all great evangelistic personalities. So the question becomes, What sort of church-centered evangelistic ministry does the Bible put its stamp of approval on?

BIBLICAL EVANGELISM IS CHURCH-CENTERED

That the church stands central in evangelism is axiomatic. This precipitates the question, What constitutes the true nature of the church? In *Baker's Dictionary of Theology*, Willliam Robinson defines the church: "The one church of God is not an institutional but a supernatural entity which is in the process of growth toward the world to come. It is the sphere of all the action of the risen and ascended Lord. All its members are in Christ and are knit together by a supernatural kinship."[7]

This definition falls right in line with the New Testament term that biblical writers employed to describe the church: *ecclesia,* meaning "a called-out people." This definition implies that God, by the Holy Spirit, calls people out of their sin and spiritual death, and as they respond they become God's own personal people, set apart for ministry and His glory. That is a high and holy calling indeed. The apostle Paul expressed in beautiful words the position and privilege of the church. He wrote to the Ephesians, "Christ . . . loved the church and gave Himself up for her; that He might sanctify her, having cleansed her by the washing of water with the word, that He might present to Himself the church in all her glory, having no spot or wrinkle or any such thing; but that she should be holy and blameless" (5:25–27).

THE CHURCH UNIVERSAL

In the important passage above, Paul presents the church in its eternal, all-inclusive, worldwide perspective. Believers of all ages make up its composition. Many graphic, biblical metaphors describe the various aspects of the universal church: "a royal priesthood" (1 Pet. 2:9), "a holy nation" (1 Pet. 2:9), "the bride, the wife of the Lamb" (Rev. 21:9), "the body of Christ" (1 Cor. 12:27 NIV), and "God's building" (1 Cor. 3:9). We rightly call it the "church universal."

Several significant truths emerge from these metaphors and similar scriptural passages. In the first place, the church is made up of a distinct, "peculiar" people (Titus 2:14 KJV). That is to say, believers in Christ are a "people for God's own possession" (1 Pet. 2:9). They hold that unique position because they have been bought by God at the price of the "precious blood of Christ" (1 Pet. 1:19 KJV). Belonging to God, they are thus expected to do His will, follow His leading, faithfully serve Him, and bring glory to His name. They are His *personal people.*

Moreover, the church in its universal configuration stands as something of a mediator, a "royal priesthood" (1 Pet. 2:9). In this priestly role, the church offers up sacrifices to God (Heb. 8:3), officiates in worship (Lev. 23), and comes before God to intercede for people. That fact implies the church's worldwide mission, which is the real meaning of the "priesthood of all believers." God's "priests" serve Christ to impact the world with the saving gospel of Christ; they evangelize.

THE UNIVERSAL CHURCH AS NEW
COVENANT LIFE IN CHRIST

Finally, the church, as the "fellowship of the ministering to the saints" (2 Cor. 8: 4 KJV), stands as God's model of what the ideal society should be. God's ideal for humanity has been warped and perverted by sin, but God's love in Christ stepped in to redeem the wayward world (John 3:16). Thus, the church draws the world by word, example, and service to Christ. This forms the essence of the covenant and its ministry. God designed the church as a living organism of new covenant life to bring glory to Jesus Christ and thus inspire and lead people to faith in our Lord.

An important implication of the covenant concept centers in the fact that all believers are merged into a dynamic fellowship with all who share in it. Not only are Christ's covenant people vertically related to God, they are horizontally related to others who share in the same relationship (1 John 1:3). All who are part of the covenant family are vitally connected to each other. Believers become one in Christ regardless of age, country, culture, denomination, gender, time, race, or any human category. All who are "born again" (John 3:3 KJV) participate in the covenant and thus become brothers and sisters who together receive the grace of God.

The covenant principle actually constitutes the essence of what the Bible implies by the Greek word *laos*, "the people of God." Often misunderstood, some tend to set the "laity" over against the "clergy," as touched upon in an earlier chapter. *Laos* simply means "people." The *laos* of God are comprised of all redeemed men and women, regardless of their role in the structured life of their local church. It includes the professional, ordained leaders as well as those who hold no leadership positions whatsoever. In the new covenant, all are one in Christ (Gal. 3:28).

These realities delineate the essential meaning of the church in its universal configuration. There is, however, the practical outworking of these principles, which are effected in the other New Testament aspect of the church—its local, limited manifestations. This fact is most important for evangelism.

THE LOCAL ASPECT OF THE CHURCH

The church in its local historical setting becomes the place where all the principles of the church's universal nature are pragmatically realized. The reason for that is obvious: A local congregation of like-minded believers can be seen, can worship, and can minister. True fellowship is realized on that practical, local level. Christians who wish to minister in fellowship with God's covenant people must in some sense relate to the local church. Hence, it becomes vitally necessary to be involved in a local congregation in the kingdom's evangelistic enterprise—the *misseo dei*.

Therefore, a local church stands at the fountainhead of proclamation and makes its impact with the gospel. This does not mean that witnessing the good news of God goes on only inside the four walls of a church building. On the contrary, a true Christian church carries its witness to the marketplaces of daily life. The local church gathered becomes the place where believers meet to worship, to grow in knowledge and grace, to be inspired and guided to higher Christian living and godliness, to devise programs, to preach the gospel, and then go out into the world to minister. A church scattered in the world and ministering in Christ's name is just as much the church as when it is gathered together in worship.

MINISTERS

Thus, ministry becomes a central aspect of the local congregational life. This means the church is to respond to all needs of all people as much as possible. Wherever any kind of problem arises, God intends the church to step in regardless of race, economic background, or other distinction and attempt to meet the real needs of people to the best of its ability and resources. Let it be made clear again that no conflict exists between evangelism and social involvement. The blending of the two is often the secret of successful cross-cultural evangelism—all kinds of evangelism for that matter.

All this points to the fact that the general nature and purpose of the church of Jesus Christ center primarily in evangelism. This has hopefully now become evident. The church is God's covenant people involved in worship, proclamation, and ministry. It has a mission and message as a unified whole. This is true in principle on a universal level and pragmatically workable on the local scene. Because the divine commission is given to the entire church, the whole church (the *laos*) is to engage in it. All are responsible to serve and become witnesses (Acts 1:8), because all have been brought into covenant life by the free grace of

God. That constitutes the nature of the covenant and thus the nature of the church and its ministry. Obviously, the entire *laos* of God possess a most profound evangelistic calling. That truth demands a closer look.

THE CHURCH'S PRIMARY MINISTRY TO AN ALIENATED WORLD: EVANGELISM

The church stands as God's agent in a needy world. Jesus said, as we have seen so often, "All authority in heaven and on earth has been given to me. Go therefore and make disciples of all nations, baptizing them in the name of the Father and of the Son and of the Holy Spirit, teaching them to observe all that I have commanded you; and lo, I am with you always, to the close of the age" (Matt. 28:18–20 RSV). At the heart of the oft-quoted Great Commission, the church's primary task stands out in bold relief. There is much to be found in the Commission, as it encompasses the entire spectrum of the church's life and ministry. However, central to the call of Christ is the fact that believers are to become witnesses (Acts 1:8) and make disciples of all nations.

Churches must be absolutely clear in their understanding concerning their task and message. Covenant people are to realize God has given them a heaven-sent message (*kerygma*), and He places a premium stamp on communicating it and winning the lost. Actually, one cannot be a balanced biblical believer and come to any other conclusion. This entire volume has hopefully made that obvious. Of course, there have been shallow, superficial evangelistic activities, but that does not excuse anyone for not giving evangelism first priority in individual and covenant church life. Let it once more be said, this must be recognized by the entire *laos* of God, not just the "professional" evangelist or preacher.

SOCIAL DIMENSIONS OF THE GOSPEL

Giving evangelism priority does not mean there are no other ministries to perform in the covenant life of the local church. There are many worthy and needed social and family services in which to engage, as seen in the chapter on St. Francis. To these things the church should give itself. To sever evangelism from social concern and action becomes a real tragedy.

Still, evangelism must be seen as the priority; it comes first because it meets the deepest need—salvation. That attitude wins the world to Jesus Christ, and that sets the church's goal. The church obviously has a great responsibility that demands every resource the local congregation can muster.

But why do so many believers appear apathetic in introducing people to Jesus Christ? There are many probable reasons. For example, some embrace faulty theological views and thus feel no real compulsion to evangelize. More often, however, the Lord's people simply do not grasp the practical principles of how to engage in God's scheme of world outreach, and through fear or ignorance (or both) fail as a witness. The need of the hour centers in setting out Spirit-inspired principles as found in the Word of God and preparing believers to engage in world evangelization, thus bringing the fruits of their labors to the church.

SUMMARY AND CONCLUSION

It has now been made evident that the New Testament and history teach that evangelism—at least in its finest expressions—should be church-centered. One can point to many instances of evangelists going into an area "on their own" and often registering "great results." But what happens to the converts? Often they are left on their own with no leadership, spiritual guidance, or opportunity for spiritual maturity. Evangelists should invade all areas of the earth to be sure; but it must be remembered that the local church can best nurture and care for the new converts and play a vital role in the ministry of follow-up, as well as undergirding the evangelist in his or her ministry.

Consequently, the local church makes a significant contribution. The wise evangelist realizes this truth and thus relates to the local church as much as possible. As one observes the course of the moving of the Spirit through the ages, the closer evangelism is tied into church life, the more effective that evangelism becomes. One can sense the favor of God upon such an approach in the process of reaching the world for Christ. Therefore, let it be stressed again, when itinerant evangelists and parachurch organizations center their work, as much as possible, in and through local churches, the more positive the final results become.

The teaching of the Scriptures and the history of effective evangelism make it obvious: The local church must assume a central role in evangelism. And the ripple effect goes through the entire universal church until finally the kingdom of God itself is significantly enhanced. Thus the contribution is made. That principle, along with the others this book has set forth, represents a vital phase of historical authenticity in evangelism. It presents a biblical, historical criterion for the evaluation of Billy Graham's ministry and his contribution and legacy to the church local and universal.

PART II:
BILLY GRAHAM AND THE CHURCH

Jesus delivered to the church its immediate, compelling commission . . . evangelization.
—BILLY GRAHAM

INTRODUCTION

"Of all the many groups in which humans have collected themselves, of all the tribes, clans, organizations, and societies throughout history, none has been so powerful, so far-reaching, or more universal than the Church."[8] So said evangelist Billy Graham. He particularized and personalized this general statement by stating, "I was brought up as a Presbyterian and later became a Baptist. In later years I have felt that I belonged to all churches."[9] John Yarbrough, director of evangelism for Southern Baptists—the denomination of which Billy is a member—much admires Billy Graham's reaching out to the whole church as he does in his evangelization.[10]

Billy Graham obviously holds real regard for the church of the Lord Jesus Christ. As Baptist World Alliance leader Denton Lotz has said, "Billy is a great churchman and his influence has spread across denominational lines."[11] Although Graham would be the first to say that when we stand before God, the question concerning salvation will not be what church we have faithfully attended; rather, what we have done with God's Son, the Lord Jesus Christ; He is the prime issue. Nonetheless, Graham does hold the church in high esteem, and he makes serious effort to enlist and involve the church in all he undertakes as a world evangelist. Ralph Bell, associate evangelist, readily admits,

"Our work could not go on without the church support. Billy Graham and the team see themselves as servants of the church."[12] In like manner, Sterling Huston, crusade director, has said, "The BGEA must function in ways that honor, serve and build up the church or we are not biblical."[13] With these statements Billy Graham heartily agrees. But how does the evangelist understand the church? What makes up his doctrinal position concerning the "bride, the wife of the Lamb" (Rev. 21: 9)?

BILLY GRAHAM AND HIS VIEW OF THE CHURCH

Billy Graham, as expected, assumes a basic, biblical approach. He understands the church in a twofold sense; namely, the church in its universal aspect and the church as a local body of believers. Concerning the life of the church, Graham has made a number of definitive statements in his work *Billy Graham Answers Your Questions*. He has written, "Being a member of Christ's church involves more than an outward attachment. . . . Church membership, in the true sense, is being a real part of a company of people who have staked their all on the belief that all that Jesus said was true. . . . A member of Christ's church is one who has made Christ central in his life."[14]

On the local level, he describes the Bride of Christ in saying, "The Church is the family of believers (Eph. 2:19)."[15] And what is true in its local aspect is likewise true on the universal level; the church in every sense stands as the great family of believers. Putting it together he declares that the church, "on the local limited scale, like the universal Church, is the body of Christ." He bases this statement on Ephesians 1:22–23, in which Paul wrote, "And He put all things in subjection under His feet, and gave Him as head over all things to the church, which is His body, the fulness of Him who fills all in all." Graham goes on from there to delineate in more detail his doctrine of the church from this twofold perspective.

THE CHURCH UNIVERSAL

From the above quotations concerning the universal church, Billy Graham obviously sees the church as composed of the entire body of all believers, as he puts it, from the Day of Pentecost until the return of Christ when God's people shall be resurrected. Admittance to the church in this broad sense comes about through hearing the gospel, responding positively to the message through repentance and faith, and thus being granted entrance into the body of Christ. As he has said, "Those who are counted part of this one, true, universal Church of God are those who have repented of their sins, sought God's pardon, and accepted the Lord Jesus Christ as their personal Savior."[16] Graham sees no delay in membership into the church universal through a process of indoctrination, catechism, or any restriction that a local church may enact relative to receiving its members. He stresses, "You become a member of this church—the universal church—the moment you become a believer."[17]

Of importance in Graham's ecclesiology is his conviction that the church universal—or local for that matter—is not the result of human work or organizational effort. He has said, "The Church is the only institution organized by Christ . . . the Church is the result of Christ's death and resurrection." In a word, "Jesus Christ Himself founded the church."[18] Furthermore, when a person becomes a "member" of the universal congregation of God's redeemed people, obligations are immediately forthcoming. In Graham's *Peace with God*, he has said to those who respond to the gospel imperative:

> Now that you have accepted Christ as your Savior and put your trust and confidence in Him, you have already become a member of the great universal Church. You are a member of the household of faith. You are a part of the body of Christ. Now you are called upon to obey Christ, and if you obey Christ, you will follow His example of joining with others in the worship of God.[19]

Graham then emphasizes, "It is to the Church and its Christ that you owe allegiance."[20] All of this implies that the church, in both aspects of its manifestations, rests upon Jesus Christ as the chief cornerstone, and He is thus the Head in the fullest sense of the word. Graham stated,

> He [Jesus Christ] is the great cornerstone upon which the Church is built. He is the foundation of all Christian experience, and the Church is founded upon Him . . . Jesus proclaimed Himself to be the founder of the Church, the builder of the Church, and the Church belongs to Him alone. He has promised to live with, and in, all those who are members of this Church. Here is not only an

organization but an organism which is completely unlike anything else that the world has ever known: God Himself living with, and in, ordinary men and women who are members of His Church.[21]

Graham believes it is important to realize that we do not unmistakably know who composes the true universal body of Christ. He tells us that the members of the one true body of Christ are ultimately known only to God. They are the ones who have their names written in the Lamb's Book of Life (Rev. 21:27). God has designated them as the "called-out" ones. And against this true church, the gates of hell will never prevail (Matt. 16:18).

One note that should be addressed centers in the fact that, as pointed out above, Graham sees the universal church as being comprised of those who have come to a living faith in God from the Day of Pentecost onward. This implies a "dispensational" approach. He was influenced by the Scofield Reference Bible in his Bible school and Wheaton days. Scofield espoused a typical dispensational view. But that point need not be particularly pressed; Graham does see the church in its broad aspect to which most Bible scholars eventually agree. This now leads to Billy Graham's views on the purpose of the church in its local manifestation.

THE LOCAL CHURCH

The evangelist begins by stating that "membership in a Christ-centered local church is . . . vitally important."[22] Ira Craft, businessman and supporter of the Graham ministry, commends Graham's attitude toward the local church. In an interview Craft stated, "Billy never left the local church out of his ministry."[23] Billy Graham does view the church as most important, because the local church is a group of people joining together "for worship, fellowship, and instruction." This, in turn, the evangelist says, will "strengthen one's walk with God and make it possible to have a more positive and effective testimony for Christ."[24] That is vital to historical Christianity. Graham thus puts strong stress on the importance of the local church, seeing it as the tangible manifestation of the church universal and that to which one should give oneself. The local church serves as an expression of faith and commitment to Jesus Christ.

Graham, as mentioned, cautiously warns people that membership in a local church will not in itself produce salvation. God's redemption comes solely by grace through faith in Jesus Christ (Eph. 2:8). He has said, "Membership in a local church does not save a person." He goes on by declaring, "Nowhere in the Bible do we find on teaching that we are saved by uniting with a church."[25] Yet at the same time, he wants it to be fully understood that those who are saved should definitely identify themselves with a local body of believers. He said the Bible declares, "Christ, loved the church and gave Himself for it. If our Lord loved it enough to die for it; then we should respect it enough to support and attend it."[26] He goes on, "Christians have always required a living relationship with such assemblies."[27] This leads to another important principle in Graham's grasp of the local church, namely, the biblical prerequisites for membership in a congregation.

Billy Graham first of all unequivocally declares, "A member of Christ's church is one who has made Christ central in his life; who thinks in terms of eternity, and who is committed to Him, who is the Way, the Truth, and the Life."[28] Graham is also very explicit that a high ethical standard for local church membership should be maintained. And when members fail, they should be disciplined, but always for redemptive purposes. He outlines the scriptural pattern for discipline. A question was put to him about a woman who had openly flaunted God's moral laws. Graham answered with this counsel:

> The Bible prescribes a formula for dealing with the situation. . . . First, someone who is a member of the church should go to her and confront her in private with her sin. Then, if she does not repent, two or three others are to confront her in private. If she will still not repent, she is to be taken before the entire congregation. If she still refuses to repent, she is to be put out of the church. The emphasis is on repentance, not judgment, except as a last resort—and even then God still cares about her redemption and restoration. This was the pattern quite clearly that Christ laid out.[29]

Graham rightly emphasizes that discipline is always to be administered with redemptive and restorative views in mind. The wayward church member should hopefully be brought back into the fold and fellowship restored. And, of course, the classic case is outlined by Paul in his letter to the Corinthian church concerning the man who was living an incestuous lifestyle. Paul rejoiced when the wayward church member was restored through repentance.

Then Paul urged the church to receive him back into the full fellowship of believers (2 Cor. 2:5–11). That constitutes the goal of discipline. The church must be kept pure; Billy Graham is insistent upon that.

But the church obviously exists for much more than disciplinary purposes. Graham outlines his grasp of the nature and primary purpose of the local church. The evangelist well understands that the church has a *mission* to perform and that members of the church should give themselves to that purpose and the many implications of the church's rationale for its existence—and that is quite extensive. What, therefore, constitutes those various goals that grow out of the mission purpose of a local congregation?

The foundational purpose for the gathering of God's people together in corporate life centers in worship. Graham has said, "In church we come together with the believers to worship God."[30] He emphasizes again, "The purpose of this Christian society called the 'Church' is, first: to glorify God by our worship. We do not go to church just to hear a sermon. We go to church to worship God."[31] Graham stresses that the church is for fellowship and that fellowship must be in mutual harmony and for the glorifying of God in worship.

Graham also states that as the church gathers for worship they also "come together to learn more about God and His word."[32] He elaborates on that thought as he urges believers to "seek to live each day for Christ." Then he goes on to say, "An important part of that is growing in your relationship to God by having fellowship with other believers in hearing His word taught, which is why the Church is important."[33]

Elaborating on this last purpose, Graham sees as an important factor that "the Church is for the strengthening of faith."[34] The Scriptures place in high profile the fact that "faith comes from hearing, and hearing by the word of Christ" (Rom. 10:17). As believers come together in fellowship and hear the Word of God, their faith is strengthened and encouraged. The faithful proclamation of the essential truths of Jesus Christ in the context of church worship deeply moves hearers and strengthens their faith and commitment to the Lord Jesus. Of course, that immediately implies that the church plays a central role in the spreading of the gospel. Billy Graham has said, "The church is commanded to go."

Actually, the evangelist sees the *primary mission* of the church in its service to the world as centering in proclaiming Christ to that lost world. That is the core of the issue. In that setting the church submits to God's command and fulfills the Great Commission. And that includes the encouragement of all members to become a witness to Christ's saving grace. Operation Andrew, the BGEA's witnessing program begun in London's Harringay crusade in 1954, has made a significant contribution to that end. In faithful witnessing, God's people become pleasing to their Lord and Head, Jesus Christ. That is why Graham states, "The church is a medium of service. We are saved to serve. There are a thousand and one tasks to be done for Christ. This work can best be accomplished through the fellowship of a local church. A virile Christianity has never existed apart from the church. The church is the organization of Christ on earth."[35] He develops that theme by declaring, "I am convinced that the cluster of believers . . . these brothers and sisters in Christ where you join to pray and study, give and witness, is the basic unit through which God is working to redeem the world."[36] High role for the church to fulfill! Thus believers who join together for worship and praise occupy a very vital place in the evangelistic mandate of the church.

BEING BUILT UP IN THE FAITH

Moreover, the church exists not only for the purpose of bringing people to faith in Christ, but also for building up believers in the faith. As Graham has said, "I believe the changing of people's hearts is the primary mission of the Church."[37] And that means not only evangelization, but the maturation of those who have been evangelized as well. Graham stated, "The Church has a very specific assignment, and only the church provides the nurture for spiritual growth."[38] The reason being, according to Billy, "through joint prayers, testimonies and the preaching and teaching . . . faith will be strengthened."[39] The church can furthermore be the avenue, as Graham expressed it, "that our humanitarianism finds its widest expression."[40]

Billy loves the church for that very reason. He recalled his early days in his church with these words: "I remember how I loved to be with the members of my church for worship and fellowship." Today, concerning the rich fellowship of the church, Billy said, "I feel that I belong to all the churches. I am equally at home in an Anglican or Baptist church or a Brethren assembly. . . . To me, the most important part, of course, is the Communion service, when I have the opportunity to fellowship at the Lord's Table and take of this wine that is representative of His blood and of the bread that represents His body."[41] It must be remembered that Billy was pastor of a local church for a period. This was most influential in his attitude toward the church, not only regarding fellowship but in his evangelism also. As one scholar said, "Graham's pastoral [work] . . . climaxed his concept that evangelism must be church centered."[42]

Of course, fellowship is not the only reason Billy Graham loves the church, but it does rank high on the list. The fellowship of believers can obviously be a dynamic spiritual experience. At the same time, Graham does not have a "Pollyanna" attitude toward the church; he knows it has its failings. He has said, "The church is not perfect. Some within the churches . . . have even departed from the basic truths of the Christian faith. But God has His people and the church is essential to His plan."[43]

Furthermore, the church that enjoys a rich fellowship must minister in a holistic sense. In an earlier chapter we have seen Graham's insistence and practice of this principle. As an example, he stated that during one of his evangelistic crusades they literally gathered tons of food for the needy. Graham holds that holistic evangelism is applicable and actually essential to the life of any local congregation. As Jesus ministered in that manner, so must His "body."[44]

Being in a definite geographical, cultural situation, a local church can reach out in ways that bring glory to God and the alleviation of many problems and pains to multitudes of people. Graham places strong emphasis on the importance of the church in that aspect of ministry. The evangelist has said, "Jesus stated that his true followers would be those who cared for the hungry and others in need (Matt. 25:31–46). The Bible also declares, 'If a brother or sister is without clothing and in need of daily food, and one of you says to them, "Go in peace, be warmed and be filled," and yet you do not give them what is necessary for their body, what use is that?' (Jas. 2:15-16)."[45] Billy also urges, "The Church should be the means of channeling your funds for Christian work."[46] God's people can by faithful stewardship to their church do much to help needy people and further the mission cause. Graham is thus very pragmatic in his views of the place of the local church in the breadth of Christian ministry.

THE HEAD: JESUS CHRIST

Foundational to all of these principles of Graham's doctrine of the church is the fact that Jesus Christ stands as the Head of the body. This truth must be seen as central. As has been set forth earlier, Graham places a significant emphasis upon that reality. He has said, "Jesus Christ is the head of this great universal Church. From Him must spring all the activities and teachings of the Church, for He is the fountainhead of all Christian religious experience."[47] Graham unequivocally declares, "He is the great cornerstone on which the Church is built."[48] That is why Graham feels most strongly, "When a person experiences the new birth, he or she . . . should seek to identify immediately with a local church which honors the Lord and His Word."[49] Therefore, as a logical deduction, Graham holds that every activity of the church should be carried on to glorify God. If all these things are true concerning the church, how does Graham see the local church in its ordered, structured life?

ORGANIZATIONAL PRINCIPLES

Billy Graham insists that the church must maintain a strong leadership structure. He sees the pastor as the primary leader with its attending responsibilities. Graham has said, "The Bible tells us that we should submit to those who have such responsibility [because] 'they keep watch over you as men who must give an account. Obey them so their work will be a joy, not a burden, for that would be of no advantage to you' (Heb. 13:17)."[50] He does not elucidate a complex church administrative structure, however. He simply sees the local church as led by pastors who teach, preach, and minister God's Word as Christ's "undershepherds." He leaves the details of structures up to the local church with its doctrinal, denominational views.

Now, in light of all that has been said, Graham states, "The Church is a family of believers, Christ died not only for the individual, but for the [whole] Church."[51] Therefore, it is interesting to see how he deals with this reality as an interdenominational evangelist when he attempts to enlist all churches in his work. This is an important point for Graham. He has several things to say.

THE EVANGELIST AND THE EVANGELIZING CHURCH

Graham points out first that most of the major denominations, when it comes to evangelism, normally exhibit a gracious spirit of cooperation, not condemning others for their deviation from their own system of church structure and government. In the final analysis, Graham believes "that most of the major denominations have basically the same Christian doctrines. At least this would hold true for the more evangelical denominations." Elaborating on that point he states, "It is true that some are much closer to their original beliefs than others . . . [But] remember that there is no perfect church and no perfect congregation."[52]

Therefore, Graham contends, differences—at least in evangelical churches—should not deter them from throwing their time and energy into evangelistic efforts together. Graham, of course, is insistent that such cooperation does not mean anyone should forsake loyalty to their own church and denomination. He has said, "I believe in denominational loyalty."[53] And he is essentially correct when he states, as seen above, that most major evangelical denominations adhere to basically the same theology as far as the gospel is concerned. Graham has said, "I have found that non-essentials separate people more often than essentials. In reading the history of denominations, it is interesting to note that . . . divisions have always resulted from somewhat minor differences . . . I made up my mind to fellowship with all those who love Jesus Christ with all their heart, and are seeking to serve Him."[54]

He confesses, "I have sometimes been criticized for doing this, but I would rather lose a few friends than the blessing and favor of my Lord."[55] In that same spirit, he also feels he must submit to the church. Citing the apostle Paul's spirit in this regard he states, "Scripture indicates that first he earned the confidence of the church by his submission to it and his service to it."[56] That is Graham's attitude and approach, showing his respect for the church and their evangelistic endeavors.

At the same time, as mentioned earlier, Billy Graham is a faithful Southern Baptist and a supporting member of the First Baptist Church of Dallas, Texas. Graham emphasizes the fact that "the Bible says . . . that it was Christ's love for the Church [and] I must love it too. I must pray for it, defend it, work in it, pay my tithes and offerings to it, help to advance it, promote holiness in it, and make it the functional, and witnessing body our Lord meant it to be."[57] As the evangelist said in his autobiography, "One of my objectives was to build the church in the community. . . . I wanted to leave something behind in the very churches themselves."[58] All this being the case, what does Graham do to help people into the life of the church when they make decisions in his evangelistic crusades?

THE CHURCH IN BILLY GRAHAM'S
EVANGELISTIC FOLLOW-UP

In the evangelist's assimilation work, Billy is well aware that "without the cooperation of the local churches and their pastors not only would attendance [at the crusades] suffer, but so would follow-up of new Christians."[59] For many years, Charles Riggs, along with Tom Phillips, directed the program of Counseling and Church Assimilation of those who make a decision in the crusades. In that office, they worked essentially through local churches. As stated above, Billy Graham has always nourished a deep concern to integrate new converts into a local church and thus into a life of usefulness for Christ.

To this end a comprehensive program has been developed. The program has been touched upon previously; but one or two more words are appropriate here. It all begins the moment a person makes a public commitment to Christ during the invitation time in a Graham crusade. As previously shown, names of inquirers are sent to local churches the same night the decision is made. Moreover, contact is kept with decision-makers for, in most instances, at least a year. The Graham team does all in its power to involve the inquirer into a local church. It seems conclusive that anyone who makes any kind of commitment in a Graham crusade is honestly cared for and nurtured in the context of the local church. He reminds his fellow evangelists in *A Biblical Standard for Evangelists:* "Proclaiming Christ must be linked to building His church, the importance of which is clearly taught in the New Testament."[60] He elaborates, "A further aspect of the evangelist's responsibility . . . to the Church is that the fruits of an evangelistic ministry which serves Christ should be directed to biblically based churches."[61]

It does go without saying, of course, that for the program of any evangelist to be successful, the local church must respond. Here the record has not been as positive as one would hope. Many churches do rise to the occasion and carry on the ministry of integration, but there are those, sadly, who do not. Congregations that do fully cooperate with the Graham program normally see a good influx of new members, not to mention the enhancement of the spiritual lives of many of their own constituents. Churches that do not involve themselves usually fail to see many positive results from the crusade, and in such instances they tend to be critical because they do not see much significance in their own corporate life.

A SPIRITUAL BATTLE

Graham is very conscious of the fact that satanic opposition will be encountered, not only in follow-up programs, but also in the entire evangelistic enterprise. As he said, "Satan does not want to build a church and call it, 'the First Church of Satan,' he is far too clever for that. He invades the Sunday School, the youth department, the Christian education program, the pulpit and the seminary classroom."[62] And, it could be added, a good follow-up program. The devil's ploy is to get believers, especially new believers, into theological or practical error and destroy their faith and service. And the devil will often use church leaders, if he can. Satan is a liar and a deceiver. Billy calls him the "great imitator." Further, Graham does not hesitate to label men like the more liberal John A. T. Robinson and Paul Tillich as departing from the essential truth of the gospel.[63] It does seem incredible, but as Graham states, "It is difficult for us to accept the fact that Satan can use a preacher or clergyman as one of his tools, proclaiming another gospel than the gospel of Jesus Christ. Yet that can be the case . . . We 'test the spirits' as we compare their teaching with the truth of God's Word, the Bible."[64] A good word of warning!

When failure in the battle is encountered, and churches reap little or no harvest from a Graham crusade, it thus seems correct and fair to say that in such instances the fault is especially their own. They have simply failed to use the facilities and the programming provided by the BGEA that have brought positive results to other local congregations. It is possible for a church to fall into Satan's trap and ignore or pervert the Holy Spirit's work in a crusade. That may sound rather harsh, but it is the truth.

It would seem wise at this stage to present a statistical analysis of the general impact of a Graham crusade in a community. When churches throw themselves into a crusade, positive results are basically forthcoming. But at times, some dynamics are somewhat disappointing.

CRUSADE STATISTICS

Not all evaluations of Graham crusades have been completely positive. A study of the effectiveness of an earlier Graham crusade was undertaken by Frank Fitt. Concerning the Detroit meetings, Fitt stated in an article in the *Christian*

Century, "On the basis of the usual replies received from almost 30 per cent of the Protestant pastors of metropolitan Detroit, twelve months after the Graham campaign, it is possible to state, first, that the lasting significance of the card-signing phase at present organized is vastly exaggerated; and second, that extremely few local churches were strengthened spiritually by the campaign."[65]

This crusade obviously did not receive as positive an evaluation as the Harringay crusade in London of 1954. In the Harringay effort, Stanley High gave the results of a poll taken by the *British Weekly*. The poll investigated British clergyman of all denominations on "What's Left of Harringay?" It found that of the outsiders (neither church members nor regular churchgoers) converted at Harringay, 64 percent "are still attending church and taking part in church life regularly." Other positive results occurred according to Stanley High: "Since the Harringay Crusade, England's Scripture Union, an interdenominational organization to promote regular Bible-reading, has had the largest one-year increase in membership in its history. Subscriptions to his Scripture-reading 'helps' have grown by 60,000. London's bookstores report record Bible sales."[66]

Another study took some issue with the results of the research that High reported. Cecil Northcott, in the *Christian Century*, a liberal publication, pointed out that another London newspaper, the *Evening Standard*, conducted a survey of what was left eight months after the London meetings of 1954.[67] Twenty vicars of large London parishes were asked where the converts sent to them had gone. These twenty churches reported that 336 people were referred to them. Of the 336 referred, 226 were old churchgoers and 110 were "outsiders." Of the 110 outsiders, the *Standard* reported that only 45 (41 percent) were still coming to church eight months after the meetings. There were about thirty-six thousand who made "decisions for Christ" at the Harringay crusade. As a result of a sample test, it was reported that twenty-four thousand were old faithfuls and of the other twelve thousand, some four thousand were still in the churches. These figures have not been seriously challenged. High's figure of 64 percent did not correspond with this study; however, it remains whose figures one chooses.

A study was conducted concerning the New York City crusade of 1957. Four months after the meetings, 504 Protestant clergymen in New York, Nassau, and Westchester Counties were polled. Three questions were asked:

(1) How many referrals did you receive? (2) How many of these were new names? (3) How many of these referrals are now attending services regularly? The list of ministers who received the questionnaires was "picked at random from the 1957–58 directory published by the Protestant Council of the City of New York and represented about 25% of all churches in the directory."[68] About one-third of those queried, or 159 ministers, replied. There were 3,997 referrals to the churches; 2,522 (64 percent) were already church members. Replies to the third question "were inconclusive because many ministers left that answer blank. Some reported that they had no way to check and others said the time was too short to give a fair figure. Enough replies were received, however, to indicate that the 'pillars of the church' stayed on, but many of the new names went to another church or dropped out of sight."[69]

It would seem from these surveys that Billy Graham had at least reasonable success, even in these very early crusades. He certainly was as "successful" as the average church in receiving and integrating new members regardless of the methods the local church used. And, one must not forget the point made earlier in this book concerning the parable of the sower. Not all the "seed" cast falls on fertile ground and produces "fruit." Moreover, it should be emphasized that the crusades have grown in effectiveness through the years. For example, in the St. Louis crusade of 1999, 6.4 percent of attendees made decisions for Christ. In the crusade in Indianapolis, the same year, 7.9 percent made decisions; and in the Washington, D.C., crusade in 1986, 6 percent of attendees became inquirers. These types of statistics can be recorded over and again.

Furthermore, an interesting phenomenon occurs: Some inquirers do not really get settled in a church for some time. Four or five years after their decisions, the statistics are quite improved. That may sound paradoxical, but it is true. The reason has been speculated that the pure "outsider" who makes a decision in a Graham crusade needs time to settle into a church where he or she feels "at home."

Be that as it may, Graham has been increasingly effective in church assimilation through the years. This, it would seem, is especially true as the follow-up procedures have improved. Moreover, one cannot evaluate the lasting impact in a Graham crusade by the immediate results in numbers alone. With rare exceptions, a crusade creates an atmosphere in a community that continues on in the lives of many people and pastors for years. That does impact churches most positively in the long run. Moreover, Graham reaches certain people in a crusade setting who most likely would rarely if ever go to a church. That fact cannot be overlooked or minimized.

In the setting of these circumstances, Billy Graham always exhibits a gracious spirit to his pastoral critics. Bev Shea tells the story of a pastor in a crusade who strongly opposed the effort. Yet many of his church members were attending and being helped tremendously. The pastor was on the liberal side theologically and could say few good things about Billy Graham. Near the end of the series of services, Billy called up the pastor and asked him to come and sit on the platform. The pastor asked Billy if he played golf; Billy answered in the affirmative, and they spent a few hours on the greens. The pastor came to the next service and sat on the platform, and Billy invited him to lead the vast audience in prayer. The pastor's life and ministry were transformed. The next Sunday he went into his own pulpit and said, "I have never given an invitation to receive Christ in the fifteen years I have been your pastor, but I am giving one now." Several people came forward. The pastor was so changed he became a pastor-evangelist, going about during the week evangelizing. And such stories happen quite often in the crusades. Billy is concerned and committed to pastors and the local church, and most agree that many congregations are helped significantly in the crusades.

BILLY GRAHAM'S GENERAL IMAGE AMONG LOCAL PASTORS AND CHURCHES

Billy Graham has received a quite favorable acceptance in most churches and by their leadership. As Bev Shea has said, "Billy urges people to love their pastors."[70] He is generally appreciated because of his genuine concern to enhance the local church and pastors through the crusades. As Billy Graham has said, his entire association attempts to "lay the foundation of the careful crusade preparation as that the churches will be mobilized to reach their communities for Christ."[71]

In his book *A Catholic Looks at Billy Graham*, Charles W. Dullea compliments Graham's attempts to involve the churches, especially in the area of helping the new converts to be integrated in the life of a local congregation. He said, "[In] follow-up by the Graham organization, 'the crusade organizer' makes every effort after the crusade to see that the inquirer is put in contact with a suitable ministry so they can get active in the Church."[72]

Graham's basic philosophy concerning his role in such an emphasis can be seen when he said, in something of the spirit of President John Kennedy, "Don't ask what your church can give you, but what you can give your church."[73] At the same time, Billy Graham urges his fellow evangelists, "The visible body, to which the evangelist is responsible, for which he conducts his ministry, and to which he directs its fruits, is the local church."[74] The evangelist is convinced that means involvement in the church for all true believers. Churches normally respond positively to that approach and philosophy.

CRITICISM

As perhaps could be expected, when Billy Graham holds a crusade in a community, the bulk of criticism arises from churches and pastors. One criticism that comes to Graham was expressed by Charles Dullea, who is basically positive to Graham but feels Graham leaves some doctrines unaffirmed, saying nothing about the sacraments and little about the church.[75] There may be some semblance of truth in that criticism. Billy Graham would be the first to acknowledge that he does not hold a crusade to elucidate all the doctrines of the Christian faith. As pointed out several times, he does not see himself as a theologian or as one to indoctrinate his listeners in a full-orbed biblical theology. Nor does he delineate his views on church policy and practice. As an evangelist, he preaches only the doctrinal elements that emerge out of the *kerygma:* the proclamation of the life, death, resurrection, and ascension of Jesus Christ and the call to repentance and faith. He refuses to go into secondary doctrinal issues concerning the details of ecclesiology. Perhaps he should say more, but such issues have been dividers among believers and an evangelistic crusade is not a time to precipitate divisions. Thus he restricts himself to preaching the basic content of the gospel. But, as pointed out previously, he certainly does all he can do to integrate inquirers into a local church of their choice. They can then adhere to the doctrines of the church of their choice. Graham obviously feels that as his ministry centers in preaching the gospel, the maturation process becomes the basic responsibility of the local church where fellowship and spiritual nourishment can be found. This has been historically true of many evangelists. In America, Charles G. Finney, D. L. Moody, Billy Sunday, and many other mass evangelists have taken this approach. And it can be traced throughout church history.

Others have criticized Billy Graham because he does not hold his crusades in church buildings. Leaning on historical precedents, Graham answers his critics with these words: "In almost every generation God has raised up evangelists, who have often had to pursue their calling outside the structured church."[76] Furthermore, the pragmatic problem arises out of where a church building could be found to hold tens of thousands who attend the crusades. Not only that, many unbelievers feel far more comfortable in a stadium than in a church building; and they are the ones whom Graham is concerned to reach. It took some time, but even John Wesley, the Anglican priest, finally learned the lesson and took to the open fields. History books abound with such accounts.

This raises another church issue. Graham has been charged with turning over his inquirers for instruction and counsel to ministers and churches lacking certain Christian beliefs. Again, an element of truth resides in this criticism. This attack normally comes from critics who feel their particular doctrines on certain secondary issues are vital. But Graham would argue that whenever inquirers make decisions, they are encouraged to go to a local church of their preference. Graham honors their decisions and does not attempt to stop them from going to the church they wish. He feels he cannot dictate to people what church they should affiliate with. Thus he could possibly be turning over some inquirers for instruction and counseling to ministers and churches lacking certain important beliefs. But that would be in a quite limited sense. Furthermore, if a person does not have a church preference, the counselors always encourage the inquirer to attend a local church that truly believes the Bible and is committed to the evangelical faith. They make very definite recommendations of certain congregations in such cases and turn over the decision card and information to that evangelical church for follow-up ministry. So though it may be possible that some may find their way into churches with which Graham himself would not be happy, the vast majority do get directed to a solid evangelical congregation.

A further criticism that has been leveled against Graham accuses him of saying that the church should not concern itself with the temporal lot of man.

This negative word falls to the ground. To say that Billy Graham is not concerned about the social and physical needs of people is simply not true. His Love in Action program proves that. Graham is vitally concerned about a holistic approach to evangelism, as has been made amply clear. Along this same line, Reinhold Niebuhr reacts negatively to Graham's position that lives must be changed before society can be transformed. Yet Billy Graham would be the last one to say that Christians should not involve themselves in social structures and elect officials who would help bring about reform. Nonetheless, Graham's philosophy and approach holds that society will only be reformed *in depth* as individuals who make up that society are themselves reformed. Much discussion revolves around this issue today. Billy Graham contends tenaciously for his position, and it does have historical precedent through many centuries. Moreover, when appropriate, he has often spoken out on certain social issues and even given counsel to presidents. He does feel governments have a significant role to play. But still, "big government" cannot solve the problems of materialism, greed, avarice, selfishness, and sin. And that constitutes the real problem as to why hunger, homelessness, and privation abound in this world. People do need transformation, and that Graham seeks above all.

POSITIVE WORDS

In spite of this criticism of Billy Graham and his church views, many positive words of affirmation concerning the impact of the Graham crusade on the local church stand in order. As a case in point, as this particular chapter is being composed, the American Broadcasting Corporation's television network showed a Billy Graham World Wide dramatic film relating the true story of a company executive who gave up his position to care for his seriously ill wife. It was a quite moving film with the gospel clearly presented. That appeared on prime-time network television in America. Such efforts as this by the Graham organization may not directly fill any one particular local church, but they cast forth the seed of the gospel that ultimately can bring forth much fruit and enhance the ministry of many churches.

The BGEA's efforts in the crusades themselves and these broad-based ministries lay a positive foundation for churches to rise to the opportunity and thus lead people to Christ and into the fellowship of their church. Graham has had a positive influence and real concern for building up the church, and a host of ministers understand this and give proper acclaim to Billy Graham's contribution to the church and its development. A brief, further look at this will be our final area of investigation.

GRAHAM'S CONCERN AND CONTRIBUTION FOR BUILDING UP THE CHURCH

It has surely been made evident that Billy Graham is very emphatic as to the importance and uniqueness of the church of Jesus Christ. The church, as Graham sees it, "is not only an organization but an organism which is completely unlike anything that the world has ever known: God Himself living with, and in, ordinary men and women who are members of His church."[77] Of course, Graham does not see the church in itself as a panacea for every ill. As he has said, "All the church can ever do is to direct you to the One who imparts His peace by coming into our lives."[78] His concern is that a person does not rely on attendance in church or joining a Christian organization to experience what only Jesus Christ Himself can impart. But all of this does give profile to Graham's concern for the importance of the local congregation.

Perhaps one of the primary reasons for Graham's interest and success in building up the church is because of his grasp of its breadth and universality. He said in 1960, "Ten years ago my concept of the Church tended to be narrow and provincial, but after a decade of intimate contact with Christians the world over, I am now aware that the family of God contains people of various ethnological, cultural, class, and denominational differences."[79] He also said, "I am far more tolerant about the kinds of Christians than I once was. My contact with Catholic, Lutheran, and other leaders—people far removed from my Southern Baptist tradition, has helped me, hopefully, to move in the right direction."[80] This approach of Billy Graham to the ministry of the church universal actually led him to say in 1966, "I find myself closer to Catholics than the radical Protestant."[81] There may well be those who would take serious issue with this, but it does show something of the fact that Billy Graham is concerned about building up the *entire* body of Jesus Christ. And the evangelist has been very pragmatic in his work for the churches.

A PRACTICAL HELP

As a single example among many that could be cited, one of the most practical contributions Billy Graham has made to the church centers in the Schools of Evangelism that the BGEA sponsors. These conferences are designed with the pastor in mind to help church leaders become more informed and adept at developing effective outreach in their congregations. Much good has been forthcoming. Actually, Billy Graham feels these schools may be making the most profound contributions to world evangelization as any work he or the entire BGEA undertakes.

The schools began quite early on when Lowell Berry, a concerned and dedicated layman, financially underwrote the enterprise. For several years the conferences were held in conjunction with the crusades. The conference program would be held during the day, and then the attendees would attend the crusade meeting at night. And this approach was used around the world. In recent years, however, schools of evangelism are held in different venues at various times. They are something of a smaller version of the conferences for evangelists held in Amsterdam, but they are geared to local church leadership, not just evangelists. And they have been well received and have "revived" more than one church to be sure.

A BRIEF SUMMARY

There have obviously been those who have registered complaints of Graham's understanding of—and involvement in—the church generally. Yet the overwhelming number of churchmen have been quite positive to the Graham ministry and the practical help he has afforded them. Therefore, seeing all Billy Graham has done to aid pastors and churches, it does seem fair to say that the local church has by and large profited considerably by the Graham effort.

Of further significance, as mentioned, creating an atmosphere in which Billy Graham has declared the gospel has fostered an openness and receptivity to the message of Jesus Christ that many communities did not enjoy prior to the crusade. In these cases, certainly such an endeavor is worthwhile. Moreover, the criticism directed toward Graham does not invalidate the receptivity he receives from the general populace when he conducts a crusade. Such commendations and affirmations from church laypeople should not be laid aside because they may seem to some naive. Graham impacts lives, and many are dramatically changed by the power of Christ through his preaching of the gospel. Homes have been rescued, families reunited, and multitudes saved from lives of virtual destruction. That is profound and significant. The kingdom of God has been established in many lives, and that matters most. That is no small legacy for an evangelist to leave in a community.

CONCLUSION AND HISTORICAL CONTRIBUTION OF BILLY GRAHAM TO THE CHURCH

So the work goes on, and even though Graham is now in his later years, communities and cities and countries receive him warmly. Furthermore, one finds it difficult to argue against the fact that the church of Jesus Christ has been enhanced by the Graham ministry. It must be granted that in some areas the church is more positive in its attitude and hence more strengthened by a crusade than in other settings. Nonetheless, rare is the community that fails to be positively impacted with the gospel of Jesus Christ when Billy Graham holds a crusade. And that being true, the church is built up in the faith. Just as his Lord, Graham loves the church and has given himself to it. And that is historical evangelism that contributes to the kingdom, the church, society, the home, and *people.*

But now that Billy Graham is older and suffering from various illnesses, how much longer will he be with us to carry on his historical ministry? That is the question many are asking. Therefore, an epilogue stands in order to raise that question and then to present an overall evaluation of Graham's place in history, his contribution to God's kingdom and the world, and the legacy he leaves.

CHAPTER 14

THE LASTING LEGACY

~∽

IT WAS NOT EASY GETTING THERE. THE TRAFFIC jammed the roads leading to the Alltel Stadium in Jacksonville, Florida, home of the Jacksonville Jaguars professional football team. As we drove in that Thursday night, we wondered if Florida would keep its promise of warm weather that first weekend in November of the new millennium. But we made it, and it was pleasantly warm in the large football stadium. The crowd was great. It boded for a good beginning, but not for a football game; it was a Billy Graham evangelistic crusade.

As we sat there waiting for Cliff Barrows to kick off the service, we could not but wonder if this would be Billy's last crusade. We could scarce refrain from asking it—at least to ourselves. A few were "brave" enough to query their friends, but no one wanted to make any pronouncements. Billy Graham, the evangelist, had overcome many barriers in his fifty-plus years of crusade evangelism. Still, we all realized this could be the last time we would see him, at least in the role of a full crusade program. Billy had just spent three months at the Mayo Clinic in Rochester, Minnesota. He had undergone three surgeries for hydrocephalus, the last one a very precarious surgery that lasted three and one-half hours. Not only that, he suffers from Parkinson's disease, and two days after the crusade closed (November 7, 2000) he would turn eighty-two years old. Could he really go on, even if he made it through the next four days? We would see.

As the service began, we could not but reflect that it was much like Los Angeles in 1949. Of course, on the surface, it was different. The music certainly was unlike 1949. Still, there was the traditional choir, five thousand strong. They also had the typical piano and organ as Cliff led the singing and "Bev" Shea—now ninety-one—sang. Remarkable! When you think about it, it did look much like the great crusades of the 1950s, 1960s, and 1970s. But then the new generation took stage. CeCe Winans, along with the Bill Gaither Vocal Band, sang. We all heard "Because He Lives" and other choruses, and it was as contemporary—gospel style—as MTV; well, almost. That was different. Moreover, there were broader emphases; people were challenged to take part in the benevolent program to help needy people. Actually, the contemporary and traditional blended quite well. Then the mayor of Jacksonville, Jack Delony, spoke and gave Billy Graham a key to the city. Governor Jeb Bush of Florida also gave a testimony, saying, "We need the Savior's help."

As the service progressed, Bev sang and Billy got up to preach. Would he be the Billy of 1949? Yes and no. He was not the "hot gospeler" of earlier years. His physical condition precluded that. But the gospel he preached had not changed one iota, at least in essence. He believes today as he did back in the 1940s that Christ *alone* is God's way to salvation. He did use current illustrations and terminology; he has always been good at that. He said once, "I try to contextualize the gospel, it becomes a pathway into their hearts for the gospel."[1] Still, the core of the *kerygma*, "the proclamation," was communicated in all its fullness; and it was done with great power: the power of the Holy Spirit.

On that Thursday night Billy preached from Luke 4:16ff. His theme centered on "Who was Jesus?" He gave six reasons that Jesus came: (1) to preach the gospel to the poor, (2) to heal the brokenhearted, (3) to preach deliverance according to the Scriptures, (4) to bring sight to the blind, (5) to set at liberty those bruised, and (6) to preach the acceptable year of the Lord. Billy presented Jesus as the creative, compassionate, crucified Christ.

It has been said many times that Billy Graham begins his invitation for inquirers as soon as he starts preaching. In a dynamic sense, that is true. But when it comes to the time of the actual appeal to step forward, he does so in a most restrained, unemotional manner. And people stream onto the turf. This author must confess, as often as I have witnessed the scene, the magnitude of the response is always deeply moving and inspiring. No pressure, no emotional stories, no haranguing, people are simply moved by the Holy Spirit, and they respond by the literal thousands.

This might not be the last crusade after all. But then, we have three nights to go.

Friday came; we gathered again—larger in number than the first night—and we wondered once more how Billy would do. The service unfolded in the normal fashion. Charlie Daniels and his country-style band thrilled the crowd. Especially exciting was his rendition of "I'll Fly Away." The coliseum seemed to fly with Charlie, a fine musician with a powerful testimony for Christ. Cliff and the choir did a great job, Bev sang exceedingly well, and Billy stood up to preach. How would he do?

Billy preached on Isaiah 53. He shared the story of Stuart Hamblen's conversion in the Los Angeles 1949 crusade. Billy stressed, "We will only be saved if we come by the way of the cross." He went on, saying, "There are many religious roads, but only *one* to the kingdom of God, and that is the way of the cross." He then stressed the resurrection of Christ. The sermon had great effect. Again, many responded to the simple invitation.

Saturday morning saw the "Kids' Gig." This service is designed for children. It reminds one of a sort of gospel *Sesame Street*. With dynamic music and skits, it has great appeal to children. Some twenty thousand kids attended. Care is taken not to exploit children in any manner. A wholesome, spiritual program unfolds simply to acquaint children with the truths of the Christian life and faith. The kids have a great time, and many are touched by the Lord.

Then came Saturday night! Now that was different. To begin with, the largest number to attend came, some seventy thousand, and it seemed that two-thirds of them were teenagers. They stood in front of the podium on the football field with many more thousands in the stands. It was a sight to see. Gospel rock stars Jars of Clay, Kirk Franklin, and DC Talk sang, and the crowd was wild with excitement. They jumped up and down, waved their hands, and squealed. For the older generation it almost seemed a puzzle.

But could God work in all this? It was a new experience to be sure. The music, the excitement, and the spirit all but baffled some folks. But as Ruth Graham has said, the gospel rock groups stock the pool so her husband can go fishing. Well put!

The response that night proved to be unbelievable. When Billy stood up to preach—after all the incredible excitement—a holy hush fell over the entire stadium. The young people who had been singing, jumping, and waving their arms stood there as if mesmerized, hanging on every word of the evangelist. Billy preached from John 3 on being "born again." He stressed the atonement of Christ on the cross and the resurrection. It was a clear scriptural presentation of the full gospel. The kids were spellbound, and 3,642 responded to the invitation.

When the last service began on Sunday night, there was a bit of sorrow in the air—yet real hope. Sorrow because this could be Billy Graham's last full crusade service, but hope because he seemed stronger than when he began. Each night he appeared to increase in vigor. Billy was clearer and more lucid, and his thoughts and words came tumbling out almost like the "old days." Though he is not in the best of health or as young as he once was, on that last night he rose to the occasion.

The music again was very good, with Take 6 and Michael W. Smith. Mark Brunell, quarterback for the Jacksonville Jaguars, and Renaldo Wynn of the Jaguars both gave great testimonies for Christ.

During Bev Shea's solo just before Billy was to preach, Bev made a bit of a bobble and took a second or two to get back on track. When Billy came to the pulpit, he called attention to Bev's mistake and called him back to the pulpit. Then Billy got Cliff Barrows there as well and three of the original team stood together. It was a great picture. But then to the surprise of all, Billy suggested they sing a trio. And all three—Billy, Bev, and Cliff—sang the little children's gospel song, "This Little Light of Mine." When the chorus was sung, "Hide it under a bushel? *NO!*" Billy shouted the "NO." It was something to behold. This had never been done before. It all but "brought down the house." That made a large color picture article on the front page of the Jacksonville paper the next morning.

But then the serious moment came and Billy preached to the huge crowd a sermon on Luke 17:32 entitled "Remember Lot's Wife." Billy gave the exclusive gospel and urged us all to pray for revival. As often as has been said, he "rang the bell." Many came forward, realizing that Jesus alone must be received by repentance and faith (Acts 4:12), and the crusade ended on a high, authentic evangelical note.

It truly was a high hour. The city of Jacksonville had responded tremendously. More than seven hundred churches from forty-four denominations cooperated in the event. The crusade preparation by the Jacksonville churches was really quite remarkable. The BGEA itself carried on its usual preparation and follow-up programs. In a word, the entire crusade unfolded in typical fashion, and God honored the work most significantly. The cumulative attendance was 242,000 with 10,200-plus responding to the invitation. The newspaper coverage was the most complete seen in some time; it was like the early days. Every issue of the *Florida Times-Union* gave full coverage with color photos, often on the front page.

It really was a great time and the final service a rich experience. We all began to feel that perhaps Billy Graham can carry on—at least for a time. The Jacksonville crusade might be the last full effort, but time will tell. Most hope the crusade work will continue until health or circumstances bring down the curtain. The *Florida Times-Union* in a lead article on Monday after the crusade wrote, "The legendary evangelist, who turns 82 tomorrow, temporarily put to rest any concerns about his health not allowing him to continue preaching. He looked and sounded strong despite his years and lengthy hospitalization this summer."

We all hope the paper is right. Nonetheless, the work will surely go on; it will go on for many years because of the historical contribution the evangelist has made. This book must not end without a summary look at that significant legacy of the Graham ministry.

THE HISTORICAL CONTRIBUTION OF BILLY GRAHAM

It has been contended that Billy Graham's ministry basically falls in line with historical evangelical evangelism and therein makes its contribution. This is certainly not to imply that Graham or his ministry has been perfect. There have been mistakes. When the evangelist was interviewed concerning aspects of his work, he said, "Don't forget the 'warts.'" There have been some: the calendar error before the London Harringay crusade of 1954, Billy's experience with

President Harry Truman, the "secret" twenty-three-million-dollar fund, the accusations of denying the gospel by inviting all who will to cooperate in the crusades, and the overstatement—or understatement—of Christ's exclusiveness. For example, in the 1990s during a television interview, Billy left the impression that a person could be saved apart from the gospel of Christ. When Billy realized what had transpired he was shocked and immediately completely repudiated it. He believes and preaches the absolute exclusiveness of Jesus Christ for salvation. These and other criticisms constitute the "warts," as it were. Billy's ministry has not been free from them, but then, none have. All have flaws and make errors in judgment. At the same time, however, when Graham's ministry is honestly and fairly analyzed, as has been attempted in this work, he comes through as essentially and basically in line with historical evangelicalism and with today's emphasis called the "new evangelicalism." A final brief run-through of this positive evaluation should make this rather sweeping statement clear.

HISTORICAL EVANGELICAL ATTESTATION

It would seem incontestable that Billy Graham does adhere to historical, evangelical evangelism. Granted, his methodologies may differ quite dramatically from others in the historical chain we have attempted to put together. But then, the twelve sterling personalities presented as personifying various principles of evangelical evangelism differed in methods one from the other. It has been something of the genius of evangelicals to retain the essence of the gospel and yet be adaptable in methods and means of communication to the culture and time in which each has ministered. It could hardly be expected, for example, that Billy Graham and Athanasius would use the same approach in sharing the gospel. The good news remains unchangeable, but it must be culturalized to be relevant to contemporary societies as so often stated. And the historical authenticity and contribution of Graham's evangelical position and approach to preaching the gospel, regardless of his particular methodologies, seem basically impeccable. A brief review of his ministry should make that rather categorical statement self-evident. This evaluation can be grasped from the twelve different perspectives presented.

The Holy Spirit in Evangelism. To quote the evangelist once more, "Without the Holy Spirit, the work would die . . . the Holy Spirit in contextualizing the gospel is what makes it come alive to people."[2] Graham sees the Spirit of God at the very core of the entire enterprise of evangelism, and he recognizes his utter dependence upon His work to bring the gospel home relevantly to the human heart. This dynamic work of God's Spirit inevitably makes a positive contribution to the kingdom of God and hence to society generally.

The Call and the Gospel in Evangelism. Few if any argue that Billy Graham fails to declare the full historical, biblical, evangelical gospel. As he stated, "I feel the *whole* content (of the *kerygma*) must be in every sermon."[3] Moreover, it has surely become obvious that as an evangelist he feels called to that particular task. Graham's struggle at the eighteenth green on the golf course at Temple Terrace should settle that aspect of biblical, historical evangelism. It certainly did for Billy. And remembering Paul's word that the gospel is the "power of God unto salvation" (Rom. 1:16 KJV), many have come to faith in Jesus Christ. That leaves a tremendous legacy to the individual and to the very structure of current culture. Franklin Graham concurs; he stated in a personal correspondence that his "[Billy Graham's] single focus on the proclamation of the gospel of the Lord Jesus Christ" will be Graham's lasting legacy.

The Sovereignty of God in Evangelism. Again, Billy Graham's essential theology concerning the attributes of God puts him in the notable historic line of such giants of the faith as Augustine, Calvin, Luther, Whitefield, Spurgeon, and a host of others—not to mention many contemporaries. In a personal interview, Billy said, "I believe God has prepared the hearts of certain people in every audience I speak to. I never think about the results. I know there are people that God has prepared their hearts, and in that sense they are chosen by God. I have total relaxation, I just know something is going to happen that God has planned."[4] He goes on to use the oft-repeated illustration of a person walking up to the gate of salvation and seeing on the threshold a sign reading, "Whosoever will may come." The eager soul enters, turns around, and sees another sign on the inside of the threshold he or she just entered: "Chosen from the foundations of the world." Billy gladly confesses he lives in the tension of divine sovereignty and human responsibility. To this paradox, he says he is absolutely committed. Further, as he has said, "I have sensed the sovereignty of God in my life, ministry, in all."[5] That's sovereignty; and few would deny that ministry predicated on that biblical historical principle makes a positive contribution to the well-being of many.

Christology in Evangelism. Little needs to be said on this issue. That Graham holds to a high evangelical view of the person of Jesus Christ is evident in his entire life and ministry. He places Christ first and foremost in all he undertakes in evangelism. To quote Graham again, "He [Jesus Christ] is the centrality of evangelism and all else."[6] That quite well covers the issue, and Jesus made it clear that when He is exhalted He will draw people to Himself and transform lives.

Holistic Ministry in Evangelism. Concerning this area of an evangelical approach to evangelism, Graham has excelled, at least in comparison with many evangelists. As a single case in point, few people know how much money and effort the evangelist put into rescuing Jewish people from the Soviet Union in communist days. Graham succeeded in getting many out of the hands of the oppressive Soviets. And such stories can be multiplied over and over again. He does care for the total person regardless of his image as an evangelist. That too is biblical, historical, and Christ-honoring, not to mention contributing to needy lives and inspiring the evangelical world to bring social action and evangelism back together again.

Suffering in Evangelism. It goes without saying that Billy Graham has paid a price for his ministry of evangelism. But such has been the lot of God's faithful servants down through history. What commends the evangelist so highly in this regard centers in his reaction to the slings and arrows that have been hurled his way. He tells of one such occasion when he was savagely attacked by a churchman. He said, "I felt the Lord wanted me to be quiet and not say too much in reply and rebuttal." He wrote a letter to his detractor and simply said, "Dear Dr. _____, thank you for your letter. . . . I'll think carefully about what you have written. May God bless you in your work."[7] Such an approach to suffering for the Savior is certainly biblical and Christlike. Moreover, that approach wins in the end, as history has verified many times. And it becomes a source of inspiration, help, and encouragement to those who do suffer for Christ.

The Bible in Evangelism. Billy Graham's well-known phrase "the Bible says," has become the hallmark of his preaching, writing, witnessing, and all communication. Actually, his time-honored phrase says it all: He truly does believe the Bible, preach the Bible, and live the Bible. The encounter with God and the Scriptures at Forest Home in 1949 settled that issue once and for all. And who could argue that such an approach is not historical evangelicalism? Again, Graham falls in line and in step with that army of God's faithful ministers. Further, the pure communication of Holy Scriptures always makes its contribution, and it does so on a broad scale.

Boldness in Evangelism. Again, few words are demanded on this point. Fifty-plus years of evangelism, never compromising the message, enduring a thousand temptations to "cut corners," staying strong in every conceivable situation he found himself in—it all speaks well for the evangelist. Of course, he has not been perfect and at times has been seriously misunderstood. But he has stood, and that constitutes boldness in the finest tradition of the gospel. As a consequence he has touched many lives and strengthened the church generally to stand in the time of conflict.

Godliness in Evangelism. In this regard it will be well to recall a statement of Anne Graham Lotz, Billy's daughter. She describes her father as "sweetness and gentleness when under pressure."[8] And she knows him well. When under pressure one's genuine godliness is best revealed. To say that Billy Graham has been under pressure on countless occasions is an understatement. But in it all, his integrity, Christian spirit, and utter commitment to God's will and purpose have been evident to all. This no doubt accounts for the fact that he has been admired around the world for decades. Moreover, it has surely become clear that Graham has a deep desire not only for personal holiness, but for all those on the team and for everyone who makes a decision in the context of his ministry. And not to sound too repetitive, but that also is historical, evangelical evangelism—not to mention the central emphasis the Bible itself places on the discipline. Moreover, when the church actually practices being the "salt of the earth," society is greatly blessed. Therein Graham has made one of his great contributions in demonstrating and challenging God's people to that high level of godly living and service. That leaves a legacy to be sure.

Revival in Evangelism. The question is often raised, Do the crusades of Billy Graham actually produce revival? Some affirm they do; others disagree. Perhaps a word from the evangelist will help here. Again in a personal interview, he said, "I think when one person surrenders their life as best they can . . . that is revival in that person. And that happens all the time."[9] Such seems essentially true.

But Graham also goes beyond that principle and expands the vision. Recall, his brother Melvin stated that Billy prayed for revival in the broad, sweeping sense more than anything else. In that spirit, Billy Graham pointed out that in the early days of crusade work the theme song of his crusades was "Send a Great Revival." It would appear he has a heart for real revival, be it on a personal basis or in the broad, historical sense of a widespread move of the Holy Spirit. And he recognizes that it all rests in the sovereignty of God. Along with his fellow historical evangelicals, he longs to see just that take place again. Any contribution toward real revival is a contribution indeed. America—the world—desperately needs to experience a true spiritual awakening.

Worldwide Ministry in Evangelism. The worldwide consciousness that clearly grips Graham's heart began during his first visit to Europe, but the vision of the Great Commission saw a profound deepening the first time he went to Korea and Japan. He said that experience was "the first time I saw the mission field."[10] Since those days, Billy's world consciousness—and commitment—has become legendary. The fact that he has ministered in more than eighty countries, crossed social and cultural barriers, and reached people in every conceivable context has become an inspiration and contribution to virtually the whole church of Jesus Christ. Billy Graham is, indeed, a *world* evangelist. It must grieve him now that his travel has to be restricted because of health. But the entire evangelical world owes him a debt of gratitude for his historical contribution to the kingdom of God and to many nations and societies he has touched.

The Church in Evangelism. There is little doubt that Charles Spurgeon, the pastor-evangelist, would smile on Billy Graham's approach to coaching his evangelistic ministry in the setting of the local church. When asked if he needed the church in his evangelistic ministry he strongly replied, "Absolutely." This fact becomes evident in several areas: He always goes to a city only at the invitation of the churches; he always enlists the many workers, such as the counselors, from the churches; he does all he can to get the inquirers into a church; and many other aspects of his ministry speak of his church involvement. Billy as churchman well realizes "Christ . . . loved the church, and gave himself for it" (Eph. 5:25 KJV). And again, not to appear unduly repetitive, that too is biblical, historical, evangelical contributory evangelism.

What can be thus concluded from all these pages attempting to analyze the ministry of evangelist Billy Graham? This author concludes, hopefully from an objective perspective, that Billy Graham and the Billy Graham Evangelistic Association have strived to maintain an integrity and honesty that emerge out of a basic evangelical, historical understanding of the Christian faith and evangelistic ministry. Have they *always* been successful? There have been minor slips here and there—as pointed out—but in a quite incredible fashion the foundation of a biblical, evangelistic integrity has been kept. That can only be attributed to the grace of God and His sovereign power. And Billy Graham is the first to admit that salient fact. Thus we can conclude the evangelist does fit, and fit quite well, in the historical line of true evangelical evangelism and thus made his contribution.

THE HISTORICAL CONTRIBUTION AND LEGACY OF BILLY GRAHAM

Once again, the question must be asked, Have all the time, effort, resources, and labor put into the Graham ministry really made a significant contribution, to his day—and to the future? Will he leave a positive legacy? Obviously the answer to these prime questions has already been outlined in the twelve principles of evangelical evangelism presented above. But in closing, this central issue must be answered more directly, if only briefly.

It would appear that the Graham phenomenon, relative to its contribution, could be evaluated from a fivefold perspective. That is not to say that Graham has "failed" in some of the twelve areas of evangelism discussed. To the contrary, but in something of a summary fashion, five aspects of his ministry stand out in bold relief. First, the fact that literally millions have come to faith in Jesus Christ speaks for itself. To put it rather bluntly, Billy Graham has been used of the Holy Spirit to "populate" the kingdom of God significantly. That does not mean he did it single-handedly; by no means. As seen, multiplied thousands have contributed and shared in the effective evangelism of the BGEA. But it must be granted that many will spend eternity with Christ as a consequence of Graham's ministry. And in the final analysis, that is what evangelism is all about. This, no doubt, epitomizes the evangelist's greatest, single contribution, and constitutes a vital aspect of his lasting legacy.

Second, many churches have profited in myriad ways because of the ministry of Billy Graham. Pastors have been emboldened to be more biblical and evangelistic. Consequently, the ripple effect throughout many churches has been most positive. And that stands true not only for pastors and leaders, but in the lives of multitudes of church members as well. Those who have worked in crusades, read Graham's many writings, or heard him preach have often come into a deeper experience of Jesus Christ. As Sterling Huston, crusade director, has pointed out, "The gift of the evangelist . . . functions best in the church."[11] Billy has certainly grasped that principle and has geared his ministry on that basis. His contributions to the church have thus been most helpful.

In this same context, Billy Graham has exerted a most positive influence on his fellow evangelists. This impact centers in the godliness of his personal life perhaps more than in any other aspect of his ministry. As Baptist evangelist Bailey Smith has said, Graham has shown that "you can be successful and have integrity and humility." That in itself constitutes a genuine contribution to the cause of evangelism and then in turn to the churches and hence the world.

At the same time, regarding Graham's contribution to the church, his influence in theological education and training has proved most significant. The schools of evangelism, the Cove, and the great conferences he sponsored through the years have aided in fostering a sound theology and integrity in methodologies. Those programs have served pastors, evangelists, and church leaders in a most positive manner on a worldwide scale. Some of the comments of attendees at Amsterdam 2000, for example, have been recorded in a previous chapter. It would appear evident that much help was derived from such endeavors by Graham's ministry. That is no insignificant historical contribution to the life of the church and to the entire kingdom of God.

Third, Billy has clearly made a contribution to society generally. The integrity and authenticity of the man and his methods have helped create a favorable view of evangelism and the Christian faith generally. Moreover, his influence on world leaders has benefited society perhaps more than can be realized. People in high places have looked to the evangelist for guidance in moral, ethical issues. That is no insignificant contribution. And then there is the holistic approach Billy Graham has taken. Many a hungry mouth has been fed; many a desperate, despairing person encouraged; actually, many a life saved. Society owes a debt of gratitude to Billy Graham for his impact in many nations and needs worldwide. Few fail to appreciate this aspect of his ministry.

Fourth, Billy Graham has elevated the image of the evangelist in society in a most helpful way. True, there have been the "Elmer Gantry" types in his day, but by the sheer godliness and integrity of his life, Billy has restored the integrity of the title "evangelist" in the minds of many. That contribution ripples through the church and society and ultimately contributes to the salvation of people and the vindication of the faith.

Fifth, and in summary, Billy Graham has brought true glory to God. He would be the last to say it was because of him that such "success" has been forthcoming in his ministry. Billy's humility always causes him to give all credit to the Holy Spirit. It stands as testimony to his realization that it is all of God. His sincere wish that God be glorified is clearly evident. As Paul said, "Whatever you do, do all to the glory of God" (1 Cor. 10:31). That expresses the spirit of Billy Graham and becomes the final judgment on the man.

Billy Graham has lived a contributory life and conducted a ministry that has influenced his time profoundly and will no doubt continue to impact the future. But right at this moment an important thing took place.

While writing this last chapter, the word came that during the BGEA board meeting following the Jacksonville crusade, Billy Graham will retain the title of Chairman of the Board, and his son Franklin will become the new Chief Executive Officer of the Billy Graham Evangelistic Association. And of significant importance, Billy will continue to engage in crusades, as health permits. After all, there were 242,000 attendees at the Jacksonville crusade and Billy's health seemed improved. Just before this book went to print the Louisville crusade was undertaken and finished with over 190,000 people attending, with some 10,000 decisions for Christ recorded. So, once again, we look forward to Fresno, California, in the autumn of 2001, and hopefully, he will be able to carry on as God gives him strength. In this light, Graham's many admirers are most gratified for the continuing ministry of the evangelist.

The crusades yet to come by God's grace will very likely follow the pattern of the Jacksonville and Louisville meetings. Also, some crusades are in the planning stage with Franklin Graham and Billy Graham sharing the pulpit. Regardless of the method employed, the actual "last crusade" will hopefully be a long time in the future as God grants health and strength to His herald of the gospel. And beyond doubt, through the media, the ministry of Billy Graham will continue on for many years and into the future.

CONCLUSION

Regardless of Billy Graham's age and health issues and regardless of whether the future of his continuing ministry is long or short, Graham's historical contribution and legacy will go on for many, many years. Perhaps the best way to conclude this work on Billy Graham the evangelist would be to hear what he wanted to leave with young evangelists who will follow in his train—and what he has said applies to all true believers. Billy stated, "I would say, study the Word night and day, pray without ceasing, cut the TV off as much as possible, and put emphasis on the one person as much as the big audience, witnessing to that person by the life you lead as well as speaking to them verbally about Christ."

Evangelist Billy Graham has set the example himself, as the discerning world knows. Those principles move right into the heart of the man and create the contribution and historical authenticity of the evangelist. No doubt history—and eternity—will verify it. And for posterity that is what matters most.

APPENDIX A:
BOOKS AND BOOKLETS BY BILLY GRAHAM

America's Hour of Decision—Van Kampen Press, 1951

Angels: God's Secret Agents—1ˢᵗ edition, Doubleday, 1975; revised and expanded, Word Books, 1985

Answers to Life's Problems—Word Books, 1988

Approaching Hoofbeats—Word Books, 1983

A Biblical Standard for Evangelists—World Wide Publications, 1984

Billy Graham Answers Your Questions—World Wide Publications, 1960

Billy Graham Talks to Teenagers—Zondervan, 1958

Calling Youth to Christ—Zondervan, 1947

The Challenge—Doubleday, 1969

Facing Death and the Life After—Word Books, 1987

Freedom from the Seven Deadly Sins—Zondervan, 1955

The Holy Spirit—Word Books, 1978

Hope for the Troubled Heart—Word Books, 1991

How to be Born Again—Word Books, 1977

I Saw Your Sons at War—Billy Graham Evangelistic Association, 1953

The Jesus Generation—Zondervan, 1971

Just As I Am—HarperCollins, 1997

My Answer—Doubleday, 1960

Peace with God—1ˢᵗ edition, Doubleday, 1953; revised and expanded, Word Books, 1984

The Secret of Happiness—1ˢᵗ edition, Doubleday, 1955; revised and expanded, Word Books, 1985

Storm Warning—Word Books, 1992

Till Armageddon—Word Books, 1981

Unto the Hills—Word Books, 1986

World Aflame—Doubleday, 1965

APPENDIX B:
THE LAUSANNE COVENANT[1]

INTRODUCTION

We, members of the Church of Jesus Christ, from more than 150 nations, participants in the International Congress on World Evangelization at Lausanne, praise God for his great salvation and rejoice in the fellowship he has given us with himself and with each other. We are deeply stirred by what God is doing in our day, moved to penitence by our failures and challenged by the unfinished task of evangelization. We believe the Gospel is God's good news for the whole world, and we are determined by his grace to obey Christ's commission to proclaim it to all mankind and to make disciples of every nation. We desire, therefore, to affirm our faith and our resolve, and to make public our covenant.

1. The Purpose of God

We affirm our belief in the one eternal God, Creator and Lord of the world, Father, Son and Holy Spirit, who governs all things according to the purpose of his will. He has been calling out from the world a people for himself, and sending his people back into the world to be his servants and his witnesses, for the extension of his kingdom, the building up of Christ's body, and the glory of his name. We confess with shame that we have often denied our calling and failed in our mission, by becoming conformed to the world or by withdrawing from it. Yet we rejoice that even when borne by earthen vessels the Gospel is still a precious treasure. To the task of making that treasure known in the power of the Holy Spirit we desire to dedicate ourselves anew.

(Isa. 40:28; Matt. 28:19; Eph. 1:11; Acts 15:14; John 17:6,18; Eph. 4:12; I Cor. 5:10; Rom. 12:2; II Cor. 4:7)

2. The Authority and Power of the Bible

We affirm the divine inspiration, truthfulness and authority of both Old and New Testament Scriptures in their entirety as the only written word of God, without error in all that it affirms, and the only infallible rule of faith and practice. We also affirm the power of God's Word to accomplish his purpose of salvation. The message of the Bible is addressed to all mankind. For God's revelation in Christ and in Scripture is unchangeable. Through it the Holy Spirit still speaks today. He illumines the minds of God's people in every culture to perceive its truth freshly through their own eyes and thus discloses to the whole church ever more of the many-colored wisdom of God.

(II Tim. 3:16; II Pet. 1:21; John 10:35; Isa. 55:11; I Cor. 1:21; Rom. 1:16; Matt. 5:17-18; Jude 3; Eph. 1:17,18; 3:10,18)

3. The Uniqueness and Universality of Christ

We affirm that there is only one Savior and only one Gospel, although there is a wide diversity of evangelistic approaches. We recognize that all men have some knowledge of God through his general revelation in nature. But we deny that this can save, for men suppress the truth by their unrighteousness. We also reject as derogatory to Christ and the Gospel every kind of syncretism and dialogue which implies that Christ speaks equally through all religions and ideologies. Jesus Christ, being himself the only God-man, who gave himself as the only ransom for sinners, is the only mediator between God and man. There is no other name by which we must be saved. All men are perishing because of sin, but God loves all men, not wishing that any should perish but that all should repent. Yet those who reject Christ repudiate the joy of salvation and condemn themselves to eternal separation from God. To proclaim Jesus as "the Savior of the world" is not to affirm that all men are either automatically or ultimately saved, still less to affirm that all religions offer salvation in Christ. Rather it is to proclaim God's love for a world of sinners and to invite all men to respond to him as Savior and Lord in the wholehearted personal commitment of repentance and faith. Jesus Christ has been exalted above every other name; we long for the day when every knee shall bow to him and every tongue shall confess him Lord.

(Gal. 1:6-9; Rom. 1:18-32; I Tim. 2:5-6; Acts 4:12; John 3:16-19; II Pet. 3:9; II Thess. 1:7-9; John 4:42; Matt. 11:28; Eph. 1:20,21; Phil. 2:9-11)

4. The Nature of Evangelism

To evangelize is to spread the good news that Jesus Christ died for our sins and was raised from the dead according to the Scriptures, and that as the reigning Lord he now offers the forgiveness of sins and the liberating gift of the Spirit to all who repent and believe. Our Christian presence in the world is indispensable to evangelism, and so is that kind of dialogue whose purpose is to listen sensitively in order to understand. But evangelism itself is the proclamation of the historical, biblical Christ as Savior and Lord, with a view to persuading people to come to him personally and so be reconciled to God. In issuing the Gospel invitation we have no liberty to conceal the cost of discipleship. Jesus still calls all who would follow him to deny themselves, take up their cross, and identify themselves with his new community. The results of evangelism include obedience to Christ, incorporation into his church and responsible service in the world.

(I Cor. 15:3,4; Acts 2:32-39; John 20:21; I Cor. 1:23; II Cor. 4:5; 5:11,20; Luke 14:25-33; Mark 8:34; Acts 2:40,47; Mark 10:43-45)

5. Christian Social Responsibility

We affirm that God is both the Creator and the Judge of all men. We therefore should share his concern for justice and reconciliation throughout human society and for the liberation of men from every kind of oppression. Because mankind is made in the image of God, every person, regardless of race, religion, color, culture, class, sex or age, has an intrinsic dignity because of which he should be respected and served, not exploited. Here too we express penitence both for our neglect and for having sometimes regarded evangelism and social concern as mutually exclusive. Although reconciliation with man is not reconciliation with God, nor is social action evangelism, nor is political liberation salvation, nevertheless we affirm that evangelism and socio-political involvement are both part of our Christian duty. For both are necessary expressions of our doctrines of God and man, our love for our neighbor and our obedience to Jesus Christ. The message of salvation implies also a message of judgment upon every form of alienation, oppression and discrimination, and we should not be afraid to denounce evil and injustice wherever they exist. When people receive Christ they are born again into his kingdom and must seek not only to exhibit but also to spread its righteousness in the midst of an unrighteous world. The salvation we claim should be transforming us in the totality of our personal and social responsibilities. Faith without works is dead.

(Acts 17:26,31; Gen. 18:25; Isa. 1:17; Psa. 45:7; Gen. 1:26,27; Jas. 3:9; Lev. 19:18; Luke 6:27,35; Jas. 2:14-26; John 3:3,5; Matt. 5:20; 6:33; II Cor. 3:18; Jas. 2:20)

6. The Church and Evangelism

We affirm that Christ sends his redeemed people into the world as the Father sent him, and that this calls for a similar deep and costly penetration of the world. We need to break out of our ecclesiastical ghettos and permeate non-Christian society. In the church's mission of sacrificial service evangelism is primary. World evangelization requires the whole church to take the whole Gospel to the whole world. The church is at the very center of God's cosmic purpose and is his appointed means of spreading the Gospel. But a church which preaches the Cross must itself be marked by the Cross. It becomes a stumbling block to evangelism when it betrays the Gospel or lacks a living faith in God, a genuine love for people, or scrupulous honesty in all things including promotion and finance. The church is the community of God's people rather than an institution, and must not be identified with any particular culture, social or political system, or human ideology.

(John 17:18; 20:21; Matt. 28:19,20; Acts 1:8; 20:27; Eph. 1:9,10; 3:9-11; Gal. 6:14,17; II Cor. 6:3,4; II Tim. 2:19-21; Phil. 1:27)

7. Cooperation in Evangelism

We affirm that the church's visible unity in truth is God's purpose. Evangelism also summons us to unity, because our oneness strengthens our witness, just as our disunity undermines our gospel of reconciliation. We recognize, however, that organizational unity may take many forms and does not necessarily forward evangelism. Yet we who share the same biblical faith should be closely united in fellowship, work and witness. We confess that our testimony has sometimes been marred by sinful individualism and needless duplication. We pledge ourselves to seek a deeper unity in truth, worship, holiness and mission. We urge the development of regional and functional cooperation for the furtherance of the church's mission, for strategic planning, for mutual encouragement, and for the sharing of resources and experience.

(John 17:21,23: Eph. 4:3,4; John 13:35; Phil. 1:27; John 17:11-23)

8. Churches in Evangelistic Partnership

We rejoice that a new missionary era has dawned. The dominant role of western missions is fast disappearing. God is raising up from the younger churches a great new resource for world evangelization, and is thus demonstrating that the responsibility to evangelize belongs to the whole body of Christ. All churches should therefore be asking God and themselves what they should be doing both to reach their own area and to send missionaries to other parts of the world. A re-evaluation of our missionary responsibility and role should be continuous. Thus a growing partnership of churches will develop and the universal character of Christ's Church will be more clearly exhibited. We also thank God for agencies which labor in Bible translation, theological education, missions, church renewal and other specialist fields. They too should engage in constant self-examination to evaluate their effectiveness as part of the Church's mission.

(Rom. 1:8; Phil. 1:5; 4:15; Acts 13:1-3; I Thess. 1:6-8)

9. The Urgency of the Evangelistic Task

More than 2,700 million people, which is more than two-thirds of mankind, have yet to be evangelized. We are ashamed that so many have been neglected; it is a standing rebuke to us and to the whole church. There is now, however, in many parts of the world an unprecedented receptivity to the Lord Jesus Christ. We are convinced that this is the time for churches and parachurch agencies to pray earnestly for the salvation of the unreached and to launch new efforts to achieve world evangelization. A reduction of foreign missionaries and money in an evangelized country may sometimes be necessary to facilitate the national church's growth in self-reliance and to release resources for unevangelized areas. Missionaries should flow ever more freely from and to all six continents in a spirit of humble service. The goal should be, by all available means and at the earliest possible time, that every person will have the opportunity to hear, understand, and receive the good news. We cannot hope to attain this goal without sacrifice. All of us are shocked by the poverty of millions and disturbed by the injustices which cause it. Those of us who live in affluent circumstances accept our duty to develop a simple life-style in order to contribute more generously to both relief and evangelism.

(John 9:4; Matt. 9:35-38; Rom. 9:1-3; I Cor. 9:19-23; Mark 16:15; Isa. 58:6,7; Jas. 1:27; 2:1-9; Matt. 25:31-46; Acts 2:44,45; 4:34,35)

10. Evangelism and Culture

The development of strategies for world evangelization calls for imaginative pioneering methods. Under God, the result will be the rise of churches deeply rooted in Christ and closely related to their culture. Culture must always be tested and judged by Scripture. Because man is God's creature, some of his culture is rich in beauty and goodness. Because he has fallen, all of it is tainted with sin and some of it is demonic. The Gospel does not presuppose the superiority of any culture to another, but evaluates all cultures according to its own criteria of truth and righteousness, and insists on moral absolutes in every culture. Missions have all too frequently exported with the Gospel an alien culture, and churches have sometimes been in bondage to culture rather than to the Scripture. Christ's evangelists must humbly seek to empty themselves of all but their personal authenticity in order to become the servants of others, and churches must seek to transform and enrich culture, all for the glory of God.

(Mark 7:8,9,13; Gen. 4:21,22; I Cor. 9:19-23; Phil. 2:5-7; II Cor. 4:5)

11. Education and Leadership

We confess that we have sometimes pursued church growth at the expense of church depth, and divorced evangelism from Christian nurture. We also acknowledge that some of our missions have been too slow to equip and encourage national leaders to assume their rightful responsibilities. Yet we are committed to indigenous principles, and long that every church will have national leaders who manifest a Christian style of leadership in terms not of domination but of service. We recognize that there is a great need to improve theological education, especially for church leaders. In every nation and culture there should be an effective training program for pastors and laymen in doctrine, discipleship, evangelism, nurture and service. Such training programs should not rely on any stereotyped methodology but should be developed by creative local initiatives according to biblical standards.

(Col. 1:27,28; Acts 14:23; Tit. 1:5,9; Mark 10:42-45; Eph. 4:11,12)

12. Spiritual Conflict

We believe that we are engaged in constant spiritual warfare with the principalities and powers of evil, who are seeking to overthrow the church and frustrate its task of world evangelization. We know our need to equip ourselves with

God's armor and to fight this battle with the spiritual weapons of truth and prayer. For we detect the activity of our enemy, not only in false ideologies outside the church, but also inside it in false gospels which twist Scripture and put man in the place of God. We need both watchfulness and discernment to safeguard the biblical Gospel. We acknowledge that we ourselves are not immune to worldliness of thought and action, that is, to a surrender to secularism. For example, although careful studies of church growth, both numerical and spiritual, are right and valuable, we have sometimes neglected them. At other times, desirous to insure a response to the Gospel, we have compromised our message, manipulated our hearts through pressure techniques, and become unduly preoccupied with statistics or even dishonest in our use of them. All this is worldly. The church must be in the world; the world must not be in the church.

(Eph. 6:12; II Cor. 4:3,4; Eph. 6:11, 13-18; II Cor. 10:3-5; I John 2:18-26; 4:1-3; Gal. 1:6-9; II Cor. 2:17; 4:2; John 17:15)

13. Freedom and Persecution

It is the God-appointed duty of every government to secure conditions of peace, justice, and liberty in which the church may obey God, serve the Lord Christ, and preach the Gospel without interference. We, therefore, pray for the leaders of the nations and call upon them to guarantee freedom of thought and conscience, and freedom to practice and propagate religion in accordance with the will of God and as set forth in The Universal Declaration of Human Rights. We also express our deep concern for all who have been unjustly imprisoned, and especially for our brethren who are suffering for their testimony to the Lord Jesus. We promise to pray and work for their freedom. At the same time we refuse to be intimidated by their fate. God helping us, we too will seek to stand against injustice and to remain faithful to the Gospel, whatever the cost. We do not forget the warnings of Jesus that persecution is inevitable.

(I Tim. 1:1-4; Acts 4:19; 5:29; Col. 3:24; Heb. 13:1-3; Luke 4:18; Gal. 5:11; 6:12; Matt. 5:10-12; John 15:18-21)

14. The Power of the Holy Spirit

We believe in the power of the Holy Spirit. The Father sent his Spirit to bear witness to his Son; without his witness ours is futile. Conviction of sin, faith in Christ, new birth and Christian growth are all his work. Further, the Holy Spirit is a missionary spirit; thus evangelism should arise spontaneously from a Spirit-filled church. A church that is not a missionary church is contradicting itself and quenching the Spirit. Worldwide evangelization will become a realistic possibility only when the Spirit renews the church in truth and wisdom, faith, holiness, love, and power. We, therefore, call upon all Christians to pray for such a visitation of the sovereign Spirit of God that all his fruit may appear in all his people and that all his gifts may enrich the body of Christ. Only then will the whole church become a fit instrument in his hands, that the whole earth may hear his voice.

(I Cor. 2:4; John 15:26,27; 16:8-11; I Cor. 12:3; John 3:6-8; II Cor. 3:18; John 7:37-39; I Thess. 5:19; Acts 1:8; Psa. 85:4-7; 67:1-3; Gal. 5:22,23; I Cor. 12:4-31; Rom. 12:3-8)

15. The Return of Christ

We believe that Jesus Christ will return personally and visibly in power and glory, to consummate his salvation and his judgment. This promise of his coming is a further spur to our evangelism, for we remember his words that the Gospel must first be preached to all nations. We believe that the interim period between Christ's ascension and return is to be filled with the mission of the people of God, who have no liberty to stop before the end. We also remember his warning that false Christs and false prophets will arise as precursors of the final Antichrist. We, therefore, reject as a proud, self-confident dream the notion that man can ever build a utopia on earth. Our Christian confidence is that God will perfect his kingdom, and we look forward with eager anticipation to that day, and to the new heaven and earth in which righteousness will dwell, and God will reign forever. Meanwhile, we rededicate ourselves to the service of Christ and of men in joyful submission to his authority over the whole of our lives.

(Mark 14:62; Heb. 9:28; Mark 13:10; Acts 1:8-11; Matt. 28:20; Mark 13:21-23; John 2:18; 4:1-3; Luke 12:32; Rev. 21:1-5; II Pet. 3:13; Matt. 28:18)

CONCLUSION

Therefore, in the light of this our faith and our resolve, we enter into a solemn covenant with God and with each other, to pray, to plan, and to work together for the evangelization of the whole world. We call upon others to join us. May God help us by his grace and for his glory to be faithful to this our covenant! Amen, Alleluia!

APPENDIX C:
THE AMSTERDAM DECLARATION

The Amsterdam Declaration is presented as a joint report of the three task groups of mission strategists, church leaders, and theologians gathered at Amsterdam 2000. It has been reviewed by hundreds of Christian leaders and evangelists from around the world. It is commended to God's people everywhere as an expression of evangelical commitment and as a resource for study, reflection, prayer, and evangelistic outreach.

THE AMSTERDAM DECLARATION
A CHARTER FOR EVANGELISM IN THE 21ST CENTURY

PREAMBLE

As a renewal movement within historic Christian orthodoxy, transdenominational evangelicalism became a distinct global reality in the second half of the twentieth century. Evangelicals come from many churches, languages and cultures but we hold in common a shared understanding of the gospel of Jesus Christ, of the church's mission, and of the Christian commitment to evangelism. Recent documents that express this understanding include the Berlin Statement (1966), the Lausanne Covenant (1974), the Amsterdam Affirmations (1983), the Manila Manifesto (1989), and The Gospel of Jesus Christ: An Evangelical Celebration (1999).

At the invitation of Dr. Billy Graham, some 10,000 evangelists, theologians, mission strategists and church leaders from more than 200 countries have assembled in Amsterdam in the year 2000 to listen, pray, worship and discern the wisdom of the Holy Spirit for the unfinished task of world evangelization. We are stirred and encouraged by the challenges we have heard and the fellowship we have shared with so many brothers and sisters in Christ. More than ever, we are resolved to make Christ known to all persons everywhere.

This Amsterdam Declaration has been developed as a framework to surround the many action plans that are being made for the evangelization of the world. It is based on the principles set forth in the documents referred to above, and includes these three parts: A charter of commitments, definitions of key theological terms used in the charter, and a prayer of supplication to our Heavenly Father.

CHARTER OF COMMITMENTS

This charter is a statement of tasks, goals and ideals for evangelism in the 21st century. The order of topics reflects the range of our concerns, not the priority of these themes.

1. *Mission Strategy and Evangelism* The mission of the church has at its heart world evangelization. We have from our Lord a mandate to proclaim the good news of God's love and forgiveness to everyone, making disciples, baptizing, and teaching all peoples. Jesus made it clear in his last teachings that the scope of this work of evangelism demands that we give attention not only to those around us but also to the despised and neglected of society and to those at the ends of the earth (Matthew 28:19; Acts 1:8). To do anything less is disobedience. In addition, we affirm the need to encourage new initiatives to reach and disciple youth and children worldwide; to make fuller use of media and technology in evangelism; and to stay involved personally in grass-roots evangelism so that our presentations of the biblical gospel are fully relevant and contextualized. We think it urgent to work toward the evangelization of every remaining unreached people group.

   We pledge ourselves to work so that all persons on earth may have an opportunity to hear the gospel in a language they understand, near where they live. We further pledge to establish healthy, reproducing, indigenous churches among every people, in every place, that will seek to bring to spiritual maturity those who respond to the gospel message.

2. *Leadership and Evangelism* We affirm that leadership is one of Christ's gifts to the church. It does not exist for itself; it exists to lead the people of God in obedience to our Heavenly Father. Leaders must submit themselves in humility to Christ, the Head of the church, and to one another. This submission involves the acceptance of the supreme authority of scripture by which Christ rules in his church through his Spirit. The leaders' first task is to preserve the biblical integrity of the proclamation of the church and serve as vision carriers of its evangelistic vocation. They are responsible to see that vocation implemented by teaching, training, empowering and inspiring others. We must give special attention to encouraging women and young leaders in their work of evangelism. Leaders must always be careful not to block what God is doing as they exercise their strategic stewardship of the resources which Christ supplies to his body (Ephesians 4:11-13; Mark 10:42-45; Colossians 1:18).

   We *pledge ourselves* to seek and uphold this model of biblical servant-leadership in our churches. We who are leaders commit ourselves afresh to this pattern of leadership.

3. *Theology and Evangelism* Christian theology is the task of careful thinking and ordering of life in the presence of the triune God. In one sense, all Christians are theologians and must labor to be good ones rather than bad ones. This means that everyone's theology must be measured by biblical teaching from which alone we learn God's mind and will (Mark 7:13; II Timothy 2:15; 3:16). Those called to the special vocations of evangelism, theology, and pastoral ministry must work together in the spread of the gospel throughout the world. Evangelists and pastors can help theologians maintain an evangelistic motivation, reminding them that true theology is always done in the service of the church. Theologians can help to clarify and safeguard God's revealed truth, providing resources for the training of evangelists and the grounding of new believers in the faith (I Timothy 6:20; II Timothy 1:14).

   We *pledge ourselves* to labor constantly in learning and teaching the faith according to the Scriptures, and in seeking to ensure (1) that all who preach the gospel are theologically equipped and resourced in adequate

ways for the work they have in hand, and (2) that all professional teachers of the faith share a common concern for evangelism.

4. *Truth and Evangelism* Under the influence of modern rationalism, secularism, and humanism (modernity), the Western intellectual establishment has largely reacted into a relativistic denial that there is any global and absolute truth (postmodernity). This is influencing popular culture throughout the world (Romans 15:16). By contrast (Galatians 1:7; 2:14), the gospel which is the authoritative word of the one, true and living God, comes to everyone everywhere at all times as truth in three senses: its affirmations are factually true, as opposed to false; it confronts us at every point with reality, as opposed to illusion; and it sets before us Jesus Christ, the co-Creator, Redeemer, and Lord of the world, as the Truth (that is, the one universally, real, accessible, authoritative, truth-telling, trustworthy Person), for all to acknowledge (I Corinthians 9:12; II Thessalonians 1:8). There is a suspicion that any grand claim that there is one truth for everyone is inevitably oppressive and violent. But the gospel sets before us one who, though he was God, became man and identified with those under the bondage of sin to set them free from its enslavement. This gospel of God is both true for everyone and truly sets people free (John 8:31-32). It is therefore to be received in trust, not suspicion.

We pledge ourselves to present and proclaim the biblical gospel and its Christ, always and everywhere, as fully sufficient and effective for the salvation of believers. Therefore, we oppose all skeptical and relativizing or syncretizing trends, whether rationalist or irrationalist, that treat that gospel as not fully true, and so as unable to lead believers into the new divine life that it promises them. We oppose all oppressive and destructive uses of God's wonderful truth.

5. *Human Need and Evangelism* Both the law and the gospel uncover a lost human condition that goes beyond any feelings of pain, misery, frustration, bondage, powerlessness, and discontent with life. The Bible reveals that all human beings are constitutionally in a state of rebellion against the God who made them, and of whom they remain dimly aware; they are alienated from him, and cut off from all the enjoyment of knowing and serving him that is the

true fulfillment of human nature (Romans 1:18-32; 5:12; 18a; I Corinthians 15:22). We humans were made to bear God's image (Genesis 1:26) in an endless life of love to God and to other people, but the self-centeredness of our fallen and sinful hearts makes that impossible. Often our dishonesty leads us to use even the observance of religion to keep God at a distance, so that we can avoid having him deal with us about our ungodly self-worship. Therefore all human beings now face final condemnation by Christ the Judge, and eternal destruction, separated from the presence of the Lord (II Thessalonians 1:9).

We pledge ourselves to be faithful and compassionate in sharing with people the truth about their present spiritual state, warning them of the judgment and hell that the impenitent face, and extolling the love of God who gave his Son to save us.

6. *Religious Pluralism and Evangelism* Today's evangelist is called to proclaim the gospel in an increasingly pluralistic world. In this global village of competing faiths and many world religions, it is important that our evangelism be marked both by faithfulness to the good news of Christ and humility in our delivery of it. Because God's general revelation extends to all points of his creation, there may well be traces of truth, beauty and goodness in many non-Christian belief systems (Romans 1:18-20). But we have no warrant for regarding any of these as alternative gospels or separate roads to salvation (John 14:6; Acts 4:12). The only way to know God in peace, love and joy is through the reconciling death of Jesus Christ the risen Lord. As we share this message with others, we must do so with love and humility, shunning all arrogance, hostility and disrespect (Mark 10:41-45; James 1:20). As we enter into dialogue with adherents of other religions, we must be courteous and kind. But such dialogue must not be a substitute for proclamation. Yet because all persons are made in the image of God (Genesis 1:26), we must advocate religious liberty and human rights for all.

We pledge ourselves to treat those of other faiths with respect and faithfully and humbly serve the nation in which God has placed us, while affirming that Christ is the one and only Savior of the world.

7. *Culture and Evangelism.* By the blood of the Lamb, God has purchased saints from every tribe and language and people and nation (Revelation 5:9; I Corinthians 6:19). He saves people in their own culture. World evangelization aims to see the rise of churches that are both deeply rooted in Christ and closely related to their culture. Therefore, following the example of Jesus and Paul, those who proclaim Christ must use their freedom in Christ to become all things to all people (I Corinthians 9:19-23). This means appropriate cultural identification while guarding against equating the gospel with any particular culture. Since all human cultures are shaped in part by sin, the Bible and its Christ are at key points counter-cultural to every one of them.

> *We pledge ourselves* to be culturally sensitive in our evangelism. We will aim to preach Christ in a way that is appropriate for the people among whom we witness and which will enrich that culture in all appropriate ways. Further, as salt and light we will seek the transforming of culture in ways that affirm gospel values.

8. *Scripture and Evangelism* The Bible is indispensable to true evangelism. The Word of God itself provides both the content and authority for all evangelism. Without it there is no message to preach to the lost (I Thessalonians 2:13; Acts 2:14-39; 13:16-41). People must be brought to an understanding of at least some of the basic truths contained in the Scriptures before they can make a meaningful response to the gospel. Thus we must proclaim and disseminate the Holy Scriptures in the heart language of all those we are called to evangelize and disciple.

> *We pledge ourselves* to keep the Scriptures at the very heart of our evangelistic outreach and message, and to remove all language and cultural barriers to a clear understanding of the gospel on the part of our hearers.

9. *The Church and Evangelism* There is no dispute that in established congregations regular teaching for believers at all stages in their pilgrimage must be given, and appropriate pastoral care must be provided (I Corinthians 14:13-17). But these concerns must not displace ongoing concern for mission, which involves treating evangelistic outreach as a continuing priority. Pastors in conjunction with other qualified persons should lead their congregations in the work of

evangelism. Further, we affirm that the formation of godly, witnessing disciples is at the heart of the church's responsibility to prepare its members for their work of service (Matthew 28:19; II Timothy 2:2). We affirm that the church must be made a welcoming place for new believers.

> *We pledge ourselves* **to urge all congregations in and with which we serve to treat evangelism as a matter of priority at all times, and so to make it a focus of congregational praying, planning, training and funding.**

10. *Prayer and Evangelism* God has given us the gift of prayer so that in his sovereignty he may respond in blessing and power to the cries of his children. Prayer is an essential means God has appointed for the awakening of the church and the carrying of the gospel throughout the world. From the first days of the New Testament church, God has used the fervent, persistent praying of his people to empower their witness in the Spirit, overcome opposition to the Lord's work and open the minds and hearts of those who hear the message of Christ (Acts 1:14; 2:42; 4:23-30; 6:4; 12:5). At special times in the history of the church, revivals and spiritual breakthroughs have been preceded by the explicit agreement and union of God's people in seasons of repentance, prayer and fasting. Today, as we seek to carry the gospel to unreached people groups in all the world, we need a deeper dependence upon God and a greater unity in prayer (Ephesians 6:18).

> *We pledge ourselves* **to pray faithfully to the Lord of the harvest to send out workers for his harvest field (Matthew 9:37-38). We also pray for all those engaged in world evangelization and to encourage the call to prayer in families, local churches, special assemblies, mission agencies and transdenominational ministries.**

11. *Social Responsibility and Evangelism* Although evangelism is not advocacy of any social program, it does entail social responsibility for at least two reasons. First, the gospel proclaims the kingship of the loving Creator who is committed to justice, to human life and the welfare of his creation (Psalm 47:7; I Timothy 6:15; Revelation 17:14). So evangelism will need to be accompanied by obedience to God's command to work for the good of all in a way that is

fitting for the children of the Father who makes his sun shine on the evil and the good and sends his rain on the righteous and the unrighteous alike (Galatians 6:10; Matthew 5:45). Second, when our evangelism is linked with concern to alleviate poverty, uphold justice, oppose abuses of secular and economic power, stand against racism, and advance responsible stewardship of the global environment, it reflects the compassion of Christ and may gain an acceptance it would not otherwise receive (Deuteronomy 24:10-13, 14-15; Luke 1:52-53; 4:18-19; James 5:1-6).

We pledge ourselves **to follow the way of justice in our family and social life, and to keep personal, social and environmental values in view as we evangelize.**

12. *Holiness and Evangelism* The servant of God must adorn the gospel through a holy life (I Timothy 3:2-13; Titus 1:6-9). But in recent times God's name has been greatly dishonored and the gospel discredited because of unholy living by Christians in leadership roles. Evangelists seem particularly exposed to temptations relating to money, sex, pride, power, neglect of family and lack of integrity. The church should foster structures to hold evangelists accountable for their lives, doctrine and ministries. The church should also ensure that those whose lives dishonor God and the gospel will not be permitted to serve as its evangelists. The holiness and humility of evangelists gives credibility to their ministry and leads to genuine power from God and lasting fruit (I Corinthians 5:1-13; II Thessalonians 3:14-15; I Timothy 5:11-13, 19-20).

We pledge ourselves **to be accountable to the community of faith for our lives, doctrine and ministry, to flee from sin, and to walk in holiness and humility (I Corinthians 6:18; II Timothy 2:2).**

13. *Conflict, Suffering and Evangelism* The records of evangelism from the apostolic age, the state of the world around us today, and the knowledge of Satan's opposition at all times to the spread of the gospel, combine to assure us that evangelistic outreach in the twenty-first century will be an advance in the midst of opposition (Acts 13:6-12; Ephesians 6:11-13). Current forms of opposition, which Satan evidently exploits, include secular ideologies that see

Christian faith as a hindrance to human development; political power structures that see the primacy of Christians' loyalty to their Lord as a threat to the regime; and militant expressions of non-Christian religions that are hostile to Christians for being different. We must expect, and be prepared for, many kinds of suffering as we struggle not against enemies of blood and flesh, but against the spiritual forces of evil in the heavenly places (Ephesians 6:14-18).

We pledge ourselves ever to seek to move forward wisely in personal evangelism, family evangelism, local church evangelism, and cooperative evangelism in its various forms, and to persevere in this despite the opposition we may encounter. We will stand in solidarity with our brothers and sisters in Christ who suffer persecution and even martyrdom for their faithful gospel witness.

14. *Christian Unity and Evangelism* Jesus prayed to the Heavenly Father that his disciples would be one so that the world might believe (Ephesians 4:1-6; John 17:21-23). One of the great hindrances to evangelism worldwide is the lack of unity among Christ's people, a condition made worse when Christians compete and fight with one another rather than seeking together the mind of Christ. We cannot resolve all differences among Christians because we do not yet understand perfectly all that God has revealed to us (Romans 11:24; II Peter 3:15). But in all ways that do not violate our conscience, we should pursue cooperation and partnerships with other believers in the task of evangelism, practicing the well-tested rule of Christian fellowship: "In necessary things, unity; in non-essential things, liberty; in all things, charity" (Romans 14:14, 23).

We pledge ourselves to pray and work for unity in truth among all true believers in Jesus and to cooperate as fully as possible in evangelism with other brothers and sisters in Christ so that the whole church may take the whole gospel to the whole world.

DEFINITIONS OF KEY TERMS

The message we proclaim has both a propositional and an incarnational dimension—"the Word became flesh" (John 1:14). To deny either one is to bear false witness to Christ. Because the relation between language and reality is much debated today, it is important to state clearly what we mean by what we say. To avoid confusion and misunderstanding, then, we here define the following key words used in this Declaration. The definitions are all Trinitarian, Christocentric, and Bible-based.

1. *God* The God of whom this Declaration speaks is the self-revealed Creator, Upholder, Governor and Lord of the universe (Genesis 1:1; Exodus 20:11; Psalm 24:1-2; 33:6; Acts 4:24-30). This God is eternal in his self-existence and unchanging in his holy love, goodness, justice, wisdom, and faithfulness to his promises (Psalm 90:2; 119:42). God in his own being is a community of three coequal and coeternal persons, who are revealed to us in the Bible as the Father, the Son, and the Holy Spirit (Matthew 28:19; II Corinthians 13:14). Together they are involved in an unvarying cooperative pattern in all God's relationships to and within this world. God is Lord of history, where he blesses his own people, overcomes and judges human and angelic rebels against his rule, and will finally renew the whole created order (Daniel 7:1-28; Acts 2:23-24; 4:28; Ephesians 1:9-10).

2. *Jesus Christ* The Declaration takes the view of Jesus that the canonical New Testament sets forth and the historic Christian creeds and confessions attest. He was, and is, the second person of the triune Godhead, now and forever incarnate. He was virgin-born, lived a life of perfect godliness, died on the cross as the substitutionary sacrifice for our sins, was raised bodily from the dead, ascended into heaven, reigns now over the universe and will personally return for judgment and the renewal of all things. As the God-man, once crucified, now enthroned, he is the Lord and Savior who in love fulfills towards us the threefold mediational ministry of prophet, priest and king. His title, "Christ," proclaims him the anointed servant of God who fulfills all the Messianic hopes of the canonical Old Testament (Romans 9:5; Titus 2:13; Hebrews 1:8; John 1:1-14; Hebrews 4:15; Romans 3:21-26; II Corinthians 5:21; I Corinthians 15:3-4; I Timothy 3:16; Philippians 2:9-11; II Thessalonians 1:7-10; Acts 2:26; Romans 1:1-3).

3. *Holy Spirit* Shown by the words of Jesus to be the third divine person, whose name, "Spirit," pictures the energy of breath and wind, the Holy Spirit is the

dynamic personal presence of the Trinity in the processes of the created world, in the communication of divine truth, in the attesting of Jesus Christ, in the new creation through him of believers and of the church, and in ongoing fellowship and service (John 3:8; 14:16-17, 26; 16:13-15). The fullness of the ministry of the Holy Spirit in relation to the knowledge of Christ and the enjoyment of new life in him dates from the Pentecostal outpouring recorded in Acts 2. As the divine inspirer and interpreter of the Bible, the Spirit empowers God's people to set forth accurate, searching, life-transforming presentations of the gospel of Jesus Christ, and makes their communication a fruitful means of grace to their hearers (Acts 2:14; II Timothy 3:16; II Peter 1:21; I Thessalonians 1:5). The New Testament shows us the supernatural power of the Spirit working miracles, signs and wonders, bestowing gifts of many kinds, and overcoming the power of Satan in human lives for the advancement of the gospel (Acts 2:43; 5:12; 6:8; 14:3; 15:12). Christians agree that the power of the Holy Spirit is vitally necessary for evangelism and that openness to his ministry should mark all believers.

4. **Bible** The 66 books of the Old and New Testaments constitute the written Word of God. As the inspired revelation of God in writing, the Scriptures are totally true and trustworthy, and the only infallible rule of faith and practice. In every age and every place, this authoritative Bible, by the Spirit's power, is efficacious for salvation through its witness to Jesus Christ (II Timothy 3:16; II Peter 1:21; Luke 1:1-4; John 14:26; I John 1:3).

5. **Kingdom** The kingdom of God is his gracious rule through Jesus Christ over human lives, the course of history, and all reality (Daniel 7:14; Luke 11:20). Jesus is Lord of past, present, and future, and Sovereign ruler of everything (Hebrews 13:8). The salvation Jesus brings and the community of faith he calls forth are signs of his kingdom's presence here and now, though we wait for its complete fulfillment when he comes again in glory (Luke 22:29). In the meantime, wherever Christ's standards of peace and justice are observed to any degree, to that degree the kingdom is anticipated, and to that extent God's ideal for human society is displayed (Luke 6:20; Matthew 5:3).

6. **Gospel** The gospel is the good news of the Creator's eternal plan to share his life and love with fallen human beings through the sending of his Son Jesus Christ,

the one and only Savior of the world. As the power of God for salvation, the gospel centers on the life, death, resurrection and return of Jesus and leads to a life of holiness, growth in grace and hope-filled though costly discipleship in the fellowship of the church (Romans 1:16-17; I Corinthians 15:2; Acts 2:14-39; 13:16-41; Romans 1:1-5). The gospel includes the announcement of Jesus' triumph over the powers of darkness and of his supreme lordship over the universe (Colossians 2:15; I Peter 3:22).

7. *Salvation* This word means rescue from guilt, defilement, spiritual blindness and deadness, alienation from God, and certainty of eternal punishment in hell, that is everyone's condition while under sin's dominion. This deliverance involves present justification, reconciliation to God and adoption into his family, with regeneration and the sanctifying gift of the Holy Spirit leading to works of righteousness and service here and now, and a promise of full glorification in fellowship with God in the future. This involves in the present life joy, peace, freedom and the transformation of character and relationships and the guarantee of complete healing at the future resurrection of the body. We are justified by faith alone and the salvation faith brings is by grace alone, through Christ alone, for the glory of God alone (Ephesians 2:8-9; Romans 5:9; 3:21-26; 8:30; Ephesians 2:10; Philippians 2:12-13; 3:21; I Corinthians 15:43; II Thessalonians 1:9-10; Mark 4:42-48; Romans 4:4-6; Ephesians 2:8-9; Titus 3:4-7; Romans 11:36; 15:9; Philippians 1:11).

8. *Christian* A Christian is a believer in God who is enabled by the Holy Spirit to submit to Jesus Christ as Lord and Savior in a personal relation of disciple to master and to live the life of God's kingdom (Acts 11:26; 26:28). The word Christian should not be equated with any particular cultural, ethnic, political, or ideological tradition or group (I Peter 4:16). Those who know and love Jesus are also called Christ-followers, believers and disciples.

9. *Church* The church is the people of God, the body and the bride of Christ, and a temple of the Holy Spirit. The one, universal church is a transnational, transcultural, transdenominational and multi-ethnic family, the household of faith (I Corinthians 12:27; Ephesians 5:25-27, 32). In the widest sense, the church includes all the redeemed of all the ages, being the one body of Christ extended

throughout time as well as space (Matthew 28:19; Romans 3:27-30; Revelation 7:9-10). Here in the world, the church becomes visible in all local congregations that meet to do together the things that according to Scripture the church does (I Corinthians 1:2). Christ is the head of the church. Everyone who is personally united to Christ by faith belongs to his body and by the Spirit is united with every other true believer in Jesus.

10. *Mission* Formed from *missio,* the Latin word for "sending," this term is used both of the Father's sending of the Son into the world to become its Savior and of the Son's sending the church into the world to spread the gospel, perform works of love and justice, and seek to disciple everyone to himself (John 17:18; 20:21).

11. *Evangelism* Derived from the Greek word *euangelizesthai,* "to tell glad tidings," this word signifies making known the gospel of Jesus Christ so that people may trust in God through him, receiving him as their Savior and serving him as their Lord in the fellowship of his church (Luke 4:18; Romans 1:15-17). Evangelism involves declaring what God has done for our salvation and calling on the hearers to become disciples of Jesus through repentance from sin and personal faith in him.

12. *Evangelist* All Christians are called to play their part in fulfilling Jesus' Great Commission, but some believers have a special call to, and a spiritual gift for, communicating Christ and leading others to him. These we call evangelists, as does the New Testament (II Timothy 4:5; Ephesians 4:11).

PRAYER

Gracious God, our Heavenly Father, we praise you for the great love that you have shown to us through the redeeming death and triumphant resurrection of your Son, our Lord Jesus Christ. We pray that you would enable us by the power of your Holy Spirit to proclaim faithfully the good news of your kingdom and your love. Forgive us for failing to take the gospel to all the peoples of the world. Deliver us from ignorance, error, lovelessness, pride, selfishness, impurity, and cowardice. Enable us to be truthful, kind, humble, sympathetic, pure, and courageous. Salvation belongs to you, O God, who sits on the throne, and to the Lamb. We ask you to make our gospel witness effective. Anoint our proclamation with the Holy Spirit; use it to gather that great multitude from all nations who will one day stand before you and the Lamb giving praise (Revelation 7:9-10). This we ask by the merits of our Lord Jesus Christ. Amen.

CRUSADE	DATES	ATTENDANCE	INQUIRERS
	1947		
Grand Rapids, MI	Oct	6,000	500
Charlotte, NC	Nov (2 wks)	42,000	1,200
		48,000	1,700
	1948		
Augusta, GA	Oct (16 days)	65,000	1,400
Modesto, CA	Nov		
Birmingham, England		———	6,000
		65,000	7,400
	1949		
Miami, FL	Feb/Mar		
Baltimore, MD	May		
Altoona, PA	June		
Los Angeles, CA	Sept/Nov	350,000	3,000
	1950		
Boston, MA	Dec/Jan (3 wks)	105,000	3,000
Columbia, SC	Feb/Mar	190,000	12,000
Tour-			
New England States	Mar/Apr (4 wks)	160,000	6,000
Portland, OR	July/Sept	520,000	9,000
Minneapolis, MN	Sept/Oct	282,000	5,700
Atlanta, GA	Oct/Dec (5 wks)	500,000	8,000
		1,757,000	43,700

1951

Tour - Southern States	Jan/Feb	125,000	
Fort Worth, TX	Feb/Mar (4 wks)	336,300	4,000
Shreveport, LA	Apr (3 wks)	223,000	5,446
Cincinnati, OH	May	21,000	
Memphis, TN	May/June (4 1/2 wks)	317,700	4,648
Seattle, WA	July/Sept	443,500	6,785
Hollywood, CA	Sept/Oct (2 1/2 wks)	135,000	2,120
Greensboro, NC	Oct/Nov (6 wks)	391,050	6,443
Raleigh, NC	Nov	<u>34,000</u>	<u>1,450</u>
		2,026,550	30,892

1952

Washington, DC	Jan/Feb (5 wks)	307,000	6,244
Tour - American Cities	Apr/May	41,000	
Houston, TX	May/June (5 wks)	462,500	7,754
Jackson, MS	June/July (4 wks)	362,300	5,927
Tour - American Cities	Aug	126,000	
Pittsburgh, PA	Sept/Oct (4 wks)	263,500	5,986
Albuquerque, NM	Nov	<u>133,030</u>	<u>3,011</u>
		1,695,330	28,922

1953

Tour - Florida Cities	Jan/Feb	120,000	
Chattanooga, TN	Mar/Apr (4 wks)	283,300	4,406
St. Louis, MO	Apr/May (4 wks)	318,400	3,065
Dallas, TX	May/June (4 wks)	513,000	5,869
Tour - West Texas	July	77,000	
Syracuse, NY	Aug (4 wks)	105,200	2,630
Detroit, MI	Sept/Nov (5 wks)	363,030	6,980
Asheville, NC	Nov (2 wks)	<u>112,100</u>	<u>2,653</u>
		1,892,030	25,603

1954

London, England	Mar/May (12 wks)	2,047,333	38,447

Tour - Europe	June	303,800	
Nashville, TN	Aug/Sept (4 wks)	652,000	9,067
New Orleans, LA	Oct (4 wks)	319,300	4,932
Tour - West Coast	Nov	87,500	2,650
		3,409,933	55,096

1955

Glasgow, Scotland	Mar/Apr (6 wks)	2,647,365	52,253
Tour - Scotland Cities			1,289
London, England	May (1 wk)	450,000	23,806
Paris, France	June (4 days)	43,619	2,153
Zurich, Switzerland	(1 day)	50,000	5,000
Geneva, Switzerland	(2 days)	40,000	3,000
Mannheim, Germany	(1 day)	40,000	1,500
U.S. Service Bases		25,000	7,000
Stuttgart, Germany	(1 day)	60,000	2,400
Nurnberg, Germany	(1 day)	65,000	2,500
Dortmund, Germany	(1 day)	30,000	1,800
Frankfurt, Germany	(1 day)	40,000	2,000
Rotterdam, The Netherlands	(1 day)	65,000	2,000
Oslo, Norway	(2 days)	77,000	1,000
Gothenburg, Sweden	(1 day)	26,000	150
Aarhus, Denmark	(1 day)	10,000	200
Toronto, Canada	Sept/Oct (3 wks)	356,000	7,436
		4,024,984	115,487

1956

Tour - India & Far East	Jan/Feb (8 wks)	800,000	29,034
Richmond, VA	Apr/May (3 wks)	298,370	6,209
Oklahoma City, OK	June/July (4 wks)	464,139	7,148
Louisville, KY	Sept/Oct (4 wks)	492,740	6,870
		2,055,249	49,261

	1957		
New York City, NY	May/Sept (16 wks)	2,397,400	61,148

	1958		
Tour - Caribbean	Jan/Feb (3 wks)	1,000,000 +	20,000 +
San Francisco, CA	Apr/June (7 wks)	721,725	28,898
Sacramento, CA	June/July (1 wk)	149,600	4,965
Fresno, CA	July (2 days)	51,000	1,550
Santa Barbara, CA	July (1 day)	12,000	671
Los Angeles, CA	July (1 day)	40,000	2,117
San Diego, CA	July (2 days)	55,000	3,284
San Antonio, TX	July (1 day)	30,000	1,903
Charlotte, NC	Sept/Oct (5 wks)	423,387	17,853
		2,482,712	81,241

	1959		
Melbourne, Australia	Feb/Mar (4 wks)	719,000	26,440
Auckland, New Zealand	Mar/Apr (1 wk)	163,000	6,890
Sydney, Australia	Apr/May(4 wks)	980,000	56,780
Perth, Australia	May (1 wk)	106,800	5,396
Brisbane, Australia	May (2 wks)	246,000	10,661
Adelaide, Australia	May (2 wks)	253,000	11,992
Relay Services		650,440	15,650
Wellington, New Zealand	June (1 wk)	59,000	4,740
Christ Church, New Zealand	June (1 wk)	133,000	4,693
Canberra, Launceston & Hobart	(1 day each)	52,000	3,492
AUSTRALIA TOUR TOTAL		3,362,240	146,734

Little Rock, AR	Sept (2 days)	50,000	1,438
Wheaton, IL	Sept/Oct (1 wk)	101,000	2,812
Indianapolis, IN	Oct/Nov (4 wks)	328,127	9,320
		3,841,367	160,304

1960

Monrovia, Liberia	Jan (5 days)	12,800	1,297
Accra, Ghana	Jan (1 wk)	32,500	2,827
Kumasi	Jan (3 days)	12,500	453
Lagos, Nigeria	Jan (1 wk)	128,600	4,559
Ibadan	Feb (10 days)	32,905	2,151
Kaduma	Feb (1 wk)	22,450	1,595
Enugu	Feb (9 days)	41,400	1,565
Jos	Feb (1 wk)	25,770	1,535
Brazzaville, Congo	Feb (1 day)	***	***
Bulawayo, S. Rhodesia	Feb (1 wk)	42,000	2,345
Salisbury	Feb (9 days)	36,000	2,214
Kitwe, N. Rhodesia	Feb (1 wk)	28,000	1,497
Moshi, Tanganyika	Feb (2 days)	40,000	5,211
Kisumu, Kenya	Mar (5 days)	22,300	3,406
Nairobi	Mar (1 wk)	39,300	1,349
Usumbura, R. U.	Mar (1 wk)	26,650	1,551
Addis Ababa, Ethiopia	Mar (2 days)	18,000	739
Cairo, Egypt	Mar (1 day)	7,000	453
Jersualem, Jordan	Mar (1 day)	<u>2,000</u>	<u>137</u>
AFRICAN/MIDEAST TOUR TOTAL		570,175	34,884
Washington, DC	June (1 wk)	139,000	4,971
Rio de Janeiro, Brazil	July (1 day)	143,000	2,193
Bern, Switzerland	Aug (1wk)	29,250	1,260
Zurich, Switzerland	Aug (2 days)	25,000	1,243
Basel, Switzerland	Aug (1 wk)	34,750	1,830
Lausanne, Switzerland	Sept (1 wk)	79,000	3,226
Essen, Germany	Sept (1 wk)	155,000	4,175
Hamburg, Germany	Sept (1 wk)	297,000	7,192
Berlin, Germany	Sept/Oct (1 wk)	<u>197,000</u>	<u>5,269</u>
EUROPEAN TOUR TOTAL		817,000	24,195
New York City (Spanish)	Oct (3 days)	<u>43,500</u>	<u>1,139</u>
		1,712,675	67,382

1961

Jacksonville, FL	Jan (2 days)	28,000	912
Orlando, FL	Jan (2 days)	23,000	714
Clearwater, FL	Jan (1 day)	9,000	282
St. Petersburg, FL	Jan (1 day)	19,800	291
Bradenton-Sarasota, FL	Feb (1 day)	13,700	305
Tampa, FL	Feb (1 day)	20,000	629
Tallahassee, FL	Feb (1 day)	14,000	395
Gainesville, FL	Feb (1 day)	22,000	407
Miami, FL	Mar (3 wks)	250,380	8,062
Cape Canaveral, FL	Mar (1 day)	9,000	446
West Palm Beach, FL	Mar (1 day)	12,000	515
Vero Beach, FL	Mar (1 day)	6,000	97
Peace River, FL	Apr (1 day)	20,000	350
Boca Raton, FL	Apr (1 day)	11,000	510
Ft. Lauderdale, FL	Apr (1 day)	<u>10,000</u>	<u>100</u>
FLORIDA MEETINGS TOTAL		467,880	14,015
Manchester, England	May/June (3 wks)	416,500	17,769
Glasgow, Scotland	June (1 day)	40,000	600
Belfast, Ireland	June (1 day)	55,000	900
Relays - Manchester		400,000	6,000
Minneapolis, MN	July (1 wk)	44,672 +	555 +
Minneapolis, MN	July (1 wk)	308,000	6,678
Philadelphia, PA	Aug/Sept (4 wks)	<u>550,000</u>	<u>16,244</u>
		2,282,052	62,761

1962

Tour - South American	Jan/Feb (5 wks)	255,125	9,228
Raleigh, NC	Mar (1 day)	9,000	352
Jacksonville, NC	Mar (1 day)	17,000	426
Chicago, IL	May/June (3 wks)	704,900	16,597
Seattle, WA	July (1 day)	35,000	609
Fresno, CA	July (1 wk)	161,200	6,820
Redstone Arsenal, AL	Aug (1 day)	35,000	473
Tour - South American	Sept/Oct (4 wks)	572,500	12,469

El Paso, TX	Nov (1 wk)	<u>86,500</u>	<u>3,821</u>
		1,876,225	50,795

1963

Paris, France	May (8 days)	40,000	1,147
Lyon, France	Assoc. 4 days-BG2	*18,800	*417
Mulhouse, France	Assoc. 7 days-BG1	*18,500	*650
Toulouse, France	Assoc. 9 days-BG1	*12,200	*287
Montauban, France	Assoc. 9 days	*1,850	*95
Nancy, France	Assoc. 1 wk	*2,000	*62
Douai, France	Assoc. 6 days	*2,500	*40
Nurnberg, Germany	June (6 days)	117,000	2,611
Stuttgart, Germany	June (6 days)	138,000	3,967
Los Angeles, CA	Aug/Sept (3 1/2 wks)	<u>910,445</u>	<u>36,487</u>
		*1,261,295	*45,763

1964

Birmingham, AL	Mar (1 day)		1,227
Phoenix, AR	Apr (3 days)	103,500	4,239
San Diego, CA	May (9 days)	180,000	8,664
Columbus, OH	July (10 days)	316,500	12,149
Omaha, NE	Sept (10 days)	183,170	10,724
Boston, MA	Sept (10 days)	209,150	9,012
Boston, MA	Oct (1 wk)	83,500	5,209
Manchester, NH	Oct (1 day)	7,300	500
Portland, ME	Oct (1 day)	6,500	600
Bangor, ME	Oct (1 day)	7,500	514
Providence, RI	Oct (1 day)	10,000	600
Louisville, KY	Nov (1 day)	<u> </u>	<u>860</u>
		1,107,120	54,298

1965

Honolulu, HI	Feb (8 days)	65,182	2,907
Kahului Maui, HI	Feb (1 day)	2,800	383
Hilo, HI	Feb (1 day)	2,688	353
Lihue, Kauai, HI	Feb (1 day)	1,886	244

Dothan, AL	Apr (1 day)	7,500	239
Tuscaloosa, AL			
(University of Alabama)	Apr (1 day)	15,000	
Auburn, AL			
(Auburn University)	Apr (1 day)	16,000	
Tuskegee, AL			
(Tuskegee Institute)	Apr (1 day)	10,000	
Copenhagen, Denmark	May (8 days)	65,700	681
Copenhagen, Denmark	May (8 days)		
Montgomery, AL	June (8 days)	98,500	4,414
Vancouver, BC,			
Canada	July (3 days)	77,800	1,751
Seattle, WA	July (1 day)	25,000	
Denver, CO	Aug/Sept (10 days)	277,300	10,251
Houston, TX	Nov (10 days)	<u>379,159</u>	<u>14,063</u>
		1,044,515	35,286
	1966		
Greenville, SC	Mar 4-13	278,700	7,311
London, England	June 1–July 2	1,055,368	42,487
Berlin, Germany	Oct 16-23	<u>90,000</u>	<u>2,749</u>
		1,424,068	52,547
	1967		
Ponce, Puerto Rico	Mar 18	7,500	326
San Juan, Puerto Rico	Mar 19-26	105,700	4,355
Winnipeg, Manitoba,			
Canada	May 28–June 4	126,300	3,470
Great Britain	June 23–July 1	1,006,254	34,367
Turin, Italy	July 5	3,000	**
Zagreb, Yugoslavia	July 8-9	10,000	**
Toronto, Ontario,			
Canada	Sept 3	40,000	**
Kansas City, MO	Sept 8-17	364,000	11,379
Tokyo, Japan	Oct 20-29	<u>191,950</u>	<u>15,854</u>
		1,854,704	69,751

1968			
Brisbane, Australia	Apr 5-7	167,397	7,618
Sydney, Australia	Apr 20-28	516,111	24,191
Portland, OR	May 17-26	227,797	7,950
San Antonio, TX	June 13-16	99,500	4,326
Pittsburgh, PA	Aug. 30–Sept 8	280,100	12,414
		1,290,905	56,499
1969			
Auckland, New Zealand	Feb 27–Mar 2	128,000	6,080
Dunedin, New Zealand	Mar 9	20,000	976
Melbourne, Australia	Mar 14-23	333,250	12,194
New York City, NY	June 13-22	234,000	10,852
Anaheim, CA	Sept 26–Oct 5	384,000	20,336
		1,099,250	50,438
1970			
Dortmund, Germany	Apr 5-12	838,023	15,742
Knoxville, TN	May 22-31	552,000	12,303
New York City, NY	June 24-28	139,500	6,025
Baton Rouge, LA	Oct 21-25	197,000	9,076
		1,726,523	43,146
1971			
Lexington, KY	Apr 25-28	77,500	2,100
Chicago, IL	June 3-13	326,300	11,889
Oakland, CA	July 23–Aug 1	367,200	21,670
Dallas-Fort Worth, TX	Sept 17-26	456,400	12,830
		1,227,400	48,489
1972			
Charlotte, NC	Apr 5-9	72,100	4,709
Birmingham, AL	May 14-21	373,300	9,788
Cleveland, OH	July 14-23	372,440	19,608
Kohima, Nagaland, India	Nov 20-22	500,000	***
		1,317,840	34,105

1973			
Durban, South Africa	Mar 17	45,000	4,000
Johannesburg, South Africa	Mar 25	60,000	4,200
Seoul, Korea (South)	May 30–June 3	3,210,000	****72,365
Atlanta, GA	June 18-24	266,500	9,735
Minneapolis-St. Paul, MN	July 13-22	318,350	16,520
Raleigh, NC	Sept 23-30	237,500	10,568
St. Louis, MO	Nov 2-11	224,400	5,814
		4,361,750	123,202
1974			
Phoenix, AZ	May 5-12	240,195	9,718
Los Angeles, CA (25th Anniversary Celebration)	Sept 19-21	40,600	1,644
Rio de Janeiro, Brazil	Oct 2-6	590,000	****31,039
Norfolk-Hampton, VA	Nov 1-10	175,850	6,296
		1,046,645	48,697
1975			
Albuquerque, NM	Mar 16-23	122,300	8,657
Jackson, MS	May 11-18	281,100	7,335
Brussels, Belgium	July 24–Aug 2	101,805	2,557
Lubbock, TX	Aug 31–Sept 7	272,000	7,071
Taipei, Taiwan	Oct 29–Nov 2	250,000	11,607
Hong Kong	Nov 12-16	217,230	20,522
		1,244,435	57,749
1976			
Seattle, WA	May 9-16	434,100	18,136
Williamsburg, VA	June 24-25	18,900	514
San Diego, CA	Aug 13-20	254,800	10,215
Detroit, MI	Oct 15-24	365,768	14,039
Nairobi, Kenya	Dec 13	50,000	985
		1,123,568	43,889

<u>1977</u>

Gothenburg, Sweden	Jan 12-16	58,632	867
Asheville, NC	Mar 23-27	51,200	1,342
South Bend, IN	May 11-15	95,600	3,421
Hungary	Sept 3-10	30,000	***
Cincinnati, OH	Oct 21-30	160,572	7,075
Manila, Philippines	Nov 23-27	412,000	22,512
Good News Festivals in India	Nov 29–Dec 11	<u>676,000</u>	<u>13,291</u>
		1,484,004	48,508

<u>1978</u>

Las Vegas, NV	Feb 1-5	63,000	3,144
Memphis, TN	May 7-14	298,600	4,512
Toronto, Ontario, Canada	June 11-18	209,000	9,305
Kansas City, MO	Aug 27–Sept 4	143,592	3,334
Oslo, Norway	Sept 24	20,000	89
Stockholm, Sweden	Sept 27–Oct 1	45,800	547
SATELLITE LOCATIONS:			
Sweden		70,353	472
Norway		80,170	764
Iceland		3,450	40
Poland	Oct 6-16	25,000	***
Singapore	Dec 6-10	<u>337,000</u>	<u>19,631</u>
		1,295,965	41,838

<u>1979</u>

Sao Paulo, Brazil	Feb 4	60,000	3,000
Tampa, FL	Mar 21-25	175,000	6,366
Sydney, Australia	Apr 29–May 20	491,500	21,331
Nashville, TN	June 24–July 1	222,550	4,259
Milwaukee, WI	Aug 8-12	151,500	10,418
Halifax, Nova Scotia, Canada	Oct 26-30	<u>50,400</u>	<u>2,705</u>
		1,150,950	48,079

	1980		
Oxford, England	Jan 30–Feb 3	13,350	312
Cambridge, England	Feb 9-16	17,450	1,565
Indianapolis, IN	May 2-11	141,300	5,863
Edmonton, Alberta, Canada	Aug 10-17	126,000	4,358
Wheaton, IL	Sept 14	10,000	322
Okinawa, Japan	Oct 3-5	34,612	4,434
Osaka, Japan	Oct 7-12	115,500	7,264
Fukuoka, Japan	Oct 17-19	36,000	1,983
Tokyo, Japan	Oct 21-26	131,800	11,190
Reno, NV	Nov 13-16	28,000	2,648
Las Vegas, NV	Nov 19-23	<u>41,800</u>	<u>2,823</u>
		695,812	42,762

	1981		
Mexico City, Mexico	Mar 1-5	95,500	6,874
Villahermosa, Mexico	Mar 12-15	107,000	10,899
Boca Raton, FL	Apr 12	8,500	275
Baltimore, MD	June 7-14	234,100	12,244
Calgary, Alberta, Canada	Aug 23-30	164,000	7,309
San Jose, CA	Sept 27–Oct 4	197,000	10,387
Houston, TX	Nov 8-15	<u>220,000</u>	<u>8,312</u>
		1,026,100	56,300

	1982		
Blackpool, England	Mar 2-3	18,800	1,035
Providence, RI	Apr 17	19,000	1,925
Burlington, VT	Apr 23	7,500	739
Portland, ME	Apr 25	9,250	893
Springfield, MA	Apr 30	10,500	1,314
Manchester, NH	May 1	10,600	1,063
Moscow, Russia	May 7-13	***	***
Hartford, CT	May 23	16,500	1,952
New Haven, CT	May 24	10,000	1,322

SUMMARY OF NEW ENGLAND UNIVERSITY
AND COLLEGE LECTURE TOUR 4/15– 5/26

Boston, MA			
(Northeastern University)	Apr 15	1,600	180
Amherst, MA			
(University of			
Massachusetts)	Apr 16	2,100	252
New Haven, CT			
(Yale University)	Apr 19	1,100	78
Cambridge, MA			
(Harvard University)			
JFK School of			
Government	Apr 20	800	
Memorial Chapel	Apr 21	1,100	118
Newton, MA			
(Boston College)	Apr 22	600	108
Cambridge, MA			
(Massachusetts Institute			
of Technology)	Apr 28	1,100	226
South Hamilton			
(Gordon-Conwell			
Seminary)	May 21	1,700	
Hanover, NH			
(Dartmouth College)	May 26	<u>4,000</u>	<u>596</u>
LECTURE TOUR TOTAL		14,100	1,558
Boston, MA	May 30–June 6	136,000	8,619
New Orleans, LA	June 13	42,000	***1,025
Boise, ID (Southern			
Baptist Convention			
Evangelistic Rally)	Aug 8-15	101,900	4,988
Spokane, WA	Aug 22-29	223,500	12,936
Chapel Hill, NC	Sept 27–Oct 1	30,700	3,252
German Democratic			
Republic (GDR)		***	***
Wittenberg	Oct 17		

Dresden (Saxony)	Oct 17		
Gorlitz	Oct 18		
Stendal	Oct 20		
Stralsund	Oct 21		
Berlin	Oct 23-24		
Czechoslovakia		***	***
Prague	Oct 30-31		
Brno	Nov 1		
German Democratic Republic (GDR)		***	***
Bratislava	Nov 2		
Nassau, Bahamas	Nov 24	<u>25,000</u>	<u>2,215</u>
		675,350	44,836

1983

Orlando, FL	Apr 10-17	203,700	6,025
Tacoma, WA	May 15-22	211,100	8,811
Sacramento, CA	Sept 11-18	203,600	9,343
Oklahoma City, OK	Oct 23-30	<u>130,800</u>	<u>3,086</u>
		749,200	27,265

1984

Anchorage, AK	Mar 11-18	68,750	3,666

SUMMARY OF MISSION ENGLAND

Bristol, England	May 12-19	243,500	20,444
Sunderland, England	May 26–June 2	124,097	11,785
Norwich, England	June 9-12	62,700	3,702
Birmingham, England	June 30–July 7	257,015	26,181
Liverpool, England	July 14-21	247,989	27,412
Ipswich, England	July 24-28	<u>90,363</u>	<u>7,458</u>
MISSION ENGLAND TOUR TOTAL		1,025,664	96,982

Seoul, Korea (South)	Aug 19	1,000,000	***
Union of Soviet Socialist Republics		***	***

Leningrad, Russia	Sept 10-12		
Tallinn, Estonia	Sept 12-14		
Moscow, Russia	Sept 14-16		
Novosibirsk, Siberia	Sept 17-19		
Moscow, Russia	Sept 19-21		
Vancouver,			
British Columbia	Oct 14-21	<u>229,200</u>	<u>10,784</u>
		2,323,614	111,432
	<u>1985</u>		
Fort Lauderdale, FL	Feb 17-24	166,500	8,735
Hartford, CT	May 19-26	98,650	8,747
Sheffield, England	June 22-29	257,900	26,131
Livelink Satellite			
Centers (51 Venues)		181,356	8,186
Anaheim, CA	July 19-28	536,600	33,627
Romania	Sept 8-15	150,000	***
Suceava	Sept 8		
Cluj-Napoca	Sept 9		
Oradea	Sept 10		
Arad	Sept 11		
Timisoara	Sept 12		
Sibiu	Sept 13		
Bucharest	Sept 14-15		
Hungary			
Pecs	Sept 21	22,000	***
Budapest	Sept 22	<u>14,000</u>	***
EASTERN EUROPEAN TOUR TOTAL		<u>186,000</u>	***
		1,427,006	85,426
	<u>1986</u>		
Washington, DC	Apr 27–May 4	150,550	8,993
France	Sept 20-27		
Paris		100,500	7,094

Satellite Centers			
(31 Cities)		<u>173,615</u>	<u>6,257</u>
MISSION FRANCE TOUR TOTAL		274,115	13,351
Tallahassee, FL	Nov 2-9	<u>119,300</u>	<u>3,659</u>
		543,965	26,003

<u>1987</u>			
Columbia, SC	Apr 25–May 2	287,100	11,915
Cheyenne, WY	June 14	9,450	804
Fargo, ND	June 19-21	65,850	4,070
Billings, MT	June 24	13,500	1,165
Sioux Falls, SD	June 27-28	49,000	1,856
Denver, CO	July 17-26	438,250	24,794
Helsinki, Finland	August 25-30	<u>183,000</u>	<u>9,460</u>
		1,046,150	54,064

<u>1988</u>			
People's Republic of China	Apr 12-28	***	***
Beijing	Apr 12-28		
Hualyin	Apr 19-20		
Nanjing	Apr 21-22		
Shanghai	Apr 23-26		
Guangzhou	Apr 27-28		
Union of Soviet Socialist Republics	June 8-17	***	***
Moscow, Russia	June 8		
Zagorsk, Russia	June 9		
Moscow, Russia	June 10-13		
Kiev, Ukraine	June 14-16	12,000	
Moscow, Russia	June 17		
Buffalo, NY	Aug 1-7	126,950	6,937
Rochester, NY	Sept 11-18	143,780	11,394
Hamilton, Ontario, Canada	Oct 26-30	<u>90,030</u>	<u>4,264</u>
		372,760	22,595

1989

Syracuse, NY	Apr 25-30	103,157	8,518
London, England	June 14–July 8		
	(13 days)	379,950	34,408
Livelink Centers,			
Great Britain	June 26–July 1	817,000	46,111
Budapest, Hungary	July 29	110,000	35,000
Little Rock, AK	Sept 17-24	282,800	6,677
		1,692,907	130,714

1990

Berlin, West Germany	Mar 10	15,000	1,800
Montreal, Quebec,			
Canada	June 3-10	*86,000	*3,033
Albany, NY	July 8-15	79,500 +	5,223 +
Uniondale, NY	Sept 19-23	98,700	8,703
Hong Kong	Nov 14-18	331,000	23,810
		610,200	42,569

1991

Seattle and Tacoma, WA	April 4-7	150,211	8,807
Scotland			
Edinburgh	May 25-26	62,000	4,070
Aberdeen	May 30–June 1	37,000	2,870
Glasgow	June 4-8	57,500	11,670
Livelink Centers		88,726	4,061
East Rutherford, NJ	Sept 3-7	106,100	8,951
New York City, NY			
(Central Park)	Sept 22	250,000	***
Buenos Aires,			
Argentina	Nov 14-17	259,500	15,500
		786,037	45,929

1992

Pyongyang, Korea			
(North)	Mar 31–Apr 4	***	***

Philadelphia, PA	June 24-28	200,700	13,512
Portland, OR	Sept 23-27	304,000	15,084
Moscow, Russia	Oct 23-25	<u>155,500</u>	<u>42,686</u>
		660,200	71,282

1993

Essen, Germany	Mar 17-21		
ProChrist - '93		1,000,000	80,000
Mission World-Europe		7,200,000	250,000
Pittsburgh, PA	June 2-6	171,500	14,897
Columbus, OH	Sept 22-26	<u>173,500</u>	<u>11,032</u>
		8,545,000	355,929

1994

People's Republic of China, Beijing	Jan	125,000	12,101
Pyongyang, Korea (North)	Jan 27–Feb 1	***	***
Cleveland, OH	June 8-12	257,000	24,605
Atlanta, GA	Oct 26-30	<u>332,500</u>	<u>19,059</u>
		714,500	55,765

1995

San Juan, Puerto Rico	Mar 14-18	175,500	4,652
Global Mission	Mar 16-18	***	***
Toronto, Ontario, Canada	June 7-11	261,500	15,759
Sacramento, CA	Oct 18-22	<u>177,600</u>	<u>11,483</u>
		614,600	31,894

1996

Minneapolis, MN	June 19-23	348,000	33,194
Charlotte, NC	Sept 26-29	<u>336,100</u>	<u>22,249</u>
		684,100	55,443

	1997		
San Antonio, TX	Apr 3-6	247,250	22,576
San Jose, CA	Sept 26-28	71,500	4,926
San Francisco, CA	Oct 9-11	51,200	2,903
Oakland, CA	Oct 25-26	123,600	10,213
		493,550	40,618
	1998		
Ottawa, Ontario, Canada	June 25-26	106,000	8,634
Tampa Bay, FL	Oct 22-25	283,000	22,250
		389,000	30,884
	1999		
Indianapolis, IN	June 3-6	193,500	15,328
St. Louis, MO	Oct 14-17	200,000	12,820
		393,500	28,148
	2000		
Nashville, TN	June 1-4	227,000	9,429
Jacksonville, FL	Nov 2-5	242,000	10,539
		469,000	19,968
	2001		
Louisville, KY	June 21-24	191,500	10,321
		660,500	30,289
GRAND TOTALS		**82,194,995**	**3,130,802**

+ Includes Associate Meetings

* Other evangelists preached because Mr. Graham was unable to attend.

** Information based on available source data. Statistics not available from some earlier meetings.

*** Official count unknown. Unable to count or estimate.

**** Actual number of cards received. Because of the magnitude of the crowds, many decisions were made without the benefit of personal counseling and decision cards.

Source: Billy Graham Evangelistic Association

APPENDIX E:
CORPORATE STATEMENTS OF THE BGEA

FINANCIAL INTEGRITY

How can we be sure that our organization will remain true and authentic in the matter of financial integrity? That question is asked constantly at the Billy Graham Evangelistic Association.

Given our biblical understanding of the fallen nature of humankind, there is no way to be absolutely certain of achieving this worthy goal. But there are some very specific things we've done at BGEA (which can be done by almost any organization big or small) in order to maximize our oversight of finances with the greatest care.

At a prayer day retreat in Modesto, California, early in the Team's history, Mr. Graham, Mr. Barrows, and Mr. Shea prayed and discussed the great problems that evangelists had been plagued by: immorality, greed, lies by overstatements, and a proud, critical spirit. So, they formed what is now referred to as "The Modesto Manifesto." It has four parts:

1. We will never criticize, condemn, or speak negatively about other pastors, churches, or other Christian workers.

2. We will be accountable, particularly in handling finances, with integrity according to the highest business standards.

3. We will tell the truth and be thoroughly honest, especially in reporting statistics.

4. We will be exemplary in morals—clear, clean, and careful to avoid the very appearance of any impropriety.

While all of these points are a part of our corporate culture, financial accountability is one of the major issues. Here are some of the things we've done to develop a high level of confidence and integrity:

Board of Directors: All of BGEA is accountable to a strong Board which has full authority to control the financial operations, including the ability to say "no" when necessary and enforce that decision. The thirty-one members are made up of executives and businessmen, balanced by ministers; a limited number of Team employees; and including members with diversity in race, gender, geographical region and theological viewpoints.

Executive Committee: Comprised of all outside Board Members (with no employees—including Mr. Graham, who is not on the Executive), the finances are under the control of the Executive Committee with recommendations and oversight of a strong Finance Committee.

Audit Review Committee of the Board: An active Committee that recommends the engagement of outside auditors each year, meets with them independent of management and reviews every conceivable issue which could allow some difficulty. Minutes are maintained and circulated to appropriate Board members so that all are apprised of their activity.

Annual Report: Publication of the full, audited statement for the Association is made available to all who request it. Though not required by law, it is another step toward accountability in full disclosure of all the Association's finances.

Outside Auditors: A "big eight" firm of professionals is engaged each year to audit the Association and its affiliates. Their statement is another verification that appropriate accounting and business practices are being practiced and that BGEA is fully accountable.

Internal Auditor: A full-time employee, answerable directly and independently to the Audit Review Committee, assures the Board and Management of the highest levels of accountability. Efficiency and effectiveness are constantly scrutinized and improved in the still-expanding experience of the ministry.

Checks-and-Balances: Procedures within the day-to-day operations of BGEA reveal the same sensitivity to avoiding the appearances of wrong by providing for the normal business checks and balances. This allows for constant, daily accountability to one another within the work teams and provides for protective safeguards in the full range of prudent activities. Examples of this principle are independent verifications by persons not in the regular functional process, dual signers required, etc.

Other Ideas: Management constantly monitors our systems and watches for exposures. Regular compliance testing is a way of life using such concepts as surveillance cameras, security systems, field tests, employee training, and professional monitoring services.

Commitment Authority Policy: Making spending commitments in line with the preapproved budget is done by policy at four levels and by those designated on an annually-approved listing of management personnel. Specific authorization is by policy with an established procedure that incorporates the best control and flow techniques.

Conflict of Interest Policy: BGEA asks its Board and employees to sign a disclosure statement each year. Carefully reviewed by management and the Audit Review Committee, the policy requires disclosures and avoidance of perceptions of conflict in all transactions.

Policies: Financial policy is taken seriously, and while too extensive to report fully in this document, here are some of the most important matters for which we have established policy guidelines.

We do not borrow money but are committed to operate with the funding which the Lord's people provide in support of our objectives. Also, we do not loan money.

We do not use professional fund-raisers nor their techniques. We do not pay commission for funds received, use a "gift of" for a premium, ask for upgraded percentage increases, telephone calling pressure tactics, nor any of the product-commissions-type schemes such as percentage of royalties, percent of phone calls, etc. We avoid these to be totally non-commercial and to be completely dependent on God's supply from His people.

We have a graded scale of compensation and job evaluations . . . along with a Corporate Compensation Committee of the Board. All officers elected by the Board and officers' salaries are set by the Executive Committee. There are no bonuses and no salary incentive programs for any employees or officers.

All employees are salaried and receive reimbursement for appropriate business expenses of their assignments. All business travel is pre-approved by the employee's supervisor before the expenses are paid. Full documentation is required from all employees and carefully monitored.

All "love gifts" and honoraria of the evangelists, Associates and officers are assigned to the Association, and no individual personally profits by those gifts. All contributions are receipted and accounted for on a daily basis.

BGEA does not employ fundraisers and thus does not pay outside consultants, firms, nor persons to represent the ministry to donors. Field staff assist donors when requested, but do not accept on-the-spot gifts of cash.

Investments: Our Board has an annual appointment of a committee that drafts our Investment Policy; then the Investment Committee monitors the performance and compliance of outside professional management firms who handle investments for the Association.

We do not co-mingle investment funds but maintain simpler records of each investment source for increased accountability.

Budgets: Funding allocations are approved by the Board in the annual Operating Budget and an annual Capital Budget. Monthly reports to the Board track the compliance to the approved budget and variances are dealt with by the Board.

IRS Audit: We have more than once had agents of the Internal Revenue Service call on us at BGEA and carefully audit our records. Everything has been found to be fully disclosed, appropriately reported and accounted for to their satisfaction.

Organizations: BGEA is a member in good standing with the Evangelical Council for Financial Accountability (ECFA) and with the Christian Charitable Council in Canada (CCCC). We are locally members of the Chamber of Commerce and other regional and professional groups. Additionally, our executive management team are encouraged to belong to professional associations in their specialized field.

VALUES OF BILLY GRAHAM EVANGELISTIC ASSOCIATION

Inclusive Fellowship

1. Capacity to convene God's people.
2. True to biblical fundamentals yet openly including those sincerely holding different theological positions.

3. Stay inclusive on race, gender, politics, ideology, theology and sociological issues,

4. Loyalty to old friends in time, commitments.

Moral Purity

5. Avoid even the appearance of evil in moral/sexual matters.
6. Pursue righteousness; be intolerant of evil.
7. Be careful/conservative in reporting statistics.
8. Money is handled by local committee, not by Team.

Sincere Spirituality

9. Prayer is the priority.
10. Centrality of Christ.
11. Authority and use of Scripture.
12. A sense of urgency—imminency of return of Christ.
13. Single-minded concentration to evangelism in all ways.
14. Global perspective from the outset.
15. Contemporary issues awareness.
16. "Team" effort instead of individual stars.

Preformance Quality of Excellence

17. Business-like operations.
18. Commit to personnel and trust them to operate.
19. Quality first-class whenever prudent.
20. Media have a unique power we can benefit from.
21. Willingness to risk at all levels.
22. Use of non-team top-quality talent personnel.
23. Diversification into radio, film, TV, magazine, etc.
24. Use of modern transportation—flights, Europe.
25. Association with greatness—places, people, possessions.

To Honor the Local Church

26. Non-competitive with the local church.
27. Origins: By invitation only of the total local church.

28. Full recognition of God's place for church—temporary permanency.
29. Non-critical of other servants or institutions.
30. Total concept of evangelism through discipleship and follow-up.

Financial Intregrity
31. High integrity in fundraising.
32. Full disclosure on finances.
33. Pay as you go—no debt.
34. Be generous in giving to others.

VALUES OF BILLY GRAHAM EVANGELISTIC ASSOCIATION

INCLUSIVE FELLOWSHIP

1. Capacity to convene God's people.

There is a magnetism that God has given to draw the Lord's people together under the ministry of Mr. Graham and the BGEA. It is partly the heritage of trust built up over years of consistency. BGEA has been able to get the people of God to rally together and put their distinctives aside in order to accomplish a greater good together. To convene for evangelistic purposes is a divine gift to BGEA.

2. True to biblical fundamentals yet openly including those sincerely holding different theological positions.

Broad acceptance of God's people and a willingness to work practically with people who were willing to work with us . . . that is part of the Graham movement. Not insisting on a theological consensus but rather maintaining the personal privilege to speak the truth as Mr. Graham understood it without apology. . . but also without rancor. Maintaining his own belief in the fundamental truths of the Scripture and declaring the gospel authoritatively was the evangelist's job. Not squeezing all others in the same mold and allowing the Holy Spirit to work in His time—this permitted the inclusion of many and the hostility of few.

3. *Stay inclusive on race, gender, politics, ideology, theology and sociological issues.*

Beyond being "politically correct," there is concern to balance the matters in such a way that all feel a part and none are excluded. As much as possible, BGEA strives to be non-offensive in the questions of the day and issues of the times.

4. *Loyalty to old friends in time, commitments.*

Mr. Graham has a special love and loyalty to friends of long standing. They are not forgotten, nor easily forsaken in the heat of the battle. Time is committed to old friends even when busy. Appointments are undertaken and events committed to the schedule often (not on the merits of the activity) because of the old friend who requested. Loyalty to those who helped in the past is a part of the Graham Team. Friends are remembered and cherished, honored and respected.

MORAL PURITY

5. *Avoid even the appearance of evil in moral/sexual matters.*

Constant watchfulness and careful attention to appearances are daily alerts for all BGEA. Care is taken to eliminate situations where persons could be suspected of any impropriety between the sexes. Avoiding the situations by which rumors and suspicions could be spawned has been a regular watchword for BGEA.

6. *Pursue righteousness; be intolerant of evil.*

It is our corporate intent to follow not only the letter of the law but also the spirit of that law. We want to be as close as we can to righteousness and proactively seek ways to be conformed to His ways. While avoiding the showy patterns in order to be seen by men, we know we are accountable to God and to one another. When evil exists, we purpose to repent, to correct, and to purge out the leaven of wickedness, to cleanse ourselves of all unrighteousness of the soul and spirit, perfecting holiness in the sight of God. Rigid watchfulness in little things keeps us from being scandalized in major matters.

7. Be careful/conservative in reporting statistics.

We choose to err on the down side whenever numbers are reported. Recognizing that bigness is not the same as godliness, BGEA would report numbers on the conservative side, especially as regards crowd sizes and estimated results.

8. Money is handled by local committee, not by Team.

Financial policies that create integrity by process, disclosure, reporting, and accountability. Early on it was the goal to leave no sad questions about finances. Among the helpful steps: commitment to have the finances handled by the local committee, put the Team on salary instead of the traditional "love gifts," and the adoption of many good common-sense business practices. With money not a driving force of motivation, the Team was free to serve the Lord without the pressure of finding ways to pay the bills on a day-to-day basis.

SINCERE SPIRITUALITY

9. Prayer is the priority.

Prayer has received more than lip-service attention. It has been given prominence in what is said about ministry activities, but more than that it has pervaded offices, committees, boards, conferences, consultations, etc., as well as constantly utilized individually, in groups, and in every conceivable method

10. Centrality of Christ.

The banner of most Crusades was "Jesus said, 'I am the Way, the Truth, and the Life.'" Christianity is Christ, His uniqueness as Savior and His sufficiency as Lord of All, Head of His Church. Truth issues are all related to Him and our lives and ministry anchored by our being "in Christ."

11. Authority and use of Scripture.

"The Bible Says" became a characteristic phrase of Mr. Graham's preaching. Full authority of Scripture as our rule of faith, beliefs, and for our practical directions has provided solid rock foundation to BGEA ministry. Not only has Mr. Graham preached the Word, but we have published copies of the Bible and Bible portions, Bible studies, guides, commentaries, and study helps to saturate our own hearts and minds with the treasures of God's Word.

12. A sense of urgency—imminency of return of Christ.

In the beginning, the imminent return of Christ had high profile. Mr. Graham's preaching over the years on the coming of Christ holds the concern for the immediate possibility that He will come today. Urgency to bring others to the Savior is motivated by the sense that we are at the end of times—the night cometh when no man can work. Mr. Graham once commented about a struggling evangelist, "he may not have a sense of urgency" (thought to be a qualifying necessity for an evangelist).

13. Single-minded concentration to evangelism in all ways.

Focus on the primary task and specific calling of the evangelist has been maintained. Determined and dogged pursuit of one calling of God has not wavered: to evangelize. Temptations have come along the way to make major commitments for education, churchmanship, entertainment, business enterprise, youth specialization, etc. Part of the BGEA culture is to stay in a focused, single-minded, this-one-thing-I-do mode for evangelistic outreach. Everything else is secondary to this consuming passion and concentration.

14. Global perspective from the outset.

National vision was clearly not enough. Mr. Graham had a world on his heart from the start. The Switzerland conference and the world conferences evidence this heartbeat. Perhaps the early trips to England in the '40s and the World War's end had its impact upon the Team, but global concerns have been a part of the Graham ministry.

15. Contemporary issues awareness.

Early *Hour of Decision* broadcast messages began with a reflection of current news items that led to Mr. Graham's sermon week after week. Matters of public concern have often formed the basis for capturing attention and leading on to the deeper issues of spiritual life. Avoiding controversy for controversy's sake, steering clear of political issues, etc., the Team have always tried to keep abreast of issues of the day and use them to bring attention to the gospel facts.

16. "Team" effort instead of individual stars.

Billy Graham is the acknowledged personality of the ministry—there is no other rivaling his stature. But it is his desire and deference that, supporting all BGEA activities, the whole "team" effort of cooperation should be acknowledged and acclaimed. Much positive testimony has been born to a watching world by the positive, affirming, and loving relationship of being "team" players together in the Lord's harvest.

PERFORMANCE QUALITY OF EXCELLENCE

17. Business-like operations.

Recognizing the spiritual gifts to God's servants, the business of the BGEA has been guided by common sense and normal, wise practices of the commercial world. Refusing to allow slip-shod or spiritualized excuses for sloppiness has resulted in crisp, clear, clean operations that achieve with professionalism and excellence. Business, as well as programs, are part of the ministry of pleasing our Lord.

18. Commit to personnel and trust them to operate.

Beginning with Mr. Graham himself and throughout the company, workers are given responsibility and then, without undue interference, allowed to operate in a highly-trusted, though accountable, fashion. It is a satisfying relationship for the employee and an effective pattern for achievement.

19. Quality first-class whenever prudent.

The resources are guided toward use of excellence in all forms. This applies to use of talented personnel and to the use of physical equipment and practical means for our work and ministry. Our choice is for quality over quantity whenever a decision between the two must be made.

20. Media have a unique power we can benefit from.

Media have been both favorable and adversarial to BGEA over the years—with far more positive coverage given. Care is taken to accommodate the news media. Recognizing the powerful impact of the general population hearing about the ministry through news outlets, BGEA seeks to harness and aid the news media personnel in getting their story. And, we have been careful to see that activities would be non-offending if reported so that there is no fear of the truth being told.

21. Willingness to risk at all levels.

Flamboyant Youth for Christ "stunts" were considered and utilized. Media was a risk for a young team. In later years, the new use of youth-oriented music is risky—not only on the platform, but in the sites, preparations, programs of involvement, and personalities. Capacity to put achievement ahead of reputation and status quo have led the Team to significant strides of progress and success.

22. Use of non-team top-quality talent personnel.

Teams have been close-knit family in spirit. Outside guests are used only when their talented competence is matched with spiritual integrity. High-quality ability and achievement must be paralleled by a corresponding quality of character development. If a testimony is blurred or non-established, BGEA has elected to present only those whose witness is verified and firm.

23. Diversification into radio, film, TV, magazine, etc.

From the beginning, technology and varied methods have been used to communicate the message and to expand the scope of proclaiming the Word. National radio programs were few when the *Hour of Decision* began. Christian western musicals in films were unheard of when Mr. Texas came from the Graham ministry. Television, computers, satellite, etc., are all utilized in a Global Mission strategy. The capacity to innovate and utilize new technology is a hallmark of the BGEA.

24. Use of modern transportation—flights, Europe.

Travel by air was rather rare as Mr. Graham began. Trains, autos, and buses were much more common for travel. The capacity to fly across the country, and across the ocean to Europe, greatly enhanced his itinerating evangelism. Now as resources allow the Team to fly to appointments freely, a standard of travel prevails that is foreign to most evangelists in our time.

25. Association with greatness—places, people, possessions.

A relationship with popular and well-known persons began with the celebrities finding the Lord in LA '49. It continued with well-known places such as the early rally on the steps of the United States Capitol. Political personalities all the way to Presidents. Hollywood types such as Cecil B. DeMille, etc. Sports stars, media magnets, educators, philanthropists, business leaders. Most did very little directly for the Graham work, but their association with the Team gave an aura of success and credibility in the early days.

TO HONOR THE LOCAL CHURCH

26. Non-competitive with the local church.

We always begin from the perspective of the local congregation as a source of the force for evangelism and end with the benefit being incorporated into the local body of believers. BGEA does nothing that denigrates or minimizes the local church, but rather honors her place as God's institution without being <u>dominated</u> by any single congregation,

27. Origins: By invitation only of the total local church.

Much has been gained by the insistence of beginning with the local invitation. BGEA does not superimpose its program upon the community nor its churches. Rather, Billy Graham comes only upon their invitation. At times, BGEA has had to work to develop that local consensus, but without it, we are not able to proceed with effectiveness.

28. Full recognition of God's place for church—temporary permanency.

BGEA remains non-competitive with the permanent organizations of a community. Organizational structures and program entities are temporary. This allows temporary subjugation of distinctives within the Body while the cooperative effort of BGEA is achieved. Knowing that the BGEA event is temporary encourages local bodies to participate for the short-term. They know from years of track record, that BGEA will not continue to be there to draw away resources and attention for the continual longer term. Temporary permanence is really limited permanence for the extent of the <u>ministry</u> event of BGEA—after that, the local structures and BGEA-supporting bodies will incorporate the harvest into the mainstream of church/community life.

29. Non-critical of other servants or institutions.

Our policy is that we do not comment on other organizations nor other

Christian workers. Especially, we avoid criticism of them, their methods, and their ministries. We seek to never speak negatively of others.

Mr. Graham's personal temperament is non-confrontive, and so for BGEA. We are not lighters—even to "defend" ourselves—not because we are gutless, but because we desire to "live peaceably with all men" for "as much as you can."

30. Total concept of evangelism through discipleship and follow-up.

Decisions alone are not the objective . . . rather, fulfillment of the Great Commission in its broader and fuller implications. Disciples are the goal—believers incorporated into the life of the Church and making a wholesome contribution to the development of His Body. We have believed that evangelism is not complete until the evangelized become evangelistic. Care is taken to see that appropriate follow-up and "linking" activity takes place so that evangelism is integrated into mainstream church life. It is thought to be irresponsible to "win'em and leave'em."

FINANCIAL INTEGRITY

31. High integrity in fund-raising.

No gimmicks to fund-raising. No professional fund-raisers are used. No cheap-shot offers. No pressure tactics such as the telemarketing phone callers. No "for-a-gift-of" offers. Premiums have been kept to ministry items that are valid messages by themselves. No one has a job description that includes the task of raising funds.

32. Full disclosure on finances.

Openness to discuss and reveal financial matters has added to the respect for Mr. Graham. Willingness to disclose his own personal situation of salary, organizational accountability and public reporting, even beyond what is legally required, has resulted in the aura of financial integrity.

33. Pay as you go—no debt.

Believing that God's work done in God's way does not want for God's supply, debt is unnecessary. By avoiding the pressures of financial bonds, the ministry has the freedom to be immediate, free and spontaneous.

34. Be generous in giving to others.

BGEA has shown generosity from the outset in providing (sharing) funding for other organizations' benefit. Whatever we have—personnel, funds, expertise, information—has been shared most freely. It has been "give and it shall be given unto you." Like Mr. Graham, the organization has never been stingy, though often restrained by necessity.

NOTES

Foreword

1. Billy Graham, *Just As I Am* (San Francisco: HarperCollins, 1997), 160.
2. See John Stott, ed., *Making Christ Known: Historic Mission Documents from the Lausanne Movement, 1974–1989* (Grand Rapids: Eerdmans, 1996), xiv.
3. Ibid., 240.

Chapter 1: The Epic Begins

1. John Pollock, *Billy Graham: The Authorized Biography* (Grand Rapids: Zondervan, 1966), 55.
2. Ibid., 12.
3. Ibid., 53.
4. Ibid., 55.
5. Ibid., 56–59.
6. Ibid., 60.
7. Ibid.
8. Ibid.
9. Ibid., 61.
10. Ibid., 64.
11. Timothy Dudley-Smith, *John Stott: The Making of a Leader* (Downers Grove, Ill.: InterVarsity, 1999), 15.
12. D. A. Carson, *The Gagging of God* (Grand Rapids: Zondervan, 1996), 445.

Chapter 2: The Holy Spirit in Evangelism

1. John Polhill, *The New American Commentary* (Nashville: Broadman, 1992), vol. 26, 64.
2. Frank Stagg, *Commentary on Acts* (Nashville: Broadman & Holman, 1955).
3. William Barclay, *The Acts of the Apostles* (Philadelphia: Westminster Press, 1953), 82.
4. Polhill, *The New American Commentary*, 72.
5. Ibid., 71.
6. Ibid., 256.
7. Ibid., 264.
8. James D. G. Dunn, *Jesus and the Spirit* (Philadelphia: Westminster Press, 1975), 63.
9. Leon Morris, *New Testament Theology* (Grand Rapids: Zondervan, 1986), 193.

10. R. A. Torrey, *The Holy Spirit: Who He Is and What He Does and How to Know Him in all the Fullness of His Gracious and Glorious Ministry* (New York: Revell, 1927), 12.

11. Raymond E. Brown, *The Gospel According to John* (XIIOXXI), The Anchor Bible, 44 vols. (Garden City, N.J.: Doubleday, 1970), 29A:711.

12. Rudolf Schnackenburg, *The Gospel According to St. John* (New York: Crossroads, 1982), 3:149.

13. Ibid., 149.

14. Leon Morris, *Commentary on the Gospel of John,* The New International Commentary, F. F. Bruce, ed. (Grand Rapids: Eerdmans, 1971), 697.

15. C. H. Spurgeon, *Twelve Sermons on the Holy Spirit* (Grand Rapids: Baker, 1973), 23.

16. C. H. Dodd, *The Interpretation of the Fourth Gospel* (Cambridge: University Press, 1953), 414.

17. Ethelbert Stauffer, *New Testament Theology* (London: SCM Press Ltd., 1955), 167, emphasis added.

18. Brown, *The Gospel According to John,* 712.

19. Morris, *Commentary on the Gospel of John,* 698.

20. Ibid., 699.

21. Edwyn Clement Hoskyns, *The Fourth Gospel,* rev. ed. Francis Noel Davey, ed. (London: Faber and Faber, 1947), 484.

22. Leon Morris, *Commentary on the Gospel of John,* 699.

23. George R. Beasley-Murray, *Word Biblical Commentary—John,* vol. 36 (Nashville: Word, 1987), 282.

24. Ibid.

25. Brown, *The Gospel According to John,* 714.

26. W. T. Conner, *The Work of the Holy Spirit* (Nashville: Broadman, 1949), 57–58.

27. Torrey, *The Holy Spirit.*

28. Spurgeon, *Twelve Sermons on the Holy Spirit.*

29. W. H. Griffith Thomas, *The Holy Spirit of God,* 3rd ed. (Grand Rapids: Eerdmans, 1955), 196–97.

30. Pollock, *Billy Graham: The Authorized Biography,* 38.

31. Ibid., 38–39.

32. William Martin, *A Prophet with Honor: The Billy Graham Story* (New York: W. Morrow, 1991), 98.

33. Pollock, *Billy Graham: The Authorized Biography,* 39.

34. Ibid., 39.

35. Martin, *A Prophet with Honor,* 98.

36. Ibid.

37. Ibid.

38. Ibid., 98–99.

39. Ibid., 99.

40. Ibid.

41. Ibid.

42. Billy Graham, *The Holy Spirit* (Nashville: Word, 1978), 11.

43. Ibid.

44. Ibid., 12.

45. Ibid., 20.

46. Ibid., 23.

47. Ibid.

48. Ibid., 28.

49. Ibid., 29.

50. Beasley-Murray, *World Biblical Commentary—John,* 56.

51. Graham, *The Holy Spirit,* 42.

52. Ibid., 45.

53. Ibid., 46.

54. Ibid.

55. Ibid., 47.

56. Ibid.

57. David Frost, *Billy Graham: Personal Thoughts of a Public Man* (Colorado Springs: Chariot Vector, 1997), 64.

58. Billy Graham, *How to Be Born Again* (Nashville: Word, 1977), 163.

59. Ibid.

60. T. S. Settel, ed. *The Faith of Billy Graham* (New York: Wing Books, 1968), 72.

61. Billy Graham, *Unto the Hills* (Nashville: Word, 1996), 401.

62. Beasley-Murray, *Word Biblical Commentary—John,* 271.

63. Billy Graham, *Approaching Hoofbeats: The Four Horsemen of the Apocalypse* (Minneapolis: Grayon, n.d.), 233.

64. Billy Graham, *A Biblical Standard for Evangelists* (Minneapolis: World Wide Publications, 1984), 65.

65. Graham, *The Holy Spirit,* 59.

66. Ibid., 62.

67. Ibid.

68. Ibid., 65.

69. Ibid., 71.

70. Ibid., 97.

71. Graham, *Unto the Hills,* 254.

72. Graham, *The Holy Spirit,* 110.

73. Billy Graham, *Hope for the Troubled Heart* (New York: Bantam, 1973), 173.

74. Graham, *The Holy Spirit,* 99.

75. Ibid., 103.

76. Billy Graham, interview by author, Montreat, N.C., October 2000.

77. Graham, *The Holy Spirit,* 106.

78. Billy Graham, interview.

79. Graham, *The Holy Spirit*, 108.

80. Ibid.

81. Ibid., 119.

82. Ibid., 125.

83. Frost, *Personal Thoughts of a Public Man*, 72.

84. Janet Lowe, *Billy Graham Speaks* (New York: John Wiley, 1999), 68.

85. Billy Graham, *Peace with God* (New York: Pocket Books, 1953), 200.

86. Graham, *The Holy Spirit*, 144.

87. Billy Graham, *Storm Warning* (Nashville: Word, 1992), 21–22.

88. Graham, *The Holy Spirit*, 148.

89. Billy Graham, *Breakfast with Billy Graham* (Ann Arbor, Mich.: Servant Publications, 1996), 85.

90. Billy Graham and Charles G. Ward, ed., *The Christian Workers Handbook* (Minneapolis: World Wide Publications, n.d.), 158.

91. Ibid.

92. Ibid., 293.

93. Billy Graham, *Angels: God's Secret Agents* (Garden City, N.J.: Doubleday, 1975), 18.

94. Ibid., 15.

95. Ibid., x.

96. Ibid.

97. Ibid.

98. Sterling Huston, *Crusade Evangelism and the Local Church* (Minneapolis: World Wide Publications, 1984), 49.

99. David Bruce, interview by author, Montreat, NC., October, 2000.

Chapter 3: The Call and the Gospel in Evangelism

1. Os Guinness, *The Call* (Nashville: Word, 1998), 76.

2. Polhill, *The New American Commentary*, 325.

3. Gerhard Friedrich, *Theological Dictionary of the New Testament*, vol. 3 (Grand Rapids: Eerdmans, 1964), 714.

4. This is not meant necessarily to rule out the "signs and wonders" that took place throughout Acts and take place today, even if some have overemphasized the fact.

5. Friedrich, *Theological Dictionary of the New Testament*, 716.

6. Douglas Webster, *Yes to Mission* (London: SCM Press, 1966), 20, italics in original.

7. The concern here is not with the strengths and weaknesses of Dodd's "realized eschatology." The help Dodd gives is in the study of the *kerygma*. His systematizing of the various elements of the proclamation and the subsequent impact of his findings is most significant.

8. The author follows here his own work: *Leading Your Church in Evangelism* (Nashville: Broadman, 1975), 95–106.

9. C. H. Dodd, *Apostolic Preaching and Its Development* (London: Hodder and Stoughton, 1936), 8.

10. Ibid., 24.
11. James S. Stewart, *A Faith to Proclaim* (New York: Charles Scribner's Sons, 1953), 14–15.
12. Ibid., 18.
13. Ibid., 50.
14. Ibid., 82.
15. Ibid., 104.
16. Hans Conzelmann, *An Outline of the Theology of the New Testament* (London: SCM Press, 1969), 88. Interestingly, Conzelmann does not see the sermons in Acts as primitive preaching.
17. Ibid.
18. T. F. Glasson, "The Kerygma: Is Our Version Correct? The Gospel and Its Meaning," *The Hibbert Journal* 51 (October 1952–July 1953): 129, 132.
19. Bertil Gardner, *The Areopagus Speech and Natural Revelation* (Ubsalat: C.W. K. Gleerup, 1955), 33.
20. David Lockard, *The Unheard Billy Graham* (Nashville: Word, 1971) 16.
21. Graham, *Just As I Am*, 62–63.
22. Lockard, *The Unheard Billy Graham*, 18.
23. Ibid.
24. Beasley-Murray, *Word Biblical Commentary—John*, 75.
25. Graham, *Just As I Am*, 490.
26. Billy Graham, *Billy Graham Answers Your Questions* (Minneapolis: World Wide Publications, n.d.), 156.
27. Graham, *How to Be Born Again*, 34.
28. Ibid., 37.
29. Ibid., 47.
30. Ibid., 39.
31. Tom Phillips, interview by author, Warsaw, Poland, September 1999, quoting Billy Graham.
32. Graham, *A Biblical Standard for Evangelists*, 8.
33. Phillips, interview.
34. Frost, *Personal Thoughts of a Public Man*, 163.
35. Bruce, interview.
36. Graham, *Peace with God*, 96.
37. Graham and Ward, ed., *The Christian Workers Handbook*, 61.
38. Graham, *Approaching Hoofbeats*, 70.
39. Ibid., 139.
40. Lowe, *Billy Graham Speaks*, 136.
41. Beasley-Murray, *Word Biblical Commentary—John*, 33.
42. Graham, *Approaching Hoofbeats*, 30.
43. Graham, *Billy Graham Answers Your Questions*, 230.
44. Graham, *Answers to Life's Problems* (Nashville: Word, 1988), 284.

45. Billy Graham, interview.

46. Stephen Olford, interview by author, Amsterdam, July 2000.

47. T. W. Wilson, interview by author, Montreat, NC., June 2000.

48. Graham, *How to Be Born Again*, 115.

49. Ibid., 111.

50. Ibid., 110.

51. Ibid., 111.

52. Graham, *Peace with God*, 51–52.

53. Graham, *How to Be Born Again*, 131–32.

54. Ibid., 133.

55. Ibid., 136.

56. Ibid.

57. Graham and Ward, ed., *The Christian Workers Handbook*, 183.

58. Graham, *Peace with God*, 51–52.

59. Graham and Ward, ed., *The Christian Workers Handbook*, 239–40.

60. Ibid.

61. Ibid.

62. Ibid.

63. Ibid.

64. Ibid.

65. Ibid.

66. Ibid.

67. Ibid.

68. Graham, *Peace with God*, 119.

69. Ibid., 121.

70. Ibid.

71. Ibid., 131–34.

72. Ibid., 136–39.

73. Graham, *How to Be Born Again*, 114.

74. Ibid., 171–72.

75. Graham and Ward, ed., *The Christian Workers Handbook*, 155–56.

76. Billy Graham, *The Secret of Happiness* (Garden City, N.J.: Doubleday, 1955), 201–2.

77. Billy Graham, *Facing Death and the Life After* (Nashville: Word, 1980), 159.

78. Ibid., 160.

79. Ibid., 164.

80. Ibid.

81. Ibid.

82. Ibid., 169.

83. Ibid., 175.

84. Ibid., 178.

85. Ibid., 180–81.

86. Billy Graham, *The Challenge* (Garden City, N.J.: Doubleday, 1969), 157.

87. Ibid., 153.

88. Graham, *Peace with God*, 71.

89. Graham, *How to Be Born Again*, 90.

90. Graham, *Answers to Life's Problems*, 151.

91. Graham, *Peace with God*, 44–47.

92. Ibid., 51–53.

93. Ibid., 53.

94. Billy Graham, *Billy Graham Talks to Teenagers* (Grand Rapids: Zondervan, 1958), 64.

95. Graham, *How to Be Born Again*, 150–51.

96. Ibid., 156.

97. Ibid.

98. Graham, *Billy Graham Answers Your Questions*, 228.

99. Graham, *Facing Death and the Life After*, 128.

100. Wilson, interview.

101. Lowe, *Billy Graham Speaks*, 70.

102. Video script produced by the Billy Graham Evangelistic Association. Used by permission.

103. William Thomas, "An Assessment of Mass Meetings as a Method of Evangelism: Case Study of Eurofest '75 and the Billy Graham Crusade in Brussels" (Ph.D. diss., Free University of Amsterdam, Holland, 1977), 65.

104. Russ Busby, *Billy Graham: God's Ambassador* (Alexandria, Va.: Time-Life Books, 1999), 23.

Chapter 4: The Sovereignty of God in Evangelism

1. Gerald Bray, *Creeds, Councils and Christ* (Leicester, England: InterVarsity, 1984), 43.

2. Phillip Levine, *Augustine*, James J. O'Donnell, ed. (Boston: Twayne, 1985), 101.

3. Ibid., 39.

4. Timothy George, *The Theology of the Reformers* (Nashville: Broadman, 1988), 73–74.

5. D. A. Carson, *Divine Sovereign and Human Responsibility* (Atlanta: John Knox, 1981), 205.

6. *Confessions of Saint Augustine*, Book 1, 1.

7. James M. Wall, ed., *Theologians in Transition* (New York: Crossroad, 1981), 77.

8. Norman Pittenger, *Catholic Faith in a Process Perspective* (Maryknoll, N.Y.: Orbis, 1981), 21–22. This brief quotation from Pittenger is not to imply that Pittenger's entire approach is found in such few words.

9. Ibid., 15. It seems clear that Pittenger uses the term "fundamentalist" far too broadly and glibly.

10. Paul Tillich, *The Protestant Era* (Chicago: University of Chicago Press, 1983), 202.

11. Remember, Einstein has shown us that time and space are interrelated, relative aspects of reality. Human beings are in a "space-time capsule," in Einstein's words. Thus if God created space, He created time.

12. Karl Barth, *Credo* (London: Hodder and Stoughton, 1936), 22.

13. Norman Geisler, *Chosen but Free* (Minneapolis: Bethany House, 1999), 15.

14. Graham, *Approaching Hoofbeats*, 37.

15. John Pollock, *The Crusades: 20 Years with Billy Graham* (Minneapolis: World Wide Publications, 1969), 276.

16. Ibid., 277.

17. Maurice Rowlandson, *Life with Billy* (London: Hodder and Stoughton, 1992), 168.

18. Martin, *A Prophet with Honor*, 25.

19. Ibid., 94.

20. Graham, *Unto the Hills*, 90.

21. Martin, *A Prophet with Honor*, 461.

22. Billy Kim, interview by author, Melbourne, Australia, July 2001.

23. Martin, *A Prophet with Honor*, 592.

24. Pollock, *Billy Graham: The Authorized Biography*, 252.

25. Ibid., 253.

26. Pollock, *The Crusades: 20 Years with Billy Graham*, 190.

27. Graham, *Unto the Hills*, 180.

28. Graham, *Peace with God*, 140.

29. Billy Graham, *World Aflame* (Garden City, N.J.: Doubleday, 1965), 142.

30. Pollock, *Billy Graham: The Authorized Biography*, 125.

31. Billy Graham, *The Messages 2* (Baguio City, Philippines: Philippine Theological Seminary Press, 1979), 4–5.

32. Billy Graham, *Blow Wind* (Old Tappan, N.J.: Revell, 1975, 1977), 88.

33. Graham, *Just As I Am*, 235.

34. Marshall Frady, *A Parable in American Righteousness* (Boston: Little, Brown and Co., 1979), 315.

35. Pollock, *The Crusades: 20 Years with Billy Graham*, 190.

36. Ibid., 277.

37. Graham, *Just As I Am*, 220.

38. Alan Street, *The Effective Invitation* (Old Tappan, N.J.: Revell, 1984), 122.

39. J. I. Packer, *Evangelism and the Sovereignty of God* (London: InterVarsity, 1961), 125.

40. C. H. Spurgeon, *New York Street Pulpit* (London: Passmore and Alabaster, 1862), 86.

41. Graham, *Peace with God*, 28.

42. Graham, *How to be Born Again*, 30–31.

43. Lowe, *Billy Graham Speaks*, 38.

44. Frost, *Personal Thoughts of a Public Man*, 166–67.

45. Graham, *Billy Graham Answers Your Questions*, 207.

46. Ibid., 213.

47. Graham, *The Holy Spirit*, 75.

48. Graham, *Peace with God*, 25.

49. Ibid., 30–31.

50. Wayne Stanley Bonde, "The Rhetoric of Billy Graham: A Description, Analysis, and Evaluation" (Ph.D. diss., Southern Illinois University, 1973), 45.

51. John Calvin, *Instruction in Faith*, quoted in Bonde, "The Rhetoric of Billy Graham," 48–49.

52. Bonde, "The Rhetoric of Billy Graham," 45.

53. Billy Edward Vaughn, "A Rhetorical Study in Adaptation," (Ph.D. diss., University of Kansas, 1972), 193.

54. Graham, *Facing Death and the Life After*, 38.

55. Ibid., 54.

56. Packer, *Evangelism and the Sovereignty of God*, 16.

57. Ibid., 10.

58. John Newport, *The Lion and the Lamb* (Nashville: Broadman and Holman, 1986), 201.

59. Graham, *Storm Warning*, 50.

60. Ibid., 119.

61. Beasley-Murray, *Word Biblical Commentary—John*, 190.

62. Pollock, *The Crusades: 20 Years with Billy Graham*, 120.

63. Dick Jensen, *The Billy Pulpits* (Memphis: Riverside Printing, 1996), 55.

64. Graham, *World Aflame*, 139.

65. Ibid., 85.

66. Graham, *Just As I Am*, 213.

67. Ibid., 225.

68. Pollock, *Billy Graham: The Authorized Biography*, 252.

69. Graham, *Just As I Am*, 680.

70. Frost, *Personal Thoughts of a Public Man*, 64.

71. Graham, *Just As I Am*, 225.

72. John Pollock, *Billy Graham: Evangelist to the World* (San Francisco: Harper and Row, 1979), 111.

73. Pollock, *Billy Graham: The Authorized Biography*, 251.

74. Pollock, *The Crusades: 20 Years with Billy Graham*, 145.

75. Graham, *Just As I Am*, 246.

76. Frady, *A Parable in American Righteousness*, 315.

Chapter 5: Christology in Evangelism

1. Bray, *Creeds, Councils and Christ*, 107.

2. Stephana Dan in a comment to author, June 1999.

3. Bray, *Creed, Councils and Christ*, 115.

4. Ibid., 110.

5. Ibid., 111.

6. From personal correspondence.

7. This is how Donald Baillie in *God Was in Christ* interpreted Brunner. There are other versions of the anhypostasia concept as well, for example, views expressed by H. M. Retton, Leonard Hodgson, etc. They cannot be approached in this limited space; however, it is correct to say they are all variations of the same basic idea.

8. Donald Baillie, *God Was in Christ* (Minneapolis: World Wide Publications, 1984), 89.

9. Vincent Taylor, *The Person of Christ in the New Testament Teaching* (London: Macmillan, 1958), 270.

10. Donald Baillie made three very good points in his setting out the weakness of *kenosis* ideas as the full answer to the incarnation problem.

11. Baillie, *God Was in Christ*, 97.

12. Ibid., 65. Donald Baillie agreed that our faith is full of the paradox. The incarnation is the peak of the issue. But believers have learned this is inevitable because they are faced with the suprarational God.

13. William Temple said, "If any man says that he understands the relation of Deity to humanity in Christ, he only makes it clear he does not understand at all what is meant by Incarnation." William Temple, *Christus Veritas* (London: Macmillan, 1924), 139.

14. Saint Athanasius, *The Incarnation,* ed. A. Robertson (London: D. Nutt, 891), 14–15.

15. G. I. Williamson, *The Westminster Confession of Faith for Study Classes* (Philadelphia: Presbyterian and Reformed Publishing Co., 1964), 72–73.

16. The author follows Erickson on the following positive points regarding the incarnation. Erickson's treatment seems most helpful and satisfying.

17. Carl F. H. Henry "Our Lord's Virgin Birth," *Christianity Today*, 7 December 1959, 20.

18. Millard J. Erickson, *Christian Theology* (Grand Rapids: Baker, 1983, 1985), 738.

19. Graham, *A Biblical Standard for Evangelists*, 11.

20. Graham, *Storm Warning*, 80.

21. Billy Graham, interview.

22. Huston, *Crusade Evangelism and the Local Church*, 21.

23. Graham, *Storm Warning*, 80.

24. Lockard, *The Unheard Billy Graham*, 35.

25. Graham, *Storm Warning*, 80.

26. Billy Graham, "Jesus Christ, Superstar," sermon preached in Birmingham, Ala., 16 May 1972.

27. Graham, *Storm Warning*, 76.

28. Graham, *Answers to Life's Problems*, 156–57.

29. Lowe, *Billy Graham Speaks*, 39.

30. Ibid., 169.

31. Graham, *World Aflame*, 111.

32. Martin, *A Prophet with Honor*, 407.

33. Graham, *The Secret of Happiness*, 10.

34. Graham, *Facing Death and the Life After*, 37.

35. Ibid.

36. Graham, *Peace with God*, 93.

37. Ibid.

38. Graham, *Facing Death and the Life After*, 38.

39. Graham, *Peace with God*, 91.

40. Graham, "Jesus Christ, Superstar."

41. Ibid.

42. Ibid.

43. Ibid.

44. Ibid.

45. Graham, *The Secret of Happiness*, 12.

46. E. M. B. Green, ed., *Truth of God Incarnate* (Grand Rapids: Eerdmans, 1977), 80.

47. Billy Graham, *America's Hour of Decision* (Wheaton, Ill.: Van Kampen Press, 1951), 124.

48. John R. W. Stott, *The Cross of Christ* (Downers Grove, Ill.: InterVarsity, 1986), 89.

49. Ibid.

50. Billy Graham's sermon preached in Nashville, Tennessee, crusade on 9 September 1954.

51. Ibid.

52. Billy's Graham, "Did Christ Die for You?" sermon quoted in William Dale Apel, "The Understanding of Salvation and the Evangelistic Message of Billy Graham" (Ph.D. diss., Northwestern University, 1993), 91.

53. Graham, *World Aflame*, 122.

54. Graham, *Peace with God*, 85.

55. Lectures by evangelist Billy Graham at Union Theological Seminary, New York, 17 February 1954.

56. Billy Graham, *Decision*, April 1999, 1.

57. Ibid.

58. Ibid.

59. Billy Graham, "Facts, Faith and Feeling," radio sermon #27, *Hour of Decision*, 1953.

60. "Sick Society," message published by BGEA, 1967.

61. Billy Graham, "Three Keys to Youthfulness," sermon, 1962.

62. George Beasley-Murray, *Jesus and the Kingdom of God* (Grand Rapids: Eerdmans, 1986), 73.

63. "Sick Society," message published by BGEA, 1967.

64. Stettel, *The Faith of Billy Graham*, 18.

65. Graham, *The Secret of Happiness*, 10.

66. Graham, *World Aflame*, 59.

67. Ibid.

68. Ibid. 123.

69. Ibid., 104.

70. Graham, *The Challenge*, 111.

71. *Living in Christ* (Minneapolis: Billy Graham Evangelistic Association, 1980), 5.

72. Ibid., 7.

73. Ibid., 8.

74. Ibid., 9.

75. Ibid., 19.

76. Ibid.

77. Bruce, interview.

78. Billy Graham, *The Seven Deadly Sins* (Grand Rapids: Zondervan, 1955), 52.

Chapter 6: Holistic Ministry in Evangelism

1. James Burns, *Revivals: Their Laws and Leaders* (Grand Rapids: Baker, 1960), 78.

2. Ibid., 80.

3. Ibid., 25.

4. Ibid., 86.

5. Ibid., 104.

6. Lockard, *The Unheard Billy Graham*, 120.

7. Tom Allan, quoted in Lockard, *The Unheard Billy Graham*, 20.

8. Graham, *World Aflame*, 177.

9. Lockard, *The Unheard Billy Graham*, 8.

10. Aruth Smith in the London Paper, *Daily Sketch*.

11. Lockard, *The Unheard Billy Graham*, 27.

12. Billy Graham, "My Personal Use of the Bible," *Christianity Today*, 22 November 1953, 166.

13. E. S. James, "Billy Graham and the Bible," *The Baptist Standard*, 21 April 1965, 4.

14. T. B. Maston, *Christianity and World Issues* (New York: Macmillan, 1957), 326–27.

15. Graham, *World Aflame*, 142.

16. Ibid., 18.

17. Ibid., 120.

18. Lockard, *The Unheard Billy Graham*, 92.

19. Ibid., 93.

20. Graham, *World Aflame*, 187.

21. Ibid.

22. Pollock, *The Crusades: 20 Years with Billy Graham*, 281.

23. Billy Graham, Spoken at the World Congress on Evangelism, Berlin, 4 November 1966.

24. Graham, *Billy Graham Answers Your Questions*, 125.

25. Ibid., 128.

26. Graham, *Approaching Hoofbeats*, 160.

27. Rick Marshall, interview by author, St. Louis, Mo., October 1999.

28. John Stott, interview by author, Amsterdam, Netherlands, July 2000.

29. "Graham Now Favors War on Poverty," *The Baptist Standard*, 21 June 1967, 17.

30. Billy Graham, interview.

31. Graham, *World Aflame*, 142.

32. "Graham Now Favors War on Poverty," 17.

33. Lockard, *The Unheard Billy Graham*, 142.

34. Ibid., 144.

35. Graham, *Hope for the Troubled Heart*, introduction.

36. Graham, *World Aflame*, 178.

37. Billy Graham, "God and the Nations," from a sermon preached in 1964.

38. Billy Graham, *My Answer* (New York: Doubleday, 1960), 177.

39. Lockard, *The Unheard Billy Graham*, 139.

40. Jay Walker, *Billy Graham: A Life in Word and Deed* (New York: Avon, 1998), 142.

41. Frost, *Personal Thoughts of a Public Man*, 48.

42. Ibid., 54.

43. Cliff Barrows, interview by author, Birmingham, Ala., 1999.

44. Lowe, *Billy Graham Speaks*, 116–17.

45. Graham, *Storm Warning*, 51.

46. Personal interview, August, 2000.

47. Graham, *Approaching Hoofbeats*, 129.

48. Lockard, *The Unheard Billy Graham*, 28.

49. Billy Graham, "What Ten Years Have Taught Me," *Christian Century*, 17 February 1960, 189.

50. Jensen, *The Billy Pulpits*, 83.

51. Lowe, *Billy Graham Speaks*, 66.

52. Stanley High, *Billy Graham* (Kingwood-Surrey: The World's Work, 1957), 61.

Chapter 7: Suffering in Evangelism

1. Burns, *Revivals: Their Laws and Leaders*, 123.

2. Ibid., 124.

3. Ibid., 138–39.

4. Ibid., 144.

5. Ibid., 149.

6. Ibid.

7. Ibid., 149–50.

8. Ibid., 156.

9. Charles R. Erdman, *The Epistle of Paul to the Galatians* (Philadelphia: The Westminster Press, 1930), 95.

10. Graham, *The Secret of Happiness*, 179–80.

11. Graham, *Storm Warning*, 28.

12. Billy Graham, *Till Armageddon* (Nashville: Word, 1981), 83–89.

13. Graham, *The Secret of Happiness*, 183.

14. Graham, *Approaching Hoofbeats*, 92

15. Graham, *The Secret of Happiness*, 183.

16. Ibid., 94.

17. Ibid., 184.

18. Curtis Mitchell, *Billy Graham: Saint or Sinner* (Old Tappan, N.J.: Revell, 1979), 66.

19. Graham, *The Secret of Happiness*, 190.

20. Ibid., 188–89.

21. High, *Billy Graham*, 64.

22. Graham, *The Secret of Happiness*, 190–91.

23. Ibid., 192.

24. Ibid.

25. Ibid.

26. Ibid., 193.

27. Ibid.

28. Ibid., 195.

29. Ibid., 198.

30. Ibid., 199.

31. Grady Wilson, *Count It All Joy* (Nashville: Broadman, 1984), introduction.

32. Stott, interview.

33. Martin, *A Prophet with Honor*, 218.

34. Ibid., 317–18.

35. Lowe, *Billy Graham Speaks*, 164.

36. Graham, *Hope for the Troubled Heart*, 115.

37. Ibid., 47.

38. Martin, *A Prophet with Honor*, 335.

39. Lowe, *Billy Graham Speaks*, 135.

40. Robert Ferm, *Cooperative Evangelism: Is Billy Graham Right or Wrong?* (Grand Rapids: Zondervan, 1958), 13.

41. Ibid., 21.

42. Ibid., 51.

43. Ibid., 56.

44. Ibid., 57.

45. Ibid., 59.

46. Ibid., 69.

47. Ibid., 70.

48. Ibid., 76.

49. Ibid., 81.

50. Ibid., 87.

51. Graham, *Billy Graham Answers Your Questions*, 158.

52. Martin, *A Prophet with Honor*, 223.

53. Lowe, *Billy Graham Speaks*, 49.

54. Pollock, *Billy Graham: Evangelist to the World*, 78.

55. Ibid., 225.

56. Pollock, *The Crusades: 20 Years with Billy Graham*, 172.

57. Graham, *Unto the Hills*, 137.

58. Graham, *Just As I Am*, 187.

59. Lowe, *Billy Graham Speaks*, 167.

60. Ibid.

61. Ibid., 168.

62. Ibid.

63. Ibid., 169.

64. Eugene S. Todd, "Just Promotionalism," *The Christian Century*, 16 January 1957, 81.

65. "In the Garden," *The Christian Century*, editorial, 15 May 1957.

66. Billy Graham, "Does a Religious Crusade Do Any Good?" *US News and World Report*, 27 September 1957.

67. Martin, *A Prophet with Honor*, 175.

68. Ibid.

69. Graham, *Just As I Am*, 249–50.

70. Martin, *A Prophet with Honor*, 175.

71. Ibid., 176.

72. Ibid.

73. Frost, *Personal Thoughts of a Public Man*, 120.

74. High, *Billy Graham*, 203.

75. John Corts, interview by author, Jacksonville, Fla., October 2000.

76. Pollock, *Billy Graham: Evangelist to the World*, 38.

77. Graham, *Till Armageddon*, 9.

78. Frank Harbor, interview by author, Amsterdam, Netherlands, July 2000.

79. Graham, *Hope for the Troubled Heart*, 118.

80. Frost, *Personal Thoughts of a Public Man*, 156.

81. Ibid., 87–88.

82. Graham, *Storm Warning*, 111–12.

83. Lowe, *Billy Graham Speaks*, 146.

84. Frost, *Personal Thoughts of a Public Man*, 83–84.

85. Ibid., 86.

86. Graham, *Unto the Hills*, 265.

87. Ibid., 354.

88. Frost, *Personal Thoughts of a Public Man*, 87–88.

89. Graham, *The Secret of Happiness*, 186–87.

90. Mitchell, *Billy Graham: Saint or Sinner*, 216.

91. Billy Graham, interview.

92. Ibid.

93. Ibid.

Chapter 8: The Bible in Evangelism

1. Martin Luther, *Commentary on Genesis*, vol. 1, J. Theodore Mueller, trans. (Grand Rapids, 2. Zondervan, 1958), 298.

2. Roland H. Bainton, *Here I Stand: A Life of Martin Luther* (New York: Abingdon-Cokesbury 4. Press, 1950), 185.

3. George, *The Theology of the Reformers*, 53.

4. Ibid., 54.

5. Ibid., 55.

6. Bainton, *Here I Stand: A Life of Martin Luther*, 34.

7. Ibid., 41.

8. Ibid., 45.

9. Ibid., 51.

10. Ibid., 56.

11. Ibid., 59.

12. Ibid., 60.

13. Ibid., 60–62.

14. Ibid.

15. Ibid., 63.

16. Ibid., 65.

17. Dewey M. Beegle, *Scripture, Tradition, and Infallibility* (Grand Rapids: Eerdmans, 1973), 98.

18. Clark H. Pinnock, *Biblical Revelation* (Chicago: Moody, 1971), 153–54.

19. Ibid., 139.

20. Ibid., 211.

21. Robert M. Grant, *The Bible in the Church: A Short History of Interpretation* (New York: Macmillan, 1954), 110.

22. Martin Luther, *Bondage of the Will* (Old Tappan, N.J.: Revell, 1957), 125.

23. Ibid.

24. Bainton, *Here I Stand: A Life of Martin Luther*, 185.

25. Lewis A. Drummond, "The Point for Theology," *Word of the Cross* (Nashville: Broadman, 1992), 35–38, 43–54, 57–63.

26. J. I. Packer, *Keep in Step with the Spirit* (Old Tappan, N.J.: Revell, 1984), 38.

27. Stott, interview.

28. Graham, *The Holy Spirit*, 42.

29. Graham, *Just As I Am*, 46.

30. Graham, *The Holy Spirit*, 39.

31. Donald A. White, "Evangelistic Preaching of Billy Graham," (Ph.D. diss., Purdue University, 1961).

32. Graham, *World Aflame*, 99.

33. Billy Graham, "Ambassadors," *Decision*, May 1977, 3.

34. Billy Graham, interview.

35. Graham, *The Holy Spirit*, 43.

36. Ibid., 40.

37. Billy Graham, interview.

38. Olford, interview.

39. Graham, *World Aflame*, 40.

40. Richard Els Woods, ed., *To God Be the Glory* (New York: Walker and Co., 1984), 31.

41. Graham, *How to be Born Again*, 26.

42. Graham, *Billy Graham Answers Your Questions*, 132.

43. Lowe, *Billy Graham Speaks*, 41.

44. Frost, *Personal Thoughts of a Public Man*, 73.

45. Graham, *Billy Graham Answers Your Questions*, 130.

46. Luther, *Commentary on Genesis*, vol. 1, 150.

47. Billy Graham, "Why I Believe the Bible Is the Word of God," *Decision*, November 1968, 14.

48. John Calvin, *Institutes of the Christian Religion*, vol. 4, trans. F. L. Battles Collins, vol. 4: 8–9.

49. Luther, *Commentary on Genesis*, vol. 1, 169–70.

50. Graham, *The Holy Spirit*, 44.

51. Ibid.

52. Ibid.

53. Ibid., 47.

54. Curtis Mitchell, *Billy Graham: The Making of a Crusader* (Philadelphia: Chilton, 1966), 54.

55. Court R. Flint, *The Faith of Billy Graham* (Anderson, S.C.: Drake House, 1968), 28.

56. Ibid., 40.

57. Billy Graham, "Can God Bring Revolution to Your Heart?" *Decision,* no. 22 (July 1981), 7.

58. Luther, *Commentary on Genesis*, vol. 1, 155.

59. Lowe, *Billy Graham Speaks*, 40–41.

60. Settel, *The Faith of Billy Graham*, 118.

61. Billy Graham, *Our Bible* (Minneapolis: World Wide Publications, 1993), tract.

62. Graham, *Billy Graham Answers Your Questions*, 114.

63. Frost, *Personal Thoughts of a Public Man*, 28.

64. Billy Graham, interview.

65. Graham, *How to Be Born Again*, 39.

66. Marshall, interview.

67. Billy Graham, "Ambassadors," *Decision* no. 5 (May 1977), 26.

68. Roger Elwood, ed., *To God Be the Glory* (New York: Walker, 1984), 31.

69. Flint, *The Faith of Billy Graham*, 28.

70. Graham, *The Holy Spirit*, 47.

71. Graham, *Billy Graham Answers Your Questions*, 156.

72. Phillips, interview.

73. Frost, *Personal Thoughts of a Public Man*, 145.

74. Billy Graham, interview.

75. Flint, *The Faith of Billy Graham*, 24.

76. Graham, *Hope for the Troubled Heart*, 14.

77. Flint, *The Faith of Billy Graham*, 118.

78. Ibid., 5–6.

79. Billy Graham, interview.

80. Graham, *Just As I Am*, 126.

81. Curtis Mitchell, *Billy Graham: The Making of a Crusader*, 18.

82. Larry Walker, interview by author, Amsterdam, Netherlands, July 2000.

83. Graham, *Just As I Am*, 324.

84. Billy Graham, "Your Spiritual Survival Kit," *Decision*, November 2000.

85. Ben Siamlie, "I Can Go No Further," *Christianity Today*, 26 September 1966, 53.

86. Larry Davis, "Interpretation of Scripture in the Evangelistic Preaching of William Franklin Billy Graham" (Ph.D. diss., Southern Baptist Theological Seminary, 1986).

87. Luther, *Commentary on Genesis*, 155.

88. Graham, *World Aflame*, xiv.

89. Graham, *Unto the Hills*, 313.

90. Robert Ferm, *Persuaded to Live* (Westwood, N.J.: Revell, 1958), 192.

91. Henry Holley, interview by author, St. Louis, October 1999.

92. Luther, *Commentary on Genesis*, vol. 1, 143.

Chapter 9: Boldness in Evangelim

1. George, *The Theology of the Reformers*, 160.

2. Ibid., 110.

3. Ibid., 111.

4. Ibid., 113.

5. Ibid.

6. Ibid., 117.

7. Ibid.

8. Ibid., 121.

9. Ibid., 135–36.

10. "Boldness," *Funk and Wagnall's Desk Standard Dictionary*.

11. Joseph Henry Thayer, *Greek-English Lexicon of the New Testament* (New York: American Book, n.d.), 491.

12. Curtis Mitchell, *Billy Graham: Saint or Sinner* (Old Tappan, N.J.: Revell Co., 1979), 135.

13. Ibid.

14. Ibid., 137.

15. Ibid., 138.

16. Harbor, interview.

17. Graham, *Just As I Am*, 172.

18. Ibid.

19. Frost, *Personal Thoughts of a Public Man*, 132.

20. Martin, *A Prophet with Honor*, 145.

21. Ibid., 246.

22. Ibid., 247.

23. Ibid.

24. Ibid., 249–50.

25. Ibid., 250.

26. Ibid., 248.

27. Ibid.

28. Holley, interview.

29. Martin, *A Prophet with Honor*, 402.

30. Ibid., 403.

31. Ibid., 406.

32. Ibid., 422.

33. Ibid.

34. Frost, *Personal Thoughts of a Public Man*, 131.

35. Billy Graham, interview.

36. Ibid.

Introduction to the Puritan/Piestistic-Revival Age

1. Ernest Stoeffler, *The Rise of Evangelical Pietism* (Leeden, Netherlands: E. J. Brill, 1971), 27.

Chapter 10: Godliness in Evangelism

1. Marcus L. Loane, *Makers of Religious Freedom in the Seventeenth Century* (Grand Rapids: Eerdmans, 1961), 167.

2. Ibid., 169.

3. Ibid., 171.

4. Ibid., 173.

5. Benjamin Fawcett, *The Saint's Everlasting Rest* (New York City: American Tract Society,), ii.

6. Ibid. (The historian quoted is the honorable Robert Boyle.)

7. Loane, *Makers of Religious Freedom in the Seventeenth Century*, 193.

8. Fawcett, *The Saint's Everlasting Rest*, ii.

9. Bainton, *Here I Stand: A Life of Martin Luther*.

10. Graham, *Just As I Am*, 32.

11. Pollock, *Billy Graham: The Authorized Biography*, 4.

12. Graham, *Unto the Hills*, 65.

13. Ibid.

14. Ibid., 38.

15. Ibid., 43.

16. Ibid., 69.

17. Billy Graham, "You Can't Cover Up Sin," *Decision*, September 1999.

18. Ibid.

19. Ibid.

20. Graham, *The Secret of Happiness*, 90.

21. Ibid., 103.

22. Ibid., 69.

23. Ibid., 103.

24. Graham, "You Can't Cover Up Sin."

25. Graham, *The Secret of Happiness*, 43.

26. Ibid., 78.

27. Ibid., 133.

28. Denton Lotz, interview by author, Amsterdam, July 2000.

29. Graham, *Approaching Hoofbeats*, 98.

30. Graham, *The Secret of Happiness*, 101–102.

31. Frost, *Personal Thoughts of a Public Man*, 28–29.

32. Ibid., 173.

33. Graham, *Unto the Hills*, 172.

34. Frost, *Personal Thoughts of a Public Man*, 145.

35. Ibid.

36. Billy Graham, interview.

37. Graham, *Hope for the Troubled Heart*, 143.

38. Ibid., 166.

39. Billy Graham, "The Power of Prayer: Turning the Tide of History," *Decision*, July/August 1999.

40. Ibid.

41. Ibid.

42. Ibid.

43. Ibid.

44. Ibid.

45. Ibid.

46. Barrows, interview.

47. Graham, *The Secret of Happiness*, 208.

48. Graham, *Storm Warning*, 127–28.

49. "Operation Andrew" Prayer Card.

50. Martin, *A Prophet with Honor*, 595.

51. Graham, *The Seven Deadly Sins*, 27.

52. Martin, *A Prophet with Honor*, 598.

53. Graham, *The Seven Deadly Sins*, 56.

54. Martin, *A Prophet with Honor*, 595.

55. Ibid., 596.

56. Ibid., 598.

57. Martin, *A Prophet with Honor*, 599.

58. Graham, *Help for the Troubled Heart*, 22.

59. Ibid.

60. Graham, *Unto the Hills*, 51–52.

61. Anne Graham Lotz, interview by author, St. Louis, Mo., October 1999.

62. Busby, *God's Ambassador*, 240–41.

63. Ibid., 232.

64. Graham, *The Seven Deadly Sins*, 17.

65. Denton Lotz, interview.

66. Martin, *A Prophet with Honor*, 602.

67. Graham, *Approaching Hoofbeats*, 58.

68. Flint, *The Faith of Billy Graham*, 34.

69. Ibid., 70.

70. Ibid., 71.

71. Graham, *The Secret of Happiness*, 202–12.

72. Flint, *The Faith of Billy Graham*, 84.

73. Graham, *How to Be Born Again*, 127.

74. Graham, *Hope for the Troubled Heart*, 135.

75. Melvin Graham, interview by author, St. Louis, October 1999.

76. Martin, *A Prophet with Honor*, 595.

77. Ibid.

78. Ibid., 603.

79. Graham, *A Biblical Standard for Evangelists*, 74.

80. Martin, *A Prophet with Honor*, 107.

81. Material furnished by Cliff Barrows.

82. Sterling Huston, interview by author, Indianapolis, Ind., June 1999.

83. Lowe, *Billy Graham Speaks*, 102.

84. Graham, *A Biblical Standard for Evangelists*, 109.

85. Ibid., 110.

86. Frost, *Personal Thoughts of a Public Man*, 71–72.

87. *Christian Life and Witness Course*, Christian Growth Series (Minneapolis: World Wide Publications, year?), page?.

88. *Living in Christ* (Minneapolis: World Wide Publications, 1998), 1–2.

89. *Friendship Evangelism* (Minneapolis: World Wide Publications, 1998).

90. Frost, *Personal Thoughts of a Public Man*, 173.

Chapter 11: Revival in Evangelism

1. James Burns, *Revivals: Their Laws and Leaders* (Grand Rapids: Baker, 1960), 287.

2. Ibid.

3. Ibid., 283.

4. Mandell Taylor, *Exploring Evangelism* (Kansas City, Mo.: Beacon Hill, 1964), 250.

5. Burns, *Revivals: Their Laws and Leaders*, 301.

6. Ibid., 304.

7. Ibid., 307.

8. Ibid., 309–10.

9. Ibid., 310–11.

10. Ibid., 319.

11. Ibid.

12. Ibid.

13. Ibid., 247.

14. Ibid., 28.

15. Ibid., 38.

16. Ibid., 85.

17. Ibid., 44.

18. Lowe, *Billy Graham Speaks*, 31.

19. Graham, *Storm Warning*, 307–8.

20. Aubrey Morris, "A Study of Psychological Factors in the Evangelistic Preaching of Billy Graham" (Ph.D. diss., Southern Baptist Theological Seminary, 1966), 158.

21. Lowe, *Billy Graham Speaks*, 31.

22. Bonde, "The Rhetoric of Billy Graham," 85.

23. Ibid., 386.

24. Billy Graham, *Revival in Our Time* (Wheaton, Ill.: Van Kamper, 1950), 73.

25. Ibid., 77.

26. Graham, *Storm Warning*, 47.

27. Ibid.

28. D. A. Waite, *The Evangelistic Speaking of Billy Graham1949–1959.* (Ph.D. diss., Purdue University, 1961), 91.

29. Ian H. Murray, *Revival and Revivalism* (Carlisle, Pa.: The Banner of Truth Trust, 1994), 23.

30. Graham, *The Holy Spirit*, 220.

31. Lockard, *The Unheard Billy Graham*, 97.

32. Graham, *A Biblical Standard for Evangelism*, 124.

33. Ibid.

34. Pollock, *Billy Graham: Evangelist to the World*, 217.

35. Pollock, *Billy Graham: The Authorized Biography*, 124.

36. Apel, "The Understanding of Salvation," 41.

37. Graham, *Unto the Hills*, 178.

38. Graham, *A Biblical Standard for Evangelists*, 178.

39. Melvin Graham, interview.

40. Graham, *Storm Warning*, 200.

41. Ibid.

42. Huston, interview.

43. Pollock, *Billy Graham: The Authorized Biography*, 173.

44. Ibid., 175.

45. John Yarbrough, interview by author, Nashville, August 2000.

46. Pollock, *Billy Graham: The Authorized Biography*, 173.

47. Frost, *Personal Thoughts of a Public Man*, 23.

48. Sherwood Eliot Wirt, *Crusade at the Golden Gate* (New York: Harper and Brothers, 1959), 146–47.

49. Anne Graham Lotz, interview.

50. Graham, *Storm Warning*, 307–8.

51. Graham, *World Aflame*, 23–24.

Chapter 12: Worldwide Ministry in Evangelism

1. Timothy George, *Faithful Witness: The Life and Mission of William Carey* (Birmingham, Ala.: New Hope, 1991), 137.
2. Ibid., 4.
3. Ibid., 6.
4. Ibid., 8.
5. Ibid., 16.
6. Ibid., 18.
7. Ibid.
8. Ibid., 30.
9. Bill O'Brien, "The Biblical Basis and Priority for Frontier Missions," *International Journal of Frontier Missions* (1996): 13.
10. Ibid.
11. Graham, *Breakfast with Billy Graham*, 38.
12. Jensen, *The Billy Pulpits*, 121.
13. Barrows, interview.
14. Graham, *Just As I Am*, 622.
15. Frost, *Personal Thoughts of a Public Man*, 133–34.
16. Ibid., 152.
17. Graham, *A Biblical Standard for Evangelists*, 23.
18. Beasley-Murray, *Jesus and the Kingdom of God*, 3.
19. Graham, *Storm Warning*, 301.
20. Ibid.
21. Pollock, *The Crusades: 20 Years with Billy Graham*, 168.
22. Martin, *A Prophet with Honor*, 97.
23. Barrows, interview.
24. Ibid.
25. Martin, *A Prophet with Honor*, 319.
26. Jensen, *The Billy Pulpits*, 21.
27. Martin, *A Prophet with Honor*, 439.
28. Kim, interview.
29. Rowlandson, *Life with Billy*, 254.
30. Billy Graham, "Extending the Kingdom of God," *Decision*, October 2000, 4.
31. Denton Lotz, interview.
32. Martin, *A Prophet with Honor*, 449.
33. Billy Graham, interview.
34. Graham, *Just As I Am*, 182.
35. Ibid., 453.
36. Frost, *Personal Thoughts of a Public Man*, 144–45.
37. Billy Graham, interview.

38. Graham, *Storm Warning*, 301.

39. Billy Graham, "My Greatest Concern for 1974," *Eternity*, January 1974, 16.

Chapter 13: The Church in Evangelism

1. *Spurgeon's Autobiography*, vol. 1 (London: Passmore and Alabaster, 1898), 22–23.

2. W. Y. Fullerton, *Biography of Spurgeon* (London: Williams and Norgate, 1920), 14.

3. Lewis A. Drummond, *Spurgeon: Prince of Preachers* (Grand Rapids: Kregel, 1992), 22–23.

4. Ibid., 162.

5. Ibid.

6. Charles R. Erdman, *The Pastoral Epistles of Paul* (Philadelphia: Westminster Press, 1923), 1.

7. *Baker's Dictionary of Theology* (Grand Rapids: Baker, 1960), 122–23.

8. Graham, *Peace with God*, 188.

9. Graham, *Death and Life After*, 163.

10. Yarbrough, interview.

11. Denton Lotz, interview.

12. Ralph Bell, interview by author, Indianapolis, June 1999.

13. Sterling Huston, interview by author, Indianapolis, Ind., June 1999.

14. Graham, *Billy Graham Answers Your Questions*, 73.

15. Letter to Allison Barker, Christian Guidance Department, 13 April 1999.

16. Ibid.

17. Ibid.

18. Graham, *Peace with God*, 190.

19. Ibid., 191–92.

20. Ibid., 194.

21. Ibid., 190.

22. Letter to Allison Barker, Christian Guidance Department, 13 April 1999.

23. Ira Craft, interview by author, Winchester, U.K., December 1999.

24. Letter to Allison Barker, Christian Guidance Department, 13 April 1999.

25. Graham, *Answers to Life's Problems*, 68.

26. Ibid., 67.

27. Ibid., 69.

28. Ibid., 73.

29. Ibid., 112.

30. Ibid., 109.

31. Graham, *Peace with God*, 194.

32. Graham, *Answers to Life's Problems*, 109.

33. Ibid., 110.

34. Graham, *Peace with God*, 196.

35. Ibid.

36. Graham, *Approaching Hoofbeats*, 43.

37. Billy Graham, "Challenge for Today's Church," audiocassette by Dale Randolph.

38. Graham, *Answers to Life's Problems*, 114.

39. Graham, *Peace with God*, 196.

40. Ibid., 201.

41. Graham, *Storm Warning*, 100.

42. Frost, *Personal Thoughts of a Public Man*, 74.

43. Ibid., 76.

44. Aubrey Morris, "A Study of Psychological Factors in the Evangelistic Preaching of Billy Graham," 82.

45. Graham, *Approaching Hoofbeats*, 90.

46. Graham and Ward, ed., *The Christian Workers Handbook*, 71.

47. Graham, *Peace with God*, 121.

48. Ibid., 186.

49. Ibid., 190.

50. Ibid.

51. Graham and Ward, ed., *The Christian Workers Handbook*, 71.

52. Graham, *Answers to Life's Problems*, 110.

53. Ibid., 116.

54. Ibid., 118.

55. Ibid.

56. Graham, *A Biblical Standard for Evangelists*, 90.

57. Graham and Ward, ed., *The Christian Workers Handbook*, 72.

58. Graham, *Just As I Am*, 169.

59. Ibid.

60. Graham, *A Biblical Standard for Evangelists*, 103.

61. Ibid., 105.

62. Graham, *Approaching Hoofbeats*, 106.

63. Graham, "What Ten Years Have Taught Me," 186–89.

64. Graham, *Approaching Hoofbeats*, 106.

65. Frank Fitt, "In the Wake of Billy Graham," *Christian Century*, 1 December 1954.

66. Stanley High, "Do Billy Graham's Crusades Have Lasting Effect?" *Reader's Digest*, September 1955, 67–77, 82.

67. Ibid.

68. Cecil Northcott, "Needed: Evangelism in Depth," *Christian Century*, 26 June 1957.

69. George Dugan, "Graham's Impact Held Fleeting as Ministers Appraise Crusade," *New York Times*, 26 January 1958.

70. George Beverly Shea, interview by author, St. Louis, October 1999.

71. Huston, *Crusade Evangelism and the Local Church*, 10.

72. Charles Dullea, *A Catholic Looks at Billy Graham* (New York: Paulist Press, 1974), 48.

73. Graham, *Billy Graham Answers Your Questions*, 67.

74. Graham, *A Biblical Standard for Evangelists*, 106.

75. Dullea, *A Catholic Looks at Billy Graham*, 144.

76. Lowe, *Billy Graham Speaks*, 68.

77. Graham, *Peace with God*, 190.

78. Ibid., 70.

79. Lowe, *Billy Graham Speaks*, 127.

80. Ibid.

81. Ibid., 128.

Chapter 14: The Lasting Legacy

1. Billy Graham, interview.

2. Ibid.

3. Ibid.

4. Ibid.

5. Ibid.

6. Ibid.

7. Ibid.

8. Anne Graham Lotz, interview.

9. Billy Graham, interview.

10. Ibid.

11. Huston, interview.

Appendix B

1. The Lausanne Covenant is reprinted here by permission of Leighton Ford, Leighton Ford Ministries.

INDEX

DATE DUE